Catalogue

OF

THE VALUABLE LIBRARY

OF

HENRY B. HUMPHREY, Esq.

TO BE SOLD BY AUCTION,

ON TUESDAY, MAY 9TH, 1871, AND FOLLOWING DAYS,

IN THE LIBRARY SALESROOM OF

LEONARD AND COMPANY,

No. 50 BROMFIELD STREET, BOSTON.

SALE EACH DAY AT 10 AND 3 O'CLOCK.

The sale will be wholly without reserve, by order of JOSEPH DORR, *Esq., Guardian.*

CAMBRIDGE:
Printed at the Riverside Press.
1871.

Catalogue, price One Dollar each. . . . . . . Large Paper, Five Dollars.

CONDITIONS OF SALE.

I. The highest bidder to be the buyer; and if any question arise between bidders, the lot so disputed shall be immediately put up again, provided the auctioneer cannot decide the said dispute.

II. The purchasers to give in their names and residences, and to make a deposit, if required, in part-payment of the purchase-money; in default of which, the lot or lots purchased to be immediately put up again and resold.

III. The lots to be taken away at the buyer's expense, within three days after the conclusion of the sale, and the remainder of the purchase-money to be paid previous to the delivery of the goods.

IV. Upon failure to comply with the above conditions, any money that may have been deposited will be forfeited, and all goods not removed within the time named may be resold by public or private sale, on account of the purchaser, and any deficiency occurring at such resale to be made good by the said purchaser.

V. The books are presumed to be perfect, unless otherwise expressed. All notices of imperfections must be made within a week from the last day of sale. No allowance will be made for stained, soiled, or short leaves.

VI. To prevent inaccuracy in delivery, and inconvenience in the settlement of the purchases, no lot can, on any account, be delivered during the sale.

LEONARD & CO.

Gentlemen who cannot attend the sale may have their purchases faithfully executed by the auctioneers, at a charge of five per cent. on the amount of bills.

NOTICE.

In submitting the present library to public competition, a few words will suffice as an introduction to what is, we believe, the most valuable collection of books ever offered by public sale in this city.

The books are mostly in good condition, a large portion of them in fine bindings, and the description of the books in the catalogue is believed to be unusually accurate.

The catalogue has been prepared by Lawrence Rhoades, Esq., of Newport, R. I., who has taken especial care in collating the plates, and in the description of the condition of the books.

The titles have been taken very fully from the books themselves; more so, perhaps, than might generally be considered necessary, but it is a fault, if one at all, on the right side.

Mr. Rhoades says, in a note to Mr. Dorr: "I have taken unusual care. I feel confident that few catalogues have ever been made with the same degree of accuracy. The mere collation of 11,000 volumes is no small thing in itself, and that has been very thoroughly done, and I can guarantee the books as described. The examination of the numerous engravings, in the illustrated works, and the description of their state, besides giving the names of celebrated designers and engravers (all of which has been carefully attended to), occupies much time, and requires both experience and judgment. All these facts add much to the value of a catalogue, especially to those who have not the leisure to examine for themselves. I have been obliged to depend, almost entirely, upon the bibliographical works, which the library itself affords, to verify facts; and having to derive most of the information in the catalogue from the works themselves, I feel the more confident that the statements are correct." L. R.

"With very few exceptions the BOOKS in this catalogue are placed under the *names* of the *authors*, *compilers*, etc., when known; under the *pseudonyms* when the *autonyms* have not been ascertained; and under the *first word of the title* (*not an article*), when the author's name of an *anony-mous* work is unknown. When the *initials only* of an *un-known author* appear, the work has been treated as *anonymous*, and *polysyngraphic* works are placed either under the *author's name which first appears*, or under the *first word*, on the title. Among the exceptions to these general rules are *biographies* containing writings of the subject, which have *generally* been placed under the *name of the subject*, instead of under that of the biographer; a *few pseudonymous* publications, which have been treated as *anonymous*; a *few collections*, forming uniform sets, — such as *society publications*, under the *name of the society*, '*Life and Times*' of Napoleon, under *Napoléon I.*, etc.; some *state*, *city*, etc., publications placed under the *name of the state*, *city*, etc.; and some '*galleries*' — 'Dres-den,' 'Florence,' 'Houghton,' 'Stafford,' etc. — under the names by which they are generally known. The *catalogues* have been placed together in C, the *maps* in M, the *photo-graphs* in P, and the *engravings* at the end of the catalogue of books. The number of *pamphlets* being small they have *generally* been treated as *books*. In some cases the *contents of polygraphic* works are given, and in others references to bibliographical works in which the *contents* may be found."

"The library is particularly rich in *books of prints* and other works which contain engravings by *celebrated engravers*, ancient and modern, after the *most eminent artists*, but it is useless to call attention to any particular work, or class, in a collection so MISCELLANEOUS AND VALUABLE; for, in the most casual glance over these pages, the eye will meet with *stand-ard, rare, and elegant* works in all departments of literature."

Catalogue.

1 ABBOTT, Rev. Jacob. History of Mary Queen of Scots. *With engravings. 16mo, cloth.* New York, 1848

2 ABBOTT, Rev. Jacob. History of Julius Cæsar. *With engravings. 16mo, cloth.* New York, (1849)

3 ABBOTT, Rev. John Stevens Cabot. The History of Napoleon Bonaparte. *Portraits, maps, and wood-cuts. 2 vols., royal 8vo, half calf, marbled edges.* New York, 1855

4 ABBOTT, Rev. John Stevens Cabot. The History of the Civil War in America; comprising a Full and Impartial Account of the Origin and Progress of the Rebellion, etc., etc. *Illustrated with maps, diagrams, and numerous steel engravings of battle scenes, from original designs by Darley and other eminent artists, and portraits of distinguished men. 2 vols., royal 8vo, roan.* New York, 1866

5 ABBOTT, Rev. John Stevens Cabot. Lives of the Presidents of the United States of America, from Washington to the Present Time. *Portraits, views, etc., on steel and wood. 8vo, half calf, extra, gilt edges.* Boston, 1867

6 ABDY, Edward Strutt. Journal of a Residence and Tour in the United States of North America, from April 1833, to October 1834. *3 vols., crown 8vo, cloth, uncut.* J. Murray, London, 1835

7 ABEKEN, Bernard Rudolf. An Account of the Life and Letters of Cicero, translated from the German. Edited by Charles Merivale. *12mo, half calf, very neat; with autograph of Rufus Choate.* London, 1854

8 ABELARD and Héloïse. Letters of Abelard and Eloisa; with Several Poems by Mr. Pope & other Authors (and the History of Abelard and Eloisa). *Engraved title and 6 plates by Sharp, Heath, etc., after Stothard, Wale, etc. Crown 8vo, old calf.* W. Lowndes, London, 1802

9 ABERCROMBIE, John, M. D. Inquiries concerning the Intellectual Powers. *12mo, half calf.* New York, 1833

10 ABOUT, Edmond François Valentin. The Roman Question. Translated by Mrs. Annie T. Wood; edited, with Introduction, by Rev. E. N. Kirk, D. D. *12mo, cloth.* Boston, 1859

11 ABOUT, EDMOND FRANÇOIS VALENTIN. ROME OF TO-DAY. *12mo, paper.* New York, 1861

12 ABSTRACT (AN) OF THE SUFFERINGS OF THE PEOPLE CALL'D QUAKERS, for the Testimony of a Good Conscience, from the Time of their being first distinguished by that Name; taken from Original Records, and other Authentic Accounts. (A. D. 1650–1666, with Alphabetical Lists of Names of the Sufferers.) *3 vols., 8vo, calf.* London, 1733–38

13 ACCOUNT OF THE CENTENNIAL CELEBRATION IN DANVERS (MASS.), June 16, 1852; together with the Proceedings of the Town in Relation to the Donation of George Peabody, Esq. *Portraits. 8vo, cloth, gilt edges. Presented to Rufus Choate by the Publishing Committee.* Boston, 1852

14 ACCOUNTS AND EXTRACTS OF THE MANUSCRIPTS IN THE LIBRARY OF THE KING OF FRANCE; published under the Inspection of a Committee of the Royal Academy of Sciences at Paris. Translated from the French [by William Tooke]. *2 vols., 8vo, old mottled calf, yellow edges; with book-plates of John Waddington, Chr. Pegge, and F. S. Bang.* R. Faulder, London, 1789

15 ACERBI, JOSEPH. TRAVELS THROUGH SWEDEN, FINLAND, AND LAPLAND, to the North Cape, in the Years 1798 and 1799. *Portrait, map, and 15 plates (those of natural history colored), with 12 engraved pages of music. 2 vols., 4to, old calf.* London, 1802

16 ADAMS, ABIGAIL, wife of JOHN ADAMS. LETTERS OF. With an Introductory Memoir; by her Grandson, Charles Francis Adams. *Portrait, and fac-simile of hand-writing. 2 vols., post 8vo, cloth.* Boston, 1840

17 ADAMS, ABIGAIL. JOURNAL AND CORRESPONDENCE OF; written in France and England, in 1785. Edited by her Daughter. *Portrait after painting by Copley. 2 vols., 12mo, cloth.* New York, 1841–42

18 ADAMS, HANNAH. AN ALPHABETICAL COMPENDIUM OF THE VARIOUS SECTS, which have appeared in the World, from the Beginning of the Christian Æra to the Present Day; with an Appendix, containing a Brief Account of the Various Schemes of Religion now embraced among Mankind. *8vo, sheep.* Boston, 1784

19 ADAMS, HANNAH. THE HISTORY OF THE JEWS, from the Destruction of Jerusalem to the Nineteenth Century. *2 vols., 12mo, half sheep; with autograph of Gorham Parsons.* Boston, 1812

20 ADAMS, JOHN. THE WORKS OF. With a Life of the Author, Notes, and Illustrations; by his Grandson, Charles Francis Adams. *Portraits and plates. 10 vols., imperial 8vo, cloth, uncut.* LARGE PAPER. Boston, 1850–56

21 ADAMS, JOHN. ANOTHER COPY: *small paper. Portraits, etc.* 10 *vols.*, 8*vo, cloth.* Boston, 1850–56

22 ADAMS, JOHN. A DEFENCE OF THE CONSTITUTIONS OF GOVERNMENT OF THE UNITED STATES OF AMERICA (in Answer to M. Turgot and others). 3 *vols.*, 8*vo, old calf, yellow edges.* C. Dilly and J. Stockdale, London, 1787–88

23 ADAMS, JOHN, and WILLIAM CUNNINGHAM. CORRESPONDENCE BETWEEN; beginning in 1803, and ending in 1812. 8*vo, paper, rough edges.* Boston, 1823

24 ADAMS, JOHN, and THOMAS JEFFERSON. A SELECTION OF EULOGIES, pronounced in the Several States, in Honor of those Illustrious Patriots and Statesmen. 8*vo, boards, rough edges.* Hartford, 1826

25 ADAMS, JOHN QUINCY. AN INAUGURAL ORATION, delivered at the Author's Installation as Boylston Professor of Rhetoric and Oratory, at Harvard University, in Cambridge, 12 June, 1806. 8*vo, pp.* 28, *clean.* Boston, 1806

26 ADAMS, JOHN QUINCY. ORATION ON THE LIFE AND CHARACTER OF LAFAYETTE, delivered at the Request of Both Houses of the Congress of the United States, at Washington, 31st December, 1834. 8*vo, pp.* 94, *clean.* Washington, 1835

27 ADAMS, JOHN QUINCY. SPEECH [SUPPRESSED BY THE PREVIOUS QUESTION] on the Removal of the Public Deposites. 8*vo, pp.* 43, *clean.* Washington, 1834

28 ADDISON, JOSEPH. THE WORKS; with a Complete Index. *Portrait by Miller, after Kneller, and plates by Grignion, after Hayman, etc.* 4 *vols., royal* 4*to, marbled calf, gilt, yellow edges.* BASKERVILLE'S ELEGANT EDITION: *fine clean copy.* Birmingham, 1761

Baskerville's books are seldom found so free from stains as this copy.

29 ADDISON, JOSEPH. THE MISCELLANEOUS WORKS, IN PROSE AND VERSE, with some Account of the Life and Writings of the Author, by Mr. Tickell. *Portrait and plates after Hayman, etc.* 4 *vols.*, 8*vo, marbled calf, gilt, yellow edges; with bookplate of Geo. Hen. Barnett.* J. & R. Tonson, London, 1765

30 ADDISON, JOSEPH. Another copy. *Same title. Portrait and plates.* 3 *vols.*, 12*mo, old calf.* London, 1777

31 ADOLPHUS, JOHN. MEMOIRS OF JOHN BANNISTER, COMEDIAN. *Two portraits of Bannister.* 2 *vols.*, 8*vo, cloth, uncut.* London, 1839

32 ADVENTURES (THE) OF CATULLUS, AND HISTORY OF HIS AMOURS WITH LESBIA; intermixt with Translations of his Choicest Poems. By Several Hands: done from the French. *Frontispiece by M. Vander Gucht.* 12*mo, old calf.* J. Chantry, London, 1707

33 ADVENTURES (THE) OF UNCLE SAM, IN SEARCH AFTER HIS LOST HONOR; by Frederick Augustus Fidfaddy, Esq., Member of the Legion of Honor, Scratch-etary to Uncle

Sam, and Privy Counsellor to Himself. *12mo, boards, rough edges.* Middletown, 1816

34 ÆSOP, THE FABLES OF; paraphras'd in Verse, adorn'd with Sculpture, and illustrated with Annotations. The Second Edition. By John Ogilby, Esq. *Portrait of Ogilby by Faithorne, besides the other plates by Hollar. Folio, old calf.* Printed by T. Roycroft for the Author, London, 1668

35 ÆSOP. FABLES AND STORYES MORALIZED; being a Second Part of the Fables of Æsop, and other Eminent Mythologists, etc. By Sir Roger L'Estrange, Kt. (With Life of Æsop.) *Title to first part wanting. Frontispiece. 2 vols., folio, old calf.* London, (1694)–99

36 AGASSIZ, LOUIS JEAN RUDOLF. CONTRIBUTIONS TO THE NATURAL HISTORY OF THE UNITED STATES OF AMERICA. *Plates. Vols. I.–IV., 4to, cloth.* Boston, 1857–62

37 AIKIN, JOHN. LETTERS FROM A FATHER TO HIS SON, relative to Literature and the Conduct of Life; written in the Years 1792 and 1793 (with a Second Volume of Letters written in the Years 1798 and 1799). *Third and second editions. 2 vols., crown 8vo, old calf.* London, 1796–1803

38 AINSWORTH, WILLIAM HARRISON. THE TOWER OF LONDON. *Illustrated by George Cruikshank. 8vo, half calf, extra, marbled edges.* London, 1840

39 AINSWORTH, WILLIAM HARRISON. WINDSOR CASTLE. *Illustrated by George Cruikshank and Tony Johannot, with Designs on Wood by W. Alfred Delamotte. 8vo, half calf, extra, marbled edges.* London, 1844

40 AKENSIDE, MARK. THE POEMS OF. *Printed on writing-paper by Bowyer and Nichols. Profile portrait by E. Fisher. 4to, marbled calf, green edges, fine copy.* J. Dodsley, London, 1772

41 ALCIATI, ANDREA. EMBLEMATA V. CL. ANDREAE ALCIATI CŪ IMAGINIBUS PLERISQUE RESTITUTIS AD MENTEM AUCTORIS; adjecta Compendiosâ Explicatione Claudii Minois Divionensis, et Notulis Extemporariis Laurentii Pignorii Patavini. *Plate title, and fine impressions of the numerous wood-cuts. Small 8vo, calf, neat.* Apud P. P. Tozzium, Patavii, 1622 (?)

42 ALCOCK, SIR RUTHERFORD. THE CAPITAL OF THE TYCOON: a Narrative of a Three Years' Residence in Japan. *Maps, colored plates, and wood-cuts, illustrative of manners, costumes, etc. 2 vols., 8vo, cloth, uncut.* London, 1863

43 ALEMAN, MATEO. HISTOIRE DE L'ADMIRABLE DON GUZMAN D'ALFARACHE. *Plates. 3 vols., small 12mo, half morocco, red edges.* M. Cramoisy, Paris, 1695

This work, which was originally written in Spanish, about the middle of the sixteenth century, may be considered, in a measure, as the parent of "Gil Blas." It has also been translated ("purgée des moralités superflues") by Le Sage.

44 ALEXANDER, SIR JAMES EDWARD. TRAVELS TO THE SEAT OF WAR IN THE EAST, through Russia and the Crimea,

in 1829; with Sketches of the Imperial Fleet and Army, Personal Adventures, and Characteristic Anecdotes. *Map, plates, and wood-cuts; the plates of military uniform, colored.* 2 *vols. in* 1, 8*vo, half morocco.* London, 1830

45 ALEXANDER, SIR JAMES EDWARD. L'ACADIE, or Seven Years' Explorations in British America. *Plates.* 2 *vols.*, 12*mo, cloth, uncut.* London, 1849

46 ALEXANDER, WILLIAM, M. D. THE HISTORY OF WOMEN, from the Earliest Antiquity to the Present Time; giving some Account of almost every Interesting Particular concerning that Sex, among all Nations, Ancient and Modern. 2 *vols.*, 8*vo, marbled calf, gilt, green edges.* Dublin, 1779

47 ALISON, REV. ARCHIBALD. ESSAYS ON THE NATURE AND PRINCIPLES OF TASTE. From the Edinburgh Edition of 1811. 8*vo, old calf.* Boston, 1812

48 ALISON, REV. ARCHIBALD. ESSAYS ON THE NATURE AND PRINCIPLES OF TASTE. The Fifth Edition. 2 *vols.*, 8*vo, boards, rough edges.* Edinburgh, 1817

49 ALISON, SIR ARCHIBALD. TRAVELS IN FRANCE, during the Years 1814–15; comprising a Residence at Paris during the Stay of the Allied Armies, and at Aix, at the Period of the Landing of Bonaparte. Second Edition. 2 *vols. in* 1, 8*vo, half calf, extra.* Edinburgh, 1816

50 ALISON, SIR ARCHIBALD. HISTORY OF EUROPE; from the Commencement of the French Revolution in 1789, to the Restoration of the Bourbons in 1815. 4 *vols.*, 8*vo, cloth.* New York, 1844–45

51 ALKEN, HENRY. THE NATIONAL SPORTS OF GREAT BRITAIN; with Descriptions in English and French. *A series of* 50 *large colored plates, of racing, hunting, shooting, fishing, prize-fighting, cock-fighting, bull-baiting, etc., etc. Royal folio, morocco extra, gilt edges.* London, 1823

52 ALL THE YEAR ROUND; a Weekly Journal, conducted by Charles Dickens; with which is incorporated Household Words. *Oct.* 29, 1859–*March* 23, 1861. 4 *vols.*, 8*vo, first two, cloth; rest in numbers.* London, 1859–61

53 ALLAN, JOHN H. A PICTORIAL TOUR IN THE MEDITERRANEAN; including Malta, Dalmatia, Turkey, Asia Minor, Grecian Archipelago, Egypt, Nubia, Greece, Ionian Islands, Sicily, Italy, and Spain. *Illuminated title,* 40 *large tinted plates, and wood-cut vignettes. Imperial* 4*to, cloth.* London, 1843

54 ALLASON, THOMAS. PICTURESQUE VIEWS OF THE ANTIQUITIES OF POLA, IN ISTRIA; with Remarks on the Ancient and Modern History of Istria and Dalmatia elucidatory of the Origin, Manners, and Customs of their Present Inhabitants. *With plates engraved by W. B. and G. Cooke, H. Moses, and C. Armstrong, after J. M. W. Turner, etc. Imperial folio, boards, leather back, rough edges.* J. Murray, London, 1819

55 ALLEN, William. An American Biographical and Historical Dictionary; containing an Account of the Lives, Characters, and Writings of the most Eminent Persons in North America, from its First Discovery to the Present Time, and a Summary of the History of the Several Colonies and of the United States. *Portrait of Washington inserted. Royal 8vo, boards, rough edges.* Cambridge, 1809

56 ALLIBONE, Samuel Austin. A Critical Dictionary of English Literature, and British and American Authors, Living and Deceased, from the Earliest Accounts to the Middle of the Nineteenth Century; containing Thirty Thousand Biographies and Literary Notices, with Forty Indexes of Subjects. *Vol. I., imperial 8vo, cloth.* Philadelphia, 1863

Vols. II. and III., which complete the work, are just published.

57 ALUMNI HALL: an Appeal to the Alumni and Friends of Harvard College. *Plan and description. 8vo, pp.* 23. Cambridge, 1866

58 AMERICA: the Second Part, containing the Topographicall Description of the Several Provinces, both of the Northern and Southern Part ; with some Observations incident thereunto. By N. N. Both parts. 1 *vol., small 8vo, half calf.* E. Dod, London, (1655)

The title to the first part ("America, or an Exact Description of the West Indies," etc.) is wanting; otherwise a perfect copy.

59 AMERICAN (The) Almanac and Repository of Useful Knowledge. *Complete from the commencement in* 1830 *to* 1861, *inclusive.* 32 *vols.*, 12*mo, half green morocco.* Fine set. Boston, 1830–61

60 AMERICAN (The) Almanac, etc. *For the year* 1847. 12*mo, half russia.* Boston, 1846

61 AMERICAN (The) Almanac, etc. *For the year* 1861. 12*mo, half green morocco.* Boston, 1861

62 AMERICAN (The) Freemason; an Organ of Ancient Craft Masonry. [Edited by R. Morris, F. M. King, and Dr. Mackey.] *Oct.* 15, 1855–*Feb.* 1858, 37 *nos. (newspaper)*, 8 *pp. each, and* 2 *nos.* (8*vo*), 80 *pp. each.* Louisville, 1856–58

63 AMERICAN (The) Quarterly Observer. *July*, 1833–*Oct.* 1834, 3 *vols.*, 8*vo, half morocco.* Boston, 1833–34

64 AMERICAN (The) Quarterly Register and Magazine: conducted by James Stryker. *May*, 1848–*July*, 1850. 4 *vols.*, 8*vo, half russia.* Philadelphia, (1848–50)

65 AMERICAN (The) Quarterly Review of Freemasonry and its Kindred Sciences; edited by Albert G. Mackey, M. D., etc. *Vol. I., July, A. L.* 5857–*April, A. L.* 5858. 8*vo, half morocco.* New York, 1858

66 AMERICAN (The) Traveller; being a New Historical Collection carefully compiled from Original Memoirs in Several Languages, and the most Authentic Voyages and Travels; con-

taining a Compleat Account of that Part of the World, now called the West Indies, from its Discovery by Columbus to the Present Time. Illustrated with Heads of the most Eminent Admirals, Commanders, and Travellers, neatly engraved. To which is prefixed an Introduction, shewing the Rise, Progress, and Improvement of Navigation; the Use and Properties of the Loadstone; and an Enquiry concerning the First Inhabitants of America: With an Account of Admiral Vernon's taking Porto-Bello, Fort Chagre, and Carthagenna; as also of the Damages done on Each Side, and the Number of British Ships taken by the Spaniards and Spanish Ships taken by the English since the Commencement of the War. *With a frontispiece, portraits of Cortes and Drake, and a plate lettered "Spanish Gratitude: Cortes orders Montezuma to be Fetter'd." Small 8vo, new sprinkled calf, gilt.* J. Fuller, London, 1743

This edition is not mentioned by Rich. The edition of 1741 does not contain the "Account of Admiral Vernon's taking Porto Bello," etc., which has been added to this in a smaller type, commencing at p. 391.

67 AMES, FISHER. WORKS OF; compiled by a Number of his Friends. To which are prefixed Notices of his Life and Character. *Portrait after Stuart. 8vo, old calf.* Boston, 1809

68 AMES, FISHER. WORKS OF; with a Selection from his Speeches and Correspondence. Edited by his Son, Seth Ames. *Portrait. 2 vols., 8vo, tree calf, gilt, marbled edges, by Riviere.* Boston, 1854

69 AMORY, THOMAS. THE LIFE OF JOHN BUNCLE, ESQ. A New Edition. *3 vols., crown 8vo, half calf, neat. Best edition.* S. Prowett, London, 1825

70 AMOS, ANDREW. THE GREAT OYER OF POISONING: the Trial of the Earl of Somerset for the Poisoning of Sir Thomas Overbury, in the Tower of London, and Various Matters connected therewith; from Contemporary MSS. *Portraits. 8vo, cloth, uncut.* London, 1846

71 ANACREON. ΑΝΑΚΡΕΟΝΤΟΣ ΤΗΙΟΥ ΜΕΛΗ, praefixo Commentario quo Poëtae Genus traditur et Bibliotheca Anacreonteia adumbratur. Additis Var. Lect. *Small square 8vo, dark blue morocco, gilt edges. Vellum paper, printed in capital letters.* In Aedibus Palatinis (Bodoni), Parmae, 1791

Only a few copies of this beautiful edition were printed upon vellum paper.

72 ANACREON, ODES OF, translated into English Verse, by Thomas Moore, Esq. Fourth Edition. *Portrait of Moore by Heath, and medallion of Anacreon by H. Richter. 2 vols., foolscap 8vo, half morocco, gilt tops.* J. Carpenter, London, 1804

73 ANDERDON, JOHN LAVICOUNT. THE RIVER DOVE; with some Quiet Thoughts on the Happy Practice of Angling. [By J. L. Anderdon.] *Foolscap 8vo, cloth, uncut.* W. Pickering, London, 1847

74 ANDERSEN, Hans Christian. Tales for Children. Translated by Alfred Wehnert. *With* 105 *Illustrations by E. H. Wehnert, W. Thomas, and others. Crown* 8*vo, cloth, gilt edges.* New York, 1861

75 ANDERSEN, Hans Christian. Stories and Tales, Translated by H. W. Dulcken. *With* 80 *Illustrations by A. W. Baynes, engraved by the Brothers Dalziel. Square* 8*vo, cloth.* London, 1865

76 ANDERSEN, Hans Christian. What the Moon Saw, and other Tales. Translated by H. W. Dulcken. *With* 80 *Illustrations by A. W. Baynes, engraved by the Brothers Dalziel. Square* 8*vo, cloth.* London, 1866

77 ANDERSON, Christopher, D. D. The Annals of the English Bible. *Portrait of Tyndale and fac-similes.* 2 *vols.,* 8*vo, polished calf, gilt, gilt tops.* W. Pickering, London, 1845

78 ANDERSON, Christopher, D. D. The Annals of the English Bible. *Portrait, etc.* 2 *vols.,* 8*vo, half morocco, gilt tops.* W. Pickering, London, 1845

Both copies contain the "Historical Index."

79 ANDERSON, D. Belle Scott, or the Crisis of Freedom. Fourth Edition. 12*mo, cloth.* Boston, s. a.

80 ANDERSON, James. The Constitutions of the Free-Masons: containing the History, Charges, Regulations, etc., of that most Ancient and Right Worshipful Fraternity. For the Use of the Lodges. [Compiled by James Anderson.] *Fac-simile reprint of the London edition of* 1723. 4*to, cloth.* New York, 1855

81 ANDERSON, Brig.-Gen. Robert. Evolutions of Field Batteries of Artillery. *Plates.* 18*mo, cloth.* New York, 1860

82 ANDREANA: containing the Trial, Execution, and Various Matter connected with the History of Major John Andre, Adjutant General of the British Army in America, A. D. 1780. (With an Introduction by Horace W. Smith.) *With* 12 *plates of portraits, fac-similes, etc.* 8*vo, half green morocco, neat, gilt top.* Only 175 copies printed: 25 *in folio,* 50 *in quarto,* 100 *in octavo.* Philadelphia, 1865

83 ANDREW, John Albion. Valedictory Address, to the Legislature of Massachusetts, January 4, 1866. 8*vo, pp.* 42. Boston, 1866

84 ANDREWS, Alexander. The History of British Journalism, from the Foundation of the Newspaper Press in England to the Repeal of the Stamp Act in 1855; with Sketches of Press Celebrities. *Index.* 2 *vols., crown* 8*vo, half green calf, extra.* London, 1859

85 ANDREWS, Ethan Allen. A Copious and Critical Latin-English Lexicon, founded on the Larger Latin-Ger-

man Lexicon of Dr. William Freund; with Additions and Corrections from the Lexicons of Gesner, Facciolati, Scheller, Georges, etc. *Thick royal 8vo, sheep.* New York, 1856

86 ANDREWS, ETHAN ALLEN, and S. STODDARD. A GRAMMAR OF THE LATIN LANGUAGE, etc. *12mo, half roan.* Boston, 1852

87 ANDREWS, HENRY C. THE HEATHERY, or a Monograph of the Genus Erica; containing Coloured Engravings, with Latin and English Descriptions, Dissections, etc., of all the Known Species of that Extensive and Distinguished Tribe of Plants. Second Edition, corrected and enlarged. *Engraved title and 300 plates. 6 vols., royal 8vo, cloth.* H. G. Bohn, London, 1845

88 ANDREWS, LANCELOT, BISHOP OF WINCHESTER, ETC. ΑΠΟΣΠΑΣΜΑΤΙΑ SACRA, or a Collection of Posthumous and Orphan Lectures; delivered at St. Pauls and St. Giles his Church. Never before extant. *Folio, calf, gilt; portrait wanting.* London, 1657

"The most popular of all his productions." — *Lowndes.*

89 ANECDOTES OF POLITE LITERATURE. *5 vols., small 8vo, old calf; with book-plate of Mr. Horatio Walpole.* G. Burnett, London, 1764

"An amusing and judicious selection, very neatly printed." — *Lowndes.*

90 ANICETUS. (*Pseudonym.*) OUR MODERN ATHENS, or Who is First? A Poem. *12mo, cloth.* Boston, 1860

91 ANICETUS. (*Pseudonym.*) THE LEARNED WORLD. A Poem. *12mo, cloth.* Boston, 1864

92 ANNIVERSARY (THE) CALENDAR, NATAL BOOK, AND UNIVERSAL MIRROR; embracing Anniversaries of Persons, Events, Institutions, and Festivals of all Denominations, Historical, Sacred, and Domestic, in every Period and State of the World, from the Creation to the Present Age. *Printed by Whittingham, with a border around each page. 2 vols., royal 8vo, boards, rough edges.* LARGE PAPER. W. Kidd, London, 1832

93 ANNUAL (THE) REGISTER, or a View of the History, Politicks, and Literature, for the Year. *From* 1758 *to* 1782, *inclusive.* 25 *vols.*, 8*vo*; 22 *old calf*, 3 *half bound. Book-plate of Francis Enys in some of the volumes.* J. Dodsley, London, 1760–91

For full account of this valuable publication see Bohn's "Lowndes," p. 48.

94 ANTHON, CHARLES. A CLASSICAL DICTIONARY, containing an Account of the Principal Proper Names mentioned in Ancient Authors, etc. Together with an Account of Coins, Weights, Measures, etc. *Thick royal 8vo, sheep.* New York, 1841

95 ANTI-JACOBIN. POETRY OF THE ANTI-JACOBIN: comprising the Celebrated Political & Satirical Poems, Parodies, and Jeux-d'Esprit of the Right Hon. George Canning; the

Earl of Carlisle; Marquis Wellesley; the Right Hon. J. H. Frere; W. Gifford, Esq.; the Right Hon. W. Pitt; G. Ellis, Esq., and others. With Explanatory Notes, by Charles Edmonds. Second Edition, considerably enlarged; with six Etchings by the Famous Caricaturist, James Gillray. *Foolscap 8vo, cloth, uncut.* G. Willis, London, 1854

96 ANTIQUARIAN (The) Repertory; a Miscellany intended to Preserve and Illustrate Several Valuable Remains of Old Times. [Compiled by, or under the Direction of, Francis Grose, Thomas Astle, and other Eminent Antiquaries.] Adorned with Elegant Sculptures. *Fine impressions of the plates. 4 vols. in 2. 4to, cloth.* Original edition. London, 1775–84

97 ANTIQUARIAN (The) Repertory; a Miscellaneous Assemblage of Topography, History, Biography, Customs, and Manners, intended to Illustrate and Preserve Several Valuable Remains of Old Times: chiefly compiled by, or under the direction of, Francis Grose, Esq., F. R. & A. S.; Thomas Astle, Esq., F. R. & A. S.; and other Eminent Antiquaries. Adorned with Numerous Views, Portraits, and Monuments. A New Edition, with many Valuable Additions, [edited by Edward Jeffery]. *4 vols., royal 4to, half russia.*
E. Jeffery, London, 1807–09

The fourth volume contains the Earl of Northumberland's Household-Book, edited by Bp. Percv, two portraits (dressed and undressed) of Jane Shore, a copious General Index, etc.

98 ANTIQUITÉS Mexicaines. Relation des Trois Expéditions du Colonel Dupaix, ordonnées en 1805, 1806, et 1807, par le Roi Charles IV. pour la Recherche des Antiquités du Pays, notamment celles de Mitla et de Palenque; avec les Dessins de Castañeda, Dessinateur en Chef des Trois Expeditions, &c., et une Carte des Pays explorés; suivie d'un Parallèle de ces Monuments avec ceux de l'Égypte et de l'Inde, par M. Alexandre Lenoir; d'une Dissertation sur l'Origine et sur la Linguistique des Populations Primitives des Deux Amériques, d'un Historique des Diverses Antiquités et des Fossiles du Double Continent, par M. Warden; avec un Discours Préliminaire des Travaux et Documents Divers, de MM. de Chateaubriand, Farcy, Galindo, de Humboldt et de St. Priest, et plusieurs autres Voyageurs qui ont visité l'Amérique. *Index to each part. Plates large and finely colored. 2 vols., imperial folio, half crimson morocco.* Fine copy of this valuable work. Paris, 1834–44

99 ANTOMMARCHI, Francesco, M. D. The Last Days of Napoleon: Memoirs of the Last Two Years of Napoleon's Exile, by F. Antommarchi; forming a Sequel to the Journals of Dr. O'Meara and Count Las Cases. Second Edition. *2 vols. in 1, 8vo, cloth, uncut.* London, 1826

100 APPULEIUS, Lucius. The Metamorphosis, or Golden

Ass; and Philosophical Works of. Translated from the Original Latin, by Thomas Taylor. *8vo, boards, rough edges.* R. Triphook, London, 1822

This copy contains, at the end, the suppressed passages.
"An esteemed version by the translator of Plato and Aristotle."—*Lowndes.*

101 APPULEIUS, LUCIUS. THE BIRTH OF PLEASURE; the Story of Cupid and Psyche. *From the "Golden Ass." Post 8vo, cloth.* New York, 1867

102 ARABIAN TALES, OR A CONTINUATION OF THE ARABIAN NIGHTS ENTERTAINMENTS; consisting of Stories related by the Sultana of the Indies, to divert her Husband from the Performance of a Rash Vow, exhibiting a most Interesting View of the Religion, Laws, Manners, Customs, Arts, and Literature, of the Nations of the East. Newly translated from the Original Arabic into French, by Dom Chavis and M. Cazotte; and translated from the French into English, by Robert Heron [John Pinkerton?]. *4 vols., 12mo, old calf.* Edinburgh, 1792

103 ARAGO, JACQUES ÉTIENNE VICTOR. SOUVENIRS D'UN AVEUGLE VOYAGE DU MONDE. Nouvelle Édition, revue et augmentée; *illustrée de 22 Grandes Vignettes, Portraits, et de 150 Gravures dans le Texte.* Enrichée de Notes Scientifiques, par M. François Arago; et précédée d'une Introduction, par M. Jules Janin. Fourth Edition. *2 vols. in 1, half crimson morocco, very neat, gilt edges.* Lebrun, Paris, s. a.

104 ARBLAY, MADAME D'. DIARY AND LETTERS OF; edited by her Niece. *2 vols., 8vo, half calf; with autograph of Rufus Choate.* Philadelphia, 1842

105 ARCHER, JOHN WYKEHAM. VESTIGES OF OLD LONDON: a Series of Etchings from Original Drawings, illustrative of the Monuments and Architecture of London, in the First Fourth, Twelfth, and Six Succeeding Centuries; with Descriptions and Historical Notes. *Contains 37 plates. Imperial 4to, half morocco.* London, 1851

106 ARCHITECTURE. MODERN COTTAGE AND VILLA ARCHITECTURE; *consisting of 19 colored plates of elevations, with landscapes after drawings by G. F. Bragge and F. Sexton Without title. 2 vols. oblong folio, cloth.* Williams & Co. (London), s. a.

107 ARIOSTO, LODOVICO. ORLANDO FURIOSO. Translated from the Italian, with Notes, by John Hoole. *Portraits of Hoole and Ariosto, and plates by Bartolozzi, Heath, etc., after Stothard, Aug. Kauffmann, etc. 5 vols., royal 8vo, old marbled calf, gilt, yellow edges.* LARGE PAPER: *fine copy.* London, 179[illegible]

108 ARIOSTO, LODOVICO. ANOTHER COPY: *the same, small paper; with 10 additional plates, by Hall after Mortimer, inserted in first volume. 5 vols., old mottled calf.* London, 179[illegible]

109 ARIOSTO, LODOVICO. ROLAND FURIEUX; Poëme Héroïque: avec Figures. Traduction Nouvelle, par M. le Comte de Tressan. EXTRAIT DE ROLAND L'AMOUREUX de Matheo-Maria Boyardo, Comte de Scandiano; par M. le Comte de Tressan. *Fine portrait of Ariosto, and* 46 *of the plates engraved by Ponce, after Cochin, for the translation by d' Ussieux. Together,* 4 *vols.,* 4*to, diamond calf, neat.* LARGE PAPER: *fine copy.* Paris, (1804)

110 ARIOSTO, LODOVICO. L'ORLANDO FURIOSO; con le Dichiarazioni di Giovannandrea Barotti, e d'altri: e gli Argomenti dei Quattro Comentatori, Anguillara, Ammirato, Dolce, e Verdizzotti; preceduto per la Prima Volte da molte Illustrazioni Storiche e Romanzesche su Carlo Magno, i Paladini di Francia ed altri Personaggi Distinti rammentati nel Poema, Necessaie per la Perfetta Intelligenza del medesimo; e corredato d'un Discorso sul Blasone e sull' Arte Araldica, proseguito da un Vocabulario di tutte le Armi ed Armature Antiche. Edizione adorna di 100 Tavole in Rame, designate di Giuseppe Gozzini. 3 *vols., royal* 8*vo, half morocco.*
A. & S. Batelli, Firenze, 1844–50

111 ARISTOTLE. TREATISE ON POETRY, TRANSLATED: with Notes on the Translation and on the Original; and Two Dissertations, on Poetical, and Musical, Imitation. By Thomas Twining. The Second Edition, by Daniel Twining. 2 *vols.,* 8*vo, tree calf, gilt, marbled edges.*
T. Cadell, etc., London, 1812

"Of this translation all the literary journals have spoken in terms of very high and justly-merited praise." — *Lowndes.*

112 ARISTOTLE. ETHICS AND POLITICS, comprising his Practical Philosophy, translated from the Greek: illustrated by Introductions and Notes; the Critical History of his Life; and a New Analysis of his Speculative Works; by John Gillies, LL. D., etc. The Third Edition. 2 *vols.,* 8*vo, tree calf, gilt, marbled edges.* T. Cadell, etc., London, 1813

"A translation executed with strict fidelity and great classical taste."—*Lowndes.*

113 ARISTOTLE. RHETORIC, with an Introduction and Appendix, Explaining its Relation to his Exact Philosophy, and Vindicating that Philosophy, by Proofs that all Departures from it have been Deviations into Error; by John Gillies, LL. D., etc. 8*vo, tree calf, gilt, marbled edges.*
T. Cadell, London, 1823

"An excellent translation." — *Lowndes.*

114 ARMY (THE) LISTS OF THE ROUNDHEADS AND CAVALIERS, containing the Names of the Officers in the Royal and Parliamentary Armies of 1642; edited by Edward Peacock, F. S. A. *Handsomely printed, with head-pieces and ornate initials, at the Chiswick Press. Foolscap* 4*to, half morocco, red paper sides, gilt top. Very few copies printed.*
J. C. Hotten, London, 1863

Reprint of a comparatively unknown tract, in the Bodleian Library, entitled

"A Catalogue of the Names of the Dukes, Marquesses, Earles and Lords, that have absented themselves from the Parliament, and are now with his Majesty, etc., etc. Printed 1642."

115 ARNAULD, ANTOINE. LA LOGIQUE, OU L'ART DE PENSER; contenant outre les Règles Communes, plusieurs Observations Nouvelles, propres à former le Jugement. Sixiéme Édition, revûe & de nouveau augmentée. *12mo, old calf; with autograph of J. G. Percival.* G. Desprez, Paris, 1730

116 ARNOLD, AUGUSTUS C. L. THE RATIONALE AND ETHICS OF FREEMASONRY, or the Masonic Institution considered as a Means of Social and Individual Progress. *12mo, cloth.* New York, 1858

117 ARNOLD, GEORGE. DRIFT; A SEA-SHORE IDYL; and other Poems. (Edited, with a Memoir, by Will. Winter.) *Portrait. Square post 8vo, cloth, gilt top.* Boston, 1866

Arnold was author of the "McArone" papers, which appeared in "Vanity Fair," etc.

118 ARNOLD, HOWARD PAYSON. EUROPEAN MOSAIC. *Post 8vo, cloth, gilt top.* Boston, 1864

119 ARNOLD, RICHARD. THE CUSTOMS OF LONDON, OTHERWISE CALLED ARNOLD'S CHRONICLE; containing among Divers other Matters, the Original of the celebrated Poem of the Nut-Brown Maid. Reprinted from the First Edition with Additions included in the Second. *Royal 4to, russia neat, marbled edges. Uniform with Fabyan, Froissart, Grafton, Hall, Hardyng, Holinshed, Monstrelet, and Rastell.* London, 1811

"A faithful reprint with a judicious introduction, by Francis Douce, Esq. Warton observes of this work, that it is perhaps the most heterogeneous and multifarious miscellany that ever existed." — *Lowndes.*

120 ARNOLD, THOMAS, D. D. INTRODUCTORY LECTURES ON MODERN HISTORY, delivered in Lent Term, MDCCCXLII; with the Inaugural Lecture delivered in December, MDCCCXLI. Second Edition. *8vo, calf, gilt, marbled edges.* London, 1843

121 ARNOLD, THOMAS, D. D. HISTORY OF ROME. Third Edition. *3 vols, 8vo, calf, gilt, marbled edges.* London, 1844–45

122 ARNOLD, THOMAS, D. D. THE LIFE AND CORRESPONDENCE OF. By Arthur Penrhyn Stanley, M. A.; etc. Fourth Edition. *Portrait. 2 vols., 8vo, calf, gilt, marbled edges.* London, 1845

The above six volumes are uniformly bound.

123 ARNOULT, EMILE. PRONOUNCING READING BOOK OF THE FRENCH LANGUAGE; Part First. *Royal 8vo, cloth.* Boston, 1857

124 ARROWSMITH, H. W. AND A. THE HOUSE DECORATOR AND PAINTER'S GUIDE; containing a Series of Designs for decorating Apartments, suited to the Various Styles of Architecture. *Letter-press, pp. 120, and 61 plates, chiefly colored. 4to, cloth.* London, (1840)

125 ART (THE) OF CONVERSATION, with Directions for Self Education. *12mo, cloth.* New York, 1864

126 ARTHUR OF LITTLE BRITAIN. THE HISTORY OF THE VALIANT KNIGHT ARTHUR OF LITTLE BRITAIN; a Romance of Chivalry. Originally translated from the French by John Bourchier, Lord Berners. A New Edition (edited by E. V. Utterson); with a Series of Plates, from Illuminated Drawings contained in a Valuable MS. of the Original Romance. *Plates engraved in outline, by C. Heath. Post 4to, boards, rough edges. Only 200 copies printed: 25 of which on large paper.* London, 1814

127 ARTHUR, TIMOTHY SHAY. ADVICE TO YOUNG MEN, AND TO YOUNG LADIES, on their Duties and Conduct in Life. 2 *vols., 16mo, cloth.* Boston, 1858

128 ART UNION AND ART JOURNAL. *From* 1843 *to* 1864, *inclusive; with the "Illustrated Catalogue,"* 1851. *Many hundred beautiful plates and wood-cuts.* 23 *vols.; 4to, and royal 4to, half morocco, marbled edges.* FINE SET, *commencing with Vol. V., "Art Union."* London, 1843–64

129 ARVINE, KAZLITT. THE CYCLOPÆDIA OF ANECDOTES OF LITERATURE AND THE FINE ARTS. The Third Edition. *Numerous wood-cuts. Royal 8vo, cloth.* Boston, 1856

130 ASIATIC (THE) ANNUAL REGISTER; or, a View of the History of Hindustan, and of the Politics, Commerce, and Literature of Asia. [Edited by Lawrence Dundas Campbell and E. Samuels.] *From* 1799 *to* 1810–11, *inclusive.* 12 *vols. in* 13, *8vo, russia, very neat, green edges.* London, 1801–11

The volume for 1806 is bound in two vols.

131 ASTLE, THOMAS. THE ORIGIN AND PROGRESS OF WRITING, as well Hieroglyphic as Elementary; also some Account of the Origin and Progress of Printing. Second Edition, with Additions. *Printed by T. Bensley. Portrait and numerous plates taken from ancient and modern marbles, manuscripts, and charters. Large folio, calf, very neat, marbled edges.* LARGE PAPER: *plates not folded.* London, 1803

132 ATHENÆUM (THE): Journal of Literature, Science, and the Fine Arts. *From Jan.* 3, 1857 (*No.* 1523) *to Dec.* 27, 1862 (*No.* 1835), *inclusive, except No.* 1784 (*Jan.* 4, 1862). 10 *vols., 4to, half morocco, extra, marbled edges; and* 2 *vols. in numbers.* London, 1857–62

133 ATKINSON, CAPTAIN GEORGE FRANCKLIN. THE CAMPAIGN IN INDIA, 1857–58; from Drawings made during the Eventful Period of the Great Mutiny, illustrating the Military Operations before Delhi and its Neighborhood: with Descriptive Letter-Press. *A series of* 26 *large tinted plates. Imperial folio, cloth, emblematically gilt, gilt edges. Slightly injured by water.* London, 1859

134 ATKINSON, THOMAS WITLAM. ORIENTAL AND WESTERN

SIBERIA; a Narrative of Seven Years' Explorations and Adventures in Siberia, Mongolia, the Kirghis Steppes, Chinese Tartary, and Part of Central Asia. *Plate and wood-cuts. 12mo, cloth.* Philadelphia, 1859

135 ATLANTIC (THE) MONTHLY: a Magazine of Literature, Art, and Politics. *From Nov.* 1857 *to Feb.* 1868, *inclusive.* 10 *vols.* (*including Dec.*, 1862), *half morocco, rest in numbers.* Boston, 1857-68

136 AUBREY, JOHN. MISCELLANIES UPON VARIOUS SUBJECTS. The Fourth Edition. *Handsomely printed by Whittingham. Portrait and view of birth-place. Foolscap 8vo, cloth, uncut.* J. R. Smith, London, 1857

Best edition of this very curious work.

137 AUDUBON, JOHN JAMES. ORNITHOLOGICAL BIOGRAPHY, or an Account of the Habits of the Birds of the United States of America; accompanied by Descriptions of the Objects represented in the Work entitled "The Birds of America," and interspersed with Delineations of American Scenery and Manners. *Wood-cuts.* 5 *vols., imperial 8vo, half morocco, neat, gilt edges.* Philadelphia and Edinburgh, 1832-39

The first volume of this copy was printed in Philadelphia, the others in Edinburgh.

138 AUDUBON, JOHN JAMES. THE BIRDS OF AMERICA, from Drawings made in the United States and their Territories. *Descriptive letter-press and* 500 *elegantly colored plates, representing the birds in their most characteristic attitudes, and in many instances both male and female.* 7 *vols., imperial 8vo, half morocco, extra, gilt edges.* ORIGINAL OCTAVO EDITION: *published for subscribers in* 100 *parts.* J. J. Audubon, New York, 1840-44

139 AUGUSTINUS, AURELIUS. DE TRINITATE, ET DE CIVITATE DEI CUM COMMENTO. *Initials painted in red. Together in* 1 *vol., 4to,* 12×8 *inches, boards; with book plate of Thomas Morong.* **Black letter:** *in good condition.* In Friburga, 1494

140 AUSTEN, JANE. PRIDE AND PREJUDICE, a Novel. *Frontispiece and vignette on the engraved title. Foolscap 8vo, cloth, uncut.* London, 1833

141 AUSTEN, JANE. NOVELS: Sense and Sensibility; Pride and Prejudice; Mansfield Park; Emma; Northanger Abbey, and Persuasion (in one vol.). *Frontispieces and vignette titles.* 5 *vols., foolscap 8vo, calf, gilt, marbled edges.* London, 1856

142 AUSTIN, BENJAMIN. CONSTITUTIONAL REPUBLICANISM, in Opposition to Fallacious Federalism; as published Occasionally in the "Independent Chronicle," under the signature of Old-South. To which is prefixed a Prefatory Address to the Citizens of the United States, never before published. *8vo, old marbled calf, yellow edges.* Adams & Rhoades, Boston, 1803

143 AUSTIN, Benjamin. Another copy: *the same.* *8vo, boards, rough edges.* Boston, 1803

144 AUSTIN, Sarah. Fragments from German Prose Writers, translated by Sarah Austin; illustrated with Notes. *12mo, cloth, uncut.* J. Murray, London, 1841

145 AUTHENTIC Memoirs of the Green-Room: including Sketches, Biographical, Critical, and Characteristic, of the Performers of the Theatres Royal, Drury-Lane, Covent-Garden, and the Haymarket; containing Original Lives and Anecdotes, never before published. *Portrait of Miss Stephens ("Miss Young").* *12mo, half green morocco, extra.* J. Roach, London, (1814)

146 AYER, J. C., m. d. Some of the Usages and Abuses in the Management of our Manufacturing Corporations. *8vo, pp.* 24. Lowell, 1863

147 BABES (The) in the Wood. *Ten fine etchings, with the verses.* *Royal 4to, cloth.* J. Cundall, London, 1849

148 BACON, Francis. The Works of Francis Bacon, Baron of Verulam, Viscount St. Albans, and Lord High Chancellor of England: collected and edited by James Spedding, M. A.; Robert Leslie Ellis, M. A.; and Douglas Denon Heath, Barrister-at-Law, etc. *Portraits, fac-similes, etc.* *7 vols., thick 8vo, cloth, uncut; with Autograph of Rufus Choate.* London, 1857–59

149 BACON, Francis. Another copy: *Reprint of the above, with some corrections and additions by Mr. Spedding, and more copious indexes. Portraits on India paper and the arms of Bacon in gold and colors on each title.* *15 vols., half morocco, red paper sides, gilt tops, rough edges.* Large paper: *only* 100 *copies printed for subscribers.* Riverside Press, Cambridge, 1863

Best edition of Bacon's Works, and one of the most beautiful specimens of American typography.

150 BADGER, Mrs. C. M. Floral Belles from the Green-House and Garden; painted from Nature, by Mrs. C. M. Badger. *Consisting of 16 finely colored plates, with poetical selections.* *Royal folio, dark green levant morocco, extra, gilt edges.* New York, 1867

151 BAIARDI, Ottavo Antonio. Le Pitture Antiche d'Ercolano, e Contorni incise; con qualche Spiegazione [da Baiardi]. Tomo Primo. *Engraved title; portrait of Charles III. of Spain, etc.; map; 50 large plates; and numerous vignettes and initials; engraved by F. Morghen, etc.* *Royal folio, old mottled calf, gilt, red edges.* Regia Stamperia, Napoli, 1757

First volume of the original edition of "Le Antichita di Ercolano Esposte."

152 BAILEY, Nathaniel. Dictionarium Britannicum, or a more Compleat Universal Etymological English Dictionary

than any Extant; etc., etc. Illustrated with near Five Hundred Cuts, etc. By N. Bailey, assisted by G. Gordon, P. Miller, and T. Lediard. The Second Edition, with Numerous Additions and Improvements. *Folio, old calf.*
T. Cox, London, 1736

Before the publication of Johnson's this was the standard dictionary, and is still valuable to some students, as it contains many words now become obsolete.

153 BAILLIE, JOANNA. THE DRAMATIC AND POETICAL WORKS OF. *Portrait and engraved title. Thick 8vo, cloth.*
London, 1851

154 BAKER, DAVID ERSKINE. BIOGRAPHIA DRAMATICA, OR A COMPANION TO THE PLAYHOUSE: containing Historical and Critical Memoirs, and Original Anecdotes, of British and Irish Dramatic Writers, from the Commencement of our Theatrical Exhibitions, among whom are some of the most Celebrated Actors; also an Alphabetical Account, and Chronological Lists, of their Works, the Dates when printed, and Observations on their Merits. Together with an Introductory View of the Rise and Progress of the British Stage. Originally compiled, to the Year 1764, by David Erskine Baker; continued thence to 1782, by Isaac Reed; and brought down to the End of November, 1811, with very Considerable Additions and Improvements Throughout, by Stephen Jones. *3 vols. in 4, 8vo, half russia.* London, 1812

155 BALDWIN, JOHN LORAINE. THE LAWS OF SHORT WHIST; edited by J. L. Baldwin. And a Treatise on the Game, by J. C. [James Clay, M. P.] First American Edition, with an Introduction. *16mo, cloth.* New York, 1866

156 BALFOUR, JOHN HUTTON. CLASS BOOK OF BOTANY; being an Introduction to the Study of the Vegetable Kingdom. With upwards of 1,000 Illustrations. (Part I., Structural and Morphological Botany.) *8vo, cloth.*
Edinburgh, 1852

The article "Botany" in the last edition of the "Encyclopædia Britannica" was written by Professor Balfour.

157 BALL, JOHN. PEAKS, PASSES, AND GLACIERS; a Series of Excursions by Members of the Alpine Club. Edited by John Ball, President. Second Edition. *Colored maps, etc., and wood-cuts. 8vo, half morocco.* London, 1859

158 BALLARD, REV. EDWARD. MEMORIAL VOLUME OF THE POPHAM CELEBRATION, August 29, 1862, commemorative of the Planting of the Popham Colony on the Peninsula of Sabino, August 19, O. S., 1607, Establishing the Title of England to the Continent. *Maps, and fac-simile of signature of Sir John Popham. 8vo, cloth.* Portland, 1863

159 BALZAC, HONORÉ DE. ŒUVRES ILLUSTRÉES DE BALZAC. 200 Dessins par MM. Tony Johannot, Staal, Bertall, E. Lampsonius, H. Monnier, Daumier, Meissonnier, etc. *Double columns. 8 vols., 4to, half calf.*

 Maresq & Cie., Paris, 1852–54

160 BALZAC, HONORÉ DE. PETITES MISÈRES DE LA VIE CONJUGALE; illustrées par Bertall. *Imperial 8vo, half green morocco, extra, gilt edges.* Chlendowski, Paris, s. a.

161 BALZAC, HONORÉ DE. THE PETTY ANNOYANCES OF MARRIED LIFE. Translated by O. W. Wight and F. B. Goodrich. *12mo, cloth.* New York, 1861

162 BANCROFT, GEORGE. HISTORY OF THE UNITED STATES; from the Discovery of the American Continent to the Present Time. *Portraits, maps, etchings, etc. 9 vols., 8vo, half morocco, neat.* Boston, 1834–66

The above title is from the first volume, first edition, the words "to the Present Time" having been struck out in the other volumes and also in subsequent editions of this volume.

163 BANCROFT, GEORGE. ANOTHER COPY: *Portraits, etc. Vols. I.–VI., 8vo, calf, very neat.* Boston, 1845–56

164 BANCROFT, GEORGE. ANOTHER COPY: *Photographic portrait, with autograph, of the author; the other portraits on India paper. Vols. I.–VIII., imperial 8vo, cloth, rough edges.* LARGE PAPER: *only 50 copies printed, for C. B. Richardson & Co., New York.* Boston, 1861

Two copies of this large paper edition were destroyed by fire at Mr. Richardson's store in New York, September, 1864. The ninth volume has not yet been issued in this style.

165 BARBAULD, ANNA LÆTITIA. THE WORKS OF; with a Memoir by Lucy Aikin. *Portrait. 2 vols., 8vo, half calf, extra.* London, 1825

166 BARBER, JOSEPH. CRUMBS FROM THE ROUND TABLE; a Feast for Epicures. *Post 8vo, cloth, gilt top.* New York, 1866

167 BARCLAY'S UNIVERSAL DICTIONARY, OR CYCLOPÆDIA OF USEFUL KNOWLEDGE; conformed to the Present State the Arts, Science, and Statistics, by Wm. Willmore Darling, Esq. *Numerous fine plates. 4to, cloth, uncut.* W. Sprent, Hull, s. a.

168 BARCLAY, JOHN. JO. BARCLAII ARGENIS, nunc Primum Illustrata. *Frontispiece (title) and portrait. Small 8vo, vellum.* Ex Officina F. Hackii, Lugd. Bat., 1659

Above the portrait, which is well executed, is engraved "Jo. Barclaius, natus 28 January, 1582, obiit 12 Aprilis, 1621;" and below, "Gente Caledonius, Gallus natalibus, hic est, Romam Romano qui docet ore loqui. — *H. Grotius.*"
["A Scott by blood, — and French by birth, — this man,
At Rome speaks Latin as no Roman can."]

169 BARCLAY, ROBERT. AN APOLOGY FOR THE TRUE CHRISTIAN DIVINITY, as the same is held forth and preached by the People called, in Scorn, Quakers; being a Full Explanation and Vindication of their Principles and Doctrines, by many Arguments, deduced from Scripture and Right Reason, etc., etc. The Sixth Edition in English. *8vo, old calf.* London, 1736

170 BARHAM, REV. RICHARD HARRIS. THE INGOLDSBY LEGENDS, or Mirth and Marvels; by Thomas Ingoldsby, Es-

quire [Barham]. First, Second, and Third Series. *Engraved titles, portraits, plates, and wood-cuts, after George Cruikshank, John Leech, etc. 3 vols., 12mo, cloth, uncut. Fine copy.* Bentley, London, 1855

171 BARHAM, Rev. Richard Harris. Another copy: with a Memoir of the Author. Reprinted from the Tenth English Edition. *Illustrations by Cruikshank and Leech. 2 vols., 12mo, cloth.* Philadelphia, 1860

172 BARLOW, Joel. The Columbiad, a Poem. *Fine portrait, after painting by Fulton, and 11 plates, after paintings by Smirke, engraved by Anker Smith, Schiavonetti, Heath, etc. 4to, calf; with autograph of Dr. Winslow Lewis.* Philadelphia, 1807

173 BARRÉ, Louis. Herculanum et Pompéi: Recueil Général des Peintures, Bronzes, Mosaïques, etc., découverts jusqu' à ce Jour, et reproduits d'après le Antichità di Ercolano, il Museo Borbonico, et tous les Ouvrages Analogues, augmenté de Sujets Inédits; gravés au Trait sur Cuivre, par H. Roux Ainé (et Adr. Bouchet), et accompagné d'un Texte Explicatif par M. L. Barré. Complete, *including the "Musée Secret." 8 vols., royal 8vo, boards, uncut.* Paris, 1839–40

174 BARRÉ, Louis. Another copy: *the same. 8 vols., royal 8vo, half morocco, marbled edges.* Paris, 1839–40

175 BARRERA, Madame A. de. Gems and Jewels: their History, Geography, Chemistry, and Ana; from the Earliest Ages, down to the Present Time. (With a Few Words on Precious Stones, àpropos of this Work, by M. Babinet.) *Crown 8vo, cloth, uncut.* London, 1860

176 BARRETT, Eaton Stannard. The Rising Sun, a Serio-Comic Satiric Romance; by Cervantes Hogg, F. S. M. [Barrett]. *Colored frontispiece. 2 vols., 12mo, sprinkled calf, very neat.* London, 1807

177 BARRETT, Eaton Stannard. Another copy. Fifth Edition; revised, corrected, and enlarged. *Colored frontispieces. 3 vols., 12mo, half calf.* London, 1809

178 BARRETT, Samuel, D. D. Memoir of; with a Selected Series of his Discourses. By Lewis G. Pray. *Post 8vo, cloth.* Boston, 1867

179 BARRI, Giraldus de. The Itinerary of Archbishop Baldwin through Wales, A. D. MCLXXXVIII. Translated into English, and illustrated with Views, Annotations, and a Life of Giraldus; by Sir Richard Colt Hoare, Bart., F. R. S., etc. *Large colored map and 59 plates, comprising portraits, monuments, views, inscriptions, architecture, etc. 2 vols., royal 4to, russia, extra, marbled edges; with book-plate of Charles Chatfield.* London, 1806

"The learned editor's annotations and notes are peculiarly valuable." — *Lowndes.*

180 BARROW, SIR GEORGE. CEYLON; PAST AND PRESENT. With a Map by John Arrowsmith. *Post 8vo, cloth, uncut.* J. Murray, London, 1857

181 BARROW, ISAAC, D. D. THE THEOLOGICAL WORKS OF. *Portrait. 8 vols., 8vo, dark blue turkey morocco, neat, gilt edges.* BEST EDITION. University Press, Oxford, 1830

For contents of this edition see Darling's "Cyclopædia Bibliographica," col. 181–183.

182 BARROW, ISAAC, D. D. A TREATISE ON THE POPE'S SUPREMACY; to which is added, a Discourse concerning the Unity of the Church. A New Edition, corrected. *Portrait. 8vo, cloth.* London, 1851

183 BARRY, JOHN STETSON. THE HISTORY OF MASSACHUSETTS. (Three Periods: Colonial, Provincial, and Commonwealth.) *3 vols., 8vo, cloth.* Boston, 1855–57

184 BARTAS, GILLAUME DE SALLUSTE DU. DU BARTAS HIS DIVINE WEEKES AND WORKES; with a Compleate Colectiō of all the other most Delight-full Workes translated and written by y^t Famous Philomusus, Josuah Sylvester, Gent. *Fine portrait of Sylvester by Corn. v. Dalen, frontispiece (title) by R. Elstracke, and other embellishments. Folio, old calf, red edges.* VERY FINE COPY. R. Young, London, 1633

This edition contains "Tobacco Battered and the Pipes Shattered," etc., "Panthea," "Lachrymæ Lachrymarum," "The Wood-man's Bear," "Monodia," and many other pieces of the "Silver-tong'd Sylvester."

185 BARTHELEMY, JEAN JACQUES. TRAVELS OF ANACHARSIS THE YOUNGER IN GREECE, during the Middle of the Fourth Century before the Christian Æra. Translated from the French [by William Beaumont]. The Fourth Edition, carefully revised, corrected, etc.; with Memoirs of the Life of J. J. Barthelemy, written by himself. *With an atlas containing portrait and maps, plans, views, coins, etc., illustrative of the geography and antiquities of ancient Greece; with critical observations on the maps by M. Barbié du Bocage. 7 vols., 8vo, russia, very neat; and 1 vol., 4to, half russia.* London, 1806

"A faithful and elegant translation of a most interesting work." — *Lowndes.*

186 BARTHÉLEMY, JEAN JACQUES. ANOTHER COPY; Second Edition. *Portrait, maps, etc. 7 vols. 8vo, old marbled calf, yellow edges; and 1 vol., 4to, half calf.* London, 1794

187 BARTHÉLEMY, JEAN JACQUES. VOYAGE DU JEUNE ANACHARSIS, vers le Milieu du Quatrième Siècle avant l'Ère Vulgaire; Nouvelle Édition, ornée du Portrait de l'Auteur, et accompagnée d'un Atlas de 39 Planches, gravées par M. Tardieu. *Seventh volume and atlas wanting. 6 vols., 8vo, sheep, gilt, marbled edges.* Ledoux, Paris, 1821

188 BARTLETT, JOHN RUSSELL. DICTIONARY OF AMERICANISMS: A Glossary of Words and Phrases usually regarded

as peculiar to the United States. Second Edition, greatly improved and enlarged. *Royal 8vo, cloth.* Boston, 1859

189 BARTLETT, JOHN RUSSELL. BIBLIOGRAPHY OF RHODE ISLAND: a Catalogue of Books and other Publications relating to the State of Rhode Island, with Notes, Historical, Biographical, and Critical. *Imperial 8vo, boards, cloth back, red paper sides.* LARGE PAPER: *only 150 copies printed.* Providence, 1864

190 BARTLETT, WILLIAM H. THE NILE BOAT, or Glimpses of the Land of Egypt. Second Edition. *Maps, numerous plates and wood-cuts. Royal 8vo, cloth, gilt, uncut.* London, 1850

191 BARTLETT, WILLIAM H. GLEANINGS, PICTORIAL AND ANTIQUARIAN, ON THE OVERLAND ROUTE. *Maps, plans, numerous plates and wood-cuts. Royal 8vo, cloth, gilt top, uncut.* London, 1851

192 BARTLETT, WILLIAM H. JERUSALEM REVISITED. *Folding view and numerous vignette plates and wood-cuts. Imperial 8vo, cloth, gilt top, uncut.* London, 1855

193 BARTOL, C. A. PICTURES OF EUROPE; framed in Ideas. *12mo, cloth.* Boston, 1855

194 BARTON, BERNARD. HOUSEHOLD VERSES. *Vignettes. Foolscap 8vo, cloth, uncut.* G. Virtue, London, 1845

195 BASAN, PIERRE FRANÇOIS COLLECTION DE CENT-VINGT. ESTAMPES, GRAVÉES D'APRÈS LES TABLEAUX ET DESSINS QUI COMPOSOIENT LE CABINET DE M. POULLAIN; précédée d'un Abrégé Historique de la Vie des Auteurs qui la composent: dédiée à M. le Comte d'Orsay. Cette Suite a été exécutée, sous la Direction du Sieur Fr. Basan, Graveur; par Jeunes Artistes des Deux Sexes, dont les Talens se sont Connoître & Accroissent de Jour en Jour. Le St. Moitte, Peintre, en avoit fait les Dessins, d'après les Tableaux, avant la Mort de ce Célèbre Amateur. ORIGINAL IMPRESSIONS. *4to, half calf, extra; with book-plate of James Thomson.* Paris, 1781

196 BATES, MRS. D. B. INCIDENTS ON LAND AND WATER, or Four Years on the Pacific Coast; etc. Seventh Edition. *Wood-cuts. 12mo, cloth.* Boston, 1858

197 BATES MEMORIAL. A MEMORIAL OF JOSHUA BATES, from the City of Boston. *Portrait and view of the "Bates' Hall," Boston Public Library. 4to, cloth.* Boston, 1865

198 BATES, WILLIAM, D. D. THE HARMONY OF THE DIVINE ATTRIBUTES, in the Contrivance and Accomplishment of Man's Redemption by the Lord Jesus Christ; or Discourses wherein is shewed how the Wisdom, Mercy, Justice, Holiness, Power, and Truth of God are glorified in that Great and Blessed Work. *Small 4to, old calf.* Printed by J. Darby, for N. Ranew, etc., London, 1674

199 BATMAN, STEPHEN, D. D. THE GOLDEN BOOKE OF THE LEADEN GODDES, wherein is described the Vayne Imaginations of Heathē Pagans and Counter-faict Christians; with a Description of their Several Tables, what ech of their Pictures signified. By Stephan Batman, Student in Divinitie. *Engraved title (neatly repaired), and leaves (numbered) 1–36. Small 4to, purple calf; with book-plate of W. P. Turnbull.* **Black Letter.** T. Marshe, London, 1577

"Shakespeare is supposed to have consulted this book, which may be considered as the first attempt towards a Pantheon, or description of the Heathen Gods. A copy is in the British Museum." —*Lowndes.*

200 BATTY, ROBERT. SCENERY OF THE RHINE, BELGIUM, AND HOLLAND; from Drawings by Captn. Batty, of the Grenadier Guards, F. R. S., etc. *Vignette on title,* 61 *fine plates, and* 62 *wood-cut vignettes, engraved by Goodall, Wallis, Finden, and other eminent artists; with descriptions in English and French. Imperial* 8*vo, half morocco, gilt top.*

R. Jennings, London, 1826

See EUROPEAN SCENERY.

201 BAUTAIN, LOUIS EUGÈNE MARIE. THE ART OF EXTEMPORE SPEAKING: Hints for the Pulpit, the Senate, and the Bar. With Additions by a Member of the New York Bar. *Post* 8*vo, cloth.* New York, 1859

202 BAXTER, ANDREW. MATHO, OR THE COSMOTHEORIA PUERILIS; a Dialogue in which the First Principles of Philosophy and Astronomy are accommodated to the Capacity of Young Persons, or such as have yet no Tincture of the Sciences; hence the Principles of Natural Religion are deduced. Translated and enlarged by the Author [Baxter]. *Plates.* 2 *vols.,* 12*mo, old calf.* Dublin, 1742

203 BAXTER, RICHARD. GILDAS SALVIANUS; THE REFORMED PASTOR: shewing the Nature of the Pastoral Work, especially in Private Instruction and Catechizing; with an Open Confession of our too Open Sins. Prepared for a Day of Humiliation kept at Worcester, Decemb. 4, 1655, by the Ministers of that County, who subscribed the Agreement for Catechizing and Personal Instruction, at their Entrance upon that Work; by their Unworthy Fellow-Servant, Richard Baxter, Teacher of the Church at Kederminster. The Second Edition, with an Appendix in Answer to some Objections. *Small thick* 8*vo, old calf; with autographs of Wensley Hobby, præceptor [of George Washington].*

Printed by R. White for N. Simmons, etc., London, 1657

204 BAY PSALM BOOK. A LITERAL REPRINT OF THE BAY PSALM BOOK: being the Earliest New England Version of the Psalms, and the First Book printed in America. 8*vo, cloth, uncut.* PRIVATELY PRINTED: *only* 50 *copies,* 3 *of which were destroyed by fire in* 1864.

Cambridge; printed for C. B. Richardson, New York, 1862

This PERFECT FAC-SIMILE of the original edition (1640) of the "New England

Version of the Psalms" was printed at the Riverside Press. Dr. Shurtleff, who owns a copy of the original and superintended this reprint through the press, in his preface says — after mentioning the literal manner (as regards the copying of defects, errors, etc.) in which it has been executed — "Let the reader, then, give to the printer the credit justly his due; for in this instance he has produced a reprint, such as a reprint of curious old books should be."

205 BAYLE, PIERRE. DICTIONAIRE HISTORIQUE ET CRITIQUE. Troisième Édition; revue, corrigée, et augmentée, par l'Auteur. *Plates on titles by G. Vander Gouwen, after A. Vander Werf, and the* TWO LIVES OF DAVID. *4 vols., folio, old sprinkled calf, gilt, marbled edges.* BEST EDITION : *fine copy.* M. Bohm, Rotterdam, 1720

"Édition la plus belle et qui a été long temps la plus recherchée de ce dictionnaire." — *Brunet.*

206 BEALE, ANNE. SIMPLICITY AND FASCINATION. Third Edition. 12*mo, cloth.* Boston, 1866

207 BEATTIE, JAMES, LL. D., and WILLIAM COLLINS. THE POETICAL WORKS OF. With Memoirs of their Lives and Writings, by Thomas Miller; and Engravings, by Samuel Williams, etc., from Drawings by John Absolon. *Crown 8vo, half morocco, marbled edges.* D. Bogue, London, 1846

208 BEATTIE, WILLIAM. SWITZERLAND. Illustrated in a Series of Views taken expressly for this Work, by W. H. Bartlett, Esq. *Above* 100 *plates.* 2 *vols., 4to, half green morocco, very neat.* London, 1836

209 BEATTIE, WILLIAM. THE CASTLES AND ABBEYS OF ENGLAND; from the National Records, Early Chronicles, and other Standard Authors. *Portrait and above* 200 *engravings on steel and wood. Imperial* 8*vo, cloth, uncut. First series.* London and New York, s. a.

210 BEAUMONT, FRANCIS, and JOHN FLETCHER. THE WORKS OF BEAUMONT and FLETCHER; the Text formed from a New Collation of the Early Editions: with Notes and a Biographical Memoir by the Rev. Alexander Dyce. *Portraits.* 11 *vols., 8vo, tree calf, gilt, marbled edges, by Riviere.* BEST EDITION : *elegant copy.* E. Moxon, London, 1843–46

211 BEAUMONT AND FLETCHER. ANOTHER COPY: *Reprint of the above. Portraits.* 2 *vols., royal 8vo, half calf, extra, marbled edges.* Boston, 1854

212 BEAUTIES (THE) OF ENGLAND AND WALES; or Original Delineations, Topographical, Historical, and Descriptive, of Each County. (By Britton, Brayley, Nightengale, Brewer, Evans, Hodgson, Laird, Shoberl, Bigland, and Rees.) Embellished with Engravings. *Above* 700 *beautiful engravings,* PROOF IMPRESSIONS. *With the* INTRODUCTION, *by J. Norris Brewer.* 19 *vols. in* 26, *royal 8vo, half green turkey morocco, extra, marbled edges. Uniform with "Beauties of Scotland."* LARGE PAPER : *elegant copy.* London, 1801–18

Collation may be found in Bohn's "Lowndes," pp. 139–140. See FORSYTH, ROBERT.

213 BEAUTIES (THE) OF THE BRITISH SENATE; taken from Debates of the Lords and Commons, from the Beginning of the Administration of Sir Robert Walpole, to the End of the Second Session of the Administration of the Right Hon. William Pitt: being an Impartial Selection of, or Faithful Extracts from, the most Eminent Speeches, delivered in the Course of a most Important and Truly Interesting Period of more than Fifty Years; severally arranged under their Respective Heads, with the Names of the Members to whom they are ascribed, annexed thereto. To which is prefixed, the Life of Sir Robert Walpole. *2 vols., 8vo, old marbled calf, green edges.* J. Stockdale, London, 1786

214 BECHSTEIN, JOHANN MATTHAUS, M. D. CAGE AND CHAMBER-BIRDS; their Natural History, Habits, Food, Diseases, Management, and Modes of Capture. Translated from the German; with Considerable Additions on Structure, Migration, and Economy, compiled from Various Sources by H. G. Adams: incorporating the Whole of Sweet's British Warblers. *Plates and wood-cuts. Post 8vo, half calf, extra, marbled edges.* H. G. Bohn, London, 1864

215 BECK, WILHELMINA, BARONESS VON. PERSONAL ADVENTURES DURING THE LATE WAR OF INDEPENDENCE IN HUNGARY. *Portrait of Kossuth. 12mo, cloth.* London, 1851

216 BECKWITH, REV. JOHN H. IMMERSION NOT BAPTISM. *12mo, cloth.* Boston, 1858

217 BEECHER, HENRY WARD. STAR PAPERS, or Experiences of Art and Nature. *12mo, cloth.* New York, 1855

218 BEECHER, HENRY WARD. LIFE THOUGHTS, gathered from the Extemporaneous Discourses of Henry Ward Beecher; by One of his Congregation [Edna Dean Proctor]. *12mo, cloth.* Boston, 1858

219 BELGIUM, THE RHINE, ITALY, GREECE, AND THE SHORES AND ISLANDS OF THE MEDITERRANEAN; with Historical, Classical, and Picturesque Descriptions, by the Rev. G. N. Wright, M. A., and L. F. A. Buckingham, Esq. *A series of 154 finely executed engravings after drawings by Allom and others. 2 vols., 4to, morocco, antique, gilt edges.* P. Jackson, London, s. a.

2 0 BELL, SIR CHARLES. THE ANATOMY AND PHILOSOPHY OF EXPRESSION as connected with the Fine Arts. Third Edition, enlarged. *Plates. Imperial 8vo, cloth.* J. Murray, London, 1844

221 BELL, JOHN. NEW PANTHEON, or Historical Dictionary of the Gods, Demi-Gods, Heroes, and Fabulous Personages of Antiquity, also of the Images and Idols adored in the Pagan World; together with their Temples, Priests, Altars, Oracles, Fasts, Festivals, Games, etc., as well as Descriptions of their Figures, Representations, and Symbols, collected from

Statues, Pictures, Coins, and other Remains of the Ancients. The Whole designed to facilitate the Study of Mythology, History, Poetry, Painting, Statuary, Medals, etc., etc., and compiled from the Best Authorities. Richly embellished with Characteristic Prints. *Fine impressions of the numerous plates, engraved by Grignion, Cook, Condé, etc. 2 vols. in 1, royal 4to, half russia, neat; with book-plate of Edward B. Lewin.* London, 1790

"An excellent and useful compilation." —*Lowndes.*

222 BELL, ROBERT. WAYSIDE PICTURES THROUGH FRANCE, HOLLAND, BELGIUM, AND UP THE RHINE. *Numerous woodcuts by the Dalziels, etc., after Birket Foster and George Measom, including some designs by the author. Post 8vo, cloth.* London, 1858

223 BELLAMY, DANIEL. ETHIC AMUSEMENTS, by Mr. Bellamy; revised by his Son, D. Bellamy. *Frontispiece and 48 curious plates by G. Bickham. 4to, old mottled calf, yellow edges.* London, 1768

There should be 50 plates, but one (numbered 26) is wanting.

224 BELLAMY, GEORGE ANNE, Actress. AN APOLOGY FOR THE LIFE OF; written by herself. To which is annexed, her Original Letter to John Calcraft, Esq., advertised to be published in October, 1767, but which was then Violently Suppressed. The Second Edition. *2 vols., 12mo, old calf; with book-plate of Aaron Putnam, Medford.* Dublin, 1785

225 BELLORI, GIOVANNI PIETRO. PICTURÆ ANTIQUÆ CRYPTARUM ROMANARUM ET SEPULCRI NASONUM, delineatæ & expressæ ad Archetypa a Petro Sancti Bartholi et Francisco ejus Filio; descriptæ vero, & illustratæ a Joanne Petro Belloro et Michaele Angelo Causseo. Opus nunc Primum Latine redditum, proditque absolutius & exactius. *With 75 plates of ancient frescoes, mosaics, arabesques, vases, etc., besides numerous vignettes and initials. Folio, half bound.* Romæ, 1738

226 BELOE, REV. WILLIAM. ANECDOTES OF LITERATURE AND SCARCE BOOKS. *6 vols., half calf; with autograph and book-plate of Henry Thomas Buckle.* London, 1807–12

"A work containing much bibliographical information, and extracts from curious works." — *Lowndes.*

227 BELOE, REV. WILLIAM. THE SEXAGENARIAN, or the Recollections of a Literary Life. [By Beloe.] *2 vols., 8vo, half calf, extra, marbled edges; with autograph of John Clowes.* ORIGINAL EDITION. London, 1817

In the second edition, 1818, much was suppressed.

228 BEMIS, GEORGE. REPORT OF THE CASE OF JOHN W. WEBSTER, indicted for the Murder of George Parkman, before the Supreme Judicial Court of Massachusetts; including the Hearing of the Petition for a Writ of Error, the Prisoner's Confessional Statements and Application for a Com-

mutation of Sentence, and an Appendix containing Several Interesting Matters never before published. By George Bemis, Esq. *View of Mass. Medical College, plans, etc. Royal 8vo, cloth.* Boston, 1850

229 BEMIS, GEORGE. AMERICAN NEUTRALITY; its Honorable Past, its Expedient Future. A Protest against the proposed Repeal of the Neutrality Laws, and a Plea for their Improvement and Consolidation. *8vo, pp.* 211, *paper.* Boston, 1866

230 BENDEMANN, EDUARD. DIE WANDGEMAELDE IM BALL- UND CONCERT-SAAL DES KOENIGLICHEN SCHLOSSES ZU DRESDEN; erfunden und ausgefuehrt von E. Bendemann. 12 Blaetter, in $\frac{1}{16}$ der Natuerl. Groesse, radirt von Hugo Buerkner; mit Erklaerendem Text, von Joh. Gust. Droysen. *Text in English and German. Oblong royal 4to, boards.* E. Arnold, Dresden, s. a.

231 BENEDICT, DAVID, D. D. A GENERAL HISTORY OF THE BAPTIST DENOMINATION IN AMERICA, and other Parts of the World. 2 *vols., 8vo, sheep.* Boston, 1813

232 BENTIVOGLIO, GUIDO, CARDINAL. THE HISTORY OF THE WARRS OF FLANDERS, written in Italian; Englished by Henry Earl of Monmouth. The Whole Work. *Large portrait of Bentivoglio by T. Cross, "Mapp of the XVII. Provinces," and* 23 *other portraits by R. Vaughan, etc. Folio, half calf.* D. Newman, London, 1678

To this edition is prefixed "A Continuation of the History of the Wars of Flanders," 1671–75.

233 BENTLEY'S MISCELLANY; 1837–1859. *Portraits, and numerous plates by "Phiz" (H. K. Browne), Cruikshank, Leech, and others.* 45 *vols., 8vo, dark diamond calf, neat.* London, 1837–59

234 BÉRANGER, PIERRE JEAN DE. THE SONGS OF BÉRANGER, IN ENGLISH; with a Sketch of the Author's Life. [Edited by R. W. Griswold, D. D.] *Crown 8vo, boards.* Philadelphia, 1844

First collection of Béranger's writings published in America.

235 BÉRANGER, PIERRE JEAN DE. ŒUVRES. CHANSONS: Édition revue par l'Auteur, contenant cinquante-trois Gravures sur Acier, les Dix Chansons publiées en 1847, et le Facsimile d'une Lettre de Béranger. 2 *vols.* — DERNIÈRES CHANSONS, de 1834 à 1851; avec une Préface de l'Auteur: illustrées de 14 Dessins. 1 *vol.* — ŒUVRES POSTHUMES: Ma Biographie, écrite par Béranger; avec un Appendice et des Notes. Ornée d'un Portrait en Pied dessiné par Charlet, d'une Photographie d'après le Marbre de M. Geoffroy-Dechaume, et de huit Gravures. 1 *vol. Together,* 4 *vols., 8vo, half morocco, extra, gilt edges.* Perrotin, Paris, 1859–60

The plates are engraved by Durond, Massart, Lalaisse, Nargeot, Ruhierre, etc., after Charlet, A. de Lemud, Johannot, De Rudder, Sandoz, d'Aubigny, Wattier, etc., etc.

236 BERESFORD, REV. JAMES. THE MISERIES OF HUMAN LIFE, or the Groans of Samuel Sensitive, and Timothy Testy; with a Few Supplementary Sighs from Mrs. Testy. In Twelve Dialogues. The Seventh Edition. THE MISERIES OF HUMAN LIFE, or the Last Groans of Timothy Testy and Samuel Sensitive; with a Few Supplementary Sighs from Mrs. Testy: with which are now for the First Time interspersed, Varieties, incidental to the Principal Matter, in Prose and Verse. In Nine Additional Dialogues, as overheard, etc. *Colored frontispiece by W. H. Pyne, and two other plates ("Miseries Personified") by the author, folded, besides numerous wood-cuts. 2 vols., foolscap 8vo, old mottled calf, yellow edges.* W. Miller, London, 1807

237 BERESFORD, REV. JAMES. ANOTHER COPY: *Third edition of Vol. I. and first edition of Vol. II. Colored frontispiece, plates, and wood-cuts. 2 vols., foolscap 8vo, marbled calf extra, yellow edges.* W. Miller, London, 1806–07

In this copy the author's name does not appear on the title of first volume, the sixth edition being the first which bears his name.

238 BERLÈSE, L'ABBÉ. ICONOGRAPHIE DU GENRE CAMELLIA, ou Collection des Camellia les Plus Beaux et les Plus Rares, peints, d'après Nature dans les Serres de M. l'Abbé Berlèse, par M. J. — J. Jung; avec la Description Exacte de Chaque Fleur, accompagnée d'Observations Pratiques sur la Culture de cette Plante, et des Soins qu'elle exige pour Fleurir Abondamment, par M. l'Abbé Berlèse. *With 96 elegant colored plates. 1 vol., 4to, green turkey morocco, extra, gilt edges.* H. Cousin, Paris, s. a.

239 BERNARD, JOHN, Actor. RETROSPECTIONS OF THE STAGE. *2 vols., 12mo, half calf, neat.* London, 1830

240 BERNARD, JOHN, Actor. ANOTHER COPY: *American edition. 2 vols. in 1, 12mo, half calf, neat.* Boston, 1832

241 BERNARDI, MAJOR JOHN. A SHORT HISTORY OF THE LIFE OF; written by himself in Newgate, where he has been for near 33 Years a Prisoner of State, without any Allowance from the Government, and could never be admitted to his Tryal. To which is added, by Way of Appendix, a True Copy of the Diploma, or Patent of Count of the Empire, granted to the Author's Grand-Father in the Year 1629, and a Translation of it into English: as also Copies of the Major's Several Commissions, etc. *Small 8vo, old calf.* London, 1729

242 BERNERS, JULIANA. THE TREATYSE OF FYSSHYNGE WYTH AN ANGLE; attributed to Dame Juliana Berners, reprinted from the Book of St. Alban's. *Fac-simile wood-cuts. Printed with the types of John Baskerville. Crown 8vo, half morocco, carmine edges.* ONLY 100 COPIES PRINTED. W. Pickering, London, 1827

243 BERRY, MARY. A COMPARATIVE VIEW OF THE SOCIAL LIFE OF ENGLAND AND FRANCE, FROM THE RESTORATION OF CHARLES THE SECOND TO THE FRENCH REVOLUTION; by the Editor of Madame du Deffand's Letters [Miss Berry]. *8vo, half calf, very neat.* London, 1828

244 BERRY, MARY. EXTRACTS FROM THE JOURNALS AND CORRESPONDENCE OF MISS BERRY, FROM THE YEAR 1783 TO 1852; edited by Lady Theresa Lewis. Second Edition. *Portrait and plates. 3 vols., thick 8vo, cloth, uncut.* London, 1866

245 BESCHERELLE, LOUIS NICOLAS. GRAND DICTIONNAIRE DE GÉOGRAPHIE UNIVERSELLE, ANCIENNE ET MODERNE, ou Description Physique, Ethnographique, Politique, Historique, Statistique, Commerciale, Industrielle, Scientifique, Littéraire, Artistique, Morale, Religieuse, etc. de toutes les Parties du Monde; par M. Bescherelle Aîné, Bibliothécaire au Louvre, etc., et M. G. Devars, avec la Collaboration de plusieurs Géographes Français et Étrangers. *4 vols., royal 4to, paper, uncut.* Paris, 1859

246 BESLER, BASIL. HORTUS EYSTETTENSIS, sive Diligens et Accurata omnium Plantarum, Florum, Stirpium, ex Variis Orbis Terræ Partibus, Singulari Studio collectarum, quæ in celeberrimis Viridariis Arcem Episcopalem ibidem cingentibus, hoc Tempore conspiciuntur Delineatio ad Vivum Repræsentatio. *Fine impressions of the engraved title and 370 large plates. 2 vols., square imperial folio, old calf, red edges.* ORIGINAL EDITION; COMPLETE *and in good condition.* (Nuremberg), 1613

247 BETHUNE, GEORGE W., D. D. THE BRITISH FEMALE POETS; with Biographical and Critical Notices. *Portrait of Mrs. Norton, vignette on the engraved title, and 10 plates, by W. & E. Finden, J. C. Armytage, etc. 8vo, sheep, marbled edges.* Philadelphia, (1848)

248 BETTERTON, THOMAS. THE HISTORY OF THE ENGLISH STAGE; including the Lives, Characters, and Amours of the most Eminent Actors and Actresses. With Instructions for Public Speaking; wherein the Action and Utterance of the Bar, Stage, and Pulpit are distinctly considered. Revised, with Additional Notes, by Charles L. Coles. (Followed by Memoirs of Miss Anne Oldfield.) *8vo, half morocco.* Boston, 1814

In Bohn's "Lowndes," p. 166, this work is said to be by Wm. Oldys.

249 BEVERIDGE, WILLIAM, BISHOP OF ST. ASAPH. TWENTY-SIX SERMONS, on Various Subjects, selected from the Works of. *8vo, cloth.* London, 1850

250 BEVERLEY, ROBERT. THE HISTORY AND PRESENT STATE OF VIRGINIA. By R: B: Gent: *Frontispiece and*

12 plates (reduced from De Bry), by S. Gribelin. Title and plates numbered 4 and 5 wanting, otherwise perfect.
(R. Parker, London, 1705)

COLLATION: Frontispiece, 1 leaf. Epistle Dedicatory, 2 leaves. Preface, 3 leaves. Book I., pp. 104. Book II., pp. 40. Book III., pp. 64. Book IV., pp. 83. Folding sheet of the Census of 1703. Table and Errata, pp. 20. The above short title is from the frontispiece.

251 BHAGVAT-GEETA (LE), OU DIALOGUES DE KREESHNA ET D'ARJOON; contenant un Précis de la Religion & de la Morale des Indiens. Traduit du Sanscrit, la Langue Sacrée des Brahmes, en Anglois, par M. Charles Wilkins; et de l'Anglois en François, par M. Parraud. *8vo, old mottled calf, gilt, marbled edges.* Londres (Paris), 1787

252 BIBLE. BIBLIA HEBRAICA, secundum Ultimam Editionem Jos. Athiae, a Johanne Leusden Denuo recognitam, recensita atque ad Masoram, et Correctiores Bombergi, Stephani, Plantini, aliorumque Editiones, exquisite adornata Variisque Notis illustrata; ab Everardo Van der Hooght, V. D. M. Editio longe accuratissima. *Engraved titles on copper (first vol.) and wood (second vol.).* 2 *vols.,* 8*vo, diamond russia, very neat.* Amstelaedami, 1705

"Édition belle et recherchée." —*Brunet.*

253 BIBLE. THE HOLY BIBLE, containing the Old and New Testaments. *With above* 200 *engravings by J. Cole. Crown* 4*to, old red morocco, extra, gilt edges.* ILLUSTRATED COPY: *with Apocrypha.* J. Baskett, Oxford, 1733

Bound in this copy are,—"The Book of Common Prayer; *printed by the University Printer, Oxford,* 1731:" and, "A Brief Concordance, etc., by John Downame, B. D.; *printed for R. Ware, London,* 1732." The title to the engraved illustrations reads: "The Historical Part of the Holy Bible, or the Old and New Testament Exactly and Compleatly Describ'd in above Two Hundred Historys, Curiously Engrav'd by J. Cole, from Designs of y[e] best Masters."

254 BIBLE. AN ILLUSTRATION OF THE HOLY SCRIPTURES, BY NOTES AND EXPLICATIONS ON THE OLD AND NEW TESTAMENT: in which the Useful Observations of Former Commentators will be made Use of; the Different Translations of the Bible into Various Languages taken Notice of, to explain Difficult Texts; and the Observations of the most Learned Men applied; with such Notes added, as will greatly explain the Nature and Spirit of the Holy Scriptures. The Sixth Edition. *Maps and numerous plates.* 3 *vols., folio, old calf; backs cracked.* GOADBY'S: *with Apocrypha.*
Printed for R. Goadby, in Sherborne: London, 1759

255 BIBLE. THE ROYAL BIBLE, OR A COMPLETE BODY OF CHRISTIAN DIVINITY; containing the Holy Scriptures at Large, and a Full and Clear Explanation of all the Difficult Texts, from the Various Readings of Authors, Antient and Modern: together with Critical Notes and Observations on the Whole. By Leonard Howard, D. D., etc. Second Edi-

tion. *Portrait and numerous plates, after Houbraken, Picart, etc. 2 vols., folio, rough calf.* HOWARD'S: *with Apocrypha.* I. Pottinger, London, 1761–62

256 BIBLE. THE CHRISTIAN'S FAMILY BIBLE; containing the Old and New Testaments at Large, and the Apocrypha: with Comments and Annotations, Theological, Historical, Critical, and Moral; by the Reverend W. Rider, A. B. etc., etc. *Maps and numerous fine plates engraved by C. Grignion, etc., after Salvator Rosa, Paul Veronese, etc. 2 vols., folio, half sheep; third volume (New Testament) wanting.* RIDER'S: *with plates after the "Great Masters."* London, 1763–67

257 BIBLE. OLD TESTAMENT, NEW TESTAMENT, AND APOCRYPHA; embellished with Engravings from Pictures and Designs by the most Eminent English Artists. *Elegantly printed, by T. Bensley, with exceedingly large type. Fine impressions of the plates, engraved by Bartolozzi, Sharp, Fittler, Heath, etc. 7 vols., royal folio, blue morocco, very neat, gilt edges.* MACKLIN'S SUPERB EDITION: *fine copy.* London, 1800–16

In this edition, for the sake of typographical elegance, the words introduced by the translators (which in other editions are printed in italics) are designated by a dot placed under the first vowel, thereby preserving the beauty of the page by its uniformity, yet allowing such words to be as readily distinguished as by the usual method.

The Apocrypha was published (1816), at £18.18, by Cadell and Davies; the other volumes (1800) were published in 70 numbers, at £1.1 each, by T. Macklin.

258 BIBLE. THE HOLY BIBLE, CONTAINING THE OLD AND THE NEW TESTAMENT, AND APOCRYPHA; with Critical, Philological, and Explanatory Notes, by the Rev. John Hewlett, B. D., etc., etc. Illustrated with One Hundred and Twenty Engravings, from the Best Pictures of the Great Masters in the Various Schools of Painting. *3 vols. in 4, royal 4to, diamond calf, gilt.* HEWLETT'S: *fine impressions of the plates.* London, 1811

259 BIBLE. THE HOLY BIBLE, CONTAINING THE OLD AND NEW TESTAMENTS, AND THE APOCRYPHA; embellished with Engravings by Charles Heath, from Designs by Richard Westall, R. A. *3 vols., imperial 8vo, half morocco, very neat, gilt tops.* A VERY ELEGANT EDITION. London (Oxford), 1815

260 BIBLE. THE COMPREHENSIVE BIBLE; containing the Old and New Testaments, according to the Authorized Version, with the Various Readings and Marginal Notes usually printed therewith: a General Introduction, containing Disquisitions on the Genuineness, Authenticity, and Inspiration of the Holy Scriptures; the Various Divisions and Marks of Distinction in the Sacred Writings; Ancient Versions; Coins, Weights, and Measures; the Various Sects among the Jews: Introductory and Concluding Remarks to each

Book: the Parallel Passages contained in Rev. T. Scott's Commentary, Canne's Bible, Rev. J. Brown's Self-Interpreting Bible, Dr. Adam Clarke's Commentary, and the English Version of Bagster's Polyglot Bible, systematically arranged; with numerous Philological and Explanatory Notes; a Table of Contents, arranged in Historical Order; an Analysis and Compendium of the Holy Scriptures; an Index of the Subjects contained in the Old and New Testaments; a Chronological Index, with Synchronisms of the most Important Epochs and Events in Profane History; and an Index to the Notes, Introductions, and Concluding Remarks. *Colored maps. 4to, dark blue levant morocco, gilt edges.* BAGSTER'S COMPREHENSIVE: DEMY PAPER.

S. Bagster & Sons, London, s. a.

This valuable Bible contains 4,000 notes, which by a simple index are made to illustrate 40,000 passages; they are exclusively philological and explanatory, and consequently contain nothing of a doctrinal or controversial nature. It is handsomely and accurately printed, and for general utility not surpassed.

261 BIBLE. LA SAINTE BIBLE, QUI CONTIENT LE VIEUX ET LE NOUVEAU TESTAMENT; imprimée sur l'Édition de Paris, de l'Année 1805. *Thick 12mo, sheep.* New York, 1820

262 BIBLIOGRAPHIE DES PRINCIPAUX OUVRAGES RELATIFS À L'AMOUR, AUX FEMMES, AU MARIAGE, indiquant les Auteurs de ces Ouvrages, leurs Éditions, leur Valeur, et les Prohibitions ou Condamnations dont certains d' entre eux ont été l'Objet. Par M. Le C. D'I * * * . *8vo, half green crushed morocco, neat, marbled edges.* J. Gay, Paris, 1861

263 BIBLIOMANE (LE). *Nos. I. and II. (January and July,* 1861). Trübner & Cie., Londres, 1861

264 BICKHAM, GEORGE. THE UNIVERSAL PENMAN. *Consisting of above 200 finely engraved plates containing specimens of penmanship in all its branches, embellished with numerous vignettes after Watteau and others. Folio, old calf, gilt, red edges.* London, (1733–41)

265 BIGELOW, JACOB, M. D. AMERICAN MEDICAL BOTANY; being a Collection of the Native Medicinal Plants of the United States, containing their Botanical History and Chemical Analysis, and Properties and Uses in Medicine, Diet and the Arts. *With 60 colored plates. 3 vols., royal 8vo, half morocco, very neat, marbled edges.* Boston, 1817–20

266 BIGELOW, JACOB, M. D. FLORULA BOSTONIENSIS: a Collection of Plants of Boston and its Vicinity, with their Generic and Specific Characters, Principal Synonyms, Descriptions, and Occasional Remarks. Second Edition, greatly enlarged; to which is added, a Glossary of the Botanical Terms employed in the Work. *8vo, morocco, neat, gilt edges.* Boston, 1824

267 BIGELOW, JACOB, M. D. MODERN INQUIRIES: Classical, Professional, and Miscellaneous. *Post 8vo, cloth.* Boston, 1867

268 BIGLAND, John. Letters on the Study and Use of Ancient and Modern History; containing Observations and Reflections on the Causes and Consequences of those Events which have produced Conspicuous Changes in the Aspect of the World, and the General State of Human Affairs. *8vo, sheep; with book-plate of Winthrop Sargent.* Whitehall (Penn.), 1806

269 BINGHAM, Joseph. Origines Ecclesiasticæ: the Antiquities of the Christian Church; with Two Sermons and Two Letters on the Nature and Necessity of Absolution. Reprinted from the Original Edition, MDCCVIII.–MDCCXXII., with an enlarged Analytical Index. *2 vols., imperial 8vo, cloth, uncut.* H. G. Bohn, London, 1852–56

270 BIOGRAPHICAL (The) Dictionary of the Society for the Diffusion of Useful Knowledge. *Vols. I.–III. (Aa–Atkyns) in 6 parts, 8vo, cloth, uncut.* London, 1842–44

271 BIOGRAPHICAL (The) Magazine; containing Portraits of Eminent and Ingenious Persons of Every Age and Nation, with their Lives and Characters. *Contains 96 medallion portraits in each volume. 2 vols., royal 8vo, half morocco, neat.* Complete. E. Wilson, etc., London, 1819–20

272 BIRCH, Thomas, D. D. The Heads of Illustrious Persons of Great Britain, engraved by Mr. Houbraken and Mr. Vertue; with their Lives and Characters, by Thomas Birch. A New Edition. *With the 108 portraits after Holbein, Vandyck, Kneller, etc. Folio, russia extra, gilt edges; back cracked.* London, 1813

273 BLACK'S Economical Guide through Edinburgh; with a Plan of the City and a Description of its Environs. Second Edition. *Fine plates besides the map and plan. 16mo, paper.* Edinburgh, 1840

274 BLACK'S General Atlas of the World. New Edition; containing the Latest Discoveries, New Boundaries, and Introductory Description. *Frontispiece containing the flags of all nations, etc.; 56 fine large colored maps; and an index of 65,000 names, giving the latitude, longitude, and number of map. Large folio, half crimson morocco, neat, gilt edges.* Edinburgh, 1865

275 BLACKIE, W. G. The Imperial Gazetteer: a General Dictionary of Geography, Physical, Political, Statistical, and Descriptive; compiled from the Latest and Best Authorities. *With seven hundred illustrations, views, costumes, maps, plans, etc. 2 vols., thick imperial 8vo, calf, neat, gilt edges.* Glasgow, 1855

276 BLACKWELL, Elizabeth. A Curious Herbal, containing Five Hundred Cuts of the Most Useful Plants which are now used in the Practice of Physick; Engraved on Folio Copper Plates, after Drawings taken from the

Life, by Elizabeth Blackwell: to which is added a Short Description of yᵉ Plants, and their Common Uses in Physick. *Engraved throughout, the plates finely colored. 2 vols., folio, old mottled calf.* London, 1739

The title to the second volume is dated 1737.

277 BLACKWELL, THOMAS. AN ENQUIRY INTO THE LIFE AND WRITINGS OF HOMER. [By Thomas Blackwell.] *Portrait, map, and plates, by Vander Gucht, Scotin, etc., after Gravelot. 8vo, old mottled calf, red edges.* LARGE PAPER: ORIGINAL EDITION. London, 1735

278 BLACKWOOD'S EDINBURGH MAGAZINE. *April,* 1817–*December,* 1862. 92 *vols., 8vo, half calf, extra, marbled edges.* FINE SET. Edinburgh, 1817–62

This set contains (Vol. II. pp. 89–96) the "Translation from an Ancient Chaldee Manuscript," a celebrated *jeu-d'esprit* by James Hogg, "the Ettrick Shepherd," which was suppressed after a few numbers had been issued, on account of its personalities and alleged immorality.

279 BLAEU, JEAN. LE GRAND ATLAS, OU COSMOGRAPHIE BLAVIANE. *Fine copy of the* GEOGRAPHY, *with the maps and plates colored.* 12 *vols., imperial folio, vellum, extra, gilt edges.* Amsterdam, 1667

280 BLAGDON, FRANCIS WILLIAM. A BRIEF HISTORY OF ANCIENT AND MODERN INDIA, from the Earliest Periods of Antiquity to the Termination of the Late Mahratta War. *With* 68 *finely colored plates after pictures painted by Mr. Daniell, Col. Ward, and Lieut. James Hunter. Atlas folio, half russia, extra.* E. Orme, London, 1805

281 BLAINE, JAMES GILLESPIE. THE WAR DEBTS OF LOYAL STATES. Speech of Mr. Blaine, of Maine, in the House of Representatives, April 21, 1864. *8vo, pp.* 8. Washington, 1864

282 BLAIR, HUGH, D. D. LECTURES ON RHETORIC AND BELLES LETTRES. 3 *vols., crown 8vo, half calf.* Basil, 1801

283 BLAIR, HUGH, D. D. ANOTHER COPY: Fourteenth Edition. *8vo, half calf, extra, marbled edges.* London, 1825

284 BLAIR, HUGH, D. D. SERMONS: to which is annexed (Vol. V.) a Short Account of the Life and Character of the Author, by James Finlayson, D. D. A New Edition. *Portrait.* 5 *vols., 8vo, half morocco.* London, 1817

285 BLAIR, JOHN. THE CHRONOLOGY AND HISTORY OF THE WORLD, FROM THE CREATION TO THE YEAR OF CHRIST 1814. Illustrated in LVII. Tables, of which IV. are Introductory and include the Centuries prior to the 1st Olympiad; and each of the remaining LIII. contain, in One Expanded View, 50 Years or Half a Century. *Vignette, after Eisen, on title. Engraved throughout (except the preface and index), and printed on writing-paper. Royal folio, paper.* London, 1814

286 BLAIR, ROBERT. THE GRAVE, A POEM. *With portrait of, and* 11 *illustrations by, William Blake* ("*Pictor Ignotus*"). *4to, half morocco, gilt edges.* New York, 1858

287 BLAND, Col. Theodorick, Jun. The Bland Papers: being a Selection from the Manuscripts of Colonel Theodorick Bland, Jr., of Prince George County, Virginia; to which are prefixed an Introduction, and a Memoir. Edited by Charles Campbell. 2 *vols. in* 1, 8*vo*, *half morocco*.
Petersburg, 1840–43
Important Revolutionary History.

288 BLESSINGTON, Marguerite Power, Countess of. The Idler in Italy. 2 *vols.*, 12*mo*, *cloth*.
Philadelphia, 1839

289 BOADEN, James. An Inquiry into the Authenticity of Various Pictures and Prints, which, from the Decease of the Poet to our own Times, have been offered to the Public as Portraits of Shakspeare: containing a Careful Examination of the Evidence on which they claim to be received; by which the Pretended Portraits have been rejected, the Genuine confirmed and established. Illustrated by Accurate and Finished Engravings, by the Ablest Artists, from such Originals as were of Indisputable Authority. 4*to*, *green morocco*, *extra*, *gilt edges*. Large paper: *India proofs of the five portraits*.
R. Triphook, London, 1824

290 BOADEN, James. Another copy. *Fine impressions of the portraits*. 8*vo*, *half morocco*. London, 1824

291 BOADEN, James. Another copy: the same. 8*vo*, *boards*, *uncut*. London, 1824

292 BOADEN, James. Memoirs of the Life of John Philip Kemble; including a History of the Stage, from the Time of Garrick to the Present Period. 8*vo*, *sheep*.
Philadelphia, 1825

293 BOCCACCIO, Giovanni. Il Decamerone. *Printed on Holland paper, with a very wide margin and no titles except those engraved. Above* 100 *plates and numerous vignettes, after Gravelot, Eisen, Cochin, etc.* 5 *vols.*, *crown* 8*vo*, *half green morocco*. Londra (Parigi), 1757

294 BOCCACCIO, Giovanni. The Decameron, or Ten Days' Entertainment of Boccaccio; translated from the Italian. To which are prefixed, Remarks on the Life and Writings of Boccaccio; and an Advertisement, by the Author of Old Nick, a Piece of Family Biography, &c. [E. Dubois.] 8*vo*, *cloth*, *uncut*. London, 1845

295 BOCCACCIO, Giovanni. The Decameron, or Ten Days' Entertainment of Boccaccio; with Eighteen Steel Engravings. 12*mo*, *cloth*. New York, 1858

296 BOETHIUS. Anicius Manlius Severinus. Consolation of Philosophy; in Five Books. Made English and illustrated with Notes, by Richard, Lord Viscount Preston. The Second Edition, corrected. *Small* 12*mo*, *old calf*.
J. Tonson, London, 1712

297 BOILEAU DESPRÉAUX, NICOLAS. OEUVRES DE : avec des Éclaircissemens Historiques donnez par lui-meme. Nouvelle Édition, revuë, corrigée, & augmentée de Diverses Remarques [par Cl. Brossette et du Monteil]. Enrichée de Figures gravées par Bernard Picart. *Each page printed within a border, and fine impressions of the plates. 2 vols., folio, old calf, red edges.* D. Mortier, Amsterdam, 1718

"Primière édition de luxe que l'on ait donnée de ce grande poëte. [Elle se recommande et par sa belle exécution typogr. et par d'assez bonnes estampes ou vignettes." — *Brunet.*

298 BOISGELIN, LOUIS DE. ANCIENT AND MODERN MALTA: containing a Full and Accurate Account of the Present State of the Islands of Malta and Goza, the History of the Knights of St. John of Jerusalem; also a Narrative of the Events which attended the Capture of these Islands by the French, and their Conquest by the English; and an Appendix, containing Authentic State-Papers and other Documents. Illustrated with a Large Chart of the Islands, Views, Portraits, Antiques, etc 2 *vols., 4to, half morocco, marbled edges.* R. Phillips, London, 1805

The second volume is in two parts.

299 BOLDENYI, J. LA HONGRIE, ANCIENNE ET MODERNE: Histoire, Arts, Littérature, Monuments; par une Société de Littérateurs, sous la Direction de M. J. Boldenyi. Dessinateurs: Janet-Lange, V. Beaucé, E. Breton, Catenacci, De Bar, Freeman; Graveurs: Trichon, Brevière, Fagnion, Etherington, E. Deschamps, Blaise, Hildibrand, Montigneul, Pathey, Rose. *Numerous fine wood-cuts of views, portraits, costumes, etc., etc. Imperial 8vo, half morocco, neat.* H. Lebrun, Paris, 1853

300 BONAPARTE, LUCIEN. GALLERY. CHOIX DE GRAVURES À L'EAU FORTE, d'après les Peintures Originales et les Marbres de la Galerie de Lucien Bonaparte. *Contains 142 fine etchings after the " Great Masters " in the various schools. Imperial 4to, citron morocco, extra, gilt edges.* Londres, 1812

301 BONSTETTEN, CHARLES VICTOR DE. THE MAN OF THE NORTH, AND THE MAN OF THE SOUTH; or, the Influence of Climate. Translated from the French. *16mo, cloth, red edges.* New York, 1864

302 BOOK (THE) OF COMMON PRAYER, AND ADMINISTRATION OF THE SACRAMENTS; and other Rites and Ceremonies of the Church, according to the Use of the Protestant Episcopal Church in the Confederate States of America: together with the Psalter, or Psalms of David. *Long primer 24mo (16mo), morocco, gilt edges.* J. W. Randolph, Richmond, Va., 1863

This edition was printed by Eyre & Spottiswoode, London, with the above imprint, for use in the "Confederate States." For an instance of the errors in this edition see the first " Prayer to be used at Sea," where the words *United States* have been printed in place of *Confederate States.*

303 BOOK (THE) OF COSTUME, OR ANNALS OF FASHION, from the Earliest Period to the Present Time; by a Lady of Rank. Illustrated with upwards of Two Hundred Engravings on Wood, by the most Eminent Artists. New Edition. *8vo, cloth, gilt edges.* H. Colburn, London, 1847

304 BOOK (THE) OF FAMILIAR QUOTATIONS; being a Collection of Popular Extracts and Aphorisms from the Works of the Best Authors. Second Edition. *Fac-simile wood-cuts. Foolscap 8vo, cloth, carmine edges.* Whittaker & Co., London, 1860

305 BOOK (THE) OF SHAKESPEARE GEMS: in a Series of Landscape Illustrations of the most Interesting Localities of Shakespeare's Dramas. (With Historical and Descriptive Accounts, by Washington Irving, E. Jesse, W. Howitt, C. Wordsworth, etc.) *Engraved title and 45 fine plates, by Woods, Hinchcliff, Varrall, Winkles, Radcliffe, etc., after drawings chiefly by G. F. Sargent. 8vo, turkey morocco, extra, tooled edges.* London, 1850

306 BOOK (THE) OF THE SIGNERS: CONTAINING FAC-SIMILE LETTERS OF THE SIGNERS OF THE DECLARATION OF INDEPENDENCE; illustrated also with Sixty-one Engravings, from Original Photographs and Drawings, of their Residences, Portraits, etc. From the Collections of an Association of American Antiquaries. Edited by William Brotherhead. *All the illustrations are India proofs. Royal folio, half morocco, gilt top, rough edges.* LARGE PAPER: *only 99 copies printed.* Philadelphia, 1861

307 BOOK (THE) OF VAGABONDS AND BEGGARS, WITH A VOCABULARY OF THEIR LANGUAGE; edited by Martin Luther in the Year 1528. Now first translated into English, with Introduction and Notes, by John Camden Hotten. *Fac-simile wood-cut and typographical embellishments. Printed at the Chiswick Press. Small 4to, half morocco, red paper sides, gilt top.* J. C. Hotten, London, 1860

308 BOOK (THE) OF WAVERLEY GEMS: in a Series of Engraved Illustrations of Incidents and Scenery in Sir Walter Scott's Novels. (With Illustrative Letter-press.) *Engraved title and 64 plates and vignettes, by Heath, Finden, Rolls, etc., after Leslie, Stothard, Cooper, Howard, and other eminent artists. 8vo, turkey morocco extra, tooled edges.* London, 1848

309 BORGET, AUGUSTE. SKETCHES OF CHINA AND THE CHINESE; from Drawings by Auguste Borget. *A series of 32 views, lithographed by Cicéri; with descriptive letter-press in English. Imperial folio, half morocco.* London (Paris, 1842)

309a BORGET, AUGUSTE. ANOTHER COPY: *views numbered 1–4 and 27–32 wanting, the others somewhat stained. Imperial folio, half morocco.* London (Paris, 1842)

310 BOSSI, GIUSEPPE. DEL CENACOLO DI LEONARDO DA VINCI, Libri Quattro. *Printed on vellum paper. With 6 plates. Imperial 4to, boards, rough edges.* Milano, 1810

311 BOSTON, Massachusetts. Annual Reports of the School Committee. For 1860 and 1861. *Views and plans.* 2 *vols.*, 8*vo, cloth.* Boston, 1860–61

312 BOSTON, Massachusetts. Report of the Standing Committee on Music of the Public Schools: September 10, 1861. 8*vo, pp.* 28. Boston, 1861

313 BOSTON, Massachusetts. City Document No. 97. Occupation of the South Boston Flats. *Colored plan.* 8*vo, pp.* 19. (Boston), 1866

314 BOSTON, Massachusetts. Report of the Evidence and other Matter presented before a Joint Committee of the City Council upon the Subject of Gas. Phonographically reported by Mr. J. M. W. Yerrinton. 8*vo, pp.* 464, *paper.* Boston, 1867

315 BOSTON Common. 12*mo, pp.* 63, *cloth.* H. B. Williams, Boston, 1842

316 BOSTON (The) Directory; containing the Names of the Inhabitants, their Occupations, Places of Business, and Dwelling Houses. With Lists of the Streets, Lanes, and Wharves; the Town-Officers, Public Offices, and Banks; of the Stages, which run from Boston, with the Times of their Arrival and Departure; and a General Description of the Town, illustrated by a Plan drawn from Actual Survey. 16*mo, paper.* Boston, 1807

317 BOSWELL, James. The Life of Samuel Johnson, LL. D., including a Journal of his Tour to the Hebrides; with Numerous Additions and Notes, by the Right Hon. John Wilson Croker, M. P. To which are added, Two Supplementary Volumes of Johnsoniana, by Hawkins, Piozzi, Murphy, Tyers, Reynolds, Malone, Nichols, Steevens, Cumberland, and others; and Notes by Various Hands: also, upwards of Fifty Engraved Illustrations. 10 *vols., foolscap* 8*vo, calf, extra, marbled edges.* London, 1853

The only edition which contains the "Johnsoniana."

318 BOTTA, Anne C. Lynch. Hand-Book of Universal Literature, from the Best and Latest Authorities; designed for Popular Reading and as a Text-Book for Schools and Colleges. 12*mo, cloth.* New York, 1860

319 BOTTA, Carlo Giuseppe Guglielmo. History of the War of the Independence of the United States of America. Translated from the Italian, by George Alexander Otis, Esq. Seventh Edition, revised and corrected. *Maps, plate (frontispiece), and wood-cuts.* 2 *vols.*, 8*vo, russia, very neat, marbled edges.* New Haven, s. a.

320 BOTTARELLI, F. The New Italian, English, and French Pocket-Dictionary; to which is prefixed a New Compendious Italian Grammar. The Third Edition, corrected and improved. 3 *vols., square* 12*mo, sheep.* London, 1795

321 BOUCHETTE, JOSEPH. THE BRITISH DOMINIONS IN NORTH AMERICA, or a Topographical and Statistical Description of the Provinces of Lower and Upper Canada, New Brunswick, Nova Scotia, the Islands of Newfoundland, Prince Edward, and Cape Breton; including Considerations on Land-Granting and Emigration. To which are annexed Statistical Tables, and Tables of Distances, etc. 2 *vols.* A TOPOGRAPHICAL DICTIONARY of the Province of Lower Canada. 1 *vol. Portrait, and numerous plates of views, plans, etc. Together,* 3 *vols.,* 4*to, half calf, neat.*
London, 1832

322 BOURRIENNE, LOUIS ANTOINE FAUVELET DE. MEMOIRS OF NAPOLEON BONAPARTE; to which are now first added, an Account of the Important Events of the Hundred Days, of Napoleon's Surrender to the English, and of his Residence and Death at St. Helena: with Anecdotes and Illustrative Notes, from the most Authentic Sources. *Portraits and other engravings.* 4 *vols.,* 8*vo, cloth, uncut.* London, 1836

323 BOUTELL, REV. CHARLES. THE MONUMENTAL BRASSES OF ENGLAND: a Series of Engravings upon Wood from Every Variety of these Interesting and Valuable Memorials, accompanied with Brief Descriptive Notices, by the Rev. Charles Boutell, M. A., etc., etc. The Engravings drawn and executed by Mr. R. B. Utting. *Imperial* 8*vo, half calf.*
G. Bell, London, 1849

From the library of the late W. E. Burton, Comedian, lettered on back "History of the Stage:— Costumes.— Boutell's Monumental Brasses; — 150 Engravings: 1849, London. — W. E. Burton" (fac-simile of signature).

324 BOUTERWEK, FRIEDRICH. HISTORY OF SPANISH AND PORTUGUESE LITERATURE. Translated from the Original German, by Thomasina Ross. 2 *vols.,* 8*vo, half calf, extra.* BEST EDITION. Boosey & Sons, London, 1823

325 BOUTERWEK, FRIEDRICH. HISTORY OF SPANISH LITERATURE. Translated from the Original German, by Thomasina Ross; with Additional Notes, by the Translator. *Portrait of Cervantes. Post* 8*vo, cloth, uncut.*
D. Bogue, London, 1847

326 BOWDITCH, NATHANIEL INGERSOLL. MEMOIR OF NATHANIEL BOWDITCH, LL. D. *Portraits of Dr. Bowditch and his wife.* 4*to, boards.* PRINTED FOR PRESENTATION: *and only a few copies.* Boston, 1839

This memoir (a small edition of which was separately printed for the author) forms a part of the fourth volume of Dr. Bowditch's translation of the "Mécanique Céleste" of La Place. This copy was presented to "Mr. & Mrs. Jereh S. Boies, with the regards of the Author, Boston, May 8, 1839."

327 BOWDITCH, NATHANIEL INGERSOLL. A HISTORY OF THE MASSACHUSETTS GENERAL HOSPITAL. *Portraits of Dr. John C. Warren and Dr. James Jackson, and views of the Hospital and McLean Asylum. Royal* 8*vo, cloth; with autograph of author.* PRIVATELY PRINTED: *presentation copy.*
Boston, 1851

328 BOWDITCH, NATHANIEL INGERSOLL. SUFFOLK SURNAMES. Third Edition. *Handsomely printed with large type, by John Wilson & Son. Portrait on India paper. Thick 8vo, cloth.* London (Boston), 1861

329 BOWLES, SAMUEL. ACROSS THE CONTINENT: a Summer's Journey to the Rocky Mountains, the Mormons, and the Pacific States, with Speaker Colfax. *Map. 12mo, cloth.* Springfield, Mass., 1865

330 BOWRING, SIR JOHN. POETRY OF THE MAGYARS; preceded by a Sketch of the Language and Literature of Hungary and Transylvania. *Crown 8vo, cloth, uncut.* London, 1830

331 BOWYER, WILLIAM. THE ORIGIN OF PRINTING; in Two Essays: I. The Substance of Dr. Middleton's Dissertation on the Origin of Printing in England. II. Mr. Meerman's Account of the First Invention of the Art. An Appendix is annexed: 1. On the First printed Greek Books. 2. On the First printed Hebrew Books, with Observations on some Modern Editions; and a Collation, from Walton's Polyglott, of a Remarkable Passage as printed in Kings and Chronicles. 3. On the Early Polyglotts. [By William Bowyer.] *8vo, half morocco. Fine copy.* London, 1774

332 BOWYER, WILLIAM. ANOTHER COPY: the Second Edition with Improvements. (1776.) *With* SUPPLEMENT (1781), *containing "Dr. Ducarel's Letter to Mr. Meerman, with the Doctor's Notes," answers, with translations, etc., etc. 8vo, sprinkled calf, yellow edges; with book-plate of Sir Henry Mainwaring, Bart.* BEST EDITION: *with a rare tract added.* London, 1776–81

Bound in this copy is the Memoir (by John Nichols, 1781) of the unsuccessful inventor of stereotyping, entitled, — "Biographical Memoirs of William Ged, including a Particular Account of his Progress in the Art of Block-Printing."

333 BOYD, REV. A. K. H. THE RECREATIONS OF A COUNTRY PARSON. Second Series. [By Rev. A. K. H. Boyd.] *12mo, cloth, gilt top.* Boston, 1861

334 BOYD, REV. A. K. H. THE GRAVER THOUGHTS OF A COUNTRY PARSON; by the Author of "the Recreations of a Country Parson," etc., etc. *Post 8vo, cloth.* Boston, 1863

335 BOYD, REV. A. K. H. THE EVERY-DAY PHILOSOPHER, IN TOWN AND COUNTRY; by the Author of the Recreations of a Country Parson. *Post 8vo, cloth, gilt top.* Boston, 1863

336 BOYDELL, JOHN AND JOSIAH. A COLLECTION OF PRINTS FROM PICTURES PAINTED, FOR THE PURPOSE OF ILLUSTRATING THE DRAMATIC WORKS OF SHAKSPEARE, BY THE ARTISTS OF GREAT-BRITAIN. *Contains* 100 *large and beautiful engravings by Thew, Schiavonetti, Bartolozzi, Fittler, Middiman, Sharp, etc., after Fuseli, Smirke, Opie, Hamilton, Westall, Reynolds, Northcote, Stothard, West, and other eminent artists; including the large portraits of George III. and Queen Charlotte, Smirke's "Seven Ages," and the plate of "Shakspeare nursed by Tragedy*

and Comedy" after Romney. 2 vols., elephant folio (26 × 20 *inches), half crimson morocco, gilt edges.* ORIGINAL EDITION: THE "LARGE SET." London, 1803

337 BOYER, ABEL. FRENCH DICTIONARY; comprising all the Additions and Improvements of the Latest Paris and London Editions, etc., etc., with the Pronunciation of Each Word, according to the Dictionary of the Abbé Tardy, etc., etc. AN ENGLISH-FRENCH DICTIONARY, designed as a Second Part to the Boston Edition of Boyer's French Dictionary, etc. *Together in* 1 *vol.,* 8*vo, sheep.* Boston, 1830–31

338 BOYLE, HENRY. THE CHRONOLOGY OF THE EIGHTEENTH AND NINETEENTH CENTURIES; comprehending every Important Transaction from the Year 1700, to the Year 1835. *Thick* 8*vo, boards, uncut.* London, 1835

339 BOYNTON, CAPTAIN EDWARD C. HISTORY OF WEST POINT, AND ITS MILITARY IMPORTANCE DURING THE AMERICAN REVOLUTION; and the Origin and Progress of the United States Military Academy. *Folding view of West Point,* 1780, *and numerous plans and plates, colored and tinted, besides wood-cuts in the text. Imperial* 8*vo, cloth, rough edges.* LARGE PAPER: *only* 100 *copies printed, for E. French.* New York, 1864

340 BRACE, CHARLES L. HOME LIFE IN GERMANY. 12*mo, cloth.* New York, 1853

341 BRADFORD, REV. WILLIAM. SKETCHES OF THE COUNTRY, CHARACTER, AND COSTUME, IN PORTUGAL AND SPAIN, made during the Campaign, and on the Route of the British Army, in 1808 and 1809: engraved and colored from the Drawings; with Incidental Illustration, and Appropriate Descriptions, of Each Subject. (With a Supplement of Military Costume.) *Contains* 54 *plates. Imperial folio, half dark blue calf, very neat, gilt top; with book-plate of Shrewsbury.* LARGE PAPER. London, 1809

342 BRADFORD, REV. WILLIAM. ANOTHER COPY: *with Supplement; the letter-press in English and French. Contains* 51 *plates. Imperial* 4*to, crimson morocco extra, gilt edges; with book-plate of Lord Farnham.* London, s. a.

343 BRADSTREET, ANNE. THE TENTH MUSE LATELY SPRUNG UP IN AMERICA, OR SEVERALL POEMS, COMPILED WITH GREAT VARIETY OF WIT AND LEARNING, FULL OF DELIGHT; wherein especially is contained a Compleat Discourse and Description of the Four Elements, the Four Constitutions, the Four Ages of Man, the Four Seasons of the Year: together with an Exact Epitomie of the Four Monarchies, viz: the Assyrian, the Persian, the Grecian, the Roman. Also a Dialogue between Old England and New, concerning the Late Troubles: with Divers other Pleasant and Serious Poems. *Small* 8*vo, old calf, back cracked.* ORIGINAL EDITION. S. Bowtell, London, 1650

Collation: Title (repaired); 1 leaf. — "Kind Reader;" 1 leaf. — Verses by "N. Ward," "her sister," "I. W.," "A Knowne Friend," "C. B.," "R. Q.," "N. H.," "C. B.," "H. S.," and two anagrams; 5 leaves. — pp. 1–207. The preliminary leaves in the Boston edition, 1678, differ somewhat from those in this edition.

344 BRAND, Lieut. Charles, R. N. Journal of a Voyage to Peru; a Passage across the Cordillera of the Andes, in the Winter of 1827, performed on Foot in the Snow; a Journey across the Pampas. *Plates. 8vo, half crimson morocco.* London, 1828

345 BRAND, John. The History and Antiquities of the Town and County of the Town of Newcastle-upon-Tyne, including an Account of the Coal Trade of that Place. *Portrait of Sir Walter Blackett, Bart., engraved titles, plans, and numerous views of public buildings, etc., engraved by Fittler. 2 vols., royal 4to, old marbled calf; with book-plate of W. W. Atkinson, Burton in Kendal.* London, 1789

346 BRAND, John. Another copy: *the same. 2 vols., royal 4to, old calf, backs broken; with book-plate of William Bell.* London, 1789

347 BRANTÔME, Pierre de Bourdeille, l'Abbé de. Œuvres Complètes du Seigneur de Brantôme, accompagnées de Remarques Historiques et Critiques. Nouvelle Édition, collationnée sur les Manuscrits Autographes de la Bibliothèque du Roi, et Augmentée de Fragmens Inédit. *8 vols., 8vo, half calf, neat, marbled edges.* Foucault, Paris, 1822–23

348 BRATHWAITE, Richard. Essays upon the Five Senses; revived by a New Supplement, with a Pithy One upon Detraction, continued with Sundry Christian Resolves and Divine Contemplations. Reprinted from the Edition of 1625. *4to, half calf.* Only 200 copies printed. Private Press of Longmans & Co., London, 1815

This volume forms part VI. (or Part III. of the second volume as generally bound) of "Archaica," edited by Sir S. E. Brydges, which was published with "Heliconia," edited by T. Park. See Heliconia.

349 BRATHWAITE, Richard. Barnabæ Itinerarium, or Drunken Barnaby's Four Journeys to the North of England; in Latin and English Metre: wittily and merrily (tho' an Hundred Years ago) composed; found among some Old Musty Books that had lain a Long Time by in a Corner, and now at last made Public. Together with Bessy Bell: to which is now added (never before published), the Ancient Ballad of Chevy Chase; in Latin and English Verse. By Richard Brathwait; with a Life of the Author, Copious Notes, and Index. *Frontispiece, 12mo, cloth, red edges.* T. Gent, York, 1852

350 BRAYLEY, Edward Wedlake; and William Herbert. A Concise Account, Historical and Descriptive, of Lambeth Palace. *Engraved title, and 20 plates representing*

its most interesting antiquities in buildings, portraits, stained glass, etc.; the portraits and plate of arms colored. Imperial 4to, boards, rough edges. London, 1806

351 BRAYLEY, Edward Wedlake. Historical and Descriptive Accounts of the Theatres of London; illustrated with a View of Each Theatre, drawn and engraved by the late Daniel Havell. *4to, cloth.* London, 1833

352 BREAKFAST, Dinner, and Tea: viewed Classically, Poetically, and Practically; containing Numerous Curious Dishes and Feasts of all Times and all Countries, besides Three Hundred Modern Receipts. *Square crown 8vo, cloth, gilt top.* New York, 1859

353 BRETON, Nicholas. Cornu-copiæ: Pasquil's Night-Cap, or Antidot for the Head-ache. [By Breton.] London, printed for Thomas Thorp, 1612. *Reprinted from the editions of 1612 and 1623, by Whittingham. 8vo, boards, rough edges.* Privately printed: *and only 100 copies.* (R. Triphook, London), 1819

354 BRIDGENS, R., and Henry Shaw. Furniture, with Candelabra, and Interior Decoration. *A series of 60 fine plates, all beautifully colored. Imperial 4to, half morocco, uncut.* Large paper: *few copies printed.* W. Pickering, London, 1838

355 BRIDGES, Rev. Charles. An Exposition of the Book of Proverbs. *8vo, cloth.* New York, 1854

356 BRIDGMAN, Thomas. Epitaphs from Copp's Hill Burial Ground, Boston; with Notes. *12mo, cloth.* Boston, 1851

357 BRIDGMAN, Thomas. Memorials of the Dead in Boston; containing Exact Transcripts of Inscriptions on the Sepulchral Monuments in the King's Chapel Burial Ground, in the City of Boston; with Copious Historical and Biographical Notices of many of the Early Settlers of the Metropolis of New England. *Plates and wood-cuts. 12mo, cloth, gilt edges.* Boston, 1853

358 BRIDGMAN, Thomas. The Pilgrims of Boston and their Descendants; with an Introduction by Hon. Edward Everett, LL. D. Also, Inscriptions from the Monuments in the Granary Burial Ground, Tremont Street. *Portraits, views, arms, pedigrees, etc. Royal 8vo, cloth.* New York, 1856

359 BRINLEY, Francis. Life of William T. Porter. *Portrait. 12mo, cloth.* New York, 1860

360 BRISTED, Rev. John. America and her Resources; or, a View of the Agricultural, Commercial, Manufacturing, Financial, Political, Literary, Moral, and Religious Capacity and Character of the American People. *8vo, half calf.* London, 1818

361 BRITISH Almanac and Companion. The British

ALMANAC OF THE SOCIETY FOR THE DIFFUSION OF USEFUL KNOWLEDGE; with the COMPANION TO THE ALMANAC, or Year-Book of General Information. *For the years* 1828–1864. 37 *vols.*, 12*mo, cloth.* London, (1828–64)

362 BRITISH DRAMA. THE BRITISH DRAMA; comprehending the Best Plays in the English Language. (A Collection of 124 Tragedies, Comedies, Operas, and Farces by Various Authors, from 1598 to 1776.) *Plates* (3) *on titles, by J. Fittler, etc., after Smirke, etc.* 3 *vols. in* 5, *royal* 8*vo, diamond russia extra, marbled edges; with book-plate of John Hume Spry, M. A.* W. Miller, London, 1804

363 BRITISH DRAMA. THE ANCIENT BRITISH DRAMA. (A Collection of 57 Plays by Various Authors, from 1547 to 1778; reprinted, with 9 Exceptions, from Dodsley's Old Plays.) *Plates on titles.* 3 *vols., royal* 8*vo, old sprinkled calf, gilt, green edges.* W. Miller, London, 1810

The dates of these plays are from 1547 to 1667, except the last, Middleton's "Witch," which was first printed in 1778 from an old manuscript.

364 BRITISH DRAMA. THE MODERN BRITISH DRAMA. (A Collection of 155 Tragedies, Comedies, Operas, and Farces by Various Authors from 1598 to 1788.) *Plates* (5) *on titles, by J. Fittler, etc., after Smirke, etc.* 5 *vols., royal* 8*vo, old marbled calf, gilt.* W. Miller, London, 1811

This edition differs from the "British Drama" (1804) above, not only in the titles, but in the prefaces and contents also. Each contains pieces not in the other.

All the above three editions were printed by James Ballantyne, and they are said to have been edited by Sir Walter Scott.

365 BRITISH ESSAYISTS; WITH PREFACES, HISTORICAL AND BIOGRAPHICAL, BY ALEXANDER CHALMERS, F. S. A. *Portraits.* 38 *vols., foolscap* 8*vo, calf, gilt, marbled edges.* Boston, 1856–64

CONTENTS.

THE TATLER	4 vols.	THE CONNOISSEUR	2 vols.
THE SPECTATOR	8 vols.	THE IDLER	1 vol.
THE GUARDIAN	3 vols.	THE MIRROR	2 vols.
THE RAMBLER	3 vols.	THE LOUNGER	2 vols.
THE ADVENTURER	3 vols.	THE OBSERVER	3 vols.
THE WORLD	3 vols.	THE LOOKER-ON	3 vols.
INDEX,	1 vol.		

366 BRITISH NOVELISTS; WITH AN ESSAY, AND PREFACES, BIOGRAPHICAL AND CRITICAL, BY MRS. BARBAULD. 50 *vols.*, 12*mo, half morocco, contents lettered, marbled edges.* London, 1810

This collection comprises works of the most esteemed novelists, including the best novels of Miss Burney (Madame D'Arblay), DeFoe, Fielding, Goldsmith, Johnson, Richardson, Smollett, etc., etc.

367 BRITISH POETS. THE WORKS OF THE BRITISH POETS; WITH PREFACES, BIOGRAPHICAL AND CRITICAL, BY ROBERT ANDERSON, M. D. *Engraved titles.* 13 *vols., royal* 8*vo, old sprinkled calf, contents lettered, with book-plate of John Risdon.* London, 1795. (Edinburgh, 1793, etc.)

CONTENTS: Vol. I. Chaucer, Surrey, Wyatt, Sackville. Vol. II. Spenser,

Shakespeare, Davies, Hall. Vol. III. Drayton, Carew, Suckling. Vol. IV. Donne, Daniel, W. Browne, P. Fletcher, G. Fletcher. B. Jonson, Drummond, Crashaw, Davenant. Vol. V. Milton, Cowley, Waller, Butler, Denham, Vol. VI. Dryden, Rochester, Roscommon, Otway, Pomfret, Dorset. Stepney, J. Philips, Walsh, E. Smith, Duke, King, Sprat, Halifax. Vol. VII. Parnell, Garth, Rowe, Addison, Hughes, Sheffield, Prior, Congreve, Blackmore, Fenton, Granville. Yalden. Vol. VIII. Pope, Gay, Pattison, Hammond, Savage, Hill, Tickell, Somerville, Broome, Pitt, Blair. Vol. IX. Swift, J. Thomson, Watts, A. Philips, Hamilton, G. West, Collins, Dyer, Shenstone, Mallet, Akenside, Harte. Vol. X. Young, Gray, B. West, Lyttleton, Moore, Boyce, W. Thompson, Cawthorne, Churchill, Falconer, Lloyd, Cunningham, Green, Cooper, Goldsmith, P. Whitehead, J. Brown, Grainger, Smollett, Armstrong. Vol. XI. Wilkie, Dodsley, Smart, Langhorne, Bruce, Chatterton, Græme, Glover, Shaw, Lovibond, Penrose, Mickle, Jags, J. Scott, S. Johnson, W. Whitehead, Jenyns, Logan, Warton, Cotton, Blacklock. Vol. XII. Pope's Homer; West's Pindar; Dryden's Virgil, Persius, and Juvenal; Pitt's Æneid; Rowe's Lucan. Vol. XIII. Cooke's Hesiod; Fawkes's Theocritus, Anacreon, Sappho, Bion, Moschus, Musæus, and Appolonius Rhodius (with C——'s Coluthus Lycopolites); Creeche's Lucretius; Grainger's Tibullus, and Sulpicia.

"Your edition of the Poets of Great Britain does so much honor to their biographer and critic, that every friend to literature should assist his candid and ingenious labours; this, I hope, will serve as my apology for addressing a letter to you, without a more regular introduction." — *Bp. Percy.* (See Nichols' "Literary Illustrations," Vol. VII.)

368 BRITISH POETS. THE ALDINE EDITION OF THE BRITISH POETS. (With Memoirs and Notes, by Sir N. Harris Nicolas, J. Mitford, A. Dyce, and others.) PICKERING'S BEAUTIFUL EDITION. *Elegantly printed by Whittingham. Portraits.* 53 *vols., foolscap* 8*vo, maroon turkey morocco, gilt edges, by Hayday.* SPLENDID COMPLETE SET.
W. Pickering, London, 1830–53

CONTENTS.

AKENSIDE	1 vol.	MILTON	3 vols.
BEATTIE	1 vol.	PARNELL	1 vol.
BURNS	3 vols.	POPE	3 vols.
BUTLER	2 vols.	PRIOR	2 vols.
CHAUCER	6 vols.	SHAKESPEARE	1 vol.
CHURCHILL	3 vols.	SPENSER	5 vols.
COLLINS	1 vol.	SURREY	1 vol.
COWPER	3 vols.	SWIFT	3 vols.
DRYDEN	5 vols.	THOMSON	2 vols.
FALCONER	1 vol.	WHITE	1 vol.
GOLDSMITH	1 vol.	WYATT	1 vol.
GRAY	1 vol.	YOUNG	2 vols.

The most beautiful edition of poets ever printed, containing many pieces of each author not before published. Complete sets are now very difficult to make up.

369 BRITISH POETS. A COMPLETE COLLECTION OF THE BRITISH POETS; WITH BIOGRAPHICAL, HISTORICAL, AND CRITICAL NOTICES. *The whole thoroughly revised and corrected, especially for this edition. Portraits on India paper.* 130 *vols., crown* 8*vo, boards, green cloth backs, red sides, uncut.* LARGE PAPER: *only* 100 *copies printed.* Boston, 1865–66

CONTENTS.

AKENSIDE	1 vol.	CHURCHILL	3 vols.
BALLADS	8 vols.	COLERIDGE	3 vols.
BEATTIE	1 vol.	COLLINS	1 vol.
BURNS	3 vols.	COWPER	3 vols.
BUTLER	2 vols.	DONNE	1 vol.
BYRON	10 vols.	DRYDEN	5 vols.
CAMPBELL	1 vol.	FALCONER	1 vol.
CHATTERTON	2 vols.	GAY	2 vols.

GOLDSMITH	1 vol.	SHAKESPEARE	1 vol.
GRAY	1 vol.	SHELLEY	4 vols.
HERBERT	1 vol.	SKELTON	3 vols.
HERRICK	2 vols.	SOUTHEY	10 vols.
HOOD	5 vols.	SPENSER	5 vols.
KEATS	1 vol.	SURREY	1 vol.
MARVELL	1 vol.	SWIFT	3 vols.
MILTON	3 vols.	THOMSON	2 vols.
MONTGOMERY	5 vols.	VAUGHAN	1 vol.
MOORE	6 vols.	WATTS	1 vol.
PARNELL & TICKELL	1 vol.	WHITE	1 vol.
POPE	3 vols.	WORDSWORTH	7 vols.
PRIOR	2 vols.	WYATT	1 vol.
SCOTT	9 vols.	YOUNG	2 vols.

This collection, edited by Child, Lowell, and other eminent scholars, is the most complete ever printed.

370 BRITISH THEATRE. BELL'S BRITISH THEATRE. (Consisting of the most esteemed English Plays; and containing 69 Tragedies and 70 Comedies.) *Numerous fine plates after Smirke, Fuseli, Opie, etc., including portraits of eminent actors in their favorite characters. 3 vols., 18mo, old mottled calf, gilt, contents lettered.* J. Bell, London, 1791, etc.

371 BRITISH THEATRE. PLATES TO COOKE'S BRITISH THEATRE, *consisting of 55 fine engravings by Heath, Fittler, etc., after Smirke, Opie, and other eminent artists. No title. Imperial 8vo, boards.* LARGE PAPER: PROOF IMPRESSIONS. (C. Cooke, London, 1816–21)

372 BROCKEDON, WILLIAM. ILLUSTRATIONS OF THE PASSES OF THE ALPS BY WHICH ITALY COMMUNICATES WITH FRANCE, SWITZERLAND, AND GERMANY. *General map and 108 fine engravings, by E. Finden and other celebrated engravers, including a separate map of each pass; with historical and descriptive letter-press. 2 vols., 4to, half crimson morocco, gilt edges.* London, s. a.

373 BRONTË, CHARLOTTE, "CURRER BELL." JANE EYRE, a Novel. *Frontispiece. 12mo, cloth.* New York, 1864

374 BROOKES, JOSHUA. AN ADDRESS DELIVERED AT THE ANNIVERSARY MEETING OF THE ZOÖLOGICAL CLUB OF THE LINNEAN SOCIETY, November 29, 1828. *8vo, pp. 30, boards; with book-plate of Robert Balmanno, F. S. A.* London, 1828

375 BROOKS, EDWARD. AN ANSWER TO THE PAMPHLET OF MR. JOHN A. LOWELL, entitled "Reply to a Pamphlet recently circulated by Mr. Edward Brooks;" with New Facts and Further Proofs. *Royal 8vo, pp. 836, cloth.* Boston, 1851

376 BROUGHAM, HENRY, LORD. POLITICAL PHILOSOPHY. Part I. Principles of Government. Monarchical Government. Part II. Of Aristocracy. Aristocratic Government. Part III. Of Democracy. Mixed Monarchy. *3 vols., 8vo, half calf, extra, with autograph of Rufus Choate.* C. Knight, London, 1846

This edition was published under the superintendence of the Society for the Diffusion of Useful Knowledge.

377 BROUGHTON, HUGH. A SHORT VIEW OF THE PERSIAN MONARCHIE, AND OF DANIELS WEEKES; being a Peece of Bervaldus Workes, with a Censure in some Points. [By Broughton.] *Somewhat stained, but perfect copy. Small 4to, pp.* 46, *half morocco.* Imprinted by T. Orwin, London, 1590

378 BROUSSAIS, FRANÇOIS JOSEPH VICTOR. ON IRRITATION AND INSANITY; a Work, wherein the Relations of the Physical with the Moral Conditions of Man, are established on the Basis of Physiological Medicine. Translated by Thomas Cooper, M. D., etc. To which are added Two Tracts on Materialism, and an Outline of the Association of Ideas. *Portrait of Dr. Cooper. Royal 8vo, boards, rough edges.* Columbia, S. C., 1831

379 BROWN, CHARLES BROCKDEN. THE NOVELS OF: Wieland, Arthur Mervyn, Ormond, Edgar Huntly, Jane Talbot, and Clara Howard. With a Memoir of the Author. 6 *vols.*, 16*mo, half roan.* Boston, 1827

380 BROWN, JOHN, D. D., Vicar of St. Nicholas, NEWCASTLE. AN ESTIMATE OF THE MANNERS AND PRINCIPLES OF THE TIMES; by the Author of Essays on the Characteristics, etc. [Dr. Brown.] The Third Edition. *Parts I.–III., pp.* 221, *crown 8vo, sprinkled calf, neat.* London, 1757

"This work on its first publication excited uncommon attention, and ran through seven editions in one year." — *Lowndes.*

381 BROWN, JOHN, M. D. THE WORKS OF; to which is prefixed a Biographical Account of the Author, by William C. Brown. 3 *vols.*, 8*vo, old marbled calf, gilt.* London, 1804

This author was the founder of the once popular "Brunonian System" of medicine.

382 BROWN, THOMAS N. THE LIFE AND TIMES OF HUGH MILLER. 12*mo, cloth.* New York, 1858

383 BROWNE, CHARLES F. ARTEMUS WARD, HIS BOOK. With many Comic Illustrations. 12*mo, cloth.* New York, 1864

384 BROWNE, JUNIUS HENRI. FOUR YEARS IN SECESSIA; Adventures within and beyond the Union Lines, embracing a great Variety of Facts, Incidents, and Romance of the War, etc., etc. 8*vo, cloth.* Hartford, 1865

385 BROWNE, SIR THOMAS. PSEUDODOXIA EPIDEMICA, OR ENQUIRIES INTO VERY MANY RECEIVED TENENTS, AND COMMONLY PRESUMED TRUTHS; by Thomas Browne, Dr. of Physick. *Small folio, half calf; back cracked.* ORIGINAL EDITION OF THE "VULGAR ERRORS." E. Dod, London, 1646

386 BROWNE, SIR THOMAS. WORKS, INCLUDING HIS LIFE AND CORRESPONDENCE; edited by Simon Wilkin, F. L. S. *Portrait, pedigree, and plates.* 4 *vols., royal 8vo, tree calf, gilt, marbled edges.* BEST EDITION. LARGE PAPER: *only* 50 *copies printed.* W. Pickering, London, 1835–36

387 BROWNING, W. S. THE HISTORY OF THE HUGUENOTS, DURING THE SIXTEENTH CENTURY. 2 *vols., 8vo, half calf.* W. Pickering, London, 1829

388 BRUCE, JAMES. TRAVELS TO DISCOVER THE SOURCE OF THE NILE, in the Years 1768–1773. — ACCOUNT OF THE LIFE AND WRITINGS OF JAMES BRUCE; by Alexander Murray. *Portrait by Heath, maps, and numerous plates. Together,* 6 *vols., royal 4to, half morocco, rough edges.* FINE COPY: *with very wide margins.* Edinburgh, 1790–1808

TWELVE copies of this work were printed on LARGE PAPER.

389 BRUMOY, PIERRE. THE GREEK THEATRE OF FATHER BRUMOY; translated by Mrs. Charlotte Lennox [assisted by Boyle, Earl of Cork and Orrery, and Dr. Johnson]. 3 *vols., 4to, old calf, backs cracked; with book-plate of John Symmons.* London, 1759

390 BRUNET, JACQUES CHARLES. MANUEL DU LIBRAIRE ET DE L'AMATEUR DE LIVRES; contenant, 1°. Un Nouveau Dictionnaire Bibliographique, etc., etc. 2°. Une Table en Forme de Catalogue Raisonné, etc., etc. Cinquième Édition Originale, entièrement refondue, et augmentée d'un Tiers, par l'Auteur. 6 *vols., royal 8vo, half morocco, neat.* LAST AND BEST EDITION. Paris, 1860–65

This is an entirely new edition of this valuable bibliographical work, very much enlarged and improved. It is handsomely printed, on a fine paper, by Firmin Didot Frères, Fils & Cie., and contains numerous wood cut fac-similes of the devices of early printers, etc. The author spent the greater part of a long life in the study of bibliography, and lived to see this edition completed. It is invaluable to the collector, and only a small edition was printed.

391 BRUNTON, MARY. SELF-CONTROL, a Novel. *Frontispiece and vignette on the engraved title. Post 8vo, cloth, uncut.* London, 1832

392 BRYANT, JACOB. A NEW SYSTEM, OR AN ANALYSIS OF ANCIENT MYTHOLOGY; wherein an Attempt is made to divest Tradition of Fable, and to reduce the Truth to its Original Purity. In this Work is given an History of the Babylonians, Chaldeans, Egyptians, Canaanites, Helladians, Ionians, Leleges, Dorians, Pelasgi; also of the Scythæ, Indo-Scythæ, Ethiopians, Phenicians. The whole contains an Account of the Principal Events in the First Ages, from the Deluge to the Dispersion; also, of the Various Migrations which ensued, and the Settlements made afterwards in Different Parts; Circumstances of great Consequence, which were Subsequent to the Gentile History of Moses. *With* 33 *plates, including the* 3 *maps and* 3 *tail-pieces.* 3 *vols., royal 4to, diamond russia, neat, marbled edges. Very fine copy.* London, 1774–76

393 BRYANT, JACOB. ANOTHER COPY: *the same. Same plates.* 3 *vols., 4to, old mottled calf, marbled edges.* London, 1775–76

The "Marlborough Gem" in both these copies is engraved by Sherwin.

394 BRYANT, WILLIAM CULLEN. LETTERS OF A TRAVELLER. Second Series. (From Spain, etc.) *12mo, cloth.* New York, 1859

395 BRYDGES, SIR SAMUEL EGERTON. RESTITUTA; OR TITLES, EXTRACTS, AND CHARACTERS OF OLD BOOKS IN ENGLISH LITERATURE REVIVED. *Printed by T. Bensley. 4 vols., 8vo, half russia, rough edges.* FINE COPY: *only 250 printed.* London, 1814–16

396 BRYDGES, SIR SAMUEL EGERTON. ANOTHER COPY; *the same. 4 vols., 8vo, half morocco, marbled edges; with book-plate of Henry Thomas Buckle.* London, 1814–16

397 BRYDGES, SIR SAMUEL EGERTON. THE AUTOBIOGRAPHY, TIMES, OPINIONS, AND CONTEMPORARIES OF. *Portraits. 2 vols., 8vo, half calf, extra.* London, 1834

398 BRYDONE, PATRICK. A TOUR THROUGH SICILY AND MALTA; in a Series of Letters to William Beckford, Esq., of Somerly, in Suffolk. *12mo, sheep.* New York, 1813

399 BUCK, SIR GEORGE. THE HISTORY OF THE LIFE AND REIGNE OF RICHARD THE THIRD; composed in Five Books, by Geo. Buck, Esquire. *Portrait by Cross. Small folio, old calf.* London, 1647

"Sir George Buck, contrary to all historians before him, doth make King Richard 3 an admirable man, and not at all that man that other histories make him to be. He condemns the history of Sir Tho. More who follows his quondam master Dr. John Moreton, archbishop of Canterbury, a favourer of King Henry the 7th." — *Ant. à Wood.*

400 BUCKINGHAM, JOSEPH T. SPECIMENS OF NEWSPAPER LITERATURE; with Personal Memoirs, Anecdotes, and Reminiscences. *Portraits of I. Thomas and B. Russell, and woodcuts. 2 vols., 12mo, cloth.* Boston, 1852

401 BUCKINGHAMSHIRE, JOHN SHEFFIELD, DUKE OF. THE WORKS OF. *Portrait by Vertue, and plates. 2 vols. in 1, 4to, old sprinkled calf.* London, 1723

402 BUCKINGHAMSHIRE, JOHN SHEFFIELD, DUKE OF. ANOTHER COPY: *the same. Portrait and title to first volume wanting. 2 vols., old calf, backs cracked; with book-plate of William Austen of Hernden in Kent.* London, 1723

403 BUCKINGHAMSHIRE, JOHN SHEFFIELD, DUKE OF. ANOTHER COPY; the Fourth Edition. *2 vols., post 8vo, half morocco.* London, 1753

404 BUCKLE, HENRY THOMAS. HISTORY OF CIVILIZATION IN ENGLAND. From the Second London Edition; to which is added, an Alphabetical Index. *2 vols., 8vo, cloth.* New York, 1860–61

405 BUDDEUS, CARL. VOLKSGEMÄLDE UND CHARAKTERKÖPFE DES RUSSISCHEN VOLKS; ein Beytrag zur Nähern Kenntniss der Sitten und Gebräuche, der Wohnungen, Beschäftigungen, und Vergnügungen desselben. *2 Nos. (I. and II.), containing 8 colored plates each, imperial 4to, boards.* Leipzig, 1820

406 BUDGEN, Miss L. M. Episodes of Insect Life; by Acheta Domestica, M. E. S. [Miss Budgen.] Three Series, *with numerous pleasing and grotesque wood-cuts, finely executed after designs by the author. 3 vols., square crown 8vo, half calf, very neat, marbled edges.* Original edition: *fine impressions of the cuts.* London, 1849–51

407 BUELOW, Joseph de. Historical Sketches of Europe, containing Accounts of Interesting Events, Distinguished Actions, etc., etc. *Parts I.–XII., with 47 lithographic plates. 4to.* New York, (1860, etc.)

408 BUFF, Heinrich. Familiar Letters on the Physics of the Earth; treating of the Chief Movements of the Land, the Waters, and the Air, and the Forces that give rise to them. Edited by A. W. Hofmann. *Foolscap 8vo, cloth, uncut.* London, 1851

409 BULFINCH, Thomas. Works. The Age of Fable, or Beauties of Mythology. — The Age of Chivalry, or Legends of King Arthur. — Legends of Charlemagne, or Romance of the Middle Ages. — Oregon and Eldorado, or Romance of the Rivers [Columbia and Amazon]. *Wood-cuts. Together, 4 vols., crown 8vo, crimson morocco, gilt edges.* Boston, 1863–66

410 BULWER, John. Anthropometamorphosis: Man Transformed, or the Artificial Changeling; Historically presented in the Mad and Cruel Gallantry, Foolish Bravery, Ridiculous Beauty, Filthy Finenesse, and Loathsome Lovelinesse of most Nations, fashioning & altering their Bodies from the Mould intended by Nature. With a Vindication of the Regular Beauty and Honesty of Nature; and an Appendix of the Pedigree of the English Gallant. By J. B., sirnamed the Chirosopher [John Bulwer]. *Frontispiece. 12mo, calf. First edition.* J. Hardesty, London, 1650

411 BUNBURY, Henry. Twenty-two Plates, Illustrative of Various Interesting Scenes in the Plays of Shakspeare, engraved by Bartolozzi, Tomkins, Cheesman, Meadows, etc., etc.; from the Designs of the late Henry Bunbury, Esq., in the Possession of her Royal Highness the Duchess of York. *Fine impressions, two without letters. Atlas folio, half calf.* London, s. a.

412 BUNBURY, Henry. An Academy for Grown Horsemen, containing the Completest Instructions for Walking, Trotting, Cantering, Galloping, Stumbling, and Tumbling. The Annals of Horsemanship: containing Accounts of Accidental Experiments and Experimental Accidents, both Successful and Unsuccessful; communicated by Various Correspondents to the Author, Geoffrey Gambado, Esq., Riding Master, Master of the Horse, and Grand Equerry to

the Doge of Venice. [By H. Bunbury.] *Colored plates by Rowlandson, after the author's designs.* 1 *vol.*, 8*vo, half morocco; with book-plate of Rev*[d.] *Fred. Ekins.* London, 1809

413 BUNN, ALFRED. THE STAGE, BOTH BEFORE AND BEHIND THE CURTAIN; from "Observations taken on the Spot." 2 *vols.*, 12*mo, half morocco.* Philadelphia, 1840

414 BUNYAN, JOHN. THE PILGRIM'S PROGRESS FROM THIS WORLD TO THAT WHICH IS TO COME. With Memoir of the Author, by George Cheever, D. D.; and Engravings on Wood by G., E., and J. Dalziel, from Designs by William Harvey. *Crown* 4*to, calf, extra, gilt edges.* LARGE PAPER: PROOF IMPRESSIONS OF THE CUTS. Bogue, London, 1850

This edition is very rare in this state, as only 50 copies were printed on this size paper before any others were struck off, and dated one year earlier than those on small paper. A *large paper* edition was published in 1859 (without date), but the cuts were then very much worn.

415 BUNYAN, JOHN. THE PILGRIM'S PROGRESS; with a Memoir of the Author's Life, by the Rev. Thomas Scott, and Illustrative Notes by the Editor. *Portrait, fac-simile of Bunyan's will. Plates, and wood-cuts. Imperial* 4*to, cloth.* London, s. a.

416 BUNYAN, JOHN. THE PILGRIM'S PROGRESS. A New Edition, with a Memoir by J. M. Hare. *Wood-cuts, after J. R. Clayton and J. L. Williams. Post* 8*vo, cloth.* London, 1853

417 BUNYAN, JOHN. THE PILGRIM'S PROGRESS FROM THIS WORLD TO THAT WHICH IS TO COME. A New Edition, with a Memoir and Notes by George Offor. Illustrated with One Hundred and Ten Designs by J. D. Watson, engraved on Wood by the Brothers Dalziel. *Foolscap* 4*to, cloth, gilt edges.* London, 1861

418 BURCHELL, WILLIAM JAMES. TRAVELS IN THE INTERIOR OF SOUTHERN AFRICA. With an Entirely New Map, and Numerous Engravings. *Vol. I. only; the large plates finely colored.* 4*to, half calf extra.* London, 1822

The second volume was published in 1824. In the subsequent issues the plates were not so well colored.

419 BURGES, SIR JAMES BLAND, BART. THE BIRTH AND TRIUMPH OF LOVE; A POEM. PROOF IMPRESSIONS, *of the* 24 *fine plates by Tomkins, from the designs of the Princess Elizabeth.* 4*to, old marbled calf, gilt, yellow edges.* London, 1796

420 BURGHLEY, WILLIAM CECIL, LORD. MEMOIRS OF THE LIFE AND ADMINISTRATION OF WILLIAM CECIL, LORD BURGHLEY, Secretary of State in the Reign of King Edward VI. and Lord High Treasurer of England in the Reign of Queen Elizabeth; containing an Historical View of the Times in which he lived, and of many Eminent and Illustrious Persons with whom he was connected: with Extracts

from his Private and Official Correspondence and other Papers, now first published from the Originals. By the Rev. Edward Nares, D. D., etc. *Fine portraits and plates.* *3 vols., 4to, blue calf, marbled edges.* London, 1828–31

"The present work is the production of an author well qualified to do justice to his subject; and in composition and arrangement he has exhibited incalculable industry and talents. Nothing seems to have escaped him that could tend to illustrate the life and times of this great statesman." — *Gent's Mag.*

421 BURGOYNE, Lieut. Gen. John. The Dramatic and Poetical Works of; to which is prefixed Memoirs of the Author. Embellished with Copper-Plates. *Handsomely printed by Whittingham.* *2 vols., 8vo, tree calf, gilt, marbled edges, by Riviere.* Large paper: *fine copy.* London, 1808

422 BURKE, Edmund. The Works of. *9 vols., 8vo, cloth, uncut.* Boston, 1839

"That great master of eloquence, Edmund Burke! . . . . . in aptitude of comprehension and richness of imagination, superior to every orator, ancient or modern." — *Macaulay.*

423 BURKE, Edmund. A Philosophical Inquiry into the Origin of our Ideas of the Sublime and Beautiful; with an Introductory Discourse concerning Taste. *Frontispiece and vignette by C. Heath, after H. Corbould.* *18mo, cloth.* London, 1839

424 BURKE, Edmund, and French Laurence. The Epistolary Correspondence of the Right Hon. Edmund Burke and Dr. French Laurence; published from the Original Manuscripts. *8vo, cloth, uncut.* London, 1827

425 BURLEIGH, J. B. The Legislative Guide; containing all the Rules for conducting Business in Congress, Jefferson's Manual, and the Citizens' Manual, including a Concise System of Rules of Order founded on Congressional Proceedings, etc., etc. Fourth Edition, revised. *8vo, sheep.* Philadelphia, 1853

426 BURN, Lieut. Col. Robert. A Naval and Military Technical Dictionary of the French Language; in Two Parts: French-English, and English-French. *Thick crown 8vo, cloth, uncut.* Boston (London), 1853

427 BURNET, Gilbert, Bishop of Salisbury. The History of the Reformation of the Church of England. A New Edition, with Numerous Illustrative Notes and a Copious Index; *and embellished with forty-seven portraits.* *2 vols., imperial 8vo, cloth, uncut.* London, 1841

428 BURNEY, Charles. An Account of the Musical Performances in Westminster-Abbey and the Pantheon, May 26th, 27th, 29th, and June the 3d and 5th, 1784; in Commemoration of Handel. (With Life, etc., of Handel, and a List of his Works.) *Fine plates, engraved by Bartolozzi, Sherwin, etc.* *4to, half morocco.* London, 1785

429 BURNEY, FRANCES, afterwards MADAME D'ARBLAY. CECILIA, or Memoirs of an Heiress; by the author of Evelina [Miss Burney]. The Eighth Edition. *5 vols., 12mo, sheep.* London, 1802

430 BURNS, ROBERT. THE WORKS OF; with an Account of his Life, and a Criticism on his Writings: to which are prefixed some Observations on the Character and Condition of the Scottish Peasantry. [By Dr. James Currie.] Sixth Edition, 1809. RELIQUES OF ROBERT BURNS, consisting chiefly of Original Poems, and Critical Observations on Scottish Songs; collected and published by R. H. Cromek, 1808. *Together, 5 vols., 8vo, russia extra, gilt edges.* ILLUSTRATED COPY. T. Cadell, etc., London, 1808–09

This fine copy is from the library of the late John Allan, and contains, neatly inserted, 89 portraits and plates executed by the best engravers, including Vertue, Bartolozzi, Schiavonetti, etc., etc., all fine impressions, some proofs before letters, and many of them very rare.

431 BURNS, ROBERT. THE WORKS OF; with his Life, by Allan Cunningham. *Portrait and* 15 *plates, by E. Goodall, W. J. Cooke, and others.* 8 *vols., foolscap* 8*vo, cloth, uncut.* London, 1834

432 BURNS, ROBERT. THE POETICAL WORKS OF (with Memoir and Notes, by Sir N. Harris Nicolas). *Portrait; glossary and indexes.* 4 *vols., foolscap* 8*vo, cloth, uncut.* ALDINE EDITION. W. Pickering, London, 1839

433 BURNS, ROBERT. THE WORKS OF; with Life, by Allan Cunningham. New Edition. *Engraved title and dedication, portrait and fac-similes. Royal* 8*vo, morocco extra, gilt edges.* London, 1845

434 BURNS, ROBERT. THE SOLDIER'S RETURN. Illustrated by John Faed, R. S. A.—AULD LANG SYNE. Illustrated by George Harvey, R. S. A. *Published for the members of the "Royal Association for the Promotion of the Fine Arts in Scotland." Plates engraved by Lemon, Stocks, and Stephenson.* 2 *vols., folio, cloth.* Edinburgh, 1857–59

435 BURNS, ROBERT. POEMS, CHIEFLY IN THE SCOTTISH DIALECT. Kilmarnock: Printed by John Wilson, MDCCLXXXVI. *Fac-simile reprint of the original edition.* 8*vo, boards, uncut.* ONLY 600 COPIES PRINTED.

(J. McKie, Kilmarnock, 1867.)

436 BURTON, JOHN HILL. THE BOOK-HUNTER, ETC. (Part I. His Nature. Part II. His Functions. Part III. His Club. Part IV. Book-Club Literature.) *Handsomely printed, with ornate initials and other embellishments. Foolscap* 4*to, half olive turkey morocco, red cloth sides, rough edges.* LARGE PAPER: *only* 25 *copies printed.* Edinburgh, 1862

437 BURTON, JOHN HILL. ANOTHER COPY: *American edition*

with additional notes by Richard Grant White. Crown 8vo, cloth, gilt top. New York, 1863

Mr. White in his "Prefatory Note" says: "The following desultory dissertation on books, book-collecting, and book-collectors, cannot fail to be welcome, for it is always interesting, often serviceable, and sometimes amusing information."

438 BURTON, JOHN HILL. THE HISTORY OF SCOTLAND, FROM AGRICOLA'S INVASION TO THE REVOLUTION OF 1688. *Vols. I.-IV., 8vo, cloth, uncut.* Edinburgh, 1867

439 BURTON, RICHARD, or ROBERT, alias NATHANIEL CROUCH. ADMIRABLE CURIOSITIES, RARITIES, AND WONDERS, IN ENGLAND, SCOTLAND, AND IRELAND; being an Account of many Remarkable Persons and Places, and likewise of Battles, Sieges, Earthquakes, Inundations, Thunders, Lightnings, Fires, Murders, and other Considerable Occurrences and Accidents, for Several Hundred Years Past: with the Natural and Artificial Rarities in Every County, and many other Observable Passages, as they are recorded by Credible Historians of Former and Latter Ages. A New Edition; with Additional Wood-cut Portraits, and a Copious Index [Edited by Machell Stace]. *Duplicates of many of the portraits, surrounded by borders, with biographical notices beneath.* LARGE PAPER: *only* 50 *copies printed.* M. Stace, Westminster, 1811

There were five other volumes issued in this set of reprints, comprising the following works of this author: "Wars in England, Scotland, and Ireland;" "Historical Remarks on the Ancient and Present State of London and Westminster;" "History of Ireland:" "History of Scotland;" and "History of the House of Orange."

The original editions bear imprint of "N. Crouch;" and John Dunton in his "Life and Errors" speaks of the author as "Nat. Crouch."

Dr. Johnson, in a letter to "Mr. Dilly in the Poultry, January 6, 1784," says: "There is in the world a set of books which used to be sold by the booksellers on the bridge, and which I must entreat you to procure for me. They are called BURTON'S *Books:* the title of one is 'Admirable Curiosities, Rarities, and Wonders in England' . . . . . . they seem very proper to allure backward readers."

440 BURTON, ROBERT. THE ANATOMY OF MELANCHOLY, WHAT IT IS, WITH ALL THE KINDS, CAUSES, SYMPTOMES, PROGNOSTICS, AND SEVERAL CURES OF IT; in Three Partitions, with their Several Sections, Members and Subsections Philosophically, Medicinally, Historically opened and cut up. By Democritus Junior [Burton]. With a Satyrical Preface conducing to the following Discourse. The Tenth Edition corrected, to which is now first prefixed an Account of the Author. *Frontispieces after Thurston, etc. 2 vols., royal 8vo, diamond russia, neat, marbled edges.* LARGE PAPER: *fine copy.* London, 1804

441 BURTON, ROBERT. ANOTHER COPY: The Sixteenth Edition, printed from the authorized copy of 1651, with the Author's last Corrections, Additions, etc., etc. *Frontispiece. 8vo, calf, very neat, marbled edges.* London, 1836

442 BURTON, William E. Cyclopædia of Wit and Humor, containing Choice and Characteristic Selections from the Writings of the most Eminent Humorists of America, Ireland, Scotland, and England. Edited by William E. Burton. *With 24 portraits and nearly 600 wood-cuts. 2 vols., royal 8vo, cloth.* New York, 1858

443 BUSK, Hans. The Navies of the World; their Present State, and Future Capabilities. *Wood-cuts. Post 8vo, cloth, uncut.* London, 1859

444 BUSK, M. M. The History of Spain and Portugal, from B. C. 1000 to A. D. 1814. *8vo, cloth, uncut; with autograph of Rufus Choate.* London, (1832)

445 BUSSY-RABUTIN, Roger, Comte de. The Amorous History of the Gauls; containing the Intrigues and Gallantries of the Court of France, during the Reign of Louis XIV. Written in French by Roger de Rabutin; and now translated into English. The Second Edition. *12mo, new sprinkled calf, gilt, red edges.* London, 1727

446 BUSY (The) Hives around us: a Variety of Trips and Visits to the Mine, the Workshop, and the Factory. *Wood-cuts by the Dalziels, after Harvey. Foolscap 8vo, cloth.* London, s. a.

447 BUTLER, Henry D. The Family Aquarium, or Aqua Vivarium; a "New Pleasure" for the Domestic Circle, etc. *Colored frontispiece and wood-cuts. 12mo, cloth.* New York, (1858)

448 BUTLER, Joseph, Bishop. The Analogy of Religion, Natural and Revealed, to the Constitution and Course of Nature. With an Introductory Essay, by Albert Barnes. *12mo, cloth.* New York, 1840

449 BUTLER, Joseph, Bishop. The Works of. To which is prefixed a Preface, giving some Account of the Character and Writings of the Author; by Samuel Halifax, D. D. A New Edition. *2 vols., 8vo, tree calf, gilt.* University Press, Oxford, 1844

450 BUTLER, Joseph, Bishop. Another copy: *the same. 2 vols., 8vo, calf, gilt, marbled edges.* University Press, Oxford, 1849–50

451 BUTLER, Samuel. Hudibras: the First and Second Parts, written in the Time of the late Wars; corrected and amended, with Several Additions and Annotations. The Third and Last Part, written by the Author of the First and Second Parts. *Anonymous; the first and second parts printed for John Martyn and Henry Herringman, the third part for Simon Miller. 1 vol., small 8vo, old calf, red edges, back cracked; with autographs.* London, 1678

On a fly-leaf is this note: "This is the most complete edition of Hudibras that exists, revised and corrected by the author himself." (Signed) George W. Erving, Lincolns Inn, Feby. 23d, 1792."

452 BUTLER, SAMUEL. HUDIBRAS, in Three Parts, written in the Time of the late Wars [by Butler]; corrected and amended. With large Annotations and a Preface, by Zachary Grey, LL. D. *Portrait by Vertue, and 16 plates after Hogarth. 2 vols., 8vo, sprinkled calf, gilt, yellow edges, by Riviere; uniform with "Remains."* BEST EDITION: *elegant copy.* Cambridge, 1744

The second volume has, inserted, the title (on India paper) engraved by Thompson for Baldwin's edition of 1819.

453 BUTLER, SAMUEL. THE GENUINE REMAINS, IN VERSE AND PROSE, OF MR. SAMUEL BUTLER, AUTHOR OF HUDIBRAS; published from the Original Manuscripts, formerly in the Possession of W. Longueville, Esq., with Notes by R. Thyer. *2 vols., 8vo, sprinkled calf, gilt, yellow edges, by Riviere; uniform with the above copy of "Hudibras."* ELEGANT COPY. J. & R. Tonson, London, 1759

454 BUTLER, SAMUEL. HUDIBRAS, in Three Parts, written in the Time of the late Wars, by Samuel Butler, Esq. With large Annotations and a Preface, by Zachary Grey, LL. D. *Printed by T. Bensley. Portrait, after Sir P. Lely, and plates after Hogarth, engraved by Ridley; with wood-cut vignettes, by C. Nesbit. 2 vols., royal 8vo, old marbled calf, extra.* LARGE PAPER: *fine copy.* London, 1799

455 BUTLER, SAMUEL. HUDIBRAS. With Notes by the Rev. Treadway Russel Nash, D. D. A New Edition illustrated. *Numerous portraits, plates, and wood-cuts. 2 vols., post 8vo, morocco, extra, gilt edges.* London, 1847

456 BUTLER, WILLIAM ALLEN. NOTHING TO WEAR; an Episode of City Life. *Illustrated by Hoppin. 12mo, cloth.* New York, 1857

457 BUTLER, WILLIAM ALLEN. TWO MILLIONS. *12mo, boards.* New York, 1858

458 BUTTS, I. R. THE UNITED STATES BUSINESS MAN'S LAW CABINET; containing Practical Forms, and Commercial and Domestic Laws applicable to almost every Possible Circumstance and Situation in which Persons can be placed in the Ordinary Occurrences of Trade and Social Life. By I. R. Butts, assisted by Members of the Bar. *Thick 12mo, sheep.* Boston, 1860

459 BYRON, GEORGE ANSON, LORD. VOYAGE OF H. M. S. BLONDE TO THE SANDWICH ISLANDS, IN THE YEARS 1824–1825; Captain the Rt. Hon. Lord Byron, Commander. *Maps and plates. 4to, half green calf, neat.* J. Murray, London, 1826

460 BYRON, GEORGE NOEL GORDON, LORD. THE WORKS OF: with his Letters and Journals, and his Life by Thomas Moore, Esq. *Portrait and 33 plates by W. and E. Finden, fac-similes, etc. 17 vols., foolscap 8vo, cloth, uncut.* J. Murray, London, 1832–33

461 BYRON, GEORGE NOEL GORDON, LORD. THE POETICAL WORKS OF; collected and arranged, with Illustrative Notes, by Thomas Moore [and others]. *Portrait, engraved title and dedication, fac-similes, etc. Royal 8vo, morocco, gilt edges.* J. Murray, London, 1845

462 BYSSHE, EDWARD. THE ART OF ENGLISH POETRY; containing, I. Rules for making Verses. II. A Collection of the most Natural, Agreeable, and Sublime Thoughts, etc. III. A Dictionary of Rhymes. The Seventh Edition, corrected and enlarged. 2 *vols., R. Wilkin, etc.* 1725.—VOL. THE III[d] AND IVth which, with the Two Former Volumes, make a Compleat Common-Place-Book of English Poetry, etc. Alphabetically digested and brought down to the Present Time. 2 *vols., W. Taylor,* 1718. *Together,* 4 *vols.,* 12*mo, old calf.* London, 1718–25

463 CABINET (THE) OF GENIUS; containing Frontispieces and Characters adapted to the most Popular Poems, etc., with the Poems, etc., at large. *Engraved title and* 70 *plates; engraved, chiefly, by C. Taylor, after paintings by S. Shelley. Foolscap 4to, citron morocco, extra, gilt edges.* London, 1792

Some of the plates are engraved by Ogborne.

464 CAIRNES, JOHN E. THE SLAVE POWER, ITS CHARACTER, CAREER, AND PROBABLE DESIGNS; being an Attempt to explain the Real Issues involved in the American Contest. *8vo, cloth.* New York, 1862

465 CALAMY, EDMUND, D. D. THE NONCONFORMIST'S MEMORIAL; being an Account of the Lives, Sufferings, and Printed Works, of the Two Thousand Ministers ejected from the Church of England, chiefly by the Act of Uniformity, Aug. 24, 1666. Originally written by Edmund Calamy, D. D.; abridged, corrected, and methodized, with many Additional Anecdotes and Several New Lives, by Samuel Palmer. The Second Edition. *Numerous fine portraits.* 3 *vols., 8vo, sprinkled calf, gilt, marbled edges.* London, 1802–03

466 CALDCLEUGH, ALEXANDER. TRAVELS IN SOUTH AMERICA, DURING THE YEARS 1819–20–21; containing an Account of the Present State of Brazil, Buenos Ayres, and Chile. *Maps and plates in aqua-tinta.* 2 *vols., 8vo, cloth; with a MS. page of statistics and numerous pencil-notes.* J. Murray, London, 1825

467 CALEDONIAN (THE) MUSICAL REPOSITORY; a Choice Selection of Esteemed Scottish Songs, adapted for the Voice, Violin, and German Flute. *Frontispiece and vignette on the engraved title. Post 8vo, sheep; with autograph of Rufus Choate.* CROSBY'S COLLECTION. Oliver & Boyd, Edinburgh, 181[illegible]

468 CALEF, ROBERT, AND COTTON MATHER, D. D. SALEM WITCHCRAFT: comprising more Wonders of the Invisible World, collected by Robert Calef; and Wonders of the Invisible World, by Cotton Mather. Together with Notes and Explanations, by Samuel P. Fowler. *Portrait of Mather, on India paper, and typographical embellishments. 4to, cloth, rough edges.* LARGE PAPER: *only* 100 *copies printed.*
W. Veazie, Boston, 1865

469 CALKINS, N. A. PRIMARY OBJECT LESSONS FOR A GRADUATED COURSE OF DEVELOPMENT; a Manual for Teachers and Parents, with Lessons for the Proper Training of the Faculties of Children. *Colored frontispiece and woodcuts.* 12*mo, cloth.* New York, 1861

470 CALMET, AUGUSTIN. DICTIONARY OF THE BIBLE, TAYLOR'S EDITION, WITH THE BIBLICAL FRAGMENTS. *Above* 200 *plates.* 5 *vols.,* 4*to, half levant morocco, gilt tops, rough edges.* VERY FINE COPY. Charlestown (Mass.), 1812–17

"Calmet's truly valuable Dictionary of the Bible has formed the basis of all modern works of the kind. In the edition by Taylor many alterations were made and much additional matter added. It was the principal occupation of the life of that industrious editor, and contains a vast fund of Biblical illustration." — *Darling.*

471 CALVERT, GEORGE H. THE GENTLEMAN. *Post* 8*vo, cloth.* Boston, 1863

472 CALVERT, GEORGE H. SCENES AND THOUGHTS IN EUROPE. First and Second Series. 2 *vols., post* 8*vo, cloth, gilt tops.* Boston, 1863

473 CAMOENS, LUIS DE. THE LUSIAD. Books I. to V., translated by Edward Quillinan, with Notes by John Adamson. *Portrait.* 12*mo, cloth, uncut.*
E. Moxon, London, 1853

474 CAMPAN, JEANNE L. H. G. CONVERSATIONS OF MADAME CAMPAN, comprising Secret Anecdotes of the French Court, with Correspondence, etc.; edited by M. Maigne. 8*vo, cloth, uncut.* London, s. a.

475 CAMPAN, J. L. H. G. MEMOIRS OF THE COURT OF MARIE ANTOINETTE, QUEEN OF FRANCE. New Edition. *Portraits.* 2 *vols.,* 8*vo, cloth, uncut.* London, 1843

476 CAMPBELL, HUGH. THE LOVE LETTERS OF MARY QUEEN OF SCOTS, to James Earl of Bothwell; with her Love Sonnets and Marriage Contracts (being the Long-Missing Originals from the Gilt Casket): explained by State Papers, and the Writings of Buchanan, Goodall, Robertson, Hume, Lord Hailes, Lord Ellibank, Tytler, Horace Walpole, Whitaker, Laing, Chalmers, Brantome, Ronsard, Miss Benger, and a Host of Authors; forming a Complete History of the Origin of the Scottish Queen's Woes and Trials, before Queen Elizabeth. *Portrait.* 8*vo, half calf, neat.*
London, (1824)

477 CAMPBELL, John, LL. D. Memoirs of the Lives and Conduct of those Illustrious Heroes, Prince Eugene of Savoy and John Duke of Marlborough; wherein is included a Full, Particular, and Impartial Account of their Behaviour in the Late Wars, as likewise the Military and Gallant Actions of the Duke of Argyle, the Earl of Stair, the Lord Cobham, the Earl of Cadogan, and many other Generals, both English and Foreign. The Whole being a Compleat and Regular History of the Wars in all Parts of Europe, from the Beginning of the Reign of Queen Anne to the Time of the Last General Peace. The Whole illustrated with a great Number of Large Copper Plates representing the Principal Battles, etc.; together with the Effigies of Prince Eugene, and the Duke of Marlborough. To which is added a Compleat Index. *Folio, old calf.* London, 1742

478 CAMPBELL, Rev. John. Travels in South Africa; undertaken at the Request of the Missionary Society. *Portrait, map, and plates. Royal 8vo, half calf, extra.* First journey: *large paper.* London, 1815

"In his First Journey, he considerably enlarged the sphere of our knowledge of Southern Africa; but we cannot say much in favor of the result of his Second Expedition." — *Quarterly Review, Vol. XXVII. p.* 365.

479 CAMPBELL, Thomas. The Poetical Works of. New Edition. *Portrait, after Sir T. Lawrence, and 7 plates by C. Heath, after Westall. 2 vols., foolscap 8vo, boards, uncut.* London, 1833

480 CAMPBELL, Thomas. Life of Mrs. Siddons. *Portrait and wood-cuts. 2 vols., 8vo, calf, neat.* London, 1834

481 CANOVA, Antonio. The Works of Antonia Canova in Sculpture and Modelling, engraved in Outline by Henry Moses; with Descriptions from the Italian of the Countess Albrizzi, and a Biographical Memoir by Count Cicognara. *Portrait and 154 plates. 3 vols., imperial 4to, half morocco, neat, gilt tops.* Large paper: *proof impressions.* London, 1824–28

482 CANTICUM Canticorum, reproduced in Fac-Simile from the Scriverius Copy in the British Museum; with an Historical and Bibliographical Introduction, by J. Ph. Berjeau. *With 16 plates printed in brown ink, the whole on a very heavy paper. Imperial 4to, white vellum, gilt top.* Only 150 copies printed. Trübner & Co., London, 1860

483 CANTU, Cesare. Histoire Universelle, par César Cantu; soigneusement remaniée par l'Auteur, et traduite sous ses Yeux, par Eugène Aroux, et Piersilvestro Léopardi. *19 vols., 8vo, half green calf, neat, with autograph of Rufus Choate.* Paris, 1853–55

484 CAPE COD (The) Centennial Celebration at Barnstable, Sept. 3, 1839, of the Incorporation of that Town, Sept. 3, 1639. A Discourse pronounced at Barnstable on

the Third of September, 1839, at the Celebration of the Second Centennial Anniversary of the Settlement of Cape Cod; by John G. Palfrey. *F. Andrews, Boston,* 1840. *Together, 8vo, pp.* 92 *and* 71, *binding broken.* Boston, 1840

485 CAPICIUS, Scipio. De Principiis Rerum Libri Duo. Ejusdem de Vate Maximo (S. Joanne Baptista) Libri Tres. *Small 8vo, vellum.* Apud Aldi Filios, Venetiis, 1546

486 CAPPE, Catharine. Memoirs of the Life of; written by herself. (Edited by her Daughter, Mary Cappe.) *Portrait. 8vo, half morocco, neat.* London, 1822

487 CARACCIOLUS, Galeacius. The Italian Convert: News from Italy of a Second Moses, or the Life of Galeacius Caracciolus, the Noble Marquess of Vico; containing the Story of his Admirable Conversion from Popery, and Forsaking a Rich Marquesdom for the Sake of the Gospel of Jesus Christ. Written first in Italian, thence translated into Latin by Reverend [Theodore] Beza, and for the Benefit of Our People, put into English, and now published by W. C[rashaw].

Printed and sold by Thomas Fleet, etc., Boston, 1751

488 CARCANET (The): being Select Passages from the most Distinguished Writers. *18mo, cloth, gilt edges.*

W. Pickering, London, 1830

489 CAREW, Thomas. The Poetical Works of. (With Cœlum Britannicum, a Masque; as performed at Whitehall, in the Banqueting-Room, on Shrove Tuesday Night, the 18th of February, 1633: by Tho. Carew and Inigo Jones.) *16mo, half morocco, neat.* London, 1845

490 CAREY, Mathew. The Olive Branch, or Fault on Both Sides, Federal and Democratic; a Serious Appeal on the Necessity of Mutual Forgiveness and Harmony, to save our Common Country from Ruin. Third Edition, greatly enlarged and improved. *12mo, boards, rough edges.*

Boston, Feb., 1815

491 CARICATURES. A Collection of Caricatures, Political and Humorous, by Gillray, Cruikshanks, etc., etc. *Nearly* 300 *prints, mounted, in a scrap-book. Atlas folio, half crimson morocco.* Very curious collection.

(London)

492 CARLETON, William. Traits and Stories of the Irish Peasantry: with an Autobiographical Introduction, Explanatory Notes; and Numerous Illustrations, on Wood and Steel, by Harvey, Phiz (H. K. Browne), Franklin, Macmanus, Gilbert, and other Artists of Eminence. 2 *vols., 8vo, half calf, extra.* Dublin, 1843–44

493 CARLETON, William; Samuel Lover; and, Anna Maria Hall. Tales and Stories of Ireland. With Etchings by Kirkwood. *16mo, boards.* Halifax, 1854

494 CARLIER, AUGUSTE. MARRIAGE IN THE UNITED STATES. Translated from the French by B. Joy Jeffries. *Post 8vo, cloth.* Boston, 1867

495 CARLISLE, CHARLES HOWARD, EARL OF. A RELATION OF THREE EMBASSIES from his Sacred Majestie Charles II. to the Great Duke of Muscovie, the King of Sweden, and the King of Denmark; performed by the Earl of Carlisle in the Years 1663 and 1664. Written by an Attendant on the Embassies, and published with his L[ps] Approbation. *Portrait by Faithorne. Small 8vo, sprinkled calf.* London, 1669

The "Epistle Dedicatory" is signed "G. M."

496 CARLYLE, ALEXANDER, D. D. AUTOBIOGRAPHY; containing Memorials of Men and Events of his Own Time. [Edited by J. H. Burton.] *Portrait. Crown 8vo, cloth.* Boston, 1861

497 CARLYLE, THOMAS. LATTER-DAY PAMPHLETS. *12mo, cloth.* Boston, 1850

498 CARLYLE, THOMAS. THE LIFE OF JOHN STERLING. Second Edition. *Crown 8vo, cloth, uncut.* London, 1852

499 CARLYLE, THOMAS. HISTORY OF FRIEDRICH II. OF PRUSSIA, called Frederick the Great. *Portraits, plates, maps, etc. 6 vols., 8vo, half calf, extra, marbled edges.* London, 1858–65

500 CARR, SIR JOHN. A NORTHERN SUMMER, or Travels round the Baltic, through Denmark, Sweden, Russia, Prussia, and Part of Germany, in the Year 1804. *With 11 tinted plates by T. Medland, after drawings by the author. 4to, half calf; with autograph and book-plate of Thomas Huxley, and book-plate of Parks.* London, 1805

501 CARR, SIR JOHN. ANOTHER COPY: *the same. With same plates. 4to, half calf.* London, 1805

502 CARR, SIR JOHN. DESCRIPTIVE TRAVELS IN THE SOUTHERN AND EASTERN PARTS OF SPAIN AND THE BALEARIC ISLES, in the Year 1809. *With 6 plates drawn by the author. 4to, half calf.* London, 1811

503 CARTER, JOHN. SPECIMENS OF THE ANCIENT SCULPTURE AND PAINTING, now remaining in this Kingdom, from the Earliest Period to the Reign of Henry y[e] VIII.: consisting of Statues, Basso-relievos, Brasses, etc.; Paintings on Glass, and on Walls, etc.; a Description of Each Subject, some of which by Gentlemen of Literary Abilities and well versed in the Antiquities of this Kingdom, whose Names are prefixed to their Essays. This Work is designed to shew the Rise and Progress of Sculpture and Painting in England, to explain Obscure and Doubtful Parts of History, and preserve the Portraits of Great and Eminent Personages. The Drawings made from the Original Subjects and engraved by John Carter. *Contains 120 fine large plates (including titles),*

some of which are colored. 2 vols. in 1, *royal folio, half morocco, very neat, red edges.* ORIGINAL EDITION: *before the plates were retouched.* London, 1780–87

504 CARTER, N. H. LETTERS FROM EUROPE; comprising the Journal of a Tour through Ireland, England, Scotland, France, Italy, and Switzerland, in the Years 1825, '26, and '27. 2 *vols.*, 8*vo, half calf, extra, marbled edges.* New York, 1827

505 CASSIN, JOHN. UNITED STATES EXPLORING EXPEDITION, during the Years 1838–1842, under the Command of Charles Wilkes, U. S. N. MAMMALOGY AND ORNITHOLOGY, by John Cassin. *Contains* 53 *large and finely colored plates. Text,* 2 *vols., royal* 4*to, cloth; plates,* 1 *vol., imperial folio, half morocco.* LARGE PAPER: *fine copy.* Philadelphia, 1858

The text of this copy ranges with the "Narrative" in large paper. See WILKES, CHARLES.

This work supplies the place of Peale's "Mammalia," which was suppressed.

506 CASSIN, JOHN. ILLUSTRATIONS OF THE BIRDS OF CALIFORNIA, TEXAS, OREGON, BRITISH AND RUSSIAN AMERICA: intended to contain Descriptions and Figures of all North American Birds not given by Former American Authors, and a General Synopsis of North American Ornithology. 1853 to 1855. *Printed on tinted paper, with* 50 *finely colored plates. Imperial* 8*vo, cloth.* Philadelphia, 1862

507 CASTI, GIAN BATTISTA. THE COURT AND PARLIAMENT OF BEASTS; freely translated from the Animali Parlanti of Giambattista Casti, a Poem in Seven Cantos, by William Stewart Rose. *Foolscap* 8*vo, boards, rough edges.* J. Murray, London, 1819

508 CATAFAGO, JOSEPH. AN ENGLISH AND ARABIC DICTIONARY; in Two Parts; Arabic and English, and English and Arabic; in which the Arabic Words are represented in the Oriental Character, as well as their Correct Pronunciation and Accentuation shewn in English Letters. By Joseph Catafago, of Aleppo, in Syria, Secretary to Soliman Pasha. *Thick* 8*vo, half crimson morocco, gilt top, rough edges.* LARGE PAPER. London, 1858

This is the *first* Arabic and English Dictionary ever published, of which the "Athenæum" (Jan. 29, 1859) says: "On the whole the work is a most acceptable contribution to Oriental literature; and the English and Arabic part especially will be an invaluable aid to travellers in the East, and to all Englishmen who have occasion to study Arabic."

CATALOGUES OF PUBLIC AND PRIVATE LIBRARIES, BOOKSELLERS, SALES BY AUCTION, ETC., ETC.

509 ABBOTSFORD. CATALOGUE OF THE LIBRARY AT ABBOTSFORD. [As formed and arranged by Sir Walter Scott; with his Notes, and References to his Works. Compiled, with a Copious Index, by J. G. Cochrane. 4*to, boards, uncut.* Edinburgh, 1838

Handsomely printed for the "Maitland Club;" presented by J. G. Lockhart.

510 ALLEN. BIBLIOTHECA ALLENIANA: a Catalogue of the Curious, Elegant, and very Valuable Library of Thomas Allen, Esq.; Monday, June 1, 1795, and the Nine following Days. *Contains* 1,585 *lots.* — ELEGANT BOOKS; a Catalogue of a very Valuable Library of Books, the Property of a Gentleman [Thomas Allen], many of them in most Splendid Binding, etc., etc.; Wednesday, June 24, 1807, and Seven following Days. *Contains* 1,488 *lots.* — A CATALOGUE OF A CHOICE COLLECTION OF HISTORICAL AND FANCY PRINTS, containing Extra fine Specimens of the Ancient and Modern Schools, etc., etc.: the Whole assembled at a great Expense, by Thomas Allen, Esq., F. A. S.; Wednesday, May 13, 1807, and Two following Days. *Contains* 351 *lots.* — A CATALOGUE OF A CHOICE COLLECTION OF BRITISH PORTRAITS, by the most Eminent English Artists: the Whole assembled, at a great Expense, by Thomas Allen, Esq.; Saturday, May 16, 1807, and Three following Days. *Contains* 500 *lots.* *Four catalogues in* 1 *vol., royal* 8*vo, half russia, rough edges.* LARGE PAPER: PROBABLY UNIQUE. (London, 1795–1807)

On a fly-leaf is the following autograph note by William Upcott: "With prices and purchasers' names by the late George Baker of St. Paul's Ch: Yard."

511 ANGLING. BIBLIOTHECA PISCATORIA: a Catalogue of Books upon Angling. *Fac-simile wood-cut. Foolscap* 8*vo, half green turkey morocco, very neat, gilt edges.* (W. Pickering), London, 1836

This catalogue is formed upon Sir Henry Ellis's corrected copy of the list which he contributed to the "British Bibliographer" in 1811, and some editions are noticed the existence of which was then unknown.

512 ASKEW. BIBLIOTHECA ASKEVIANA, sive Catalogus Librorum Rarissimorum Antonii Askew. *Contains* 3,570 *lots.* — BIBLIOTHECA ASKEVIANA MANU SCRIPTA, sive Catalogus Librorum Manuscriptorum Antonii Askew, M. D., his adduntur, ex eâdem Bibliothecâ, Auctores Classici in quorum Marginibus Scriptæ sunt, suis ipsorum Manibus, Doctissimorum Virorum Notæ atque Observationes, nempe Bentleii Magni, Chandleri, Chishulli, Joannis Taylori, Antonii Askæi, aliorum. *Contains* 633 *lots.* *Together in* 1 *vol., with prices and names. Royal* 8*vo, half russia, rough edges; with autograph of William Upcott.* LARGE PAPER: *few printed.* (London, 1775–85)

513 ASKEW. ANOTHER COPY: *the first sale only. Small paper, priced.* 8*vo, half morocco, neat.* (London, 1775)

514 BAKER. A CATALOGUE OF THE VERY CHOICE AND SELECT LIBRARY OF THE LATE GEORGE BAKER, ESQ., of St. Paul's Churchyard, etc., etc.; sold by Auction, Monday, June 6, 1825, and Two following Days. *Contains* 855 *lots.* *Ruled and priced, with names of purchasers. Imperial* 8*vo, paper, rough edges.* LARGE PAPER. (London, 1825)

Baker was the "Quisquillius" of Dibdin in his "Bibliomania."

515 BAKER. ANOTHER COPY: *small paper, trimmed.* 8*vo.* (London, 1825)

516 BARNARD. CATALOGUE OF THE SUPERB AND ENTIRE COLLECTION OF PRINTS, AND BOOKS OF PRINTS, OF JOHN BARNARD, ESQ., of Berkeley Square, deceased, formed with Infinite Taste and Judgment during a Period. exceeding Fifty Years: comprehending the Choicest Works of the Greatest Masters, from the Earliest Period to the Present Time; and almost Entire Works of the most Esteemed Artists, particularly Rembrandt, Hollar, Marc Antonio, Parmegiano, Vandyck, Rubens, etc., etc.; which will be sold by Auction, Monday, the 16th of April, 1798, and Twenty-six following Days. *Contains* 2,620 *lots, exclusive of portfolios. Portrait of Correggio inserted. Partly priced.* 8*vo, half sheep, rough edges.* (London, 1798)

517 BAYNES & SON. BIBLIOTHECA SELECTISSIMA: a Catalogue of Books printed in the Fifteenth Century, Productions of the Presses established by Schoiffer, Caxton, Ulric Zell, etc., etc., and most other Illustrious Typographers; including several Editiones Principes, and Volumes unknown to Bibliographers: to which is added, a large Collection of Works printed by the Alduses; a Selection of Curious and Rare Books, in History, Biography, Theology, Facetiæ, Romance, and Poetry, in the English, French, Spanish, Italian, Latin, and other Languages; comprehending Books printed on Vellum, Numerous Specimens of the Giunta, Giolito, Elzevir, Bodoni, Baskerville, and other celebrated Presses; with a number of Ancient Manuscripts, upon a Variety of Subjects, chiefly on Vellum. *Contains* 1,281 *lots, priced.* (London), 1826

In this catalogue the works are very fully described with numerous long notes.

518 BEAUCLERK. BIBLIOTHECA BEAUCLERKIANA: a Catalogue of the Large and Valuable Library of the late Honourable Topham Beauclerk, F. R. S., etc., etc.; sold by Auction, Monday, April 9, 1781, and the Forty-nine following Days. *First part contains* 5,959 *lots. Second part contains* 3,297 *lots. Ruled and priced. Royal* 8*vo, half morocco, gilt top, uncut.* (London, 1781)

519 BLANDFORD. CATALOGUS LIBRORUM QUI IN BIBLIOTHECÂ BLANDFORDIENSI REPERIUNTUR. [Compiled by Robert Triphook.] 4*to, half morocco.* PRIVATELY PRINTED; *and only very few copies.* (London), 1812

At the sale of this collection (the "White Knights"), in 1819, the famous Valdarfer Boccaccio, which was purchased for £2,260 at the Roxburgh sale, passed into the hands of Earl Spencer (through Longman & Co.) for the sum of £918 15, although seven years previous he had offered £2,250 for the same in competition with the Marquis of Blandford.

520 BOHN. HENRY G. BOHN'S CATALOGUE OF BOOKS. Vol. I.; containing Natural History, Books of Prints, Science, Language, Bibliography, Oriental and Northern Literature,

Old English Historians, Early Voyages, etc., Games, etc. *pp.* 467 *and* 108. *Royal 8vo, half crimson morocco, marbled edges.* London, 1847

521 BOOKSELLERS' CATALOGUES. PARCEL OF; *chiefly English.* London, etc., 1861–66

522 BOSSANGE. LIVRES ESPAGNOLES. Second Supplement. *Lots* 27,253–27,419. — LIVRES FRANÇAIS, Grecs, Latins, Allemands, Anglais, Espagnols, Italiens, Portugais, Orientaux. Troisième Supplement. *Lots* 27,465–30,839. — LISTE ALPHA BÉTIQUE DES OUVRAGES PÉRIODIQUES; Journaux Religieux, Scientifique, Politiques, Littéraires, et des Beaux-Arts publiés à Paris. Cinquième Supplement. *Lots* 30,908–31,243. *Three supplements to the general catalogue of Hector Bossange, bookseller.* 2 *vols., royal* 8*vo, half morocco.* Paris, 1848–53

523 BOSTON ATHENEUM. CATALOGUE OF BOOKS IN THE; to which are added the By-Laws of the Institution, and a List of its Proprietors and Subscribers. 8*vo, cloth.* Boston, 1827

524 BRAND. BIBLIOTHECA BRANDIANA: a Catalogue of the Unique, Scarce, Rare, Curious, and numerous Collection of Works on the Antiquity, Topography, and Decayed Intelligence of Great Britain and Ireland, from the First Invention of Printing down to the Present Time, etc., etc.; being the Entire Library of the late Rev. John Brand: sold by Auction, Wednesday, May 6, 1807, and Thirty-six following Days. *Contains* 8,854 *lots.* 8*vo, boards, rough edges.* (London, 1807)

525 BURTON. BIBLIOTHECA DRAMATICA: Catalogue of the Theatrical and Miscellaneous Library of the late William E. Burton, comprising an Immense Assemblage of Books relating to the Stage, etc., etc.: also, a Small but Select Collection of Curiosities, Antiquities, Shakspearian Models, etc., etc.; Oil Paintings, etc. Sold at Auction, New York, Monday, October 8, 1860, and following Days. *Contains* 6,154 *lots. Portrait. Imperial* 8*vo, paper, rough edges.* LARGE PAPER: *few printed.* (New York, 1860)

Mr. Burton's library was one of the largest collections of dramatic literature ever assembled by a single individual, and in this catalogue the works are very thoroughly and accurately described, by Mr. Sabin, with many valuable notes.

526 CAPEL. A CATALOGUE OF A PART OF THE LIBRARY OF THE HON. JOHN THOMAS CAPEL, etc., etc.; sold by Leigh and Sotheby, on Thursday, July 4, 1811, and Two following Days. *Contains* 574 *lots; pp.* 20. *Interleaved copy, ruled and priced.* 8*vo, half calf.* (London, 1811)

527 CHOATE. CATALOGUE OF THE LIBRARY OF THE LATE HON. RUFUS CHOATE; sold by Auction, Oct. 18–20, and 25–28, 1859. *Contains* 2,672 *lots.* 8*vo, half morocco, neat.* Boston, 1859

528 COCKBURN. CATALOGUE OF THE VALUABLE LIBRARY OF THE LATE LORD COCKBURN, consisting of an Extensive Collection of Books in English and Scottish History and Antiquities, the Belles Lettres, Law and General Literature, etc., etc.: the Sale also includes, Ten of the Celebrated Stirling Heads, being the highly interesting Ancient Scottish Carvings in Oak, from the Roof of the King's Room at Stirling Castle; Antique Indian China Vases, etc.; sold by Auction, Wednesday, November 22, 1854, and Four following Days. *Contains* 1,495 *lots. With* 10 *plates of the "Stirling Heads." Royal* 8*vo, half olive morocco, gilt top.*

(Edinburgh, 1854)

529 CREVENNA. CATALOGUE DES LIVRES DE LA BIBLIOTHÉQUE DE M. PIERRE-ANTOINE-BOLONGARO-CREVENNA. 5 *parts in* 4 *vols.*, 8*vo, half calf. Vol. II. wanting.*

This copy contains the supplement ("Collection concernant les Jesuites") at the end of the fourth volume, pp. 54; and the table of prices at the end of the fifth volume, pp. 46.

530 CROWNINSHIELD. CATALOGUE OF THE VALUABLE PRIVATE LIBRARY OF THE LATE EDWARD A. CROWNINSHIELD, embracing in the Collection a Large Number of Valuable and Rare Books; Choice Editions, or Elegant Large Paper Copies of Standard English Authors; Rare Works on the Early History of America; Early Voyages and Travels, including First Editions of Purchas and Hakluyt; etc., etc.: sold by Auction, on Tuesday, Nov. 1, 1859, and Three following Days, by Leonard & Co. *Contains* 1,156 *lots of books, and* 116 *of autographs.* 8*vo, half morocco, neat, gilt top.*

Boston, 1859

This collection was not sold as advertised, but was purchased intact, by Henry Stevens, of London, for $8,500. No. 878 is a copy of the original edition of the "Bay Psalm Book," one of the earliest books printed in North America (printed by Stephen Daye, Cambridge, 1640), for which in 1867, Mr. Stevens' price was 150 guineas. See BAY PSALM BOOK.

531 DAVIS. CATALOGUE OF THE ENTIRE PRIVATE LIBRARY OF THE LATE MR. WILLIAM J. DAVIS; sold at Auction, Monday Evening, April 17th, 1865, and the following Evenings, until all are sold. *Contains* 1,766 *lots. Royal* 4*to, paper, rough edges.* LARGE PAPER: *with "Memorial."*

New York, 1865

The "Memorial," by Henry B. Dawson, is separate, and contains a photographic portrait.

532 EVANS & SONS. THE FINE ART CIRCULAR AND PRINT COLLECTOR'S MANUAL: Catalogue of nearly Six Thousand Etchings and Engravings, by Artists of every School and Period, comprising the Best Examples of every Eminent Engraver, from the Earliest Period to the Present Time, with the Size and Price of each Print, and References to the Works of those Authors who have made the Art of Engraving their Study. With an Appendix, consisting of a Catalogue

Raisonnée of nearly 400 Prints unknown to Bartsch. *Alphabetically arranged under the names of the engravers. 8vo, boards.* (London, 1857)

533 FOWLE. Catalogue of the Choice Collection of Books belonging to William F. Fowle, Esquire, of Boston, Mass. *Contains* 818 *lots. Ruled and priced. Imperial 8vo, half morocco, neat, gilt top, rough edges.* Large paper: *only 85 copies printed, chiefly for presentation.* Riverside Press, Cambridge, 1865

The sale of this collection probably bears the same relation to American, that Colonel Stanley's (1813) does to English, sales. Of the latter Brunet says: "This sale appears to be that in which the thermometer of Bibliomania reached its highest point in England."

534 FOWLE. Catalogue of the very Choice Collection of Books forming the Library of William F. Fowle, Esquire, of Boston, Mass. *Ruled and priced. 8vo, paper, rough edges.* Riverside Press, Cambridge, 1864

There is a difference, both in the titles and numbers, between the large and small paper copies; in the former No. 642 has been added, and an error (No. 751 repeated in the latter) corrected.

535 FRIENDS' Library, Philadelphia. Catalogue of the Books belonging to the Library of the Four Monthly Meetings of Friends of Philadelphia; with the Rules for the Government of the Library. 12*mo, half morocco.* Philadelphia, 1831

536 FRENCH Sale Catalogues of Vertu: Comprising some of the most Important Sales of Paintings, Marbles, Bronzes, Porcelains, Furniture, Curiosities, etc., etc., which took place at Paris in 1851 and 1852, including the Soult Gallery, etc., etc. *Plates in outline of many of the Paintings.* 33 *catalogues in* 1 *vol., thick 8vo, half morocco; with newspaper cuttings and prices.* Paris, 1850–52

Some of the paintings, etc., in these collections were purchased by the late Mr. Augustus Thorndike, and were included in the sale (Boston, Oct. 25, 1860) of his collection.

537 GARRICK. A Catalogue of the Library, Splendid Books of Prints, Poetical and Historical Tracts, of David Garrick, Esq., removed from his Villa at Hampton, and House on the Adelphi Terrace, with the Modern Works added thereto by Mrs. Garrick; sold by Auction, Wednesday, April 23d, 1823, and 9 following Days. *Contains* 2,678 *lots. Ruled and priced, with names of purchasers. 4to, half calf.* Large paper: *portrait and biographical notice inserted.* (London, 1823)

538 GOSSETT. A Catalogue of the Extensive and very Valuable Library of the Late Rev. Is. Gossett, D. D., sold by Auction, Monday, June 7, 1813, and Twenty-two following Days. *Contains* 5,740 *lots. Ruled and priced. 8vo, half calf, rough edges; with a long autograph ("Sketch of the Character of Dr. Gossett, composed in* 1804*"), by William Upcott, written on cover and fly-leaves.* (London, 1813)

Dr. Gossett was the "Lepidus" of Dibdin in his "Bibliomania."

539 HALL. CATALOGUE OF THE VALUABLE LIBRARY OF FITZ EDWARD HALL, ESQ., sold by Auction [at Boston] on Tuesday, February 5, 1867, and following Days. *Contains above 2,700 lots. Royal 8vo, paper, rough edges.* Munsell, Albany, (1866)

540 HAZEWELL. CATALOGUE OF A VALUABLE PRIVATE LIBRARY, comprising an Extensive and Select Collection of Choice Books, in every Department of Literature, etc., etc.; a Work of Great Value, the only Copy in this Country, and the only known Copy in the World for Sale, a Rare and Rich Treasury of Engravings comprised in the Chalcographie du Musee Royal, etc., etc.; the Whole forming the Private Library of a Gentleman [G. R. Hazewell], etc., etc.: sold at Auction, Monday, May 16 [1859], etc. *Contains* 5,106 *lots; pp.* 324. *Interleaved copy, priced. Royal* 8*vo, half morocco, rough edges.* New York, (1859)

541 HEBER. BIBLIOTHECA HEBERIANA. Catalogue of the Library of the late Richard Heber, Esq. *Sold by Auction,* TWO HUNDRED AND EIGHT DAYS' SALE, *between April* 10, 1834, *and February* 28, 1837. THIRTEEN PARTS, CONTAINING 54,235 LOTS. 5 *vols.,* 8*vo, half maroon turkey morocco, gilt tops, rough edges, by Clarke & Bedford.* RULED AND PRICED THROUGHOUT. (London, 1834–37)

Copies priced *throughout* are seldom met with, and this copy, which is thoroughly priced and in the neatest manner (priced by Thomas Rodd for Zelotes Hosmer), is probably the finest in this country.

This collection, which *filled eight houses* (*perhaps more!*) was the most extensive ever made by any one individual; and, when sold, it realized the immense sum of £56,759 3*s.* 6*d.* which, however, was not more than one half what it cost the collector. Mr. Heber was elder half-brother of Bp. Heber, and figures as "ATTICUS" in Dibdin's "Bibliomania," the first edition of which is in the form of an Epistle addressed to him.

542 HOSMER. CATALOGUE OF THE CHOICE COLLECTION OF BOOKS, FORMING THE LIBRARY OF ZELOTES HOSMER, ESQ., of Cambridge, Mass., illustrative of Early English Literature and Standard Authors; Fine Editions, Choice Copies, and Rare Books in Bibliography, History, Poetry, the Drama, Antiquities, Illustrated Works, etc. Together with Rare Editions of the Greek and Latin Classics, from the Aldine, Elzevir, and Junta Presses, and other Early Printed Books. All in the finest possible Condition; sold by Auction, Tuesday, May 7, 1861, and Three following Days. *Contains* 1,192 *lots. Prices in pencil. Imperial* 8*vo, dark blue turkey morocco, extra, gilt top.* LARGE PAPER: *only* 100 *copies printed.* Boston, 1861

543 HOSMER. ANOTHER COPY. *Small paper. Prices in red ink. Royal* 8*vo, half dark brown levant morocco, very neat, gilt top, rough edges.* Boston, 1861

544 JOSSELYN. CATALOGUE OF A FINE COLLECTION OF BOOKS, including Scarce Reprints, Large Paper Copies, Pri-

vately Printed Books, etc., etc.; Superbly Illustrated Volumes, etc., etc. (forming the Library of Freeman M. Josselyn, Esq., of Boston, Mass): sold by Auction, on Wednesday, March 27, 1867. *Contains 339 lots. Royal 8vo, paper, rough edges.* Boston, 1867

545 LIBRI. CATALOGUE OF THE CHOICER PORTION OF THE MAGNIFICENT LIBRARY, FORMED BY M. GUGLIELMO LIBRI, so eminent as a Collector; amongst which will be found Unknown Block-Books; Specimens of Early Typography and Art, comprising an Unknown Kalendarium with the Earliest Engravings on Copper; etc., etc.; Early Productions of the English Press; Manuscripts and Books with Autograph Notes; etc., etc.; a most Superb, Interesting, and Perfectly Unique Collection of Historical Bindings; etc., etc.; sold by Auction, Monday, 1st of August, 1859, and Twelve following Days. *Contains 2,824 lots; pp. 380. Imperial 8vo, half morocco, neat, gilt top, rough edges.* (London, 1859)

This Catalogue comprises some of the most valuable books of the most extensive collection which has been dispersed since that of Mr. Heber. It is particularly valuable for the vast amount of bibliographical information which it contains.

546 LONDON ATHENÆUM. A CATALOGUE OF THE LIBRARY OF THE ATHENÆUM. *Printed for the members. Royal 8vo, half morocco.* London, 1845

547 LONDON INSTITUTION. A CATALOGUE OF THE LIBRARY; systematically classed. Preceded by an Historical and Bibliographical Account of the Establishment. *Vol. I., with engraved plans accompanied by a descriptive account of the arrangement of the Library. Thick imperial 8vo, cloth, rough edges.* NOT PUBLISHED. (London), 1835

This volume, compiled chiefly by William Upcott, is valuable for giving the contents of long sets of books, etc.

548 LOUIS PHILIPPE. CATALOGUE DE LIVRES PROVENANT DES BIBLIOTHÈQUES DU FEU ROI LOUIS PHILIPPE, dont le Vente aura lieu le 8 Mars, 1852, et les 26 Jours suivants, par le ministère de m[e] bonne-fons de Lavialle. Bibliothéques du Palais-Royal et de Neuilly. Première Partie. *Contains 3,042 lots. 8vo, paper.* Paris, 1852

549 M'KIE. BIBLIOTHECA BURNSIANA: Life and Works of Burns; Title-Pages and Imprints of the Various Editions in the Private Library of James M'Kie, Kilmarnock, Prior to Date 1866. (With an Addenda, containing List of Editions not in his Possession.) *Contains 252 and 191 titles; pp. 43. 8vo, boards.* Kilmarnock, 1866

550 MUNSELL. VALUABLE PRIVATE LIBRARY: Catalogue of a Rare and Extensive Collection of Books principally relating to America, comprising a Portion of the Private Library of Joel Munsell, of Albany, N. Y., and embracing Works of Great Value, of Small Editions, and Large Paper Copies, etc.; sold at Auction, April 11, 1865, and the following

Days. *Contains* 1,491 *lots. Imperial* 8*vo, half morocco, neat, gilt top, rough edges.* LARGE PAPER : *only* 50 *copies printed.* (J. Munsell, Albany, 1865)

551 NASSAU. CATALOGUE OF THE CHOICE, CURIOUS, AND EXTENSIVE LIBRARY OF THE LATE GEORGE NASSAU, ESQ.; etc., etc.; sold by Auction, Monday, February 16, and Eleven following Days (and on Monday, March 8, and Seven following Days), 1824. *Two parts, containing* 2,603 *and* 1,661 *lots. Ruled and priced.* 8*vo, half russia, neat.* (London), 1824

552 NEWCASTLE REPRINTS. REPRINTS OF RARE TRACTS, AND IMPRINTS OF ANTIENT MSS., chiefly illustrative of the History of the Northern Counties, etc., etc.; from the Press of M. A. Richardson, Newcastle. *With a list of works on sale, etc., and some fac-similes. Crown* 8*vo ; with book-plate of Robert Balmanno, F. S. A.* Newcastle, 1844

553 NUTT. A CATALOGUE OF THEOLOGICAL BOOKS IN FOREIGN LANGUAGES, INCLUDING THE SACRED WRITINGS; Fathers, Doctors of the Church, Schoolmen, and Ecclesiastical Historians, to the Death of Boniface VIII. A. D. 1303; Jewish and Rabbinical Commentators, Works of the Reformers, and of more Recent Divines, Ascetical, Dogmatical, Polemical, and Exegetical; Liturgies, Rituals, and Liturgical Literature; Councils, Synods, and Confessions of Faith; Monastic History and Rule; Canon and Ecclesiastical Law; Church Polity and Discipline; Hebrew and Syriac Literature; etc., etc. WITH APPENDIX. *Contains* 7,166 *lots.* 2 *vols.,* 8*vo, half morocco.* London, 1857

554 PARKER. CATALOGUE OF THE EXTENSIVE COLLECTION OF SPLENDID, RARE, AND IMPORTANT BOOKS, FORMING THE PRIVATE LIBRARY OF THE LATE GEORGE PHILLIPS PARKER; etc., etc.; sold at Auction, Tuesday, March 1 (1859), etc. *Contains* 2,620 *lots. Interleaved copy, priced. Royal* 8*vo, half morocco, rough edges.* New York, 1859

555 PARR. BIBLIOTHECA PARRIANA: a Catalogue of the Library of the late Reverend and Learned Samuel Parr, LL. D. [Compiled by Henry G. Bohn] *Fine portrait by W. Skelton. Thick imperial* 8*vo, cloth, rough edges.* LARGE PAPER: *only* 40 *copies printed.* J. Bohn, London, 1827

This catalogue, which contains Dr. Parr's notes from the fly leaves of his books, was prepared after his death, not for a sale catalogue, but at his request, for — as he often remarked, — "the world would then see what sort of a collection of books had been made by a country parson."

556 PHILADELPHIA LIBRARY. THE CHARTER, LAWS, AND CATALOGUE OF BOOKS OF THE LIBRARY COMPANY OF PHILADELPHIA. (With a Short Account of the Library, and the Medals, and a List of Members, February, 1765.) *Crown* 8*vo, half morocco.* PRINTED BY FRANKLIN. Philadelphia, 1764

This library was the *first chartered* in this country, and the *second established* The "Redwood Library," Newport, R. I., was established one year earlier (1730), but was not chartered until five years later (1747) than this.

557 REDWOOD LIBRARY. A CATALOGUE OF THE REDWOOD LIBRARY AND ATHENÆUM, IN NEWPORT, R. I.; together with a Supplement, Addenda, and Index of Subjects and Titles: showing all the Books belonging to the Company on the First of June, 1860. To which is prefixed a Short Account of the Institution; with the Charter, Laws, and Regulations. *Royal 8vo, half roan.*
Printed by J. Wilson & Son, Boston, 1860

This library was *established* in 1730 and *chartered* in 1747; it is, therefore, *one of the two oldest* libraries in this country [the Philadelphia Library was established in 1731 and chartered in 1742]. It contains many valuable works.

558 ROYAL INSTITUTION OF GREAT BRITAIN. A CATALOGUE OF THE LIBRARY; including a Complete List of all the Greek Writers, by the late Rev. Charles Burney, D. D.: methodically arranged, with an Alphabetical Index of Authors; by William Harris, Keeper of the Library. The Second Edition, considerably enlarged and improved. *Royal 8vo, half calf, marbled edges; with book-plate of George Phillips Parker.* London, 1821

559 ROXBURGHE. A CATALOGUE OF THE LIBRARY OF THE LATE JOHN, DUKE OF ROXBURGHE; sold by Auction, Monday, 18th May, 1812, and the Forty-one following Days (and on Monday, the 13th of July, 1812, and the Three following Days). *With* SUPPLEMENT, *etc., and prices. Contains* 9,353, *and* 767 *lots.* *8vo, calf, very neat.*
Printed by W. Bulmer & Co., London, 1812

No. 6,292, the celebrated Valdarfer Boccaccio of 1471, the only known copy, was purchased by the Marquis of Blandford for £2,260, the highest price ever paid for a single volume, and which caused the formation of the "Roxburghe Club." Dibdin gives (*more suo*) a long account of the contest for this volume in his "Bibliographical Decameron," Vol. III. pp. 62–65.

560 SALE CATALOGUES. BOOKS, PAMPHLETS, ENGRAVINGS, PAINTINGS, PORCELAINS, BRONZES, COINS AND MEDALS, AUTOGRAPHS, FURNITURE, CURIOSITIES, etc., etc. *Parcel of catalogues of sales by Leonard & Co., Boston; including, the miscellaneous libraries of Zelotes Hosmer, J. G. Percival, James Hayward, C. H. Stedman, Thomas Wetmore, etc., etc.; the law libraries of Rufus Choate and L. S. Cushing; the stocks of Lafayette Burnham and other booksellers; the collection of paintings, porcelains, bronzes, etc., of Augustus Thorndike; etc., etc., etc.* Boston, 1858–66

561 SALE AND EXHIBITION CATALOGUES. PAINTINGS, COINS AND MEDALS, BOOKS, etc., etc. *Parcel of catalogues comprising a collection of paintings, made by Judge Lee, sold at Baltimore,* 1860; *first exhibition of the Allston Club, Boston,* 1866; *second exhibition of the French Etching Club, Boston,* 1866, *etc., etc.; sales of books, etc., at Boston and New York, including a collection of books entirely relating to America, many of which were from Mr. S. G. Deeth's library; W. E.*

Woodward's sale of coins and medals, selected from the "Finotti Collection," New York, Nov., 1862, etc., etc.
Balt^{o}., Bost., N. Y., and Cincin^{i}., 1859–68

562 SMITH. BIBLIOTHECA AMERICANA: a Catalogue of a Valuable Collection of Books and Pamphlets relating to the History and Geography of North and South America, and the West Indies; altogether forming the most Extensive Collection ever offered for sale, containing many Curious Articles unknown to American Bibliographers. On sale by John Russell Smith, London. *Contains* 3,372 *lots, and index. 8vo, half green turkey morocco, gilt top.* London, 1853

563 SOMERBY. CATALOGUE OF THE VERY CHOICE COLLECTION OF BOOKS FORMING THE LIBRARY OF GUSTAVUS A. SOMERBY, ESQUIRE, of Boston, Mass.; sold by Auction, Boston, Tuesday, Wednesday, and Thursday, the 25th, 26th, and 27th of May (1869). *Contains* 725 *and* 31 *lots. 8vo, paper, rough edges.* Riverside Press, Cambridge, 1869

A collection very similar to that of Mr. W. F. Fowle. This catalogue was prepared by Mr. Fowle in the same manner as that of his own library, and the works are very thoroughly and accurately described.

564 SOUTHGATE. MUSEUM SOUTHGATIANUM, being a Catalogue of the Valuable Collection of Books, Coins, Medals, and Natural History, of the late Rev. Richard Southgate, A. B., F. A. S., etc. To which is prefixed, Memoirs of his Life. *Sold by auction,* 12 *days' sale, Monday, April* 27, 1795. *Portrait. Ruled and priced. Imperial 8vo, half russia, rough edges; with autograph of William Upcott.* LARGE PAPER.
London, 1795

565 STEVENS. CATALOGUE OF MY ENGLISH LIBRARY, COLLECTED AND DESCRIBED BY HENRY STEVENS, G. M. B., F. S. A., ETC. *Foolscap 8vo, cloth, gilt top, rough edges.* FOR PRIVATE DISTRIBUTION: *only* 150 *copies printed.*
London, Nov., 1853

This little volume is beautifully printed by Whittingham, and contains the titles of the best editions of the principal standard authors sufficient to form a library of about 6,000 volumes. The contents of the several volumes of the chief polygraphic works are given; also, the dates of birth and death of most of the deceased authors.

566 STEVENS. HISTORICAL NUGGETS: BIBLIOTHECA AMERICANA, or a Descriptive Account of my Collection of Rare Books relating to America. *Contains* 2,934 *lots.* 2 *vols., foolscap 8vo, cloth, gilt tops, rough edges.* London, 1862

This catalogue is particularly valuable for containing full and exact titles, all the works being very carefully described. It is handsomely printed by Whittingham, and only a small edition was struck off, several copies of which were destroyed by fire in New York.

567 STRANGE. BIBLIOTHECA STRANGEIANA: a Catalogue of the General, Curious, and Extensive Library of that Distinguished Naturalist and Lover of the Fine Arts, the late John Strange, Esq., LL. D.; digested by Samuel Paterson, sold by Auction, Monday, March 16, 1801, etc. *Two parts,* 56

days' sale, containing 12,663 *lots. Ruled and priced.* 8*vo*, *half russia.* (London, 1801)

568 STRAWBERRY HILL. A CATALOGUE OF THE CLASSIC CONTENTS OF STRAWBERRY HILL, COLLECTED BY HORACE WALPOLE. *Sold by auction, by Mr. George Robins ;* 24 *days' sale, commencing Monday, April* 25, 1842. *Wood-cut title, portrait on India paper, etc. The sale catalogue, partly priced in pencil.* 4*to, calf, gilt, marbled edges, by Riviere.* LARGE PAPER : *very few printed.* (London, 1842)

569 SYKES. CATALOGUE OF THE SPLENDID, CURIOUS, AND EXTENSIVE LIBRARY OF THE LATE SIR MARK MASTERMAN SYKES, BART. PART I., *eleven days' sale, commencing May* 11, 1824; *contains* 1,676 *lots.* PART II., *six days' sale, commencing May* 28, 1824; *contains* 825 *lots.* PART III., *eight days' sale, commencing June* 21, 1824: *contains* 1,190 *lots. Portrait.* 1 *vol., imperial* 8*vo, half morocco, very neat, gilt top, rough edges ; with book-plate of John Trotter Brockett, F. S. A.* (London), 1824

This eminent collector was the "LORENZO" of Dibdin in his "Bibliomania."

570 THORNDIKE. CATALOGUE OF THE LIBRARY OF THE LATE AUGUSTUS THORNDIKE, ESQ.; sold by Auction, Boston, May 29th, and following Days, 1860. *Contains* 1,325 *lots.* 8*vo, paper.* Boston, 1860

571 WAKEFIELD. A CATALOGUE OF THE VERY ELEGANT CLASSICAL AND CRITICAL LIBRARY OF THE LATE REV. GILBERT WAKEFIELD, A. M., Editor of Lucretius, Pope's Homer, etc., etc.; sold by Auction, Thursday, March 25, 1802, and Six following Days. *Contains* 1,493 *lots. Ruled, and partly priced.* 8*vo, half morocco, rough edges; with autograph of William Upcott.* (London), 1802

572 WEST. BIBLIOTHECA WESTIANA: a Catalogue of the Curious and Truly Valuable Library of the late James West, Esq., President of the Royal Society; comprehending a Choice Collection of Books in Various Languages, etc., etc.; more especially such as relate to the History of Great Britain and Ireland; their Early Navigators, Discoverers, and Improvers, and the Ancient English Literature, etc., etc.; digested by Samuel Paterson: sold by Auction, Monday, the 29th of March, 1773, and the Twenty-three following Days. *Contains* 4,653 *lots. Priced.* 8*vo, half russia.* (London, 1773)

573 WILLIAMS. A CATALOGUE OF THE SPLENDID AND VALUABLE LIBRARY OF THE REV. THEODORE WILLIAMS, containing a most Extraordinary Collection of Early Biblical and Theological Manuscripts; Books printed on Vellum, from the Aldine, Junta, and other Celebrated Presses; the Best Editions of the Classics, etc., etc ; sold by Auction, Thursday, April 5th, 1827, and Five following Days; on Monday, April

23, 1827, and Eight following Days. *Contains* 1,948 *lots. Royal* 8*vo, half calf; with book-plate of E. A. Crowninshield.* (London, 1827)

574 CATHERINE II., OF RUSSIA. MEMOIRS, written by herself; with a Preface by A. Herzen. Translated from the French. 12*mo, cloth.* New York, 1859

This autobiography, found among her papers after her death, and of which several copies were made, was carefully suppressed by her family; but, in some way, a copy escaped, from which this work was printed.

575 CATLIN, GEORGE. ILLUSTRATIONS OF THE MANNERS, CUSTOMS, AND CONDITION OF THE NORTH AMERICAN INDIANS; with Letters and Notes written during Eight Years of Travel and Adventure among the Wildest and most Remarkable Tribes now existing. Ninth Edition. *Maps, and* 360 *engravings from the author's original paintings.* 2 *vols., royal* 8*vo, cloth, uncut.* H. G. Bohn, London, 1857

576 CATLIN, GEORGE. THE BREATH OF LIFE; or, Mal-Respiration, and its Effects upon the Enjoyments and Life of Man. *Wood-cuts.* 8*vo, boards.* New York, 1864

577 CAULFIELD, JAMES. BLACKGUARDIANA, or a Dictionary of Rogues, Bawds, Pimps, etc., etc. Interspersed with many Curious Anecdotes, Cant Terms, Flash Songs, etc., etc. *With* 21 *portraits of remarkable (for villany) characters.* 8*vo, old calf.* London, (1793?)

578 CAULFIELD, JAMES. PORTRAITS, MEMOIRS, AND CHARACTERS OF REMARKABLE PERSONS, FROM THE REIGN OF EDWARD THE THIRD TO THE REVOLUTION; collected from the most Authentic Accounts extant. A New Edition, completing the Twelfth Class of Granger's Biographical History of England; with many Additional Rare Portraits. *Contains* 110 *portraits.* 3 *vols.,* 4*to, boards, rough edges.* LARGE PAPER: *fine copy.* London, 1813

579 CAULFIELD, JAMES. PORTRAITS, MEMOIRS, AND CHARACTERS OF REMARKABLE PERSONS, FROM THE REVOLUTION, IN 1688, TO THE END OF THE REIGN OF GEORGE III.; collected from the most Authentic Accounts extant. *Contains* 155 *portraits.* 4 *vols.,* 4*to, half morocco, neat, gilt tops.* LARGE PAPER: *fine copy.* London, 1819–20

Although this work is sometimes described as containing 157 portraits, the compiler of this catalogue has never seen a copy with the portraits of "Cardinal" Carstairs, and William Ellis. The author says that "not a life or character is recorded, but is accompanied by a portrait of unquestioned authenticity."

580 CAULFIELD, JAMES. THE HIGH COURT OF JUSTICE; comprising Memoirs of the Principal Persons who sat in Judgment on King Charles the First, and signed his Death-Warrant, together with those Accessaries, excepted by Parliament in the Bill of Indemnity. Illustrated with their portraits, Autographs, and Seals, collected from Authentic Materials. *Fine impressions of the* 24 *portraits,* 23 *of them*

surrounded with an emblematical border. 4to, diamond russia; with book-plate of William Smith Hesleden. London, 1820

581 CAUSEUS DE LA CHAUSSE, MICHAEL ANGELO. ROMANUM MUSEUM, sive Thesaurus Eruditæ Antiquitatis in quo proponuntur, ac dilucidantur Gemmæ, Idola, Insignia Sacerdotalia, Instrumenta Sacrificiis inservientia, Lucernæ, Vasa, Bullæ, Armillæ, Fibulæ, Claves, Annuli, Tesseræ, Styli, Strigiles, Vota, Signa Militaria, Marmora, etc.; adjectis in hac Tertia Romana Editione plurimis Annotationibus, & Figuris. 2 *vols., folio, half morocco, rough edges.* Romæ, 1746

582 CAVENDISH, GEORGE. THE LIFE OF CARDINAL WOLSEY; from the Original Autograph Manuscript. With Notes and other Illustrations, by Samuel Weller Singer, F. S. A. Second Edition. *Portraits and plates. 8vo, tree calf, gilt, marbled edges.* London, 1827

"One of the most interesting and valuable specimens of biography in the English language." — *Lowndes.*

583 CÉRÉMONIES ET COUTUMES RELIGIEUSES DE TOUS LES PEUPLES DU MONDE, REPRESENTÉES PAR DES FIGURES DESSINÉES DE LA MAIN DE BERNARD PICART; avec une Explication Historique, & quelques Dissertations Curieuses. Vols. I.–V. — SUPERSTITIONS ANCIENNES ET MODERNES: Prejugés Vulgaires qui ont induit les Peuples à des Usages & à des Pratiques contraires à la Religion. *Vol. I. Fine impressions of the plates. Together,* 6 *vols., folio, half calf.* ORIGINAL EDITION. Amsterdam, 1723–33

584 CEREMONIES (THE) AND RELIGIOUS CUSTOMS OF THE VARIOUS NATIONS OF THE KNOWN WORLD; together with Historical Annotations and Several Curious Discourses, equally Instructive and Entertaining. Written originally in French, and illustrated with a large Number of Folio Copper Plates, all beautifully designed by Mr. Bernard Picart, and curiously engraved by most of the Best Hands in Europe; faithfully translated into English by a Gentleman, some time since of St. John's College, in Oxford. *Vols. I.–IV., large folio, old calf, gilt.* London, 1733–34

585 CERVANTES SAAVEDRA, MIGUEL DE. TWO HUMOROUS NOVELS, viz. I. A Diverting Dialogue between Scipio and Bergansa, Two Dogs belonging to the Hospital of the Resurrection, in the City of Valladolid, giving an Account of their Lives and Various Adventures; interspers'd with their Reflexions and Sentiments on the Lives, Characters, Humours, and Employments of the Different Masters they liv'd with. II. The Comical History of Rinconete and Cortadillo. Both written by the celebrated Author of Don Quixote, and now first translated from the Spanish Original. The Second Edition. 12*mo, new sprinkled calf, gilt, red edges.* Printed by H. Kent, for W. Sandby, London, 1742

586 CERVANTES SAAVEDRA, MIGUEL DE. THE HISTORY AND ADVENTURES OF THE RENOWNED DON QUIXOTE, translated from the Spanish; to which is prefixed, some Account of the Author's Life. By T. Smollett. Illustrated with Copper-Plates. *4 vols. in 2, 8vo, old calf, green edges.* Dublin, 1783

587 CERVANTES SAAVEDRA, MIGUEL DE. THE ADVENTURES OF THE RENOWNED DON QUIXOTE DE LA MANCHA; translated from the Original Spanish, by T. Smollett. To which is prefixed a New Life of Cervantes. *Portrait and frontispieces. 4 vols., 12mo, crimson morocco, extra, gilt edges.* London, 1803

588 CERVANTES SAAVEDRA, MIGUEL DE. DON QUIXOTE DE LA MANCHA; translated from the Spanish by Charles Jarvis, Esq. Carefully revised and corrected. *Above 800 fine humorous wood-cuts, after designs by Tony Johannot, and others. 2 vols., royal 8vo, half morocco, neat; with autograph of Rufus Choate.* London, 1842

589 CHALLAMEL, AUGUSTIN. HISTOIRE-MUSÉE DE LA RÉPUBLIQUE FRANÇAISE; DEPUIS L'ASSEMBLÉE DES NOTABLES, JUSQU'À L'EMPIRE. *Numerous plates, and wood-cuts of views, portraits, caricatures, costumes, medals, fac-similes, etc. 2 vols., imperial 8vo, half morocco, marbled edges.* Challamel, Paris, 1842

590 CHAMBERLAIN, JOSHUA L. ADDRESS TO THE LEGISLATURE OF THE STATE OF MAINE, January, 1867. *8vo.* Augusta, 1867

591 CHAMBERS, ROBERT. THE SCOTTISH SONGS, COLLECTED AND ILLUSTRATED BY. *3 vols., 12mo, cloth, rough edges; with autograph of the compiler and newspaper cuttings.* W. Tait, Edinburgh, 1829

Among the cuttings inserted in this copy are several songs not in the collection, including Scott's "Bonnets of Bonnie Dundee," which is in the table of contents, but not in the work.

592 CHAMBERS, ROBERT. A BIOGRAPHICAL DICTIONARY OF EMINENT SCOTSMEN; edited by Robert Chambers. New Edition, revised and continued to the Present Time. *Numerous fine portraits and engraved titles for binding in 5 vols. 9 vols., royal 8vo, cloth, uncut; with autograph of Rufus Choate.* Glasgow, 1853–55

593 CHAMBERS, WILLIAM AND ROBERT. CHAMBERS'S INFORMATION FOR THE PEOPLE; edited by William and Robert Chambers. New and improved Edition. *Numerous wood-cuts. 2 vols., royal 8vo, cloth.* Philadelphia (Edinburgh), 1860

594 CHAMBERS' REPOSITORY OF INSTRUCTIVE AND AMUSING PAPERS. *Wood-cuts. Vols. I.–IV. in 1 vol., thick 16mo, half calf.* Boston, 1853

595 CHANDLER, MARY G. THE ELEMENTS OF CHARACTER Second Edition. *16mo, cloth.* Boston, 1854

596 CHANDLER, RICHARD, D. D. THE LIFE OF WILLIAM WAYNFLETE, Bishop of Winchester, Lord High Chancellor of England in the Reign of Henry VI., and Founder of Magdalen College, Oxford; collected from Records, Registers, Manuscripts, and other Authentic Evidences. *Portrait, plates, and index. Imperial 8vo, morocco, neat, gilt edges.* LARGE PAPER: *only 50 copies printed.* London, 1811

597 CHANDLER, RICHARD, D. D. TRAVELS IN ASIA MINOR AND GREECE, or an Account of a Tour made at the Expense of the Society of Dilettanti. Third Edition. *Maps, plans, etc. 2 vols., 4to, boards, uncut.* London, 1817

598 CHANNING, GEORGE G. EARLY RECOLLECTIONS OF NEWPORT, R. I., from the year 1793 to 1811. *Post 8vo, cloth. Printed by J. Wilson & Son, Cambridge, Mass.* Newport, 1868

599 CHANNING, WILLIAM ELLERY, D. D. THE WORKS OF. Tenth complete Edition, with an Introduction. *6 vols., 12mo, half green morocco.* G. G. Channing, Boston, 1849

600 CHAPEL (THE) OF ST. MARY; by the Author of "The Rectory of Moreland." *12mo, cloth.* Boston, 1861

601 CHAPLIN, REV. JEREMIAH. THE EVENING OF LIFE, or Light and Comfort amid the Shadows of Declining Years. *12mo, cloth.* Boston, 1856

602 CHAPMAN, GEORGE, and JAMES SHIRLEY. THE BALL, A COMEDY; as it was presented by her Majesty's Servants, at the Private House in Drury Lane. *Interleaved and bound in 1 vol., 4to, half calf; with crest and initials J. L. G., gilt on sides. MS. notes.* ORIGINAL EDITION. London, 1639

603 CHAPONE, HESTER. THE POSTHUMOUS WORKS OF MRS. CHAPONE; containing her Correspondence with Mr. Richardson, a Series of Letters to Mrs. Elizabeth Carter, and some Fugitive Pieces never before published; together with an Account of her Life and Character, drawn up by her own Family. *2 vols., foolscap 8vo, green morocco, neat, gilt edges.* J. Murray, London, 1807

604 CHAPPE D'AUTEROCHE, JEAN. VOYAGE EN SIBÉRIE, FAIT PAR ORDRE DU ROI EN 1761; contenant les Mœurs, les Usages des Russes, et l'État Actuel de cette Puissance; la Description Géographique & le Nivellement de la Route de Paris à Tobolsk; l'Histoire Naturelle de la même Route; des Observations Astronomiques, & des Expériences sur l'Electricité Naturelle. *Numerous plates, representing the customs, manners, idols, costumes, etc., of the Russians, besides many relating to the natural history of the country, etc. 2 vols. in 3, royal 4to, old mottled calf, gilt, gilt edges.* Paris, 1768

The second volume of this work contains the Description of Kamtschatka by Kracheninnikow, translated into French from the original edition published at St. Petersburg, 1755.

605 CHAPPE D'AUTEROCHE, JEAN. ANOTHER COPY: *the same. 2 vols. in 3, old mottled calf, gilt, marbled edges.* Paris, 1768

CHARLES I., OF ENGLAND. ΒΑΣΙΛΙΚΑ: THE WORKS OF KING CHARLES THE MARTYR; with a Collection of Declarations, Treaties, and other Papers concerning the Differences betwixt his said Majesty and his Two Houses of Parliament (including ΕΙΚΩΝ ΒΑΣΙΛΙΚΗ). With the History of his Life [by Richard Perrinchiefe], as also of his Tryal and Martyrdome. *Frontispiece (arms) by J. Sturt, engraved title (with portrait) by A. Hertochs, and two other plates, one of which (Jotham's Parable) is by J. Neefs, after P. Fruytiers. Folio, old calf, red edges.* Ric. Chiswell, London, 1687

607 CHARLES, ELIZABETH R. CHRONICLES OF THE SCHÖNBERG-COTTA FAMILY; with Introduction by Bishop M'Ilvaine. *Frontispiece. Crown 8vo, half calf, extra, marbled edges.* T. Nelson & Son, New York, 1864

608 CHARLES, ELIZABETH R. CHRONICLES OF THE SCHÖNBERG-COTTA FAMILY; by Two of Themselves. *12mo, cloth.* M. W. Dodd, New York, 1864

609 CHARLEVOIX, PIERRE FRANÇOIS XAVIER DE. THE HISTORY OF PARAGUAY, containing, amongst other New, Curious, and Interesting Particulars of that Country, a Full and Authentic Account of the Establishments formed there by the Jesuits; Establishments allowed to have realized the Sublime Ideas of Fenelon, Sir Thomas More, and Plato. *2 vols., 8vo, old calf, neat.* Dublin, 1769

610 CHARNOCK, JOHN. BIOGRAPHIA NAVALIS, or Impartial Memoirs of the Lives and Characters of Officers of the Navy of Great Britain, from the Year 1660, to the Present Time; drawn from the most Authentic Sources, and disposed in a Chronological Arrangement. *With the* CONTINUATION. *Portrait of Sir Charles Saunders by Shipster, and folding plate of naval engagement, but the portraits and other engravings by Bartolozzi are wanting. 6 vols., 8vo, half calf.* London, 1794–98

611 CHARRON, PIERRE. OF WISDOME, THREE BOOKES, written in French, by Peter Charrõ, Doct. of Lawe, in Paris. Translated by Samson Lennard. *Engraved title (by Hole) only. Small 4to, old calf.* Printed by R. B. for W. Aspley, London, 1640

COLLATION: Engraved title; 1 leaf. To the Reador; 1 leaf. Table; 3 leaves. Preface; 10 leaves. Subject and Order of the Books; 1 leaf. Text; pp. 588. Alphabetical Table; 18 leaves.

612 CHASE, GEORGE W. THE MASONIC HARP; a Collection of Masonic Odes, Hymns, Songs, etc., for the Public and Private Ceremonies and Festivals of the Fraternity. — THE MASONIC MONITOR; containing the Monitorial Prayers, Charges, Explanations, etc., used in Conferring the Degrees in Lodge, Chapter, Council, and Encampment. *Together in 1 vol., square 12mo, cloth.* Boston, (1859)

613 CHASLES, PHILARÈTE. ÉTUDES SUR L'ANTIQUITÉ; précédées d'un Essai sur les Phases de l'Histoire Littéraire, et sur les Influences Intellectuelles des Races. 12*mo, half calf; with autograph of Rufus Choate.* Paris, 1847

614 CHATEAUBRIAND, RENÉ FRANÇOIS AUGUSTE, VICOMTE DE. ATALA. Avec les Dessins de Gustave Doré. *Elegantly printed on a very fine thick paper, with* 30 *full-page engravings and many smaller ones. Folio, half morocco, very neat, gilt top.* ORIGINAL EDITION: *fine impressions of the cuts.* Paris, 1863

615 CHATFIELD, PAUL. THE TIN TRUMPET, or Heads and Tails for the Wise and Waggish. A New American Edition, with Alterations and Additions. 12*mo, cloth, gilt top.* New York, 1859

616 CHATTERTON, THOMAS. THE WORKS OF; with Life by G. Gregory, D. D. [Edited by Robert Southey and Amos Cottle.] *Views of Redcliff Church, fac-similes, etc.* 3 *vols.,* 8*vo, old sprinkled calf, gilt; backs cracked.* London, 1803

617 CHATTO, WILLIAM A. THE ANGLER'S SOUVENIR, by P. Fisher, Esq. [W. A. Chatto]; assisted by Several Eminent Piscatory Characters. With Illustrations by Beckwith & Topham. *In addition to the fine plates each page is enclosed within a different emblematical wood-cut border. Post* 8*vo, cloth, gilt top.* C. Tilt, London, 1835

A remarkably pretty volume.

618 CHAUCER, GEOFFREY. THE CANTERBURY TALES OF CHAUCER; to which are added, an Essay on his Language and Versification, and an Introductory Discourse: together with Notes and a Glossary. By the late Thomas Tyrwhitt, Esq., F. R. S. The Second Edition. *Portrait of Tyrwhitt.* 2 *vols.,* 4*to, half calf, extra; with autograph of Rufus Choate.* Clarendon Press, Oxford, 1798

"This edition was printed by the University of Oxford as a tribute of respect for the Editor." — *Lowndes.*

619 CHAUCER, GEOFFREY. THE CANTERBURY TALES OF CHAUCER; with an Essay on his Language and Versification, an Introductory Discourse, Notes, and a Glossary, by Thos. Tyrwhitt, Esq. *Portrait, and fine plate of the Canterbury Pilgrimage after Stothard.* 5 *vols., crown* 8*vo, green turkey morocco, neat, gilt edges.* ONLY 250 COPIES PRINTED. W. Pickering, London, 1830

620 CHAUCER, GEOFFREY. CHAUCER'S ROMAUNT OF THE ROSE, TROILUS AND CRESSIDA, AND THE MINOR POEMS; with Life of the Poet, by Sir Harris Nicolas. 3 *vols., crown* 8*vo, green turkey morocco, neat, gilt edges.* ONLY 250 COPIES PRINTED. W. Pickering, London, 1846

621 CHAUNCY, CHARLES, D. D. SEASONABLE THOUGHTS ON THE STATE OF RELIGION IN NEW ENGLAND, a Treatise in Five Parts. I. Faithfully pointing out Things of a Bad and

Dangerous Tendency in the Late and Present Religious Appearance in the Land. II. Representing the Obligations which lie upon the Pastors of these Churches in Particular, and upon all in General, to use their Endeavours to suppress Prevailing Disorders, with the Great Danger of a Neglect in so Important a Matter. III. Opening, in many Instances, wherein the Discouragers of Irregularities have been injuriously treated. IV. Shewing what ought to be corrected, or avoided, in Testifying against the Evil Things of the Present Day. V. Directing our Thot's, more positively, to what may be judged the Best Expedients to promote Pure and Undefiled Religion in these Times. With a Preface giving an Account of the Antinomians, Familists, and Libertines who infected these Churches above an Hundred Years ago; very Needful for these Days, the like Spirit and Errors prevailing now as did then. The whole being intended and calculated to serve the Interest of Christ's Kingdom. *Small 8vo, old calf.*

Printed by Rogers & Fowle, for S. Eliot, Boston, 1743

622 CHAUNCY, CHARLES, D. D. A COMPLEAT VIEW OF THE EPISCOPACY, as exhibited from the Fathers of the Christian Church, until the Close of the Second Century; containing an Impartial Account of them, of their Writings, and of what they say concerning Bishops and Presbyters: with Observations and Remarks tending to shew that they esteemed these One and the Same Order of Ecclesiastical Officers. In answer to those who have represented it as a Certain Fact, universally handed down, even from the Apostles' Days, that Governing and Ordaining Authority was exercised by such Bishops only as were of an Order superior to Presbyters. *Small 8vo, old calf.*

Printed by D. Kneeland, for T. Leverett, Boston, 1771

623 CHÉNIER, MARIE JOSEPH DE. THÉATRE DE; précédé d'une Notice, et orné du Portrait de l'Auteur. *Portrait and third volume wanting.* 2 *vols.*, 8*vo, old marbled calf, gilt, marbled edges.* Paris, 1818

624 CHESNUT, JAMES, JUN. RELATIONS OF STATES: Speech delivered in the Senate of the United States, April 9, 1860, on the Resolutions submitted by Jefferson Davis, on 1st March, 1860. 8*vo, pp.* 24. Baltimore, 1860

625 CHESTERFIELD, PHILIP DORMER STANHOPE, EARL OF. THE LETTERS OF, including Numerous Letters now First Published from the Original Manuscripts. Edited, with Notes, by Lord Mahon [now Earl Stanhope]. *Portraits.* 5 *vols.*, 8*vo, green calf, gilt, marbled edges.* ONLY COMPLETE EDITION. R. Bentley, London, 1845–53

"In Lord Mahon's case the work of 'editing' is not confined to putting his name on the title-page, and adding a stray note here and there. He supplies the elucidatory information required by the text, and employs conscientious care in seeing that the text is critically perfect."—*Athenæum.*

626 CHESTERFIELD, PHILIP DORMER STANHOPE, EARL OF. ANOTHER COPY: *the same.* 5 *vols.*, 8*vo*, *cloth*, *uncut.* London, 1845–53

627 CHEVALIER, MICHEL. SOCIETY, MANNERS, AND POLITICS IN THE UNITED STATES; being a Series of Letters on North America. Translated from the Third Paris Edition [by T. G. Bradford]. 8*vo*, *cloth.* Boston, 1839

628 CHEVREUL, MICHEL EUGÈNE. THE PRINCIPLES OF HARMONY AND CONTRAST OF COLOURS, AND THEIR APPLICATIONS TO THE ARTS; including Painting, Interior Decoration, Tapestries, Carpets, Mosaics, Coloured Glazing, Paper-Staining, Calico-Printing, Letter-press Printing, Map-Colouring, Dress, Landscape, and Flower Gardening, etc. Translated from the French by Charles Martel. Third Edition, illustrated. *Post* 8*vo*, *cloth*, *uncut.* London, 1859

629 CHILD, FRANCIS JAMES. FOUR OLD PLAYS: Three Interludes — Thersytes, Jack Jugler, and Heywood's Pardoner and Frere; and Jocasta, a Tragedy, by Gascoigne and Kinwelmarsh. With an Introduction and Notes [by F. J. Child]. *Fac-simile wood-cut*, *glossary and index.* 12*mo*, *cloth*, *uncut.* Cambridge (Mass.), 1848

These old plays, published by Prof. Child, soon after leaving college, are very accurately reprinted.

630 CHILD, FRANCIS JAMES. ENGLISH AND SCOTTISH BALLADS; Edited (with Notes, Glossaries, etc.) by Francis James Child. 8 *vols.*, *crown* 8*vo*, *half morocco*, *red paper sides*, *gilt tops* BEST COLLECTION: LARGE PAPER. Boston, 1860

631 CHILLINGWORTH, WILLIAM. THE WORKS OF (with some Additions and Corrections, and Life of the Author). 3 *vols.*, 8*vo*, *calf.* University Press, Oxford, 1838

"I should propose the constant reading of Chillingworth, who by his example will teach both perspicuity, and the way of right reasoning, better than any book that I know; and therefore will deserve to be read upon that account, over and over again; not to say anything of his argument." — *Locke.*

632 CHINA: IN A SERIES OF VIEWS DISPLAYING THE SCENERY, ARCHITECTURE, AND SOCIAL HABITS OF THAT ANCIENT EMPIRE; drawn, from Original and Authentic Sketches, by Thomas Allom, Esq. With Historical and Descriptive Notices by the Rev. G. N. Wright. *Vignettes on the engraved titles*, *and* 124 *fine plates.* 4 *vols. in* 2, *morocco*, *extra*, *gilt edges.* London, (1844)

633 CHINESE (THE) REPOSITORY. *From May*, 1832, *to Dec.* 1851, *inclusive*, *and* GENERAL INDEX. *Printed on India paper*, *with maps and plates.* 20 *vols.*, 8*vo*, *blue Chinese cloth.* COMPLETE AND FINE SET: VERY FEW EXTANT. Canton, 1833–51

This valuable repository of history, statistics, language, etc., was commenced by the Rev. Dr. Robert Morrison, the learned Chinese scholar and father of Protestant Missionary effort in China. It contains the most reliable and valuable information relative to the Celestial Empire. This copy is probably the ONLY COMPLETE SET in this country, and it is so extremely scarce that very few *complete sets* can be found in England, and probably none on the continent, as Remusat, in the preface to his Chinese grammar, complains that he could not see a copy.

The following note (signature erased) is attached to a fly-leaf of the first volume: "This set of the 'Chinese Repository,' was bought for me in 1857, by R. P. Dana, at Canton, China. It is the *only copy* which escaped destruction from the burning of the foreign factories, set on fire by the natives Dec. 14–16, 1856, in consequence of the troubles with England. Some 7,000 volumes of the Repository, etc., and the entire fonts of Chinese types were destroyed with the printing-office."

634 CHOATE, RUFUS. THE WORKS OF ; with a Memoir of his Life, by Samuel G. Brown. *Portrait.* 2 *vols.*, 8*vo*, *cloth.* Boston, 1862

635 CHODERLOS DE LA CLOS, PIERRE AMBROISE FRANÇOIS. LES LIAISONS DANGEREUSES: Lettres recueillies dans une Société, et publiées pour l'Instruction de quelques autres. Par C * * * de L * * * . *The second edition with the* 14 *plates after Monnet and Mlle. Gérard.* 2 *vols.*, 8*vo*, *half calf.* Londres (Paris), 1796

636 CHOISEUL-GOUFFIER, M. G. F. A. COMTE DE. VOYAGE PITTORESQUE DE LA GRÈCE. *Vol. I., containing maps of Ancient and Modern Greece,* 126 *beautiful large plates, and numerous vignettes. Imperial folio, crimson morocco, extra, gilt edges.* Paris, 1782

"Le premier volume de cet ouvrage, à l'époque où il parut pour la première fois était incontestablement, sous le rapport de la gravure, la plus belle production en ce genre qu'on eût encore vue." —*Brunet.*

637 CHORLEY, HENRY F. THE AUTHORS OF ENGLAND : a Series of Medallion Portraits of Modern Literary Characters, engraved from the Works of British Artists, by Achille Collas; with Illustrative Notices, by Henry F. Chorley. *Royal* 4*to*, *half morocco.* London, 1838

638 CHRISTIAN (THE) EXAMINER AND THEOLOGICAL REVIEW. *From Jan.* 1824, *to Nov.* 1862, *inclusive.* 73 *vols.*, 8*vo*, *half sheep.* Boston, 1824–26

639 CHRISTIAN (THE) SCHOLAR; by the Author of "the Cathedral." *Foolscap*, 8*vo*, *cloth*, *uncut.* J. H. Parker, Oxford, 1849

640 CHRISTIAN'S (THE) GUIDE TO HEAVEN, OR A MANUAL OF SPIRITUAL EXERCISES; with the Evening Office of the Church, in Latin and English, and a Selection of Pious Hymns. 18*mo*, *morocco*, *gilt edges.* Boston, 1845

641 CHRISTMAS WITH THE POETS: A COLLECTION OF SONGS, CAROLS, AND DESCRIPTIVE VERSES, RELATING TO THE FESTIVAL OF CHRISTMAS, from the Anglo-Norman Period to the Present Time. Embellished with Fifty-three tinted Illustrations by Birket Foster, and with Initial Letters and other Ornaments. *The borders and initials printed in gold. First edition. Royal* 8*vo*, *olive morocco*, *extra*, *gilt edges.* D. Bogue, London, 1855

642 CHRONICLES (THE) OF THE BASTILE; an Historical Romance. Fifth Edition. *Frontispiece and* 39 *plates after R. Cruikshank.* 1 *vol.* — THE EMBASSY, or the Key to a Mystery; an Historical Romance: being the Second Series of the Chronicles of the Bastile. 3 *vols. Together,* 4 *vols.,* 8*vo, cloth.* London, 1846 and 1847

643 CHRONOLOGIE DES EMPÉREURS OTTOMANS. *With colored portraits of the* 31 *Sultans from the foundation of the monarchy, to the late Sultan Abdul-Medjid. Folio, half morocco.* s. l. s. a.

644 CHURCH, EDWARD. NOTICE ON THE BEET SUGAR; containing a Description of the Culture, Preservation, and Process of Extracting its Sugar. Preceded by a Few Remarks on the Origin and Present State of the Indigenous Sugar Manufactories of France. Translated. 12*mo, boards.* Northampton (Mass.), 1837

645 CHURCH, JOHN. A CABINET OF QUADRUPEDS, CONSISTING OF HIGHLY-FINISHED ENGRAVINGS BY TOOKEY, FROM DRAWINGS BY JULIUS IBBETSON; with Historical and Scientific Descriptions by John Church. *Fine impressions of the* 84 *plates.* 2 *vols., imperial* 4*to, old calf, gilt.* London, 1805.

646 CHURCHILL, AWNSHAM and JOHN. A COLLECTION OF VOYAGES AND TRAVELS, some now first printed from Original Manuscripts, others translated out of Foreign Languages and now first publish'd in English; to which are added, some few that have formerly appear'd in English, but do now for their Excellency and Scarceness deserve to be reprinted. With a General Preface, giving an Account of the Progress of Navigation from its First Beginning to the Perfection it is now in, etc. *Numerous maps and plates.* 4 *vols., folio, half russia, backs cracked; with book-plate of Julius Charles Hare.* A. and J. Churchill, London, 1704

647 CHURCHILL, CHARLES. THE POETICAL WORKS; with Copious Notes and a Life of the Author, by W. Tooke, F. R. S. *Portrait.* 3 *vols., foolscap* 8*vo, half calf, extra, marbled edges.* Boston, 1854

648 CHURCHILL, COLONEL CHARLES HENRY. MOUNT LEBANON: a Ten Years' Residence, from 1842 to 1852, describing the Manners, Customs, and Religion of its Inhabitants; with a Full & Correct Account of the Druse Religion, and containing Historical Records of the Mountain Tribes. 3 *vols.,* 1853. — THE DRUZES AND THE MARONITES; under the Turkish Rule, from 1840 to 1860. 1 *vol.,* 1862. *Portraits.* 4 *vols.,* 8*vo, cloth, uncut.* London, 1853–62

The later published work contains an index to both.

649 CIBBER, COLLEY. THE DRAMATIC WORKS OF. *Portrait*

and plates. 4 vols., 12mo, old marbled calf; with newspaper cuttings, autograph of W. Forsyth and other MS. notes. London, 1760, etc.

This copy has had the following pieces bound with it, namely, "Cæsar in Egypt," 1736; "Perolla and Isadora," 1736; "Xerxes," 1736; "The School-Boy," 1761; "Venus and Adonis," and "Myrtillo," 1736.

650 CIBBER, COLLEY. AN APOLOGY FOR THE LIFE OF; written by himself. *Portrait. 12mo, half morocco.* London, 1826

651 CIBBER, THEOPHILUS. THE LIVES OF THE POETS OF GREAT BRITAIN AND IRELAND, TO THE TIME OF DEAN SWIFT; compiled from Ample Materials scattered in a Variety of Books, and especially from the MS. Notes of the late Ingenious Mr. Coxeter and others, collected for this Design, by Mr. Cibber (and other Hands). *5 vols., 12mo, half calf; bindings broken.* London, 1753

652 CICERO. M. TULLII CICERONIS OPERA, cum Indicibus et Variis Lectionibus. CLAVIS CICERONIANA, sive Indices Rerum et Verborum Philologico-Critici in Opera Ciceronis; accedunt Græca Ciceronis Necessariis Observationibus illustrata. *10 vols., royal 4to, old sprinkled calf, gilt, green edges; with book-plate of the Marquis of Blandford.* E Typographeo Clarendoniano, Oxonii, 1783

This edition is a careful reprint of the text of Olivet, but without the notes. The "Various Readings" are from MSS., collated by Thomas Hearne, from the public and private libraries of Oxford, and from other MSS. in the library of York Cathedral. The Index is reprinted from that of Ernesti.

Gibbon, in speaking of the writings of Cicero, says: "The most perfect Editions, that of Olivet, which may adorn the shelves of the rich, that of Ernesti, which should lie on the table of the learned, were not in my power." —*Miscel. Wks.* (Vol. I., p. 62, of the Dublin Edition, 1796.)

653 CICERO. THREE BOOKES OF DUTIES, TO MARCUS HIS SONNE; tourned out of Latine into English, by Nicolas Grimald. Whereunto the Latin is adjoyned. *Wood-cut title. The two versions in parallel columns, the Latin in Roman type. Small square 8vo, new tree calf, gilt, carmine edges.* **Black letter**: *fine copy.* R. Tottell, London, 1583

654 CICERO. CATO MAJOR, OR THE BOOK OF OLD AGE; first written by M. T. Cicero, and now Excellently Englished by William Austin, of Lincolns Inne, Esquire. With Annotations upon the Names of the Men and the Places. *Engraved title, by J. Goddard. 12mo, half calf, red edges.* ORIGINAL EDITION: *fine clean copy.* W. Leake, London, 1648

655 CICERO. ESSAYS ON OLD AGE AND FRIENDSHIP; with Remarks, by William Melmoth, Esq. *8vo, sheep; with autograph of Rufus Choate.* London, 1807

656 CICERO. LETTERS TO SEVERAL OF HIS FRIENDS; with Remarks, by William Melmoth, Esq. The Sixth Edition, to which is now added a General Index. *Portrait. 3 vols., 8vo, half calf, extra; with autograph of Rufus Choate.* London, 1803–04

"An elegant translation of more than ordinary merit." — *Lowndes.*

657 CICERO. LETTERS; with Remarks, by William Melmoth, Esq. 5 *vols., foolscap 8vo, marbled calf, extra, marbled edges.* Printed by J. Ballantyne & Co., Edinburgh, 1808

658 CICERO. THE POLITICAL WORKS; comprising his Treatise on the Republic, and his Treatise on the Laws. Translated from the Original, with Dissertations and Notes; by Francis Barham, Esq. 2 *vols., 8vo, half calf, neat; with autograph of Rufus Choate.* E. Spettigue, London, 1841–42

659 CLARENDON, EDWARD HYDE, EARL OF. THE LIFE OF; in which is included a Continuation of his History of the Grand Rebellion. Written by himself. A New Edition, exhibiting a Faithful Collation of the Original MS., with all the Suppressed Passages. 3 *vols., 8vo, tree calf, gilt, marbled edges.* Clarendon Press, Oxford, 1827

660 CLARENDON, EDWARD HYDE, EARL OF. THE HISTORY OF THE REBELLION AND CIVIL WARS IN ENGLAND, TOGETHER WITH AN HISTORICAL VIEW OF THE AFFAIRS OF IRELAND; now for the First Time carefully printed from the Original MS. preserved in the Bodleian Library. To which are subjoined the Notes of Bishop Warburton. 7 *vols., royal 8vo, calf, gilt, marbled edges; with autograph of Rufus Choate.* University Press, Oxford, 1849

661 CLARK, DANIEL. PROOFS OF THE CORRUPTION OF GEN. JAMES WILKINSON, AND OF HIS CONNEXION WITH AARON BURR; with a Full Refutation of his Slanderous Allegations in Relation to the Character of the Principal Witness against him. *8vo, half morocco, neat, gilt top.* Philadelphia, 1809

662 CLARK, JOHN HEAVISIDE. A PRACTICAL ILLUSTRATION OF GILPIN'S DAY, representing the Various Effects on Landscape Scenery from Morning till Night, in Thirty Designs from Nature, by the late Rev. William Gilpin, A. M., etc.; with Instructions in, and Explanations of the improved Method of Colouring and Painting in Water Colours. *Plates finely colored by hand. Imperial 4to, half morocco, uncut.* London, 1824

663 CLARK, WILLIAM. PELOPONNESUS; NOTES OF STUDY AND TRAVEL. *Maps and plans. 8vo, cloth, uncut; with autograph of Rufus Choate.* London, 1858

664 CLARKE, EDWARD D. TRAVELS IN VARIOUS COUNTRIES OF EUROPE, ASIA, AND AFRICA. (Part the First: Russia, Tahtary, and Turkey. Part the Second: Greece, Egypt, and the Holy Land; to which is added a Supplement respecting the Author's Journey from Constantinople to Vienna, containing his Account of the Gold Mines of Transylvania and Hungary. Part the Third: Scandinavia.) *Portrait by Fry after*

Opie, and numerous maps, plates, and wood-cuts. 11 *vols.*, 8*vo, half russia, marbled edges.* London, 1816–24

"Perhaps the most instructive and engaging book of travels ever published in this country." — *Lowndes.*
"If HUMBOLDT be the first, CLARKE is the second Traveller of his age."—*Dibdin.*

665 CLARKE, JAMES STANIER, D. D. NAUFRAGIA; or, Historical Memoirs of Shipwrecks, and of the Providential Deliverance of Vessels. *Chart of the North Pole, etc.* 2 *vols.*, 12*mo, half morocco, extra.* London, 1805–06

666 CLARKE, JAMES STANIER, D. D.; and JOHN M'ARTHUR. THE LIFE OF ADMIRAL LORD NELSON, K. B., from his Lordship's Manuscripts. *Numerous fine plates by C. Heath, J. Fittler, etc., after West, Smirke, Westall, etc.* 2 *vols., imperial* 4*to, polished calf, gilt.* LARGE PAPER: *early impressions of the plates.*
Printed by T. Bensley, London, 1809

667 CLARKE, MARY ANN. AUTHENTIC MEMOIRS OF MRS. CLARKE; in which is pourtrayed the Secret History and Intrigues of many Characters in the First Circles of Fashion and High Life: and containing the Whole of her Correspondence during the Time she lived under the Protection of his Royal Highness the Duke of York, the Gallant Duke's Love Letters, and other Interesting Papers never before published. By Miss Elizabeth Taylor. Second Edition. *Colored portrait.* 12*mo, half red morocco.* T. Tegg, London, 1809

668 CLARKE, SAMUEL, D. D. A LETTER TO MR. DODWELL; wherein all the Arguments in his Epistolary Discourse against the Immortality of the Soul are particularly answered, and the Judgment of the Fathers concerning that Matter truly represented. The Second Edition. 8*vo, old calf, gilt, red edges; with autograph of Rufus Choate.*
London, 1706

669 CLARKE, SAMUEL, D. D. A DISCOURSE CONCERNING THE BEING AND ATTRIBUTES OF GOD, the Obligations of Natural Religion, and the Truth and Certainty of the Christian Revelation; in Answer to Mr. Hobbs, Spinoza, and other Deniers of Natural and Revealed Religion. The Seventh Edition, corrected: there is inserted in this Edition, a Discourse concerning the Connexion of the Prophesies in the Old Testament, and the Application of them to Christ; there is also added, an Answer to a Seventh Letter, concerning the Argument, *à priori*, in Proof of the Being of God. 8*vo, old calf; with autographs of Jonathan Mayhew, and Rufus Choate, etc.* London, 1728

670 CLARKE, SAMUEL, D. D. SERMONS: published from the Author's Manuscript, by John Clarke, D. D., Dean of Sarum. With a Preface, giving some Account of the Life, Writings, and Character of the Author; by Benjamin [Hoadly],

now Lord Bishop of Winchester. The Sixth Edition, corrected. *Portrait by Vertue, and indexes.* 10 *vols.*, 8*vo, old sprinkled calf.* London, 1743–44

For contents see Darling's "Cyclopædia Bibliographica," col. 684, etc.

671 CLARKE, STEPHEN REYNOLDS. VESTIGIA ANGLICANA, or Illustrations of the more Interesting and Debatable Points in the History and Antiquities of England; from the Earliest Ages to the Accession of the House of Tudor. *Portraits of Queen Elizabeth and George I., inserted.* 2 *vols., imperial* 8*vo, cloth, uncut.* LARGE PAPER. London, 1862

672 CLARKE, WILLIAM. REPERTORIUM BIBLIOGRAPHICUM, or some Account of the most Celebrated British Libraries. [By William Clarke, Bookseller.] *Frontispiece on India paper, and portrait (inserted) of White Kennet, Bp. of Peterborough.* 2 *vols., imperial* 8*vo, calf, extra, marbled edges, by Riviere.* LARGE PAPER: *only* 59 *copies printed.* London, 1810

673 CLARKE, WILLIAM. ANOTHER COPY. *Frontispiece, and* 11 *portraits of eminent collectors, etc., including* 1 *of Francis I., King of France, engraved by W. Behnes (the celebrated portrait sculptor), which is the "first and only specimen of his engraving." Royal* 8*vo, calf, gilt.* London, 1819

674 CLASSICAL (THE) MUSEUM; a Journal of Philology, and of Ancient History and Literature. *Maps, plans, and other plates.* 7 *vols.,* 8*vo, half green morocco.* London, 1844–50

675 CLAY, HENRY. THE LIFE, CORRESPONDENCE, AND SPEECHES OF; by Calvin Colton, LL. D. *Portraits and views.* 6 *vols.,* 8*vo, cloth.* New York, 1857

676 CLEGHORN, GEORGE. ANCIENT AND MODERN ART; Historical and Critical. Second Edition, corrected and enlarged. 2 *vols., post* 8*vo, cloth, uncut.* Edinburgh, 1848

677 CLEVELAND, HENRY. A SELECTION FROM THE WRITINGS OF; with a Memoir, by George S. Hillard. *Post* 8*vo, crushed morocco, extra, gilt edges.* PRIVATELY PRINTED. (Boston, 1844)

678 CLINTON, GEORGE. MEMOIRS OF THE LIFE AND WRITINGS OF LORD BYRON. *Portrait and wood-cuts.* 8*vo, calf, gilt.* London, 1825

679 CLINTON, HENRY FYNES. AN EPITOME OF THE CIVIL AND LITERARY CHRONOLOGY OF GREECE, from the Earliest Accounts to the Death of Augustus. 8*vo, half calf, extra; with autograph of Rufus Choate.* University Press, Oxford, 1851

680 COBB, JONATHAN H. A MANUAL CONTAINING INFORMATION RESPECTING THE GROWTH OF THE MULBERRY TREE, with Suitable Directions for the Culture of Silk. New Edition. *Plates, those representing the leaves and insects are colored.* 12*mo, boards.* Boston, 1833

681 COBBETT, William. Selections from Cobbett's Political Works; being a Complete Abridgement of the 100 Volumes which comprise the Writings of "Porcupine" and the "Weekly Political Register." With Notes Historical and Explanatory, by John M. Cobbett and James P. Cobbett. *6 vols., 8vo, half calf, extra; with autograph of Rufus Choate.* (London, 1835, or 1837)

682 COCHIN, Augustin. The Results of Slavery. Translated by Mary L. Booth. *12mo, cloth.* Boston, 1863

683 COCHIN, Augustin. The Results of Emancipation. Translated by Mary L. Booth. *12mo, cloth.* Boston, 1863

684 COCKBURN, Henry Thomas, Lord. Memorials of his Time. *12mo, cloth.* New York, 1856

685 CODMAN, John, Charles R., and Francis. An Exposition of the Pretended Claims of William Vans on the Estate of John Codman; with an Appendix of Original Documents, Correspondence, and other Evidence. *8vo, cloth; with book-plate of T. H. Perkins.* Boston, 1837

686 COFFIN, Charles Carleton. Four Years of Fighting; a Volume of Personal Observation with the Army and Navy, from the First Battle of Bull Run to the Fall of Richmond. *Portrait, plans, and wood-cuts, after Nast. 8vo, sheep.* Boston, 1866

687 COFFIN, Robert Barry. My Married Life at Hillside; by Barry Gray [R. B. Coffin]. *Wood-cuts. Post 8vo, cloth.* New York, 1865

688 COFFIN, Robert. Matrimonial Infelicities, with an Occasional Felicity, by Way of Contrast; by an Irritable Man: to which are added, as being Pertinent to the Subject, my Neighbors, and Down in the Valley. *Crown 8vo, cloth.* New York, 1865

689 COFFIN, Robert. Out of Town, a Rural Episode; with Illustrations. *Post 8vo, cloth.* New York, 1866

690 COLEMAN, Edward. Observations on the Structure, Economy and Diseases of the Foot of the Horse, and on the Principles and Practice of Shoeing. Second Edition. *Plates. Vol. I., 4to, old marbled calf.* Printed for the author, London, 1798

The second volume was published in 1802. "An Esteemed Work." — *Lowndes.*

691 COLEMAN, William. A Collection of Facts relative to the Death of Major-General Alexander Hamilton, with Comments; together with the Various Orations, Sermons, and Eulogies, that have been published or written on his Life and Character. *8vo, sheep.* New York, 1804

692 COLERIDGE, Hartley. Poems; with a Memoir of his Life, by his Brother. *Portrait. 2 vols., foolscap 8vo, cloth, uncut.* E. Moxon, London, 1851

693 COLERIDGE, SAMUEL TAYLOR. WORKS. (Edited by his Son-in-Law and Nephew, H. N. Coleridge, and by his Daughter, Sara.) *Portrait on India paper, and view of his study.* 19 *vols., foolscap* 8*vo, green turkey morocco, gilt, contents lettered, gilt edges, by Clarke & Bedford.* ELEGANT SET.
J. Murray and W. Pickering, London, 1835–50

CONTENTS : Table Talk (with portrait and plate) ; 2 *vols., Murray,* 1835. — On the Constitution of Church and State, with Lay Sermons ; 1 *vol., Pickering,* 1839. — The Friend ; 3 *vols., Pickering,* 1844. — Poetical and Dramatic Works ; 3 *vols., Pickering,* 1847. — Biographia Literaria ; 2 *vols., Pickering,* 1847. — Aids to Reflection ; 2 *vols., Pickering,* 1848. — Notes and Lectures upon Shakespeare, etc. ; 2 *vols., Pickering,* 1849. — Confessions, etc. ; 1 *vol., Pickering,* 1849. — Essays on his Own Times ; 3 *vols., Pickering,* 1850.

694 COLERIDGE, SAMUEL TAYLOR. THE LITERARY REMAINS OF ; collected and edited by Henry Nelson Coleridge, Esq., M. A. 4 *vols.,* 8*vo, cloth, uncut.*
W. Pickering, London, 1836–39

695 COLERIDGE, SAMUEL TAYLOR. THE LITERARY REMAINS OF ; collected and edited by Henry Nelson Coleridge, Esq., M. A. 3 *vols.,* 8*vo., half morocco, neat.*
W. Pickering, London, 1836–38.

The fourth volume (1839) is wanting, but as the first two volumes are the scarce ones, this copy can easily be completed.

696 COLERIDGE, SAMUEL TAYLOR. NOTES AND LECTURES UPON SHAKESPEARE, and some of the Old Poets and Dramatists ; with other Literary Remains of S. T. Coleridge. Edited by Mrs. H. N. Coleridge. 2 *vols., foolscap* 8*vo, cloth, uncut.*
W. Pickering, London, 1849

697 COLERIDGE, SAMUEL TAYLOR. THE DRAMATIC WORKS OF ; edited by Derwent Coleridge. A New Edition. *Foolscap* 8*vo, cloth uncut.* E. Moxon, London, 1852

698 COLES, ELISHA. A DICTIONARY, ENGLISH–LATIN AND LATIN–ENGLISH ; containing all Things Necessary for the Translating of either Language into the other, to which End many Things that were Erroneous are rectified, many Superfluities retrenched, and very many Defects supplied, etc., etc. The Second Edition, enlarged. *Foolscap* 4*to, old calf, red edges ; with an old book-plate of Sir John Hussey Delaval, Bart.*
London, 1679

699 COLLECTION (A) OF ENGRAVINGS FROM PAINTINGS AND DRAWINGS BY THE MOST CELEBRATED MASTERS, containing a Series of Fine Specimens after Vandyke, Annibal Caracci, Murillo, Carlo Dolci, Salvator Rosa, Teniers, Rembrandt, Vander-Velde, Brauwer, Netcher, etc., etc. ; engraved and etched in the Best Manner by the most Eminent Artists. *A series of* 173 *fine plates.* 2 *vols., royal folio, half russia, neat.*
London, s. a.

700 COLLECTION (A) OF THE MOST ESTEEMED FARCES AND ENTERTAINMENTS PERFORMED ON THE BRITISH STAGE. (By Garrick, Murphy, Ravenscroft, Fielding, Foote, Coleman, Mendez, etc.) 12*mo, old calf.* C. Elliot, Edinburgh, 1782

701 COLLECTION (A) OF POEMS; by Several Hands. — A COLLECTION OF THE MOST ESTEEMED PIECES OF POETRY, that have appeared for Several Years, with Variety of Originals; by the late Moses Mendez, Esq., and other Contributors to Dodsley's Collection, to which this is intended as a Supplement. *Plates, 7 vols., post 8vo, half calf, yellow edges.* DODSLEY'S COLLECTION: *with Mendez's Supplement.*
London, 1766–70

702 COLLECTION (A) OF POEMS; by Several Hands. *Plates. 6 vols., post 8vo, old mottled calf, green edges.*
J. Dodsley, London, 1775
Same as the above, without the supplement.

703 COLLECTION (A) OF POEMS; by Several Hands. (Consisting of Valuable Pieces not inserted in Mr. Dodsley's Collection, or published since; with Several Originals, by Eminent Writers.) *Vignettes. 4 vols., post 8vo, old calf, gilt, yellow edges.* Printed for G. Pearch, London, 1775
This collection, called Pearch's, was designed as a continuation to the above.

704 COLLECTION (A) OF VOYAGES AND TRAVELS, some now first printed from Original Manuscripts, others now first published in English; to which is prefixed, an Introductory Discourse (supposed to be written by the celebrated Mr. Locke), intitled, the Whole History of Navigation from its Original to this Time. Illustrated with near Three Hundred Maps and Cuts curiously engraved on Copper. The Third Edition. Printed by Assignment from Messrs. Churchill. 6 *vols., H. Lintot and J. Osborn,* 1744–46. — A COLLECTION OF VOYAGES AND TRAVELS, consisting of Authentic Writers in our own Tongue, which have not before been collected in English, or have only been abridged in other Collections, and continued with others of Note that have published Histories, Voyages, Travels, Journals, or Discoveries in other Nations and Languages, relating to any Part of the Continent of Asia, Africa, America, Europe, or the Islands thereof; from the Earliest Account to the Present Time: with Historical Introductions to each Account, containing either Lives of the Authors, or what else could be discovered, and was supposed capable of entertaining and informing the Curious Reader; and with great Variety of Cuts, Prospects, Ruins, Maps, and Charts. Compiled from the Curious and Valuable Library of the late Earl of Oxford: interspersed and illustrated with Notes, containing either a General Account of the Discovery of those Countries, or an Abstract of their Histories, Government, Trade, Religion, etc.; collected from Original Papers, Letters, Charters, Letters Patents, Acts of Parliament, etc., not to be met with, and proper to explain many Obscure Passages, in other Collections of this kind. 2 *vols., T. Osborne,* 1745. *Together, 8 vols., folio, half morocco.* CHURCHILL AND HARLEIAN COLLECTIONS: FINE SET.
London, 1744–46

705 COLLIER, JANE. AN ESSAY ON THE ART OF INGENIOUSLY TORMENTING, with Proper Rules for the Exercise of that Pleasant Art; humbly addressed, in the First Part, to the Master, Husband, etc., in the Second Part, to the Wife, Friend, etc. With some General Instructions for Plaguing all your Acquaintance. [By Miss Collier.] The Second Edition, corrected. *Frontispiece (a cat tormenting a mouse) by Hogarth. 8vo, old calf.* A. Millar, London, 1757

Allibone says, "What a subject for a lady's pen!" "What a subject for a dean's pen!" would be equally applicable to Swift's "Rules that Concern all Servants in General," both being fine examples of irony.

706 COLLIER, JEREMY. A SHORT VIEW OF THE IMMORALITY AND PROFANENESS OF THE ENGLISH STAGE; together with the Sense of Antiquity upon this Argument. The Second Edition. *8vo, old calf.* London, 1698

See Allibone's "Dictionary of Authors," Vol. I. pp. 408–410.

707 COLLIER. JEREMY. ANOTHER COPY: The Third Edition. *8vo, old calf.* London, 1698

708 COLLIER, JOHN, "TIM BOBBIN." HUMAN PASSIONS DELINEATED, in about 120 Figures, Droll, Satyrical, and Humourous; designed in the Hogarthian Style, very Useful for Young Practitioners in Drawing. By Timothy Bobbin [John Collier]. *Portrait of "Tim Bobbin" and 45 plates, including title, with explanations in verse, partly in the Lancashire dialect. Oblong 4to, half calf.* Rochdale, 1773

709 COLLIER, JOHN. THE MISCELLANEOUS WORKS OF TIM BOBBIN, ESQ.; containing his View of the Lancashire Dialect, with large Additions and Improvements: also, his Poem of the Flying Dragon, and the Man of Heaton; together with other Whimsical Amusements in Prose and Verse (a Glossary of Lancashire Words and Phrases, the Black-Bird, the Goose, Letters, etc., etc.). To which is added, a Life of the Author, by Richard Townley, Esq. *Portrait and 9 plates. 12mo, new sprinkled calf, gilt, red edges.* London, 1806

710 COLLIER, JOHN. THE WORKS OF TIM BOBBIN, ESQ. (in the Lancashire Dialect), in Prose and Verse; with a Memoir of the Author, by John Corry. To which is added a Rendering into Simple English of the Dialogue of Tummus and Meary, with the Idioms and Similes retained, and Explanatory Notes, etc.; by Elijah Ridings. *Portrait and 10 other humorous plates by the author. 8vo, cloth, uncut.* Manchester, 1862

711 COLLIER, JOHN PAYNE. REASONS FOR A NEW EDITION OF SHAKESPEARE'S WORKS, containing Notices of the Defects of Former Impressions, and pointing out the lately acquired Means of Illustrating the Plays, Poems, and Biography of the Poet. (With Preface to his Edition of Shakespeare's Works.) *pp. 52 and viii. 8vo, boards, gilt top; with book-plate of Robert Balmanno, F. S. A.* London, 1841–44

712 COLLIER, JOHN PAYNE. SHAKESPEARE'S LIBRARY; a Collection of the Romances, Novels, Poems, and Histories used by Shakespeare as the Foundation of his Dramas. Now first collected, and accurately reprinted from the Original Editions; with Introductory Notices. *Title in black only. 2 vols., 8vo, cloth, uncut.* T. Rodd, London, (1843)

713 COLLIER, JOHN PAYNE. SHAKESPEARE'S LIBRARY; a Collection of the Ancient Novels, Romances, Legends, Poems, and Histories used by Shakespeare as the Foundation of his Dramas. Now first collected, and accurately reprinted from the Original Editions; with Introductory Notices. *Title in red and black. 2 vols., 8vo, cloth, uncut.* London, 1850

714 COLLIER, JOHN PAYNE. A BOOK OF ROXBURGHE BALLADS; edited by John Payne Collier, Esq. *Fac-simile woodcuts. Foolscap 4to, dark brown smooth morocco, extra, gilt over carmine edges, by Riviere.* London, 1847

715 COLLIER, JOHN PAYNE. ANOTHER COPY: *the same. Foolscap 4to, half olive morocco, red paper sides, uncut.* London, 1847

716 COLLIER, JOHN PAYNE. NOTES AND EMENDATIONS TO THE TEXT OF SHAKESPEARE'S PLAYS, from Early Manuscript Corrections in a Copy of the Folio, 1632, in the Possession of J. Payne Collier, Esq., F. S. A.; forming a Supplemental Volume to the Works of Shakespeare by the same Editor, in Eight Volumes, Octavo. *Fac-simile. 8vo, cloth, uncut.* Printed for the Shakespeare Society, London, 1852

This work was afterwards withdrawn from the list of publications of the Shakespeare Society, and published in 1853, as the "second edition" For an account of the work, and the controversy occasioned by it, see Bohn's "Lowndes," pp. 2335, etc.

717 COLLIER, JOHN PAYNE. A REVIEW OF "AN INQUIRY INTO THE GENUINENESS OF THE MANUSCRIPT CORRECTIONS IN MR. J. PAYNE COLLIER'S ANNOTATED SHAKSPERE, FOLIO, 1632; and of Certain Shaksperian Documents likewise published by Mr. Collier;" by N. E. S. A. Hamilton [Bentley]. Also, the Reply of Mr. J. Payne Collier, to the "Inquiry." Reprinted from the Athenæum of the 18th of February, 1860. *8vo, pp. 32.* New York, 1860

"Printed for private circulation by Charles W. Fredericksar."

718 COLLIER, REV. W. POEMS ON VARIOUS OCCASIONS, with Translations from Authors in Different Languages. *2 vols., post 8vo, red morocco, gilt, gilt edges.* London, 1800

From the Duke of Gloucester's library, with arms and book-plate.

719 COLLINS, LT. COL. DAVID. AN ACCOUNT OF THE ENGLISH COLONY IN NEW SOUTH WALES, from its first Settlement in January, 1788, to August, 1801; with Remarks on the Dispositions, Customs, Manners, etc., of the Native Inhabitants of that Country. To which are added,

some Particulars of New Zealand; and an Account of a Voyage performed by Captain Flinders and Mr. Bass, by which the Existence of a Strait separating Van Dieman's Land from the Continent of New Holland was ascertained. The Second Edition. *Portraits, charts, views, etc., engraved by J. Heath, etc.; the plates of birds colored. 4to, half calf.* London, 1804

"A singularly curious and painfully interesting journal, which may be considered as a sort of Botany Bay Calendar." — *Quarterly Review.*

720 COLLINS, JOHN. A DICTIONARY OF SPANISH PROVERBS, compiled from the Best Authorities in the Spanish Language, translated into English; with Explanatory Illustrations from the Latin, Spanish, and English Authors. *12mo, cloth, uncut.* London, 1823

721 COLLINS, WILKIE. THE CROSSED PATH, OR BASIL; a Story of Modern Life. *12mo, cloth.* Philadelphia, s. a.

722 COLLINS, WILKIE. THE WOMAN IN WHITE; a Novel. Illustrated by John McLenan. *8vo, cloth.* New York, 1860

723 COLLINS, WILKIE. NO NAME; a Novel. Illustrated by John McLenan. *8vo, cloth.* New York, 1863

724 COLLINS, WILLIAM. THE POETICAL WORKS. (With Memoir, by Sir N. Harris Nicolas; Essay on his Genius, by Sir S. E. Brydges; and Observations on the Eclogues and Odes, by Dr. Langhorne.) *Portrait. Foolscap 8vo, cloth, uncut.* ALDINE EDITION. W. Pickering, London, 1830

725 COLLINS, WILLIAM. ANOTHER COPY: *the same. Foolscap 8vo, turkey morocco, gilt edges, by Hayday; with autograph of Rufus Choate.* London, 1830

726 COLLINS, WILLIAM. THE POETICAL WORKS OF. (With Memoir, etc.) *Portrait. Foolscap 8vo, half calf, extra.* Boston, 1853

727 COLMAN, BENJAMIN, D. D. PRACTICAL DISCOURSES ON THE PARABLE OF THE TEN VIRGINS, being a Serious Call and Admonition to Watchfulness and Diligence in Preparing for Death and Judgment. By Benjamin Colman, D. D., Pastor of the Church in Brattle-Street, Boston. The Second Edition. *8vo, half calf, antique.* Rogers & Fowle, and J. Edwards, Boston, N. E., 1747

728 COLMAN, GEORGE, JUN. POSTHUMOUS LETTERS, from Various Celebrated Men addressed to Francis Colman, and George Colman, the Elder; with Annotations and Occasional Remarks, by George Coleman, the Younger. Exclusive of the Letters are, an Explanation of the Motives of William Pulteney (afterwards Earl of Bath) for his Acceptance of a Peerage, and Papers tending to elucidate the Question relative to the Proportional Shares of Authorship to be attributed to the Elder Colman and Garrick in the Comedy of the Clandestine Marriage. *4to, half calf, very neat.* London, 1820

729 COLEMAN, George, Jun. The Poetical Works of. *Wood-cuts. 24mo, cloth.* London, 1840

730 COLLYER, Rev. Robert. Nature and Life: Sermons by Robert Collyer, Pastor of Unity Church, Chicago. *12mo, cloth.* Boston, 1867

731 COLQUHOUN, John. Life in Italy and France in the Olden Time. *12mo, cloth, uncut; with autograph of Rufus Choate.* London, 1858

732 COLTON, Rev. C. C. Lacon, or Many Things in Few Words; addressed to those who Think. A New Edition complete in One Volume. *Post 8vo, cloth, uncut.* W. Tegg & Co., London, 1851

"In 1820 he created a considerable sensation in the literary world by the publication of 'Lacon,' one of the most valuable works in the English language. . . . Returning to Europe after a sojourn of some years in America, he took up his abode in Paris, where he became acquainted with the *habitués* of the gaming-saloons of the Palais Royal, and so successful was he in his speculations that, in the course of a year or two, he acquired a considerable fortune, but it was soon dissipated. . . . He blew out his brains at Fontainebleau in April, 1832; and this was the act of him who, in his 'Lacon,' proclaims this aphorism: 'The gamester, if he die a martyr to his profession, is doubly ruined. He adds his soul to every other loss, and by the act of suicide, renounces earth to forfeit heaven.'" —*Edwin Beedell.*

733 COLTON'S Atlas of the World, illustrating Physical and Political Geography. By George W. Colton; accompanied by Descriptions, Geographical, Statistical, and Historical, by Richard Fisher, M. D. *Engraved titles and above* 100 *large colored maps, plans, etc.* 2 *vols., large folio, half morocco, marbled edges.* New York, 1856

734 COMMERCE and Navigation: Reports of the Secretary of the Treasury, transmitting a Report from the Register of the Treasury, of the Commerce and Navigation of the United States for the Year(s) ending June 30, 1855 (and 1857). 2 *vols., 8vo, cloth.* Washington, 1855–57

735 COMPANION (A) to Wallace Hill; containing a Description of the Statue of Sir William Wallace, with a Sketch of his Life, and an Illustration of the Surrounding Scenery of the Country, interspersed with Historical Events, etc. *Etching of the statue. 12mo, pp.* 36, *boards; with book-plate of Robert Balmanno, F. S. A.* Alnwick, 1829

736 COMPENDIUM (A) of the most approved Modern Travels; containing a Distinct Account of the Religion, Government, Commerce, Manners and Natural History of Several Nations. 4 *vols., 12mo, old calf.* Dublin, 1757

Contains Wafer's "Isthmus of Darien" and Pelham's "Greenland," besides Maundrell, Mandeville, Pococke, Hanway, Drummard, etc., etc.

737 COMPLETE (The) Atlas of Modern, Classical, and Celestial Maps, together with Plans of the Principal Cities of the World; constructed, and engraved on Steel, under the Superintendence of the Society for the Diffusion of Useful

Knowledge, and including all the Recent Geographical Discoveries, compiled from the Latest and most Authentic Sources: accompanied by an Alphabetical Index to the Modern Maps. *With 218 colored maps, including the 6 maps of stars.* COMPLETE *in 1 vol., elephant 4to, half russia, neat, gilt edges.* London, 1857

738 CONGREVE, RICHARD. THE ROMAN EMPIRE OF THE WEST: Four Lectures delivered at the Philosophical Institution, Edinburgh, February, 1855. *Crown 8vo, half morocco, neat; with autograph of Rufus Choate.*
London, 1855

739 CONGREVE, WILLIAM. THE WORKS OF; consisting of his Plays and Poems (with Life). *Portrait by T. Chambers after Kneller, and plates by Grignion after Hayman. 3 vols., royal 8vo, calf, extra.* BASKERVILLE'S EDITION: *clean copy.*
Birmingham, 1761

Copies are seldom met with so free from stains.

740 CONGREVE, WILLIAM. THE WORKS OF (containing the Old Batchelor, the Double Dealer, Love for Love, the Mourning Bride, the Way of the World, the Judgment of Paris, Semele, with Poems on Several Occasions). The Seventh Edition; to which is prefixed, the Life of the Author. *Portrait by M. Vander Gucht after Kneller, and plates by Grignion after Hayman. 2 vols., 12mo, calf, gilt, green edges; with autograph of Rufus Choate.*
T. Lowndes, etc., London, 1774

741 CONLIN, JOHANN RUDOLF. ROMA SANCTA, sive Benedicti XIII. Pontificis Maximi & Eminentissimorum & Reverendissimorum S. R. E. Cardinalium Viva Virtutum Imago Æri & Literis in perennaturam Virtutum Memoriam incisa; continentur Vitæ, Familiæ, Patriæ, Legationes, aliáque scitu & memoratu Digna Omnium S. R. E. Cardinalium qui Ultimo Conclavi Anno 1724 interfuêre. Præter eos qui à Sanctissimo Patre Benedicto XIII. neo-denominati fuêre; quibus Supplementi Loco in Singulos 6 Menses post Creationem accedent, quotquot S. R. E. Cardinales denominari contigerit. Omnia desumpta ex Fidis Manuscriptis, Relationibus, Publicis Monumentis; Historicam Relationem adumbrante Joan, Rudolph. Conlin, Canonico ad S. Petrum Augustæ; Icones cælante Joanne Christophoro Kolb, Calcographo Augustano. *With two supplements. Frontispiece, 93 portraits, vignettes, etc. Folio, half calf, neat.*
Augustæ Vindelicorum, 1726–30

742 CONSTABLE, JOHN. ENGLISH LANDSCAPE SCENERY: A Series of Forty Mezzotinto Engravings on Steel by David Lucas, from Pictures painted by John Constable, R. A. *Folio, half crimson morocco, extra, gilt edges.*
London, 1855

743 CONSTANT, BENJAMIN. CURSO DE POLITICA CONSTITUTIONAL, escrito por Mr. Benjamin Constant; traducido libremente al Español, por D. Marcial Antonio Lopez. Segunda Edicion. *3 vols., 12mo, sheep, marbled edges.* Burdeos (Paris), 1823

744 CONSTANTIN, ROBERT. LEXICON GRAECO-LATINUM. Secunda hac Editione, Partim ipsius Authoris, Partim Francisci, Porti & aliorum Additionibus plurimum Auctum, tum quanta fieri potuit Diligentia recognitum, ita ut jam Studiosis possit esse Græcæ Linguæ Thesaurus. *2 vols. in 1, thick folio, old calf, gilt; with autograph of Rufus Choate.* CLEAN AND PERFECT COPY. (Genevæ), 1592

"Ouvrage estimé et dont il n'est pas facile de trouver des exemplaires bien conservés." —*Brunet.*

745 CONTARINI, GASPARE, CARDINAL. THE COMMONWEALTH AND GOVERNMENT OF VENICE; written by the Cardinall Gaspare Contareno, and translated out of Italian into English by Lewes Lewkenor, Esquire. With Sundry other Collections, annexed by the Translator for the more cleere and Exact Satisfaction of the Reader; with a Short Chronicle in the End, of the Lives and Raignes of the Venetian Dukes, from the very Beginninge of their Citie. *The second and third leaves of the address "to the reader" torn and a few words wanting, otherwise perfect. Small 4to, half calf, red edges* Imprinted by J. Windet, for E. Mattes, London, 1599

746 CONTINENTAL (THE) MONTHLY; devoted to Literature and National Policy. *January,* 1862–*December,* 1862. *Vols. I. and II., 8vo, half morocco.* New York & Boston, 1862

747 CONVERSATIONS ON CHEMISTRY; in which the Elements of that Science are familiarly explained and illustrated by Experiments. The Tenth Edition, considerably enlarged and corrected. *Plates. 2 vols., 12mo, boards, uncut.* London, 1825

748 CONVERSATIONS ON VEGETABLE PHYSIOLOGY; comprehending the Elements of Botany, with their Application to Agriculture, etc.; by Rev. J. L. Blake. *Colored plates. 12mo, sheep.* Boston, 1830

749 CONWAY, MONCURE D. THE REJECTED STONE, OR INSURRECTION VS. RESURRECTION IN AMERICA. Third Edition. *12mo, cloth.* Boston, 1862

750 CONYBEARE, JOHN. ILLUSTRATIONS OF ANGLO-SAXON POETRY. Edited, together with Additional Notes, Introductory Notices, etc., by his Brother, William Daniel Conybeare. *8vo, half calf, neat.* London, 1826

751 CONYBEARE, REV. WILLIAM J. and REV. J. S. HOWSON. THE LIFE AND EPISTLES OF ST. PAUL. *Maps, plates, and wood-cuts. 2 vols., 4to, half morocco; with autograph of Rufus Choate.* Longman & Co., London, 1853

752 CONYBEARE, Rev. William. Perversion, or the Causes and Consequences of Infidelity; A Tale for the Times. *3 vols., crown 8vo, cloth, uncut.* London, 1856

753 COOK, Captain James. An Account of the Voyages undertaken by the Order of his Present Majesty, for making Discoveries in the Southern Hemisphere, and successively performed by Commodore Byron, Captain Wallis, Captain Carteret, and Captain Cook, in the Dolphin, the Swallow, and the Endeavour: drawn up from the Journals which were kept by the Several Commanders, and from the Papers of Joseph Banks, Esq.; by John Hawkesworth, LL. D. Illustrated with Cuts, and a great Variety of Charts and Maps relative to Countries now first discovered, or hitherto imperfectly known. *3 vols., 4to, half calf, extra.* Original edition.
W. Strahan & T. Cadell, London, 1773

In the subsequent edition the paging recommences at Vol. III., but in this it runs consecutively through the second and third volumes.

754 COOKE, Captain James. A Voyage towards the South Pole, and Round the World; performed in His Majesty's Ships the Resolution and Adventure, in the Years 1772, 1773, 1774, and 1775: written by James Cook, Commander of the Resolution; in which is included, Captain Furneaux's Narrative of his Proceedings in the Adventure, during the Separation of the Ships. Illustrated with Maps and Charts, and a Variety of Portraits of Persons and Views of Places, drawn during the Voyage by Mr. Hodges, and engraved by the most Eminent Masters. The Second Edition. *2 vols., 4to, half calf, extra; backs cracked.*
W. Strahan & T. Cadell, London, 1777

755 COOK, Captain James. A Voyage to the Pacific Ocean, for making Discoveries in the Northern Hemisphere; performed under the Direction of Captains Cook, Clerke, and Gore, in His Majesty's Ships the Resolution and Discovery, in the years 1776, 1777, 1778, 1779, and 1780. Vol. I. and II. written by Captain James Cook, R. F. S.; Vol. III., by Captain James King, LL. D. Published by Order of the Lords Commissioners of the Admiralty. *Maps, charts, plates, etc. 3 vols., 4to, old marbled calf, gilt, yellow edges; and an imperial folio atlas (with maps and 59 large plates not folded, engraved by Bartolozzi, J. K. Sherwin, etc.), half russia.*
G. Nicol & T. Cadell, London, 1784

The above *three titles* form a fine set of the Three Voyages of Captain Cook.

756 COOKE, Captain James. A New, Authentic and Complete Collection of Voyages Round the World, undertaken and performed by Royal Authority; containing a New, Authentic, Entertaining, Instructive, Full, and Complete Historical Account of Captain Cook's First, Second,

Third, and Last Voyages, etc., etc., etc. The Whole of these Voyages of Captain James Cook, etc., being newly written by the Editors from the Authentic Journal of Several Principal Officers, and other Gentlemen of the most distinguished Naval and Philosophical Abilities, who sailed in the Various Ships, and now publishing under the Immediate Direction of George W. Anderson, Esq., etc. *Portrait, maps, and numerous plates. Folio, old calf.* London, (1795)

This edition contains accounts of the voyages of Byron, Wallis, Carteret, Lord Mulgrave, Lord Anson, and Sir Francis Drake.

757 COOKE, EDWARD. A JUST AND SEASONABLE REPREHENSION OF NAKED BREASTS AND SHOULDERS, written by a Grave and Learned Papist; translated by Edward Cooke, Esquire, with a Preface by Mr. Richard Baxter. *Small 8vo, morocco antique, gilt over red edges.* J. Edwin, London, 1678

758 COOKE, GEORGE FREDERICK. MEMOIRS OF; by William Dunlap, Esq. Composed principally from the Personal Knowledge of the Author, and from the Manuscript Journals left by Mr. Cooke; comprising Original Anecdotes of his Theatrical Contemporaries, his Opinions on Various Dramatic Writings, etc. *Portrait by Cooper. 2 vols. in 1, 8vo, half crimson morocco, extra.* London, 1813

759 COOKE, GEORGE WINGROVE. THE HISTORY OF PARTY; from the Rise of the Whig and Tory Factions, in the Reign of Charles II., to the Passing of the Reform Bill. (1666–1832.) *3 vols., 8vo, half calf, very neat; with autograph of Rufus Choate.* London, 1836–37

760 COOKE, WILLIAM. THE ELEMENTS OF DRAMATIC CRITICISM, containing an Analysis of the Stage under the following Heads: Tragedy, Tragi-Comedy, Comedy, Pantomime, and Farce. With a Sketch of the Education of the Greek and Roman Actors; concluding with some General Instructions for Succeeding in the Art of Acting. *8vo, sheep; back cracked.* London, 1775

761 COOKE, WILLIAM B. ROME AND ITS SURROUNDING SCENERY, illustrated with Engravings by W. B. Cooke, from Drawings by Eminent Artists; accompanied by Literary Sketches, by H. Noel Humphreys, Esq. *Engraved title, containing 8 views and 30 fine plates, 4to, cloth, gilt edges.* London, 1840

762 COOMBE, WILLIAM. THE TOURS OF DR. SYNTAX: in Search of the Picturesque; in Search of Consolation; in Search of a Wife. *Three poems in Hudibrastic verse, with 80 colored plates, by Rowlandson. 3 vols., royal 8vo, half calf, extra.* ORIGINAL COPIES. R. Ackermann, London, 1812–21

763 COOMBE, WILLIAM. THE ENGLISH DANCE OF DEATH, from the Designs of Thomas Rowlandson; with Metrical

Illustrations. *Frontispiece, engraved title, and 72 other colored plates. 2 vols., royal 8vo, calf, gilt, marbled edges.* R. Ackermann, London, 1815–16

764 COOMBE, William. The Dance of Life, a Poem. *With 26 colored plates by Rowlandson. Royal 8vo, half russia; back cracked.* R. Ackermann, London, 1817

765 COOMBE, William. Another copy: *the same. Royal 8vo, calf, gilt, marbled edges.* R. Ackermann, London, 1817

766 COOMBE, William. The History of Johnny Quæ Genus, the Little Foundling of the late Dr. Syntax, a Poem. *With 24 colored plates by Rowlandson. Royal 8vo, half calf, extra.* R. Ackermann, London, 1822

767 COOPER, James Fenimore. The History of the Navy of the United States of America, abridged, in One Volume. *Wood-cuts. 8vo, roan, gilt, marbled edges.* Richmond, Va., s. a.

768 COOPER, James Fenimore. The Choice Works of. Revised and Corrected Series, with New Introductions, Notes, etc. *20 vols., 12mo, cloth.* New York, 1856

Contents: The Spy; The Deerslayer; The Last of the Mohicans; The Pathfinder; The Pioneers; The Prairie; The Pilot; Lionel Lincoln; The Red Rover; The Wept of Wish-Ton-Wish; The Water-Witch; The Bravo; The Headsman; Homeward Bound; Home as Found; The Two Admirals; Wing-and-Wing; Wyandotte; Jack Tier; The Sea Lions.

769 COOPER, R.; and R. Page. Fifty Wonderful Portraits; engraved by R. Cooper and R. Page from Authentic Originals. *4to, boards.* London, 1824

770 COOPER, Thomas Sidney. Groups of Cattle, drawn from Nature. *Frontispiece (title) and 25 fine plates, selected from Cooper's most celebrated cattle pictures, drawn upon the stone by himself. Imperial folio, half morocco, extra, gilt edges.* London, 1839

771 COPELAND, R. M. Country Life; a Handbook of Agriculture, Horticulture, and Landscape Gardening. *Numerous wood-cuts. 8vo, cloth, red edges.* Boston, 1859

772 COPERNICUS, Nicolas. De Revolutionibus Orbium Cœlestium, Libri VI.; in quibus Stellarum et Fixarum et Erraticarum Motus, ex Veteribus atque Recentibus Observationibus, restituit hic Autor. Præterea Tabulas Expeditas Luculentasque addidit, ex quibus eosdem Motus ad quodvis Tempus Mathematûm Studiosus facillime calculare poterit. Item, de Libris Revolutionum Nicolai Copernici Narratio Prima, per M. Georgium Joachimum Rheticum ad D. Joan. Schonerum scripta. *Small folio, old calf, red edges; with book-plate of Sir George Shuckburgh, Bart.* Second edition: *clean and in good condition, except binding.* Henric. Petrina, Basileae, 1566

773 COPPING, Edward. Alfieri and Goldoni; their Lives and Adventures. *Post 8vo, cloth, uncut.* London, 1857

774 CORNARO, LUIGI. DISCOURSES ON A SOBER AND TEMPERATE LIFE, by Lewis Cornaro, a Noble Venetian; wherein is demonstrated, by his own Example, the Method of preserving Health to Extreme Old Age. Translated from the Italian Original. A New Edition, corrected. *Foolscap 8vo, vellum, neat, yellow edges.* BEST EDITION. London, 1779

This edition is the one mentioned by Sir John Sinclair as the best English translation. The author lived to the great age of *ninety-eight years*, and part of this work was written at the age of *ninety-five.*

775 CORNEILLE, PIERRE. ŒUVRES DE. Édition illustrée de 85 Vignettes par Pauquet; augmentée d'une Vie de Corneille, et de Notices sur chaque Pièce, par Émile de la Bédollière. *Imperial 8vo, cloth.* Paris, s. a.

776 COSMO III., De MEDICI. TRAVELS OF COSMO THE THIRD, Grand Duke of Tuscany, through England, during the Reign of King Charles the Second (1669); translated from the Italian Manuscript in the Laurentian Library at Florence. To which is prefixed, a Memoir of his Life. Illustrated with a Portrait of his Highness, and Thirty-nine Views of the Metropolis, Cities, Towns, and Noblemen's and Gentlemen's Seats as delineated at that Period by Artists in the Suite of Cosmo. *Royal 4to, cloth, uncut.* London, 1821

777 COSTELLO, LOUISA STUART. SPECIMENS OF THE EARLY POETRY OF FRANCE; from the Time of the Troubadours and Trouveres to the Reign of Henri Quatre. *Plates. Crown 8vo, cloth, uncut.* W. Pickering, London, 1835

778 COSTIGAN, ARTHUR WILLIAM. SKETCHES OF SOCIETY AND MANNERS IN PORTUGAL; in a Series of Letters from Arthur William Costigan, Esq., late Captain of the Irish Brigade in the Service of Spain, to his Brother in London. *2 vols., post 8vo, sheep, yellow edges.* (London), 1787

779 COSTUME DE L'EMPIRE RUSSE, représenté en plus de Soixante-dix Gravures superbement colorées; dédiées à son Altesse Royale la Princesse Elizabeth. *Text in English and French. Imperial 4to, russia, extra.* FINE ORIGINAL COPY. E. Harding, London, 1803

780 COTMAN, JOHN SELL. ARCHITECTURAL ANTIQUITIES OF NORMANDY; accompanied by Historical and Descriptive Notices by Dawson Turner, Esq. *Above 100 fine etchings, comprising views, elevations, and details of various ancient edifices. 2 vols. in 1, royal folio, half crimson morocco, extra, gilt edges.* London, 1822

"A highly valuable and faithful delineation of hitherto inedited monuments." — *Lowndes.*

781 COTTON, CHARLES. THE GENUINE POETICAL WORKS OF; containing, I. Scarronides, or Virgil Travestie. II. Lucian Burlesqu'd, or the Scoffer Scofft. III. The Wonders of the Peake. Illustrated with many Curious Cuts, all new-design'd,

and engraved by the Best Artists. The Second Edition, corrected. *The plates engraved by M. Vander Gucht. 12mo, half morocco, red edges.* London, 1725

782 COTTON, CHARLES. ANOTHER COPY: the Third Edition, corrected. *Plates by M. Vander Gucht. 12mo, half calf.* London, 1734

783 COUES, S. E. OUTLINES OF A SYSTEM OF MECHANICAL PHILOSOPHY. *12mo, cloth.* Boston, 1851

784 COURT-TALES, OR A HISTORY OF THE AMOURS OF THE PRESENT NOBILITY; to which is prefixed a Compleat Key. The Second Edition. *Small 8vo, old calf.* E. Curll, London, 1720

At the end of this copy is a catalogue (pp. 14) of works issued by this publisher.

785 COURTENAY, THOMAS P. COMMENTARIES ON THE HISTORICAL PLAYS OF SHAKSPEARE. *2 vols., crown 8vo, cloth, uncut.* London, 1840

786 COUSIN, VICTOR. COURS DE L'HISTOIRE DE LA PHILOSOPHIE MODERNE. Deuxième Série. Nouvelle Édition, revue et corrigée. *3 vols., 12mo, half calf; with autograph of Rufus Choate.* Paris, 1847

787 COUSIN, VICTOR. LECTURES ON THE TRUE, THE BEAUTIFUL, AND THE GOOD. Increased by an Appendix on French Art. Translated, with the Approbation of M. Cousin, by O. W. Wight. *12mo, cloth.* New York, 1854

788 COWLES, MARIAN. RUTLEDGE. *12mo, cloth.* New York, 1860

789 COWLEY, ABRAHAM. THE WORKS OF; consisting of those which were formerly printed and those which he design'd for the Press: now published out of the Author's Original Copies. The Seventh Edition (with Life, by Bishop Sprat, addressed to Martin Clifford). *Portrait by Faithorne. Small folio, old calf.* H. Herringman, London, 1681

790 COWLEY, ABRAHAM. THE WORKS OF; in Prose and Verse. A New Edition; pointing out the Pieces selected by Richard Hurd, D. D., late Bishop of Worcester, and including his Lordship's Notes, and Dr. Johnson's Life of the Author. *Portrait on the engraved titles. 3 vols., 8vo, calf, gilt, marbled edges; with autograph of Rufus Choate.* LARGE PAPER: *fine copy.* J. Sharpe, London, 1809

791 COWPER, WILLIAM. THE WORKS OF; comprising his Poems, Correspondence, and Translations. With a Life of the Author, by the Editor, Robert Southey, Esq., LL. D. *Portraits, plates, and vignettes. 15 vols., foolscap 8vo, cloth, uncut.* London, 1835–37

792 COWPER, WILLIAM. THE POETICAL WORKS OF; edited by the Rev. H. F. Cary, A. M., with a Biographical Notice of the Author. *Vignette on the engraved title. Royal 8vo, half calf, extra, marbled edges.* London, 1839

793 COWPER, WILLIAM. POEMS; with a Biographical and Critical Introduction, by the Rev. Thomas Dale. *With 75 wood-cuts by J. Orrin Smith after John Gilbert. 2 vols., square crown 8vo, morocco, gilt, gilt edges.* London, 1841

794 COWPER, WILLIAM. THE POETICAL WORKS OF. (With a Memoir, by Sir N. Harris Nicolas.) *Beautifully printed, with large type, by Whittingham. Portrait. 2 vols., 8vo, tree calf, gilt, marbled edges, by Riviere.* ELEGANT EDITION: *only 350 copies printed.* W. Pickering, London, 1853

795 COX, FRANCIS AUGUSTUS, D. D. SACRED HISTORY AND BIOGRAPHY, from the Antediluvian Period to the Time of the Prophet Malachi, A. M. 1 to A. M. 3607, B. C. 397; edited and partly written by F. A. Cox, D. D. Second Edition, revised. *Post 8vo, cloth, uncut.* London, 1850

796 COX, FRANCIS AUGUSTUS, D. D. BIBLICAL ANTIQUITIES, with some Collateral Subjects, illustrating the Language, Geography, and Early History of Palestine. *Colored maps, and numerous wood-cuts. Post 8vo, cloth, uncut.* London, 1852

The above two volumes form a part of the "Cabinet Edition of the Encyclopædia Metropolitana."

797 COX, REV. THOMAS. MAGNA BRITANNIA ET HIBERNIA, Antiqua & Nova, or a New Survey of Great Britain; wherein to the Topographical Account given by Mr. Cambden, and the late Editors of his Britannia, is added a more large History, not only of the Cities, Boroughs, Towns, and Parishes mentioned by them, but also of many other Places of Note, and Antiquities since discovered. Together with the Chronology of the most Remarkable Actions of the Britains, Romans, Saxons, Danes, and Normans; the Lives and Constitutions of the Bishops of all our Sees, Founders and Benefactors to our Universities and Monasteries, the Sufferings of Martyrs, and many Ecclesiastical Matters; the Acts and Laws of our Parliaments, with Place of their Meeting; a Character of such Eminent Statesmen and Churchmen as have signalized themselves by their Wise Conduct and Writings; and the Pedigrees of all our Noble Families and Gentry, both Ancient and Modern, according to the Best Relations extant. Collected and composed by an Impartial Hand [Rev. Thomas Cox]. *Maps, etc. Vols. I. and II., 4to, russia, red edges; with book-plate of S[r] John Anstruther, of that ilk Baronet.* In the Savoy (London), 1720

Vol. I. contains the Introduction, and the counties of Bedford, Berks, Buckingham, Cambridge, Chester, Cornwall, Cumberland, Derby, Devon, Dorset, Durham, and Essex; Vol. II., the counties of Gloucester, Southampton, Hereford, Hertford, Huntingdon, Kent, Leicester, and Lincoln.

798 COXE, PETER. THE SOCIAL DAY; a Poem, in Four Cantos. *Engraved title, portrait, and 30 plates, after Wilkie, Smirke,*

Stothard, etc. Imperial 8vo, boards, rough edges. LARGE PAPER: SUBSCRIBER'S COPY. London, 1823

At page 288 will be found the beautiful plate of the "Broken China Jar," by Wilkie, engraved by C. Warren.

799 COXE, WILLIAM. TRAVELS IN SWITZERLAND, AND IN THE COUNTRY OF THE GRISONS; in a Series of Letters to William Melmoth, Esq. The Third Edition. *Large colored map, plans, and numerous plates in aquatinta. 2 vols., imperial 4to, diamond russia, very neat, gilt over marbled edges.* LARGE PAPER: *fine copy.* T. Cadell, London, 1794

The plates are found only in the quarto and large paper octavo editions, being too large for the ordinary size. This copy has, inserted after page 88 of the second volume, a curious plate (neatly inlaid) containing 16 portraits, each figure numbered to correspond with the names of the characters which are written on the back.

800 COXE, WILLIAM. TRAVELS IN POLAND, RUSSIA, SWEDEN, AND DENMARK; illustrated with Charts and Engravings. The Fifth Edition [with Considerable Additions]. *Good impressions of the numerous portraits, plates of costume, maps, etc. 5 vols., 8vo. half calf.* London, 1802

801 COXE, WILLIAM. MEMOIRS OF JOHN, DUKE OF MARLBOROUGH, with his Original Correspondence; collected from the Family Records at Blenheim, and other Authentic Sources. Illustrated with Portraits, Maps, and Military Plans. *With an additional plate inserted (mounted on reverse of the plate of arms), engraved by Bartolozzi after a painting by Sam[l]. Shelley. 3 vols., 4to, sprinkled calf, gilt; with bookplate and autograph of John Arden.* London, 1818–19

Written in pencil beneath the added plate is this note: "A Private Print by Bartolozzi, of the Duke and Duchess of Marlborough, and their Infant Son, the Present Duke. Given by Sir Henry Lawson, Bart., to John Arden, Esquire; 1822."

802 CRABB, GEORGE. UNIVERSAL TECHNOLOGICAL DICTIONARY, or Familiar Explanation of the Terms used in all Arts and Sciences; containing Definitions drawn from the Original Writers, and illustrated by Plates, Diagrams, Cuts, etc. *2 vols., 4to, half morocco, neat.* London, 1823

803 CRABB, GEORGE. ENGLISH SYNONYMES; with Copious Illustrations and Explanations, drawn from the Best Writers. A New Edition, enlarged. *8vo, sheep.* New York, 1830

804 CRABBE, REV. GEORGE. THE POETICAL WORKS OF; with his Letters and Journals, and his Life, by his Son. [Edited by Wright.] *Portrait after T. Phillips, and frontispieces and vignettes after C. Stanfield, engraved by E. Finden. 8 vols., foolscap 8vo, half morocco, neat.* J. Murray, London, 1834

805 CRABBE, REV. GEORGE, VICAR OF BREDFIELD. AN OUTLINE OF A SYSTEM OF NATURAL THEOLOGY. *8vo, cloth, uncut.* W. Pickering, London, 1840

806 CRAIG, JOHN. A NEW UNIVERSAL ETYMOLOGICAL, TECHNOLOGICAL, AND PRONOUNCING DICTIONARY OF THE ENGLISH LANGUAGE; embracing all the Terms used in Arts, Science, and Literature. *Frontispiece and engraved titles. 2 vols., thick royal 8vo, cloth.* London, 1852

807 CRAIG, W. MARSHALL. SPORTS OF LOVE, in Six Poems and Six Etchings. *Frontispiece and wood-cut vignettes in addition to the six plates. 4to, half calf.* ORIGINAL EDITION. London, 1807

808 CRAIG, W. MARSHALL. ANOTHER COPY: *Frontispiece and the six plates, colored, but without the vignettes. 4to, morocco, extra, gilt edges.* London, 1818

809 CRAIK, GEORGE LILLIE. THE ROMANCE OF THE PEERAGE, or Curiosities of Family History. *Portraits. 4 vols., crown 8vo, cloth, uncut.* London, 1848–50

810 CRAIK, GEORGE LILLIE. THE ENGLISH OF SHAKESPEARE, illustrated in a Philological Commentary on his Julius Cæsar. *Foolscap 8vo, cloth, uncut.* London, 1857

811 CRAIK, GEORGE LILLIE. A COMPENDIOUS HISTORY OF ENGLISH LITERATURE, AND OF THE ENGLISH LANGUAGE, from the Norman Conquest; with Numerous Specimens. *2 vols., 8vo, cloth, uncut.* London, 1861

812 CRAMER, JOHN ANTHONY, D. D. A GEOGRAPHICAL AND HISTORICAL DESCRIPTION OF ANCIENT GREECE. *Plan of Ancient Athens and its harbors. 3 vols., 8vo, half calf, extra; with autograph of Rufus Choate.* Clarendon Press, Oxford, 1828

813 CRAMER, JOHN ANTHONY, D. D. A GEOGRAPHICAL AND HISTORICAL DESCRIPTION OF ASIA MINOR. *2 vols., 8vo, half calf, extra; with autograph of Rufus Choate.* University Press, Oxford, 1832

The maps which should accompany the two above works are wanting. They were published separately.

814 CRANE, ANNE M. EMILY CHESTER; a Novel. *12mo, cloth.* Boston, 1864

815 CRANMER, THOMAS, ARCHBISHOP OF CANTERBURY. A SHORT INSTRUCTION INTO CHRISTIAN RELIGION, being a Catechism set forth by Archbishop Cranmer in MDXLVIII.; together with the same in Latin, translated from the German by Justus Jonas, in MDXXXIX. [Edited by the Rev. Edward Burton.] *Numerous fac-simile wood-cuts. 8vo, dark blue morocco, neat, gilt edges.* University Press, Oxford, 1829

816 CRANMER, THOMAS, ARCHBISHOP OF CANTERBURY. THE REMAINS OF. Collected and arranged (with Preface and Notes) by the Rev. Henry Jenkyns, M. A. *Portrait and fac-similes. 4 vols., 8vo, dark blue morocco, neat, gilt edges.* University Press, Oxford, 1833

817 CRASHAW, RICHARD. THE COMPLETE WORKS OF Richard Crashaw, Canon of Loretto; edited by William B. Turnbull, Esq. *Foolscap 8vo, cloth, uncut; with autograph of Rufus Choate.* J. R. Smith, London, 1858

818 CRAVEN, ELIZABETH, LADY. A JOURNEY THROUGH THE CRIMEA TO CONSTANTINOPLE; in a Series of Letters to his Serene Highness the Margrave of Brandebourg, Anspach, and Bareith, written in the Year 1786. *Map and plates, 4to, boards, uncut.* London, 1789

819 CREASY, EDWARD S. THE RISE AND PROGRESS OF THE ENGLISH CONSTITUTION. *12mo, half calf, very neat, marbled edges.* London, 1853

820 CROCKETT, HENRY CLAY. THE AMERICAN IN EUROPE; being "Guesses" and "Calculations" on Men and Manners, made during a Tour through the most Important Portions of Europe. *Above 100 plates, comprising views, portraits, paintings, etc. 4to, morocco, extra, gilt edges.* London and New York, s. a.

821 CROFT, SIR HERBERT. LOVE AND MADNESS, a Story too True; in a Series of Letters between Parties whose Names would perhaps be mentioned were they less known or less lamented. Third Edition. *Engraved title, and portrait (inserted) of Miss Ray. 12mo, half calf.* London, 1780

A mixture of fact and fiction founded upon the murder of Miss Martha Ray, Actress, by the Rev. James Hackman.

822 CROKER, THOMAS CROFTON. THE POPULAR SONGS OF IRELAND; collected and edited, with Introductions and Notes. *12mo, cloth, uncut.* London, 1839

823 CRONYCKE (DIE) VAN HOLLANDT, ZEELANDT EÑ VRIESLANT; behinnende vã Adams Tiden tot die Geboerte ons Heren Jhũ; voertgaende tot dẽ Jare M.CCCCC. ende XVII.: met dẽ Rechten Oerspronchoe Hollandt eerst bgrepen eñ bewoent is gheweest vã dẽ Troyanẽ. Eñ is inhoudende vã die Hertogen vã Beyerẽ, Henegonwẽ, eñ Bourgõgen; die Tiit dat si ant Graefscap geweest hebbẽ: met die Cronike der Biscoppen van Utrecht seer suuerlic geertẽdeert eñ int Lange Vhaelt. *Numerous wood-cuts, clear impressions. Two preliminary leaves, 436 leaves (numbered), and register of 4 leaves. The last four leaves closely trimmed, good margins to the rest. 4to, vellum, extra, gilt edges.* "DIVISIE-CHRONIJK": *fine copy.* Jan Seuerst, Leyden, An. xv.c. eñ xvii.

Many of the cuts in this volume are engraved by LUCAS VAN LEYDEN, of whom Strutt says: "At a period when Albert Durer had carried the art of engraving to such perfection in Germany, and Marc Antonio exercised it with the greatest reputation in Italy, Lucas disputed the palm with those celebrated competitors, in the Low Countries. . . . . He engraved on wood as well as on copper, but his cuts are not very numerous."

824 CROSS, JEREMY L. THE TEMPLAR'S CHART, or Hieroglyphic Monitor; containing all the Emblems and Hieroglyphics explained in the Valiant and Magnanimous Orders

of Knights of the Red Cross, Knights Templars, and Knights of Malta, or Order of St. John of Jerusalem: designed and duly arranged, agreeably to the Mode of Work and Lecturing, by Jeremy L. Cross, K. R. C., K. T., K. M., etc. To which are added, Lessons, Exhortations, Prayers, Charges, Songs, etc. *Plates. 18mo, sheep.* New Haven, 1821

825 CROSS, JEREMY L. THE TRUE MASONIC CHART, or Hieroglyphic Monitor; containing all the Emblems explained in the Degrees of Entered Apprentice, Fellow-Craft, Master Mason, Mark Master, Past Master, Most Excellent Master, Royal Arch, Royal Master, and Select Master: designed and duly arranged, agreeably to the Lectures, by R. W. Jeremy L. Cross, G. L. To which are added, Illustrations, Charges, Songs, etc., with Additions and Emendations; also, a History of Freemasonry, by a Brother. Sixteenth Edition. *12mo, cloth.* New York, 1851

826 CROWE, J. A., and G. B. CAVALCASELLE. A NEW HISTORY OF PAINTING IN ITALY, from the Second to the Sixteenth Century; drawn up from Fresh Materials and Recent Researches in the Archives of Italy, as well as from Personal Inspection of the Works of Art scattered throughout Europe. *Nearly 100 plates, in outline. 3 vols., 8vo, cloth, uncut.* J. Murray, London, 1864–66

827 CRUDEN, ALEXANDER. A COMPLETE CONCORDANCE TO THE HOLY SCRIPTURES OF THE OLD AND NEW TESTAMENT, etc., etc.; to which is added a Concordance to the Apocrypha. The Seventh Edition, revised and improved; with a Life of the Author by Alexander Chalmers, F. S. A. *Portrait. 4to, calf; rebacked.* London, 1824

828 CUDWORTH, RALPH, D. D. THE WORKS OF; containing the True Intellectual System of the Universe, Sermons, etc. A New Edition, with References to the Several Quotations in the Intellectual System, and a Life of the Author; by Thomas Birch, M. A., F. R. S. *Portrait by R. Cooper. 4 vols., 8vo, calf, gilt.* Oxford, 1829

829 CULLUM, MRS. ——. CHARLOTTE, or One Thousand Seven Hundred and Seventy-three; a Play. *Frontispiece after Wale. 8vo, morocco, extra, gilt edges.* Printed by Baker & Galabin, London, 1775

This piece was never intended for the stage.

830 CUMBERLAND, RICHARD, LL. D. A PHILOSOPHICAL ENQUIRY INTO THE LAWS OF NATURE, wherein the Essence, the Principal Heads, the Order, the Publication, and the Obligation of these Laws are deduced from the Nature of Things; wherein also, the Principles of Mr. Hobbes's Philosophy, both in a State of Nature, and of Civil Society, are examined into, and confuted. Written originally in Latin; and translated into English, with large Explanatory Notes, and

an Appendix, by the Reverend John Towers, D. D., etc. *Crown 4to, old calf, red edges; with autograph of Rufus Choate.* Dublin, 1750

The "Appendix" contains biography and other matters relating to the improvements in natural and moral philosophy, comprising the lives of Bacon, Bp. Cumberland, Hooke, Harvey, Willis, Robert Boyle, Hobbes, Isaac Newton, Sir Wm. Temple, and Locke, etc.

On the first cover is the following autograph note, by Rufus Choate: "'Cumberland has substantial merits.' — *Sir J. Mackintosh.*"

831 CUMBERLAND, Richard, LL. D. Memoirs of, written by himself; containing an Account of his Life and Writings, interspersed with Anecdotes and Characters of Several of the most Distinguished Persons of his Time, with whom he has had Intercourse and Connexion. *Fine portraits, including one of Bp. Cumberland, and one of Dr. Bentley. Royal 4to, calf, gilt, yellow edges.* London, 1806

832 CUMBERLAND, Richard, LL. D. The Posthumous Dramatick Works of. (Published, without Revision, by his Daughter, Frances Marianne Jansen.) *2 vols., 8vo, half calf, neat.* London, 1813

833 CUMMINS, Maria S. The Lamplighter. [By Miss Cummins.] *12mo, cloth.* Boston, 1854

834 CUNNINGHAM, Allan. The Cabinet Gallery of Pictures by the First Masters of the English and Foreign Schools, in Seventy-two Line Engravings; with Biographical and Critical Dissertations. *Fine impressions of the plates. 2 vols., royal 8vo, cloth, gilt tops, uncut.* J. Major, London, 1834

This copy is from the library of the Princess Elizabeth, daughter of George III.

835 CUNNINGHAM, Allan. The Gallery of Pictures by the First Masters of the English and Foreign Schools, with Biographical and Critical Dissertations. *Portrait, engraved title, and 96 plates. 2 vols., 4to, half morocco, marbled edges.* G. Virtue, London, s. a.

836 CUNNINGHAM, Allan. The Songs of England and Scotland. (With Introductions, Notes, etc.) *Portraits and vignettes. 2 vols., post 8vo, cloth, uncut; with autograph of Rufus Choate.* J. Cochrane & Co., London, 1835

837 CUNNINGHAM, Allan. The Life of Sir David Wilkie; with his Journals, Tours, and Critical Remarks on Works of Art, and a Selection from his Correspondence. *Portrait. 3 vols., 8vo, tree calf, gilt, marbled edges, by Riviere.* J. Murray, London, 1843

838 CUNNINGHAM, George Godfrey. A History of England in the Lives of Englishmen. *Numerous portraits. 8 vols., 8vo, cloth, uncut.* Edinburgh, 1851–52

839 CUNNINGHAM, Peter. Hand-Book of London, Past and Present. A New Edition, corrected and enlarged. *Thick crown 8vo, cloth, uncut.* J. Murray, London, 1850

840 CURRAN, JOHN PHILPOT. SPEECHES. Complete and Correct Edition. Edited, with Memoir and Historical Notices, by Thomas Davis, Esq., etc. *Portrait.* *8vo, half calf, extra; with autograph of Rufus Choate.* London, 1847

841 CURTIS, GEORGE T. AN ORATION DELIVERED ON THE FOURTH OF JULY, 1862, before the Municipal Authorities of the City of Boston. *8vo, cloth.* Boston, 1862

842 CURTIS, GEORGE W. NILE NOTES OF A HOWADJI. *12mo, cloth.* New York, 1851

843 CURTIS, GEORGE W. TRUMPS; a Novel. *Wood-cuts after Hoppin.* *12mo, cloth.* New York, 1861

844 CURTIUS. QUINTUS CURTIUS RUFUS, DE REBUS GESTIS ALEXANDRI MAGNI. Editio prioribus correctior. *Engraved title, pp.* 271, *and index.* *Small 8vo (32mo), vellum, red edges.* Apud Guil. Blaeu, Amsterodami, 1644

845 CURTIUS. Q. CURTII RUFI DE REBUS GESTIS ALEXANDRI MAGNI Libri Decem. *Frontispiece and vignettes by Lempereur after Eisen.* *12mo, wide margin, mottled calf, gilt, gilt edges.* J. Barbou, Parisiis, 1757

846 CURZON, ROBERT. A VISIT TO MONASTERIES IN THE LEVANT. *12mo, cloth.* New York, 1852

847 CUSHING, CAROLINE E. W. LETTERS, descriptive of Public Monuments, Scenery, and Manners in France and Spain. *Portrait.* *2 vols., 12mo, cloth.* PRIVATELY PRINTED. Newburyport, 1832

This copy was presented to Mrs. James Hayward by Mr. Cushing. See autograph on reverse of title.

Mrs. Cushing accompanied her husband, Hon. Caleb Cushing, to Europe in 1829, and these volumes (I. France, II. Spain,) contain her letters, addressed to her father, during her absence.

"They contain an unpretending but very well written and interesting account of the scenes that fell under the observation of the travellers, and convey a most favorable impression of the intellectual and moral qualities of the author." — *A. H. Everett.* (*N. A. Rev., Vol. xxxvii., p.* 104.)

848 CUTTER (THE); in Five Lectures upon the Art and Practice of Cutting Friends, Acquaintances, and Relations. *Colored plates.* *Small 8vo, calf, extra, marbled edges; with autograph of the author.* J. Carpenter, London, 1808

849 CUVIER, GEORGES LÉOPOLD C. F. D., BARON DE. THE ANIMAL KINGDOM, Arranged in Conformity with its Organization; with Additional Descriptions of all Species hitherto named, and of many not before noticed, by Edward Griffith, F. L. S., A. S., etc., and others. VOLS. I.–V., MAMMALIA; IX., REPTILIA; XIII., ANNELIDA, CRUSTACEA, ARACHNIDA. *These classes* COMPLETE, *with* 325 *finely colored plates, the specific descriptions by E. Griffith, Col. C. H. Smith, Edward Pidgeon, etc.* *7 vols., royal 8vo, cloth, uncut.* LARGE PAPER. G. B. Whittaker, London, 1827–33

Signature 3 B (pp. 357–372) of the "Synopsis of Mammalia," Vol. V., has been restored from a small paper copy. This set ranges with SHAW and STEPHENS.

850 CUVIER, GEORGES LÉOPOLD C. F. D., BARON DE. THE ANIMAL KINGDOM, Arranged according to its Organization, serving as a Foundation for the Natural History of Animals, and an Introduction to Comparative Anatomy; by Baron Cuvier. With Figures designed from Nature; the Crustacea, Arachnides, and Insecta, by M. Latreille. Nearly 800 Coloured Plates. PLATES ONLY. *4 vols., 8vo, half crimson morocco, extra, gilt edges.* London, 1837

851 DAELLI, G. A RELIC OF THE ITALIAN REVOLUTION OF 1849: Album of 50 Line Engravings, executed on Copper, by the most Eminent Artists at Rome in 1849, secreted from the Papal Police after the "Restoration of Order," and just imported into America. With a Preface and Index, and Appropriate Descriptions in English, Italian, and French. *Oblong 4to, cloth.* New Orleans, s. a.

852 DAGLEY, RICHARD. GEMS, principally from the Antique, drawn and etched by Richard Dagley; with Illustrations in Verse, by the Rev. George Croly, A. M., etc. *Post 8vo, half morocco, neat; with autographs of F. W. P. Greenwood and Rufus Choate.* London, 1822

853 DAGLEY, RICHARD. DEATH'S DOINGS: consisting of Numerous Original Compositions in Prose and Verse, the Friendly Contributions of Various Writers; principally intended as Illustrations of Thirty Copper-Plates, designed and etched by R. Dagley. Second Edition, with Considerable Additions. *2 vols. in 1, sprinkled calf, gilt, carmine and gilt tooled edges.* J. Andrews, London, 1827

This copy has had several engravings inserted, including some cuts after Holbein's "Dance of Death," and each page is neatly ruled with red lines.

854 DAGLEY, RICHARD. ANOTHER COPY: *the same. Fine impressions of the plates and the wood-cut vignettes. 2 vols., 8vo, half dark blue calf, extra, marbled edges.* London, 1827

855 DALLAS, E. S. POETICS; an Essay on Poetry. *Post 8vo, half calf, extra; with autograph of Rufus Choate.* London, 1852

856 DALMAZZONI, ANGELO. THE ANTIQUARIAN, or the Guide for Foreigners to go the Rounds of the Antiquities of Rome; by Angelo Dalmazzoni. *Sold only by the author. 12mo, half calf.* Rome, 1803

857 DALRYMPLE, Sir JOHN, BART. MEMOIRS OF GREAT BRITAIN AND IRELAND; from the Dissolution of the Last Parliament of Charles II., until the Capture of the French and Spanish Fleets at Vigo. *With the third part of the second volume, containing the plate (on title) of Oxenfoord Castle. 2 vols. in 3, 4to, calf, very neat.* Edinburgh, 1771–88

Part III. of the second volume, published in 1788 (containing a continuation "from the battle off La Hogue till the capture of the French and Spanish fleets at Vigo"), is very often wanting.

858 DALZEL, ANDREW. SUBSTANCE OF LECTURES ON THE ANCIENT GREEKS, and on the Revival of Greek Learning in Europe. *2 vols., 8vo, half morocco, neat; with autograph of Rufus Choate.* Edinburgh, 1821

859 DAMER, MRS. G. L. DAWSON. DIARY OF A TOUR IN GREECE, TURKEY, EGYPT, AND THE HOLY LAND. *Plates. 2 vols., 12mo, half calf, neat.* London, 1841

860 DANA, J. F. and S. L. OUTLINES OF THE MINERALOGY AND GEOLOGY OF BOSTON AND ITS VICINITY, with a Geological Map. *Imperial 8vo, half morocco, gilt top.* Boston, 1818

861 DANA, RICHARD H., Jun. THE SEAMAN'S FRIEND: containing a Treatise on Practical Seamanship, with Plates; a Dictionary of Sea Terms; Customs and Usages of the Merchant Service; Laws relating to the Practical Duties of Master and Mariners. Eighth Edition, revised and corrected. *12mo, cloth.* Boston, 1856

862 DANIEL, GEORGE. DEMOCRITUS IN LONDON, with the Mad Pranks and Comical Conceits of Motley and Robin Good-Fellow; to which are added Notes Festivious, etc. (and the Stranger-Guest). *Foolscap 8vo, cloth, uncut.* W. Pickering, London, 1852

863 DANIEL, REV. WILLIAM B. RURAL SPORTS. (Containing Treatises on Hunting, Hawking, Shooting, Fowling, Angling, etc., etc.). *Fine impressions of the numerous plates. 4 vols., royal 8vo, half calf.* ORIGINAL OCTAVO EDITION: WITH SUPPLEMENT. London, 1801–13

"The excellent engravings in this esteemed work are principally by John Scott, the best of our English engravers of animals." — *Lowndes.*

864 DANIEL, THOMAS, and WILLIAM. ORIENTAL SCENERY: Views in Hindoostan. First Series: Twenty-four Views in Hindoostan, drawn and engraved by Thomas Daniell; 1795. Second Series: Twenty-four Views in Hindoostan, from Drawings by Thomas Daniell, engraved by himself and William Daniell; 1797. Third Series: Twenty-four Views in Hindoostan, drawn and engraved by Thomas and William Daniell; 1801. Fourth Series: Twenty-four Landscapes, Views in Hindoostan, drawn and engraved by Thomas and William Daniell; 1807. Antiquities of India: Twelve (and Twelve) Views, from the Drawings of Thomas Daniell, engraved by himself and William Daniell; 1799, 1808. Hindoo Excavations in the Mountain of Ellora near Aurungabad in the Decan: Twenty-four Views, engraved from the Drawings of James Wales by, and under the Direction of, Thomas Daniell; 1803. *The plates all on the largest scale and finely colored. 3 vols., elephant folio, half morocco, extra, gilt edges.* ORIGINALLY PUBLISHED AT £210. London, 1795–1808

For a list of the plates see Henry G. Bohn's catalogue of 1848, Vol. I., p. 93.
"This is the finest work ever published on India. — *Lowndes.*

865 DANTE, ALIGHIERI. THE DIVINA COMMEDIA OF; consisting of the Inferno, Purgatorio, and Paradiso. Translated into English Verse, with Preliminary Essays, Notes, and Illustrations; by the Rev. Henry Boyd, A. M., etc. *Portrait. 3 vols., 8vo, old marbled calf, very neat.*
Cadell & Davies, London, 1802

866 DANTE, ALIGHIERI. THE VISION, or Hell, Purgatory, and Paradise of; translated by the Rev. H. F. Cary, M. A. A New Edition, corrected; with the Life of Dante, Chronological View of his Age, Additional Notes, and Index. *Portrait. Post 8vo, cloth, uncut; with autograph of Rufus Choate.*
London, 1850

867 DANTE, ALIGHIERI. THE DIVINE COMEDY, or the Inferno, Purgatory, and Paradise of; rendered into English by Frederick Pollock, Esq. With Fifty Illustrations, drawn by George Scharf, Jun., engraved by Dalziel. *8vo, cloth; with autograph of Rufus Choate.* London, 1854

868 DANTE, ALIGHIERI. THE DIVINE COMEDY OF; translated by Henry W. Longfellow. (Inferno, Purgatorio, Paradiso; with Notes, Illustrations, and Index.) *3 vols., post 4to, cloth, gilt tops, uncut.* Boston, 1867

869 DANTE, ALIGHIERI. THE FIRST TEN CANTOS OF THE INFERNO OF; newly translated into English Verse [by Thomas W. Parsons]. *With the verses "On a Bust of Dante," and portrait. 8vo, boards.* PRIVATELY PRINTED. Boston, 1843

This copy was presented to Samuel Rogers, the poet, by Abbott Lawrence, and the autograph letter which accompanied it is attached to a fly-leaf.

870 DANTE, ALIGHIERI. L'ENFER DE; avec les Dessins de Gustave Doré. Traduction Française de Pier-Angelo Fiorentino accompagnée du Texte Italien. *Elegantly printed upon a fine thick paper, with portrait and 76 full-page engravings. Folio, cloth, uncut.* ORIGINAL EDITION: *fine impressions of the cuts.* Paris, 1862

871 DARCIE, ABRAHAM. ANNALES. The True and Royall History of the Famous Empresse Elizabeth, Queene of England, France, and Ireland, etc., True Faith's Defendresse of Divine Renowne and Happy Memory; Wherein all such Memorable Things as happened during hir Blessed Raigne, with such Acts and Treaties as past betwixt hir Matie and Scotland, France, Spaine, Italy, Germany, Poland, Sweden, Denmark, Russia, and the Netherlands are exactly described. *Engraved title by Vaughan. Small 4to, calf, gilt, red edges. Portrait wanting, otherwise perfect and in fair condition.*
B. Fisher, London, 1625

This edition has no author's name upon the title, but the engraver's mark says, — "by M. Darcie's approvall and direction." The "French Epistle Dedicatory" is signed "P. D. B." (Paul de Bellegent), and the "Epistle Dedicatory" is signed "Abraham Darcie." Lowndes quotes the following statement from *Nicolson*: "A translation of Camden, from the French, by Abraham Darcie, who, according to Dr. Fuller, understood not the Latin, and has therefore committed many mistakes."

872 DARLEY, Rev. J. R. THE GRECIAN DRAMA; a Treatise on the Dramatic Literature of the Greeks. *8vo, half morocco, neat.* Dublin, 1840

873 DARLEY, Rev. J. R. ANOTHER COPY: *the same. 8vo, half calf, extra; with autograph of Rufus Choate.* Dublin, 1840

874 DARLING, JAMES. CYCLOPÆDIA BIBLIOGRAPHICA: a Library Manual of Theological and General Literature, and Guide to Books for Authors, Preachers, Students, and Literary Men; Analytical, Bibliographical, and Biographical. *Double columns* (3328); *bound in 2 vols., royal 8vo, turkey morocco, neat.* London, 1854

875 DART, Rev. JOHN. THE HISTORY AND ANTIQUITIES OF THE CATHEDRAL CHURCH OF CANTERBURY, and the Once-adjoining Monastery, containing: an Account of its First Establishment, Building, Re-edifications, Repairs, Endowments, Benefactions, Chapels, Altars, Shrines, Reliques, Chauntries, Obiits, Ornaments, Books, Jewels, Plate, Vestments, before the Dissolution of the Monastery, and the Manner of its Dissolution; a Survey of the Present Church and Cloysters, Monuments and Inscriptions, with other Things Remarkable, which, with the Several Prospects of the Church, are engraven by the Best Hands; the Lives of the Archbishops, Priors, etc. of Christ-Church, with an Account of the Learned Men there Flourishing in their Several Times; an Appendix of Ancient Charters and Writings relating to the Church and Monastery, a Catalogue of the Church-Wealth in Prior Estrey's Time, an Ancient Saxon Obituary, and a large one continu'd thence downward. *Portrait by Faber (inserted), and* 60 *other plates (some neatly inlaid), including vignettes, besides the* 9 *plates containing arms of subscribers. Imperial folio, old mottled calf, gilt, gilt edges.* LARGE PAPER: *fine copy.* London, 1726

876 DARWIN, CHARLES. THE ZOÖLOGY OF THE VOYAGE OF H. M. S. BEAGLE, under the Command of Captain Fitzroy, R. N., during the Years 1832 to 1836; edited and superintended by Charles Darwin, Esq., M. A., F. R. S., V. P. G. S., Naturalist to the Expedition. *Contains* 165 *fine large plates, those of mammalia and birds beautifully colored.* 3 *vols., royal 4to, half crimson morocco, extra, gilt tops.* FINE COPY: COMPLETE. London, 1840–43

This work is divided into five general parts, viz:—

I. FOSSIL MAMMALIA: described by Richard Owen, Esq., F. G. S., etc.; with a Geological Introduction by Mr. Darwin.

II. MAMMALIA: described by George R. Waterhouse, Esq., Curator of the Zoölogical Society of London; with a Notice of their Habits and Ranges, by Mr. Darwin.

III. BIRDS: described by John Guild, Esq., F. L. S.; with a Notice of their Habits and Ranges, by Mr. Darwin, and with Anatomical Appendix, by T. C. Eyton, Esq., F. L. S. *This part is very rare.*

IV. FISH: described by the Rev. Leonard Jenyns, F. G. S., etc.

V. REPTILIA: described by Thomas Bell, Esq., F. R. S., etc.

877 DARWIN, ERASMUS, M. D. THE BOTANIC GARDEN, a Poem; in Two Parts. Part I. containing the Economy of Vegetation. Part II. the Lives of the Plants. With Philosophical Notes. *Third and fourth editions. Plates (many colored) by W. Blake, T. Holloway, Anker Smith, etc., after Fuseli, etc. 2 vols., 4to, diamond russia, gilt, marbled edges. Fine copy.* London, 1795 and 1794

878 DARWIN, ERASMUS, M. D. THE TEMPLE OF NATURE, or the Origin of Society; a Poem with Philosophical Notes. *Plates after Fuseli, etc. 8vo, sheep, yellow edges; with autograph of John Allan.* Baltimore, 1804

879 DARWIN, ERASMUS, M. D. THE POETICAL WORKS OF. Containing the Botanic Garden, in Two Parts, and the Temple of Nature: with Philosophical Notes and Plates. *3 vols., 8vo, old marbled calf; with autograph of Rufus Choate.* London, 1806

880 DASENT, GEORGE W. POPULAR TALES FROM THE NORSE; with an Introductory Essay on the Origin and Diffusion of Popular Tales. *12mo, cloth.* New York, 1849

881 DAUNEY, WILLIAM. ANCIENT SCOTTISH MELODIES, from a Manuscript of the Reign of King James VI.; with an Introductory Enquiry illustrative of the History of the Music of Scotland. *4to, brown turkey morocco, extra, gilt top.* Edinburgh, 1838

Dedicated to the members of the Bannatyne and Maitland Clubs.

882 DAVENANT, SIR WILLIAM. THE WORKS OF; consisting of those which were formerly printed, and those which he design'd for the Press. Now published out of the Author's Originall Copies. *Portrait wanting. Folio, half calf, neat.* London, 1672–73

883 DAVENANT, SIR WILLIAM. ANOTHER COPY: *with a wider margin. Portrait wanting. Folio, old calf.* London, 1672–73

884 DAVID, FRANÇOIS ANNE. LES ANTIQUITÉS D'HERCULANUM, avec leurs Explications en François [par Sylvain Maréchal]. *Vols. I.–VIII., containing above 600 plates comprising nearly 1,100 representations of the ancient paintings, sculptures, bronzes, household goods, etc., which were discovered in the excavations of Herculaneum, Pompeii, etc. 8 vols., 4to, red russia, extra, gilt edges; arms gilt on sides, and a neatly written MS. index to the eight volumes.* Paris, 1780–89

885 DAVIDSON, LUCRETIA M., and MARGARET M. POETICAL REMAINS of the late Lucretia Maria Davidson, selected and arranged by her Mother; with a Biography by Miss Sedgwick. Biography and Poetical Remains of the late Margaret Miller Davidson; by Washington Irving. *Together, 1 vol., 12mo, cloth.* New York, 1851–54

886 DAVIES, SIR JOHN. THE POETICAL WORKS OF: consisting of his Poem on the Immortality of the Soul; the Hymns of

Astrea; and Orchestra, a Poem on Dancing, in Dialogue between Penelope and one of her Wooers. All published from a Corrected Copy, formerly in the Possession of W. Thompson, of Queen's Coll. Oxon. *Small 8vo, calf, neat; with autograph of Rufus Choate.* T. Davies, London, 1773

887 DAVIES, THOMAS. DRAMATIC MISCELLANIES, consisting of Critical Observations on Several Plays of Shakspeare; with a Review of his Principal Characters, and those of Various Eminent Writers, as represented by Mr. Garrick, and other Celebrated Comedians: with Anecdotes of Dramatic Poets, Actors, etc. *Portrait of Betterton. 3 vols., 8vo, half calf.* Printed for the Author, London, 1784

888 DAVIS, C. S. THE NORTH-EASTERN BOUNDARY OF THE UNITED STATES. [By C. S. Davis.] *Reprinted from an article in the N. A. Rev. (vol. xxxiv., p. 514, etc.), with an appendix. 12mo, pp. 104, half roan.* Boston, 1832

889 DAVIS, SIR JOHN FRANCIS. HIEN WUN SHOO: Chinese Moral Maxims, with a Free and Verbal Translation, affording Examples of the Grammatical Structure of the Language. *Printed on India paper, by P. P. Thomas, Macao, China. 8vo, cloth.* J. Murray, London; and Macao, 1823

890 DAVIS, SIR JOHN FRANCIS. THE FORTUNATE UNION; a Romance; translated from the Chinese Original, with Notes and Illustrations. To which is added, a Chinese Tragedy (entitled the Sorrows of Hān). By John Francis Davis F. R. S., etc. *Fac-simile of title to the original romance and map. 2 vols., 8vo, half morocco, extra.* London, 1829

Printed for the "Oriental Translation Fund."

891 DAVIS, NATHAN. CARTHAGE AND HER REMAINS; being an Account of the Excavations and Researches on the Site of the Phœnician Metropolis in Africa, and other Adjacent Places, conducted under the Auspices of her Majesty's Government. *Maps, plans, plates, and wood-cuts, some tinted. 8vo, cloth, uncut.* London, 1861

892 DAVIS, SARAH M. THE LIFE AND TIMES OF SIR PHILIP SIDNEY. [By Mrs. Davis.] *Portrait, view of Penshurst Castle, and fac-simile of handwriting. Post 8vo, cloth, gilt top* Boston, 1859

893 DAVY, SIR HUMPHREY. CONSOLATION IN TRAVEL, or the Last Days of a Philosopher. Sixth Edition, with Illustrations. *Foolscap, 8vo, calf, gilt.* J. Murray, London, 1853

894 DAVY, SIR HUMPHREY. SALMONIA, or Days of Fly Fishing: in a Series of Conversations; with some Account of the Habits of Fishes belonging to the Genus Salmo. Fourth Edition, with Illustrations (and Additions by his Brother, Dr. John Davy). *Foolscap 8vo, calf, gilt.* J. Murray, London, 1851

895 DAWSON, HENRY B. BATTLES OF THE UNITED STATES BY SEA AND LAND, embracing those of the Revolutionary and Indian Wars, the War of 1812, and the Mexican War; with Important Official Documents. Illustrated with Numerous Highly-finished Engravings, including Battle Scenes and Full-length Portraits, from Original Paintings by Alonzo Chappel. *2 vols., 4to, morocco, antique, gilt edges.* New York, (1858–60)

896 DAY, FRANCIS. THE FISHES OF MALABAR. *With 20 plates, engraved by the author, beautifully colored by hand. Royal 4to, half turkey morocco, extra, emblematically tooled, gilt top.* London, 1865

897 DEANE, CHARLES. BIBLIOGRAPHICAL TRACTS; Number One: Spurious Reprints of Early Books. [By Charles Deane.] *4to paper.* ONLY 131 COPIES PRINTED. Boston, 1865

An account of the large paper (4to) edition of "Salem Witchcraft, etc.; with Notes and Explanations, by Samuel P. Fowler." From the Boston "Daily Advertiser" of March 24, 1865 (under the signature of "Delta"), with additions and corrections.

898 DEANE, REV. SAMUEL. HISTORY OF SCITUATE, MASSACHUSETTS; from its First Settlement to 1831. *Royal 8vo, cloth, rough edges.* Boston, 1831

899 DEARBORN, NATHANIEL. BOSTON NOTIONS; being an Authentic and Concise Account of "that Village," from 1630 to 1847. *Plates and wood-cuts, comprising portraits, maps, views, fac-similes, etc., 18mo, roan.* Boston, 1848

900 DEBRETT, JOHN. DEBRETT'S PEERAGE OF THE UNITED KINGDOM OF GREAT BRITAIN AND IRELAND. The Fifteenth (Sixteenth ?) Edition, considerably improved. *Portrait of George IV. and numerous plates of arms, etc. 2 vols., small thick 12mo, calf, gilt.* London, 1825

901 DEBRETT, JOHN. DEBRETT'S BARONETAGE OF ENGLAND, containing their Descent and Present State, their Collateral Branches, Births, Marriages, and Issue, from the Institution of the Order in 1611; a Complete and Alphabetical Arrangement of their Mottoes, with Correct Translations; a List of Persons who have received the Honour of Knighthood, of Extinct Baronets, of such as have been advanced to the Peerage, and of British Subjects holding Foreign Orders of Knighthood. The Fifth Edition, considerably enlarged. *Numerous plates of arms, etc. 2 vols., small thick 12mo, calf, gilt.* London, 1824

902 DE FOE, DANIEL. THE HISTORY OF THE UNION BETWEEN ENGLAND AND SCOTLAND; with an Appendix of Original Papers. To which is now added a Life of the Celebrated Author [by George Chalmers], and a Copious Index. *Portrait by W. Skelton. Royal 4to, half calf, rough edges; with book-plate of George D'Oyly, D. D.* LARGE PAPER. J. Stockdale, London, 1786

903 DE FOE, DANIEL. THE LIFE AND ADVENTURES OF ROBINSON CRUSOE; written by himself. [By De Foe.] *Engraved titles and plates by Medland after Stothard. 2 vols., 4to, half morocco, gilt tops, uncut.* LARGE PAPER.
J. Stockdale, London, 1804

904 DE FOE, DANIEL. THE LIFE AND SURPRISING ADVENTURES OF ROBINSON CRUSOE, of York, Mariner; with a Biographical Account of De Foe. Illustrated with Seventy Characteristic Wood Engravings, finely executed by Harvey and Whimper. *Crown 8vo, cloth, uncut.*
London, 1846

905 DE FOE, DANIEL. MEMOIRS OF CAPT. GEORGE CARLETON, an English Officer, including Anecdotes of the War in Spain under the Earl of Peterborough, and many Interesting Particulars relating to the Manners of the Spaniards in the Beginning of the Last Century; written by himself. *Preface by Sir Walter Scott. 8vo, marbled calf, neat.*
Edinburgh, 1808

"This valuable and interesting work (a great favorite with Dr. Johnson) has been likewise attributed to Dean Swift. 'De Foe's part in this work,' says Lord Mahon in his 'War of Succession,' 'is very doubtful.'" —*Lowndes.*

906 DE FOE, DANIEL. THE NOVELS AND MISCELLANEOUS WORKS OF; with a Biographical Memoir of the Author, Literary Prefaces to the Various Pieces, Illustrative Notes, etc., including all contained in the Edition attributed to the late Sir Walter Scott, with Considerable Additions. [Edited by C. Lewis.] *Portrait (in second volume). 20 vols., foolscap 8vo, tree calf, gilt, marbled edges.*
D. A. Talboys, Oxford; T. Tegg, London, 1840–41

The "Memoir" in the first volume is by John Ballantyne, the friend and partner of Sir Walter Scott, and is taken from the Edinburgh Edition. In the last volume is a "Life" (by George Chalmers) with a list of his (174) different works, chronologically arranged; also, a general table of contents of the twenty volumes. The contents of this edition may also be found in Bohn's "Lowndes," p. 621, *et al.*

907 DE FOE, DANIEL. ANOTHER COPY: *the same. Portrait (in last volume). 20 vols., foolscap 8vo, cloth, uncut.*
Oxford and London, 1840–41

908 DE FORREST, JOHN W. SEACLIFF, or the Mystery of the Westervelts. *12mo, cloth.* Boston, 1859

909 DEKKER, THOMAS. THE HONEST WHORE. (*First Part, title wanting.*) The Second Part of the Honest Whore, with the Humors of the Patient Man, the Impatient Wife; the Honest Whore persuaded by Strong Arguments to turne Curtizan againe, her brave refuting those Arguments: and lastly, the Comicall Passages of an Italian Bridewell, where the Scene ends. Written by Thomas Dekker. Printed by Elizabeth All-de, for Nathaniel Butter, An. Dom. 1630.—THE WONDER OF A KINGDOME; written by Thomas Dekker. Printed by Robert Raworth, for Nicholas Vavafour, etc.,

1636. *Together in 1 vol., small 4to, half morocco, carmine edges.* FIRST EDITIONS: *in good condition.*
London, 1630–36

910 DELAFIELD, BRIG. GEN. RICHARD. REPORT ON THE ART OF WAR IN EUROPE in 1854, 1855, and 1856; from his Notes and Observations made as a Member of a "Military Commission to the Theatre of War in Europe," under the Orders of the Hon. Jefferson Davis, Secretary of War. *Numerous plates (many colored), comprising views of forts, arsenals, hospitals, and other prominent places and scenes; with a large number of maps, plans of fortifications, etc., besides about* 100 *wood-cuts in the text. Royal 4to, cloth.* Washington, 1861

911 DELANY, MARY GRANVILLE, MRS. THE AUTOBIOGRAPHY AND CORRESPONDENCE OF; with Interesting Reminiscences of King George the Third, and Queen Charlotte. Edited by the Right Honourable Lady Llanover. BOTH SERIES. *Numerous portraits, etc.* 6 *vols., 8vo, green calf, gilt, marbled edges.* London, 1861–62

912 DELILLE, JACQUES. SES ŒUVRES. *Illustrated with* 21 *engravings after Monsiau, J. M. Moreau, C. Guerin, etc.* 14 *vols., 8vo, half calf, neat.*
J. Decker, Basle, 1800; Giguet & Michaud, Paris, 1803–08

CONTENTS: L'Homme des Champs, ou les Géorgiques Françoises; *Basle*, 1800. — La Pitié; *Paris*, 1803. — L'Imagination (2 vols.); *Paris*, 1806. — Les Trois Règnes de la Nature (2 vols.); *Paris*, 1808. — Les Bucoliques de Virgile; *Paris*, 1806. — L'Énéide (4 vols., with the Latin text); *Paris*, 1804. — Paradis Perdu (3 vols., with the English text); *Paris*, 1805.

913 DELILLE, JACQUES. THE GARDENS, a Poem; translated from the French of the Abbé De Lille. *With* 64 *fine colored plates (added), besides the plates engraved by Bartolozzi. 4to, morocco, very neat, gilt edges.* ILLUSTRATED COPY.
Printed by T. Bensley, London, 1798

914 DELOLME, JEAN LOUIS. THE CONSTITUTION OF ENGLAND, or an Account of the English Government; in which it is compared both with the Republican Form of Government and the other Monarchies in Europe. A New Edition; with Supplemental Notes, and a Preface Biographical and Critical [by Dr. Charles Coote]. *Portrait after Stoddart, inserted. 8vo, old marbled calf, very neat.* London, 1807

915 DEMOCRATIC REVIEW. THE UNITED STATES MAGAZINE AND DEMOCRATIC REVIEW. *From commencement in* 1837 *to* 1852, *inclusive. Numerous portraits, etc.* 31 *vols., 8vo, half morocco, neat.*
Washington and New York, 1837–52

916 DE MOIVRE, ABRAHAM. THE DOCTRINE OF CHANCES, or a Method of Calculating the Probability of Events in Play. *Small 4to, old calf; back cracked.* London, 1718

917 DEMOSTHENES and ÆSCHINES. ŒUVRES COMPLETTES de Démosthène et d'Eschine; traduites en Français, avec

des Remarques sur les Harangues et Plaidoyers de ces Deux Orateurs : précédées d'un Discours Préliminaire sur l'Éloquence et autres Objets Intéressans; d'un Précis Historique sur la Constitution de la Grèce, sur le Gouvernement d'Athènes, et sur la Vie de Philippe; d'un Traité de la Jurisdiction et des Lois d'Athènes, etc.; par M. l'Abbé Auger. Nouvelle Édition. *Portrait, map, etc.* 6 *vols.*, 8*vo, sheep, gilt, marbled edges; with autograph of Rufus Choate.* Angers, 1804

918 DEMOSTHENES. THE ORATIONS OF DEMOSTHENES, pronounced to excite the Athenians against Philip, King of Macedon; translated by Thomas Leland, D. D. A New Edition. 2 *vols. in* 1, 8*vo, half calf, extra, marbled edges.* London, 1819

"A work of extraordinary merit; the translation is executed with a spirit and energy nearly equal to the original, and the notes are very valuable."—*Lowndes.*

On a fly-leaf is this autograph note of Rufus Choate: "This book formerly belonged to Hon. Benjamin Gorham."

919 DEMOUSTIER, CHARLES ALBERT. LETTRES À ÉMILIE SUR LA MYTHOLOGIE. *Portraits and* 60 *plates by Choquet.* 6 *vols.*, 18*mo, half calf.* Nicolle, etc., Paris, 1816

920 DENDY, WALTER C. THE PHILOSOPHY OF MYSTERY. 8*vo, cloth, uncut; with autograph of Rufus Choate.* London, 1841

921 DENECOURT, C. F. DESCRIPTION GÉNÉRALE DU CHATEAU DE FONTAINEBLEAU, avec la Notice des Tableaux qui ornent et décorent cette Résidence Royale; suivie du Guide dans la Forét. Nouvelle Edition. *Map and views.* 8*vo, paper.* Fontainebleau, 1842

922 DENHAM, SIR JOHN. POEMS AND TRANSLATIONS; with the Sophy, a Tragedy. The Fifth Edition. 8*vo, old calf, gilt; with book plate of W. H. Campbell.* J. Tonson, London, 1709–10

923 DENNISTOUN, JAMES. MEMOIRS OF THE DUKES OF URBINO, Illustrating the Arms, Arts, and Literature of Italy; from 1440 to 1630. *Portraits, views, medallions, fac-similes, etc.* 3 *vols.*, 8*vo.* ILLUSTRATIONS FOR THE MEMOIRS OF THE DUKES OF URBINO. *Original India proofs of the* 34 *plates (including an etching not in the other volumes) taken before the impressions were struck off for the book.* PRIVATELY PRINTED. 1 *vol.*, 4*to.* *Together,* 4 *vols.*, 8*vo, and* 4*to, polished calf, gilt, gilt edges, by Bedford.* ELEGANT COPY. London, 1851

924 DENON, DOMINIQUE VIVANT, BARON DE. VOYAGE DANS LA BASSE ET LA HAUTE ÉGYPTE, pendant les Campagnes du Général Bonaparte. VELLUM PAPER; *with* 141 *plates containing about* 500 *subjects,—inscriptions, antiquities, views, etc., etc.* 2 *vols., elephant folio* (27 × 21 *inches*), *half red morocco,*

gilt tops, uncut; with book-plate of Alexander Randall. THE LARGE GOVERNMENT EDITION. Paris, 1802

"The work of *Denon* is fairly entitled to a particular and highly commendatory notice. I perfectly remember at Mr. Dulan's when the first copies of it were imported, in 1802, in two large folio volumes, 'the learned wondered at the work, and the vulgar were enamoured of' its execution. . . . Many of the plates, in the original French folio, are by the burin of Denon himself; and exhibit much of the force and freedom, as well as of the style, of Rembrandt." —*Dibdin (Lib. Comp.)*.

This is a very fine copy of the finest edition, executed by order of the French Imperial Government.

925 DENON, DOMINIQUE VIVANT, BARON DE. EGYPT. A Series of One Hundred and Ten Engravings, exhibiting the Antiquities, Architecture, Inhabitants, Costume, Hieroglyphics, Animals, Scenery, etc. of that Country; with Accompanying Descriptions and Explanations in French and English; selected from the Celebrated Work, detailing the Expedition of the French, by Baron Vivant Denon, etc. The Engravings are by the following Artists: Middiman, Cardon, Audinet, Comte, Mitau, Newton, Cooke, Taylor, Smith, Armstrong, Dadley, Morris, Wise, Roffe, Poole, Pollard, etc. *Portrait of Denon. Imperial folio, calf.* C. Taylor, London, 1816

926 DENTON, DANIEL. A BRIEF DESCRIPTION OF NEW YORK, formerly called New Netherlands, with the Places thereunto adjoining; likewise a Brief Relation of the Customs of the Indians there. A New Edition, with an Introduction, and Copious Historical Notes; by Gabriel Furman. *Royal 4to, cloth, uncut.* LARGE PAPER: *only* 100 *copies printed.* New York, 1845

No. 1 of "Gowans' Bibliotheca Americana;" see MILLER, REV. JOHN, and WOOLEY, REV. CHARLES.

This volume is a reprint of the *first printed* (1670) description, in the English language, of New York and New Jersey (*vide Introduction*).

927 DE PORQUET, LOUIS P. R. F. FRENCH COMPARATIVELY IN NO TIME. Le Trésor de l'École Français, or the Art of Translating English into French at Sight. Thirty-third Edition. 12*mo. cloth.* London, 1849

928 DE QUINCEY, THOMAS. DE QUINCEY'S WRITINGS. *Portrait.* 22 *vols.,* 12*mo, cloth; with autographs of Rufus Choate.* Boston, 1850–59

929 DERHAM, WILLIAM, D. D. MISCELLANEA CURIOSA; containing a Collection of some of the Principal Phænomena in Nature, accounted for by the Greatest Philosophers of this Age: being the most Valuable Discourses, read and delivered to the Royal Society, for the Advancement of Physical and Mathematical Knowledge. As also, a Collection of Curious Travels, Voyages, Antiquities, and Natural Histories of Countries; presented to the same Society, etc., etc. [Edited by W. Derham.] *Frontispiece by Vander Gucht, and numerous plates.* 3 *vols.,* 8*vo, old calf.* London, 1723–27

Vol. I., "Third Edition," 1726; Vol. II., 1723; Vol. III., "Second Edition," 1727. The third volume contains "Travels, Voyages, etc.," in which are five letters "from Mr. John Clayton, Rector of Crofton, at Wakefield, in Yorkshire, to the Royal Society, May 12, 1688, giving an Account of Several Observables in Virginia, and in his Voyage thither," pp. 281–355.

930 DESCAMPS, JEAN BAPTISTE. LA VIE DES PEINTRES FLAMANDS, ALLEMANDS, ET HOLLANDOIS ; avec des Portraits gravés en Taille-douce, une Indication de leurs Principaux Ouvrages, & des Réflexions sur leurs Différentes Manieres. 4 *vols., 8vo, old mottled calf, gilt, red edges.* C. A. Jombert, Paris, 1753–64

The frontispiece is engraved by J. P. Le Bas, and the portraits are by Ficquet, Eisen, François, etc.

931 DESCRIPCIONES DE LAS ISLAS PITHIUSAS Y BALEARES. *Small 4to, red morocco, gilt edges.* Ibarra, Madrid, 1787

932 DESCRIPTION (A) OF TREMONT HOUSE [Boston, Mass.]; with Architectural Illustrations. *View of front on Tremont Street, and* 30 *plates of sections, details, etc. Royal 4to, boards.* Boston, 1830

933 DESTOUCHES, PHILIPPE NÉRICAULT. ŒUVRES DRAMATIQUES DE. Nouvelle Édition ; précédée d'une Notice sur la Vie et les Ouvrages de cet Auteur [par M. de Senone]. *Portrait, and numerous fine plates after Lafitte.* 6 *vols., 8vo, marbled calf, gilt, marbled edges ; with autograph and book-plate of Charles White.* Paris, 1811

934 DEUCHAR, DAVID. A COLLECTION OF ETCHINGS after the most Eminent Masters of the Dutch and Flemish Schools, particularly Rembrandt, Ostade, Cornelius Bega, and Van Vliet ; accompanied with Sundry Miscellaneous Pieces, and a Few Original Designs. By Dav[d] Deuchar, Seal Engraver, Edinburgh. *Nearly* 400 *plates, many very small,* PROOF IMPRESSIONS. 2 *vols., royal folio, half crimson morocco, extra, gilt edges.* Edinburgh, Dec[r] 22, 1803

The compiler of this catalogue has never seen a copy like this, neither is he able to find one described. There were two other issues of etchings by Deuchar, in 1803, one in three large quarto volumes, with nearly 300 plates and another in folio with 100 plates containing 170 subjects.

935 DEVIL (THE) UPON CRUTCHES IN ENGLAND, or Night Scenes in London ; a Satirical Work written upon the Plan of the Celebrated Diable Boiteux of Monsieur Le Sage. In Two Parts. By a Gentleman of Oxford. The Second Edition. *Both parts in* 1 *vol., 12mo, half morocco.* London, 1756

936 DIABLE (LE) À PARIS ; PARIS ET LES PARISIENS : Mœurs et Coutumes, Caractères et Portraits des Habitants de Paris ; Tableau Complet de leur Vie Privée, Publique, Politique, Artistique, Littéraire, Industrielle, etc., etc. Text par MM. George Sand, P. J. Stahl, Léon Gozlan (et Trent autres Écrivains Célèbres) ; précédé d'une Histoire et d'une Géographie de Paris, par Théophile Lavallée. *Fine impressions of the several hundred wood-cuts, comprising "Les Gens de Paris,"*

by Gavarni (P. S. Chevallier) ; "Paris Comique," by Bertall; and views, monuments, important buildings, etc., by Champin, Bertrand, d'Aubigny, and Français. 2 vols., imperial 8vo, half crimson morocco, extra, gilt edges.
J. Hetzel, Paris, 1845–46

937 DIAL (THE) ; a Magazine for Literature, Philosophy, and Religion. *From July,* 1840, *to April,* 1844, *inclusive. 4 vols., 8vo, half sheep; with book-plate of E. A. Hitchcock, U. S. Army.* Boston, 1841–44

938 DIBDIN, CHARLES. A COMPLETE HISTORY OF THE ENGLISH STAGE: introduced by a Comparative and Comprehensive Review of the Asiatic, the Grecian, the Roman, the Spanish, the Italian, the Portuguese, the German, the French, and other Theatres; and involving Biographical Tracts and Anecdotes, Instructive and Amusing, concerning a Prodigious Number of Authors, Composers, Painters, Actors, Singers, and Patrons of Dramatic Productions in all Countries. The whole written, with the Assistance of Interesting Documents, collected in the course of Five and Thirty Years, by Mr. Dibdin. 5 *vols.,* 8*vo, half calf, neat. Printed for the Author.*
London, (1797–98)

939 DIBDIN, CHARLES. OBSERVATIONS ON A TOUR THROUGH ALMOST THE WHOLE OF ENGLAND, and a Considerable Part of Scotland; in a Series of Letters, addressed to a large Number of Intelligent and Respectable Friends, by Mr. Dibdin. 2 *vols.,* 4*to, boards, rough edges.*
London, (1801–02)

940 DIBDIN, CHARLES. SONGS OF THE LATE CHARLES DIBDIN, with a Memoir; collected and arranged by [his son] T. Dibdin. With Characteristic Sketches, by G. Cruikshank. Third Edition. *Foolscap 8vo, half morocco.*
London, 1850

941 DIBDIN, CHARLES, JUN. HISTORY AND ILLUSTRATIONS OF THE LONDON THEATRES; comprising an Account of the Origin and Progress of the Drama in England, with Historical and Descriptive Accounts of the Theatres Royal, Covent Garden, Drury Lane, Haymarket, English Opera House, and Royal Amphitheatre. *With* 15 *plates. Royal* 4*to. Boards uncut.* ONLY 25 COPIES PRINTED. London, 1826

On a fly-leaf is this autograph, — "To W. H. Murray, Esq., with J. Britton's compl'ts."

942 DIBDIN, THOMAS FROGNALL, D. D. TYPOGRAPHICAL ANTIQUITIES, or the History of Printing in England, Scotland, and Ireland; containing Memoirs of our Ancient Printers, and a Register of the Books printed by them. Begun by the late Joseph Ames, F. R. & A. SS., considerably augmented by William Herbert, of Cheshunt, Herts; and now greatly enlarged, with Copious Notes, and illustrated with

Appropriate Engravings; comprehending the History of English Literature, and a View of the Progress of the Art of Engraving, in Great Britain; by the Rev. Thomas Frognall Dibdin. *Numerous portraits, fac-similes of early printing, etc.* 4 *vols., imperial* 4*to, crimson levant morocco, gilt, gilt edges, by Clarke & Bedford.* LARGE PAPER: *only* 65 *copies printed.* London, 1809–19

Of the copies on LARGE PAPER (which contain plates not found in those on small paper) there are very few in this country, and they are so much sought for in England that, a few years ago, a copy was returned thence at a very high price.

943 DIBDIN, THOMAS FROGNALL, D. D. AN INTRODUCTION TO THE KNOWLEDGE OF RARE AND VALUABLE EDITIONS OF THE GREEK AND LATIN CLASSICS; together with an Account of Polyglot Bibles, Polyglot Psalters, Hebrew Bibles, Greek Bibles, and Greek Testaments, the Greek Fathers, and the Latin Fathers. Fourth Edition, greatly enlarged and corrected. *Fac-simile plate of the "Complutensian Polyglot."* 2 *vols., imperial* 8*vo, cloth, uncut.* BEST EDITION: *entirely rewritten.* LARGE PAPER: *only* 250 *copies printed.* London, 1827

944 DIBDIN, THOMAS FROGNALL, D. D. BIBLIOMANIA, OR BOOK-MADNESS; a Bibliographical Romance. Illustrated with Cuts. New and improved Edition; to which are now added Preliminary Observations and a Supplement, including a Key to the Assumed Characters in the Drama. *Portrait of the Author, Mr. Walmsley's plate attesting number of copies printed, and numerous other engravings and typographical embellishments. Many of the engravings on India paper.* 2 *vols., imperial* 8*vo, olive levant morocco, gilt, gilt edges.* BEST EDITION: *edited by Dr. Dibdin himself.* LARGE PAPER: *only* 55 *copies printed.* London, 1842

"The Bibliomania is written in dialogues or conversations, the characters introduced are well-known book collectors of the author's acquaintance. The great value of the work is in the notes, which abound with anecdotes of Books and Book Collectors, and an account of the rarer articles in their collections, and the prices at which they were sold, extracted from the sale catalogues." — *Lowndes.*

945 DIBDIN, THOMAS FROGNALL, D. D. THE BIBLIOGRAPHICAL DECAMERON, or Ten Days Pleasant Discourse upon Illuminated Manuscripts, and Subjects connected with Early Engraving, Typography, and Bibliography. *Numerous portraits and other illustrations, many of them on India paper; with several* DUPLICATES, PROOF IMPRESSIONS. 3 *vols., imperial* 8*vo, olive morocco, gilt, gilt edges.* LARGE PAPER: *only* 50 *copies printed.* London, 1817

This copy contains the following *duplicate* and *private plate* portraits, ENGRAVER'S PROOFS, namely, one of the Earl of Sunderland; one of Michael Maittaire and Gerard Meerman; one of Bishop Percy; one of Earl Spencer (private plate); and two of Thomas Payne, Bookseller, one of which is the "EBONY-SPECTACLE PORTRAIT," which is thus mentioned on page 435 (in a note): — "*Twenty-five copies* of the original ebony-spectacle, engraved portrait — which have been eagerly snapped up by perch-like collectors, — have reimbursed this extra expense: and this *first* plate is now BROKEN UP." It contains also the fac-simile plate, by G. Lewis, from a missal executed by Francesco Veronesi. "This work may be considered as a continuation of the Bibliomania, the same characters being introduced in the dialogues. From the information which it contains, and the splendor of the decorations and printing, it will ever be considered as a model of excellence and good taste in typography and the arts. Both the copper-plates and the wood-cuts which embellished the work have been destroyed."

946 DIBDIN, THOMAS FROGNALL, D. D. BIBLIOTHECA SPENCERIANA, or a Descriptive Catalogue of the Books printed in the Fifteenth Century, and of many Valuable First Editions, in the Library of George John Earl Spencer, K. G., etc. etc. etc. *Numerous plates and wood-cuts of fac-similes, etc., many of which are on India paper. 4 vols., imperial 8vo, olive levant morocco, gilt, gilt tops, rough edges.* London, 1814–15

"This catalogue contains only the works printed in the fifteenth century and the Editiones Principes. It is compiled with the greatest care and industry, and those who have had occasion to consult its pages, can testify to its accuracy and great utility. The collection is the finest private one in Europe; the catalogue will ever be regarded as of the first importance to the theologian, the historian, and the critic, and as a perfect model for the bibliographer." — *Lowndes.*

947 DIBDIN, THOMAS FROGNALL, D. D. ÆDES ALTHORPIANÆ, or an Account of the Mansion, Books, and Pictures, at Althorp; the Residence of George John Earl Spencer, K. G. To which is added a supplement to the Bibliotheca Spenceriana. *Numerous portraits and other illustrations, some of which are on India paper. 2 vols., imperial 8vo, olive levant morocco, gilt, gilt edges.* London, 1822

This work, designed as a supplement to the above, contains accounts of the ancestors of Earl Spencer; of the Mansion at Althorp; of the gallery, with engravings of the most important pictures; and of editions of the Scriptures, Aldine Editions, and books printed in the fifteenth century, not contained in the former volumes.

948 DIBDIN, THOMAS FROGNALL, D. D. A DESCRIPTIVE CATALOGUE OF THE BOOKS PRINTED IN THE FIFTEENTH CENTURY, lately forming Part of the Library of the Duke di Cassano Serra, and now the Property of George John Earl Spencer, K. G. With a General Index of Authors and Editions contained in the Present Volume, and in the Bibliotheca Spenceriana and Ædes Althorpianæ. *Imperial 8vo, olive levant morocco, gilt, gilt top, rough edges.* London, 1823

This work forms another supplemental volume to the "Bibliotheca Spenceriana," with an index to the seven volumes.

949 DIBDIN, THOMAS FROGNALL, D. D. A BIBLIOGRAPHICAL, ANTIQUARIAN, and Picturesque Tour in France and Germany. *Portraits and numerous beautiful plates, many upon India paper, including a full set of* LEWIS'S ETCHINGS (*India proofs*), *illustrating the physiognomy, manners, etc., of the people of France and Germany. 3 vols. in 4, imperial 8vo, olive levant morocco, gilt, gilt edges.* LARGE PAPER: *only* 100 *copies printed.* London, 1821

Besides the set of Lewis's Etchings there are inserted in this copy the following portraits, namely, one of the Author which was engraved for the second edition (1829), and one of the Comte de Brienne which was published in 1824, INDIA PROOFS; also, one of Diane de Poictiers (Vol. II., p. 497), from the private plate which was destroyed after ONLY FIFTY impressions had been taken.
"This work contains much curious information respecting the MSS. and rare works in public and private libraries abroad. It is printed and embellished in the same style of excellence as the Doctor's other works." — *Lowndes.*

950 DIBDIN, THOMAS FROGNALL, D. D. A BIBLIOGRAPHICAL, ANTIQUARIAN, AND PICTURESQUE TOUR in the Northern Counties of England, and in Scotland. *Above 100 illustrations, consisting of 44 beautiful large plates, besides wood-cuts, etc.; comprising portraits, views, ancient architecture, fac-similes, etc.;* INDIA PROOFS. *3 vols., imperial 8vo, olive morocco, gilt, gilt edges.* LARGE PAPER: *only 99 copies printed.* London, 1838

A few leaves in the preface are loose, otherwise this is a very perfect and elegant copy.

951 DIBDIN, THOMAS FROGNALL, D. D. THE LIBRARY COMPANION, or the Young Man's Guide and the Old Man's Comfort, in the Choice of a Library. Second Edition. *2 vols., imperial 8vo, boards, uncut.* LARGE PAPER. London, 1825

952 DIBDIN, THOMAS FROGNALL, D. D. ANOTHER COPY: *Small paper. 1 vol., thick 8vo, half morocco; with autograph of Rufus Choate.* London, 1825

953 DIBDIN, THOMAS FROGNALL, D. D. REMINISCENCES OF A LITERARY LIFE; with Anecdotes of Books, and of Book-Collectors. WITH INDEX AND AN AUTOGRAPH LETTER. *Portraits, views, fac-similes, etc., some of which are on India paper. 2 vols., imperial 8vo, olive levant morocco, gilt, gilt edges.* LARGE PAPER: *only 39 copies printed.* London, 1836

This copy contains a long autograph letter by Dr. Dibdin, addressed to Dawson Turner (whose copy this was), bound in the first volume; and the rare index, very neatly inlaid, bound in the second volume.

954 DIBDIN, THOMAS FROGNALL, D. D. BIBLIOPHOBIA: Remarks on the Present Languid and Depressed State of Literature and the Book Trade; in a Letter addressed to the Author of the Bibliomania. By Mercurius Rusticus, with Notes by Cato Parvus [Dr. Dibdin]. *8vo, boards, uncut.* London, 1832

The above collection of Dibdin's most valuable works is one of the finest in this country.

955 DICK, THOMAS. ON THE IMPROVEMENT OF SOCIETY. *Wood-cuts. 18mo, cloth; with autograph of Rufus Choate.* New York, 1833.

956 DICK, THOMAS. THE WORKS OF. Uniform Edition. *Portrait and wood-cuts. 10 vols. in 5, 12mo, cloth.* Philadelphia, 1851

957 DICKENS, CHARLES. WORKS. *Illustrated by George Cruikshank, H. K. Brown ("Phiz"), John Leech, Marcus Stone, and others.* 24 *vols., crown* 8*vo, half dark calf, very neat, contents lettered, marbled edges.* Chapman & Hall, London, 1862–66

This handsome set comprises: Barnaby Rudge, and Hard Times (2 vols.); Nicholas Nickleby (2 vols.); Old Curiosity Shop, and Reprinted Pieces (2 vols.); Bleak House (2 vols.); Little Dorrit (2 vols.); Great Expectations; Sketches by Boz; Oliver Twist; Tale of Two Cities; Martin Chuzzlewit (2 vols.); Dombey and Son (2 vols.); David Copperfield (2 vols.); Christmas Books; Pictures from Italy, and American Notes; Pickwick Papers (2 vols.).

958 DICKENS, CHARLES. THE CHIMES; a Goblin Story of some Bells that rang an Old Year out and a New Year in. *With* 13 *illustrations by Maclise, Doyle, Leech, and Stanfield. Foolscap* 8*vo, calf, gilt, gilt edges.* London, 1845

959 DICKENS, CHARLES. THE CRICKET ON THE HEARTH; a Fairy Tale of Home. Twentieth Edition. *With* 14 *illustrations by Maclise, Doyle, Stanfield, Leech, and Landseer. Foolscap* 8*vo, calf, gilt, gilt edges.* London, 1846

960 DICKENS, CHARLES. A CHRISTMAS CAROL, in Prose; being a Ghost Story of Christmas. Eleventh Edition. *With* 8 *illustrations* (4 *colored*) *by Leech. Foolscap* 8*vo, calf, gilt, gilt edges.* London, 1846

961 DICKENS, CHARLES. THE HAUNTED MAN AND THE GHOST'S BARGAIN; a Fancy for Christmas Time. *With* 16 *illustrations by Tenniel, Stanfield, Stone, and Leech. Foolscap* 8*vo, calf, gilt, gilt edges.* London, 1848

962 DICKENS, CHARLES. A TALE OF TWO CITIES. With Beautiful Illustrations, from Original Designs by John McLenan. 2 *vols.,* 12*mo, cloth.* Philadelphia (1859)

963 DICKENS, CHARLES. CHRISTMAS BOOKS. 12*mo, cloth.* New York, 1854

964 DICKENS, CHARLES. DR. MARIGOLD'S PRESCRIPTIONS. 8*vo, paper.* New York, 1866

965 DICKSON, REV. ADAM. THE HUSBANDRY OF THE ANCIENTS. 2 *vols.,* 8*vo, half calf; with autograph of Rufus Choate.* Edinburgh, 1788

966 DICTIONARY (A) OF QUOTATIONS FROM SHAKSPEARE. Second Edition. 12*mo, cloth.* London, 1843

967 DICTIONARY (A) OF SELECT AND POPULAR QUOTATIONS, taken from the Latin, French, Greek, Spanish, and Italian Languages; together with a Copious Collection of Law Maxims and Law Terms. Sixth American Edition, corrected, with Additions. 12*mo, cloth.* Philadelphia, 1856

968 DICTIONNAIRE DE L'ACADÉMIE FRANÇAISE; Sixième Édition. COMPLÉMENT DU DICTIONNAIRE (&c.), publié sous la Direction d'un Membre de l'Académie Française [M. Dorz], avec la Coopération de MM. Bardin, Barre, Barré (et Dix-sept autres Hommes de Lettres); avec une Préface, par M. Louis Barré. 3 *vols.,* 4*to, marbled calf, very neat, marbled edges.* Paris, (1855)–1856

969 DICTIONNAIRE DE L'ACADÉMIE FRANÇAISE ET LE COMPLÉMENT. ANOTHER COPY: *the previous impression of the sixth edition.* 3 *vols.*, 4*to*, *half calf; with autograph of Rufus Choate.* Paris, (1835)–1844

970 DIDEROT, DENIS. ENCYCLOPÉDIE, ou Dictionnaire Raisonné des Sciences, des Arts, et des Métiers, par une Société de Gens de Lettres; mis en Ordre & publié par M. Diderot, & quant à la Partie Mathématique par M. D'Alembert. Nouvelle Édition. (Avec la TABLE ANALYTIQUE ET RAISONNÉE DE MATIÈRES. etc. Lyon, 1780–81.) *Portraits and numerous plates. Dictionary,* 36 *vols.; Plates,* 3 *vols.; Tables,* 6 *vols. Together,* 45 *vols.*, 4*to*, *old calf, red edges.* Genève, 1777–79; Lyon, 1780–81

In this edition the SUPPLEMENT is incorporated in the body of the work.

971 DIDOT, PIERRE. ÉPÎTRE SUR LES PROGRÈS DE L'IMPRIMERIE; par Didot, Fils Aîné. *Imprimé chez Didot l'Aîné, avec les italiques de Firmin, son second fils. Title and pp.* 20; *with* 2 *plates (inserted), engraved by Fessard after Gravelot, etc.* 8*vo*, *mottled calf, gilt, gilt edges.* PRIVATELY PRINTED. Paris, 1784

972 DIETERICHS, JOHANN GEORG NICOLAO. PHYTANTHOZA ICONOGRAPHIA, sive Conspectus aliquot Millium, tam Indigenarum quam Exoticarum, ex Quatuor Mundi Partibus, Longâ Annorum Serie Indefessoque Studio, à Joanne Guilielmo Weirmanno collectarum, Plantarum, Arborum, Fructicum, Florum, Fructuum, Fungorum, &c.: quorum Denominationes, Characteres, Genera, Species & Descriptiones ex Optimis, tam Priscis quam Neotericis Auctoribus, Ordine ac Serie Alphabetica, cum Probatissimo Usu Medico, Pharmaceutico Chirurgico ac Oeconomico, Latino & Germanico Idiomate Sincere Explicantur; à D. Joanne Georgio Nicolao Dieterico (et à D. Ambrosio Carolo Bielero). *Portraits of Weinmann and Bieler, a frontispiece, and* 1045 *finely colored plates, by B. Seuter, J. E. Ridinger, and J. J. Haid.* 8 *vols.*, *folio, old calf, gilt. In good condition.* Ratisbonæ, 1737–45

973 DILKE, CHARLES WENTWORTH. OLD ENGLISH PLAYS; being a Selection from the Early Dramatic Writers. [Edited by C. W. Dilke.] 6 *vols.*, 8*vo*, *half calf, antique, red edges.* London, 1814–15

974 DINNER (THE) QUESTION, or How to Dine Well and Economically, etc., etc. By Tabitha Tickletooth. 16*mo*, *boards.* London, 1860

975 DION CHRYSOSTOMUS. SELECT ESSAYS OF DIO CHRYSOSTOM, translated into English from the Greek, with Notes, Critical and Illustrative; by Gilbert Wakefield, B. A. 8*vo*, *old mottled calf.* London, 1800

976 DISCOVERY (A) OF NEW WORLDS: from the French, made English by Mrs. A. Behn; together with a Preface by Way of

Essay upon Translated Prose, wholly new. *Post 8vo, old calf, gilt, red edges.* London, 1688

977 DISCURSOS SOBRE UNA CONSTITUCION RELIGIOSA, considerada como Parte de la Civil Nacional; su Autor un Americano. Los da á Luz D. Juan Antonio Llorente. *12mo, marbled calf, marbled edges.* Paris, 1820

978 D'ISRAELI, ISAAC. FLIM-FLAMS! or the Life and Errors of my Uncle and his Friends! With Illustrations and Obscurities, by Messieurs Tag, Rag, and Bobtail. A Literary Romance. [By I. D'Israeli.] A New Edition, with Material Alterations and Additions. *Plates by R. Dagley, etc. 3 vols., foolscap 8vo, half blue calf, extra, marbled edges.* J. Murray, London, 1806

979 D'ISRAELI, ISAAC. CALAMITIES OF AUTHORS; including some Inquiries respecting their Moral and Literary Characters. *2 vols., crown 8vo, half purple calf, extra; with autograph of Rufus Choate.* J. Murray, London, 1812

980 D'ISRAELI, ISAAC. QUARRELS OF AUTHORS, or some Memoirs for our Literary History; including Specimens of Controversy to the Reign of Elizabeth. *3 vols., crown 8vo, half dark calf; with autograph of Rufus Choate.* J. Murray, London, 1814

981 D'ISRAELI, ISAAC. CURIOSITIES OF LITERATURE; with a View of the Life and Writings of the Author, by his Son. Fourteenth Edition. *Portraits, view of Bradenham, etc. 3 vols., 8vo, half dark calf, very neat; with autograph of Rufus Choate.* E. Moxon, London, 1849

982 D'ISRAELI, ISAAC. ANOTHER COPY: *reprint of the above. Portrait on India paper. 4 vols., 8vo, half brown morocco, gilt tops, red paper sides, rough edges.* LARGE PAPER: *only 100 copies printed.* Privately printed, Riverside Press, Cambridge, 1864

983 DITSON, GEORGE LEIGHTON. CIRCASSIA, or a Tour to the Caucasus. *Frontispiece, 8vo, cloth.* New York, 1850

984 DIVISIONARY CORPS OF CADETS: First Division, M. V. M. (Containing Roll, May, 1860, Constitution, Dress and Equipments of the "Boston Cadets," with Indexes). *Handsomely printed, at the Riverside Press, on a delicately toned paper, and on one side only. Royal 8vo, half olive morocco, red paper sides, gilt top, uncut.* LARGE PAPER: *only 30 copies printed for presentation.* Boston, 1860

985 DIX, JOHN ROSS. LIFE OF THOMAS CHATTERTON; including his Unpublished Poems and Correspondence. *Post 8vo, half green morocco; with autographs, etc.* BEST EDITION: *presentation copy from the author.* London, 1837

An AUTOGRAPH SIGNATURE of Chatterton and a piece of the ORIGINAL ROWLEY MSS. (presented to the author by Chatterton's sister), drawings of Redcliff Church, etc., are inserted in this copy.

This is the best Life of Chatterton, of which Leigh Hunt says: "Mr. Dix has, in addition to what was before known, gathered up 'all the fragments.' His biography is heart-touching." Mr. Dix was a native of Bristol, England. He was known in England, as an author, by the name of John Dix, and in America, first by the name of John Ross, and afterwards by the name of John Ross Dix. He was a very pleasing and quite talented writer, yet he died (at Brooklyn, N. Y.) from *actual starvation.*

986 DIX, JOHN ROSS. A HAND-BOOK OF NEWPORT, AND RHODE ISLAND; by the Author of "Pen and Ink Sketches," "Life of Chatterton," etc., etc. *Wood-cuts of the "Old Stone Mill," Redwood Library, etc.; and a map (inserted) of the town and island. 12mo, cloth.* Newport, R. I., 1852

Only a small edition of this entertaining little work was printed and it has long been out of print. It contains several poems, by the author, besides interesting historical information.

987 DIXON, B. HOMER. SURNAMES. *Imperial 8vo, cloth, gilt edges; with autograph of the author.* PRIVATELY PRINTED: *presentation copy.* Boston, 1855

988 DIXON, WILLIAM HEPWORTH. PERSONAL HISTORY OF LORD BACON; from Unpublished Papers. *12mo, cloth.* Boston, 1861

989 DOBBS, ARTHUR. AN ACCOUNT OF THE COUNTRIES ADJOINING TO HUDSON'S BAY, in the North-west Part of America, containing a Description of their Lakes and Rivers, the Nature of the Soil and Climates, and their Methods of Commerce, etc.; shewing the Benefit to be made by settling Colonies, and opening a Trade in these Parts, whereby the French will be deprived in a great Measure of their Traffick in Furs, and the Communication between Canada and Mississippi be cut off: with an Abstract of Captain Middleton's Journal, and Observations upon his Behaviour during his Voyage, and since his Return. To which are added, — I. A Letter from Bartholomew de Fonte, Vice-Admiral of Peru and Mexico, giving an Account of his Voyage from Lima in Peru, to prevent, or seize upon any Ships that should attempt to find a North-West Passage to the South Sea. II. An Abstract of all the Discoveries which have been publish'd of the Islands and Countries in and adjoining to the Great Western Ocean, between America, India, and China, etc., pointing out the Advantages that may be made, if a Short Passage should be found, thro' Hudson's Streight, to that Ocean. III. The Hudson's Bay Company's Charter. IV. The Standard of Trade in those Parts of America, with an Account of the Exports and Profits made annually by the Hudson's Bay Company. V. Vocabularies of the Languages of Several Indian Nations adjoining to Hudson's Bay. The Whole intended to shew the great Probability of a North-West Passage, so long desired, and which (if discovered) would be of the highest Advantage to these Kingdoms. *Map of North America, by Joseph la France. 4to, old calf, marbled edges; with book-plate of Sir Alexr. Ramsay.*

London, 1744

990 DOBRIZHOFFER, MARTIN. AN ACCOUNT OF THE ABIPONES, an Equestrian People of Paraguay. [Translated by Sara Coleridge.] 3 *vols.*, 8*vo*, *half calf*, *very neat*. J. Murray, London, 1822

"A singularly interesting and curious work, containing the most complete and extraordinary description of savage life that has ever been published." — *Lowndes*.

This translation has generally been attributed to Miss Southey, but Samuel Taylor Coleridge thus speaks of the work: "My dear daughter's translation of this book is, in my judgment, unsurpassed for pure mother English."

991 DOBSON, SUSANNAH. HISTORICAL ANECDOTES OF HERALDRY AND CHIVALRY; tending to shew the Origin of many English and Foreign Coats of Arms, Circumstances and Customs. *Plates*. 4*to*, *boards*, *rough edges*. Worcester, (1796)

992 DOBSON, SUSANNAH. THE LIFE OF PETRARCH; collected from Memoires pour la Vie de Petrarch. Third Edition. *Index, and 8 plates by Ridley after Kirk*. 2 *vols.*, *royal* 8*vo*, *boards*, *uncut*. LARGE PAPER: *printed by T. Bensley*. London, 1797

993 DOBSON, SUSANNAH. ANOTHER COPY: Fifth edition. *Same plates, and index*. 2 *vols.*, 8*vo*, *old calf*, *gilt*. London, 1803

994 DODDRIDGE, PHILIP, D. D. THE CORRESPONDENCE AND DIARY OF; illustrative of Various Particulars in his Life hitherto unknown, with Notices of many of his Contemporaries, and a Sketch of the Ecclesiastical History of the Times in which he lived. Edited, by his Great Grandson, John Doddridge Humphreys, Esq. *Handsomely printed by Whittingham; with a fine portrait by Worthington*. 5 *vols.*, 8*vo*, *half calf*, *extra*. London, 1829–31

995 DODGE, MARY ABIGAIL. COUNTRY LIVING AND COUNTRY THINKING; by Gail Hamilton. 12*mo*, *cloth*, *red edges*. Boston, 1862

996 DODGE, MARY ABIGAIL. A NEW ATMOSPHERE; by Gail Hamilton. *Post* 8*vo*, *cloth*, *red edges*. Boston, 1865

997 DODINGTON, GEORGE BUBB. THE DIARY OF THE LATE GEORGE BUBB DODINGTON, Baron of Melcombe Regis; from March 8, 1749, to February 6, 1761: with an Appendix, containing some Curious and Interesting Papers, which are either referred to, or alluded to, in the Diary. Published from his Lordship's Original Manuscripts, by Henry Penruddocke Wyndham. Fourth Edition. 8*vo*, *half calf*, *neat; with autograph of Rufus Choate*. J. Murray, London, 1823

998 DODSLEY, ROBERT. A SELECT COLLECTION OF OLD PLAYS. A New Edition; with Additional Notes and Corrections, by the late Isaac Reed, Octavius Gilchrist, and the Editor [John Payne Collier]. 12 *vols.*, *crown* 8*vo*, *half calf*, *neat*. London, 1825–27

999 DODWELL, EDWARD. VIEWS IN GREECE, from Drawings by Edward Dodwell, Esq., F. S. A., etc. *Contains* 30 *finely colored views, with descriptive letter-press in English and French.* 2 *vols. in* 1, *imperial folio, half morocco, gilt top. Plates mounted on linen guards.* London, 1821

1000 DOMENECH, EMMANUEL. SEVEN YEARS' RESIDENCE IN THE GREAT DESERTS OF NORTH AMERICA. Illustrated with Fifty-eight Wood-cuts (colored) by A. Joliet, Three Plates of Ancient Indian Music, and a Map showing the Actual Situation of the Indian Tribes and the Country described by the Author. 2 *vols.*, 8*vo, cloth, uncut.* London, 1860

1001 DON QUIXOTS AT COLLEGE; or a History of the Gallant Adventures lately achieved by the Combined Students of Harvard University; interspersed with some Facetious Reasonings. By a Senior. *Published by Etheridge and Bliss for the author.* 8*vo, pp.* 20, *stitched.* Boston, 1807

1002 DONNE, JOHN, D. D. POEMS, etc.; with Elegies on the Author's Death: to which is added Divers Copies under his Own Hand, never before printed. *Title, dedication, etc.,* 3 *leaves; and pp.* 1–414. *Small* 8*vo, old calf; with autograph of Rufus Choate.* Printed by T. N. for Henry Herringman, In the Savoy, 1669

1003 DONNE, JOHN, D. D. THE WORKS OF, 1621–1631; with a Memoir of his Life. By Henry Alford, M. A., etc. *Portrait.* 6 *vols.*, 8*vo, calf, gilt, marbled edges; with autograph of Rufus Choate.* J. W. Parker, London, 1839

1004 DONNE, JOHN, D. D. DEVOTIONS; with Two Sermons: I. On the Decease of Lady Danvers, Mother of George Herbert. II. Death's Duel, his own Funeral Sermon. To which is prefixed his Life, by Izaak Walton. *Printed by Whittingham. Fac-simile of the frontispiece by Marshall in the edition of* 1638, *and title within a wood-cut design. Foolscap* 8*vo, dark green turkey morocco, gilt edges; with autograph of Rufus Choate.* W. Pickering, London, 1840

1005 DORAN, JOHN. "THEIR MAJESTIES' SERVANTS:" Annals of the English Stage, from Thomas Betterton to Edmund Kean; Actors, Authors, Audiences. *Photographic portraits of Garrick, Betterton, Nell Gwyn, Mrs. Siddons (two), Macklin, Mrs. Abington, Kemble, Mrs. Jordan, and Kean.* 2 *vols., imperial* 8*vo, cloth, rough edges.* LARGE PAPER: *only* 161 *copies printed.* New York, 1865

1006 DORE, GUSTAVE. LA LÉGENDE DU JUIF ERRANT: Compositions et Dessins par Gustave Doré, gravés sur Bois par F. Rouget, O. Jahyer, et J. Gauchard; imprimés par J. Best. Poeme avec Prologue et Épilogue par Pierre Dupont; Préface et Notice Bibliographique par Paul Lacroix (Bibliophile Jacob); avec la Ballade de Béranger mise en Musique, par

Ernest Doré. *Early impressions of the cuts. Atlas folio, half morocco, gilt edges.* Paris, 1856

1007 DOUBLEDAY, Edward. The Genera of Diurnal Lepidoptera: comprising their Generic Characters, a Notice of the Habits and Transformations, and a Catalogue of the Species of each Genus. *Parts I.–XII., XIV.–XXIII., and XXXII.; containing 45 beautiful colored plates, and 1 plate of outlines, by Wm. C. Hewitson, M. E. S., 23 parts, imperial 4to., as issued.* London, 1846–50

1008 DOUCE, Francis. Illustrations of Shakspeare, and of Ancient Manners; with Dissertations on the Clowns and Fools of Shakspeare, on the Collection of Popular Tales entitled Gesta Romanorum, and on the English Morris Dance. The Engravings on Wood, by J. Berryman. *Title in red and black, and plates (the "Ancient Morris Dance," a folding plate, tinted), besides the wood-cuts. 2 vols., 8vo, sprinkled calf, gilt.* Original edition.
Longmans & Co., London, 1807

Dibdin, who mentions this work as "in the first and foremost rank of 'Introductory Works to the Reading of Shakspeare,'" says: "I look upon this work as a sort of *Hortus Shakesperianus*, from which fruit of every hue and flavour may be safely plucked and eaten. The research and learning bestowed upon it are immense."

Douce was the Prospero of Dibdin in his "Bibliomania." He left all his valuable MSS. to the British Museum (he was for a time keeper of the manuscripts in that institution), stipulating that the sealed box containing them should not be opened until the year 1900! This act was from pique at the manner in which the above work was reviewed, the Edinburgh reviewers, and some other critics, ridiculing the minute knowledge therein as laborious trifling. His dissertation on the Gesta Romanorum is considered far superior to Warton's.

1009 DOUCE, Francis. Another copy: a New Edition. The Engravings on Wood, by Jackson. *1 vol., 8vo, cloth, uncut.*
T. Tegg, London, 1839

In this edition the *plates*, also, are copies, and the "Ancient Morris Dance" reduced.

1010 DOW, Lieut. Col. Alexander. The History of Hindostan, translated from the Persian. A New Edition. *Vols. II. and III., 8vo, half russia.* London, 1803

1011 DOWNING, Andrew Jackson. The Fruits and Fruit Trees of America, or the Culture, Propagation, and Management, in the Garden and Orchard, of Fruit Trees generally; with Descriptions of all the Finest Varieties of Fruit, Native and Foreign, cultivated in this Country. *Numerous wood-cuts, 12mo, cloth.* New York, 1851

1012 DOWNING, Andrew Jackson. A Treatise on the Theory and Practice of Landscape Gardening, adapted to North America, with a View to the Improvement of Country Residences; comprising Historical Notices and General Principles of the Art, Directions for laying out Grounds and arranging Plantations, the Description and Cultivation of Hardy Trees, Decorative Accompaniments of the House and Grounds, the Formation of Pieces of Artificial Water, Flower Gardens, etc.: with Remarks on Rural Architecture. Sixth Edition, enlarged, revised, and newly illustrated: with a Supplement containing some Remarks about Country Places, and the Best Method of making them, also an Account of the Newer Deciduous and Evergreen Plants, lately introduced into Cultivation, both Hardy and Half-Hardy; by Henry W. Sargent. *Portrait, plates and wood-cuts. 8vo, cloth.* New York, 1859

1013 DOYLE, RICHARD. THE FOREIGN TOUR OF MESSRS. BROWN, JONES, AND ROBINSON; being the History of what they saw, and did, in Belgium, Germany, Switzerland, and Italy. *Above 170 humorous illustrations. 4to, cloth, gilt edges.* New York, 1860

1014 D'OYLEY, SIR CHARLES. THE COSTUME AND CUSTOMS OF MODERN INDIA, from a Collection of Drawings, engraved by J. H. Clark and C. Dubourg; with a Preface and Copious Descriptions, by Captain Thomas Williamson. *Contains 20 colored plates. Royal 4to, half morocco.* E. Orme, London, s. a.

1015 D'OYLEY, SIR CHARLES. ANTIQUITIES OF DACCA. *An account of the city of Dacca, the ancient capital of Bengal; with 20 fine engravings (many on India paper), and a fac-simile of an inscription in the Great Kuttra, chiefly by J. Landseer. Imperial 4to, half crimson morocco, gilt edges.* London, (1814–27)

1016 DRAKE, SIR FRANCIS. SIR FRANCIS DRAKE REVIVED, who is or may be a Pattern to stirre up all Heroicke and Active Spirits of these Times, to benefit their Countrey and eternize their Names by like Noble Attempts; being a Summary and True Relation of Foure Severall Voyages made by the said Sir Francis Drake to the West-Indies, viz: His Dangerous Adventuring for Gold and Silver with the Gaining thereof; and the Surprizing of Nombre de Dios by himself and Two and Fifty Men. — His Encompassing the World. — His Voyage made with Christopher Carleill, Martin Frobusher, Francis Knollis, and others; their taking the Townes of Saint Jago, Sancto Domingo, Carthagena, and Saint Augustine. — His last Voyage (in which he dyed) being accompanied with Sir John Hawkins, Sir Thomas Baskerfield, Sir Nicholas Clifford, with others; his Manner of Buriall, Collected out of the Notes of the said Sir Francis Drake; Master Philip Nichols, Master Francis Fletcher, Preachers; and the Notes of Divers other Gentlemen (who went in the said Voyages), carefully compared together. *Portrait, with four lines in Latin; fine impression. Small 4to, sprinkled calf, neat.* CLEAN AND PERFECT COPY. N. Bourne, London, 1653

All the titles (except the first general title) are dated 1652. The Address to the Reader is signed R. D. Collation may be found in Bohn's "Lowndes," p. 669.

1017 DRAKE, NATHAN. ESSAYS, Biographical, Critical, and Historical; illustrative of the Rambler, Adventurer, and Idler, and of Various Periodical Papers which, in Imitation of the Writings of Steele and Addison, have been published between the Close of the Eighth Volume of the Spectator, and the Commencement of the Year 1809. *Portrait of T. Warton by Schiavonetti after Sir J. Reynolds, and view of Mrs. Piozzi's house by Landseer. 2 vols., post 8vo, half morocco, neat, marbled edges; with autograph of Rufus Choate.* Buckingham, 1809–10

1018 DRAKE, NATHAN. ESSAYS, Biographical, Critical, and Historical; illustrative of the Tatler, Spectator, and Guardian. The Second Edition. *Portrait and plates. 3 vols., foolscap 8vo, crimson morocco, extra, gilt edges.* London, 1814

1019 DRAKE, NATHAN. THE GLEANER; a Series of Periodical Essays, selected and arranged from Scarce or Neglected Volumes, with an Introduction, and Notes. *4 vols., 8vo, half russia, yellow edges; with book-plates of [Edward] Norwood and John Baldwin, Esq.* London, 1811

1020 DRAKE, NATHAN. SHAKSPEARE AND HIS TIMES; including the Biography of the Poet, Criticisms on his Genius and Writings, a New Chronology of his Plays, a Disquisition on the Object of his Sonnets, and a History of the Manners, Customs, and Amusements, Superstitions, Poetry, and Elegant Literature of his Age. *2 vols., 4to, cloth, rough edges. Portrait and plate of fac-simile autographs wanting.* London, 1817

1021 DRAKE, SAMUEL GREEN. SOME MEMOIRS OF THE LIFE AND WRITINGS OF THE REV. THOMAS PRINCE, together with a Pedigree of his Family. *With a list of subscribers to the original edition of Prince's Chronological Hist. of N. E. Portraits of Thomas Prince and Joseph Sewall. 8vo, cloth.* Boston, 1851

1022 DRAKE, SAMUEL GREEN. THE HISTORY AND ANTIQUITIES OF BOSTON, from its Settlement in 1630, to the Year 1770; also, an Introductory History of the Discovery and Settlement of New England: with Notes, Critical and Illustrative. *Maps and numerous portraits, fac-similes, wood-cuts, etc. Royal 8vo, half morocco.* Boston, 1856

1023 DRAKE, SAMUEL GREEN. RESULT OF SOME RESEARCHES AMONG THE BRITISH ARCHIVES, for Information relative to the Founders of New England; made in the Years 1858, 1859, and 1860. *Map of New England, and portraits of Sir Francis Drake and Capt. John Smith. Post 4to, cloth, gilt top.* Boston, 1860

This volume contains lists of early emigrants to New England, St. Christopher, Barbadoes, etc., with index of names and places.

1024 DRAKE, Samuel Green. The Old Indian Chronicle; being a Collection of Exceeding Rare Tracts, written and published in the Time of King Philip's War. To which are now added an Introduction and Notes, by Samuel G. Drake. *Map of the "Nipmuck Country," and index. 4to, pp. ix and 333, paper, rough edges.* Large paper: *only 75 copies printed.* Boston, 1867

There was an edition (18mo, pp. 222) of about 250 copies published in 1836, under the title of "The Old Indian Chronicle," which contained a part of this work.

1025 DRAPER, James. History of Spencer, Massachusetts, from its Earliest Settlement to the Year 1860; including a Brief Sketch of Leicester, to the Year 1753. Second Edition, enlarged and improved. *Portrait, etc. Royal 8vo, boards, rough edges.* Worcester, Mass., s. a.

1026 DRAPER, John W. A History of the Intellectual Development of Europe. *8vo, cloth.* New York, 1863

1027 DRESDEN Gallery. Der Kunstverein: Neue Serie; Stahlstich-Sammlung der Vorzüglichsten Gemälde der Dresdener Gallerie, nebst Text von Adolph Görling. *Contains 136 finely executed plates by A. H. Payne, A. Schultheiss, D. J. Pound, and others. 4to, half calf, green edges.* Leipzig u. Dresden, (1851, etc.)

1028 DREW, William A. Glimpses and Gatherings; during a Voyage and Visit to London and the Great Exhibition of 1851. *Portrait. 12mo, cloth.* Augusta (Me.), 1852

1029 DRUMMOND, Alexander. Travels through Different Cities of Germany, Italy, Greece, and Several Parts of Asia, as far as the Banks of the Euphrates; in a Series of Letters, containing an Account of what is most Remarkable in their Present State, as well as in their Monuments of Antiquity. *Numerous plates by J. S. Müller. Folio, old calf, gilt, red edges.* Printed by W. Strahan, for the author, London, 1754

1030 DRUMMOND, Henry. History of Noble British Families, with Biographical Notices of the most Distinguished Individuals in Each. *Genealogies, and 82 large plates of portraits, monuments, views, etc., besides numerous illustrations of armorial bearings, seals, etc.; the arms and portraits most beautifully colored by hand. 2 vols., imperial folio, half morocco, gilt tops, by Hayday.* Privately printed: *only a few copies.* W. Pickering, London, 1842–46

This elegant work, published at the expense of the author — very few copies of which were sold — is similar to the "Famiglie Celebri di Italia" [see Litta], and contains accounts of the following families: Ashburnham, Arden, Compton, Cecil, Harley, Bruce, Perceval, Dunbar, Hume, Dundas, Drummond, and Neville. The portraits are splendidly executed (many of them colored like miniatures) after original paintings, forming a fine collection of British Worthies in the costumes of their time, with their pedigrees, arms, etc.

1031 DRURY, Anna Harriet. Eastbury; a Tale. *Post 8vo, cloth, uncut.* W. Pickering, London, 1851

1032 DRURY, Rev. Henry. Arundines Canii, sive Musarum Cantabrigiensium Lusus Canori; collegit atque edidit Henricus Drury, A. M., etc. Editio Quinta. *Post 8vo, calf, gilt, marbled edges.* Cantabrigiæ, 1860

1033 DRYDEN, John. The Comedies, Tragedies, and Operas written by John Dryden, Esq.; now first collected together, and corrected from the Originals. *Large portrait by Edelinck after Kneller. 2 vols., folio, old calf; with book-plate of John Whitelocke, Esq.* J. Tonson, London, 1701

1034 DRYDEN, John. Miscellany Poems, containing Variety of New Translations of the Ancient Poets; together with several Original Poems. By the most Eminent Hands. Publish'd by Mr. Dryden. The Fourth Edition. *Frontispiece by L. du Guernier and Kirkall. 6 vols., small 12mo, half calf; with book-plate of William Leaf.* J. Tonson, London, 1716

"This edition, according to Malone, differs very much from the former collection, many pieces being added, and several poems omitted." — *Lowndes.*

1035 DRYDEN, John. The Fables of; ornamented with Engravings from the Pencil of the Right Hon. Lady Diana Beauclerc. *Fine impressions of the 9 large plates and 15 vignettes, engraved chiefly by Bartolozzi. Printed by T. Bensley. Folio, half purple calf.* London, 1797

1036 DUBLIN (The) University Magazine; a Literary and Political Journal. *From January,* 1833, *to December,* 1858, *inclusive. Portraits, plates, etc. 52 vols., 8vo, half calf, very neat.* Very fine set. Dublin, 1833–58

1037 DUBOS, Jean Baptiste. Critical Reflections on Poetry, Painting, and Music; with an Inquiry into the Rise and Progress of the Theatrical Entertainments of the Ancients; translated into English, by Thomas Nugent. From the Fifth Edition revised, corrected, and enlarged by the Author. *3 vols., 8vo, old calf gilt, yellow edges.* London, 1748

1038 DUCHESNE, Jean, ainé. Museo di Pittura e Scultura, ossia Raccolta dei Principali Quadri, Statue, e Bassirilievi delle Gallerie Publiche e Private d' Europe; disegnati ed incisi sull' Acciaio da Réveil: con le Notizie Descrittive, Critiche, e Storiche; di Duchesne, Primogenito. Prima Traduzione Italiana. Complete; *with appendix, and biographical notices. 16 vols., 12 mo, half morocco, neat.* Firenze, 1837–45

1039 DUDEVANT, Amantine Lucile Aurore Dupin, Baronne. Jacques; par George Sand. *2 vols., 8vo, boards.* Original edition. F. Bonnaire, Paris, 1834

1040 DUFFERIN, Frederick Temple Blackwood, Baron. A Yacht Voyage: Letters from High Latitudes; being some Account of a Voyage to Iceland, Jan Mayen, and Spitzbergen, in 1856. *12mo, cloth.* Boston, 1859

1041 DUGDALE, HENRY GEAST. THE LIFE AND CHARACTER OF EDMUND GESTE; the Principal Compiler of the Liturgy of the Church of England, established at the Time of the Reformation, and now in Use amongst us as the only English Church Service; the First Protestant Bishop of Rochester, Almoner to Queen Elizabeth. *Portraits, and pedigree of the Geste and Dugdale family.* 8*vo, cloth, uncut.* W. Pickering, London, 1840

The appendix contains, besides other writings of Bp. Geste, a reprint of his "Treatise againste the Prevee Masse in the Behalfe and Furtberaunce of the Mooste Holye Communyon."

1042 DUGDALE, SIR WILLIAM. A SHORT VIEW OF THE TROUBLES IN ENGLAND, briefly setting forth their Rise, Growth and Tragical Conclusion; as also some Parallel thereof with the Barons-Wars in the Time of King Henry III., but chiefly with that in France, called the Holy League, in the Reign of Henry III. and Henry IV., late Kings of that Realm. To which is added, a Perfect Narrative of the Treaty at Uxbridge in An. 1644. *Portrait of Charles I., by Faithorne. Folio, half calf.* Oxford, 1681

1043 DUGDALE, SIR WILLIAM. MONASTICON ANGLICANUM: a History of the Abbies and other Monasteries, Hospitals, Frieries, and Cathedral and Collegiate Churches, with their Dependencies, in England and Wales; also of all such Scotch, Irish, and French Monasteries, as were in any Manner connected with Religious Houses in England. Together with a Particular Account of their Respective Foundations, Grants, and Donations, and a Full Statement of their Possessions, as well Temporal as Spiritual. Originally published in Latin, by Sir William Dugdale, Knight, Garter King at Arms. (A New Edition, enriched with a large Accession of Materials taken from Leiger Books, Chartularies, Rolls, and other Documents preserved in the National Archives, Public Libraries, and other Repositaries; the history of each Religious Foundation in English being prefixed to its Respective Series of Latin Charters. By John Caley, Esq., Sir Henry Ellis, and Bulkeley Bandinel, D. D.) *Portrait and* 250 *fine large plates by John Coney, besides numerous wood-cuts; fine impressions.* 6 *vols. in* 8, *thick folio, half morocco, gilt tops, uncut. Fine early copy.* London, 1846

This reprint of the edition of 1817–30 is very slightly altered, and the same plates were used, being very little worn, as the former edition was limited to 350 copies

1044 DUHALDE, JEAN BAPTISTE. A DESCRIPTION OF THE EMPIRE OF CHINA AND CHINESE-TARTARY, together with the Kingdoms of Corea and Tibet: containing the Geography and History (Natural as well as Civil) of those Countries; enrich'd with General and Particular Maps, and adorned with a great Number of Cuts. From the French of P. J. B. DuHalde, Jesuit; with Notes, Geographical, His-

torical, and Critical; and other Improvements, particularly in the Maps by the Translator. *Fine impressions of the plates, which are engraved by H. Fletcher, etc., including a portrait of Confucius. 2 vols., folio, rough calf.*
London, 1738–41

1045 DUHRING, HENRY, M. D. ESSAYS ON HUMAN HAPPINESS. *Foolscap 8vo, cloth, uncut.* London, (1848)

1046 DUMAS, ALEXANDRE DAVY. THE PROGRESS OF DEMOCRACY, illustrated in the History of Gaul and France. Translated by Edward S. Gould. *12mo, cloth; with autograph of Rufus Choate.* New York, 1841

1047 DUMONT, PIERRE ÉTIENNE LOUIS. RECOLLECTIONS OF MIRABEAU, and of the Two First Legislative Assemblies of France. *8vo, half calf, marbled edges.* London, 1832

1048 DUNLAP, WILLIAM. HISTORY OF THE AMERICAN THEATRE. *2 vols., 8vo, cloth, uncut.* London, 1833

1049 DUNLOP, JOHN. THE HISTORY OF FICTION; being a Critical Account of the most Celebrated Prose Works of Fiction, from the Earliest Greek Romances, to the Novels of the Present Age. Third Edition. *Royal 8vo, cloth, uncut.*
London, 1845

1050 DUNTON, REV. JOHN. DUNTON'S REMAINS, or the Dying Pastour's Last Legacy to his Friends and Parishioners; comprehending these following Treatises, viz.: I. An Affectionate Discourse upon the Parable of Dives and Lazarus. II. The Penitent Prodigal on his Knees, with the Reason and Manner of his Returning Home to his Father's House. III. His Farewell Sermon. IV. Closet Employment. V. A Looking-Glass for our English Ladies, or Daily Directions for their Dress and Apparel. VI. A Friendly Dialogue between a Moderate Conformist and one of his Parishioners, concerning Several Points of Great Moment. VII. Remarks upon the Bloody Persecution of the Duke of Guise. VIII. The Arraignment, Tryal, and Execution of Our Saviour Christ; with his Last Words upon the Cross. By John Dunton. To this Work is prefixt the Author's Holy Life and Triumphant Death; and at the Latter End of it is annext his Funeral Sermon. *Portrait by F. H. vom Hove, and 3 plates. Small 8vo, polished calf, gilt, marbled edges, by Mackenzie.* J. Dunton, London, 1684

1051 DUPIN, LOUIS ELLIES. A NEW HISTORY OF ECCLESIASTICAL WRITERS, containing an Account of the Authors of the Several Books of the Old and New Testament; and the Lives and Writings of the Primitive Fathers; an Abridgment and Catalogue of all their Works; Censures determining the Genuine and Spurious, a Judgment upon their Style and Doctrine, and the Various Editions of their Writings: to which is added, a Compendious History of the Councils;

and many Necessary Tables and Indexes. Written in French by Lewis Ellies du Pin, etc. The Third Edition, corrected. (The Translation revised, accompanied by Notes, by Dr. W. Wotton.) 15 *vols. in* 7, *old calf.*
London, 1696, etc.

For contents of the several volumes see Darling's "Cyclopædia Bibliographica," col. 985, 986. The above title is taken from the first volume.

1052 DUPIN, LOUIS ELLIES. A COMPLEAT HISTORY OF THE CANON AND WRITERS OF THE BOOKS OF THE OLD AND NEW TESTAMENT, by Way of Dissertation, with Useful Remarks on that Subject. Done into English from the French Original. 2 *vols. in* 1, *folio, old calf.*
London, 1699–1700

1053 DUPONCHEL, A. A. HISTOIRES DE GRÈCE ET D'ITALIE, depuis les Temps les plus Reculés jusqu'à nos Jours. *Plates.* 8*vo, half calf, neat, marbled edges.* Paris, 1844

Fifth volume (complete in itself) of "Le Monde, ou Histoire de Tous les Peuples."

1054 DUPPA, RICHARD. THE LIFE AND LITERARY WORKS OF MICHAEL ANGELO BUONARROTI. *Fac-simile of handwriting and* 26 *plates.* 4*to, cloth.*
J. Murray, etc., London, 1806

1055 DURDENT, RENÉ JEAN. ÉPOQUES ET FAITS MÉMORABLES DE L'HISTOIRE D'ANGLETERRE, depuis Alfred-le-Grand jusqu'à ce Jour. Deuxième Édition, revue et corrigée. *Plates.* 12*mo, marbled calf, gilt, gilt edges.*
Paris, 1820

1056 D'URFEY, THOMAS. NEW OPERA'S; with Comical Stories and Poems, on Several Occasions, never before printed: being the Remaining Pieces, written by Mr. D'Urfey. *Small* 8*vo, calf, antique.* W. Chetwood, London, 1721

This volume contains, among other pieces, Two Queens of Brentford, Grecian Heroine, Athenian Jilt, Ariadne, Plague of Impertinence, Socrates and Timandra.

1057 DUYCKINCK, EVERT A. NATIONAL HISTORY OF THE WAR FOR THE UNION, Civil, Military, and Naval; founded on Official and other Authentic Documents. *Numerous full-length portraits, and views.* 3 *vols.,* 4*to, morocco, antique, lettered on sides, gilt edges.* New York, (1861, etc.)

1058 DWIGHT, THEODORE. HISTORY OF THE HARTFORD CONVENTION; with a Review of the Policy of the United States Government, which led to the War of 1812. 8*vo, cloth.*
New York, 1833

1059 DYCE, REV. ALEXANDER. REMARKS ON MR. J. P. COLLIER'S AND MR. C. KNIGHT'S EDITIONS OF SHAKESPEARE. 8*vo, cloth, uncut.* E. Moxon, London, 1844

1060 DYER, THOMAS HENRY. THE LIFE OF JOHN CALVIN; compiled from Authentic Sources, and particularly from his Correspondence. *Portrait.* 8*vo, cloth, uncut.*
J. Murray, London, 1850

1061 EACHARD, JOHN, D. D. WORKS: Vol. I. The Grounds and Occasions of the Contempt of the Clergy and Religion enquired into, in a Letter to R. L.; with Observations on an Answer to the Enquiry, in a Second Letter to the same. Vol. II. Mr. Hobbs's State of Nature considered in a Dialogue between Philatus and Timothy; to which are added Five Letters (in Defence of the Enquiry, against Dr. Owen and others), etc. Vol. III. A Second Dialogue between Timothy and Philatus (on the Writings of Hobbs). *No general title.* 3 *vols.*, 12*mo*, *old calf.* London, 1772

1062 EATON, CYRUS. ANNALS OF THE TOWN OF WARREN (Maine); with the Early History of St. George's, Broad Bay, and the Neighboring Settlements on the Waldo Patent. (1605–1850.) 12*mo*, *cloth.* Hallowell, 1851

1063 EATON, CYRUS. HISTORY OF THOMASTON, ROCKLAND, AND SOUTH THOMASTON, Maine, from their First Exploration, A. D. 1605; with Family Genealogies. 2 *vols.*, 12*mo*, *half morocco, very neat, gilt tops, rough edges.* Hallowell, 1865

1064 EBERS, JOHN. SEVEN YEARS OF THE KING'S THEATRE. *Portraits.* 8*vo*, *calf, extra, marbled edges.* London, 1828

1065 ECCE DEUS: Essays on the Life and Doctrine of Jesus Christ; with Controversial Notes on "Ecce Homo." 12*mo*, *cloth.* Boston, 1867

1066 ECCENTRIC (THE) MAGAZINE, or Lives and Portraits of Remarkable Persons. [Edited by Henry Lemoine, and James Caulfield.] 2 *vols. in* 1, 4*to*, *half calf, extra.* LARGE PAPER. London, 1814

Many of the portraits are the same as those in Caulfield's "Remarkable Persons," and Burton's "Admirable Curiosities."

1067 ECLECTIC (THE) MAGAZINE OF FOREIGN LITERATURE, SCIENCE, AND ART. *Numerous fine portraits and plates. From January,* 1851, *to June,* 1866, *inclusive.* 45 *vols.*, 8*vo*, *half calf, extra.* New York, 1851–66

1068 ECLECTIC MAGAZINE. Duplicate Volumes: *September–December,* 1859, *and May,* 1860–*December,* 1862. 9 *vols.*, 8*vo*, *half calf, extra.* New York, 1859–62

1069 EDINBURGH POLICE REPORTS. Reports of the Interesting Proceedings in the Police Court (Edinburgh). *February* 6, *to December* 31, 1829, *inclusive. Issued daily.* 2 *vols.*, *without titles, small* 4*to*, *half russia.* (Edinburgh, 1829)

1070 EDINBURGH (THE) REVIEW, or Critical Journal. *From October,* 1802 *(commencement), to April* 1859, *inclusive; with* INDEXES *to Vols. I.–LXXX.* 109 *vols.*, *and* 3 *vols. (Indexes),* 8*vo*; *first* 79 *vols., and* 2 *vols. indexes, half calf, the rest in numbers.* New York, Boston, and Edinburgh, 1802–59

Some of the early numbers have the American imprint, but with the *same paging* as the Edinburgh edition. The fourth volume of indexes was published in 1862, and includes the 10th volume (Vols. LXXXI.-CX.) or January, 1845–October, 1859.

1071 EDINBURGH REVIEW. SELECTIONS FROM THE: comprising the Best Articles in that Journal, from its Commencement to the Present Time; with a Preliminary Dissertation, and Explanatory Notes. Edited by Maurice Cross. 4 *vols.*, 8*vo*, *half green turkey morocco, neat.* London, 1833

1072 EDMONDS, S. EMMA E. NURSE AND SPY IN THE UNION ARMY; comprising the Adventures and Experiences of a Woman, in Hospitals, Camps, and Battle-Fields. *Portrait and wood-cuts.* 8*vo*, *cloth.* Hartford, 1865

1073 EDWARDS, BRYAN. THE HISTORY, CIVIL AND COMMERCIAL, OF THE BRITISH COLONIES IN THE WEST INDIES. Third Edition, with Considerable Additions. *Portrait, maps, and plates.* 3 *vols.*, 8*vo*, *old marbled calf, very neat.* J. Stockdale, London, 1801

1074 EDWARDS, EDWARD. MEMOIRS OF LIBRARIES; including a Hand-Book of Library Economy. *Numerous plates, comprising plans, fac-similes, etc., some of which are colored.* 2 *vols.*, *royal* 8*vo*, *half morocco, gilt tops.* LARGE PAPER: *only* 50 *copies printed.* London, 1859

1075 EDWARDS, EDWARD. LIBRARIES AND FOUNDERS OF LIBRARIES. *Royal* 8*vo*, *half morocco, gilt top.* LARGE PAPER: *only* 50 *copies printed.* London, 1865

Although this is an independent work, yet it may be considered as a continuation of the above.

1076 EDWARDS, SUTHERLAND. THE RUSSIANS AT HOME: Unpolitical Sketches, showing what Newspapers they read; what Theatres they frequent; how they Eat, Drink, and Enjoy themselves; with other Matter relating chiefly to Literature and Music, and to Places of Historical and Religious Interest in and about Moscow; comprising also Four Russian Designs (on stone). 12*mo*, *cloth, uncut.* London, 1861

1077 EFFIGIES POETICÆ, or the Portraits of the British Poets (from Chaucer to Cowper); illustrated by Notes, Biographical, Critical, and Poetical. *Engraved titles and* 138 *fine portraits engraved by Fittler, Warren, Worthington, Finden, Pye, Rolls, Rhodes, and other eminent engravers; India proofs.* 2 *vols.*, *imperial* 4*to*; *Vol. I.* (*Plates*), *crimson morocco, extra, marbled edges; Vol. II.* (*Letter-Press*), *half bound to match.* LARGE PAPER: *fine copy.* London, 1824

1078 EFFIGIES POETICÆ. ANOTHER COPY: *plates only;* INDIA PROOFS *of the* 138 *portraits. Imperial* 4*to*, *claret morocco, extra, gilt edges.* LARGE PAPER: *fine copy.* (London, 1824)

1079 EFFIGIES Poeticæ. Another copy: *plates only; the 138 portraits arranged alphabetically. 4to, claret morocco, extra, gilt edges, by Wright.* (London, 1824)

1080 EGAN, Pierce. Real Life in London, or the Rambles and Adventures of Rob Tallyho, Esq., and his Cousin, the Hon. Tom Dashall, through the Metropolis; exhibiting a Living Picture of Fashionable Characters, Manners, and Amusements in High and Low Life. By an Amateur. Embellished and illustrated with a Series of Coloured Prints, designed and engraved by Heath, Alken, Dighton, Rowlandson, etc. *2 vols., thick 8vo, cloth, uncut.* London, (1821-22)

1081 EGAN, Pierce. Boxiana, or Sketches of Ancient and Modern Pugilism; comprising the Only Original and Complete Lives of the Boxers. *Numerous portraits and plates. 5 vols., 8vo, half crimson morocco, neat.* London, (1823, etc.)

1082 EGERTON, John. The Theatrical Remembrancer, containing a Complete List of all the Dramatic Performances in the English Language; their Several Editions, Dates, and Sizes, and the Theatres where they were Originally performed; together with an Account of those which have been acted and are Unpublished, and a Catalogue of such Latin Plays as have been written by English Authors: from the Earliest Production of the English Drama to the End of the year MDCCLXXXVII. To which are added Notitia Dramatica, being a Chronological Account of Events relative to the English Stage. *12mo, sheep; with book-plate of Joseph James.* London, 1788

1083 EIGHTY Years' Progress of the United States, from the Revolutionary War to the Great Rebellion; showing the Various Channels of Industry through which the People of the United States have arisen from a British Colony to their Present National Importance, giving, in an Historical Form, the Vast Improvements made in Agriculture, Commerce, and Trade; Manufacturing, Machinery, Modes of Travel and Transportation, etc. etc.; with a large Amount of Statistical Information, showing the Comparative Progress of the Different States with each other, and, to some extent, this Country with other Nations. To which are annexed, Articles on Canada. *Numerous engravings on steel and wood. Royal 8vo, roan.* New York, 1864

1084 ELDER, William. Biography of Elisha Kent Kane. *Portrait, 8vo, cloth.* Philadelphia, 1858

1085 ELEGANT Extracts: being a Copious Selection of Instructive, Moral, and Entertaining Passages from the most Eminent British Poets, Prose Writers, and Epistolary Writ-

ers. *Plates by Heath, Pye, etc.* 17 *vols.* (*Vol. I. Epistles wanting*), 18*mo, morocco, extra, gilt edges.*
J. Sharpe, London, (1810)

1086 ELLIS, GEORGE. SPECIMENS OF EARLY ENGLISH METRICAL ROMANCES, chiefly written during the Early Part of the Fourteenth Century: to which is prefixed an Historical Introduction, intended to illustrate the Rise and Progress of Romantic Composition in France and England; by George Ellis, Esq. Second Edition. 3 *vols., crown* 8*vo, half morocco.* BEST EDITION.
Longmans & Co., London, 1811

1087 ELOISA EN DISHABILLE: being a New Version of that Lady's Celebrated Epistle to Abelard; ascribed to Professor Porson. (To which is added, a Latin Version of a Well-known Ballad, by the late Dr. Glasse.) *The parody and the original* (*by Pope*) *printed on opposite pages.* 12*mo, half morocco.* ONLY 50 COPIES PRINTED.
London, 1822

1088 ELYOT, SIR THOMAS. THE BOKE NAMED THE GOVERNOUR, devised by Sir Thomas Elyot, Knyght. *Title within a wood-cut border. Small* 8*vo, sprinkled calf, gilt.* **Black letter**: *fine clean copy.* Londini, 1557

1089 EMERSON, RALPH WALDO. THE CONDUCT OF LIFE. 12*mo, cloth.* Boston, 1860

1090 EMERSON, REV. WILLIAM. AN HISTORICAL SKETCH OF THE FIRST CHURCH IN BOSTON, from its Formation to the Present Period; to which are added Two Sermons, one on Leaving the Old, and the other on Entering the New House of Worship. 8*vo, half morocco, very neat, gilt top.*
Boston, 1812

1091 EMORY, COLONEL WILLIAM H. REPORT ON THE UNITED STATES AND MEXICAN BOUNDARY SURVEY, made under the Direction of the Secretary of the Interior, by William H. Emory. *Maps, and numerous plates; the portraits, some of the views, and the birds finely colored.* 2 *vols.*, 4*to, cloth.*
Washington, 1857–59

1092 ENFIELD, WILLIAM. THE HISTORY OF PHILOSOPHY, from the Earliest Times to the Beginning of the Present Century; drawn up from Brucker's Historia Critica Philosophiæ. *Folding biographical chart.* 2 *vols., royal* 8*vo, sprinkled calf, gilt.* London, 1819

1093 ENGLISHWOMAN (THE) IN AMERICA. 12*mo, cloth, uncut.* J. Murray, London, 1856

1094 ENGLISHWOMAN (THE) IN RUSSIA: Impressions of the Society and Manners of the Russians at Home. By a Lady, Ten Years' Resident in that Country. *Wood-cuts.* 12*mo, cloth.* New York, 1855

1095 ENGRAVINGS, Portraits, Views, Maps, etc., in Holland, Flanders, etc. *A collection of about* 2,000 *prints mounted in* 4 *imperial folio scrap-books, half russia, lettered as above.*

This collection comprises some fine and rare prints (published singly, and in old chronicles and other illustrated works), illustrating the history of the Netherlands at all the important epochs. The engravings have be n selected with care, some of them being very fine, and all in good condition, but chiefly with a view to their historical interest.

1096 ——— Collection of 173 Prints engraved by Pierre Daret, Jaspar Isac, Leonard Gaultier, etc. *Mounted and bound in an atlas folio volume, half russia, lettered* "Daret."

1097 ——— Caricatures, etc., by Hogarth, Cruikshank, Ibbetson, and others; with Songs and Verses beneath many of them. 189 *prints, various sizes, as published, by R. Sayer and Laurie & Whittle, London,* 1786–1821.

This collection contains a portrait of Wm. Henry West Betty ("The Young Roscius") on his first appearance at Drury Lane — in the character of Douglas, — December 10, 1804; many popular songs of the day, as sung at the theatres; political satires; and other humorous, rare, and curious prints.

1098 ——— Illustrations of an Old (American?) Edition of Bunyan's Pilgrim's Progress. 11 *wood-cuts*, $4\frac{1}{8} \times 2\frac{5}{8}$ *inches, clean.*

1099 ——— and Lithographs: including a Fine Portrait of Gustave Doré, *India proof;* Frith's "English Merry-Making, a Hundred Years Ago," *mounted;* Two fine large Lithographs, "Marry!" and "Don't Marry!" published by W. Untze, Berlin; Views in Europe and India, etc., etc. *Most of the lithographs colored.* 24 *prints, various sizes.*

1100 EPICS (The) of the Ton, or the Glories of the Great World; a Poem, in Two Books, with Notes and Illustrations. 12*mo, half calf.* London, 1807

1101 EPICTETUS. The Works of; consisting of his Discourses, in Four Books, the Enchiridion, and Fragments. A Translation from the Greek, based on that of Elizabeth Carter, by Thomas W. Higginson. 8*vo, cloth, uncut.* Large paper: *only* 75 *copies printed.* Boston, 1866

1102 EPIPHANIUS, Bishop of Constantia. Contra Octoginta Hæreses Opus Eximium, Panarium sive Capsula Medica appellatum, & in Libros quidem Tres, Tomos verò Septem divisum. Ejusdem D. Epiphanii Liber Ancoratus Omnem de Fide Christiana Doctrinam complectens. Ejusdem contra Octoginta Hæreses Operis à se conscripti Summa. Ejusdem Libellus de Ponderibus & Mensuris. Omnia Græcè conscripta, nunc'q Primùm in Lucem edita. *Folio, old calf, red edges; with book-plate of Thomas Morong, and MS. marginal notes.* First edition: *Greek text.* Basileae (1544)

This copy is well preserved, and shows a fine clear page, the characters being remarkably handsome.

1103 ERASMUS, DESIDERIUS. MORIÆ ENCOMIUM, or the Praise of Folly; made English from the Latin of Erasmus, by W. Kennet, Bishop of Peterborough. Adorn'd with Forty-eight Copper Plates, including the Effigies of Erasmus and Sir Thomas More, all neatly engraved from the Designs of the Celebrated Hans Holbeine. To which is prefix'd a Preface by the Translator, and Divers Copies of Commendatory Verses. The Fifth Edition.' 12*mo, half calf.* London, 1735

1104 ESSAYS AND POEMS. ON THE EMPLOYMENT OF TIME. Three Essays. The Third Edition, with Additions, 1754.— THE ART OF PRESERVING HEALTH; a Poem, in Four Books: I. Air; II. Diet; III. Exercise; IV. The Passions. By John Armstrong, M. D. The Third Edition, 1748.— THE PLEASURES OF IMAGINATION; a Poem, in Three Books. By Dr. Akenside, 1754.—THE CHACE; a Poem. By William Somerville, Esq. The Fourth Edition, 1757.— HOBBINOL, or the Rural Games; a Burlesque Poem, in Blank Verse. By William Somerville, Esq. The Fourth Edition, 1757.—*Together in* 1 *vol.,* 8*vo, old calf.* London, 1748–57

1105 ESSEX INSTITUTE. PROCEEDINGS OF THE. Vol. I., 1848 to 1856; Vol. II., 1856 to 1860. 2 *vols., imperial* 8*vo, half morocco, very neat, gilt tops, uncut.* Salem, 1856–62

1106 ETHEREGE, SIR GEORGE. DRAMATIC WORKS: the Comical Revenge, or Love in a Tub; She wou'd if She cou'd; the Man of Mode, or Sir Fopling Flutter. Acted at His Highness the Duke of York's Theatre, in Lincolns Inn-Fields. 12*mo, calf.* J. Tonson, London, 1723

1107 EUROPEAN SCENERY: a Fine Set, comprised in the following Works:—

BATTY. Italian Scenery; from Drawings made in 1817 by Miss Batty. *Engraved title and* 61 *plates, with descriptions.* Rodwell & Martin, London, 1820

BATTY. French Scenery; from Drawings made in 1819 by Captain Batty. *Engraved title and* 65 *plates, with descriptions in French and English.* Rodwell & Martin, London, 1822

BATTY. Scenery of the Rhine, Belgium, and Holland; from Drawings by Captain Batty, F. R. S., etc. *Engraved title and* 61 *plates, with descriptions in French and English.* R. Jennings, London, 1826

BATTY. Hanoverian and Saxon Scenery; from Drawings by Lieut. Colonel Batty, F. R. S., etc. *Engraved title and* 61 *plates, with* 60 *wood-cut vignettes and descriptions in French and English.* R. Jennings, London, 1829

COCKBURN. Swiss Scenery; from Drawings by Major Cockburn. *Engraved title and* 61 *plates, with descriptions.* Rodwell & Martin, London, 1820

LOCKER. Views in Spain; by Edward Hawke Locker, Esq., F. R. S. *Vignette on title and* 60 *plates, with descriptions.* J. Murray, London, 1824

Together, 6 *vols., imperial* 8*vo, uniformly bound, half green morocco, marbled edges.* London, 1820–29

The plates in the above works, except the "Views in Spain" (which were drawn on stone by Westall, Harding, and Hullmandel), are engraved by Finden, Pye, H. Le Keux, Goodall, and other eminent engravers.

1108 EUSTACE, REV. JOHN CHETWODE. A CLASSICAL TOUR THROUGH ITALY, AN. MDCCCII. Sixth Edition, with an Additional Preface, and Translations of the Various Quotations from Ancient and Modern Authors. *Large map of Italy, plans of churches, index, etc.* 4 *vols.,* 8*vo, half calf, neat, marbled edges.* London, 1821

"A much admired work." — *Lowndes.*

1109 EVANS, AUGUSTA J. BEULAH. 12*mo, cloth.* New York, 1860

1110 EVANS, MARIAN. ADAM BEDE; by George Eliot. 12*mo, cloth.* New York, 1860

1111 EVANS, MARIAN. THE MILL ON THE FLOSS; by George Eliot. 12*mo, cloth.* New York, 1860

1112 EVANS, THOMAS. OLD BALLADS, Historical and Narrative, with some of Modern Date; now first collected, and reprinted from Rare Copies and MSS., with Notes, by Thomas Evans. 2 *vols., small* 8*vo, half calf.* T. Evans, London, 1784

1113 EVELYN, JOHN. MEMOIRS Illustrative of the Life and Writings of John Evelyn, Esq., F. R. S., Author of the "Sylva," etc., etc.; comprising his Diary, from the Year 1641 to 1705–6, and a Selection of his Familiar Letters: to which is subjoined the Private Correspondence between King Charles I. and his Secretary of State, Sir Edward Nicholas, whilst his Majesty was in Scotland, 1641, and at other Times during the Civil War; also between Sir Edward Hyde, afterwards Earl of Clarendon, and Sir Richard Browne, Ambassador to the Court of France, in the Time of Charles I. and the Usurpation. The Whole now first published from the Original MSS.; Edited by William Bray, Esq. Second Edition. *Portraits, views, plans, pedigree, etc.* 2 *vols., royal* 4*to, sprinkled calf, green edges.* BEST QUARTO EDITION: *fine copy.* London, 1819

1114 EVELYN, JOHN. ANOTHER COPY: *the same.* 2 *vols., royal* 4*to, original boards, rough edges.* London, 1819

1115 EVELYN, JOHN. DIARY AND CORRESPONDENCE OF; to which is subjoined the Private Correspondence between King Charles I. and Sir Edward Nicholas, and between Sir Edward Hyde, afterwards Earl of Clarendon, and Sir Richard Browne. Edited from the Original MSS. at Wotton, by William Bray, Esq., F. A. S. A New Edition, corrected, revised, and enlarged. *Portraits, etc.* 4 *vols., crown 8vo, cloth, uncut.* Colburn & Co., London, 1857

1116 EVERARD, JOANNES SECUNDUS. THE KISSES. Joannis Secundi Basia. (Latin and English, with an Essay on the Life and Writings of Secundus.) *Frontispiece and portrait (on the engraved title) by Bartolozzi. Crown 8vo, russia, very neat, gilt edges, by Mackenzie.* FINE COPY. London, 1779

1117 EVERETT, ALEXANDER H. NEW IDEAS ON POPULATION; with Remarks on the Theories of Malthus and Godwin. *8vo, half calf.* O. Everett, Boston, 1823

1118 EVERETT, EDWARD. ORATIONS AND SPEECHES, on Various Occasions. *Portrait on India paper.* 3 *vols., imperial 8vo, dark blue turkey morocco, extra, gilt edges.* LARGE PAPER: *uniform with Webster.* Boston, 1850–59

The fourth volume has not yet been issued on large paper.

1119 EVERETT, EDWARD. AN ORATION DELIVERED AT PLYMOUTH, December 22, 1824. (With Notes, pp. 63–73.) *8vo, pp.* 73, *paper, clean.* Boston, 1825

This oration is entitled "First Settlement of New England" in the "Orations and Speeches."

1120 EVERETT, EDWARD. AN ADDRESS DELIVERED AT CHARLESTOWN August 1, 1826, in Commemoration of John Adams and Thomas Jefferson. *8vo, pp.* 36, *paper, clean.* Boston, 1826

1121 EVERETT, EDWARD. EULOGY ON THOMAS DOWSE, of Cambridgeport, pronounced before the Massachusetts Historical Society, 9th December, 1858. With the Introductory Address by Robert C. Winthrop, President of the Society, and an Appendix. *Portraits of Thomas Dowse and Edward Everett, and view of the Dowse Library.* Boston, 1859

1122 EVERETT, EDWARD. ORATION DELIVERED BEFORE THE CITY AUTHORITIES OF BOSTON, on the Fourth of July, 1860; together with the Speeches at the Dinner in Faneuil Hall, and other Ceremonies at the Celebration of the Eighty-fourth Anniversary of American Independence. *8vo, cloth.* Boston, 1860

1123 EVERETT, EDWARD. THE LIFE OF GEORGE WASHINGTON. (Written for the Encyclopædia Britannica.) *Portrait of Everett from a bust, appendix, and index. 12mo, cloth.* New York, 1860

1124 EVERETT MEMORIAL. MEMORIAL OF EDWARD EVERETT (from the New-England Historic-Genealogical Society). *Two portraits (one on India paper), view of library, and view (colored) of birthplace. 4to, paper, uncut.* LARGE PAPER: *only* 75 *copies printed in this style, and* 4 *on drawing paper.* Boston, 1865

1125 EVERETT MEMORIAL. A MEMORIAL OF EDWARD EVERETT, from the City of Boston. *Two fine portraits, one on*

India paper. Printed by order of the City Council. 4to, cloth. Boston, 1865

1126 EVERY BODY'S TOAST BOOK AND CONVIVIAL COMPANION; containing the Choicest Collection ever issued, and Brimming Over with Toasts and Sentiments for all Classes and all Occasions. By an Adept. *Wood-cuts. 18mo, cloth.* Philadelphia, (1851)

1127 EVERY SATURDAY; a Journal of Choice Reading selected from Foreign Current Literature. *From January 6, 1866, to December 28, 1867, inclusive. 4 vols., imperial 8vo; first vol. cloth, rest in numbers.* Boston, 1866–67

1128 EXCELSIOR: HELPS TO PROGRESS in Religion, Science, and Literature. *Wood-cuts. 6 vols., post 8vo, half morocco, neat.* London, 1854–56

1129 EYRE, LIEUT. VINCENT, R. A. THE MILITARY OPERATIONS AT CABUL, which ended in the Retreat and Destruction of the British Army, January, 1842; with a Journal of Imprisonment in Affghanistan. *Glossary, plan, etc. 12mo, half calf, neat.* J. Murray, London, 1843

"I will ask you to read the Narrative of Lieutenant Eyre, and remind you of the description there given of the greatest disaster that ever befell a British army." — *Sir R. Peel, in the House of Commons.*

1130 FABER, JOHN. THE KIT-CAT CLUB; done from the Original Paintings of Sir Godfrey Kneller, by Mr. Faber. *Frontispiece and 47 portraits of the members, in mezzotinto, by* JOHN FABER. BRILLIANT IMPRESSIONS. *Royal folio, old mottled calf, gilt.* LARGE PAPER: *original issue.* J. Tonson and J. Faber, London, 1735

An edition was published (royal 4to) in 1821, with biographical sketches, pp. 261, of which some were printed on large paper (small folio), but it should not be mistaken for the above as it bears no comparison. Of the edition of 1821 the "Quarterly Review" (Vol. XXVI. p. 425) says: "We do not hesitate to say, that any one, however slightly acquainted with the political or literary history of the country, must pronounce it one of the most blundering pieces of patchwork that the scissors of a hackney editor ever produced."

1131 FABYAN, ROBERT. THE NEW CHRONICLES OF ENGLAND AND FRANCE, in Two Parts, by Robert Fabyan; named by himself the Concordance of Histories. Reprinted from Pynson's Edition of 1516; the First Part collated with the Editions of 1533, 1542, and 1559; and the Second with a Manuscript of the Author's Own Time, as well as the Subsequent Editions; including the Different Continuations. To which are added, a Biographical and Literary Preface, and an Index; by Henry Ellis. *Royal 4to, russia, neat, marbled edges.* London, 1811

1132 FALCONER, WILLIAM. THE POETICAL WORKS OF (with Life by the Rev. John Mitford, Notes and Illustrations). *Foolscap 8vo, cloth, uncut.* ALDINE EDITION. W. Pickering, London, 1836

1133 FAMILY (THE) TUTOR: (English Grammar, Natural Geography, Popular Geology, Popular Astronomy; and Miscellanies). *Wood-cuts, 4 vols., square 12mo, cloth.* London, (1851–52)

1134 FAMOUS (THE), PLEASANT, AND DELIGHTFUL HISTORY OF PALLADINE OF ENGLAND, discoursing of Honourable Adventures, of Knightly Deeds of Arms, and Chivalry; interlaced likewise with the Love of Sundry Noble Personages, as Time and Affection limited their Desires. Herein is no Offence offered to the Wife by Wanton Speeches, or Encouragement to thé Loose by Lascivious Matter. Translated out of French by A. M. [Anthony Munday], one of the Messengers of her Majesties Chamber. The Second Edition. Printed by J. F. and sold by John Marshall, etc. *With 2 wood-cuts. "The Printer to the Reader" signed "T. J." Small 12mo, old calf.* London, s. a.

1135 FANSHAWE, ANN, LADY. MEMOIRS OF LADY FANSHAWE. Wife of Sir Richard Fanshawe, Bart., Ambassador from Charles the Second to the Courts of Portugal and Madrid; written by herself. With Extracts from the Correspondence of Sir Richard Fanshawe. (Edited, with Preface and Introductory Memoir, by Sir N. Harris Nicolas.) New Edition. *Portrait, post 8vo, half green morocco.* London, 1830

1136 FARINI, LUIGI CARLO. THE ROMAN STATE, from 1815 to 1850. Translated from the Italian by (and under the Direction of) the Right Hon. W. E. Gladstone. 4 *vols.*, 8*vo, polished calf, gilt, marbled edges, by Hayday.* J. Murray, London, 1851–54

1137 FARIS EL-SHIDIAC. A PRACTICAL GRAMMAR OF THE ARABIC LANGUAGE, with Interlineal Reading Lessons, Dialogues, and Vocabulary; by Faris el-Shidiac. Second Edition, by the Rev. Henry G. Williams, B. D., Professor of Arabic in the University of Cambridge. *Foolscap 8vo, cloth.* London, 1866

1138 FARNHAM, LUTHER. A GLANCE AT PRIVATE LIBRARIES. *8vo, cloth, gilt edges. Presentation copy, with autograph of the author.* Boston, 1855

1139 FARRAR, MRS. JOHN. RECOLLECTIONS OF SEVENTY YEARS. *Post 8vo, cloth.* Boston, 1866

1140 FEDERALIST (THE); A COMMENTARY ON THE CONSTITUTION OF THE UNITED STATES: a Collection of Essays by Alexander Hamilton, Jay, and Madison. Also, the Continentalist, and other Papers by Hamilton. Edited by John C. Hamilton. *Portrait, 2 vols., imperial 8vo, cloth, uncut.* LARGE PAPER: *only* 100 *copies printed, for E. French, New York.* Philadelphia, 1865

1141 FEDERALIST. ANOTHER COPY: *the same. 2 vols., imperial 8vo, cloth, uncut.* Philadelphia, 1865

1142 FELLOWES, William D. Historical Sketches of Charles the First, Cromwell, Charles the Second, and the Principal Personages of that Period; including the King's Trial and Execution: to which is annexed an Account of the Sums exacted by the Commonwealth from the Royalists, and the Names of all those who compounded for their Estates; with other Scarce Documents. Illustrated by Fifty Lithographic Plates. *4to, half morocco, very neat, gilt top. Only 45 plates.* London and Paris, 1828

This work was printed for the author, at Paris, and only a limited edition. In all the copies which the compiler of this catalogue has met with the same five plates are wanting, and it is very probable that they never were issued.

1143 FELLOWES, William D. Another copy: *the same somewhat stained. 4to, half morocco, neat, gilt top.* London and Paris, 1828

1144 FELTHAM, Owen. Resolves; Divine, Moral, and Political. *Foolscap 8vo, cloth, uncut.* W. Pickering, London, 1840

This edition (reprinted from the fourth) contains the *genuine* text, no alterations having been made except in orthography. For an account of this work see "Retrospective Review," Vol. X. pp. 343–355.

1145 FELT, Joseph Barlow. An Historical Account of Massachusetts Currency. *8vo, cloth.* Boston, 1839

1146 FELTON, Cornelius Conway. Greece, Ancient and Modern. *Portrait. 2 vols., royal 8vo, cloth.* Boston, 1867

1147 FÉNELON, François de Salignac de la Mothe. Les Aventures de Télémaque. *Handsomely printed on vellum paper. Engraved title and 96 plates by Tilliard after Monnet. 2 vols., imperial 4to, half crimson morocco, extra, uncut.* Imprim. de Monsieur, Paris, 1785

1148 FÉNELON, François de Salignac de la Mothe. The Adventures of Telemachus; from the French, by the late John Hawkesworth: corrected and revised by G. Gregory, D. D. With a Life of the Author; and a Complete Index, Historical and Geographical. *With 12 plates by W. Skelton, etc., after Stothard. 2 vols. in one, 4to, calf.* London, 1795

1149 FÉNELON, François de Salignac de la Mothe. The Adventures of Telemachus; translated from the French. With Notes, by the Author of the Dissertation on the Parian Chronicle [Joseph Robertson]. *Portrait and 23 plates inserted. 2 vols., 12mo, diamond russia; with bookplate of Thos. Jolley, Esqr., F. S. A.* Illustrated copy. London, 1795

1150 FERGUSSON, Robert. The Works of. *Portrait, and vignette on title. 12mo, cloth, uncut.* Best edition. Edinburgh, (1851)

1151 FERRANA, JACQUES, M. D. ΕΡΩΤΟΜΑΝΙΑ, or a Treatise discoursing on the Essence, Causes, Symptomes, Prognosticks, and Cure of Love, or Erotique Melancholy. [Translated from the French, by Ed. Chilmead.] *Small 8vo, old calf; with autograph of Mrs. Elizabeth Corbett,* 1677, *and a curious book-plate (in rhyme) of Charles Clark, of Totham Hall, Essex.*
Printed by L. Lichfield, for E. Forrest, Oxford, 1640

1152 FERRARIO, GIULIO. IL COSTUME ANTICO E MODERNO, o Storia del Governo, della Milizia, della Religione, delle Arti, Scienze, ed Usanze di tutti i Popoli Antichi e Moderni; provata coi Monumenti dell' Antichita' e rappresentata cogli Analoghi Disegni, dal Dottor Giulio Ferrario. Edizione Seconda, riveduta ed accresciuta. *Above* 1,800 *colored plates of the costumes, habits, sports, etc., of all nations. Asia,* 8 *vols.; Africa,* 4 *vols.; America,* 4 *vols.; Europe,* 10 *vols. in* 15. *Together,* 31 *vols.,* 8*vo, half morocco, uncut.*
V. Batelli, Firenze, 1823, etc.

1153 FERRIAR, JOHN, M. D. ILLUSTRATIONS OF STERNE; with other Essays and Verses. Second Edition. 2 *vols. in* 1, *crown* 8*vo, cloth, uncut.* BEST EDITION. London, 1812
This edition contains the "Dialogue in the Shades," "The Bibliomania, and Epistle to Richard Heber, Esq.," the "Shandy Library," etc.

1154 FESSENDEN, THOMAS GREEN. TERRIBLE TRACTORATION, and other Poems; by Christopher Caustic, M. D. [T. G. Fessenden]. Fourth American Edition; to which is prefixed, Caustic's Wooden Booksellers and Miseries of Authorship. *Frontispiece.* 16*mo, cloth.* Boston, 1837

1155 FESTIVAL (THE) OF LOVE; being the Choicest Collection of Amatory Epistles ever published. New Edition. 12*mo, pp. xi. and* 418. *Half green calf, very neat.*
Published by M. Thomas, Philadelphia, 1820
A collection of songs, etc. (belonging to the class known as "Facetiæ"), with the above title and imprint.

1156 FIEFFÉ, EUGÈNE. NAPOLÉON Ier, ET LA GARDE IMPÉRIALE. Texte par Eugène Fieffé, des Archives de la Guerre; Dessins par Raffet. *Frontispiece and* 20 *colored plates. Royal* 4*to, green turkey morocco, extra, gilt edges.*
Paris, 1859

1157 FIELDING, HENRY. THE WORKS OF; with the Life of the Author [by Arthur Murphy]. *Portrait, etched by J. Basire after Hogarth, inserted in first volume.* 4 *vols.,* 4*to, diamond russia, neat.* VERY FINE COPY.
London, 1762

1158 FIELDING, HENRY. THE HISTORY OF TOM JONES, a Foundling. With a Memoir of the Author, by Thomas Roscoe, Esq., and Illustrations, by George Cruikshank. 2 *vols., post* 8*vo, boards, uncut.* London, 1831

1159 FIGUIER, GUILLAUME LOUIS. THE WORLD BEFORE THE DELUGE. A New Edition, the Geological Portion carefully revised, and much Original Matter added, by Henry W. Bristow, F. R. S., etc. Containing Thirty-four Full-page Illustrations of Extinct Animals and Ideal Landscapes of the Ancient World, designed by Riou; and Two Hundred and Two Figures of Animals, Plants, and other Fossil Remains and Restorations. *8vo, cloth, uncut.*
New York (London), 1867

1160 FIGUIER, GUILLAUME LOUIS. THE VEGETABLE WORLD; being a History of Plants, with their Botanical Descriptions and Peculiar Properties. Illustrated with 446 Engravings, interspersed through the Text, and 24 Full-page Illustrations; chiefly drawn from Nature by M. Faguet. *Thick 8vo, cloth, uncut.* New York, 1867

1161 FILANGIERI, GAETANO. CIENCIA DE LA LEGISLACION, nuevamenta traducida, por Don Juan Ribera. Segunda Edicion, revista y corregida. 6 *vols., 12mo, sheep, marbled edges.* Burdeos (Paris), 1823

1162 FILHOL, ANTOINE MICHEL. GALERIE DU MUSÉE NAPOLÉON; publiée par Filhol, Graveur, et rédigée par [Joseph] La Vallée. Dédiée à S. M. l'Empereur Napoléon Ier. *Above 720 beautiful engravings by the most eminent French engravers, comprising paintings by the great masters, sculptures, bas-reliefs, etc. 10 vols., royal 8vo, blue morocco, extra, gilt edges, arms on sides.* FINE COPY: *early impressions.*
Filhol, Paris, 1804–15

This work contains engravings of *all* the chief paintings, etc., concentrated by Bonaparte, before they were again dispersed, while no other work contains above *two thirds* of them.

1163 FINDEN, WILLIAM AND EDWARD. LANDSCAPE ILLUSTRATIONS OF THE BIBLE, consisting of [96] Views of the most Remarkable Places mentioned in the Old and New Testament; from Original Sketches taken on the Spot, engraved by W. and E. Finden. With Descriptions by the Rev. Thomas Hartwell Horne. 2 *vols., royal 8vo, morocco.*
J. Murray, London, 1836

1164 FINDEN, WILLIAM AND EDWARD. THE ROYAL GALLERY OF BRITISH ART. *Contains 48 large and beautiful engravings by the first engravers, after the best pictures of British artists; India proofs. With descriptive letter-press. 2 vols. in 1, atlas folio, morocco, inlaid and elaborately tooled.* A FINE SPECIMEN OF BIBLIOPEGISTIC ART.
J. Hogarth, London, s. a.

1165 FINLAY, HUGH. JOURNAL KEPT BY HUGH FINLAY, Surveyor of the Post Roads on the Continent of North America, during his Survey of the Post Offices between Falmouth and Casco Bay, in the Province of Massachusetts, and Savannah, in Georgia; begun the 13th September 1773, and ended 26th June 1774. (With an Introduction by Frank H. Norton.) *Fac-similes of 2 pen-and-ink maps, etc. Imperial 4to, half green morocco, gilt top.* LARGE PAPER: *Only 25 copies printed.* Brooklyn, 1867

This work is printed *verbatim et literatim* from the original MS. in the possession of Mr. Norton. (See "Introduction.")

1166 FISCHEL, DR. EDWARD. THE ENGLISH CONSTITUTION. Translated from the Second German Edition, by Richard Jenery Shee. *8vo, cloth, uncut.* London, 1863

1167 FISHER, JOHN D., M. D. DESCRIPTION OF THE DISTINCT, CONFLUENT, AND INOCULATED SMALL POX, Varioloid Disease, Cow Pox, and Chicken Pox. Illustrated by Thirteen Plates. Second Edition. *Royal 4to, boards.* Boston, 1834

1168 FISHER, THOMAS. COLLECTIONS, HISTORICAL, GENEALOGICAL, AND TYPOGRAPHICAL, FOR BEDFORDSHIRE; etched and engraved on 114 Copper Plates from the Original Drawings, by (or under the Direction of) Thomas Fisher, Esq., F. S. A., etc. *Contains 117 plates, many of which are colored, comprising churches, priories, castles, old houses, doorways, monuments, brasses, tombs, fonts, crosses, ancient sculpture, and other antiquities. Royal folio, half morocco, uncut.* LARGE PAPER: *fine impressions.* London, 1812–36

1169 FISHER, THOMAS. ANCIENT, ALLEGORICAL, HISTORICAL, AND LEGENDARY PAINTINGS, in Fresco, discovered in the Summer of 1804, on the Walls of the Chapel of the Trinity, belonging to the Gilde of the Holy Cross, at Stratford-upon-Avon, in Warwickshire; from Drawings, made at the Time of their Discovery, by Thomas Fisher, F. S. A.: also, a View and Plan of the Chapel; a View of New Place, the Residence of William Shakspeare; Fac-similes of Various Grants and Indulgences to the Gilde, with Representations of One Hundred and Fifty Ancient Seals appended to them; Fac-simile Extracts from the Register of the Gilde, the Rolls of Accounts, etc. Described by John Gough Nichols, F. S. A. *Contains 56 fine plates, many of them colored in imitation of the originals. Royal folio, half morocco.* LARGE PAPER: *fine impressions.* London, 1838

1170 FISKE, REV. SAMUEL. MR. DUNN BROWNE'S EXPERIENCES IN THE ARMY. [By the Rev. Samuel Fiske.] *Portrait. Post 8vo, cloth.* Boston, 1866

1171 FITZCLARENCE, LIEUT. COL. GEORGE. JOURNAL OF A ROUTE ACROSS INDIA, through Egypt to England, in the Latter End of the Year 1817, and the Beginning of 1818. *Folding map and 18 plates of plans, views, costumes, etc., most of them colored. 4to, half russia.* J. Murray, London, 1819

The "Quarterly Review" refers to this work as a "lively and interesting narrative." — *Vol. XXIII. p.* 230, *note.*

1172 FITZWILLIAM (THE) MUSEUM, Cambridge, being Illustrations and Descriptions of the Collection of Ancient Marbles, Specimens of Ancient Bronze, and Various Ancient Fictile Vases, in the Fitzwilliam Museum, Cambridge, formerly in the Possession of John Disney, Esq., F. R. S., at the Hyde, near Ingatestone. *Contains* 127 *plates, and descriptions by Mr. Disney and the Rev. James Tate. Three parts in* 1 *vol., imperial 4to, half olive morocco, neat, gilt top.* Longmans & Co., London, 1849

1173 FLAGG, WILSON. STUDIES IN THE FIELD AND FOREST. 12*mo, cloth.* Boston, 1857

1174 FLATTERS, J. J., SCULPTOR. THE PARADISE LOST OF MILTON; illustrated in a Series of Fifty-four Plates of the Human Figure, for the Use of Sculptors, Artists, etc. *Plates in outline. Royal folio, half morocco.* London, 1851

1175 FLEET, THOMAS AND JOHN. A POCKET ALMANACK for the Year of Our Lord 1794, being the Second after Leap Year, and Eighteenth of American Independence, calculated chiefly for the Use of the Commonwealth of Massachusetts, Boston, etc.: to which is annexed, the Massachusetts Register. 18*mo, pp.* 148, *paper.* Boston, 1793

1176 FLETCHER, GEORGE. STUDIES OF SHAKESPEARE in the Plays of King John, Cymbeline, Macbeth, As You Like it, Much Ado about Nothing, Romeo and Juliet; with Observations on the Criticism and the Acting of those Plays. 12*mo, boards.* Longmans & Co., London, 1847

1177 FLORENCE. VIEWS OF FLORENCE AND ENVIRONS. *A collection of* 29 *engravings of arches, cathedrals, squares, galleries, and other places of interest in or near Florence; colored by hand, in imitation of drawings. Without title. Oblong 4to, cloth, enclosed in case.* (Florence, cir. 1842)

1178 FLORENCE, GALLERY. TABLEAUX, STATUES, BAS-RELIEFS, ET CAMÉES, de la Galerie de Florence et du Palais Pitti; dessinés par Wicar, et gravés sons la Direction de C. L. Masquelier, avec les Explications par Mongez. *Nearly* 400 *beautiful engravings on above* 200 *plates.* 4 *vols. in* 2, *imperial folio, half crimson morocco, gilt tops, uncut.* ONLY 200 COPIES PRINTED. F. Didot Frères, Paris, 1852–56

"MM. Fermin Didot ayant acquis les cuivres de cet ouvrage [edition 1789–1821], les ont fait retoucher avec soin par le graveur le Maître et ont obtenu ainsi un tirage bien supérieur au précédent." — *Brunet.*

1179 FLORESTON, OR THE NEW LORD OF THE MANOR; comprising the History of a Rural Revolution from Vice and Misery to Virtue and Happiness. *With* 26 *engravings after J. Gilbert, etc.* 12*mo, cloth, uncut.* London, 1839

1180 FLORIST (THE), FRUITIST AND GARDEN MISCELLANY, *January–December* 1859. *Colored plates and wood-cuts.* 8*vo, half green morocco, extra, marbled edges.* London, (1859)

1181 FLÜGEL, DR. JOHN G. A PRACTICAL DICTIONARY OF THE ENGLISH AND GERMAN LANGUAGES. Part I. English-German. Part II. German-English. 2 *vols., thick crown 8vo, half morocco, neat.* Leipzig, 1847–52

1182 FOLKES, MARTIN. A TABLE OF ENGLISH SILVER COINS, from the Norman Conquest to the Present Time; with their Weights, Intrinsic Values, and some Remarks upon the Several Pieces. (With Appendix concerning the Coins minted in Scotland since the Union of the two Crowns; Addenda; and a Table of English Gold Coins, from the Eighteenth Year of King Edward the Third, when Gold was first coined in England.) *No plates. Royal 4to, old sprinkled calf, neat; with book-plate of Magens Dorrien Magens, Esqr.* Society of Antiquaries, London, 1745

1183 FOLKES, MARTIN. ANOTHER COPY: *with 7 plates. Royal folio, boards, rough edges; ruled throughout with red lines.* LARGE PAPER. London, 1745

1184 FOOTE, SAMUEL. MEMOIRS OF; with a Collection of his Genuine Bon-Mots, Anecdotes, Opinions, etc., mostly Original: and Three of his Dramatic Pieces not published in his Works. By William Cooke, Esq. *Portrait.* 3 *vols., foolscap 8vo, half morocco, neat.* R. Phillips, London, 1805

1185 FOOTE, SAMUEL. THE WORKS OF; with Remarks on Each Play, and an Essay on the Life, Genius, and Writings of the Author. By John Bee, Esq. [John Badcock]. *Portrait.* 3 *vols., 12mo, boards, uncut.* London, 1830

CONTENTS: The Knights; Taste; The Englishman in Paris; The Englishman Returned from Paris; The Author; The Minor; The Liar; The Orators; The Mayor of Garratt; The Patron; The Commissary; The Devil upon Two Sticks; The Lame Lover; The Maid of Bath; The Nabob; The Bankrupt; The Cozeners; A Trip to Calais; The Capuchin.

1186 FORBES, CHARLES STUART, R. N. ICELAND; its Volcanoes, Geysers, and Glaciers. *Map and 22 wood-cuts, 8vo, cloth, uncut.* J. Murray, London, 1860

1187 FORBES, EDWARD. LITERARY PAPERS; selected from his Writings in the "Literary Gazette." *Portrait. Post 8vo, cloth, uncut.* London, 1855

1188 FORCE, WILLIAM Q. PICTURE OF WASHINGTON AND ITS VICINITY FOR 1850; with Thirty-eight Engravings; also, the Washington Guide, containing a Congressional Directory, and much other Useful Information. *18mo, cloth.* Washington, 1850

1189 FOREIGN (THE) QUARTERLY REVIEW. *July*, 1827–*July*, 1846. 37 *vols., 8vo, half calf, neat, gilt tops, rough edges; with book-plates of David P. Kimball and T. Bigelow Lawrence.* COMPLETE SET. London, 1827–46

Incorporated with the "Westminster Review," after Vol. XXXVII.

1190 FORGUES, Emile Dauran. La Chine Ouvert: Aventures d'un Fan-Kouei dans le Pays de Tsin; par Old Nick. [E. D. Forgues.] Ouvrage illustré par Auguste Borget. *Fine impressions of the several hundred wood-cuts illustrative of the life, manners, etc., of the Chinese, comprising views, costumes, ceremonies, grotesques, etc., etc. 8vo, half morocco, very neat, gilt edges.* Paris, 1845

1191 FORREST, Thomas. A Voyage to New Guinea and the Moluccas from Balambangan, including an Account of Magindano, Sooloo, and other Islands; during 1774, 1775, and 1776, by Captain Thomas Forrest. To which is added, a Vocabulary of the Magindano Tongue. *Portrait and 31 plates, comprising maps, views, etc. 4to, old marbled calf, yellow edges.* London, 1779

"This work supplies what is wanting in Somerat, as it is full on the physical and moral character of the inhabitants, and on their language, mode of life and trade. Somerat relates to natural history, especially zoölogy and ornithology." — *Lowndes.*

1192 FORSTER, John. The Life and Adventures of Oliver Goldsmith; a Biography, in Four Books. *Portrait on title, wood-cuts, etc. 8vo, cloth.* London, 1848

1193 FORSYTH, Robert. The Beauties of Scotland: containing a Clear and Full Account of the Agriculture, Commerce, Mines, and Manufactures; of the Population, Cities, Towns, Villages, etc. of Each County. Embellished with Engravings. Proof impressions *of the numerous fine plates. 5 vols., royal 8vo, half green morocco, extra, marbled edges; uniform with "Beauties of England and Wales."* Large paper: *elegant copy.* Edinburgh, 1805–08

1194 FORSYTH, Robert. Another copy: *small paper; fine early impressions of the plates. 5 vols., 8vo, half russia, neat, gilt tops, rough edges; with book-plate of Charles Meigh.* Edinburgh, 1805–08

1195 FORSYTH, William. Life of Marcus Tullius Cicero; with Illustrations. *2 vols., imperial 8vo, cloth, rough edges.* Large paper: *only 75 copies printed.* New York, 1865

1196 FOSBROKE, Rev. Thomas Dudley. British Monachism, or Manners and Customs of the Monks and Nuns of England; to which are added, I. Peregrinatorium Religiosum, or Manners and Customs of Ancient Pilgrims. II. The Consuetudinal of Anchorets and Hermits. III. Some Account of the Continentes, or Persons who had made Vows of Chastity. IV. Four Select Poems, in Various Styles: 1. Economy of Monastic Life; Spenser. 2. Triumph of Vengeance, an Ode; Gray. 3. The Red Man, or Address of Buonaparte's Familiar Dæmon; Gray and Collins. 4. An Epitaph; the German Manner. A New Edition, very

much enlarged, and embellished with Numerous Plates. *4to, half morocco, gilt top, uncut.*
Bentley, London, 1817

Bound at the end of this copy are 21 plates of "Costumes of the Several Monastic Orders, selected from Steevens's Edition of Dugdale's 'Monasticon,'" with four pages of letter-press description.

1197 FOSBROKE, REV. THOMAS DUDLEY. ANOTHER COPY: Third Edition, with Additions. *Portrait and plates. Royal 8vo, cloth, uncut.* London, 1843

1198 FOSBROKE, REV. THOMAS DUDLEY. ENCYCLOPEDIA OF ANTIQUITIES, and Elements of Archæology, Classical and Mediæval. A New Edition, with Improvements. *Contains 107 plates. 2 vols., royal 8vo, cloth, uncut.*
London, 1843

1199 FOSTER, B. F. THE CLERK'S GUIDE, OR COMMERCIAL CORRESPONDENCE; comprising Letters of Business, Forms of Bills, Invoices, Account-Sales, Appendix, etc. *12mo, cloth.*
Boston, 1837

1200 FOX, JOHN. ACTS AND MONUMENTS OF MATTERS MOST SPECIAL AND MEMORABLE, happening in the Church, with an Universal History of the same; wherein is set forth at Large the Whole Race and Course of the Church from the Primitive Age to these Later Times of Ours, with the Bloody Times, Horrible Troubles, and Great Persecutions against True Martyrs of Christ, sought and wrought as well by Heathen Emperors, as now lately practised by Romish Prelates, especially in this Realm of England and Scotland: now again as it was recognized, perused, and recommended to the Studious Reader, by the Author, Mr. John Fox. Whereunto are annexed certain Additions of like Persecutions which have happened in these Later Times; to which also is added the Life of the Author both in Latine and English. The Ninth Edition. *Portrait, by J. Sturt, and plates. 3 vols., folio, old marbled calf; rebacked.* BEST EDITION.
London, 1684

1201 FRANÇAIS (LES) PEINTS PAR EUX-MÊMES: Encyclopédie Morale du Dix-neuvième Siècle. *Fine impressions of the many hundred wood-cuts, after Gaviran (Paul Sulpice Chevallier), Henri Monnier, etc.; the large ones colored. 5 vols., imperial 8vo, boards.* Paris, 1840–42

1202 FRANÇAIS (LES) PEINTS PAR EUX-MÊMES; Encyclopédie Morale du Dix-neuvième Siècle. PROVINCE. *Fine impressions of the numerous wood-cuts. 2 vols., imperial 8vo, half crimson morocco, neat.* Paris, 1841

1203 FRANCE, ILLUSTRATED; exhibiting its Landscape Scenery, Antiquities, Military and Ecclesiastical Architecture, etc. Drawings by Thomas Allom, Esq. Descriptions by the Rev. G. N. Wright, M. A. *Nearly 100 fine engravings by Le Keux,*

Willmore, Wallis, etc., etc. 3 *vols. in* 1, 4*to, morocco antique, gilt edges.* London, s. a.

1204 FRANCIS I., OF FRANCE. THE LIFE AND TIMES OF FRANCIS THE FIRST, King of France. *Portrait.* 2 *vols.,* 8*vo, half calf, neat.* London, 1829

1205 FRANKLIN, BENJAMIN. THE WORKS OF: containing Several Political and Historical Tracts not included in any Former Edition, and Many Letters, Official and Private, not hitherto published. With Notes and a Life of the Author, by Jared Sparks. *Portraits and plates.* 10 *vols., imperial* 8*vo, cloth, uncut.* LARGE PAPER: *subscriber's copy.* Boston, 1836–40

1206 FRANKLIN, BENJAMIN. THE LIFE OF; containing the Autobiography, with Notes and a Continuation. By Jared Sparks. *Engraved title, portraits, etc.* 8*vo, half morocco.* Boston, 1844

1207 FRANKLIN, BENJAMIN. CORRESPONDANCE INÉDITE ET SECRÈTE DU DOCTEUR B. FRANKLIN, Ministre Plénipotentiaire des États-Unis d'Amérique près la Cour de France, depuis l'Année 1753 jusqu'en 1790; offrant, en Trois Parties Complètes et Bien Distinctes, 1° les Mémoires de sa Vie Privée; 2° les Causes Premières de la Révolution d'Amérique; 3° l'Histoire des Diverses Négociations entre l'Angleterre, la France, et les États-Unis. Publiée pour la Première Fois, en France, avec des Notes, Additions, etc. *Portrait and fac-simile.* 2 *vols., crown* 8*vo, half morocco.* Paris, 1817

1208 FRANKLIN, SIR JOHN. NARRATIVE OF A JOURNEY TO THE SHORES OF THE POLAR SEA, in the Years 1819–20–21–22; by John Franklin, Capt. R. N., etc., and Commander of the Expedition. Third Edition. *Maps.* 2 *vols.,* 8*vo, calf, very neat.* J. Murray, London, 1824

1209 FRASER'S MAGAZINE FOR TOWN AND COUNTRY. *February,* 1830–*December,* 1858. *Portraits, etc.* 58 *vols.,* 8*vo, half calf, neat.* London, 1830–58

1210 FREEMAN, STRICKLAND. THE ART OF HORSEMANSHIP altered and abbreviated, according to the Principles of the late Sir Sidney Medows. *With* 16 *large and many small plates.* 4*to, cloth, uncut.* Printed for the Author, by W. Bulmer & Co., London, 1806

1211 FREEMASON'S (THE) MONITOR, OR ILLUSTRATIONS OF MASONRY; by a Royal Arch Mason, K. T., K. of M., etc., etc. In Two Parts; Part II. containing an Account of the Ineffable Degrees of Masonry. (Followed by Songs; and, the Constitution of the General Grand Royal Arch Chapter, of the Northern States of America, as ratified at Providence, January 9, 1799.) *Together in* 1 *vol.,* 16*mo, sheep.* Albany, 1797–99

1212 FREEMASON'S (THE) MONTHLY MAGAZINE. By Charles W. Moore, Grand Secretary of the Grand Lodge of Massachusetts. *Vols. XI.–XVIII., November,* 1851–*October,* 1859. 8 *vols.,* 8*vo, half morocco.* Boston, 1852–59

1213 FREESE, JOHN HENRY. EVERYBODY'S BOOK, or Gleanings Serious and Entertaining, in Prose and Verse, from the Scrap-Book of a Septuagenarian. Part I. Religion. Part II. Education. Part III. Woman, Poets of Persia, Duties of the Affluent. Part IV. United States of America, Brazil. Edited by John H. Freese, formerly a Merchant in London and Rio de Janeiro, etc., etc. *Thick crown* 8*vo, cloth, uncut.* London, 1860

1214 FRENEAU, PHILIP. POEMS, written and published during the American Revolutionary War, and now republished from the Original Manuscripts; interspersed with Translations from the Ancients, and other Pieces not heretofore in Print. The Third Edition. *Frontispieces.* 2 *vols.,* 12*mo, old calf, gilt.* Philadelphia, 1809

1215 FRIES, J. G. GUIDE OF ENGLISH AND GERMAN CONVERSATION. 12*mo, paper.* Aarau, 1836

1216 FRITH, FRANCIS. EGYPT AND PALESTINE, photographed and described by. *Portrait and* 75 *beautiful photographic views.* 2 *vols. in* 1, *crimson levant morocco, extra, gilt edges.* AN ELEGANT COPY. London, (1857)

1217 FROISSART, JEAN. SIR JOHN FROISSART'S CHRONICLES of England, France, Spain, Portugal, Scotland, Brittany, Flanders, and the Adjoining Countries, translated from the Original French, at the Command of King Henry the Eighth, by John Bourchier, Lord Berners. Reprinted from Pynson's Edition of 1523, and 1525, with the Names of Places and Persons carefully corrected. To which are added a Memoir of the Translator and a Copious Index [by E. V. Utterson]. 2 *vols., royal* 4*to, russia, neat, marbled edges.* London, 1812

See ARNOLD, RICHARD, and HUMPHREYS, H. N.

1218 FROTHINGHAM, REV. O. B. STORIES FROM THE LIPS OF THE TEACHER. *Wood-cuts. Square post* 8*vo, cloth.* Boston, 1863

1219 FROUDE, JAMES ANTHONY. HISTORY OF ENGLAND, from the Fall of Wolsey to the Death of Elizabeth. *Vols. I.–IV., imperial* 8*vo, cloth, rough edges.* LARGE PAPER: *only* 100 *copies printed.* New York, 1865–66

1220 FRYER, JOHN, M. D. A NEW ACCOUNT OF EAST INDIA AND PERSIA, in Eight Letters, being Nine Years' Travels, begun in 1672 and finished 1681; containing Observations made of the Moral, Natural, and Artificial Estate of those Countries, namely: of their Government, Religion, Laws, Customs; of the Soil, Climate, Seasons, Health, Diseases;

of the Animals, Vegetables, Minerals, Jewels; of their Housing, Cloathing, Manufactures, Trades, Commodities; and, of the Coins, Weights, and Measures used in the Principal Places of Trade in those Parts. *Portrait by R. White, maps, etc. Folio, old calf.*

Ri. Chiswell, London, 1698

1221 FULLER, REV. ANDREW. THE CALVANISTIC AND SOCINIAN SYSTEMS, examined and compared, as to their Moral Tendency; in a Series of Letters, addressed to the Friends of Vital and Practical Religion. The Second Edition, with Corrections and Additions. *8vo, half morocco.*

London, 1794

1222 FULLER, HIRAM. SPARKS FROM A LOCOMOTIVE, or Life and Liberty in Europe; by the Author of "Belle Brittan's Letters" [H. Fuller]. *12mo, cloth.*

New York, 1859

1223 FULLER, SARAH MARGARET (OSSOLI). PAPERS ON LITERATURE AND ART. *Parts I. and II. 2 vols., 12mo, cloth.*

London, 1846

1224 FULLER, THOMAS, D. D. A PISGAH-SIGHT OF PALESTINE AND THE CONFINES THEREOF; with the History of the Old and New Testaments acted thereon. *Numerous maps, plans, etc., engraved by Vaughan, Cross, Goddard, Marshall, etc. Folio, old calf, gilt, red edges; with autographs of Robert Southey on fly-leaf and title.* FINE COPY.

London, 1650

"This curious and singular book is not a mere geographical work, but contains many things relating to Jewish antiquities, and to the manners and customs of the people, and incidentally illustrates a number of passages of Scripture." — *Lowndes.*

1225 FULLER, THOMAS, D. D. THE HISTORY OF THE WORTHIES OF ENGLAND. A New Edition, containing Brief Notices of the most Celebrated Worthies of England who have flourished since the Time of Fuller, with Explanatory Notes and Copious Indexes; by P. Austin Nuttall, LL. D. *Portrait. 3 vols., 8vo, sprinkled calf, gilt, marbled edges.*

T. Tegg, London, 1840

1226 FULLER, THOMAS, M. D. INTRODUCTIO PRUDENTIAM; or, Directions, Counsels, and Cautions, tending to Prudent Management of Affairs in Common Life. The Second Part; to which is added an Appendix, concerning Sincerity and Deceit. The Whole compiled by Thomas Fuller, M. D. *12mo, calf.* S. Austen, London, 1727

1227 GAGE, THOMAS. NOUVELLE RELATION, contenant les Voyages de Thomas Gage dans la Nouvelle Espagne ses Diverses Aventures & son Retour par la Province de Nicaragua jusques à la Havane; avec la Description de la Ville de Mexique, telle qu'elle étoit Autrefois, & connue

elle est à Present, ensemble une Description Exacte des Terres & Provinces que possedent des Espagnols en toute l'Amérique, de la Forme de leur Gouvernement Ecclesiastique & Politique, de leur Commerce, de leurs Mœurs, & de celles des Criolles, des Metifs, des Mulatres, des Indiens, & des Negres. Quatrième Édition revûë & corrigée. *Maps and plates.* 2 *vols.*, 12*mo*, *old calf, red edges.*
P. Marret, Amsterdam, 1720

1228 GAIL, JEAN BAPTISTE. LE PHILOLOGUE, ou Recherches Historiques, Militaires, Géographiques, Grammaticales, Lexicographiques, etc., spécialement d'après Hérodote, Thucydide, et Xénophon (pour servir à l'Etude de l'Histoire Ancienne). *Without atlas.*—ANTHOLOGIE POÉTIQUE GRECQUE, ou Extraits de Différens Auteurs; avec la Traduction Interlinéaire Latine & Française, & Notes Grammaticales & Critiques (1801). *Together*, 25 *vols. in* 21, *with maps, fac-similes, etc.* 3 *vols.*, 8*vo*, *old calf, gilt, marbled edges;* 18 *vols.*, 8*vo*, *half calf, neat. With autographs of Jno. Pickering and Rufus Choate.* Paris, 1801–28

1229 GALIFFE, JAMES AUGUSTUS. ITALY AND ITS INHABITANTS; an Account of a Tour in that Country in 1816 and 1817, containing a View of Characters, Manners, Customs, Governments, Antiquities, Literature, Dialects, Theatres, and the Fine Arts: with some Remarks on the Origin of Rome and of the Latin Language. 2 *vols.*, 8*vo*, *half calf, neat.* J. Murray, London, 1820

1230 GALIGNANI'S NEW PARIS GUIDE: to which is added a Description of the Environs. *Map and plates.* 16*mo*, *roan.*
Paris, 1842

1231 GALIGNANI'S NEW PARIS GUIDE FOR 1854. *Plan of Paris in pocket.* 16*mo*, *roan.* Paris, (1854)

1232 GALILEI, GALILEO. LE OPERE DI; Prima Edizione Completa, condotta sugli Autentici Manoscritti Palatini, e dedicati a S. A. I. e R. Leopoldo II., Granduca di Toscana. *Portrait on India paper, and plates. Vols. I.–IV. Imperial* 8*vo*, *boards, uncut.* LARGE PAPER.
Società Editrice Fiorentina, Firenze, 1842–44

1233 GALLERY (THE) OF PORTRAITS; with Memoirs. Published under the Superintendence of the Society for the Diffusion of Useful Knowledge. *Contains* 168 *portraits with memoirs by different biographers.* 7 *vols.*, *imperial* 8*vo*, *half green morocco, neat, gilt tops, uncut, by Hering.*
C. Knight, London, 1833–37

1234 GALT, JOHN. STORIES OF THE STUDY. Second Edition. 3 *vols.*, 12*mo*, *half calf.* London, 1834

1235 GAMBA, BARTOLOMEO DA BASSANO. OMAGGIO DELLE PROVINCIE VENETE alla Maestà di Carolina Augusta, Imperatrice d'Austria. [La Presente Edizione è fatta per

Cura di Bartolomeo Gamba di Bassano Socio Onorario della R. Accademia di Belle Arti, etc.] *A series of* 18 *plates of sculptures and paintings. Royal folio, half calf.* Venezia, 1818

1236 GANDY, JOSEPH. THE RURAL ARCHITECT; consisting of Various Designs for Country Buildings, accompanied with Ground Plans, Estimates, and Descriptions. *Contains* 42 *plates. Royal 4to, boards, uncut.* J. Harding, London, 1805

1237 GARRICK, DAVID. THE DRAMATIC WORKS OF; to which is prefixed a Life of the Author. 3 *vols.*, 12*mo, sheep.* London, 1798

1238 GASPARIN, AGÉNOR ÉTIENNE, COMTE DE. AMERICA BEFORE EUROPE: Principles and Interests. Translated from Advance Sheets, by Mary L. Booth. Third Edition. 12*mo, cloth.* New York, 1862

1239 GASPARIN, MALÉRIE BOISSIER, COMTESSE DE. HUMAN SADNESS. *Foolscap* 8*vo, cloth, uncut.* London (Edinburgh), 1864

1240 GAUTIER, THÉOPHILE. WANDERINGS IN SPAIN. *Woodcuts. Crown* 8*vo, cloth.* London, 1853

1241 GAY, JOHN. POEMS, on Several Occasions. First Edition, *with* 2 *plates*, ETCHED BY W. KENT, *and other embellishments.* 2 *vols.*, 4*to, calf.* London, 1720

1242 GAY, JOHN. FABLES. *Plates, engraved by G. Scotin, Jun., and G. Vander Gucht, after Gravelot, Wootton, and Kent.* 2 *vols. in* 1, 8*vo, diamond calf, gilt, marbled edges.* London, 1753–55

Vol. I., "Seventh Edition," *J. & R. Tonson and J. Watts*, 1753; Vol. II., "Fifth Edition," *J. & P. Knapton*, 1755.

1243 GAZUL, CLARA. THE PLAYS OF CLARA GAZUL, a Spanish Comedian; with Memoirs of her Life (by Joseph L'Estrange). *Post* 8*vo, half morocco.* London, 1825

1244 GELL, SIR WILLIAM; and JOHN P. GANDY. POMPEIANA: The Topography, Edifices, and Ornaments of Pompeii. New Edition. *With* 81 *plates and many vignettes, engraved by G. Cooke, J. Le Keux, C. Heath, J. Pye, and others.* 2 *vols., imperial* 8*vo, cloth, uncut.* London, 1824

This is the second edition of the original series, containing information obtained prior to 1819, with a second title dated 1821.

1245 GELL, SIR WILLIAM; and JOHN P. GANDY. ANOTHER COPY: Third Edition. *With* 83 *plates (two being added to this edition).* 1 *vol., royal* 8*vo, morocco extra, panelled, gilt edges.* London, 1852

1246 GENEST, JOHN. SOME ACCOUNT OF THE ENGLISH STAGE, from the Restoration in 1660 to 1830. [By John Genest.] 10 *vols.*, 8*vo, cloth, uncut.* Bath, 1832

1247 GENLIS, Stéphanie Félicité Ducrest de St. Aubin, Comtesse de. Petrarch and Laura. Translated from the French. 2 *vols. in* 1, 12*mo, half calf, neat.*
London, s. a.

1248 GENLIS, Stéphanie Félicité Ducrest de St. Aubin, Comtesse de. Manuel du Voyageur, en Six Langues: Angloise, Allemande, Françoise, Italienne, Espagnole, et Russe. Cinquième Édition, revue et considerablement augmentée. *Small square 8vo, paper.*
L. Piazzini, Florence, 1831

1249 GENTLEMAN'S (The) Magazine, or Monthly Intelligencer; by Sylvanus Urban, Gent. *January*, 1731–*December*, 1853. 194 *vols.*, 8*vo, calf, yellow edges.*
London, 1731–1853

1250 GENTLEMAN'S Magazine. Duplicate volumes: *for* 1758 *and* 1759. 2 *vols.*, 8*vo, old calf.*
London, 1758–59

1251 GENTLEMAN'S Magazine. A Selection of Curious Articles from. By John Walker, LL. B., etc. Third Edition. 4 *vols.*, 8*vo, half calf.* London, 1814

Vol. I. Researches, Historical and Antiquarian.
Vol. II. 1st. Ancient and Modern Literature, Criticism, and Philology.
2d. Philosophy and Natural History.
Vol. III. 1st. Letters to and from Eminent Persons.
2d. Miscellaneous Articles, including Anecdotes of Extraordinary Persons, Useful Projects and Inventions, etc., etc.
Vol. IV. Biographical Memoirs, Literary Anecdotes, and Characters. Topographical Notices.

1252 GERANDO, Joseph Marie, Baron de. Self-Education, or the Means and Art of Moral Progress; translated from the French. *Royal 8vo, boards, rough edges.*
Boston, 1830

1253 GERHARD, Johann. Johannis Gerhardi SS. Theol. D. et in Academia Jenensi Professoris, Locorum Theologicorum cúm pro Adstruenda Veritate, túm pro Destruenda quorumvis Contradicentium Falsitate, per Theses nervosè, solidè, & copiosè explicatorum. Tomi I.–IV. *In* 1 *vol., folio, old calf, red edges; with autograph of J. G. Percival.* Genevæ, 1639

For contents see Darling's "Cyclopædia Bibliographica," col. 1237.

1254 GERMAN (The) Theatre; translated by Benjamin Thompson, Esq. Fourth Edition. 6 *vols., small* 12*mo, smooth morocco, contents lettered, marbled edges.* London, 1811

Contents: The Stranger; Rolla; Pizarro; Don Carlos; Count Benyowsky; Lovers' Vows; Deaf and Dumb; Indian Exiles; False Delicacy; Otto of Wittlesbach; Dagobert; Adelaide of Wulfingen; The Robbers; The Happy Family; Conscience; The Ensign; Count Koenigsmark; Stella; Emelia Galotti.

1255 GIBBON, Edward. The History of the Decline and Fall of the Roman Empire. 8 *vols., royal* 8*vo, half green*

morocco, neat, gilt tops. Portrait wanting. LARGE PAPER: *only* 50 *copies printed.*
Talboys, Oxford, and Pickering, London, 1827
One of the "Oxford English Classics."

1256 GIBBON, EDWARD. THE HISTORY OF THE DECLINE AND FALL OF THE ROMAN EMPIRE. With Notes by the Rev. H. H. Milman. 8 *vols.*, 8*vo, cloth, uncut.* Paris, 1840

1257 GIBBON, EDWARD. THE HISTORY OF THE DECLINE AND FALL OF THE ROMAN EMPIRE. With Notes by the Rev. H. H. Milman. Second Edition. *Colored maps and a general index.* 6 *vols.*, 8*vo, calf, gilt.*
J. Murray, London, 1846

1258 GIBSON, WILLIAM SIDNEY. THE HISTORY OF THE MONASTERY FOUNDED AT TYNEMOUTH, in the Diocese of Durham, to the Honour of God, under the Invocation of the Blessed Virgin Mary and S. Oswin, King and Martyr. *With* 19 *large plates and numerous initial letters and wood-cuts, comprising views, fac-similes, etc.; the etchings on India paper, and many of the plates and the initials* HIGHLY ILLUMINATED IN GOLD AND COLORS. 2 *vols., royal* 4*to, half morocco, uncut. Published for the author.* SUBSCRIBER'S COPY: ONE OF ONLY 12 COPIES COLORED BY HAND.
W. Pickering, London, 1846–47

1259 GIDDINGS, JOSHUA R. HISTORY OF THE REBELLION; its Authors and Causes. 8*vo, cloth.* New York, 1864

1260 GIFFARD, EDWARD. A SHORT VISIT TO THE IONIAN ISLANDS, ATHENS, AND THE MOREA. *Map.* 12*mo, half calf, neat, marbled edges.* Paris, 1838

1261 GIFFARD, REV. GEORGE. A DIALOGUE CONCERNING WITCHES AND WITCHCRAFTES; in which is laide open how craftely the Divell deceiveth not onely the Witches but many other, and so leadeth them Awrie into many great Errours. By George Giffard, Minister of God's Word in Maldon. *Small* 4*to, half calf; with book-plate of the Hon*[ble] *Frederic North.* **Black letter**; FIRST EDITION.
London, 1593
This tract was reprinted by the Percy Society.

1262 GILDON, CHARLES. THE LIFE OF MR. THOMAS BETTERTON, the late Eminent Tragedian; wherein the Action and Utterance of the Stage, Bar, and Pulpit, are distinctly considered: with the Judgment of the late Ingenious Monsieur de St. Evremond upon the Italian and French Music and Opera's, in a Letter to the Duke of Buckingham. To which is added, the Amorous Widow, or the Wanton Wife; a Comedy, written by Mr. Betterton: now first printed from the Original Copy. *Portrait by Vander Gucht, after Kneller.* 8*vo, old calf.* London, 1710
In this copy the dedication is not signed.

1263 GILDON, CHARLES. ANOTHER COPY: *with the "Epistle Dedicatory" signed "Charles Gildon." Portrait wanting. 8vo, old calf, red edges.* London, 1710

1264 GILLIES, JOHN. THE HISTORY OF ANCIENT GREECE, its Colonies, and Conquests; from the Earliest Accounts till the Division of the Macedonian Empire in the East: including the History of Literature, Philosophy, and the Fine Arts. The Second Edition. *Portrait and maps. 4 vols., 8vo, sprinkled calf, green edges.* London, 1787

1265 GILLILAND, THOMAS. THE DRAMATIC MIRROR, containing the History of the Stage from the Earliest Period to the Present Time; including a Biographical and Critical Account of all the Dramatic Writers from 1660, and also of the most Distinguished Performers, from the Days of Shakspeare to 1807: and a History of the Country Theatres in England, Ireland, and Scotland. *Portraits and plates. 2 vols., 12mo, half russia.* London, 1808

1266 GILRAY, JAMES. CARICATURES. *The 45 suppressed plates. Atlas folio, half crimson turkey morocco, extra, gilt edges, by Wright.* (London), s. a.

1267 GILRAY, JAMES; THOMAS ROWLANDSON; etc., etc. Caricatures, drawn and etched by those Celebrated Artists Gilray, Rowlandson, Cruikshanks, etc. *Nearly 300 caricatures. Atlas folio, half morocco.* (London), s. a.

This volume has no title, the above being taken from the frontispiece, which also bears this address: "Gentlemen. In presenting to your notice this Volume of Caricatures, I am desired in the names of the Publishers, Artists, etc., also from myself and large- long- and small-headed brethren, to assure you that we have at considerable trouble and expense produced a very amusing and interesting series of subjects, which we trust will contribute to dispel *ennui* by exciting the risible faculties of all who may favor them with a perusal. Sincerely hoping that our exertions will be appreciated and merit your patronage and support we respectfully take our leave."

1268 GILMAN, MRS. CAROLINE. THE POETRY OF TRAVELLING IN THE UNITED STATES. With Additional Sketches, by a Few Friends; and a Week among Autographs, by Rev. S. Gilman. *12mo, cloth.* New York, 1838

1269 GILMORE, JAMES RUSSELL. DOWN IN TENNESSEE, and Back by Way of Richmond. By Edmund Kirke [J. R. Gilmore.] *12mo, cloth.* New York, 1864

1270 GILPIN, REV. WILLIAM. AN ESSAY UPON PRINTS: containing Remarks upon the Principles of Picturesque Beauty, the Different Kinds of Prints, and the Characters of the most Noted Masters; illustrated by Criticisms upon Particular Pieces. To which are added some Cautions that may be Useful in Collecting Prints. Second Edition. *With Index. Post 8vo, sprinkled calf, gilt, green edges.* London, 1768

1271 GLEANER (THE); A MISCELLANEOUS PRODUCTION. By Constantia. *3 vols., 12mo, sheep. Bindings broken and title to first volume wanting.*
I. Thomas & E. T. Andrews, Boston, Feb., 1798

1272 GLOVER, Richard. Leonidas, a Poem (in Twelve Books). The Seventh Edition. *Portrait by Fittler, and plates by Bartolozzi, Heath, etc., after Stothard, etc. Printed by Whittingham. 2 vols., post 8vo, sprinkled calf, very neat.* London, 1804

Some plates as in the Du Roveray edition.

1273 GODEAU, Antoine, Évêque de Vence. Les Tableaux de la Penitence. Troisième Édition. *Fine plates by Chauveau, etc. 4to, old calf.* Paris, 1662

1274 GODWIN, Parke. Vala; a Mythological Tale. *Woodcuts and borders. 4to, cloth, gilt edges.* New York, 1851

1275 GODWIN, William. Life of Geoffrey Chaucer, the Early English Poet; including Memoirs of his Near Friend and Kinsman, John of Gaunt, Duke of Lancaster: with Sketches of the Manners, Opinions, Arts, and Literature of England in the Fifteenth Century. *Portrait of Chaucer by P. Condé and one of John of Gaunt by Ogbourne; also one, from a painting found in the house in which Cromwell was born, supposed to be of Chaucer. 2 vols., 4to, old tree calf, gilt.* Fine copy. London, 1803

1276 GOLD, Captain Charles, R. A. Oriental Drawings. Sketched between the Years 1791 and 1798. *A series of 50 finely colored plates, with descriptions and a glossary, illustrating manners, buildings, costumes, antiquities, etc.* London, 1806

1277 GOLDSBURY, J.; and W. Russell. The American Common School Reader and Speaker. *12mo, sheep.* Boston, s. a.

1278 GOLDSMITH, Oliver. The Miscellaneous Works of; including a Variety of Pieces now first collected. By James Prior. *Engraved titles by E. Finden. 4 vols., 8vo, calf, gilt, marbled edges.* J. Murray, London, 1837

1279 GOLDSMITH, Oliver. The Works of (printed from the Last Editions revised by the Author). Edited by Peter Cunningham, F. S. A. *Plate of monument in Westminster Abbey, and vignettes on the engraved titles. 4 vols., 8vo, calf, gilt, gilt edges.* J. Murray, London, 1854–5.

1280 GOLDSMITH, Oliver. The Traveller. With Thirty Illustrations designed expressly for the Art-Union of London. *Portrait and 30 engravings on wood by the best artists. 4to, half morocco, neat.* (London), 1851

1281 GOLDSMITH, Oliver. A History of the Earth and Animated Nature. With Numerous Notes from the Works of the most distinguished British and Foreign Naturalists. Illustrated by upwards of Two Thousand Figures. *Many of the plates colored. 2 vols., royal 8vo, half morocco, neat.* Glasgow, 1857

1282 GOMBERVILLE, Marin le Roy de. Moral Virtue Delineated. *Text both French and English, the translation by Thomas M. Gibbs. Frontispiece, portrait of Gomberville, engraved titles, and* 103 *plates, by Pierre Daret, after the plates of Otho Venius's Emblemata Horatiana. Two parts in* 1 *vol., folio, old calf, gilt.* (London, 1721 ?)

This copy has no title except "Moral Virtue Delineated" on the two engraved titles, which have been altered [apparently] from the plates used in the Paris edition of 1646. The portrait which has the first names Hellenized (" T[h]alassius Basilides a Gombervilla, ætat. suæ XLIII.") bears date of 1643. See Engravings, No. 1096.

1283 GOMEZ, Madeleine Angelica Poisson, Madame de. La Belle Assemblée, or the Adventures of Six Days; being a Curious Collection of Remarkable Incidents which happen'd to some of the First Quality in France. Written in French for the Entertainment of the King. Translated into English. Compleat in Three Parts. The Second Edition. 3 *parts in* 1 *vol., small* 8*vo, old calf.* London, 1725

1284 GOMEZ, Madeleine Angelica Poisson, Madame de. La Belle Assemblée: being a Curious Collection of some very Remarkable Incidents which happened to Persons of the First Quality in France; interspersed with Entertaining and Improving Observations made by them on Several Passages in History, both Ancient and Modern. Adorn'd with Copper-Plates. The Fourth Edition. 4 *vols.,* 12*mo, old calf.* London, 1736

This edition contains "Seventeen Days."

1285 GOOD Words; edited by Norman Macleod, D. D. *Vol. I. Royal* 8*vo, cloth.* Edinburgh, 1860

1286 GORDON, Thomas. The Pillars of Priestcraft and Orthodoxy Shaken. (Consisting of Tracts collected or written by Thomas Gordon.) The Second Edition (edited by the Rev. Richard Baron). 4 *vols., small* 12*mo, old calf.* London, 1768

1287 GORI, Antonio Francesco. Museum Etruscum exhibens Insignia Veterum Etruscorum Monumenta Aereis Tabulis CC.: nunc Primum edita et illustrata Observationibus Antonii Francisci Gorii, Publici Historiarum Professoris. 2 *vols., folio, old mottled calf, gilt, backs cracked; with book-plate of James Herbert, Esq., of Tythorpe, in the County of Oxford.* Florentiae, 1737

1288 GORI, Antonio Francesco. Antiqua Numismata Aurea et Argentea Praestantiora et Aerea, Maximi Moduli, quae in Regio Thesauro Magni Ducis Etruriae adservantur; cum Observationibus Antonii Francisci Gorii, Publici Historiarum Professoris. *Fine impressions of the plates.* 3 *vols., royal folio, old calf, red edges; with book-plate of Peter Hardy, F. R. S.* MUSEUM FLORENTINUM: MEDALS COMPLETE. Florentiae, 1740–42

1289 GORI, ANTONIO FRANCESCO. DACTYLIOTHECA SMITHIANA: Volumen Primum Gemmarum Ectypa et Antonii Francisci Gorii Enarrationes complectens; Volumen Alterum Historiam Glyptographicam Auctore Antonio Francisco Gorio exhibens. *Frontispiece, etc., and* 100 *fine plates of gems in the collection of the British consul Joseph Smith. In* 1 *vol., folio, russia, yellow edges.* FINE COPY. Venetiis, 1767

This work was published at the expense of George III.

1290 GOSS, WARREN LEE. THE SOLDIER'S STORY OF HIS CAPTIVITY AT ANDERSONVILLE, Belle Isle, and other Rebel Prisons. *Illustrated by Thomas Nast.* 12*mo, cloth.* Boston, 1867

1291 GÖTHE, JOHANN WOLFGANG VON. MEMOIRS OF GOËTHE, written by himself. *Portrait.* 2 *vols.*, 8*vo, half russia.* London, 1824

1292 GÖTHE, JOHANN WOLFGANG VON. THE WORKS OF: Autobiography, with Letters from Switzerland and Travels in Italy (2 vols.); Dramatic Works; Novels and Tales; Wilhelm Meister's Apprenticeship. (Translated by John Oxenford, A. J. W. Morrison, Anna Swanwick, Sir Walter Scott, and H. G. Bohn.) *Portraits.* 5 *vols., post* 8*vo, half calf, neat, marbled edges.* London, 1848–61

1293 GÖTHE, JOHANN WOLFGANG VON. FAUST; a Tragedy, in Two Parts. Translated into English Verse, by Jonathan Birch, Esq. INDIA PROOFS *of the* 40 *beautiful outline engravings, by John Brain, after Moritz Retzsch. Both parts in* 1 *vol., imperial* 8*vo, cloth, uncut; with book-plate of E. A. Hitchcock, U. S. Army.* LARGE PAPER. London, 1839–43

1294 GÖTHE, JOHANN WOLFGANG VON. ANOTHER COPY: *first part only, with* 29 *plates. Royal* 8*vo, half morocco.* London, 1839

1295 GÖTHE, JOHANN WOLFGANG VON. FAUST; eine Tragödie: mit Zeichnungen von Engelbert Seibertz. *Printed on a very fine thick paper; the plates engraved by Schleich, Storz, and other celebrated German engravers.* 2 *vols., atlas* 4*to, Vol. I., with plates on India paper, crimson turkey morocco, extra, emblematically tooled, carmine edges; Vol. II., crimson turkey morocco, extra, gilt edges.* Stuttgart, 1854–58

1296 GÖTHE, JOHANN WOLFGANG VON. THE MINOR POETRY OF GOETHE; a Selection from his Songs, Ballads, and other Lesser Poems. Translated by William Grassett Thomas. *Foolscap* 4*to, half olive morocco, red paper sides, rough edges.* Philadelphia, 1859

1297 GOUGH, RICHARD. SEPULCHRAL MONUMENTS IN GREAT BRITAIN, applied to illustrate the History of Families, Manners, Habits, and Arts, at the Different Periods from the Norman Conquest to the Seventeenth Century; with Introductory Observations. *Fine impressions of the plates.* 4 *vols., imperial folio, half turkey morocco, extra.* London, 1786–96

A very fine copy, almost entirely free from stains, and perfect with the exception of the Introduction to the second part, which is seldom met with, as most of that part of the work was destroyed by fire.

1298 GRAFTON, RICHARD. GRAFTON'S CHRONICLE, OR HISTORY OF ENGLAND; to which is added, his Table of the Bailiffs, Sheriffs, and Mayors, of the City of London, from the Year 1189 to 1558, inclusive. 2 *vols., royal* 4*to, neat, marbled edges.* London, 1809

See ARNOLD RICHARD.

1299 GRAHAM, MARIA. LETTERS ON INDIA. With Etchings and a Map. 8*vo, half russia, marbled edges.* London, 1814

1300 GRAHAM, MARIA. JOURNAL OF A VOYAGE TO BRAZIL, and a Residence there during Part of the Years 1821, 1822, 1823. *Plates and wood-cut vignettes.* 4*to, half calf, extra.* London, 1824

1301 GRAHAME, JAMES. THE HISTORY OF THE UNITED STATES OF NORTH AMERICA, from the Plantation of the British Colonies till their Assumption of National Independence. Second Edition, enlarged and amended. *Portrait.* 4 *vols.,* 8*vo, cloth, uncut.* Philadelphia, 1845

1302 GRANDVILLE, JEAN IGNACE ISIDORE GÉRARD. THE FLOWERS PERSONIFIED; being a Translation of Grandville's "les Fleurs Animés." By N. Cleaveland, Esq. Illustrated with Steel Engravings, beautifully colored. *Both series;* 2 *vols., imperial* 8*vo, morocco, extra, emblematically tooled, gilt edges.* New York, 1849

1303 GRANGER, REV. JAMES. A BIOGRAPHICAL HISTORY OF ENGLAND, from Egbert the Great to the Revolution; consisting of Characters disposed in Different Classes, and adapted to a Methodical Catalogue of Engraved British Heads: intended as an Essay towards reducing our Biography to a System, and a Help to the Knowledge of Portraits; interspersed with a Variety of Anecdotes, and Memoirs of a Great Number of Persons, not to be found in any other Biographical Work. With a Preface, showing the Utility of a Collection of Engraved Portraits to supply the Defect, and answer the Various Purposes, of Medals. By the Rev. James Granger, Vicar of Shiplake in Oxfordshire. Fifth Edition; with upwards of Four Hundred Additional Lives [by James Caulfield], and a Splendid Collection of Rare and Curious Portraits. *Illustrated with above* 200 *portraits, including the set of* "HOUBRAKEN'S HEADS," COMPLETE, *besides other fine ones by* VERTUE, ELSTRACKE, FAITHORNE, VAUGHN, *etc.* 3 *vols., folio, half russia, extra, marbled edges.* LARGEST PAPER: PRINTED FOR THE ILLUSTRATOR, *and but few copies.* London, (1824)

On the first appearance of this work, in 1769, the rage for illustrating became so prevalent and was carried to such an extent that, to illustrate it, fine works embellished with portraits were most unscrupulously mutilated (or "grangerized"), which gave rise to the terms "grangerite," etc.

Dr. Johnson, in a letter to Boswell, said, "I have read every word of Granger: it has entertained me exceedingly."

1304 GRANGER, REV. JAMES. ANOTHER COPY: Fourth Edition; with the Continuation, by the Rev. Mark Noble. *Illustrated with above* 400 *portraits (mounted), some of which are fine and rare, and most of them from the original plates engraved by celebrated artists.* THE LARGE PAPER (*royal* 8*vo*) EDITIONS, *interleaved with drawing paper, bound in* 14 *vols., royal* 4*to, and* 1 *vol. (indexes), royal* 8*vo, russia; with book-plate of Sir George Staunton, Bart.* London, 1804–06

1305 GRANT, CHARLES. THE LAST HUNDRED YEARS OF ENGLISH LITERATURE. (1760–1860.) *Crown* 8*vo, cloth, uncut.* London, 1866

1306 GRANVILLE, AUGUSTUS BOZZI, M. D. THE SPAS OF GERMANY. *Maps, views, etc.,* 2 *vols.,* 8*vo, calf, extra, marbled edges; with initials "B. A. L." [Lennox] in device on sides.* London, 1837

1307 GRANVILLE, AUGUSTUS BOZZI, M. D. ANOTHER COPY: Second Edition; with a Supplement, containing an Account of the Improvements effected at the Various Watering-Places since the Publication of the First Edition, and the Result of the Author's more extended Knowledge and Experience as regards the Several Mineral Waters therein mentioned. *Maps and wood-cuts,* 8*vo, cloth, uncut.* London, 1843

This edition has the author's name on title.

1308 GRASSET SAINT-SAUVEUR, JACQUES. L'ANTICA ROMA, ovvero Descrizione Storica e Pittorica di tutto ciò che riguarda il Popolo Romano ne' suoi Costumi, Militari, Religiosi, Pubblici, e Privati, da Romalo fino ad Augusto. Opera di J. Grasset Saint-Sauveur; liberamente tradotta ed arricchita di Note, da Francesco Gandini. *Portrait of Gandini and* 60 *colored plates. Royal* 4*to, half morocco.* Bergamo, 1825

1309 GRATTAN, THOMAS COLLEY. CIVILIZED AMERICA. *Map and statistical appendix.* 2 *vols., half calf, extra, marbled edges.* London, 1859

1310 GRAY, THOMAS. DESIGNS BY MR. R. BENTLEY, for Six Poems by Mr. T. Gray. *Printed on one side only of a thick paper; with* 6 *large plates and* 19 *smaller ones (including initials), engraved by J. Muller and C. Grignion.* BRILLIANT IMPRESSIONS. *Imperial* 4*to, old tree calf, gilt, yellow edges.* ORIGINAL EDITION: *fine copy.* London, 1753

1311 GRAY, THOMAS. THE CORRESPONDENCE OF THOMAS GRAY AND WILLIAM MASON; to which are added some Letters addressed by Gray to the Rev. James Brown, D. D., Master of Pembroke College, Cambridge. With Notes and Illustrations, by the Rev. John Mitford. *8vo, cloth, uncut; with autograph of Rufus Choate.* London, 1853

1312 GRAY, THOMAS. AN ELEGY WRITTEN IN A COUNTRY CHURCHYARD. *With 23 fine wood-cuts, chiefly after Birket Foster. Printed on one side only of a fine paper and interleaved. Crown 8vo, morocco, extra, gilt edges.* New YORK, 1857

1313 GREELEY, HORACE. THE AMERICAN CONFLICT, a History of the Great Rebellion in the United States of America, 1860–64. *Portraits of eminent persons, maps, plans, views, etc. 2 vols., royal 8vo, half calf, antique, marbled edges.* Hartford, 1864

1314 GREEN, JOHN. A NEW GENERAL COLLECTION OF VOYAGES AND TRAVELS, consisting of the most Esteemed Relations which have been hitherto published in any Language; comprehending everything Remarkable in its kind in Europe, Asia, Africa, and America, with Respect to the Several Empires, Kingdoms, and Provinces; their Situation, Extent, Bounds and Division, Climate, Soil and Produce; their Lakes, Rivers, Mountains, Cities, Principal Towns, Harbours, Buildings, etc.; and the Gradual Alterations that from Time to Time have happened in each: also the Manners and Customs of the Several Inhabitants; their Religion and Government, Arts and Sciences, Trades and Manufactures; so as to form a Compleat System of Modern Geography and History, exhibiting the Present State of all Nations. [Compiled by John Green.] *Maps, and numerous plates, by Grignion, etc., comprising views, antiquities, animals, costumes, customs, etc., etc. 4 vols., 4to, old calf, red edges.* T. Astley, London, 1745–47

This collection is commonly called "Astley's."

1315 GREEN, NELSON WINCH. FIFTEEN YEARS AMONG THE MORMONS; being the Narrative of Mrs. Mary Ettie V. Smith, late of Great Salt Lake City, a Sister of one of the Mormon High Priests, she having been Personally acquainted with most of the Mormon Leaders, and long in the Confidence of the "Prophet" Brigham Young. *Frontispiece 12mo, cloth.* New York, 1858

1316 GREENE, ROBERT. THE DRAMATIC WORKS OF; to which are added his Poems. With some Account of the Author, and Notes, by the Rev. Alexander Dyce, B. A. *2 vols., crown 8vo, crimson turkey morocco, gilt edges. Uniform with* PEELE *and* WEBSTER. ONLY 250 COPIES PRINTED. W. Pickering, London, 1831

Greene, who lived only to about the age of thirty-two years, was a popular poet of the Elizabethan period, and is said to have been the first author who wrote for bread, having wasted his property in dissipation. His plays are extremely rare, and have only once before been reprinted. Oldys speaks of him as "one of the greatest pamphleteers and refiners of our language in his time."

1317 GREENE, ROBERT. ANOTHER COPY: *the same.* 2 *vols., crown* 8*vo, calf, gilt, marbled edges.* W. Pickering, London, 1831

1318 GRIFFIN, REV. EDMUND DORR. REMAINS OF; compiled by Francis Griffin. With a Biographical Memoir of the Deceased, by the Rev. John McVicar, D. D. *Portrait,* 2 *vols.,* 8*vo, half russia.* New York, 1831

1319 GRIFFIN, GERALD. THE COLLEGIANS; a Tale of Garryowen. *Foolscap* 8*vo, cloth.* London, 1857

1320 GRIMALDI, JOSEPH. MEMOIRS OF; edited by "Boz" [Charles Dickens]. With Notes and Additions, revised by Charles Whitehead. *Portrait and* 10 *plates, by G. Cruikshank,* 16*mo, boards.* London, 1854

1321 GRIMM, HERMAN. LIFE OF MICHAEL ANGELO. Translated, with the Author's Sanction, by Fanny Elizabeth Bunnètt. *Portrait on India paper, and photographic plates.* 2 *vols., imperial* 8*vo, cloth, uncut.* LARGE PAPER: *only* 50 *copies printed.* Boston, 1866

1322 GROOTE (HET) TAFEREEL DER DWAASHEID, vertoonende de Opkomst, Voortgang, en Ondergang de Actie, Bubbel, en Windnegotie, in Vromkryk, Engeland, ende Nederlanden, gepleegt in den Jaare MDCCXX; zynde een Verzameling van alle de Conditien en Projectien van de Opgeregte Compagnien, van Assurantie, Navigatie, Commercie, &c. in Nederland, zo wel die in Gebruik zyn gebragt als die door de H. Staten van eenige Provintien zyn verworpen: als meede Konst-Plaaten, Comedien, en Gedigten, door Verscheide Liefhebbers uytgegeeven, tot Beschimpinge deezer Versoeijelyke en Bedrieglyke Handel, waar door in dit Jaar, Verscheide Familien en Persoonen van Hooge en Lage Stand zyn geruïneerd, en in haar Middelen verdorven, en de Opregte Negotie gestremt, zo in Vrankryk, Engeland, als Nederland. Gedrukt tot Waarschouwinge voor de Nakomelingen, in't Noodlottige Jaar, voor veel Zotte en Wyze. 1720. *Folio, boards.* (Amsterdam?) 1720

This curious collection contains eighty plates, including two portraits of John Law, one of Madame Law, caricatures, and other humorous and satirical plates illustrating the great "MISSISSIPPI BUBBLE;" with comedies, poems, etc. satirizing the same subject. The plates are all in good condition, many of them very well executed, but without engravers' marks. There is nothing to indicate by whom the collection was made, and there is no name of publisher or place of publication.

1323 GROSE, FRANCIS. THE ANTIQUITIES OF ENGLAND AND WALES, being a Collection of Views of the most Remarkable Ruins and Antient Buildings, accurately drawn on the Spot: to each View is added an Historical Account of its

Situation, when and by whom built, with every Interesting Circumstance relating thereto. Collected from the Best Authorities, by Francis Grose, Esq., F. A. S. The Second Edition, corrected and enlarged. WITH SUPPLEMENT. 8 *vols.* — ANTIQUITIES OF SCOTLAND. 2 *vols.* — ANTIQUITIES OF IRELAND. 2 *vols.* *Together*, 12 *vols.*, *imperial* 8*vo*, *half calf, very neat.* FINE IMPRESSIONS OF THE PLATES.
London, 1783, etc.

1324 GROSE, FRANCIS. ANTIQUITIES: ENGLAND AND WALES, WITH SUPPLEMENT, 8 *vols.*; SCOTLAND, 2 *vols.*; IRELAND, 2 *vols.* *Together*, 12 *vols.*, 4*to*, *half morocco, neat.*
London, 1783, etc.

This set was issued at the same time with the editions in imperial 8vo, and with equally fine impressions of the plates. The impressions of the plates in the editions published by Stockdale, some years subsequent, are very inferior, and Lowndes pronounces them "worthless."

1325 GROSE, FRANCIS. A TREATISE ON ANCIENT ARMOUR AND WEAPONS, illustrated by Plates taken from the Original Armour in the Tower of London, and other Arsenals, Museums, and Cabinets. *Very fine impressions of the plates.* 4*to*, *old marbled calf.* ORIGINAL EDITION.
London, 1786

1326 GROSE, FRANCIS. MILITARY ANTIQUITIES respecting a History of the English Army, from the Conquest to the Present Time. A New Edition, with Material Additions and Improvements. 2 *vols.*, *royal* 4*to*, *diamond calf, extra.* LARGE PAPER. London, 1812

This edition contains the "Ancient Armour."

1327 GROSE, FRANCIS. THE OLIO; being a Collection of Essays, Dialogues, Letters, Biographical Sketches, Anecdotes, Pieces of Poetry, Parodies, Bon Mots, Epigrams, Epitaphs, etc., chiefly Original. By the late Francis Grose, Esq., F. R. S., etc. Second Edition, corrected and enlarged, with a Portrait of the Author. 12*mo*, *half brown morocco, gilt top, rough edges.* VERY FINE COPY.
London, 1796

1328 GROSE, FRANCIS. A PROVINCIAL GLOSSARY; with a Collection of Local Proverbs, and Popular Superstitions. A New Edition, corrected. *Royal* 4*to*, *paper, rough edges.*
London, 1811

1329 GROTE, GEORGE. HISTORY OF GREECE: I. Legendary Greece. II. Grecian History to the Reign of Peisistratus at Athens. *Portrait, maps, plans, and index.* 12 *vols.*, 8*vo*, *cloth, uncut.* FINEST EDITION.
J. Murray, London, 1851–56

1330 GROTE, GEORGE. PLATO, AND THE OTHER COMPANIONS OF SOCRATES. 3 *vols.*, 8*vo*, *calf, gilt, marbled edges, by Hayday.* J. Murray, London, 1865

1331 GROVE, Rev. Henry. A System of Moral Philosophy, by the late Reverend and Learned Mr. Henry Grove, of Taunton; published from the Author's Manuscript, with his Latest Improvements and Corrections, by Thomas Amory. *2 vols., 8vo, old calf, gilt.* London, 1749

1332 GRUNER, Louis. Decorations de Palais et d'Eglises en Italie, peintes à Fresque ou exécutés en Stuc, dans le Coursdu XVème et du XVIème Siècle; avec Descriptions par Louis Gruner. Avec un Essai par Mons. J. J. Hittorff, sur les Arabesques des Anciens comparées à celles de Raphaël et de son École. Nouvelle Édition, considérablement augmentée. *With 56 plates after the original paintings of Raphael, Giulio Romano, Correggio, Bernardino, etc., many of them finely colored; also key-plates, highly finished in gold and colors, to illustrate the coloring of the plain engravings. Atlas folio, half crimson morocco, extra, gilt edges.* Paris et Londres, 1854

1333 GUASCO, Francesco Eugenio. Musei Capitolini Antiquae Inscriptiones; a Francisco Eugenio Guasco, ejusdem Musei Curatore P., nunc Primum conjunctim editae Notisque illustratae. *Vellum paper. Numerous fine plates. 3 vols., folio, half calf.* Romæ, 1775–78

1334 GUERCINO. (Giovanni Francesco Barbieri, called Guercino da Cento.) Eighty-two Prints, engraved by F. Bartolozzi, etc., from the Original Drawings of Guercino, in the Collection of his Majesty. *Without title. Atlas folio, cloth, rough edges.* Proofs. (J. Boydell, London, 1764)

1335 GUÉRIN, Eugénie de. Journal of; edited by G. S. Trebutien. *Post 8vo, cloth, uncut.* London, 1865

1336 GUICCIARDINI, Francesco. The Historie of Guicciardin: containing the Warres of Italie and other Partes, continued for manie Yeares under Sundrie Kings and Princes, together with the Variations and Accidents of the same; and also the Arguments, with a Table at Large, expressing the Principall Matters through the Whole Historie. Reduced into English, by Geffray Fenton. *Small folio, half calf.* London, 1599

1337 GUILD, Reuben Aldridge. The Librarian's Manual; a Treatise on Bibliography, comprising a Select and Descriptive List of Bibliographical Works: to which are added Sketches of Publick Libraries. *Wood-cuts of 16 library edifices. Printed by J. Munsell. Foolscap 4to, boards, uncut.* Only 50 copies printed: 10 *on large paper.* C. B. Norton, New York, 1858

1338 GUILLEVILLE, Guillaume de. The Ancient Poem of Guillaume de Guileville, entitled le Pelerinage de l'Homme, compared with the Pilgrim's Progress of John Bunyan; edited from Notes collected by the late Mr. Nathaniel Hill, of the Royal Society of Literature, with Illustrations and an Appendix. *Photographic portrait of Bunyan and* 40 *other illustrations on wood, copper, and stone, some of which are colored. Crown* 4*to, cloth, uncut.* London, 1858

The appendix contains part of a metrical translation made by John Lydgate, in 1426, printed from a MS. in the British Museum.

1339 GUIZOT, FRANÇOIS PIERRE GUILLAUME. CORNEILLE AND HIS TIMES. 8*vo, cloth uncut.* London, 1852

1340 GUIZOT, FRANÇOIS PIERRE GUILLAUME. SHAKSPEARE AND HIS TIMES. Second Edition. 8*vo, cloth, uncut.* London, 1852

1341 GUIZOT, FRANÇOIS PIERRE GUILLAUME. HISTORY OF THE ENGLISH REVOLUTION OF 1640, from the Accession of Charles I. to his Death. Translated by William Hazlitt. *Portrait of Charles I. Post* 8*vo, half calf, extra, marbled edges.* London, 1854

1342 GUTCH, JOHN MATTHEW. THE ROBIN HOOD GARLANDS AND BALLADS, with the Tale of the Lytell Geste: a Collection of all the Poems, Songs, and Ballads relating to this Celebrated Yeoman; to which is prefixed his History and Character, deduced from Documents hitherto unrevised. Edited by John Matthew Gutch, F. S. A.; and adorned with Cuts by F. W. Fairholt, F. S. A. 2 *vols.,* 8*vo, cloth.* London, 1850 and 1847

In the second volume is an outline portrait and memoir of Ritson. See RITSON, JOSEPH.

1343 GUTENBERG (JOHN), FIRST MASTER PRINTER; his Acts and most Remarkable Discourses, and his Death. From the German, by C. W. *Beautifully printed. Foolscap* 4*to, half olive morocco, brown paper sides, gilt top, uncut.* LARGE PAPER: *only* 100 *copies printed.* London, 1860

1344 HABINGTON, WILLIAM. THE HISTORIE OF EDWARD THE FOURTH, KING OF ENGLAND. *Portrait by Elstracke.* 4*to, half calf.* London, 1640

Anthony à Wood says that Thomas Habington, father of the author, "had a considerable hand" in this work, and that it was "written and published at the desire of K. Charles I. being then by many esteemed to have a stile sufficiently florid, and better becoming a poetical, than historical, subject."

1345 HABITS (THE) OF GOOD SOCIETY; a Handbook for Ladies and Gentlemen: with Thoughts, Hints, and Anecdotes concerning Social Observances, Nice Points of Taste and Good Manners; the Whole interspersed with Humorous Illustrations of Social Predicaments, Remarks on the History and Changes of Fashion, and the Difference of English and Continental Etiquette. 12*mo, cloth.* New York, 1864

1346 HAGHE, Louis. Portfolio of Sketches: Belgium and Germany, 1850. New series, *consisting of frontispiece and 26 large and beautiful views, colored in the manner of highly finished drawings; mounted on thick cardboard, atlas folio size, and enclosed in a portfolio; half morocco, gilt label on side.* London, 1850

1347 HALE, Charles R; S. Huntington Jones; and Henry Morton. Report of the Committee appointed by the Philomathean Society of the University of Pennsylvania to translate the Inscription on the Rosetta Stone. Second Edition. (With a Catalogue of Members of the Society.) *Finely executed in colors, the whole report being lithographed in fac-simile of the autograph copies of the committee, and each page enclosed in an appropriate and ornamental design. Foolscap 4to, cloth, gilt edges.* Philadelphia, (1859)

1348 HALES, John. The Works of the Ever-Memorable Mr. John Hales, of Eaton; now First Collected together. *3 vols., small 8vo, new sprinkled calf, gilt.* Very fine copy. R. & A. Foulis, Glasgow, 1765

"A very valuable edition, edited by Lord Hailes. Hales is styled by Wood 'the walking library!'" — *Lowndes.*

1349 HALIFAX, George Savile, Marquis of. A Character of King Charles the Second; and Political, Moral, and Miscellaneous Thoughts and Reflections. *Small 8vo, old calf.* J. & R. Tonson, London, 1750

1350 HALKETT, John. Statement respecting the Earl of Selkirk's Settlement upon the Red River in North America; its Destruction in 1815 and 1816; and the Massacre of Governor Semple and his Party. With Observations upon a Recent Publication, entitled "a Narrative of Occurrences in the Indian Countries," etc. *Map, by Arrowsmith. The enlarged edition (pp. 194) with appendix (pp. c.). 8vo, boards, rough edges.* J. Murray, London, 1817

1351 HALL, Basil. Account of a Voyage of Discovery to the West Coast of Corea, and the Great Loo-Choo Island; with an Appendix, containing Charts, and Various Hydrographical and Scientific Notices. And a Vocabulary of the Loo-Choo Language, by H. J. Clifford, Esq. *With 9 colored plates, besides the charts, of views, costumes, etc. 4to, calf, gilt, marbled edges.* J. Murray, London, 1818

"An interesting and pleasing work, extremely valuable for its maritime geography and science." — *Lowndes.*

1352 HALL, Basil. Extracts from a Journal written on the Coasts of Chili, Peru, and Mexico, in the Years 1820, 1821, 1822. Reprinted from the last London Edition. *2 vols., 12mo, half morocco.* Boston, 1824

1353 HALL, EDWARD. HALL'S CHRONICLE; containing the History of England during the Reign of Henry the Fourth, and the Succeeding Monarchs, to the End of the Reign of Henry the Eighth; in which are particularly described the Manners and Customs of those Periods. Carefully collated with the Editions of 1548 and 1550. [Edited by Sir Henry Ellis.] *Royal 4to, russia, neat, marbled edges.* London, 1809

See ARNOLD, RICHARD.

1354 HALL, JOSEPH. THE WORKS OF JOSEPH HALL, D. D., successively Bishop of Exeter and Norwich; with some Account of his Life and Sufferings, written by himself. A New Edition, revised and corrected; with Considerable Additions, a Translation of all the Latin Pieces, and a Glossary, Indices, and Notes [by the Rev. Peter Hall]. *Portrait, etc.* 12 *vols., 8vo, cloth, uncut.* BEST AND ONLY COMPLETE EDITION. D. A. Talboys, Oxford, 1837-39

For contents see Darling's "Cyclopædia Bibliographica," col. 1369-1372.

1355 HALL, NEWMAN, D. D. THE LAND OF THE FORUM AND THE VATICAN, or Thoughts and Sketches during an Easter Pilgrimage to Rome. *Foolscap 8vo, cloth, uncut.* London, 1854

1356 HALL, S. CARTER. GEMS OF EUROPEAN ART; the Best Pictures of the Best Schools. Edited by S. C. Hall, Esq., F. S. A. FIRST AND SECOND SERIES; *containing* 95 *fine plates by the best engravers.* 2 *vols., imperial 4to, half morocco.* London, 1846

1357 HALL, SAMUEL CARTER. THE BOOK OF GEMS; the Poets and Artists of Great Britain; the Modern Poets and Artists of Great Britain. Edited by S. C. Hall. *Selections from the poets, with brief memoirs and critical observations; plates of fac-simile autographs; and nearly* 150 *fine engravings, by the best engravers, after the most eminent British artists.* 3 *vols., 8vo, calf, extra, gilt edges.* London, 1848-53

1358 HALL, SAMUEL CARTER. THE BOOK OF BRITISH BALLADS. Edited by S. C. Hall, Esq. *Several hundred fine wood-cuts.* 1 *vol., 4to, cloth, gilt edges.* London, 1853

1359 HALL, S. CARTER, and ANNA MARIA. THE BOOK OF THE THAMES; from its Rise to its Fall. By Mr. and Mrs. S. C. Hall. *Numerous fine wood-cuts. Foolscap 4to, cloth, gilt edges.* London, 1859

1360 HALL, SAMUEL CARTER, and ANNA MARIA. IRELAND; its Scenery, Character, etc. By Mr. and Mrs. S. C. Hall. A New Edition. *Maps and* 550 *engravings on steel and wood.* 3 *vols., imperial 8vo, half calf, neat.* London, s. a.

1361 HALL, Mrs. Samuel Carter. Sketches of Irish Character. Illustrated Edition. *Numerous plates and wood-cuts. Royal 8vo, calf, gilt, gilt edges.* London, 1844

1362 HALL, William W., M. D. Health and Disease; a Book for the People. Third Edition. *12mo, cloth.* New York, 1860

1363 HALLAM, Henry. Historical Works. *9 vols., 8vo, tree calf, gilt, marbled edges.* J. Murray, London, 1837–48

This set comprises the following works: Introduction to the Literature of Europe, in the Fifteenth, Sixteenth, and Seventeenth Centuries; *first edition, 4 vols.*, 1837–39. View of the State of Europe during the Middle Ages; *eighth edition, 2 vols.*, 1841. Supplemental Notes to the View of the State of Europe; *1 vol.*, 1848. The Constitutional History of England from the Accession of Henry VII. to the Death of George II.; *fourth edition, 2 vols.*, 1842.

1364 HALLAM, Henry. Introduction to the Literature of Europe in the Fifteenth, Sixteenth, and Seventeenth Centuries. *4 vols. in 2, 8vo, half calf.* Paris, 1839

1365 HALLIWELL, James Orchard. The Life of William Shakespeare; including many Particulars respecting the Poet and his Family never before published. *Numerous fac-similes and wood-cuts, from drawings by F. W. Fairholt, F. S. A. 8vo, cloth, uncut.* London, 1848

1366 HALLIWELL, James Orchard. Another copy: *the same. 8vo, cloth, uncut.* London, 1848

1367 HALLIWELL, James Orchard. A Dictionary of Archaic and Provincial Words, Obsolete Phrases, Proverbs, and Ancient Customs; from the Fourteenth Century. Second Edition. *2 vols., 8vo, cloth, uncut.* London, 1850

1368 HALLIWELL, James Orchard. Some Account of the Antiquities, Coins, Manuscripts, Rare Books, Ancient Documents, and other Reliques, illustrative of the Life and Works of Shakespeare, in the Possession of James Orchard Halliwell, Esq., F. R. S. *Numerous wood-cuts, fac-similes, etc. 4to, cloth, uncut.* Printed for private circulation only; *on a very thick paper, and the edition* most strictly limited to 80 copies; *see printer's attestation.* Brixton Hill, 1852

On a fly-leaf of this copy is an autograph note of presentation by Mr. Halliwell to Zelotes Hosmer.

1369 HALLIWELL, James Orchard. Books of Characters, illustrating the Habits and Manners of Englishmen from the Reign of James I. to the Restoration; selected by James O. Halliwell, Esq., F. R. S. *Handsomely printed on a very thick paper, by J. E. Adlard. 4to, cloth, uncut.* Privately printed: only 25 copies, *see printer's attestation.* London, 1857

CONTENTS: I. The Wandering Jew telling Fortunes to Englishmen. *London*, 1649. — II. The Man in the Moone. *London*, 1609. — III. Stephens' Essayes and Characters. *London*, 1615. — IV. London and the Country Carbonadoed and Quartered. *London*, 1632. — V. Extracts from Breton's Fantasticks. *London*, 1626.

1370 HALLIWELL, JAMES ORCHARD. AN HISTORICAL SKETCH OF THE PROVINCIAL DIALECTS OF ENGLAND, illustrated by Numerous Examples. (With Specimens of the Early English Language, chronologically arranged.) *Finely printed on a tinted paper. Imperial 8vo, cloth, rough edges, wide margin.* J. Munsell, Albany, 1863

This essay forms the introduction to Mr. Halliwell's "Dictionary of Archaic and Provincial Words."

1371 HALLORAN, ALFRED LAURENCE. WAE YÀNG JIN: Eight Months' Journal, kept on Board one of her Majesty's Sloops of War, during Visits to Loochoo, Japan, and Pootoo. *Plates and wood-cuts. Crown 8vo, cloth, uncut.* London, 1856

1372 HAMERTON, PHILIP GILBERT. A PAINTER'S CAMP. Second Edition, revised. *Post 8vo, cloth, uncut.* London, 1866

1373 HAMILTON, ALEXANDER. THE WORKS OF: comprising his most Important Official Reports; an Improved Edition of the Federalist, on the New Constitution, written in 1788; and Pacificus, on the Proclamation of Neutrality, written in 1793. *Portraits of Hamilton, Jay, and Madison. 3 vols., 12mo, sheep.* New York, 1810

1374 HAMILTON, ANTHONY, COUNT. MÉMOIRES. Édition ornée de LXXII. Portraits, gravés d'après les Tableaux Originaux. *4to, crimson morocco, very neat, gilt edges.* Londres, (1793)

This edition contains 77 portraits and a view of Somer Hill; text, pp. 313; "Notes et Eclaircissemens," pp. 77; besides title, advertisement, table of names, and notice to the binder.

1375 HAMILTON, EMMA LYON, LADY. MEMOIRS OF; with Anecdotes of many of her most Particular Friends and Distinguished Contemporaries. *Portrait. Crown 8vo, sprinkled calf, extra.* London, 1815

1376 HAMILTON, SIR WILLIAM. PHILOSOPHY OF; arranged and edited by O. W. Wight. *8vo, half calf, extra; with autograph of Rufus Choate.* New York, 1853

1377 HAMMOND, WILLIAM A., M. D. ON WAKEFULNESS; with an Introductory Chapter on the Physiology of Sleep. *12mo, cloth.* Philadelphia, 1866

1378 HANCARVILLE, PIERRE FRANÇOIS-HUGUES D'. COLLECTION OF ETRUSCAN, GREEK, AND ROMAN ANTIQUITIES from the Cabinet of the Honble. W[m]. Hamilton. [Described by P. F. Hugues d'Hancarville.] *Descriptive letter-press in English and French, and above 130 plates, chiefly colored. Vols. I. and II., imperial folio, half morocco.* Naples, 1766

Sir Wm. Hamilton's valuable collection of vases, etc., was purchased by the English government, and is now in the British Museum.

1379 HANCARVILLE, PIERRE FRANÇOIS-HUGUES D'. MONUMENS DU CULTE SECRET DES DAMES ROMAINES, pour servir de Suite aux Monumens de la Vie Privée des XII. Césars. [Par P. F. Hugues d' Hancarville.] *Engraved title and* 50 *plates. 4to, old calf, gilt, yellow edges.* Sabellus, Caprée (Le Clerc, Nancy), 1784

1380 HANCARVILLE, PIERRE FRANÇOIS-HUGUES D'. VENERES ET PRIAPI, uti observantur in Gemmis Antiquis. *Engraved titles and* 70 *plates, with descriptions in English and French.* 2 *vols. in* 1, 8*vo, smooth morocco, extra, gilt edges.* LARGE PAPER. Lugd. Batavorum, s. a.

This work, which appears to have been published in London, has been attributed to M. d'Hancarville, and as many of the plates represent the same gems figured in the previous work, it has been deemed best to insert it here, although the author is not positively known.

1381 HAND-BOOK (A) FOR VISITORS TO OXFORD; illustrated by CXXVIII. Wood-cuts by Jewitt, and XXVIII. Steel Plates by Le Keux. A New Edition. *Royal* 8*vo, cloth, gilt top.* J. H. & J. Parker, Oxford, 1858

1382 HANNAH, JOHN, D. D. DISCOURSES ON THE FALL, and its Results. *Foolscap* 8*vo, cloth, uncut.* London, 1857

1383 HARBAUGH, REV. HENRY. THE TRUE GLORY OF WOMAN, as portrayed in the Beautiful Life of the Virgin Mary, Mother of Our Lord and Saviour Jesus Christ. 12*mo, cloth.* Philadelphia, 1858

1384 HARDEE, WILLIAM J. RIFLE AND LIGHT INFANTRY TACTICS. 2 *vols.*, 18*mo, cloth.* Philadelphia, 1861

1385 HARDING, CHESTER, ARTIST. MY EGOTISTIGRAPHY. Prepared for his Family and Friends, by one of his Children [Mrs. M. E. White]. 12*mo, cloth, red edges.* PRIVATELY PRINTED. Cambridge, 1866

1386 HARDINGE, CHARLES STEWART. RECOLLECTIONS OF INDIA, drawn on Stone by J. D. Harding, from the Original Drawings by Charles Stewart Hardinge. *A series of* 26 *large tinted plates, with descriptive letter-press. Complete, but without binding, atlas folio size.* London, 1847

1387 HARDY, FRANCIS. MEMOIRS OF THE POLITICAL AND PRIVATE LIFE OF JAMES CAULFIELD, Earl of Charlemont, Knight of St. Patrick, etc., etc., etc. Second Edition. *Portrait.* 2 *vols., half morocco; with autograph of Rufus Choate.* London, 1812

1388 HARDYNG, JOHN. THE CHRONICLES OF JOHN HARDYNG; containing an Account of Public Transactions from the Earliest Period of English History to the Beginning of the Reign of King Edward the Fourth; together with the Continuation by Richard Grafton, to the Thirty-fourth Year of King Henry the Eighth: the Former Part collated with Two Manuscripts of the Author's own Time; the Last, with

Grafton's Duplicate Edition. To which are added a Biographical and Literary Preface, and an Index, by Henry Ellis. *Royal 4to, russia, neat, marbled edges.* London, 1812

Best edition, collated with the Selden, Ashmole, and Lansdowne MSS." — *Lowndes.* See ARNOLD, RICHARD.

1389 HARE, J. C. and A. W. GUESSES AT TRUTH; by Two Brothers. *Portrait of J. C. Hare.* 12*mo, cloth.* Boston, 1861

1390 HARLEIAN (THE) MISCELLANY; a Collection of Scarce, Curious, and Entertaining Pamphlets and Tracts, as well in Manuscript as in Print; selected from the Library of Edward Harley, Second Earl of Oxford. Interspersed with Historical, Political, and Critical Annotations, by the late William Oldys, Esq.; and some Additional Notes, by Thomas Park, F. S. A. 10 *vols., royal 4to, half morocco, gilt tops, uncut.* BEST EDITION: *fine copy.* London, 1808–13

Vols. IX. and X. are supplementary, containing miscellaneous pieces, not included in the former edition, selected and prepared by T. Park.

"This valuable political, historical, and antiquarian record, an indispensable auxiliary in the illustration of British history, contains between 600 and 700 rare and curious tracts." —*Lowndes.*

"Let there not be a moment's hesitation in securing the enlarged reprint, under the editorial care of Mr. Park. Of this re-publication, in ten handsome quarto volumes (and now sinking gradually into a state of exhaustion), 500 copies were struck off; containing two volumes of ADDITIONAL matter, with a general index to the whole. The reprint of the *old* tracts has also the advantage of exhibiting these tracts in the *chronological* order in which they were composed." — *Dibdin.*

1391 HARPER'S NEW MONTHLY MAGAZINE. *June,* 1850–*May,* 1862. *Numerous wood-cuts.* 24 *vols., royal 8vo, half morocco, neat, except Vols. X. and XXIV., which are in numbers.* New York, 1850–62

1392 HARPER'S NEW MONTHLY MAGAZINE. DUPLICATES: Vols. IV.–IX. and XI.–XXIII. 19 *vols., in numbers.* New York, 1852–61

1393 HARRIS, JAMES. THREE TREATISES: the First, concerning Art; the Second, concerning Music, Painting, and Poetry; the Third, concerning Happiness. The Second Edition, revised and corrected. *Frontispiece. 8vo, calf, neat.* London, 1765

1394 HARRIS, JAMES. PHILOLOGICAL INQUIRIES; in Three Parts. *Portrait and plate by Bartolozzi.* 2 *vols., 8vo, old tree calf, gilt, yellow edges.* London, 1781

1395 HARRIS, JAMES. THE WORKS OF; with an Account of his Life and Character, by his Son, the Earl of Malmesbury. *Portrait by Bartolozzi, and 4 plates.* 5 *vols., 8vo, old marbled calf, gilt.* London, 1803

1396 HARRIS, JOHN, D. D. NAVIGANTIUM ATQUE ITINERANTIUM, or a Compleat Collection of Voyages and Travels: consisting of above Four Hundred of the most Authentic

Writers; beginning with Hackluit, Purchass, etc., in English; Ramusio in Italian; Thevenot, etc., in French; De Bry, and Grynæi Novus Orbis in Latin; the Dutch East-India Company in Dutch; and continued, with others of Note, that have publish'd Histories, Voyages, Travels, or Discoveries in the English, Latin, French, Italian, Spanish, Portuguese, German, or Dutch Tongues, relating to any Part of Asia, Africa, America, Europe, or the Islands thereof, to this Present Time. With the Heads of Several of our most Considerable Sea-Commanders, and a great Number of Excellent Maps of all Parts of the World, and Cuts of most Curious Things in all the Voyages: also, an Appendix of the Remarkable Accidents at Sea, and Several of our Considerable Engagements; the Charters, Acts of Parliament, etc. about the East-India Trade, and Papers relating to the Union of the Two Companies. Throughout the Whole all Original Papers are printed at Large, as the Pope's Bull to dispose of the West Indies to the King of Spain; Letters Patents for Establishing Companies of Merchants, as the Russia, East-India Companies, etc.; Letters from one Great Prince or State to another, showing their Titles, Style, etc. To which is prefixed, a History of the Peopling of the Several Parts of the World, and Particularly of America; an Account of the Ancient Shipping, and its Successive Improvements; together with the Invention and Use of the Magnet, and its Variations, etc. By John Harris, A. M., Fellow of the Royal Society. *Fine impressions of the portraits, maps and plates, engraved by Vander Gucht, etc.* 2 *vols., folio, half calf.* London, 1705

Original edition of this esteemed collection. See CHURCHILL, A. AND J.

1397 HARRIS, MOSES. AN EXPOSITION OF ENGLISH INSECTS, including the Several Classes of Neuroptera, Hymenoptera, and Diptera, or Bees, Flies, and Libellulæ; exhibiting on 51 Copper Plates near 500 Figures, accurately drawn, and highly finished in Colours, from Nature. The Whole minutely described, arranged, and named, according to the Linnean System, with Remarks: the Figures of a great Number of Moths, not in the Aurelian Collection, formerly published by the same Author, and a Plate with an Explanation of Colours, are likewise given in the Work. *The plates in this copy* COLORED BY THE AUTHOR. *Royal 4to, half morocco.* London, 1782

"A beautiful work, in great estimation." —*Lowndes.* "Moses Harris was the best painter and engraver of insects of his day, besides being a most accurate describer." — *Swainson.*

1398 HARRIS, REV. THADDEUS MASON. THE CONSTITUTIONS OF THE ANCIENT AND HONORABLE FRATERNITY OF FREE AND ACCEPTED MASONS, containing their History, Charges,

Addresses, etc.; collected and digested from their Old Records, Faithful Traditions, and Lodge Books, for the Use of Masons. To which are added, the History of Masonry in the Commonwealth of Massachusetts, and the Constitution, Laws, and Regulations of their Grand Lodge; together with a Large Collection of Songs, Epilogues, etc. [Compiled, chiefly, by the Rev. T. M. Harris.] *4to, sheep.*
Isaiah Thomas, Worcester, 1792

This work was compiled by a committee consisting of John Warren, Moses M. Hays, Paul Revere, Aaron Dexter, William Scollay, Thaddeus M. Harris, John Lowell, Samuel Dunn, James Jackson, Samuel Barret, William Little, Samuel Parkman, and John Flemming; it was published under the superintendence of Mr. Harris, then librarian of Harvard University.

1399 HARRIS, Rev. Thaddeus Mason. Discourses, delivered on Public Occasions, Illustrating the Principles, Displaying the Tendency, and Vindicating the Design of Freemasonry. *Frontispiece. 12mo, half morocco.*
Charlestown, 1801

1400 HARRIS, William Cornwallis. Portraits of the Game and Wild Animals of Southern Africa, delineated from Life in their Native Haunts, during a Hunting Expedition, from the Cape Colony as far as the Tropic of Capricorn, in 1836 and 1837; with Sketches of the Field Sports. *Engraved title and 30 large colored plates, drawn on stone by Frank Howard, with 30 vignettes of heads, skins, etc. Imperial folio, half crimson morocco, extra, emblematically tooled, gilt edges.* W. Pickering, London, 1840

1401 HARRIS, William Thaddeus. Epitaphs from the Old Burying Ground in Cambridge; with Notes. *12mo, boards, rough edges.* Cambridge, 1845

1402 HARRISSON, David, Jun. A Voice from the Washingtonian Home; being a History of the Foundation, Rise, and Progress of the Washingtonian Home. *Portrait of Dr. Albert Day, 12mo, cloth.* Boston, 1860

Presentation copy from Dr. Day, with autograph.

1403 HARTE, Rev. Walter. The History of the Life of Gustavus Adolphus, King of Sweden, Sirnamed, the Great. *Portrait by A. Walker, maps, and plans. 2 vols., 4to, old calf, with book-plate of Fred: Cornwallis.*
London, 1759

"The best military history in our language. Dr Johnson much commended Harte as a scholar, and a man of the most companionable talents he had ever known." — *Lowndes.*

1404 HARTFORD, Frances, Countess of. Correspondence between Frances, Countess of Hartford (afterwards Duchess of Somerset), and Henrietta Louisa, Countess of Pomfret, between the years 1738 and 1741. *Portrait. 3 vols., 12mo, old marbled calf, gilt.* London, 1805

5 HARTSHORNE, Rev. Charles Henry. Ancient Metrical Tales; printed chiefly from Original Sources. Edited by the Rev. Charles Henry Hartshorne, M. A. *Crown 8vo, crimson turkey morocco, gilt edges. Uniform with* Weber.
W. Pickering, London, 1829

This work, forming a supplementary collection to those of Ritson, Percy, and Ellis, contains: The Romance of King Athelstone; a Tale of King Edward and the Shepherd; The Lady that was in Dyspeyre; A Tale of the Unnatural Daughter; A Tale of Robin Hood; The Cokwold's Daunce; Doctour Doubble Ale; Willyam and the Werwolf; and several other pieces.

1406 HARTSHORNE, Rev. Charles Henry. The Book Rarities in the University of Cambridge; illustrated by Original Letters, and Notes, Biographical, Literary, and Antiquarian. *Wood-cuts, 8vo, tree calf, gilt, marbled edges.*
London, 1829

1407 HARVARD Memorial Biographies (containing Memoirs of those Graduates and Former Under Graduates of Harvard University who fell in Battle or died in Consequence of Services rendered during the Recent War). *2 vols., 8vo, cloth, gilt tops.* Original Edition. Cambridge, 1866

The first edition was not stereotyped.

1408 HARVEY, Gabriell. Pierce's Supererogation, or a New Praise of the Old Ass; by Gabriell Harvey: from the Edition of 1593. And New Letter of Notable Contents; by the same Author: from the Edition of 1593. *4to, half green morocco neat.* Only 200 copies printed.
Private Press of Longmans & Co., London, 1815

This volume is imperfect. It contains part of the eighth and ninth parts (or Part II. of the second volume, as generally bound) of "Archaica," edited by Sir S. E. Brydges, which was published with "Heliconia," edited by T. Park. It contains both titles, and the general preface, to the two volumes of "Archaica." See Heliconia.

1409 HARVEY, William Henry, M. D. Nereis Boreali-Americana; or Contributions to a History of Marine Algæ of North America. Part II.; Rhodospermeæ. *With 24 finely colored plates. Royal 4to, cloth.*
Washington, 1853

Vol. V. of "Smithsonian Contributions to Knowledge."

1410 HASLEWOOD, Joseph. The Secret History of the Green Room; containing Authentic and Entertaining Memoirs of the Actors and Actresses in the Three Theatres Royal. The Third Edition. *2 vols., 12mo, half calf, neat, marbled edges.* London, 1793

See Ritson, Joseph; and for an account of the works edited or written by this author (several of which are contained in this catalogue,) see "Gent's Mag." Nov. 1833, pp. 467, 468.

1411 HASSELL, J. Tour of the Isle of Wight; the Drawings taken and engraved by J. Hassell. *Engraved titles and 30 views in aquatinta. 2 vols., crown 4to, boards.* Large paper. London, 1790

The views in this work are after the manner of Gilpin.

1412 HASSIA, HENRICUS DE; THOMAS AQUINAS, ETC. A COLLECTION OF TRACTS, printed in the Fifteenth Century. *Six tracts in 1 vol., 4to, 8 × 6 inches vellum.* **Black letter:** *in good condition.*

C. Kacheloven, M. Lotter, etc., Lyptzck, 1496–97

CONTENTS: "Lavacrum conscientie omnium sacerdotum." 86 *leaves (numbered).* — "Secreta Sacerdotum Magistri Heinrici de Hassia," etc. ("per Doctorem Magistrum Michaelem Lochmeyr correcta," etc.). 12 *leaves.* — "Expositio canōis sacratissime misse" (in gynnasio Lypktzensi p̄ Balthesarē finit"). 20 *leaves.* — "Legenda sctīssime matrone anne genitricis v'gīs marie et jhū xp̄i avie." 24 *leaves (last leaf blank).* — "De Laudibus sanctissime matris Anne tractat perquam utilis mmī Johañis tritemii abbatis spanhemensis ordinis dmi patris benedicti." 24 *leaves.* — "Tractatulus solēnis de arte et vero modo predicandi ex diversis sacro doctorum scripturis & principaliter sacrissimi cristiane ecclesie doctoris Thome de Aquino recollectus," etc., etc. "Una cū tractaculo eximii doctoris henrici de hassia de arte predicādi." 12 *leaves (last leaf blank).*

1413 HASTINGS, WARREN. DEBATES OF THE HOUSE OF LORDS on the Evidence delivered in the Trial of; Proceedings of the East India Company in Consequence of his Acquittal; and Testimonials of the British and Native Inhabitants of India, relative to his Character and Conduct whilst he was Governor General of Fort William, in Bengal. *Portrait of Edward Lord Thurlow, by Schiavonetti, after Reynolds. 4to, old marbled calf, neat, yellow edges; with book-plates and autographs.* London, 1797

On the title is written, — Given by Mr. Hastings, to Lord & Lady Northwick."

1414 HAUFF, WILHELM. ARABIAN DAYS' ENTERTAINMENTS; translated from the German [of Wilhelm Hauff] by H. P. Curtis. *Wood-cuts after Hoppin. 12mo, cloth.*

Boston, 1858

1415 HAUGHTON, SIR GRAVES CHAMNEY. PRODROMUS, or an Inquiry into the First Principles of Reasoning; including an Analysis of the Human Mind. *8vo, half green calf, extra.*

London, 1839

1416 HAVET, ALFRED. THE FRENCH MANUAL: a New, Simple, Concise, and Easy Method of Acquiring a Conversational Knowledge of the French Language; including a Dictionary of over Ten Thousand Words. *12mo, half roan.*

New York, 1867

1417 HAWES, MARY VIRGINIA. NEMESIS. *12mo, cloth.*

New York, 1860

1418 HAWKES, JULIA S., afterwards GARDEL. CONVERSATIONS ON ITALY; in English and French. *16mo, half roan.*

Philadelphia, 1844

1419 HAWKINS, SIR JOHN. A GENERAL HISTORY OF THE SCIENCE AND PRACTICE OF MUSIC. *Frontispiece, above 50 portraits, and numerous other plates and wood-cuts, engraved by C. Grignion, etc. 5 vols., 4to, sprinkled calf, very neat.* London, 1776

1420 HAWTHORNE, NATHANIEL. THE SCARLET LETTER; a Romance. *12mo, cloth.* Boston, 1850

1421 HAWTHORNE, NATHANIEL. THE HOUSE OF THE SEVEN GABLES; a Romance. *12mo, cloth.* Boston, 1851

1422 HAWTHORNE, NATHANIEL. THE MARBLE FAUN, or the Romance of Monte Beni. *2 vols., 12mo, cloth.* Boston, 1860

1423 HAYDN, JOSEPH. DICTIONARY OF DATES, AND UNIVERSAL REFERENCE, relating to all Ages and Nations; comprehending every Remarkable Occurrence, Ancient and Modern; the Foundation, Laws, and Governments of Countries; their Progress in Civilisation, Industry and Science; their Achievements in Arms; the Political and Social Transactions of the British Empire; its Civil, Military, and Religious Institutions; the Origin and Advance of Human Arts and Inventions, with Copious Details of England, Scotland, and Ireland: from the Earliest Accounts to the Present Time. Seventh Edition, with Additions and Corrections by B. Vincent. *Thick 8vo, cloth, uncut.* E. Moxon, London, 1855

1424 HAYDON, BENJAMIN ROBERT. LIFE OF; from his Autobiography and Journals. Edited and compiled by Tom Taylor. *3 vols., crown 8vo, cloth, uncut.* London, 1853

1425 HAYES, ISAAC I., M. D. THE OPEN POLAR SEA; a Narrative of a Voyage of Discovery towards the North Pole. *Portraits, maps, and wood-cuts. 8vo, cloth.* New York, 1867

1426 HAYES, WILLIAM, AND FAMILY. PORTRAITS OF RARE AND CURIOUS BIRDS, with their Descriptions, from the Menagery of Osterly Park, in the County of Middlesex. *Frontispiece and 100 finely colored plates. 2 vols in 1, royal 4to, blue morocco, extra, gilt edges.* FINE ORIGINAL COPY: COMPLETE.

Printed by W. Bulmer & Co., London, 1794–99

This is one of the copies colored in the finest manner. Most copies in the market contain but *eighty* plates.

1427 HAYWARD, SIR JOHN. ANNALS OF THE FIRST FOUR YEARS OF THE REIGN OF QUEEN ELIZABETH. Edited from a MS. in the Harleian Collection, by John Bruce, Esq., F. S. A. *Portrait of Q. Elizabeth by W. T. Fry. Foolscap 4to, cloth, uncut.* Camden Society, London, 1840

1428 HAYWOOD, MRS. ELIZA. THE FEMALE SPECTATOR. *Frontispiece. 4 vols., 12mo, sheep.* Glasgow, 1775

1429 HEAD, SIR FRANCIS BOND. BUBBLES FROM THE BRUNNENS OF NASSAU; by an Old Man. *18mo, boards.* Frankfort o. M., 1835

1430 HEAD, SIR FRANCIS BOND. THE LIFE OF BRUCE, the African Traveller. *Portrait and maps. 16mo, morocco, extra, gilt edges.* J. Murray, London, 1844

1431 HEAD, SIR FRANCIS BOND. A FAGGOT OF FRENCH STICKS, or Paris in 1851. Two Volumes complete in One. *12mo, cloth.* New York, 1852

1432 HEADLEY, REV. PHINEAS CAMP. MASSACHUSETTS IN THE REBELLION; a Record of the Historical Position of the Commonwealth, and the Services of the Leading Statesmen, the Military, the Colleges, and the People, in the Civil War of 1861–65. *Numerous portraits. 8vo, sheep, marbled edges.* Boston, 1866

1433 HEARNE, THOMAS. ROBERT OF GLOUCESTER'S CHRONICLE; transcrib'd, and now first publish'd, from a MS. in the Harleyan Library, by Thomas Hearne. To which is added, besides a Glossary and other Improvements, a Continuation (by the Author) of this Chronicle from a MS. in the Cottonian Library. In Two Volumes. Oxford, Printed at the Theatre, M.DCC.XXIV. *Reprinted for Samuel Bagster, with a page of "Notes on Rob. of Gloucester's Chronicle obtained through the kindness of Mr. Archdeacon Churton, from a copy formerly belonging to John Loveday, Esq., of Caversham." 2 vols., royal 8vo, crimson morocco, very neat, gilt edges.* LARGE PAPER. London, 1810

1434 HEARNE, THOMAS. PETER LANGTOFT'S CHRONICLE, (as illustrated and improv'd by Robert of Brunne) from the Death of Cadwallader to the End of K. Edward the First's Reign; transcrib'd, and now first publish'd, from a MS. in the Inner-Temple Library, by Thomas Hearne. To which are added, besides a Glossary and other Curious Papers:— (1) A Roll concerning Glastonbury Abbey, being a Survey of all the Estates belonging to that House at the Dissolution, taken by King Hen. the Eighth's Order and for his Use; (2) an Account of the Hospital of St. Mary Magdalen near Scroby in Nottinghamshire, by John Slacke. (3) Two Tracts by an Anonymous Author, the First relating to Conquest in Somersetshire, the Second concerning Stonehenge. In Two Volumes. Oxford, Printed at the Theatre, M.DCC.XXV. *Reprinted for Samuel Bagster, with four pages of "Additions and Corrections appended by Hearne to three of his later publications." 2 vols., royal 8vo, crimson morocco, very neat, gilt edges.* LARGE PAPER. London, 1810

1435 HEBER, REGINALD, BISHOP OF CALCUTTA. NARRATIVE OF A JOURNEY THROUGH THE UPPER PROVINCES OF INDIA, from Calcutta to Bombay, 1824–1825 (with Notes upon Ceylon), an Account of a Journey to Madras and the Southern Provinces, 1826, and Letters written in India.—LIFE, BY HIS WIDOW; with Selections from his Correspondence, Unpublished Poems, and Private Papers: together with a Journal of his Tour in Norway, Sweden, Russia, Hungary, and Germany; and a History of the Cossaks. *Portrait by Cousins, map, plates by Finden, and wood-cuts. Together, 4 vols., 4to, half calf, extra.* J. Murray, London, 1828–30

1436 HECKER, I. T. QUESTIONS OF THE SOUL. *12mo, cloth.* New York, 1855

1437 HEDGE, FREDERIC HENRY, D. D. REASON IN RELIGION. *24mo, cloth.* Boston, 1866

1438 HEEREN, ARNOLD HERMANN LUDWIG. A MANUAL OF ANCIENT HISTORY; particularly with Regard to the Constitutions, the Commerce, and the Colonies of the States of Antiquity. Translated from the German. *8vo, tree calf, gilt, marbled edges.* Talboys, Oxford, 1829

1439 HEEREN, ARNOLD HERMANN LUDWIG. HISTORICAL RESEARCHES into the Politics, Intercourse, and Trade of the Principal Nations of Antiquity. Translated from the German. *6 vols., 8vo, tree calf, gilt, marbled edges.* Talboys, Oxford, 1833

Vols. I.–III. Asiatic Nations: Persians, Babylonians, Phœnicians, Scythians, Indians. Vols. IV.–V. African Nations: Carthaginians, Egyptians. Vol. VI. European Nations: Greece.

1440 HEEREN, ARNOLD HERMANN LUDWIG. A MANUAL OF THE POLITICAL SYSTEM OF EUROPE, and its Colonies. Translated from the Fifth German Edition. *2 vols., 8vo, tree calf, gilt, marbled edges.* Talboys, Oxford, 1834

1441 HEEREN, ARNOLD HERMANN LUDWIG. HISTORICAL TREATISE: the Political Consequences of the Reformation; the Rise, Progress, and Practical Influence of Political Theories; the Rise and Growth of the Continental Interests of Great Britain. Translated from the German. *8vo, tree calf, gilt, marbled edges.* Talboys, Oxford, 1836

The above four titles form a fine set of Professor Heeren's historical works, uniformly bound, in ten volumes.

1442 HEINE, HEINRICH. PICTURES OF TRAVEL. Translated from the German, by Charles G. Leland. Second Edition. *Portrait. 12mo, morocco antique, gilt edges.* Philadelphia, 1858

1443 HEINE, HEINRICH. THE POEMS, complete; translated in the Original Metres, with a Sketch of Heine's Life, by Edgar Alfred Bowring. *Post 8vo, cloth, uncut.* London, 1861

1444 HEINE, HEINRICH. BOOK OF SONGS. Translated by Charles G. Leland. *Foolscap 8vo, cloth, gilt top.* Philadelphia, 1864

1445 HELICONIA; comprising a Selection of English Poetry of the Elizabethan Age, written or published between 1575 and 1604. Edited by T. Park. 3 *vols., 4to, diamond calf, neat, contents lettered, marbled edges.* ONLY 200 COPIES PRINTED. Private Press of Longmans & Co., London, 1815

"Archaica," edited by Sir S. E. Brydges, was published (2 vols.) with this work, forming a collection of rare old English pieces of prose and poetry.

1446 HELMAN, ISIDORE STANISLAUS. FAITS MÉMORABLES DES EMPEREURS DE LA CHINE, tirés des Annales Chinoises. *A series of 24 plates engraved by Helman, including copies of the 16 plates engraved under the direction of Cochin for the emperor Kien-Long. Without title. Oblong folio, boards.* Paris, (1783–88)

1447 HELPER, HINTON ROWAN. THE IMPENDING CRISIS OF THE SOUTH; how to Meet it. 12*mo, cloth.* New York, 1860

1448 HELPS, REV. ARTHUR. THE CONQUERORS OF THE NEW WORLD AND THEIR BONDSMEN; being a Narrative of the Principal Events which led to Negro Slavery in the West Indies and America. 2 *vols., crown* 8*vo, cloth, uncut.* W. Pickering, London, 1848–52

1449 HELPS, REV. ARTHUR. COMPANIONS OF MY SOLITUDE. *Foolscap* 8*vo, cloth, uncut.* W. Pickering, London, 1851

1450 HELPS, REV. ARTHUR. ANOTHER COPY: *third edition. Foolscap* 8*vo, dark blue crushed morocco, gilt edges.* W. Pickering, London, 1852

1451 HEMANS, FELICIA DOROTHEA. THE WORKS OF. With a Memoir of her Life, by her Sister [Mrs. Hughes]. *Portraits of Mrs. Hemans and her mother, and vignettes on titles after drawings by the authors.* 7 *vols., foolscap* 8*vo, cloth, uncut.* Edinburgh, 1841–54

1452 HENDERSON, JOHN, COMEDIAN. LETTERS AND POEMS; with Anecdotes of his Life, by John Ireland. 8*vo, old calf.* London, 1786

1453 HENRY, CALEB SPRAGUE, D. D. DOCTOR OLDHAM AT GREYSTONES, and his Talk there. *Frontispiece,* 12*mo, cloth.* New York, 1860

1454 HENRY, CALEB SPRAGUE, D. D. CONSIDERATIONS on some of the Elements and Conditions of Social Welfare and Human Progress. 12*mo, cloth.* New York, 1861

1455 HENRY, WALTER. EVENTS OF A MILITARY LIFE; being Recollections after Service in the Peninsular War, Invasion of France, the East Indies, St. Helena, Canada, and elsewhere. *Second edition, revised and enlarged.* 2 *vols.,* 12*mo, cloth, uncut.* W. Pickering. London, 1843

1456 HERBERT, HENRY WILLIAM. FRANK FORRESTER'S FISH AND FISHING of the United States, and British Provinces, of North America. *Numerous wood-cuts.* 8*vo, half green calf, extra, marbled edges.* Bentley, London, 1849

1457 HERBERT, WILLIAM. THE HISTORY OF THE TWELVE GREAT LIVERY COMPANIES OF LONDON, principally compiled from their Grants and Records; with an Historical Essay, and Accounts of Each Company, its Origin, Constitution, Government, Dress, Customs, Halls, and Trust Estates and Charities; including Notices and Illustrations of Metropolitan Trade and Commerce, as Originally concentrated in those Societies; and of the Language, Manners, and Expenses of Ancient Times; with Attested Copies and Translations of the Companies' Charters. *Numerous wood-cuts, comprising views, arms, etc. 2 vols., 8vo, boards, rough edges.* London, 1834–37

The first part of Vol. I. appeared in 1834, but the new titles, given with the second volume, are dated 1837 and 1836.

1458 HERIOT, GEORGE. TRAVELS THROUGH THE CANADAS, containing a Description of the Picturesque Scenery on some of the Rivers and Lakes; with an Account of the Productions, Commerce, and Inhabitants of those Provinces: to which is subjoined a Comparative View of the Manners and Customs of Several of the Indian Nations of North and South America. *Illustrated with a map and numerous engravings from drawings made at the several places by the author. 4to, calf.* London, 1807

1459 HERNDON, WILLIAM L.; and LARDNER GIBBON. EXPLORATION OF THE VALLEY OF THE AMAZON; made under Direction of the Navy Department. *Maps, above 50 tinted plates, and wood-cuts. 3 vols. (one containing maps), 8vo, cloth.* Washington, 1854

1460 HERODOTUS. THE HISTORY OF; translated from the Greek, with Notes, by the Rev. William Beloe. The Second Edition, corrected and enlarged. *Map. 4 vols., 8vo, old calf.* London, 1806

1461 HERODOTUS. HERODOTI HALICARNASSENSIS MUSAE: Textum ad Gaisfordii Editionem recognovit, perpetuatum Fr. Creuzeri tum sua Annotatione instruxit, Commentationem de Vita et Scriptis Herodoti, Tabulas Geographicas, Imagines Ligno incisas, Indicesque adjecit J. C. F. Baehr. Editio Altera, emendatior et auctior. *4 vols., 8vo, half calf, extra; with autograph of Rufus Choate.* Lipsiae, 1856–59

1462 HERODOTUS. THE HISTORY OF: a New English Version, edited with Copious Notes and Appendices, illustrating the History and Geography of Herodotus, from the most Recent Sources of Information; and embodying the Chief Results, Historical and Ethnographical, which have been obtained in the Progress of Cuneiform and Hieroglyphical Discovery. By George Rawlinson; assisted by Col. Sir Henry Rawlinson, and Sir J. G. Wilkinson. *Maps and wood-cuts. 4 vols., 8vo, cloth.* New York, 1859–60

1463 HERRICK, ROBERT. HESPERIDES; or, the Works, both Humane and Divine, of Robert Herrick, Esq. [Edited, with Preface, by S. W. Singer.] *Handsomely printed by Whittingham. Portrait. 2 vols., foolscap 8vo, cloth, uncut.* BEST EDITION: *Aldine.* W. Pickering, London, 1846

1464 HERSEY, CHARLES. HISTORY OF WORCESTER, Massachusetts, from 1836 to 1861; with Interesting Reminiscences of the Public Men of Worcester. *View of the Bigelow Monument. Royal 8vo, boards, rough edges.* Worcester, (1862)

1465 HERVÈ, PETER. HOW TO ENJOY PARIS: being a Guide to the Visiter of the French Metropolis. The Second Volume contains a Chronological Account of the History of France, from the Foundation of the Monarchy to the End of the Year 1815; to which is added, a Biographical Dictionary of Eminent French Characters. An Endeavour has also been made to render this Work interesting to those Persons, who, without visiting are desirous of becoming acquainted with the Beauties of Paris. *2 vols., 18mo, boards.* London, 1816

1466 HERVEY, CHARLES. THE THEATRES OF PARIS. Illustrated with Original Portraits of Eminent Living Actresses, by Alexandre Lacauchie. *India proofs of the portraits. Imperial 8vo, cloth, gilt top.* Paris, 1846

1467 HERVEY, REV. JAMES. MEDITATIONS AND CONTEMPLATIONS: containing his Meditations among the Tombs; Reflections on a Flower-Garden, etc.; together with the Life of the Author. To which is added, Reflections on Death; by W. Dodd, LL. D. *8vo, sheep.* Philadelphia, 1835

1468 HERVEY, THOMAS KIBBLE. ILLUSTRATIONS OF MODERN SCULPTURE; with Descriptive Prose and Illustrative Poetry [by T. K. Hervey]. *Engraved title, and 18 plates, engraved by Finden, Tomkins, etc., comprising statues and groups by Westmacott, Canova, Flaxman, Chantrey, Baily, Thorwaldsen, Carew, Bienaimé, Bacon, and Manning. Folio, half morocco gilt top.* LARGE PAPER: *India proofs.* London, (1832)

1469 HESSE, LÉOPOLD AUGUSTE CONSTANTIN. BIBLIOTHÉCONOMIE, ou Nouveau Manuel Complet pour l'Arrangement, la Conservation, et l'Administration des Bibliothèques. Revue, augmentée, et ornée de Figures. *18mo, green morocco, extra, gilt edges.* Paris, 1841

1470 HEWITT, JOHN. ANCIENT ARMOUR AND WEAPONS IN EUROPE, from the Iron-Period of the Northern Nations to the End of the Thirteenth Century; with Illustrations from Cotemporary Monuments. *Numerous wood-cuts. 8vo, cloth, gilt top.* J. H. & J. Parker, Oxford, 1855

1471 HEYLYN, PETER, D.D. COSMOGRAPHIE: IN FOUR BOOKS; containing the Chorographie and Historie of the Whole World, and all the Principal Kingdoms, Provinces, Seas, and Isles thereof. By Peter Heylyn. The Second Edition. *Frontispiece, by Vaughan, and maps. Folio, half russia.* London, 1657

The second part of the fourth book treats of America, with a map dated 1663.

1472 HICKEY, WILLIAM. THE CONSTITUTION OF THE UNITED STATES OF AMERICA; the Declaration of Independence; the Articles of Confederation; the Prominent Political Acts of George Washington; Electoral Votes for all the Presidents and Vice-Presidents; the High Authorities and Civil Officers of Goverment, from March 4, 1789, to March 3, 1847, etc. 12*mo, cloth.* Philadelphia, 1854

1473 HICKS, THOMAS. EULOGY ON THOMAS CRAWFORD (with Memoir, Notes, etc.). *Portrait and 3 plates on India paper. 8vo, paper, rough edges.* PRIVATELY PRINTED: *only* 100 *copies.* New York, 1865

This volume forms No. 1 of "Local Biographical Series," published for subscribers only, by W. L. Andrews, of New York, and printed at the Riverside Press. The edition was rigidly limited to 70 copies in octavo, 25 in quarto, and 5 in octavo on India paper. "The object of this series is to preserve, in a durable and attractive form, and suitable for illustration, some of the now scattered and perishing memorials of the distinguished men of the City of New York." (See "Introductory.")

1474 HIGGINS, GODFREY. THE CELTIC DRUIDS; or, an Attempt to shew that the Druids were the Priests of Oriental Colonies who emigrated from India, and were the Introducers of the First or Cadmean System of Letters, and the Builders of Stonehenge, of Carnac, and of other Cyclopean Works, in Asia and Europe. *Frontispiece, map, 46 large, and numerous smaller, lithographic plates of Druidical monuments; some of the plates on India paper. 4to, cloth, rough edges.* London, 1839

One of the chapters in this work is devoted to the attempt to prove that the Pentateuch was "not intended to teach chronology or geology," in which the author remarks, "I have no hesitation in saying, that the general chronology as stated in the translation of Jerome, and in our Bible, is wrong, and cannot be admitted."

1475 HIGGINS, GODFREY. ANACALYPSIS; an Attempt to draw aside the Veil of the Saitic Isis, or an Inquiry into the Origin of Languages, Nations, and Religions. *2 vols., 4to, cloth, uncut.* ONLY 200 COPIES PRINTED; *see Preface, Vol. I. p. vii.* London, 1836

The first volume, pp. xxxii and 867, was completed before the death of the author (1833) but bears the above date upon title; the second volume, pp. xi and 519, was published from the author's manuscript, edited by the printer, Mr. George Smallfield.

1476 HIGGINSON, THOMAS WENTWORTH. OUT-DOOR PAPERS. *Post 8vo, cloth* Boston, 1863

1477 HILDRETH, RICHARD. DESPOTISM IN AMERICA; an

Inquiry into the Nature, Results, and Legal Basis of the Slave-Holding System in the United States. *12mo, cloth.* Boston, 1854

1478 HILL, AARON. THE WORKS OF; consisting of Letters on Various Subjects, and of Original Poems, Moral and Facetious: with an Essay on the Art of Acting. *4 vols., 8vo, old calf, gilt.* LARGE PAPER. London, 1753

1479 HILL, JOHN. ARTIS LOGICÆ RUDIMENTA; with Illustrative Observations on Each Section. Sixth Edition. *12mo, cloth, uncut.* Oxford, 1850

1480 HILLARD, GEORGE STILLMAN. SIX MONTHS IN ITALY. *2 vols., post 8vo, calf, gilt, marbled edges; with autograph of the author.* Boston, 1853

1481 HILLARD, GEORGE STILLMAN. A MEMOIR OF JAMES BROWN; with Obituary Notices and Tributes of Respect from Public Bodies. *Portrait. 8vo, cloth, uncut.* PRIVATELY PRINTED *at the Riverside Press.* Boston, 1856

1482 HILTON, JOHN. ON THE INFLUENCE OF MECHANICAL AND PHYSIOLOGICAL REST in the Treatment of Accidents and Surgical Diseases, and the Diagnostic Value of Pain. *Wood cuts. 8vo, cloth, uncut.* London, 1863

1483 HISLOP, ALEXANDER. THE PROVERBS OF SCOTLAND; collected and arranged, with Notes, Explanatory and Illustrative, and a Glossary. *Foolscap 8vo, cloth, uncut.* Glasgow, 1862

1484 HISPANIA ILLUSTRATA, or the Maxims of the Spanish Court, and most Memorable Affairs, from the Year 1667 to the Year 1678; fully laid open in Letters from the Earl of Sandwich, the Earl of Sunderland, and Sir William Godolphin, during their Embassies in Spain. Together with Several Curious Papers from Don John of Austria, the Conde de Penaranda, and other Chief Ministers there: as also a Treatise by my Lord Sandwich, concerning the Advantages of a Nearer Union with that Crown; and another by Sir William Godolphin about the Woolls of Spain. Now first published from the Respective Originals. *8vo, old calf.* London, 1703

1485 HISTOIRE UNIVERSELLE DEPUIS LE COMMENCEMENT DU MONDE JUSQU'À PRÉSENT, composée en Anglois par une Société de Gens de Lettres; nouvellement traduite en François par une Société de Gens de Lettres. Enrichie de Figures et de Cartes. *125 vols., 8vo, half calf.* Paris, 1779-91

1486 HISTORY (THE) OF THE BRITISH DOMINIONS IN NORTH AMERICA; from the First Discovery of that Vast Continent, by Sebastian Cabot in 1497, to its Present Glorious Establishment, as confirmed by the late Treaty of Peace in 1763. In Fourteen Books. *Colored map. 2 vols. in 1, 4to, half morocco.* London, 1773

1487 HISTORY (THE) OF FEMALE FAVOURITES: of Mary de Padilla, under Peter the Cruel, King of Castile; Livia, under the Emperor Augustus; Julia Farnesa, under Pope Alexander the Sixth; Agnes Soreau, under Charles VII., King of France; and Nantilda, under Dagobert, King of France. *8vo, half calf.* London, 1772

1488 HISTORY (THE) OF JEWELS, and of the Principal Riches of the East and West; taken from the Relation of Divers of the most Famous Travellers of Our Age. Attended with Fair Discoveries, conducing to the Knowledge of the Universe and Trade. *Printed by T. N. for Hobart Kemp, at the Sign of the Ship in the Upper Walk of the New Exchange. Small 8vo, old calf.* London, 1671

This little volume (pp. 128; besides title, preface, and table of chapters, 8 leaves) mentions the discoveries, and gives some account of the mines of Mexico, Peru, the West Indies, etc.

1489 HISTORY (THE) OF SIR WILLIAM HARRINGTON; written some Years ago, by a Lady, and revised and corrected by the late Mr. [Samuel] Richardson. A New Edition. *4 vols., 16mo, half morocco.* London, 1797

1490 HITTELL, JOHN S. THE EVIDENCES AGAINST CHRISTIANITY. Second Edition. *2 vols., 12mo, cloth.* New York, 1857

1491 HITTELL, JOHN S. THE RESOURCES OF CALIFORNIA, comprising Agriculture, Mining, Geography, Climate, Commerce, etc., etc.; and the Past and Future Development of the State. *12mo, cloth.* San Francisco (New York) 1863

1492 HIVE (THE), OR WEEKLY ENTERTAINING REGISTER; comprising Curious and Valuable Papers on Interesting Subjects, Choice Selections from Rare and Costly Works, the Curiosities of Literature, Anecdotes, Facetiæ, Beautiful Poetry, etc., etc. *Nos. I.–LIV. Engraved titles and woodcuts. 2 vols., 8vo, half calf, extra.* London, 1822, etc.

1493 HOARE, SIR RICHARD COLT. A CLASSICAL TOUR THROUGH ITALY AND SICILY; tending to illustrate some Districts, which have not been described by Mr. Eustace, in his Classical Tour. *4to, boards, rough edges.* London, 1819

1494 HOBBES, THOMAS. THE ENGLISH WORKS OF; now First collected and edited by Sir William Molesworth. *Portrait and plates. 11 vols., imperial 8vo, half green morocco, gilt tops.* LARGE PAPER. London, 1839–45

1495 HOBBES, THOMAS. OPERA PHILOSOPHICA, quæ Latine scripsit Omnia; in Unum Corpus nunc Primum collecta, Studio et Labore Gulielmi Molesworth. *Two portraits (duplicate in fifth volume), and plates. 5 vols., imperial 8vo, half green morocco, gilt tops.* LARGE PAPER. London, 1839–45

The above two titles form the only *complete* edition (with copious indexes) of the works of "the Philosopher of Malmesbury." The English Works are sometimes sold separately, but the Latin Works are not.

1496 HOBHOUSE, JOHN CAM. A JOURNEY THROUGH ALBANIA, and other Provinces of Turkey in Europe and Asia, to Constantinople, during the Years 1809 and 1810 [in Company with Lord Byron]. Third Edition. *With 24 plates, comprising maps, plans, views, costumes, fac-similes, and music; the views and costumes finely colored.* 2 *vols.*, 4*to*, *cloth*, *uncut.* London, 1833

There is another edition (2 vols., 8vo, 1855), called the "third," in which the plates are omitted.

"Both the general reader and the scholar may look for no small portion of information and amusement from the present volume." — *Quarterly Review*, *Vol. X. p.* 176.

1497 HOFLAND, BARBARA. SELF-DENIAL, a Tale. 16*mo*, *cloth.* Boston, 1845

1498 HOGARTH, GEORGE. MEMOIRS OF THE MUSICAL DRAMA. *Portraits of Madame Mara, Signor Farinelli, Dr. Arne, Anastasia Robinson, Mrs. Billington, Madame Catalani, Mrs. Crouch, and Charles Dibdin.* 2 *vols.*, 8*vo*, *cloth*, *uncut.* London, 1838

1499 HOGARTH, WILLIAM. A COLLECTION OF 62 PLATES, after Hogarth, engraved by E. Riepenhausen. *Without text or title. Folio, half calf.* (Berlin, 1794, etc.)

1500 HOGARTH, WILLIAM. THE GENUINE WORKS OF; illustrated with Biographical Anecdotes, a Chronological Catalogue, and Commentary, by John Nichols, and the late George Steevens. *Fine impressions of the* 160 *plates engraved by T. Cook.* 2 *vols.*, 4*to*, *calf*, *gilt.* London, 1808–10

This edition is one of the finest.

1501 HOGARTH, WILLIAM. THE WORKS OF; in a Series of One Hundred and Fifty Steel Engravings, by the First Artists: with Descriptions and a Comment on their Moral Tendency, by the Rev. John Trusler. To which are added, Anecdotes of the Author and his Works, by J. Hogarth, and J. Nichols. 2 *vols.*, 4*to*, *morocco*, *antique.* London, s. a.

1502 HOGG, THOMAS. A CONCISE AND PRACTICAL TREATISE ON THE GROWTH AND CULTURE OF THE CARNATION, Pink, Auricula, Polyanthus, Ranunculus, Tulip, Hyacinth, Rose, and other Flowers; containing Catalogues of the Finest and most Esteemed Varieties of each Flower. Fifth Edition, with Additions. *Colored plates.* 12*mo*, *cloth*, *uncut.* London, (1834)

1503 HOLBACH, PAUL HENRI THYRI, BARON D'. EL CHRISTIANISMO A DESCUBIERTO, ó Examen de los Principios y Efectos de la Religion Cristiana; escrito en Francés por Boulanger, y traducido al Castellano por S. D. V * * *. 12*mo*, *sheep*, *marbled edges.* Londres (Paris), 1821

1504 HOLBACH, PAUL HENRI THYRI, BARON D'. HISTORIA CRITICA DE JESU CRISTO, ó Analísis Razonado de los

Evangelios; traducida del Francés por el P. F. de T., ex-Jesuita. 2 *vols.*, 12*mo*, *sheep*, *marbled edges*.
Londres (Paris), 1822

1505 HOLBACH, PAUL HENRI THYRI, BARON D'. MORAL UNIVERSAL, ó Deberes del Hombre fundados en su Naturalez; Obra escrita en Francés, y traducida al Castellano por D. Manuel Diaz Moreno. Teoría de la Moral: Primera Parte. *Frontispiece.* 12*mo*, *sheep*, *marbled edges*.
Madrid (Paris), 1823

1506 HOLBACH, PAUL HENRI THYRI, BARON D'. DICCIONARIO DE LA RELIGION CRISTIANA, ó Teología Partátil; por el Abate Bergier [Baron d'Holbach]. Segunda Edicion, revista, corregida, y aumentada. 2 *vols.*, 12*mo*, *sheep*, *marbled edges*. Londres (Paris), 1824

1507 HOLBEIN, HANS. PORTRAITS OF ILLUSTRIOUS PERSONAGES OF THE COURT OF HENRY VIII., engraved in Imitation of the Original Drawings of Hans Holbein, in the Collection of his Majesty; with Biographical and Historical Memoirs, by Edmund Lodge, Esq., F. S. A. Published by John Chamberlaine, F. S. A., Keeper of the King's Drawings and Medals. *Contains* 84 *portraits; including portraits of Holbein and his wife, and the miniatures by Bartolozzi. Imperial* 4*to*, *half crimson morocco, extra, gilt edges.*
Printed by W. Bulmer & Co., London, 1828

1508 HOLBEIN, HANS. THE DANCE OF DEATH: exhibited in Elegant Engravings on Wood; with a Dissertation on the Several Representations of that Subject, but more particularly on those ascribed to Macaber and Hans Holbein, by Francis Douce, Esq. *With* 49 *faithful fac-similes of the celebrated Lyons wood-cuts, by Bomrer and Byfield, besides* 6 *other cuts in the dissertation.* 8*vo*, *calf*, *antique*, *carmine edges*. W. Pickering, London, 1833

Douce was a very industrious antiquary and collector. His printed books, illuminated MSS., etc., he left to the Bodleian Library; his *own* MSS. (for although he *published* little, he collected much material), he left to the British Museum. See DOUCE, FRANCIS.

1509 HOLBEIN, HANS. DANCE OF DEATH, with an Historical and Literary Introduction. *Frontispiece* (*ancient bedstead at Aix la-Chapelle*) *by Fairholt, and* 53 *wood-cuts on India paper. Square* 8*vo*, *cloth, gilt top, uncut.*
J. R. Smith, London, 1849

1510 HOLGATE, JEROME B. AMERICAN GENEALOGY, being a History of some of the Early Settlers of North America and their Descendants, from their First Emigration to the Present Time; with their Intermarriages and Collateral Branches: including Notices of Prominent Families, and Distinguished Individuals; with Anecdotes, Reminiscences, Traditions, Sketches of the Founding of Cities, Villages, Manors, and Progressive Improvements of the Country from its Wilderness State to the Present Era. Illustrated by Genealogical Tables. *Royal 4to, paper, rough edges.* New York, 1851

1511 HOLINSHED, RAPHAEL. HOLINSHED'S CHRONICLES of England, Scotland, and Ireland. 6 *vols., royal 4to, russia, neat, marbled edges.* London, 1807–08

In this reprint the Castrations are inserted, many chronological errata are corrected, and a copious index added. It formed the first issue of the Quarto Series of Chronicles, published by the London trade mostly from the old folios, under the editorial superintendence of Sir Henry Ellis, E. V. Utterson, R. H. Evans, F. Douce, Dibdin, and others." — *Lowndes.* See ARNOLD, RICHARD.

1512 HOLLAND, HENRY. TRAVELS IN THE IONIAN ISLES, Albania, Thessaly, Macedonia, etc.; during the Years 1812 and 1813. *Map, and 12 plates, by G. Cooke, J. Le Keux, and others, after drawings by the author. 4to, russia, very neat, gilt edges; with book-plate of the Honble. Frederic North.* London, 1815

"An excellent article on Modern Greece, with a notice of this valuable work, will be found in the 'Quarterly Review,' xxiii. 325–359." — *Lowndes.*

1513 HOLLAND, JOHN. THE HISTORY AND DESCRIPTION OF FOSSIL FUEL, the Collieries, and Coal Trade of Great Britain. Second Edition. *Wood-cuts, 8vo, cloth.* London, 1841

1514 HOLLAND, JOSIAH GILBERT, M. D. TITCOMB'S LETTERS TO YOUNG PEOPLE, Single and Married. 12*mo, cloth.* New York, 1858

1515 HOLLAND, JOSIAH GILBERT, M. D. LE[illegible] IN LIFE; a Series of Familiar Essays. 12*mo, cloth.* New York, 1861

1516 HOLLAND, JOSIAH GILBERT, M. D. PLAIN TALKS ON FAMILIAR SUBJECTS. 12*mo, cloth.* New York, 1866

1517 HOLLEY, O. L. THE PICTURESQUE TOURIST: being a Guide through the Northern and Eastern States, and Canada; giving an Accurate Description of Cities and Villages, Celebrated Places of Resort, etc. *Maps, plans, plates, and wood-cuts.* 16*mo, cloth.* New York, 1844

1518 HOLMES, ABIEL, D. D. THE LIFE OF EZRA STILES, D. D., LL. D., etc., and President of Yale College. 8*vo, paper, uncut.* Thomas & Andrews, Boston, 1798

With the exception of a few stains, this copy looks as if it were fresh from the press.

1519 HOLMES, ABIEL, D. D. THE ANNALS OF AMERICA, from the Discovery by Columbus in the Year 1492, to the Year 1826. Second Edition. 2 *vols., 8vo, boards.* Cambridge, 1829

1520 HOLMES, OLIVER WENDELL. POEMS BY. New and Enlarged Edition. *Portrait. Post 8vo, cloth.* Boston, 1852

1521 HOLT, JOSEPH. MEMOIRS OF JOSEPH HOLT, General of the Irish Rebels in 1798; edited from his Original Manuscript, in the Possession of Sir William Betham, by T. Crofton Croker, Esq. *Portrait, etc.* 2 *vols., 8vo, cloth, uncut.* London, 1838

1522 HOLTHOUSE, HENRY JAMES. A NEW LAW DICTIONARY, containing Explanations of such Technical Terms and Phrases as occur in the Works of Legal Authors, in the Practice of the Courts, and in the Parliamentary Proceedings of the Houses of Lords and Commons; to which is added an Outline of an Action at Law and of a Suit in Equity. Edited, from the Second and Enlarged London Edition, with Numerous Additions; by Henry Penington. *8vo, sheep.* Philadelphia, 1847

1523 HOLWELL, JOHN ZEPHANIAH. A GENUINE NARRATIVE OF THE DEPLORABLE DEATHS OF THE ENGLISH GENTLEMEN, and others, who were suffocated in the Black-Hole in Fort-William, at Calcutta, in the Kingdom of Bengal; in the Night succeeding the 20th Day of June, 1756. In a Letter to a Friend. *8vo, half calf.* London, 1758

This narrative, by one of the survivors — a surgeon, and Governor of Bengal, — is still the standard account of this melancholy affair.

1524 HOME, ———. SELECT VIEWS IN MYSORE, the Country of Tippoo Sultan; from Drawings taken on the Spot by Mr. Home: with Historical Descriptions. The Letter-Press by T. Bensley, from Figgins's Types. *Maps, plans, and 29 fine plates engraved by Fittler, Skelton, Lowry, etc.;* CHOICE IMPRESSIONS. *Imperial 4to, green morocco, extra, gilt edges, by Hering; with autograph of Dawson Turner.* London, 1794

1525 HOME-LIFE (THE) OF ENGLISH LADIES IN THE XVII. CENTURY; by the Author of "Magdalen Stafford." *Foolscap 8vo, cloth, uncut.* London, 1860

1526 HOMER. ILIADS TRANSLATED; adorn'd with Sculpture, and illustrated with Annotations, by John Ogilby. *Frontispiece and plates by Hollar, Lombart, etc. Royal folio, old calf, gilt.* LARGE PAPER. London, 1660

1527 HOMER. ODYSSES TRANSLATED; adorn'd with Sculpture, and illustrated with Annotations, by John Ogilby, Esq. *Frontispiece and plates by R. White, D. Loggan, etc. Royal folio, old calf, gilt.* LARGE PAPER. London, 1669

1528 HOMER. THE ILIADS OF HOMER, Prince of Poets, never before in any Language truly translated, with a Comment upon some of his Chief Places; done according to the Greek, by George Chapman. A New Edition, with Introduction and Notes, by W. Taylor, Esq. With Forty Engravings on Wood, from the Compositions of John Flaxman, R. A. *2 vols., crown 8vo, cloth, uncut.* C. Knight, London, 1843

1529 HOMER. THE ILIADS OF HOMER, Prince of Poets, never before in any Language truly translated, with a Comment on some of his Chief Places; done according to the Greek, by George Chapman. *2 vols.,* 1857.— THE ODYSSEYS OF HOMER,

translated according to the Greek, by George Chapman. 2 *vols.*, 1857. — HOMER'S BATRACHOMYOMACHIA, Hymns and Epigrams; Hesiod's Works and Days; Musæus' Hero and Leander; Juvenal's Fifth Satire: translated by George Chapman. 1 *vol.*, 1858. — With Introductions and Notes; by Richard Hooper, M. A., F. S. A. *Fac-simile plates, and other embellishments. Beautifully printed by Whittingham. 5 vols., square post 8vo, polished calf, gilt, marbled edges.*
J. R. Smith, London, 1857–58

Part of the "Library of Old Authors," and the only complete reprint of Chapman's translations. The fac-simile plates are reduced from the original folio editions.

1530 HOMES OF AMERICAN AUTHORS; comprising Anecdotical, Personal, and Descriptive Sketches by Various Writers. Illustrated with Views of their Residences, from Original Drawings, and Fac-similes of their Manuscripts (Portraits, etc.). *Square 8vo, morocco, antique, gilt edges.*
New York, 1857

1531 HOMES OF AMERICAN STATESMEN; with Anecdotical, Personal, and Descriptive Sketches, by Various Writers. Illustrated with Engravings on Wood, from Drawings by Döpler and Daguerreotypes, and Fac-similes of Autograph Letters. *Photograph of the Hancock House, Beacon Street, Boston, inserted. Square 8vo, morocco, antique, gilt edges. Fine early copy.* New York, 1854

1532 HONE, WILLIAM. ANCIENT MYSTERIES DESCRIBED: especially the English Miracle Plays, founded on Apocryphal New Testament Story, extant among the unpublished Manuscripts in the British Museum; including Notices of Ecclesiastical Shows, the Festivals of Fools and Asses, the English Boy-Bishop, the Descent into Hell, the Lord Mayor's Show, the Guildhall Giants, Christmas Carols, etc. *Plates and wood-cuts, glossary and index. 8vo, cloth.*
Printed for W. Hone, London, 1823

1533 HONE, WILLIAM. THE EVERY-DAY BOOK, AND TABLE BOOK, or Everlasting Calendar of Popular Amusements, Sports, Pastimes, Ceremonies, Manners, Customs, and Events incident to Each of the Three Hundred and Sixty-five Days, in Past and Present Times; forming a Complete History of the Year, Months, and Seasons, and a Perpetual Key to the Almanac: Remarkable and Important Anecdotes, Facts, and Notices, in Chronology, Antiquities, Topography, Biography, Natural History, Art, Science, and General Literature, with Poetical Elucidations, for Daily Use and Diversion. With Four Hundred and Thirty-six Engravings. THE YEAR BOOK of Daily Recreation and Information, concerning Remarkable Men and Manners, Times and Seasons, Solemnities and Merry-Makings, Antiquities and Novel-

ties; on the Plan of the Every-Day Book and Table Book. With One Hundred and Fourteen Engravings. *Together, 4 vols., 8vo, calf, marbled edges.*
London, 1847–48

1534 HONOURS ACADEMIE, OR THE FAMOUS PASTORALL OF THE FAIRE SHEPHEARDESSE, JULIETTA: a Work Admirable and Rare, Sententious and Grave, and no lesse Profitable than Pleasant to peruse; wherein are many Notable Discourses, as well Philosophicall as Divine, most Part of the Seven Liberall Sciences being comprehended therein; with Divers Comicall and Tragicall Histories, in Prose and Verse, of all Sorts. Done into English, by R. T. [Robert Tofte]. *Folio, half calf, red edges.*
T. Creede, London, 1610

1535 HOOD, THOMAS. THE WORKS OF (Poetical and Prose). *Portraits, and numerous wood-cuts. 6 vols., crown 8vo, half calf, extra, marbled edges.* New York, 1861

1536 HOOD, THOMAS. MEMORIALS OF; collected, arranged, and edited by his Daughter [Frances Freeling Broderip], with a Preface and Notes, by his Son [Thomas Hood]. *Numerous wood-cuts after the sketches of Hood. 2 vols., 12mo, cloth.*
Boston, 1860

1537 HOOGEVEEN, HENDRIK. DOCTRINA PARTICULARUM LINGUAE GRAECAE, auctore et editore Henrico Hoogeveen. *Handsomely printed on a heavy paper. 2 vols., royal 4to, half morocco, neat; with autograph of Rufus Choate.* LARGE PAPER: *fine original copy, see autograph of author.*
E. Typographeo Dammeano, 1769

"Ouvrage estimé malgré sa grande prolixité." — *Brunet.*

1538 HOOK, THEODORE EDWARD. ADVENTURES OF AN ACTOR, comprising a Picture of the French Stage during a Period of Fifty Years; edited [from the Journal of M. Fleury] by Theodore Hook, Esq. Second Edition. 2 *vols., 12mo, cloth, uncut.* London, 1842

1539 HOOKER, RICHARD, D. D. THE WORKS OF THAT LEARNED AND JUDICIOUS DIVINE, MR. RICHARD HOOKER; with an Account of his Life and Death, by Isaac Walton. 2 *vols., 8vo, calf, gilt, marbled edges.*
University Press, Oxford, 1850

1540 HOOKER, SIR WILLIAM JACKSON. EXOTIC FLORA; containing Figures and Descriptions of New, Rare, or otherwise Interesting Exotic Plants, especially of such as are deserving of being cultivated in our Gardens; together with Remarks upon their Generic and Specific Characters, Natural Orders, History, Culture, Time of Flowering, etc. *With 232 fine colored plates. 3 vols., royal 8vo, cloth, uncut.*
Edinburgh, 1823–27

1541 HOOKER, SIR WILLIAM JACKSON. BOTANICAL MISCELLANY; containing Figures and Descriptions of such Plants

as recommend themselves by their Novelty, Rarity, or History, or by the Uses to which they are applied in the Arts, in Medicine, and in Domestic Œconomy; together with Occasional Botanical Notices and Information (including many Valuable Communications from Distinguished Scientific Travellers). *With* 153 *fine plates, many of which are colored.* 3 *vols., royal* 8*vo, cloth, uncut.*
J. Murray, London, 1830–33

1542 HOOKER, SIR WILLIAM JACKSON; and, ROBERT KAYE GREVILLE. ICONES FILICUM; Figures and Descriptions of Ferns, principally of such as have been altogether unnoticed by Botanists, or as have not yet been correctly figured. *With* 240 *fine colored plates.* 2 *vols., folio, half green levant morocco, extra, gilt edges, by Hammond.* FINE COPY.
Londini, 1829–31

1543 HOOPER, WILLIAM. RATIONAL RECREATIONS: in which the Principles of Numbers and Natural Philosophy are clearly and copiously elucidated, by a Series of Easy, Entertaining, Interesting Experiments; among which are all those commonly performed with Cards. 4 *vols., old marbled calf.* London, 1774

1544 HOPE, THOMAS. ANASTASIUS, OR MEMOIRS OF A GREEK; written at the Close of the Eighteenth Century. (With Memoirs of the Life of Thomas Hope.) *Map.* 2 *vols. in one,* 8*vo, half calf.* Paris, 1831

1545 HOPE, THOMAS. COSTUME OF THE ANCIENTS. A New Edition, much enlarged. *A series of* 321 *plates, in outline.* 2 *vols., royal* 8*vo, cloth, uncut.* London, 1841

1546 HOPPIN, JAMES M. OLD ENGLAND; its Scenery, Art, and People. *Post* 8*vo, cloth.* New York, 1867

1547 HORACE. QUINTI HORATII FLACCI OPERA; cum Novo Commentario ad Modum, Joannis Bond. *Beautifully printed, with rubricated headings to each book; every page enclosed within, and the text and notes separated by red lines. Frontispiece,* 10 *vignettes, and* 2 *plans, photographed, besides the* 6 *photographic views in the Life.* 16*mo, crushed crimson morocco, extra, gilt over marbled edges.* ELEGANT COPY: ALL *the plates photographed.* Didot, Parisiis, 1855

"Charmante Édition présentant un excellent texte, un commentaire latin rédigé avec autant de savoir que de goût par M. Dübner, une vie d'Horace en français par M. Noël des Vergers, une préface intéressante de M. Ambroise Firmin Didot."—*Brunet.*

1548 HORACE. THE WORKS OF QUINTUS HORATIUS FLACCUS, illustrated, chiefly from the Remains of Ancient Art; with a Life, by the Rev. Henry Hart Milman, D.D. *Ornate colored titles and borders, and nearly* 500 *fine wood-cuts. Square* 8*vo, dark brown smooth morocco, very neat, gilt edges.* ELEGANT COPY OF THIS BEAUTIFUL EDITION.
J. Murray, London, 1849

1549 HORACE. ODES OF HORACE, the Best of Lyrick Poets; contayning much Morallity and Sweetnesse. Selected and translated by S[r]. T. H[awkins]. *Engraved title, reverse blank; "To the Reader," 1 leaf; verses signed "F. L.," "John Beaumont," "George Fortescue," "Hugh Holland," "G. D.," and "I. Chapperlinus," 3 leaves; odes, etc., pp. 1–67. Small 4to, half morocco, red edges.*
Imprinted by A. M. for Will. Lee, London, 1625

1550 HORACE. THE EPODES, SATIRES, AND EPISTLES of Horace; translated by the late Rev. Francis Howes. *Foolscap 8vo, calf, antique, carmine edges.*
W. Pickering, London, 1845

1551 HORACE. THE ODES OF HORACE; translated into English Verse, with a Life and Notes, by Theodore Martin. 24*mo, cloth, "blue and gold."* Boston, 1861

1552 HORAPOLLO. THE HIEROGLYPHICS OF Horapollo Nilous (which he published in the Egyptian Tongue, and which Philip translated into the Greek Language). By Alexander Turner Cory. *Printed in two columns, Greek and English, with wood-cuts of the hieroglyphics, etc.* 12*mo, cloth, uncut.* W. Pickering, London, 1840

1553 HORDYNSKI, JOSEPH. HISTORY OF THE LATE POLISH REVOLUTION, and the Events of the Campaign. *Plans. Royal 8vo, boards.* Boston, 1832

1554 HORE BEATE MARIE VIR[GI]NIS SECUNDUM USUM ROMANUM, expliciunt feliciter Parisius: impresse p Egydiū Hardouyn, cōmorātē ī Cōfinio Pontis Nostre Domine ante Templū Divi Dionysii de Carcere; ad Intersignium Roge Auree. PRINTED UPON VELLUM, *in Roman characters, with three illuminations and the capitals all painted in gold and colors. Small 8vo, 5 × 3 inches, velvet covers.* HARDOUYNS' PRESS. (Paris, cir. 1530)

The above title and imprint are from the reverse of the last leaf. A leaf (or more) following the calendar is wanting, otherwise the volume appears to be complete.

1555 HORNIUS, JOHANNES FRIDERICUS. POLITICORUM PARS ARCHITECTONICA DE CIVITATE. *Without title, except the above on the frontispiece. Frontispiece, reverse blank; dedication, 5 leaves; "Benevole Lector," 6 leaves; text, pp. 1–582; tables and errata, 2 leaves. Small 12mo, vellum.*
Typis W. Klerck, Trajecti ad Rhenum, 1664

The dedication (to Frederick III., King of Denmark and Norway) is signed "Joh. Frid. Horn., Brigâ-Silesius." The third book treats of a "free republic."

1556 HORTICULTURIST (THE) and Journal of Rural Art and Rural Taste; devoted to Horticulture, Landscape Gardening, Rural Architecture, Botany, Pomology, Entomology, Rural Economy, etc. Edited by A. J. Downing. *July,* 1846–*December,* 1852. *Numerous wood-cuts, plans, etc.* 7 *vols., 8vo, half green morocco.* Albany, 1846–52

1557 HOUBRAKEN, ARNOLD. DE GROOTE SCHOUBURGH DER NEDERLANTSCHE KONSTSCHILDERS EN SCHILDERESSEN; waar van 'er vele met hunne Beeltenissen ten Tooneel verschynen, en hun Levensgedrag en Kontswerken beschreven worden: zynde een Vervolg op het Schilderboek van K. v. Mander. Door Arn. Houbraken. BRILLIANT IMPRESSIONS OF THE PLATES. 3 *vols.*, 8*vo*, *vellum.* VERY FINE COPY. Amsterdam, 1718–21

This work is one of the chief authorities on the Dutch artists, and the admirable portraits with which it is illustrated are some of the earliest productions of the eminent engraver Jacob Houbraken, son of the author. The third part was published after the death of the author, for his widow.

1558 HOUGHTON GALLERY. A SET OF PRINTS ENGRAVED AFTER THE MOST CAPITAL PAINTINGS in the Collection of her Imperial Majesty the Empress of Russia, lately in the Possession of the Earl of Oxford, at Houghton in Norfolk; with Plans, Elevations, Sections, Chimney Pieces and Ceilings. *Engraved titles* (*with vignettes by Bartolozzi*) *and dedication ;* 28 *plans, elevations, etc.; and* 131 *fine engravings* (*by R. Earlom and other celebrated engravers*), *including portraits of Catherine II. and Robert Walpole;* PROOF IMPRESSIONS, MANY BEFORE THE LETTERS. 2 *vols.*, *atlas folio*, 27 × 21 *inches, green morocco, extra, gilt edges.* J. & J. Boydell, London, Jan. 1, 1788

1559 HOUGHTON, EDWIN B. THE CAMPAIGNS OF THE SEVENTEENTH MAINE. 12*mo*, *half crimson morocco, very neat, marbled edges.* LARGE PAPER: *rubricated title.* Portland, 1866

There were no copies of this work *published* on large paper, or with rubricated titles, but a few were *privately printed* in this form.

1560 HOUGHTON, EDWIN B. SIX OTHER COPIES; *as published.* 12*mo*, *cloth.* Portland, 1866

This work is now out of print.

1561 HOUSEHOLD (THE) OF BOUVERIE, OR THE ELIXIR OF GOLD; a Romance. By a Southern Lady. 2 *vols.*, 12*mo*, *cloth.* New York, 1860

1562 HOUZÉ, A. ATLAS UNIVERSEL HISTORIQUE ET GÉOGRAPHIQUE; composé de Cent-une Cartes, donnant les Différentes Divisions et Modifications Territoriales des Diverses Nations aux Principales Époques de leur Histoire, avec une Notice sur tous les Faits Importants, et l'Indication des Lieux où ils se sont passés: par A. Houzé. *Boundaries and principal places indicated with colors. Imperial* 4*to*, *cloth.* Paris (1853)

1563 HOVEY, C. M. THE MAGAZINE OF HORTICULTURE, Botany, and all Useful Discoveries and Improvements in Rural Affairs. *Numerous wood-cuts and colored plates. Jan.* 1835–*July*, 1868. *First* 8 *vols. half morocco, rest in numbers.* Boston, 1835–68

The titles of the first two volumes, 1835 and 1836, read, — "The American

Gardner's Magazine, and Register of Useful Discoveries and Improvements in Horticulture and Rural Affairs; conducted by C. M. Hovey, and P. P. Hovey, Jr."; afterwards as above.

1564 HOVEY, C. M. THE FRUITS OF AMERICA: containing Richly Colored Figures, and Full Descriptions of all the Choicest Varieties cultivated in the United States. *Portraits of Hovey and Sharp, and 112 fine plates drawn from nature and chromo-lithographed by William Sharp. 2 vols., royal 8vo, half morocco, extra, marbled edges.* Boston, (1852)–56

1565 HOW TO FURNISH A HOUSE AND MAKE IT A HOME. *Woodcuts. 16mo, cloth.* London, (1853)

1566 HOWARD, SIR ROBERT. THE DRAMATIC WORKS OF: viz., the Surprisal; the Committee; the Indian Queen; the Vestal Virgin; the Duke of Lerma. The Third Edition. *12mo, old calf; binding broken and portrait wanting.* J. Tonson, London, 1722

1567 HOWEL, REV. LAURENCE. A COMPLEAT HISTORY OF THE HOLY BIBLE, contain'd in the Old and New Testament; in which are inserted the Occurrences that happen'd during the Space of about Four Hundred Years, from the Days of the Prophet Malachi to the Birth of Our Blessed Saviour, and that have been omitted in all or most of the Former Works of this Nature: the Whole illustrated with Notes, explaining Several Difficult Texts, and reconciling many Seeming Contradictions in the Translations, as well English as others, of the Sacred Scriptures. Adorn'd with above 150 Cuts, engraven by J. Sturt. The Fifth Edition, corrected. *3 vols., 8vo, calf, gilt.* London, 1729

1568 HOWELL, JAMES. EPISTOLÆ HO-ELIANÆ: Familiar Letters, Domestic and Forren; divided into Four Books, partly Historical, Political, Philosophicall, upon Emergent Occasions. The Fourth Edition. *Numerous MS. notes. Small thick 8vo, old calf, red edges.* T. Guy, London, 1673

See "Retrospective Review," Vol. IV. pp 183–200.

1569 HOWELLS, WILLIAM D. VENETIAN LIFE. *Crown 8vo, cloth.* New York, 1866

1570 HOWISON, JOHN. SKETCHES OF UPPER CANADA, Domestic, Local, and Characteristic; to which are added, Practical Details for the Information of Emigrants of every Class, and some Recollections of the United States of America. *8vo, half calf, extra.* Edinburgh, 1821

1571 HOWITT, WILLIAM. VISITS TO REMARKABLE PLACES; Old Halls, Battle Fields, and Scenes illustrative of Striking Passages in English History and Poetry. *Numerous fine wood-cut vignettes.* BOTH SERIES. *2 vols., royal 8vo, cloth, uncut.* London, 1840–42

1572 HOWITT, WILLIAM. THE RURAL AND DOMESTIC LIFE OF GERMANY, with Characteristic Sketches of its Cities and Scenery; collected in a General Tour, and during a Residence in the Country in the Years 1840, 41, and 42. *With above fifty illustrations by G. F. Sargent. 8vo, half calf, neat.* London, 1842

1573 HUC, ÉVARISTE RÉGIS, L'ABBE. TRAVELS IN TARTARY, Thibet, and China, during the Years 1844–5–6; by M. Huc. Translated from the French by W. Hazlitt. *Map and woodcuts. 2 vols., crown 8vo, cloth, gilt tops.* London, s. a.

1574 HUGHES, THOMAS. SCHOOL DAYS AT RUGBY; by an Old Boy. *12mo, cloth.* Boston, 1861.

1575 HUGHES, THOMAS. TOM BROWN AT OXFORD, a Sequel to School Days at Rugby. *Portrait in second part. 2 vols., 12mo, cloth.* Boston, 1862

1576 HUGHES, T. M. AN OVERLAND JOURNEY TO LISBON, at the Close of 1846; with a Picture of the Actual State of Spain and Portugal. *2 vols., 12mo, half green morocco.* London, 1847

1577 HUGO, VICTOR MARIE. LES MISÉRABLES. Translated from the Original French, by Chas. E. Wilbour. *The 5 parts separate. 5 vols., 8vo, cloth.* New York, 1862

1578 HUISH, ROBERT. MEMOIRS OF HER LATE ROYAL HIGHNESS CHARLOTTE AUGUSTA, Princess of Wales, etc. (from Infancy to the Period of her much lamented Death, Funeral Rites, etc., etc.), and of her Illustrious Consort Prince Leopold of Saxe-Coburg Saalfeld; including a Variety of Anecdotes, hitherto unpublished, with Specimens of her Royal Highness's Compositions in Prose, Poetry, and Music, and Fac-similes of her Hand-writing; comprising also an Historical Memoir of the House of Saxe-Coburg Saalfeld. The Whole collected and arranged, from Authorized Sources only, by Robert Huish, Esq. etc. A New Edition, revised, augmented, and improved. *Portraits and plates. 8vo, old marbled calf.* London, 1819

1579 HUISH, ROBERT. MEMOIRS OF GEORGE THE FOURTH, descriptive of the most Interesting Scenes of his Private and Public Life, and the Important Events of his Memorable Reign; with Characteristic Sketches of all the Celebrated Men who were his Friends and Companions as a Prince, and his Ministers and Counsellors as a Monarch. Compiled from Authentic Sources, and Documents, etc. *Vignettes on the engraved titles, and 18 portraits and plates. 2 vols., 8vo, half crimson morocco, extra.* London, 1830

1580 HULSIUS, LEVINUS. XII. PRIMORUM CAESARUM ET LXIIII. IPSORUM UXORUM ET PARENTUM, ex Antiquis Numismatibus, in Ære incisæ, Effigies; atque eorundem earundem-

que Vitæ & Res Gestæ, ex Variis Authoribus collectæ per Levinum Hulsium, Gandavensem. Not. Imp. *Fine impressions of the engraved title and other plates. Small 4to, half calf.*
Typis J. Collitii, Sumptibus P. Brachfeldii, Francoforti ad Mœnum, 1597

1581 HUMBOLDT, FRIEDRICH HEINRICH ALEXANDER, BARON VON. COSMOS: a Sketch of a Physical Description of the Universe. Translated from the German, by E. C. Otté, B. H. Paul, and W. S. Dallas. *Portrait. 5 vols., 12mo, half morocco, very neat, marbled edges.* New York, 1860

1582 HUMBOLDT, FREIDRICH HEINRICH ALEXANDER, BARON VON. ANOTHER COPY: *the same. Portrait. 5 vols., post 8vo, half calf, extra, marbled edges.*
London, 1864

1583 HUMBOLDT, FRIEDRICH HEINRICH ALEXANDER, BARON VON; and, AIMÉ BONPLAND. VUES DES CORDILLÈRES, et Monumens des Peuples Indigènes de l'Amerique. (Atlas Pittoresque du Voyage aux Régions Équinoxiales du Nouveau Continent, fait en 1799–1804, par Humboldt et Bonpland.) VELLUM PAPER, *with 54 fine large engravings of views, costumes, hieroglyphics, etc., many of which are finely colored. 1 vol., imperial folio, half green morocco, gilt tops.*
F. Schoell, Paris, 1810

This copy wants plates 55–69, but contains the supp'ement as far as page 304, i cluding the descriptions of these plates and the letter of M. Visconti. Most copies in the market are much more deficient.

1584 HUMBOLDT, FRIEDRICH HEINRICH ALEXANDER, BARON VON; and, AIMÉ BONPLAND. MONOGRAPHIE DES MELASTOMACÉES: comprenant toutes les Plantes de cet Ordre recueillies jusqu'à ce Jour, et notamment au Mexique, dans l'Ile de Cuba, dans les Provinces de Caracas, de Cumana, et de Barcelone, aux Andes de la Nouvelle-Grenade, de Quito, et du Pérou, et sur les Bords du Rio-Negro, de l'Orénoque, et de la Rivière des Amazones. Par Al. de Humboldt et A. Bonpland. Mise en Ordre, par A. Bonpland. *The* MELASTOMA, *45 plates, and* RHEXIA *30 plates; with letter-press. Printed on vellum paper, the 75 plates finely colored. Imperial folio, boards, uncut.*
Paris, 1823

1585 HUMBOLDT, FRIEDRICH HEINRICH ALEXANDER, BARON VON; and AIMÉ BONPLAND. PERSONAL NARRATIVE OF TRAVELS to the Equinoctial Regions of America, during the Years 1799–1804. Written in French; translated and edited by Thomasina Ross. *3 vols., post 8vo, half calf, extra, marbled edges.* London, 1852–53

1586 HUME, DAVID. THE HISTORY OF ENGLAND, from the Invasion of Julius Cæsar to the Revolution in 1688 (with Life of the Author, by himself, etc.). *Portraits, and numer-*

ous fine large plates, engraved by Bartolozzi, Fittler, Skelton, Landseer, Anker Smith, etc., after Opie, Smirke, West, Hamilton, Westall, and other eminent artists. Elegantly printed by T. Bensley. 10 *vols., imperial folio, diamond russia, neat, marbled edges.* BOWYER'S SUPERB EDITION: *fine impressions of the plates.* LONDON, 1806, etc.

1587 HUME, DAVID. THE HISTORY OF ENGLAND (from the Invasion of Julius Cæsar to the Revolution, in 1688; with Life of the Author, by himself, etc.). *Portraits by Worthington, on India paper, of Hume and each of the sovereigns from William the Conqueror to James II., including Mary Queen of Scots and Cromwell.* 8 *vols., royal* 8*vo, cloth, rough edges.* LARGE PAPER: *only* 50 *copies printed.*
Talboys, Oxford, and Pickering, London, 1826

One of the "Oxford English Classics."

1588 HUMPHREYS, COLONEL DAVID, LL. D., Aide-de-Camp to Washington, etc. THE MISCELLANEOUS WORKS OF. *Portrait; other plates wanting.* 8*vo, old marbled calf.* New York, 1804

1589 HUMPHREYS, HENRY NOEL. ILLUMINATED ILLUSTRATIONS OF FROISSART. (Selected from the MSS. in the British Museum, Bibliothèque Royale, Paris, and from other Sources.) *Contains* 72 *beautiful colored fac-similes, of the size of the originals, with description of each plate and illuminated titles.* 2 *vols. in* 1, 4*to, half crimson morocco, gilt top, uncut.* London, 1844–45

1590 HUMPHREYS, HENRY NOEL. THE ILLUMINATED BOOKS OF THE MIDDLE AGES: an Account of the Development and Progress of the Art of Illumination, as a Distinct Branch of Pictorial Ornamentation, from the IVth to the XVIIth Centuries. Illustrated by a Series of Examples, of the Size of the Originals, selected from the most Beautiful MSS. of the Various Periods, executed on Stone and printed in Colours by Owen Jones. *Illuminated title, initials, and borders, and* 39 *large plates, printed in gold, silver, and colors. The plates, initials, borders, and some of the descriptions, upon India paper. Imperial folio, half crimson morocco, extra, gilt edges, by Wright.* LARGE PAPER: *fine copy.*
London, 1849

The examples are fac-similes from the most celebrated and elegant MSS. in Europe, and the initials and borders are of the same style as MSS. of the date which they represent.

1591 HUMPHREYS, HENRY NOEL. THE ART OF ILLUMINATION AND MISSAL PAINTING; a Guide to Modern Illuminators; illustrated by a Series of Specimens, from richly illuminated MSS. of Various Periods, accompanied by a Set of Outlines, to be coloured by the Student according to the Theories developed in the Work. *Post* 8*vo, white sheep, illuminated, gilt edges; with autograph of John Ross Dix.*
London, 1849

1592 HUMPHREYS, Henry Noel. The Gold, Silver, and Copper Coins of England, exhibited in a Series of Facsimiles of the most Interesting Coins of each Successive Period, printed in Gold, Silver, and Copper; accompanied by a Sketch of the Progress of the English Coinage from the Earliest Period to the Present Time. Sixth Edition. *Illuminated title and 23 plates; also, a plate with impressions on silver foil of crown and two shilling pieces. Crown 8vo, binding broken, but otherwise perfect.* London, 1849

1593 HUNGARY, and its Revolutions, from the Earliest Period to the Nineteenth Century; with a Memoir of Louis Kossuth. By E. O. S. *Portrait of Kossuth. Post 8vo, cloth, uncut.* London, 1854

1594 HUNT, Charles Havens. Life of Edward Livingston. With an Introduction, by George Bancroft. *Portraits on India paper, of Livingston and Andrew Jackson. Imperial 8vo, cloth, rough edges.* Large paper: *only* 100 *copies printed.* New York, 1864

1595 HUNT, Frederick Knight. The Fourth Estate: Contributions towards a History of Newspapers, and of the Liberty of the Press. 2 *vols., crown 8vo, cloth, uncut.* London, 1850

1596 HUNT, Freeman. Worth and Wealth; a Collection of Maxims, Morals, and Miscellanies for Merchants and Men of Business. 12*mo, cloth.* New York, 1856

1597 HUNT, Leigh. Lord Byron and some of his Contemporaries; with Recollections of the Author's Life, and of his Visit to Italy. Second Edition. *Portraits of Byron, the Countess Guiccioli, John Keats, Leigh Hunt, and Charles Lamb; and a plate of fac-similes of the handwriting of Byron, Shelley, and Keats.* 2 *vols., 8vo, half calf, very neat, marbled edges; with newspaper cuttings concerning Byron, comprising extracts from George Burgess's "Cato to Lord Byron," and three verses (signed T. S. M.), "On the Rumoured Exclusion from Westminister Abbey of a Monument to Lord Byron," with notes.* H. Colburn, London, 1828

1598 HUNT, Leigh. Another copy: *the same; with the 5 portraits and fac-similes.* 2 *vols., 8vo, cloth, uncut.* London, 1828

1599 HUNT, Leigh. A Book for a Corner, or Selections in Prose and Verse from Authors the best suited to that Mode of Enjoyment; with Comments on Each, and a General Introduction. *Engraved title and* 80 *wood-cuts after F. W. Hulme and J. Franklin.* 2 *vols. in* 1, *foolscap 8vo, half calf, extra, marbled edges.* London, (1851)

1600 HUNT, Leigh. The Town: its Memorable Characters and Events. With Forty-five Illustrations. A New Edition. *Foolscap 8vo, cloth, uncut.* Smith, Elder & Co., London, 1859

1601 HUNT, Robert. Panthea, the Spirit of Nature. *Royal 8vo, cloth, uncut.* London, 1849

1602 HUNTER, Henry, D. D. The History of London, and its Environs: containing an Account of the Origin of the City; its State under the Romans, Saxons, Danes, and Normans; its Rise and Progress to its Present State of Commercial Greatness; including an Historical Record of Every Important and Interesting Public Event, from the Landing of Julius Cæsar to the Present Period; also a Description of its Antiquities, Public Buildings and Establishments; of the Revolutions in its Government; and of the Calamities to which its Inhabitants have been subject by Fire, Famine, Pestilence, etc. Likewise an Account of all the Towns, Villages, and Country within Twenty-five miles of London. By the late Rev. Henry Hunter, D. D., and other Gentlemen. *Maps, plans, and views. 2 vols., 4to, half russia, backs cracked; with book-plate of Edward Loveden Loveden, Esq., Buscot Park, Berks.* London, 1811

1603 HUNTER, John D. Manners and Customs of Several Indian Tribes located West of the Mississippi, including some Account of the Soil, Climate, and Vegetable Productions, and the Indian Materia Medica; to which is prefixed the History of the Author's Life during a Residence of Several Years among them. *8vo, half morocco, neat.* Philadelphia, 1823

This work occasioned considerable controversy. The "London Quarterly," and other reviewers considered it "authentic and accurate," whilst General Lewis Cass pronounced the author an "impostor," and the work "a worthless fabrication."

1604 HURD, Richard, Bishop of Worcester. Moral and Political Dialogues; with Letters on Chivalry and Romance. The Third Edition. *3 vols., post 8vo, old calf, gilt, marbled edges.* London, 1765

1605 HUTCHINSON, Thomas. The History of the Colony of Massachusetts-Bay; from the First Settlement thereof, in 1628, until its Incorporation with the Colony of Plimouth, Province of Maine, etc., by the Charter of King William and Queen Mary, in 1691. By Mr. Hutchinson, Lieutenant-Governor of the Massachusetts Province. *8vo, old calf.* T. & J. Fleet, Boston, 1764

1606 HUTCHINSON, Thomas. The History of Massachusetts; from the First Settlement thereof, in 1628, until the Year 1750. By Thomas Hutchinson, Esq., late Governor of Massachusetts. The Third Edition, with Additional Notes and Corrections. *2 vols., Thomas & Andrews, Boston,* 1795. —The History of the Province of Massachusetts Bay; from the Year 1750, until June 1774. By Mr. Hutchinson, late Governor of that Province. *Forming Vol.*

III. John Murray, London, 1828. *Together,* 3 *vols.,* 8*vo, half morocco, neat, marbled edges.*
Boston, 1795, and London, 1828

1607 ILLUSTRATED (The) London News. *From* 1842 *to* 1865, *inclusive.* 24 *vols., folio, half crimson morocco, marbled edges.* London, 1842–65

1608 ILLUSTRATED (The) Parlour Miscellany. *Woodcuts.* 8*vo, cloth, uncut.* London, 1847

1609 ILLUSTRATED (An) Record of Important Events in the Annals of Europe during the Last Four Years, comprising a Series of Views of the Principal Places, Battles, etc. etc. etc. connected with those Events: together with a History of those Momentous Transactions, compiled from Official and other Authentic Documents. *Frontispiece containing* 10 *medallion portraits, plate of fac-simile autographs, and* 19 *large colored views.* — The Campaign of Waterloo, illustrated with Engravings of les Quatre Bras, la Belle Alliance, Hougoumont, la Haye Sainte, and other Principal Scenes of Action, including a correct Military Plan together with a grand View of the Battle on a Large Scale; to which is prefixed a History of the Campaign compiled from Official Documents and other Authentic Sources. *Six of the views colored, and* 2 *plates containing* 98 *medallion portraits. Together in one vol., imperial folio, half morocco. gilt top.* Printed by T. Bensley for R. Bowyer.
London, 1816

1610 IMPERIAL (The) Dictionary of Universal Biography: a Series of Original Memoirs of Distinguished Men, of all Ages and Nations; by Writers of Eminence in the Various Branches of Literature, Science, and Art. Conducted by Professor John Eadie, D. D., Professor J. B. Nichol; John Francis Waller, Esq., Edwin Lankester, Esq., M. D.; Professor Francis Bowen, United States; P. E. Dove, General Editor; J. Brown, Corresponding Editor. *Numerous fine portraits.* 3 *vols., in* 16 *parts, imperial* 8*vo, cloth, uncut.* W. Mackenzie, Glasgow, (1864–66)

The titles for the second and third volumes bear the name of John Francis Waller as editor.

1611 INAUGURATION of the Statue of Warren, by the Bunker Hill Monument Association. June 17, 1857. *View of statue, and portraits of Edward Everett and Thos. H. Perkins. Royal* 8*vo, cloth.* Boston, 1858

1612 INCHBALD, Elizabeth. Such Things Are, a Play in Five Acts; Every One has his Fault, a Comedy in Five Acts; Wives as They Were and Maids as They Are, a Comedy in Five Acts; Lovers' Vows, a Play in Five Acts, altered from the German of Kotzebue; To Marry or Not to Marry, a Comedy in Five Acts, with

Remarks by the Author. *A volume of "Inchbald's British Theatre," with plates by Worthington, Engleharte, etc., after Singleton, Howard, etc.* 12*mo, calf, neat.* London, (1808)

1613 INCHBALD, ELIZABETH. MEMOIRS OF; including her Familiar Correspondence with the most Distinguished Persons of her Time. To which are added, the Massacre, and a Case of Conscience; now First Published from her Autograph Copies. Edited by James Boaden, Esq. *Portrait.* 2 *vols., half calf, neat.* London, 1833

1614 INDISPENSABLE (THE) ENGLISH VADE MECUM, OR POCKET COMPANION TO PARIS; for the Use of the English, and more especially for the Heads of Families: containing an Exposure of the Various Frauds and Tricks daily practised upon Strangers; together with a List of all Public Institutions, Edifices, and Different Curiosities; an Account of the Customs and Laws relating to Foreigners; Directions for Killing Time; followed by a Concise Description of the Environs of Paris. By an English Resident. Sixth Edition. *Plates, etc.* 24*mo, half morocco.* Paris, s. a.

1615 INGELOW, JEAN. POEMS. *Post* 8*vo, cloth, gilt top, uncut.* Boston, 1863

1616 INSTRUCTION FOR FIELD ARTILLERY; prepared by a Board of Artillery Officers of the U. S. Army. *Thick* 12*mo, cloth.* Philadelphia, 1860

1617 INTELLECTUAL (THE) OBSERVER: Review of Natural History, Microscopic Research, and Recreative Science. Illustrated with Plates in Colours and Tints, and Numerous Engravings on Wood. *February* 1862–*July* 1866 (9 *vols.*, 8*vo*). — RECREATIVE SCIENCE: a Record and Remembrancer of Intellectual Observation. (First Series of the "Intellectual Observer," 1860–1862, with Numerous Engravings on Wood, 3 *vols., foolscap* 4*to.*) *Together,* 12 *vols., cloth, gilt edges.* London, 1860–66

1618 INTRIGUES (THE) OF THE QUEEN OF SPAIN WITH THE PRINCE OF PEACE AND OTHERS; written by a Spanish Nobleman and Patriot, who alone can be acquainted with the Intrigues and Amours of the above Personages. 12*mo, half morocco.* Boston, 1809

1619 IRELAND, JOHN B. WALL-STREET TO CASHMERE: a Journal of Five Years in Asia, Africa, and Europe; comprising Visits during 1851, 2, 3, 4, 5, 6, to the Danemora Iron Mines, the "Seven Churches," Plains of Troy, Palmyra, Jerusalem, Petra, Seringapatam, Surat, with the Scenes of the Recent Mutinies (Benares, Agra, Cawnpore, Lucknow, Delhi, etc., etc.), Cashmere, Peshawur, the Khyber Pass to Afghanistan, Java, China, and Mauritius. *Nearly* 100 *wood-cuts from sketches by the author. Royal* 8*vo, cloth.* New York, 1859

1620 IRELAND, SAMUEL. PICTURESQUE VIEWS: on the River Thames, from its Source in Glocestershire, to the Nore; on the River Medway, from the Nore to the Vicinity of its Source in Sussex; on the Upper or Warwickshire Avon, from its Source at Naseby to its Junction with the Severn at Tewkesbury; on the River Wye, from its Source at Plinlimmon Hill, to its Junction with the Severn below Chepstow. With Observations on the Public Buildings, and other Works of Art, in their Vicinity. *Numerous plates and wood-cuts, including 3 portraits and 143 fine views in aquatinta. 5 vols., royal 4to, half russia, neat.* LARGE PAPER. London, 1792–97

1621 IRELAND, WILLIAM HENRY. MISCELLANEOUS PAPERS AND LEGAL INSTRUMENTS under the Hand and Seal of William Shakspeare, including the Tragedy of King Lear, and a small Fragment of Hamlet; from the Original MSS. in the Possession of Samuel Ireland, of Norfolk Street. *Fac-similes, and other plates, some of which are colored. Large square folio, original boards, rough edges.* ONLY 138 COPIES EXTANT. London, 1796 (Dec. 1795)

These forgeries are placed under the name of the *perpetrator* instead of under the name of the *dupe* as is customary, or rather, the name by which he is known. His baptism is said to be registered by the name of William Henry Irwyn (the name of his mother who was then separated from her husband and living with Mr. Samuel Ireland, his father), and he was called by his father, Samuel William Henry.

1622 IRELAND, WILLIAM HENRY. ANOTHER COPY: *Second edition. Frontispiece. 8vo, half green morocco, extra.* London, 1796

1623 IRELAND, WILLIAM HENRY. VORTIGERN, an Historical Tragedy, in Five Acts; represented at the Theatre Royal, Drury Lane, on Saturday, April 2, 1796. — HENRY THE SECOND, an Historical Drama, supposed to be written by the Author of Vortigern. [Both by W. H. Ireland.] *Together in 1 vol., crown 8vo, half calf.* London, 1799

1624 IRELAND, WILLIAM HENRY. CHALCOGRAPHIMANIA, or the Portrait-Collector, and Printseller's Chronicle; with Infatuations of every Description: a Humorous Poem, in Four Books, with Copious Notes Explanatory. By Satiricus Sculptor, Esq. [W. H. Ireland.] *Frontispiece. 8vo, half morocco.* London, 1814

"Written by W. H. Ireland from information mostly furnished by T. Coram." — *Lowndes.*

At pages 57, 85, and 102, allusions are made to Ireland in a manner that seems to render his authorship doubtful, but they may have been inserted to avert suspicion. The note (p) on page 57, especially the closing quotation, is what might be expected from him whose "Confessions" are in the tone of one glorying in his shame rather than of penitence for his frauds.

1625 IRELAND, WILLIAM HENRY. MEMOIRS OF HENRY THE GREAT, and of the Court of France during his Reign. *Frontispiece (Henry the Great in armor) "from the very rare print by Gaultier," and plates of music.* 2 *vols.*, 8*vo, half calf, extra.* London, 1824

1626 IRELAND, WILLIAM HENRY. MEMOIRS OF JEANNE D'ARC, surnamed la Pucelle d'Orleans; with the History of her Times. *Portrait on India paper, colored frontispieces, etc.* 2 *vols., royal* 8*vo, cloth, rough edges; with autograph of Edward D. Ingraham, newspaper cuttings and manuscript notes.* LARGE PAPER: *only* 50 *copies printed.* R. Triphook, London, 1824

This work was collected from original MSS. in the libraries of Paris, etc., but principally from one containing a "Diary of the Siege of Orleans," preserved (in the "town-house") at that city.

1627 IRVING, WASHINGTON. THE WORKS OF. New Edition, revised. *Portraits and other fine engravings.* 16 *vols.*, 12*mo, green turkey morocco, extra, contents lettered, gilt edges.* "SUNNYSIDE EDITION." New York, 1860

CONTENTS: Knickerbocker; Sketch-Book; Columbus, 3 vols.; Bracebridge Hall; Traveller; Astoria; Crayon Miscellany; Bonneville; Goldsmith; Mahomet, 2 vols.; Granada; Alhambra; Wolfert's Roost.

1628 IRVING, WASHINGTON. OLIVER GOLDSMITH; a Biography. With Illustrations. *Square* 12*mo, half morocco.* FIRST ILLUSTRATED EDITION. New York, 1849

1629 IRVING, WASHINGTON. LIFE OF GEORGE WASHINGTON. Illustrated Edition. *Engraved titles, portraits, and views.* 5 *vols., imperial* 8*vo, morocco antique, gilt edges.* New York, 1856–59

1630 IRVING, WASHINGTON. THE LIFE AND LETTERS OF; by his Nephew, Pierre M. Irving. *The "National edition," with* 4 *portraits.* 4 *vols.*, 12*mo, cloth.* New York, 1862–64

1631 IRVING, WASHINGTON. SPANISH PAPERS AND OTHER MISCELLANIES, hitherto Unpublished, or Uncollected. Arranged and edited by Pierre M. Irving. *Portrait from drawing by Wilkie.* 2 *vols.*, 12*mo, cloth.* New York, 1867

1632 IRVINGIANA: A MEMORIAL OF WASHINGTON IRVING. *Three portraits (after Jarvis, Darley, and Newton), and facsimile page of MS., all on India paper.* 4*to, boards, uncut.* LARGE PAPER: ONLY 50 COPIES IN THIS STYLE; *whole edition* 110 *copies.* New York, 1860

1633 IRWIN, EYLES. A SERIES OF ADVENTURES IN THE COURSE OF A VOYAGE UP THE RED SEA, on the Coasts of Arabia and Egypt, and of a Route through the Deserts of Thebais, hitherto unknown to the European Traveller, in the Year M.DCC.LXXVII. In Letters to a Lady. Illustrated with Maps and Cuts. 4*to, old calf.* London, 1780

"Chiefly valuable for the information which his personal adventures necessarily give of the manners, etc., of the Arabians."—*Lowndes.*

1634 ITALIAN CLASSICS, ETC. A COLLECTION OF. Ariosto, 6 vols. Bernardo della Coscienza, 1 vol. Baretti Lettere, 1 vol. Dante, 3 vols. Davila, 11 vols. Denina Revoluzio

d'Italia, 9 vols. D'Agnolo Pandolfini, 1 vol. Tragedie di Eschilo, 2 vols. Manzoni i Promessi Sposi, 4 vols. Metastasi, 15 vols. Monti Tragedie, 1 vol. Monti Poesie Liriche, 1 vol. Novelle Scelte, 4 vols. Odissea di Omero, 3 vols. Iliade di Omero, 3 vols. Plutarco, 15 vols. Rime del Petrarca, 2 vols. Sofocle, 3 vols. Tasso, 3 vols. L'Eneide di Virgilio, 2 vols. *Together*, 90 *vols.*, 18*mo*, *half calf.*
G. Pomba, Torino, 1828–30

1635 ITALY; CLASSICAL, HISTORICAL, AND PICTURESQUE. Illustrated in a Series of Views from Drawings by Stanfield, Roberts, Harding, Prout, Leitch, Brockeden, Barnard, etc.; with Descriptions of the Scenes. Preceded by an Introductory Essay, on the Recent History and Present Condition of Italy and the Italians; by Camillo Mafei, D. D., etc. *Imperial 4to, morocco, antique, gilt edges.*
Glasgow, 1856

1636 IVES, JOSEPH C. REPORT UPON THE COLORADO RIVER OF THE WEST; explored in 1857 and 1858, by Lieutenant Joseph C. Ives, Corps of Topographical Engineers. *Maps, plates, and wood-cuts; the Indian portraits colored. 4to, cloth.*
Washington, 1861

1637 IVES, LEVI SILLIMAN. THE TRIALS OF A MIND IN ITS PROGRESS TO CATHOLICISM. 12*mo, cloth.*
Boston, 1855

1638 JACKSON, JAMES, M. D. LETTERS TO A YOUNG PHYSICIAN just entering upon Practice. 12*mo, cloth.* Boston, 1855

1639 JACKSON, JAMES, M. D. ANOTHER LETTER TO A YOUNG PHYSICIAN; to which are appended some other Medical Papers. 12*mo, cloth.* Boston, 1861

1640 JACKSON, JAMES GREY. AN ACCOUNT OF THE EMPIRE OF MAROCCO, and the District of Suse; compiled from Miscellaneous Observations made during a Long Residence in, and Various Journies through, these Countries: to which is added, an Accurate and Interesting Account of Timbuctoo, the great Emporium of Central Africa. *Maps, and* 11 *plates after drawings by the author; the serpents colored. Printed for the author by W. Bulmer & Co. 4to, half calf, neat, marbled edges.* London, 1809

1641 JACKSON, JOHN; and WILLIAM ANDREW CHATTO. A TREATISE ON WOOD ENGRAVING, Historical and Practical, with upwards of Three Hundred Illustrations engraved on Wood; by John Jackson: the Historical Portion by W. A. Chatto. Second Edition; with a New Chapter on the Artists of the Present Day, and 145 Additional Wood Engravings. *Contains fac-similes from the works of Durer, Bewick, etc. Imperial 8vo, half green morocco, extra, gilt top, uncut.*
London, 1861

1642 JACOB, SIR HILDEBRAND. THE WORKS OF; containing Poems on Various Subjects, and Occasions: with the Fatal Constancy, a Tragedy; and Several Pieces in Prose. The Greatest Part never before publish'd. *8vo, old mottled calf, gilt, red edges.* ONLY 150 COPIES PRINTED. W. Lewis, London, 1735

Dedicated to "His Excellency James Earl of Waldegrave, Ambassador Extraordinary and Plenipotentiary at the Court of France, etc., etc., etc."

1643 JACOB, WILLIAM. AN HISTORICAL INQUIRY INTO THE PRODUCTION AND CONSUMPTION OF PRECIOUS METALS. *2 vols., 8vo, cloth, uncut.* J. Murray, London, 1831

1644 JAMES, HENRY. THE NATURE OF EVIL; considered in a Letter to the Rev. Edward Beecher, D. D. Author of "The Conflict of Ages." *12mo, cloth.* New York, 1855

1645 JAMES, HENRY. SUBSTANCE AND SHADOW, or Morality and Religion in their Relation to Life; an Essay upon the Physics of Creation. *Crown 8vo, cloth, uncut.* Boston, 1863

1646 JAMESON, MRS. ANNA. SOCIAL LIFE IN GERMANY, illustrated in the Acted Dramas of her Royal Highness the Princess Amelia of Saxony; translated from the German, with an Introduction and Notes, explanatory of the German Language and Manners. By Mrs. Jameson. *2 vols., 12mo, half calf, extra.* London, 1840

1647 JAMESON, MRS. ANNA. MEMOIRS OF THE BEAUTIES OF THE COURT OF CHARLES THE SECOND, with their Portraits, after Sir Peter Lely and other Eminent Painters; illustrating the Diaries of Pepys, Evelyn, Clarendon, and other contemporary Writers. Third Edition, enlarged. *India proofs of the 21 fine portraits. Imperial 8vo, crimson morocco, extra, gilt edges.* London, 1851

The Portraits were re-engraved for this edition.

1648 JAMESON, MRS. ANNA. SACRED AND LEGENDARY ART. Second Edition, complete in One Volume; containing Legends of the Angels and Archangels, the Evangelists, the Apostles, the Doctors of the Church, St. Mary Magdalene, the Patron Saints, the Martyrs, the Early Bishops, the Hermits, and the Warrior Saints of Christendom, as represented in the Fine Arts. *With 17 etchings by the author, and numerous wood-cuts. Square 8vo, brown turkey morocco, neat, gilt edges.* Longmans & Co., London, 1850

1649 JAMESON, MRS. ANNA. LEGENDS OF THE MONASTIC ORDERS, as represented in the Fine Arts; forming the Second Series of Sacred and Legendary Art. Second Edition; corrected, enlarged, and with Additional Illustrations. *With 11 etchings by the author, and numerous wood-cuts. Square 8vo, brown crushed morocco, neat, gilt over carmine edges, by Holloway.* Longmans & Co., London, 1852

1650 JAMESON, Mrs. Anna. Legends of the Madonna, represented in the Fine Arts; forming the Third Series of Sacred and Legendary Art. *With* 31 *plates drawn on stone by the author, and numerous wood-cuts. Square* 8*vo, brown crushed morocco, neat, gilt over carmine edges, by Holloway.* Longmans & Co., London, 1852

1651 JAMIESON, John, D. D. A Dictionary of the Scottish Language; in which the Words are explained in their Different Senses, authorized by the Names of the Writers by whom they are used, or the Titles of the Works in which they occur, and derived from their Originals. Abridged from the Dictionary and Supplement, in Four Volumes Quarto, by John Johnstone. *Portrait of Jamieson. Thick* 8*vo, cloth, uncut.* Edinburgh, 1846

1652 JARDINE, Sir William. The Naturalist's Library. *Above* 1,200 *colored plates and* 40 *portraits.* 40 *vols., post* 8*vo, morocco, gilt, gilt edges.* Edinburgh, (1833–44)

This work comprises Birds (14 vols.), Animals (13 vols.), Insects (7 vols.), Fishes (6 vols.); each volume containing between 30 and 40 colored plates, with a memoir and portrait of some distinguished naturalist.

1653 JARVES, James Jackson. Art Studies: the "Old Masters" of Italy; Painting. Copper-plate Illustrations. *Printed on toned paper. Royal* 8*vo, cloth, uncut.* India proofs of the plates: *only* 50 *copies printed.* New York, 1861

1654 JAY, John. The Life of; with Selections from his Correspondence and Miscellaneous Papers. By his Son, William Jay. *Portrait from a bust.* 2 *vols.,* 8*vo, half calf, neat.* New York, 1833

1655 JEFFERSON, Thomas. Memoir, Correspondence, and Miscellanies, from the Papers of. Edited by Thomas Jefferson Randolph. *Portrait, and fac-simile of the original draught of the Declaration of Independence.* 4 *vols.,* 8*vo, calf, extra, marbled edges, by Pawson and Nicholson.* Charlottesville, 1829

1656 JEFFERSON, Thomas. Mélanges Politiques et Philosophiques, Extraits des Mémoires et de la Correspondance de Thomas Jefferson; précédés d'un Essai sur les Principes de l'École Américaine et d'une Traduction de la Constitution des États-Unis, avec un Commentaire tiré, pour la plus grande partie, de l'Ouvrage publié sur cette Constitution par William Rawle, LL. D. Par L.-P. Conseil. 2 *vols.,* 8*vo, half morocco.* Paulin, Paris, 1833

1657 JEFFERSON, Thomas. A Manual of Parliamentary Practice, composed Originally for the Use of the Senate of the United States; by Thomas Jefferson. With References to the Practice and Rules of the House of Representatives. The Whole brought down to the Practice of the

Present Time; to which are added the Rules and Orders, together with the Joint Rules, of Both Houses of Congress: and accompanied with Copious Indices. *12mo, cloth.* Philadelphia, 1843

1658 JEFFERYS, THOMAS. A COLLECTION OF THE DRESSES OF DIFFERENT NATIONS, Antient and Modern, particularly Old English Dresses; after the Designs of Holbein, Vandyke, Hollar, and others: with an Account of the Authorities, from which the Figures are taken; and some short Historical Remarks on the Subject. To which are added the Habits of the Principal Characters of the English Stage. *Vignettes on the titles and 480 plates, including two plates (from Bouquet's "Account of the Expedition against the Ohio Indians, in the Year 1764") after West, engraved by Grignion and Canot. Letter-press, in French and English. 4 vols., 4to, half calf.* T. Jefferys, London, 1757–72

1659 JEFFREY, FRANCIS. CONTRIBUTIONS TO THE EDINBURGH REVIEW. Second Edition. *Index. 3 vols., 8vo, polished calf, gilt, marbled edges.* London, 1846

1660 JEFFRIES, DAVID. A TREATISE ON DIAMONDS AND PEARLS, in which their Importance is considered, and Plain Rules are exhibited for ascertaining the Value of both; also the True Method of Manufacturing Diamonds. The Fourth Edition, with Large Improvements. *Plates and tables. 12mo, cloth, uncut.* E. Lumley, London, s. a.

1661 JENYNS, SOAME. THE WORKS OF; including Several Pieces never before published. To which are prefixed, Short Sketches of the History of the Author's Family, and also of his Life; by Charles Nalson Cole, Esq. *Portrait by J. Heath after Sir J. Reynolds. 4 vols., 8vo, marbled calf, gilt, yellow edges; with book-plate and autograph of S. H. L. N. Gilman.* T. Cadell, London, 1790

1662 JEPHSON, ROBERT. ROMAN PORTRAITS, a Poem in Heroick Verse; with Historical Remarks and Illustrations. *Portrait of author, and heads from antique gems, etc. 4to, half calf, yellow edges.* London, 1794

1663 JERDAN, WILLIAM. NATIONAL PORTRAIT GALLERY, of Illustrious and Eminent Personages of the Nineteenth Century; with Memoirs, by William Jerdan, Esq., F. S. A., etc. Dedicated, by Permission, to the King. *Contains 184 fine portraits. 5 vols., imperial 8vo, green morocco, extra, gilt edges.* London, 1830–34

1664 JERROLD, DOUGLAS. SPECIMENS OF DOUGLAS JERROLD'S WIT; together with Selections, chiefly from his Contributions to Journals, intended to illustrate his Opinions. Arranged by his Son, Blanchard Jerrold. *Post 8vo, cloth.* Boston, 1858

1665 JERROLD, DOUGLAS. THE BROWNRIGG PAPERS. Edited by Blanchard Jerrold. *With a colored illustration by George Cruikshank. Crown 8vo, cloth, uncut.* London, 1860

1666 JESSE, EDWARD. A SUMMER'S DAY AT HAMPTON COURT; being a Descriptive Road-Book to the Palace, and a Guide to its Picture Gallery and Gardens. *Wood-cuts.* 16*mo, boards.* J. Murray, London, 1842

1667 JESSE, JOHN HENEAGE. GEORGE SELWYN AND HIS CONTEMPORARIES; with Memoirs and Notes. *Many fine portraits. 4 vols., 8vo. half calf, extra.* London, 1843–44

1668 JESSE, JOHN HENEAGE. MEMOIRS OF THE COURT OF ENGLAND; from the Revolution, in 1688, to the Death of George the Second. *Portraits. 3 vols., 8vo, cloth, uncut.* London, 1843

1669 JESSE, JOHN HENEAGE. MEMOIRS OF THE PRETENDERS, AND THEIR ADHERENTS. *Portraits and plates. 2 vols., royal 8vo, cloth, uncut.* London, 1845

1670 JEWEL, JOHN, BISHOP OF SALISBURY. THE WORKS OF. Edited by Richard William Jelf, D. D. *8 vols., 8vo, cloth, uncut.* University Press, Oxford, 1848

1671 JEWSBURY, MARIA JANE. PHANTASMAGORIA, or Sketches of Life and Literature. *2 vols., post 8vo, half claret morocco, extra, gilt edges.* London, 1825

This work — her first — is dedicated to Wordsworth, who, in speaking of the author, said: "In one quality — quickness in the motions of her mind — she was, in the author's estimation, unrivaled."

1672 JOBSON, REV. FREDERICK JAMES. AMERICA AND AMERICAN METHODISM. With Prefatory Letters by the Rev. Thomas B. Sargent, D. D., and the Rev. John Hannah, D. D. Illustrated from Original Sketches by the Author. *Crown 8vo, cloth, uncut.* New York (London), 1857

1673 JOHNSON'S NEW ILLUSTRATED FAMILY ATLAS OF THE WORLD; with Physical Geography, and with Descriptions, Geographical, Statistical, and Historical, including the latest Federal Census, and the Existing Religious Denominations in the World. Text by Richard Swainson Fisher, M. D. *Engraved title, above* 100 *large colored maps, plans, national emblems, coats of arms, etc., and numerous wood-cuts in the text. Large folio, half morocco, gilt side, marbled edges.* New York, 1866

1674 JOHNSON, JAMES, M. D. CHANGE OF AIR, or the Diary of a Philosopher in Pursuit of Health and Recreation; illustrating the Beneficial Influence of Bodily Exercise, Change of Scene, Pure Air, and Temporary Relaxation as Antidotes to the Wear and Tear of Education and Avocation. Second Edition. *8vo, half blue calf, extra.* London, 1831

1675 JOHNSON, JOHN. TYPOGRAPHIA, or the Printers' Instructor: including an Account of the Origin of Printing, with Biographical Notices of the Printers of England, from Caxton to the Close of the Sixteenth Century; a Series of Ancient and Modern Alphabets, and Domesday Characters; together with an Elucidation of Every Subject connected with the Art. *Portraits of Caxton and the author, and the engraved titles, on India paper; numerous wood-cuts, including other portraits; and ornamental borders. 2 vols., 8vo, tree calf, gilt, gilt edges.* LARGEST PAPER. *Elegant copy.*
London, 1824

Very few copies of this size (called "Roxburgh Copies") were printed.

1676 JOHNSON, JOHN. ANOTHER COPY: *the same; with the portraits, borders, etc., as in the above. 2 vols., crown 8vo, cloth, uncut.* LARGE PAPER. London, 1824

This work was printed in *three* sizes; the *small paper* copies were printed without the borders.

1677 JOHNSON, SAMUEL. THE WORKS OF. (Including Prayers, Sermons, and Parliamentary Debates; with an Essay on his Life and Genius, etc.) *Portrait, by Worthington, on India paper. 11 vols., royal 8vo, cloth, rough edges. Vols. VII. and VIII. somewhat water-stained.* LARGE PAPER: *only 75 copies printed.*
Talboys, Oxford, and Pickering, London, 1825

One of the "Oxford English Classics."

1678 JOHNSON, SAMUEL. A DICTIONARY OF THE ENGLISH LANGUAGE; etc. With Numerous Corrections, and with the Addition of Several Thousand Words, etc. By the Rev. H. J. Todd, M. A., etc. *Portrait. 3 vols., 4to, finely bound, russia, very neat, gilt edges.* SECOND AND BEST EDITION.
London, 1827

1679 JOHNSON, SAMUEL. LIVES OF THE MOST EMINENT ENGLISH POETS, with Critical Observations on their Works. With Notes, Corrective and Explanatory, by Peter Cunningham, F. S. A. *3 vols., 8vo, calf, gilt, gilt edges.*
J. Murray, London, 1854

1680 JOHNSONIANA; OR, SUPPLEMENT TO BOSWELL: being Anecdotes and Sayings of Dr. Johnson, collected by Piozzi, Hawkins, Tyers, Hoole, Steevens, Reynolds, Cumberland, Cradock, Seward, Murphy, Beattie, Miss Hawkins, Windham, Nichols, Humphry, Hannah Moore, Parr, Mad. d'Arblay, Horne, Baretti, Lady Knight, Northcote, Percy, Stockdale, Parker, Rose, Green, Reed, Kearsley, Knowles, Smith, Warner, King, Boothby, Pepys, Carter, etc. *Fine impressions of the 45 plates, engraved by Finden, Scriven, etc., after eminent artists, comprising portraits, views, fac-similes, etc. 4to, boards, uncut.* LARGE PAPER: BEST EDITION.
J. Murray, London, 1836

This volume, intended as a supplement to all editions of Boswell, was edited by J. W. Croker, and contains selections from nearly a hundred different publications.

1681 JOHNSTON, ALEXANDER KEITH. DICTIONARY OF GEOGRAPHY, Descriptive, Physical, Statistical, and Historical; forming a Complete General Gazetteer of the World. *Thick 8vo, half russia, neat, marbled edges.* London, 1852

1682 JOHNSTON, CHARLES. CHRYSAL, OR THE ADVENTURES OF A GUINEA; by an Adept. A New Edition, to which is now prefixed a Sketch of the Author's Life. *Colored plates. 3 vols., 8vo, calf, very neat.* LARGE PAPER. London, 1821

1683 JOHNSTON, CHARLES. CHRYSAL, OR THE ADVENTURES OF A GUINEA; wherein are exhibited Views of Several Striking Scenes, with Interesting Anecdotes of the most Noted Persons in Every Rank of Life, through whose Hands it has passed. By an Adept. *Plates. 3 vols., 12mo, half blue calf, extra.* London, 1822

Same type as the above copy, but printed on a smaller paper. The plates are not colored, and are printed without the borders.

1684 JOHNSTON, DAVID C. OUTLINES ILLUSTRATIVE OF THE JOURNAL OF F****** A*** K*****. [Frances Anne Kemble]; drawn and etched by Mr. —— [Johnston]. *Consists of eight humorous and satirical illustrations with references to the pages of the "Journal" where the same may be inserted. 12mo, boards; with book-plate of Robert Balmanno.* D. C. Johnston, Boston, 1835

1685 JOHNSTONE, WILLIAM GROSART; and ALEXANDER CROALL. THE NATURE-PRINTED BRITISH SEA-WEEDS: a History, accompanied by Figures and Dissections, of the Algæ of the British Isles; Nature-printed by Henry Bradbury. *Contains 207 beautiful colored plates of the different varieties and numerous wood-cuts. 4 vols., 8vo, half green morocco, gilt tops, uncut.* London, 1859–60

1686 JONES, OWEN; and JULES GOURY. VIEWS ON THE NILE, from Cairo to the Second Cataract, drawn on Stone by George Moore, from Sketches taken in 1832 and 1833 by Owen Jones and the late Jules Goury; with Historical Notices of the Monuments by Samuel Birch. *Frontispiece, and 30 large tinted plates. Imperial folio, half morocco.* London, 1843

1687 JONSON, BEN. THE WORKS OF: with Notes, Critical and Explanatory, and a Biographical Memoir; by W. Gifford, Esq. *Portrait by Fitler. 9 vols., royal 8vo, smooth crimson morocco, very neat, contents lettered, gilt edges, by Holloway.* LARGE PAPER: ELEGANT COPY; *uniform with Massinger and Shirley.* London, 1816

"Best edition, by the ablest of modern commentators, through 'whose learned and generous labors Old Ben's forgotten works and injured character are restored to the merited admiration and esteem of the world.' — *J. P. Kemble.*" — *Lowndes.*

1688 JONSON, BEN. ANOTHER COPY: *the same; small paper. 9 vols., 8vo, old polished calf, marbled edges.*
London, 1816

1689 JONSTON, JOHANN. HISTORIÆ NATURALIS: de Insectis, Libri III.; de Serpentibus et Draconibus, Libri II.; de Quadrupetibus, Libri IV.; de Piscibus et Cetis, Libri V.; de Avibus, Libri VI.; Johannes Jonstonus, Med. Doctor, concinnavit. *Numerous plates. 4 vols., folio, vellum, extra, gilt edges; with an old book-plate, and arms gilt on sides.* ORIGINAL EDITION.
Francofurti ad Mœnum, 1650–53

1690 JORTIN, JOHN, D. D. THE LIFE OF ERASMUS. *Facsimiles of handwriting; portrait wanting. 2 vols., 4to, old calf; binding broken.*
London, 1758–60

1691 JOSEPHUS. THE GENUINE WORKS OF FLAVIUS JOSEPHUS, the learned and authentic Jewish Historian, and celebrated Warrior. Translated from the Original Greek, according to Havercamp's Accurate Edition, with Copious Notes, and Proper Observations; by William Whiston, A. M., etc. *3 vols., 8vo, sheep, blue edges.*
Printed at Thomas & Andrews, Boston, 1809

1692 JOSEPHUS. THE WORKS OF JOSEPHUS; with a Life written by himself. Translated from the Original Greek, including Explanatory Notes and Observations, by William Whiston, A. M. With a Complete Index. *Portrait. 4 vols., thick 12mo, cloth.* Philadelphia, 1859

1693 JOSSELYN, JOHN. NEW-ENGLAND'S RARITIES, discovered in Birds, Beasts, Fishes, Serpents, and Plants of that Country; by John Josselyn, Gent. With an Introduction and Notes, by Edward Tuckerman, M. A. *Fac-similes of the original cuts. Reprint of the London edition of 1672. 4to, cloth, uncut. Only 75 copies in this style.*
W. Veazie, Boston, 1865

1694 JOSSELYN, JOHN. AN ACCOUNT OF TWO VOYAGES TO NEW ENGLAND, made during the Years 1638, 1663; by John Josselyn, Gent. (With Chronological Observations of America from the Year of the World to the Year of Christ 1673.) *Pedigree of the Josselyn family. Reprint of the London editions of 1674 75. 4to, cloth, uncut. Only 75 copies in this style.* W. Veazie, Boston, 1865

1695 JUBÉ, LE GÉNÉRAL AUGUSTE, BARON DE LAPERELLE. LE TEMPLE DE LA GLOIRE, ou les Fastes Militaires de la France; depuis le Règne de Louis XIV. jusqu' à nos Jours. *Engraved titles and 38 large plates. 2 vols., folio, half morocco, rough edges.* VELLUM PAPER. Paris, (1819–20)

This copy is complete, *i. e.*, it contains all that was ever published.

1696 JUDITH, ESTHER, AND OTHER POEMS; by a Lover of the Fine Arts. *18mo, marbled calf.* Boston, 1820

1697 JUNIUS. JUNIUS: STAT NOMINIS UMBRA. THE FIRST AUTHORIZED EDITION, *printed under the au'hor's inspection; with the table of contents and index added. Engraved titles. 2 vols., 12mo, marbled calf, gilt, yellow edges; with autograph of Jno. Pickering.*
Printed for Henry Sampson Woodfall, London, (1773)

1698 JUNIUS. JUNIUS: STAT NOMINIS UMBRA. *The elegant edition, printed by T. Bensley, with engraved titles and 16 portraits. 2 vols., royal 8vo, dark blue morocco, neat, gilt edges.* LARGE PAPER. London, 1797

1699 JUNIUS. JUNIUS; including Letters by the same Writer, under other Signatures (now first collected). To which are added, his Confidential Correspondence with Mr. Wilkes, and his Private Letters addressed to Mr. H. S. Woodfall; with a Preliminary Essay [by J. Mason Good, M. D.], Notes, Fac-similes, etc. [Edited by George Woodfall.] 3 *vols., 8vo, half russia.* London, 1812

1700 JUNKIN, GEORGE, D. D. POLITICAL FALLACIES; an Examination of the False Assumptions, and Refutation of the Sophistical Reasonings, which have brought on this Civil War. *Portrait. 12mo, cloth.* New York, 1863

1701 JUSTINIAN I. CORPUS JURIS CIVILIS QUO JUS UNIVERSUM JUSTINIANEUM COMPREHENDITUR: Pandectis, ad Florentinum Archetypum expressis. Codice, cum Optimis quibusque Editionibus collato: cum Notis repètitæ Quintùm Prælectionis Dionysii Gothofredi, J. C. Quibus inter Cætera Variæ Lectiones, Leges Similes, Contrariæ, Abrogatæ: Verborum Legumque Difficilium Interpretationes, Selectæ Repetitiones, Argumenta, Compendia, atque Epitomæ, Anni Singulis Codicis Legibus additi continentur. Additæ et Institutionum, Novellarum Justiniani, Leonis, & Feudorum Epitomæ, Edictum Perpetuum. Græcæ Leges & Constitutiones in Pandectis & Codice. Leges XII. Tabul. suo Ordini restitutæ, eodem Auctore. Accesserunt Authenticæ seu Novellæ Constitutiones Græcæ, Justiniani, Leonis, Ze nonis, Tiberii, Heraclii, & aliorum Imperatorum cum Latino Sermone collatæ, quæ antea non prodierant. Item Canones Apostolorum, & Græcè & Latinè. Chronici Canones & Consulares usque ad Justiniani Mortem, nequid, quod Incuria non extitit, desideraretur. 2 *vols., royal folio, half calf, neat.* A. Vitray, Lutetiæ Parisiorum, 1628

1702 JUVENAL. SIXTEEN SATYRS, or a Survey of the Manners and Actions of Mankind; with Arguments, Marginall Notes, and Annotations, clearing the Obscure Places, out of the History, Lawes, and Ceremonies of the Romans. By Sir Robert Stapylton, Knight. *Portrait of Stapylton by W.*

Marshall, and frontispiece by T. Rawlins. Small 8vo, calf. FINE CLEAN COPY. London, 1647

1703 JUVENAL. MORES HOMINUM: the Manners of Men, described in Sixteen Satyrs, by Juvenal; as he is published in his most Authentick Copy, lately printed by Command of the King of France. Whereunto is added the Invention of Seventeen Designes in Picture, with Arguments to the Satyrs; as also Explanations to the Designes in English and Latine: together with a Large Comment, clearing the Author, in every place wherein he seemed Obscure, out of the Laws and Customes of the Romans, and the Latine and Greek Histories. By Sir Robert Stapylton, Knight. Published by Authority. *Portrait of Stapylton by Lombart, and the* 17 *plates by Hollar;* BRILLIANT IMPRESSIONS. *Royal folio, old calf.* LARGE PAPER: *very fine copy.* London, 1660

1704 JUVENAL. THE SATIRES OF JUVENAL, Persius, Sulpicia, and Lucilius; literally translated into English Prose, with Notes, Chronological Tables, Arguments, etc. By the Rev. Lewis Evans. To which is added, the Metrical Version of Juvenal and Persius; by the late William Gifford, Esq. *Portrait of Juvenal from a bust.* 12*mo, cloth.* New York, 1860

1705 KANE, ELISHA K., M.D. ARCTIC EXPLORATIONS: the Second Grinnell Expedition in Search of Sir John Franklin, 1853, '54, '55. Illustrated by upwards of Three Hundred Engravings, from Sketches by the Author; the Steel Plates executed under the Superintendence of J. M. Butler, the Wood Engravings by Van Ingen & Snyder. 2 *vols., dark blue turkey morocco, very neat, gilt edges; with newspaper cuttings, etc.* Philadelphia, 1856

1706 KANE, ELISHA K., M.D. ANOTHER COPY: *the same. Portraits, maps, and above* 300 *engravings on steel and wood.* 2 *vols.,* 8*vo, cloth.* Philadelphia, 1857

1707 KAUFFMAN, C. H. THE DICTIONARY OF MERCHANDIZE, and Nomenclature in all Languages, for the Use of Counting Houses; containing the History, Places of Growth, Culture, Use, and Marks of Excellency of such Natural Productions as form Articles of Commerce, with their Names in all European Languages. Second Edition. 8*vo, half calf.* London, 1805

1708 KEATE, GEORGE. AN ACCOUNT OF THE PELEW ISLANDS, situated in the Western Part of the Pacific Ocean; composed from the Journals and Communications of Captain Henry Wilson, and some of his Officers, who, in August 1783, were there shipwrecked in the Antelope, a Packet belonging to the Honourable East India Company. — A SUPPLEMENT TO

THE ACCOUNT OF THE PELEW ISLANDS: compiled from the Journals of the Panther and the Endeavour, and from the Oral Communications of Captain Henry Wilson; by the Rev. John Pearce Hockin. *Portraits, charts, and plates. Together in* 1 *vol., royal* 4*to, diamond russia, very neat, marbled edges.* LARGE PAPER: *original edition.*
London, 1788–1803

1709 KEIGHTLEY, THOMAS. THE FAIRY MYTHOLOGY, illustrative of the Romance and Superstition of Various Countries. *Frontispiece by G. Cruikshank. Post* 8*vo, cloth, uncut.*
London, 1850

1710 KELLY, MICHAEL. REMINISCENCES OF; including a Period of Nearly Half a Century. With Original Anecdotes of many Distinguished Persons, Political, Literary, and Musical. *Portraits and plates of music, etc.* 2 *vols.,* 8*vo, sprinkled calf, neat.* LARGE TYPE.
London, 1826

"A very amusing work, by far the best addition to our theatrical history since Colley Cibber's 'Apology.' It contains curious particulars, etc., relating not only to the British Stage, but to the Italian Opera." —*Lowndes.*

1711 KELLY, MICHAEL. ANOTHER COPY: Second Edition. *Portrait and engraved plates of music, etc.* 2 *vols., crown* 8*vo, half morocco, extra, marbled edges.* London, 1826

This copy is printed with smaller type than the above.

1712 KELLY, WALTER KEATING. SYRIA AND THE HOLY LAND, their Scenery and their People: being Incidents of History and Travel, from the Best and most Recent Authorities; including J. L. Burckhardt, Lord Lindsay, and Dr. Robinson. *Contains* 180 *wood-cuts.* 8*vo, cloth, uncut.*
London, s. a.

1713 KELTY, MARY ANNE. REMINISCENCES OF THOUGHT AND FEELING; by the Author of "Visiting my Relations." *Foolscap* 8*vo, cloth, uncut.* W. Pickering, London, 1852

1714 KELTY, MARY ANNE. VISITING MY RELATIONS, and its Results; a Series of Small Episodes in the Life of a Recluse. *Foolscap* 8*vo, cloth.*
W. Pickering, London, 1853

1715 KELTY, MARY ANNE. THE REAL AND THE BEAU-IDEAL; etc. *Post* 8*vo, cloth.* Boston, 1861

1716 KEMBLE, FRANCES ANNE. JOURNAL OF A RESIDENCE ON A GEORGIAN PLANTATION IN 1838–1839. 12*mo, cloth.*
New York, 1863

1717 KEMP, EDWARD. HOW TO LAY OUT A SMALL GARDEN; intended as a Guide to Amateurs in Choosing, Forming, or Improving a Place (from a Quarter of an Acre to Thirty Acres in extent), with Reference to both Design and Execution. 16*mo, cloth.* London, 1850

1718 KENNEDY, JOHN PENDLETON. WORKS: Swallow Barn, or a Sojourn in the Old Dominion; Horse-shoe Robinson, a Tale of the Tory Ascendency; Rob of the Bowl, a Legend of St. Inigoe's. *Portrait and wood-cuts.* 3 *vols.*, 12*mo, half calf, extra, marbled edges.* New York, 1854–56

1719 KENNEDY, JOSEPH C. G. PRELIMINARY REPORT ON THE EIGHTH CENSUS; 1860. 8*vo, cloth.* Washington, 1862

1720 KENNEDY, JOSEPH C. G. POPULATION OF THE UNITED STATES IN 1860; compiled from the Original Returns of the Eighth Census. 4*to, half russia.* Washington, 1864

1721 KERR, ROBERT. A GENERAL HISTORY AND COLLECTION OF VOYAGES AND TRAVELS, arranged in Systematic Order; forming a Complete History of the Origin and Progress of Navigation, Discovery, and Commerce, by Sea and Land, from the Earliest Ages to the Present Time. Illustrated with Maps and Charts. 18 *vols.*, 8*vo, half russia.* London, 1824

The last volume contains a catalogue of Voyages and Travels, with an Index, etc.

1722 KIDDER, REV. DANIEL P.; and REV. J. C. FLETCHER. BRAZIL AND THE BRAZILIANS, portrayed in Historical and Descriptive Sketches. *Portrait of Dom Pedro II., maps, colored plates, and wood-cuts. Thick* 8*vo, cloth.* Philadelphia, 1857

1723 KILIAN, LUCAS and WOLFGANG. DER NEAPOLITANISCHEN KONIG LEBEN UND BILDNÜSZ. *Engraved title,* 26 *portraits, and* 7 *other plates (genealogical trees, etc.), by Lucas Kilian,* 1624. — SERENISSIMORUM SAXONIÆ ELECTORUM, et quorundam Ducum Agnatorum, Genuinæ Effigies. *Engraved title,* 22 *portraits, and* 5 *other plates, by Wolfgang Kilian,* 1621. — GENEALOGIA SERENISSIMOR. BOIARIÆ DUCUM, et quorundam Genuinæ Effigies. *Engraved title, a plate inserted, and* 10 *portraits, by Wolfgang Kilian,* 1620. *Together in* 1 *vol., small folio, vellum.* Augustæ Vindelicorum, 1620–24

These two distinguished artists were the progenitors of a line highly gifted in the art of engraving. Heineken mentions twenty-one members of this family, fourteen of whom were engravers.

1724 KILLIGREW, THOMAS. COMEDIES AND TRAGEDIES. *Contains the two tragi-comedies "Claricilla" and "the Prisoners," but the portrait is wanting. Small folio, half calf.* H. Herringman, London, 1664

1725 KING, CAPTAIN PHILLIP PARKER, R. N. NARRATIVE OF A SURVEY OF THE INTERTROPICAL AND WESTERN COASTS OF AUSTRALIA, performed between the Years 1818 and 1822. With an Appendix containing Various Subjects relating to Hydrography and Natural History. *Maps, charts, plates, and wood-cuts.* 2 *vols., 8vo, diamond russia, gilt, marbled edges.* J. Murray, London, 1826

1726 KINGLAKE, ALEXANDER WILLIAM. EOTHEN, or Traces of Travel brought Home from the East. *Crown 8vo, calf, gilt edges.* New York, 1845

1727 KINGLAKE, ALEXANDER WILLIAM. ANOTHER COPY: New Edition. *12mo, cloth.* New York, 1858

1728 KINGLAKE, ALEXANDER WILLIAM. THE INVASION OF THE CRIMEA: its Origin, and an Account of its Progress, down to the Death of Lord Raglan. *Plans, etc.* 2 *vols., 8vo. cloth, uncut.* Edinburgh, 1863

1729 KINGSLEY, REV. CHARLES. ALTON LOCKE, Tailor and Poet; an Autobiography. *12mo, cloth.* New York, 1850

1730 KINGSLEY, REV. CHARLES. TWO YEARS AGO. *12mo, cloth.* Boston, 1857

1731 KINGSLEY, REV. CHARLES. HYPATIA, or New Foes with an Old Face. Eighth Edition. *12mo, cloth.* Boston, 1859

1732 KINGSLEY, HENRY. THE RECOLLECTIONS OF GEOFFRY HAMLYN. *12mo, cloth.* Boston, 1859

1733 KINGSLEY, HENRY. RAVENSHOE. Fifth Edition. *12mo, cloth.* Boston, 1862

1734 KINGSTON, WILLIAM H. G. WESTERN WANDERINGS, or a Pleasure Tour in the Canadas. *Wood-cuts.* 2 *vols., crown 8vo, cloth, uncut.* London, 1856

1735 KINSLY, REV. WILLIAM MORGAN. PORTUGAL ILLUSTRATED; in a Series of Letters. Second Edition. *Engraved title, map, plates, and* 19 *vignettes, comprising views, music, coins, portraits, and costumes;* INDIA PROOFS *of the title, and* 12 *large plates and portraits, engraved by J. and W. Skelton, and the* 9 *plates of costume* (4 *figures on each*) COLORED. *Imperial 8vo, boards, morocco back, uncut.* London, 1829

Twelve plates wanting, otherwise a fine copy.

1736 KIRK, JOHN FOSTER. HISTORY OF CHARLES THE BOLD, Duke of Burgundy. *Portraits, etc. Vols. I. and II., royal 8vo, half morocco, gilt tops.* Philadelphia, 1864

1737 KIRKLAND, MRS. CAROLINE M. MEMOIRS OF WASHINGTON. With Illustrations. *12mo, half calf, extra, marbled edges.* New York, 1857

1738 KITCHINER, WILLIAM, M. D. THE ART OF INVIGORATING AND PROLONGING LIFE, by Food, Clothes, Air, Exercise, Wine, Sleep, etc.; and Peptic Precepts, pointing out Agreeable and Effectual Methods to Prevent and Relieve Indigestion, and to Regulate and Strengthen the Action of the Stomach and Bowels. To which is added, the Pleasure of Making a Will. New Edition. *Foolscap 8vo, boards, rough edges.* London, 1824

1739 KLAPROTH, HEINRICH JULIUS VON. TRAVELS IN THE CAUCASUS AND GEORGIA, performed in the Years 1807 and

1808, by Command of the Russian Government. Translated from the German by F. Shoberl. *4to, half morocco, uncut.* London, 1814

1740 KLAUER-KLATTOWSKI, WILHELM. POPULAR SONGS OF THE GERMANS; with a Translation of all Unusual Words, and Difficult Passages, and Explanatory Notes. *12mo, cloth, uncut.* London, 1836

1741 KLOPSTOCK, FRIEDRICH GOTTLIEB. THE MESSIAH; descriptive of the Principal Events attending the Passion, Crucifixion, Resurrection, and Ascension of Our Lord and Saviour Jesus Christ. From the German, to which are prefixed Memoirs of the Life of the Author. *Plates.* 2 *vols., 8vo, half russia, extra.* R. Evans, London, (1815?)

1742 KNAPP, ANDREW; and WILLIAM BALDWIN. THE NEW NEWGATE CALENDAR; being Interesting Memoirs of Notorious Characters, who have been convicted of Outrages on the Laws of England, during the Seventeenth [Eighteenth, 1700–1812] Century, brought down to the Present Time, Chronologically arranged: comprising Traitors, Murderers, Incendiaries, Ravishers, Pirates, Mutineers, Coiners, Highwaymen, Footpads, Housebreakers, Rioters, Extortioners, Sharpers, Forgers, Pickpockets, Fraudulent Bankrupts, Money-Droppers, Imposters, and Thieves of Every Description. Containing also a Number of Interesting Cases never before published; with Occasional Original Anecdotes, the Speeches, Confessions, and Last Exclamations; to which is added, a Correct Account of the Various Modes of Punishment of Criminals in Different Parts of the World. *Numerous portraits and plates.* 5 *vols., 8vo, boards, rough edges.* London, s. a.

1743 KNAPP, SAMUEL LORENZO. A MEMOIR OF THE LIFE OF DANIEL WEBSTER. *Portrait. 12mo, boards.* Boston, 1831

1744 KNICKERBOCKER (THE), OR NEW YORK MONTHLY MAGAZINE. *January,* 1833–*December,* 1862. 60 *vols., 8vo, half morocco.* COMPLETE FROM COMMENCEMENT TO 1862. New York, 1833–62

The early numbers are difficult to find.

1745 KNIGGE, A. F. F. L., BARON DE. PRACTICAL PHILOSOPHY, or Social Life; or, the Art of Conversing with Men: after the German, by P. Will. First American Edition. *8vo, sheep.* Lansingburgh, 1805

1746 KNIGHT, CHARLES. WILLIAM SHAKSPERE; a Biography. *Numerous wood-cuts. Royal 8vo, crushed morocco, extra, gilt over marbled edges, by Riviere.* C. Knight, London, 1843

1747 KNIGHT, CHARLES. LONDON. Edited by Charles Knight. *Several hundred wood-cuts. 6 vols. in 3, thick imperial 8vo, half calf, extra, marbled edges.* London, 1851

1748 KNIGHT, CHARLES. CYCLOPÆDIA OF THE INDUSTRY OF ALL NATIONS. *Numerous wood-cuts. Thick 12mo, half morocco, neat.* C. Knight, London, 1851

1749 KNIGHT, CHARLES. THE LAND WE LIVE IN; a Pictorial and Literary Sketch-Book of the British Empire. [Conducted by Charles Knight, Author of many of the Articles.] *Frontispieces and many hundred wood-cuts and lithographs. 4 vols. in 2, imperial 8vo, cloth, uncut.* C. Knight, London, s. a.

1750 KNIGHT, CHARLES. THE OLD PRINTER AND THE MODERN PRESS. *Foolscap 8vo, cloth, uncut.* J. Murray, London, 1854

1751 KNIGHT, CHARLES. HALF-HOURS WITH THE BEST AUTHORS; with Biographical and Critical Notices. With 52 Illustrations by William Harvey. *Portraits aud wood-cuts. 2 vols., thick post 8vo, half calf, extra, marbled edges.* London, 1855

1752 KNIGHT, CHARLES. HALF-HOURS WITH THE BEST LETTER-WRITERS AND AUTOBIOGRAPHERS; forming a Collection of Memoirs and Anecdotes of Eminent Persons. *Post 8vo, cloth.* London, 1867

1753 KNIGHT, CHARLES. THE ENGLISH CYCLOPÆDIA, a New Dictionary of Universal Knowledge; conducted by Charles Knight. BIOGRAPHY. *6 vols., 4to, cloth.* London, 1856–58

1754 KNIGHT, FREDERICK. GEMS, or Device Book. Second Edition. *Engraved title and 70 plates, containing nearly 400 beautiful and humorous little designs, by C. Vining, Cipriani, A. Cooper, and others; comprising statues and portraits, animals and insects, alphabets and monograms, heraldic devices, rebuses, mottoes, grotesques, etc., etc. 8vo, half morocco; back loose and 15 plates wanting.* London, s. a.

1755 KNIGHT, SAMUEL, D. D. THE LIFE OF DR. JOHN COLET, Dean of St. Paul's in the Reigns of K. Henry VII. and K. Henry VIII. and Founder of St. Paul's School; with an Appendix, containing some Account of the Masters and more Eminent Scholars of that Foundation, and several Original Papers relating to the said Life. A New Edition. *Portraits and plates. Royal 8vo, crown turkey morocco, neat, gilt edges.* LARGE PAPER. Clarendon Press, Oxford, 1823

1756 KNIGHT, THOMAS ANDREW. A SELECTION FROM THE PHYSIOLOGICAL AND HORTICULTURAL PAPERS, published in the Transactions of the Royal and Horticultural Societies;

to which is prefixed, a Sketch of his Life. *Portrait on India paper, and 6 folded plates. Royal 8vo, half morocco.* London, 1841

1757 KNOWLES, JAMES SHERIDAN. THE DRAMATIC WORKS OF. *Portrait by Finden. 2 vols., post 8vo, cloth, uncut.* London, 1856

1758 KNOX, ROBERT. AN HISTORICAL RELATION OF THE ISLAND CEYLON, in the East Indies; together with an Account of the Detaining in Captivity the Author and Divers other Englishmen now living there, and of the Author's Miraculous Escape. Illustrated with Figures, and a Map of the Island. By Robert Knox, a Captive there near Twenty Years. *Portrait wanting. Small folio, old calf.* London, 1681

"This work, though published so long ago, still retains its character, as the fullest and most interesting account of the inhabitants of Ceylon." —*Lowndes.*

1759 KNOX, VICESIMUS, D. D. ESSAYS, Moral and Literary. *3 vols., 8vo, old sprinkled calf, gilt.* London, 1793

1760 KORFF, M., BARON. THE ACCESSION OF NICHOLAS I.; compiled, by Special Command of the Emperor Alexander II., by his Imperial Majesty's Secretary of State, Baron M. Korff, and translated from the Original Russian. Third Impression (now first published). *8vo, cloth, uncut.* J. Murray, London, 1857

1761 KRAUSSEN, JOHANN ULRICH. HISTORISCHER BILDER BIBEL. [A History of the Bible represented in finely engraved Plates, with Explanations in German Verse.] *Contains 136 plates, numbered (two numbered 60), besides engraved titles, frontispieces, etc. 6 parts in one vol., folio, old calf.* Augsburg, 1705

1762 KUGLER, FRANZ THEODOR. THE PICTORIAL HISTORY OF GERMANY, during the Reign of Frederick the Great; comprehending a Complete History of the Silesian Campaigns, and the Seven Years' War. *Fine portrait of Frederick the Great, and 500 wood-cuts after designs by A. Menzel. Royal 8vo, half morocco.* London, 1845

1763 LABICHE, E. M.; and, A. C. LARTIQUE. LES PETITS OISEAUX, Comédie en Trois Actes. With English Notes, by Ferdinand Bôcher. *12mo, paper.* Boston, 1864

1764 LABORDE, ALEXANDRE LOUIS JOSEPH, COMTE DE. VOYAGE PITTORESQUE EN AUTRICHE, par le Cte Alexandre de Laborde. (Précis Historique de la Guerre entre la France et l'Autriche en 1809. *Contains 160 plates, of plans, maps, views, etc. 3 vols., royal folio, boards, morocco backs, uncut.* Paris, 1821–22

1765 LABORDE, ALEXANDRE LOUIS JOSEPH, COMTE DE. VERSAILLES ANCIEN ET MODERNE. *Several hundred woodcuts, many on India paper. Imperial 8vo, half morocco, very neat, marbled edges.* Paris, 1841

1766 LABORDE, LÉON EMANUEL SIMON JOSEPH, COMTE DE. NOTICE DES ÉMAUX, BIJOUX, ET OBJETS DIVERS, exposés dans les Galaries du Musée du Louvre; Ire Partie; Histoire et Descriptions. *12mo, paper.* Paris, 1853

1767 LABOULAYE, ÉDOUARD RENÉ LEFÉBVRE DE. THE UNITED STATES AND FRANCE. Translated for the Boston Advertiser. *8vo, pp.* 14. Boston, 1862

1768 LABOULAYE, ÉDOUARD RENÉ LEFÉBVRE DE. PARIS IN AMERICA. Translated by Mary L. Booth. 12*mo, cloth.* New York, 1863

1769 LA BRUYÈRE, JEAN DE. AN ACCOUNT OF THE LIFE AND WRITINGS OF. (By M. Coste. Made English by Mr. Ozell. — THE MORAL CHARACTERS OF THEOPHRASTUS, made English from the Greek; with a Prefatory Discourse concerning Theophrastus, from the French. — SPEECH upon his Admission into the French Academy, June the 15th, 1693; now first made English by Mr. Ozell. — OF THE MANNER OF LIVING WITH GREAT MEN; written after the Method of Monsieur de la Bruyère, by N. Rowe, Esq. *One volume of the sixth edition of the " Works of;" title wanting.* 8*vo, old calf.* London, 1713

1770 LA CALPRENÈDE, GAUTIER DE COSTES, SIEUR DE. HYMEN'S PRÆLUDIA, OR LOVE'S MASTER-PIECE; being that so-much-admired Romance intituled Cleopatra. In Twelve Parts. Written Originally in the French [by La Calprenède], and now Elegantly rendered into English by Robert Loveday. *Folio, old calf.* London, 1687

1771 LACKINGTON, JAMES. MEMOIRS OF THE FORTY-FIVE FIRST YEARS OF THE LIFE OF JAMES LACKINGTON; written by himself. With a Tripple Dedication: 1. To the Public; 2. To Respectable, 3. To Sordid, Booksellers. Interspersed with many Original Humorous Stories, and Droll Anecdotes, to which is also added, an Index. *Portrait.* 12*mo, boards.* London, 1794

1772 LACKLAND, THOMAS. HOMESPUN, or Five and Twenty Years Ago. *Post* 8*vo, cloth.* New York, 1867

1773 LACY, JOHN. WYL BUCKE, HIS TESTAMENT: the Legacies palatably prepared for the Legatees. *Reprinted from the edition of W. Copland; with an Introduction, by Joseph Haslewood, and plates. Square foolscap* 8*vo, dark blue calf, gilt, marbled edges.* PRIVATELY PRINTED: *only* 40 *copies.* Chiswick Press, 1827

This copy is "No. 15 of 40;" see Haslewood's autograph on the reverse of half-title.

1774 LAFAYETTE, GILBERT MOTIER, MARQUIS DE. MEMOIRS, CORRESPONDENCE, AND MANUSCRIPTS OF; Published by his Family. 3 *vols., 8vo, half morocco; portrait wanting.* London, 1837

1775 LAFITAU, JOSEPH FRANÇOIS. MŒURS DES SAUVAGES AMERIQUAINS, comparées aux Mœurs des Primiers Temps; par le P. Lafitau, de la Compagnie de Jesus. *Frontispiece by Scotin and numerous plates.* 2 *vols., 4to, old mottled calf, red edges.* Paris, 1724

1776 LA FONTAINE, JEAN DE. CONTES ET NOUVELLES EN VERS. Nouvelle Édition, corrigée, augmentée, & enrichie de Tailles-Douces, dessinées par Mr. Romain de Hooge. 2 *vols. in* 1, *small 8vo, old calf, gilt.* Amsterdam, 1721

1777 LA FONTAINE, JEAN DE. CONTES ET NOUVELLES EN VERS. *Portrait by P. Savart after H. Rigaud, vignettes, and the* 80 *celebrated plates by Eisen,* PROOFS BEFORE THE LETTERS, *as issued for the edition of* 1762. 2 *vols., post 8vo, mottled calf, gilt, marbled edges.* PLATES OF THE FARMER GENERAL EDITION: FINE COPY. Amsterdam, 1764

Fine copies, with the plates in the first state, are seldom met with.

1778 LA FONTAINE, JEAN DE. CONTES ET NOUVELLES EN VERSE. *Frontispiece, and plates printed in the text.* Amsterdam, 1776

1779 LA FONTAINE, JEAN DE. FABLES CHOISIES, mises en Vers. *Fine impressions of the* 246 *plates by Bertin, Alard, Crescent, and others.* 4 *vols., 8vo, old marbled calf, gilt edges.* Bouillon, 1776

1780 LA FONTAINE, JEAN DE. LES AMOURS DE PSYCHÉ ET DE CUPIDON. Édition ornée de Figures imprimées en Couleurs, d'après les Tableaux de M. Schall. *Imperial 4to, half calf, extra, rough edges.* LARGE VELLUM PAPER. Paris, 1791

All the illustrated editions of La Fontaine issued in the last century are becoming scarce, especial y those with the plates in fine condition.

1781 LA FONTAINE, JEAN DE. FABLES OF; illustrated by J. J. Grandville. Translated from the French, by Elizur Wright, Jr. 2 *vols., 8vo, cloth.* Boston, 1841

1782 LAING, MALCOLM. THE HISTORY OF SCOTLAND; from the Union of the Crowns on the Accession of James VI. to the Throne of England, to the Union of the Kingdoms in the Reign of Queen Anne. With Two Dissertations, on the Gowrie Conspiracy, and on the supposed Authenticity of Ossian's Poems. 2 *vols., 8vo, old calf. First edition.* London, 1800

1783 LAIRESSE, GÉRARD DE. THE ART OF PAINTING IN ALL ITS BRANCHES, methodically demonstrated by Discourses and Plates, and exemplified by Remarks on the Paintings of the Best Masters, and their Perfections and Oversights laid open. Translated by John Frederick Fritsch. *4to, half calf.* London, 1778

1784 LAIRESSE, GÉRARD DE. A TREATISE ON THE ART OF PAINTING IN ALL ITS BRANCHES, accompanied by Seventy engraved Plates, and exemplified by Remarks on the Paintings of the Best Masters, illustrating the Subject by Reference to their Beauties and Imperfections; Revised, corrected, and accompanied with an Essay, by W. M. Craig. *2 vols., 4to, morocco, extra, gilt edges.* London, 1817

1785 LAMARTINE, A. M. LOUIS PRAT DE. MEMOIRS OF CELEBRATED CHARACTERS. New Edition. *Portrait of Nelson. Post 8vo, cloth, uncut.* London, 1860

1786 LAMB, CHARLES. THE WORKS OF. (With a Sketch of his Life, by Sir Thomas Noon Talfourd.) A New Edition. *Portrait by W. Finden. 4 vols., foolscap 8vo, tree calf, gilt, marbled edges, by Riviere.* E. Moxon, London, 1855

1787 LAMB, CHARLES. THE POETICAL WORKS OF. Elegantly illustrated. *Portrait and 4 fine vignette plates. 12mo, cloth, gilt edges.* Philadelphia, 1858

1788 LAMB, ROGER. AN ORIGINAL AND AUTHENTIC JOURNAL OF OCCURRENCES DURING THE LATE AMERICAN WAR; from its Commencement to the Year 1783. By R. Lamb, late Sergeant in the late Royal Welch Fuzileers. *8vo, half morocco, neat, gilt top.* Dublin, 1809

1789 LANDAIS, NAPOLÉON. DICTIONNAIRE GÉNÉRAL ET GRAMMATICAL DES DICTIONNAIRES FRANÇAIS; Extrait et Complément de tous les Dictionnaires Anciens et Modernes les plus célèbres. Septième Édition, revue et corrigée. *2 vols., 4to, half calf.* Paris, 1843

1790 LANDON, LÆTITIA ELIZABETH. POETICAL WORKS OF. *Wood-cuts on title. 2 vols., post 8vo, calf, extra, marbled edges.* London, 1853

1791 LANDSEER, THOMAS. CHARACTERISTIC SKETCHES OF ANIMALS, principally from the Zoological Gardens, Regent's Park; drawn from the Life and engraved by Thomas Landseer: with Descriptive and Illustrative Notices by John H. Barrow, Esq. *Engraved title and 64 fine plates and vignettes. Royal 4to, half morocco, uncut.* London, 1832

1792 LANGDON, WILLIAM B. "TEN THOUSAND CHINESE THINGS." A Descriptive Catalogue of the Chinese Collection, at St. George's Place, London; with Condensed Accounts of the Genius, Government, History, Literature, Agriculture, Arts, Trade, Manners, Customs, and Social Life of the People of the Celestial Empire. *Wood-cuts. 8vo, cloth.* (London), 1843

1793 LANMAN, CHARLES. DICTIONARY OF THE UNITED STATES CONGRESS, compiled as a Manual of Reference for the Legislator and Statesman. Third Edition, revised and brought down to July 28, 1866. *8vo, cloth.* Washington, 1866

1794 LANQUETTE, THOMAS. [AN EPITOME OF CHRONICLES.] COOPER'S CHRONICLE; contenynge the Whole Discourse of the Histories, as well of thys Realme as all other Countreis, with the Succession of theyr Kynges, the Tyme of theyr Raign, and what Notable Actes were done by thē: newely enlarged and augmented, as well in the First Parte wyth divers Profitable Histories, as in the Latter Ende wyth the Whole Summe of those Thynges that Paulus Jovius and Sleigdane hath written of Late Yers; that is now lately oversene and with Great Dilligence corrected and augmented, unto the VII. Yere of the Raigne of our most Gracious Quene Elizabeth, that nowe is. Anno 1565, the First Day of Auguste. *Title and "admonition," 1 leaf; preface ("To the ryght honorable Lorde Russell Earle of Bedforde," etc.), 2 leaves; table (slightly imperfect) and "Of the use and profite of histories," etc.), 27 leaves; "Lanquette's Chronicle," etc., leaves* 1–376 *(numbered), followed by* 8 *leaves (unnumbered) and a page of errata. Small* 4*to, old calf, red edges.* **Black letter**: *fine copy.*
(London, 1565)

Although Lanquette's name does not appear on the title of this edition, the heading of each leaf, almost throughout the volume, is "Lanquette's Chronicle." In the "Admonitions to the reader" Cooper says, — "certaine persons, for lukers sake contrarie to honestye, had caused my chronicle to be prynted wythout my knowledge . . . . . ; wherein did I finde almost five hundred faultes and errours. . . . . . . I cannot therefor doe otherwyse but greatlye blame theyr unhonest dealynge and openlye protest that the Edicion of this Chronicle set forth by Marshe and Ceres in the Yere of Christ 1559 is none of myne, but the attempt of certayne persones utterlye unlearned."

See reverse of leaf 263, Anno 1452, — "One named Johannes Faustius first found the crafte of printing in the city of Mens in Germanie:" also, reverse of leaf 270, Anno 1492, — "Certain new ilandes wer found in the Ocean sea first by Amerinus Tespucius, & after by Christophorus Columbanus."

1795 LANSDOWNE, GEORGE GRANVILLE, VISCOUNT. POEMS; upon Several Occasions. The Fourth Edition. 12*mo, calf.*
J. Tonson, London, 1726

1796 LAPORTE, COUNT DE. A FRENCH GRAMMAR. 8*vo, sheep.* Boston, 1844

1797 LARCOM, LUCY. BREATHINGS OF THE BETTER LIFE. *Square foolscap* 8*vo, cloth, gilt top.* Boston, 1867

1798 LARDNER, NATHANIEL, D. D. THE WORKS OF. With a Life by Dr. Kippis. 10 *vols.,* 8*vo, cloth, uncut.*
London, 1831

1799 LA ROCHEFOUCAULD, FRANÇOIS, DUC DE. MAXIMES DE. 18*mo, paper.* Paris, s. a.

1800 LA ROCHEFOUCAULT-LIANCOURT, F. A. F., DUC DE. TRAVELS THROUGH THE UNITED STATES OF NORTH AMERICA, the Country of the Iroquois, and Upper Canada, in the Years 1795, 1796, and 1797; with an Authentic Account of Lower Canada. [Translated by H. Newman.] 2 *vols.,* 4*to, old marbled calf, neat, with autograph of Cuthbert Collingwood.* London, 1799

1801 LARWOOD, JACOB; and JOHN C. HOTTEN. THE HISTORY OF SIGNBOARDS, from the Earliest Times to the Present Day. With One Hundred Illustrations in Fac-simile. *Frontispiece. Thick crown 8vo, cloth, uncut.* London, 1866

1802 LAS CASES, EMMANUEL AUGUSTIN D. M. J., MARQUIS DE. MÉMORIAL DE SAINTE HÉLÈNE: Journal of the Private Life and Conversations of the Emperor Napoleon, at Saint Helena. *Maps and plates. 4 vols., 8vo, half calf, neat.* London, 1823

1803 LATHROP, JOSEPH, D. D. SERMONS DELIVERED ON VARIOUS OCCASIONS. *8vo, sheep.* I. Thomas, Boston, 1812

1804 LAUD, WILLIAM. THE HISTORY OF THE TROUBLES AND TRYAL OF WILLIAM LAUD, Lord Arch-Bishop of Canterbury; wrote by himself, during his Imprisonment in the Tower. To which is prefixed the Diary of his own Life, faithfully and entirely published from the Original Copy; and subjoined, a Supplement to the Preceding History, the Arch-Bishop's Last Will, his Large Answer to the Lord Say's Speech concerning Liturgies, his Annual Accounts of his Province delivered to the King, and some other Things relating to the History. [Edited by the Rev. Henry Wharton.] *Portrait. Folio, old calf.* London, 1695

See "Retrospective Review," VII., pp. 49–63.

1805 LAVATER, JOHANN CASPAR CHRISTIAN. ESSAYS ON PHYSIOGNOMY, designed to promote the Knowledge and the Love of Mankind; illustrated by more than Eight Hundred Engravings accurately copied, and some Duplicates added from Originals, executed by, or under the Inspection of Thomas Holloway. Translated from the French by Henry Hunter, D. D., etc. *5 vols., imperial 4to, half calf, rough edges.* J. Murray, and J. Stockdale, London, 1789, etc.

This appears to be Stockdale's edition, although the impressions of the plates (engraved by Holloway, Bartolozzi, Blake, etc.) are good, and some of the titles bear imprint of Murray.

1806 LAW (THE) AND PRACTICE OF THE GAME OF EUCHRE. *12mo. cloth.* Philadelphia, (1862)

1807 LAWS RELATING TO THE DIRECT AND EXCISE TAXES, passed during the First and Second Sessions of the Thirty-seventh Congress. *8vo, cloth.* New York, 1862

1808 LAYARD, AUSTEN HENRY. THE MONUMENTS OF NINEVEH, from Drawings made on the Spot; FIRST SERIES: 100 *plates comprising sculptures, bas-reliefs, etc., found at Nineveh, etc.* SECOND SERIES: 70 *plates comprising sculptures, bas-reliefs, bronzes, etc., including the discoveries at the palace of Sennacherib and the ruins of Nimroud during the second expedition to Assyria. Together* 170 *plates, with descriptive letter-press, imperial folio size, in two portfolios, morocco backs.* J. Murray, London, 1853

There should be 71 plates in the second series, but plate No. 1 is wanting, otherwise it is a fine and perfect set.

1809 LEAKE, ISAAC Q. MEMOIR OF THE LIFE AND TIMES OF GENERAL JOHN LAMB, an Officer of the Revolution who commanded the Post at West Point at the Time of Arnold's Defection; and his Correspondence with Washington, Clinton, Patrick Henry, and other Distinguished Men of his Time. *Portrait and plans. 8vo, half morocco.* J. Munsell, Albany, 1850

1810 LEAKE, WILLIAM MARTIN. THE TOPOGRAPHY OF ATHENS, with some Remarks on its Antiquities. *Frontispiece. 8vo, half calf, extra, marbled edges. The volume of maps and plates wanting.* J. Murray, London, 1821

1811 LEAR, EDWARD. ILLUSTRATED EXCURSIONS IN ITALY. *Contains 25 tinted plates of views, and numerous wood-cut vignettes to illustrate costume, etc., drawn and lithographed by E. Lear; with descriptive letter-press. Imperial 4to, cloth.* London, 1846

1812 LEBLANC, ———. LE MÉCANICIEN CONSTRUCTEUR, ou Atlas et Description des Organes des Machines. Œuvre Posthume de Leblanc, Professeur et Conservateur des Collections au Conservatoire des Arts et Métiers, etc. Ouvrage à l'Usage des Écoles d'Arts et Métiers, et formant le Complément du Choix de Modèles appliqués à l'Enseignement du Dessin des Machines. Deuxième Édition, revue, corrigée et augmentée, par M. Félix Tourneux. *Contains 25 plates with 277 figures, and scales. Imperial 4to, half morocco.* Liége, 1845

1813 LE BLANC, H. THE ART OF TYING THE CRAVAT, demonstrated in Sixteen Lessons, including Thirty-two Different Styles; preceded by a History of the Cravat, from its Origin to the Present Time, and Remarks on its Influence on Society in General. *With 4 plates. 18mo, pp. 72, boards.* Philadelphia, 1828

1814 LECKY, W. E. H. HISTORY OF THE RISE AND INFLUENCE OF THE SPIRIT OF RATIONALISM in Europe. *2 vols., 8vo, cloth, uncut.* New York, 1866

1815 LEE, NATHANIEL. THE WORKS OF. *3 vols., 12mo, old calf; with book-plate of Edward D. Ingraham, and autographs.* London, 1722

1816 LEE, RICHARD HENRY. MEMOIR OF THE LIFE OF, and his Correspondence with the most Distinguished Men in America and Europe, illustrative of their Characters, and of the Events of the American Revolution; by his Grandson, Richard H. Lee. *Portrait. 2 vols. in 1, 8vo, half morocco.* Philadelphia, 1825

1817 LEE, Rev. Samuel. Eschatology, or the Scriptural Doctrine of the Coming of the Lord, the Judgment, and the Resurrection. *12mo, cloth.* Boston, 1859

1818 LEE, Sophia, and Harriet. Canterbury Tales. *& vols., 12mo, cloth.* New York, 1857

1819 LEFEBVRE-DURUFLÉ, J. N. Excursion sur les Côtes et dans les Ports de Normandie. *Contains 40 beautiful aquatinta engravings, after Bonington, Luttringhausen, Copley Fielding, etc.;* India proofs before the letters. *Atlas folio, half morocco.* Large paper. J. F. Ostervald, Paris, (1823–25)

1820 LE FEVRE, Raoul. The Destruction of Troy; in Three Books. The I. Shewing the Founders and Foundation of the said City, with the Causes and Manner how it was sacked and First Destroyed by Hercules. The II. How it was re-edified and how Hercules slew King Laomedon, and destroyed it the Second Time; and of Hercules, his Worthy Deeds, and his Death. The III. How Priamus, Son of King Laomedon, rebuilded Troy again, more strong than it was before; and for the Ravishment of Dame Helen, Wife of King Menelaus of Greece, the said City was utterly destroyed, and Priamus, with Hector, and all his Sons, slain. Also mentioning the Rising and Flourishing of Divers Kings and Kingdoms, with the Decay and Overthrow of others; with many Admirable Acts of Chivalry and Martial Prowess, effected by Valiant Knights, in Defence and Love of Distressed Ladies. The Eleventh Edition, corrected and much amended. *Small 4to, half calf.* **Black letter.** T. Passinger, London, 1684

Translated by Caxton; see end of Second Book, p. 134, and end of Third Book, p. 120. For an account of the edition printed by Caxton see Dibdin's "Ames's Typog. Antiq.," Vol. I. pp. 1–11, and "Bibl. Spencer.," Vol. IV. pp. 173–180; or, Johnson's "Typographia," Vol. I. pp. 135–138.

1821 LE GRAND, Antoine. An Entire Body of Philosophy, according to the Principles of the Famous Renate Des Cartes, in Three Books: I. the Institution, in X. Parts; II. the History of Nature, which illustrates the Institution, and consists of great Variety of Experiments relating thereto, and explained by the same Principles, in IX. Parts; III. a Dissertation of the Want of Sense and Knowledge in Brute Animals, in II. Parts. Written Originally in Latin, by the Learned Anthony Le Grand; now carefully translated from the Last Corrections, Alterations, and Large Additions of the Author, never yet published. The Whole Work illustrated with almost an Hundred Sculptures, dispersed to such places as best admit thereof, all designed, drawn, and engraven Historically, by Good Artists; besides the Figures or Schemes for the Explanation of the Philosophical Parts that require the same. Endeavoured to be so done, that it may be of Use and Delight to the Ingenious of Both Sexes; by Richard Blome. *Folio, old calf; with book-plate of Joseph Tasker, Middleton Hall, Essex.* London, 1694

1822 LEGRAND D'AUSSY, PIERRE JEAN BAPTISTE. FABLIAUX OR TALES, abridged from French Manuscripts of the XIIth and XIIIth Centuries; selected and translated into English Verse, by the late G. L. Way, Esq., with a Preface, Notes, and Appendix, by the late G. Ellis, Esq. A New Edition, corrected. *Wood-cuts by Bewick. 3 vols., crown 8vo, crimson morocco, extra, gilt edges.* London, 1815

1823 LE GROS, W. B. FABLES AND TALES (in Verse); suggested by the Frescos of Pompeii and Herculaneum. *With 24 plates, engraved in outline by F. Bromley. Foolscap 4to, cloth, uncut.* London, 1835

1824 LEIGH'S NEW PICTURE OF LONDON, or a View of the Political, Religious, Medical, Literary, Municipal, Commercial, and Moral State of the British Metropolis; to which are subjoined a Description of the Environs, and Plan for Viewing London in Eight Days. *Maps and plates. Thick 18mo, roan.* London, 1839

1825 LEIGHTON, ALEXANDER. CURIOUS STORIED TRADITIONS OF SCOTTISH LIFE. Second Edition. 1860.—A SECOND SERIES OF (the same). 1861. *Frontispieces. 2 vols., foolscap 8vo, cloth, uncut.* Edinburgh, 1860–61

1826 LEIGHTON, JOHN. THE LIFE OF MAN SYMBOLISED IN THE MONTHS OF THE YEAR, in a Series of Illustrations, pourtrayed in their Seasons and Phases; with Passages selected from Ancient and Modern Authors, by Richard Pigot. *Handsomely printed on a thick toned paper, with 25 full-page, and several hundred marginal wood-cuts, besides tail-pieces, ornate initials, and other embellishments. 4to, dark blue turkey morocco, extra, gilt edges, by Aitken.* London, 1866

1827 LEMON, REV. GEORGE WILLIAM. ENGLISH ETYMOLOGY, or a Derivative Dictionary of the English Language; in Two Alphabets, tracing the Etymology of those English Words that are derived, I. from the Greek and Latin Languages, II. from the Saxon and other Northern Tongues. *4to, half calf.* London, 1783

A very singular work.

1828 LENFANT, JACQUES. HISTOIRE DU CONCILE DE PISE, et de ce qui s'est passé de plus Mémorable depuis ce Concile jusqu' au Concile de Constance. Par Jacques Lenfant. Enrichie de Portraits. *2 vols. in 1, 4to, old calf.* Amsterdam, 1724

The portraits are by Ricart and Houbraken.

1829 LENNOX, WILLIAM PITT, LORD. DRAFTS ON MY MEMORY; being Men I have known, Things I have seen, Places I have visited. *2 vols., 8vo, cloth, uncut.* London, 1866

1830 LENORMAND, Louis Sébastien. Nouveau Manuel Complet du Relieur dans toutes ses Parties; précédé des Arts de l'Assembleur, du Satineur, de la Plieuse, de la Brocheuse, et suivi des Arts du Marbreur sur Franches, du Doreur sur Tranches et sur Cuir. Par M. Lenormand et M. R., Relieur Amateur. Orné d'un grand Nombre de Figures. Nouvelle Édition, revue, corrigée, et considérablement augmentée. 18*mo, crimson morocco, extra, gilt edges.* Paris, 1853

1831 LE POITTEVIN de Lacroix, Edmund. The Traveller's Guide in Antwerp, to every Object Worthy of Attention; including a very Particular Description of the Paintings and Various Works of Art which adorn the Churches, an Historical Account of the City and its Citadel, a Table of Foreign Coins, and a Catalogue of the Paintings composing the Museum. Third Edition. 16*mo, paper.* Antwerp, 1839

1832 LE SAGE, Alain René. The Adventures of Gil Blas of Santillane. A New Translation, by Smollett; adorned with Twelve New Cuts, neatly engraved. The Sixth Edition. *Plates by Springsguth and Skelton, after Ansell.* 4 *vols.,* 12*mo, old marbled calf, gilt.* London, 1792

1833 LE SAGE, Alain René. The Adventures of Gil Blas of Santillane. Translated from the French, by B. H. Malkin, Esq. *With* 24 *fine engravings, after pictures by Smirke, India proofs.* 4 *vols.,* 4*to, purple morocco, extra, gilt edges.* Large paper: *fine copy.* London, 1809

1834 LE SAGE, Alain René. Histoire de Gil Blas de Santillane; Vignettes, par Jean Gigoux. *Portrait on India paper, and about* 600 *wood-cuts. Thick royal* 8*vo, calf; with autograph of the princess Elizabeth (daughter of George III.) on title.* Paulin, Paris, 1836

1835 LESLIE, Charles Robert. Autobiographical Recollections; Edited, with a Prefatory Essay on Leslie as an Artist, and Selections from his Correspondence; by Tom Taylor, Esq. *Portrait. Crown* 8*vo, cloth.* Boston, 1860

1836 L'ESTOILE, Pierre de. Journal des Choses Memorables advenues durant le Regne de Henry III., Roy de France et de Pologne. Nouvelle Édition, augmentée de plusieurs Pieces Curieuses qui n'ont jamais été imprimées & enrichie de Figures & de Nottes Historiques. 4 *vols., small* 8*vo, old mottled calf, gilt.* Heritiers de P. Marteau, Cologne, 1746

1837 LETTERS to Benjamin Franklin, from his Family and Friends, 1751–1790. *Portraits of Mrs. Franklin and Mrs. Bache. Royal* 8*vo, half morocco, neat, gilt top, uncut.* Only 260 copies printed; 10 *of which in* 4*to.* New York, 1859

1838 LETTERS WRITTEN IN LONDON BY AN AMERICAN SPY, from the Year 1764 to the Year 1785. *12mo, boards, rough edges.* Printed for the Editor. London, 1786

1839 LE VAILLANT, FRANÇOIS. HISTOIRE NATURELLE DES OISEAUX DE PARADIS ET DES ROLLIERS, suivie de celle des Toucans et des Barbus. *Contains 113 beautiful colored plates, with a duplicate set, plain,* PROOFS BEFORE THE LETTERS. *2 vols., large imperial folio, half morocco, extra, gilt edges.* LARGE VELLUM PAPER. Paris, 1806

All the figures in this work were drawn from nature by Barraband, one of the most distinguished ornithological painters which France has ever produced, engraved by Pérée and Grémillier, and printed in colors by Langlois and Rousset.

1840 LEVER, CHARLES JAMES. WORKS. *Portrait and numerous wood-cuts after Phiz (H. K. Browne), and George Cruikshank. 14 vols., 8vo, half morocco, extra.* London and Dublin, 1839–52

CONTENTS: Harry Lorrequer; Charles O'Malley (2 vols.); Jack Hinton (with portrait); Tom Burke (2 vols.); Arthur O'Leary; The O'Donoghue; Knight of Gwynne (2 vols.); Roland Cashel (2 vols.); The Daltons (2 vols.).

1841 LEVER, CHARLES JAMES. ST. PATRICK'S EVE. Illustrated by Phiz. *12mo, cloth.* London, 1845

1842 LEWES, CHARLES LEE. COMIC SKETCHES, or the Comedian his Own Manager; written and selected for the Benefit of Performers in England, Ireland, Scotland, and America: inscribed to the Performers in General, by Charles Lee Lewes, Comedian. The whole forming Matter sufficient for Two Evenings' Entertainment; Originally intended for the East Indies, and as delivered by him, without an Apparatus, in Many Parts of the Three Kingdoms, with Distinguished Patronage. *Portrait. 12mo, old calf.* London, 1804

1843 LEWES, CHARLES LEE. MEMOIRS OF; containing Anecdotes, Historical and Biographical, of the English and Scottish Stages, during a Period of Forty Years. Written by himself. *4 vols., 16mo, old calf; one cover to first vol. wanting.* London, 1805

1844 LEWIS, ALONZO. THE HISTORY OF LYNN (1629–1829). *Plates. 8vo, half morocco.* Boston, 1829

1845 LEWIS, FREDERICK C. SCENERY OF THE RIVERS OF ENGLAND AND WALES, illustrated by 24 Painter's Etchings: by a Series of Studies from Pictures in the Collections of the Duke of Bedford; Lord Northwick; Sir Thos. Ackland; Lady Forbes; Count D'Orsay: B. B. Cobbell, Esqr.; R. Vernon, Esqr.; Revd Edmd Burke Lewis; Col. G. Greenwood; John Fairlie, Esqr; J. Pease, Esqr; T. Creswick,

Esqr, A. R. A. Painted and Engraved by F. C. Lewis, Engraver to Queen Victoria. THREE PARTS, *containing* 68 *plates, all etchings. Folio, half green morocco, neat, gilt edges.* London, (1854)

1846 LEWIS, MARIA THERESE, LADY. LIVES OF THE FRIENDS AND CONTEMPORARIES OF LORD CHANCELLOR CLARENDON; illustrative of Portraits in his Gallery. With Portraits. 3 *vols.*, 8*vo, calf, gilt, marbled edges, by Hayday.* J. Murray, London, 1852

1847 LEWIS, MATTHEW GREGORY. TALES OF WONDER. *Post* 8*vo, half calf, extra.* London, 1801

1848 LEWIS, MATTHEW GREGORY. JOURNAL OF A WEST INDIA PROPRIETOR, kept during a Residence in the Island of Jamaica. 8*vo, cloth, uncut.* J. Murray, London, 1834

1849 LEWIS, MATTHEW GREGORY. THE LIFE AND CORRESPONDENCE OF M. G. LEWIS, Author of "the Monk," "Castle Spectre," etc.; with many Pieces in Prose and Verse, never before published. *Portrait and fac-simile letter.* 2 *vols.*, 8*vo, cloth.* London, 1839

1850 LEWIS, THOMAS. ORIGINES HEBRÆÆ: the Antiquities of the Hebrew Republic. A New Edition. 3 *vols.*, 8*vo, cloth, uncut.* University Press, Oxford, 1835

1851 LEWIS, WINSLOW, M. D. AN ADDRESS DELIVERED BEFORE THE NEW ENGLAND HISTORIC-GENEALOGICAL SOCIETY, January 1, 1862. 8*vo, pp.* 12, *paper.* Boston, 1862

1852 LEWIS, WINSLOW, M. D. AN ADDRESS DELIVERED BEFORE THE NEW ENGLAND HISTORIC-GENEALOGICAL SOCIETY, January 4, 1865. To which is added a Report of the Proceedings at said Meeting. 8*vo, pp.* 20, *paper.* Boston, 1865

1853 LIBERTY (THE) BELL; by Friends of Freedom. *Portrait of Wendell Phillips.* 12*mo, cloth, gilt edges.* Boston, 1845

1854 LIFE (THE) AND ENTERTAINING ADVENTURES OF MR. CLEVELAND, Natural Son of Oliver Cromwell, written by himself; giving a Particular Account of his Unhappiness in Love, Marriage, Friendship, etc., and his great Sufferings in Europe and America. Intermixed with Reflections, describing the Heart of Man in all its Variety of Passions and Disguises; also, some Curious Particulars of Oliver's History and Amours, and several Remarkable Passages in the Reign of King Charles II., never before made Publick. 4 *vols.*, 12*mo, old calf, red edges.* London, 1760

1855 LILLO, GEORGE. DRAMATIC WORKS; with Memoirs of the Author, by Thomas Davies. Second Edition, improved (with some Additions). *Wood-cuts.* 2 *vols. in* 1, *small thick* 12*mo, half calf, extra.* W. Lowndes, London, 1810

CONTENTS: Preface. Life. Silvia, or the Country Burial; an Opera. George Barnwell; a Tragedy. Life of Scanderberg. The Christian Hero; a Tragedy. Fatal Curiosity; a Tragedy. Marina; a Play. Britannia and Batavia; a Masque. Elmerick, or Justice Triumphant; a Tragedy. Arden of Feversham; an Historical Tragedy.

1856 LIMBORCH, PHILIP VAN. THE HISTORY OF THE INQUISITION; translated into English, by Samuel Chandler. To which is prefixed, a large Introduction concerning the Rise and Progress of Persecution, and the Real and Pretended Causes of it. *Plates and vignettes. 2 vols. in 1, 4to, old calf.* London, 1731

1857 LINCOLN, ABRAHAM. MESSAGE OF THE PRESIDENT OF THE UNITED STATES to the Two Houses of Congress at the Commencement of the Third Session of the Thirty-seventh Congress. (With Diplomatic Correspondence, etc.) *8vo, cloth.* Washington, 1862

1858 LINCOLN, ABRAHAM. SERMONS PREACHED IN BOSTON ON THE DEATH OF ABRAHAM LINCOLN; together with the Funeral Services in the East Room of the Executive Mansion at Washington. *4to, half green morocco, very neat, rough edges.* LARGE PAPER: *only* 200 *copies printed.* Boston, 1865

1859 LINCOLN, ABRAHAM. THE LIFE AND PUBLIC SERVICES OF; together with his State Papers, including his Speeches, Addresses, Messages, Letters, and Proclamations, and the Closing Scenes connected with his Life and Death. By Henry J. Raymond. To which are added Anecdotes and Personal Reminiscences of President Lincoln, by Frank B. Carpenter. *Portrait, plate, and wood-cuts. 8vo, half morocco, extra, gilt edges.* New York, 1865

1860 LINCOLN, ABRAHAM. THE OPINIONS OF ABRAHAM LINCOLN UPON SLAVERY AND ITS ISSUES; indicated by his Speeches, Letters, Messages, and Proclamations. *8vo, pp.* 16. (Washington) s. a.

1861 LINCOLN, WILLIAM. HISTORY OF WORCESTER, MASSACHUSETTS, from its Earliest Settlement to September, 1836; with Various Notices relating to the History of Worcester County. *Portraits. Royal 8vo, boards, rough edges.* Worcester, 1862

1862 LINDEMANN-FROMMEL, KARL. SKIZZEN AUS ROM UND DER UMGEGEND. *A series of* 36 *fine tinted and colored views. Without title. Atlas 4to, half green morocco, very neat, gilt edges.* (F. Köhler, Stuttgart, 1844, etc.)

1863 LINDLEY, GEORGE. A GUIDE TO THE ORCHARD AND KITCHEN GARDEN, or an Account of the most Valuable Fruit and Vegetables cultivated in Great Britain; with Kalenders of the Work required in the Orchard and Kitchen Garden during every Month in the Year. Edited by John Lindley, F. R. S., etc. *8vo, half green morocco.* London, 1831

1864 LINDLEY, JOHN. THE THEORY OF HORTICULTURE, or an Attempt to explain the Principal Operations of Gardening upon Physiological Principles. *Numerous wood-cuts. 8vo, half green morocco.* London, 1840

1865 LINDLEY, JOHN. POMOLOGIA BRITANNICA, or Figures and Descriptions of the Most Important Varieties of Fruit cultivated in Great Britain. *Contains 152 fine colored plates, chiefly by Mrs. Withers, artist to the Horticultural Society, London, executed in a manner similar to those in the Horticultural Society's Transactions. 3 vols., royal 8vo, half crimson morocco, extra, gilt edges, by Wright.* London, 1841

1866 LINDSAY, ALEXANDER WILLIAM CRAWFORD, LORD. LETTERS ON EGYPT, EDOM, AND THE HOLY LAND. Fifth Edition; with Additional Preface and Notes, and illustrated by Numerous Engravings. *Post 8vo, half calf, extra, gilt top.* London, 1858

1867 LIN-LE. TI-PING TIEN-KWOH; the History of the Ti-Ping Revolution, including a Narrative of the Author's Personal Adventures. By Lin-Le. *With 21 tinted and colored plates, and 9 wood-cuts. 2 vols., imperial 8vo, cloth.* Day & Son, London, 1866

The preface is signed "A. F. L."

1868 LINNÉ, CARL VON. LACHESIS LAPPONICA, or a Tour in Lapland (in 1732), now first published from the Original Manuscript Journal of the Celebrated Linnæus; by James Edward Smith, M. D., F. R. S. *Wood-cuts. 2 vols., 8vo, half calf.* London, 1811

"Botany forms the principal subject; but the work is also interesting from the picture it exhibits of the character of the author and of the manners of the Laplanders." — *Lowndes.*

1869 LINNELL, JOHN. THE ROYAL GALLERY OF PICTURES; being a Selection of the Cabinet Paintings in her Majesty's Private Collection at Buckingham Palace. Published under the Superintendence of John Linnell, Esq. *Engraved dedication and 32 plates, with descriptions. Royal 4to, half morocco.* London, 1850

1870 LIPPINCOTT, SARA JANE. RECORDS OF FIVE YEARS; *Post 8vo, cloth.* Boston, 1867

1871 LITERARY AND GRAPHICAL ILLUSTRATIONS OF SHAKSPEARE, and the British Drama; comprising an Historical View of the Origin and Improvement of the English Stage, and a Series of Critical and Descriptive Notices of upwards of One Hundred of the most Celebrated Tragedies, Comedies, Operas, and Farces. *Above 200 wood-cuts, by Harvey and others. Each page surrounded by a border. 12mo, paper.* London, 1831

1872 LITERARY (THE) MISCELLANY, or Selections and Extracts, Classical and Scientific; with Originals in Prose and Verse. *Numerous portraits and plates, after Corbould, etc. 12 vols., 8mo, half calf, neat.* Stourport, 1812

1873 LITTA, POMPEO, CONTE. FAMIGLIE CELEBRI DI ITALIA. *Genealogical tables, portraits, arms, antiquities, medals, sculptures, paintings, etc.; the portraits and arms beautifully colored. 3 vols., royal folio, half russia, rough edges.* ORIGINAL COPY. Milano, 1819, etc.

These three volumes contain the following families: Accolti, Alighieri, Arcimboldi, Bojardo, Bonacolsi, Da Camino, Candiano, Cantelmi, Carraresi, Castiglioni, Cavalcabò, Cavaniglia, Cesarini, Cesi, Concini, Da Correggio, Ecelini, Facehinetti, Gaddi, Gallio, Giovio, Guicciardini, Medici, del Monte, Orseolo, Peretti, Pico, Piccolomini, Pio, Rossi, Sanvitale, Scaligeri, Sforza, Simonetta, Trinci, Trivulzio, Valori, Dal Verme, Visconti, Visconti già Aicardi Vitelli.

"Un des livres les plus remarquables qui aient paru dans ces derniers temps en Italie." — *Brunet.*

1874 LITTELL'S LIVING AGE. *From April* 11, 1844, *to March* 30, 1867, *inclusive.* 92 *vols., 8vo, cloth.* Boston, 1844–67

1875 LITTLE (THE) BLUE BOOK; a Register of Federal Offices and Salaries. *18mo, paper.* New York, 1861

1876 LITTLE HYDROGEN, OR THE DEVIL ON TWO STICKS IN LONDON; embellished with coloured Portraits. Third Edition. *12mo, half green calf, extra.* London, 1819

1877 LIVES (THE) OF THOSE EMINENT ANTIQUARIES JOHN LELAND, THOMAS HEARNE AND ANTHONY À WOOD; with an authentick Account of their Respective Writings and Publications, from Original Papers: in which are occasionally inserted, Memoirs relating to many Eminent Persons and Various Parts of Literature; also, Several Engravings of Antiquity, never before published. [Edited by T. Warton and W. Huddesford.] *Fine impressions of the portraits and plates, engraved by Vertue, Grignion, etc.* 2 *vols., royal 8vo, old marbled calf, gilt, yellow edges.* LARGE PAPER. Clarendon Press, Oxford, 1772

1878 LIVINGSTONE, DAVID. TRAVELS AND RESEARCHES IN SOUTH AFRICA; including a Sketch of Sixteen Years' Residence in the Interior of Africa, and a Journey from the Cape of Good Hope to Loanda on the West Coast, etc. *Numerous wood-cuts. 12mo, cloth.* Philadelphia, 1859

1879 LIVY. T. LIVII PATAVINI HISTORIARUM LIBRI QUI SUPERSUNT EX EDITIONE G. A. RUPERTI, cum Supplementis, Notis, et Interpretatione in Usum Delphini, Variis Lectionibus, Notis Variorum, Recensu Editionum et Codicum, Indice Locupletissimo, et Glossario Liviano, accurate recensiti. 20 *vols., 8vo, russia, neat, marbled edges.* Curate et Imprimente, A. J. Valpy, Londoni, 1828

1880 LLORENTE, JUAN ANTONIO. APOLOGIA CATÓLICA DEL PROYECTO DE CONSTITUCION RELIGIOSA, escrito por un Americano. *12mo, calf, marbled edges.* San Sebastian (Paris), 1821

1881 LLORENTE, JUAN-ANTONIO. HISTORIA CRITICA DE LA INQUISICION DE ESPAÑA; Obra Original Conforme á lo que Resulta de los Archivos del Real Consejo de la Suprema, y de los Tribunales del Santo-Oficio de las Provincias. 10 *vols., 18mo, marbled calf, marbled edges.* Madrid, 1822

1882 LLOYD, CHARLES. PRINCIPLES FOR THE CONDUCT OF LIFE. 2 *vols., 12mo, cloth, uncut.* London, 1848

1883 LLOYD, LEWIS. SCANDINAVIAN ADVENTURES, during a Residence of upwards of Twenty Years; representing Sporting Incidents, and Subjects of Natural History, and Devices for Entrapping Wild Animals: with some Account of the Northern Fauna. Second Edition. *Map, 12 colored plates, and numerous wood-cuts, 2 vols., imperial 8vo, cloth, uncut.* London, 1854

1884 LOCKE, D. R. "SWINGIN ROUND THE CIRKLE;" by Petroleum V. Nasby: his Ideas of Men, Politics, and Things, as set forth in his Letters to the Public Press, during the Year 1866. *Wood-cuts after T. Nast. 12mo, cloth.* Boston, 1867

1885 LOCKE, JOHN. THE WORKS OF. (With Preface, Life, etc.) The Tenth Edition. *Portrait and folding analysis of the Essay on Understanding. 10 vols., royal 8vo, diamond russia, extra, gilt edges.* LARGE PAPER. London, 1801
This copy has been rather closely trimmed, but still has a good margin.

1886 LOCKE, JOHN. ANOTHER COPY: the Eleventh Edition. *Same portrait, etc. 10 vols., 8vo, old calf, neat.* London, 1812

1887 LOCKE, JOHN. AN ESSAY CONCERNING HUMANE UNDERSTANDING; in Four Books. The Fifth Edition, with Large Additions. *Folio, old calf.* London, 1706

1888 LOCKE, JOHN. AN ESSAY CONCERNING HUMAN UNDERSTANDING; with Life of the Author. First American Edition. *3 vols., 12mo, sheep, yellow edges.* Boston, 1803

1889 LOCKER, EDWARD HAWKE. MEMOIRS OF CELEBRATED NAVAL COMMANDERS; illustrated by Engravings from Original Pictures in the Naval Gallery of Greenwich Hospital. *Royal 4to, crimson morocco, extra, gilt edges, by Wright.* LARGE PAPER: INDIA PROOFS. London, 1832

1890 LOCKHART, JOHN GIBSON. PETER'S LETTERS TO HIS KINSFOLK. The Third Edition. *Portrait of "Peter Morris, M. D.," 14 other portraits of the literati of the time, and 4 vignettes. 3 vols., 8vo, half calf, neat.* Edinburgh, 1819

1891 LOCKHART, JOHN GIBSON. MEMOIRS OF THE LIFE OF SIR WALTER SCOTT. A New Edition, complete in One Volume. *Fine impressions of the portraits and plates, chiefly on India paper. Royal 8vo, calf, extra, gilt edges.* ABBOTSFORD EDITION. Edinburgh, 1850

1892 LOCKHART, JOHN GIBSON. ANCIENT SPANISH BALLADS; Historical and Romantic. Translated, with an Introduction and Notes. A New Edition, revised, with a Biographical Sketch of the Author. *Portrait. 8vo, cloth, gilt top, uncut.* Boston, 1861

1893 LODGE, EDMUND. LIFE OF SIR JULIUS CÆSAR, Judge of the High Court of Admiralty, Chancellor of the Exchequer, and a Privy Councellor to King James, and Charles the First; with Memoirs of his Family and Descendants. By Edmund Lodge, Esq. Illustrated by Eighteen Portraits, after Original Pictures; with a Pedigree, and other Engravings. To which is added, Numerus Infaustus, an Historical Work; by Charles Cæsar, Esq., Grandson to Sir Julius. *Original impressions of* ALL *the plates;* WITH INDIA PROOF OF THE PORTRAIT OF ELIZA ABERDEIN, *which is usually wanting. Imperial 4to, cloth, rough edges; with bookplate of James H. Baverstock, F. S. A.* LARGE PAPER. London, 1827 (1810 ?)

This copy has (inserted) the title of the second edition, dated 1827, but the plates all appear to be of the original issue.

1894 LODGE, EDMUND. PORTRAITS OF ILLUSTRIOUS PERSONAGES OF GREAT BRITAIN, engraved from Authentic Pictures, in the Galleries of the Nobility, and the Public Collections of the Country; with Biographical and Historical Memoirs of their Lives and Actions, by Edmund Lodge, Esq. *Contains 240 fine portraits, on a* LARGER SCALE *than those of the subsequent editions, and engraved on copper instead of steel. 4 vols., folio, morocco, extra, gilt, over marbled edges.* ORIGINAL EDITION: *fine copy.* London, 1821–34

1895 LODGE, EDMUND. ANOTHER COPY: Second Edition; *with fine early impressions of the plates. 12 vols., imperial 8vo, calf, very neat, marbled edges.* London, 1823–34

1896 LODGE, EDMUND. ANOTHER COPY: *the same; without the letter-press. 4 vols., royal 4to, cloth, uncut.* LARGE PAPER: INDIA PROOFS. London, 1836

The above three copies were all issued by Harding & Co.

1897 LODGE, EDMUND. ANOTHER COPY: *Bohn's "Illustrated Library" edition; with the 240 portraits, on a reduced scale, and the entire letter-press. 8 vols., post 8vo, calf, gilt, marbled edges.* London, 1849–50

1898 LOLA MONTEZ. LECTURES; including her Autobiography. *Portrait. 12mo, cloth.* New York, 1858

1899 LONDON (THE) MAGAZINE, or Gentleman's Monthly Intelligencer. *April,* 1732–*December,* 1781; *with* GENERAL INDEX *to the first 27 vols.* (1732–58). *Numerous portraits, plates, etc.* 51 *vols.,* 8vo (32 *vols., full bound,* 18 *vols., and index, half bound*), *old calf.* London, 1732–81

1900 LONDON SOCIETY; AN ILLUSTRATED MAGAZINE of Light and Amusing Literature, for the Hours of Relaxation. *February*, 1862–*December*, 1867. 12 *vols.*, 8*vo*; *first* 2 *vols. cloth, rest in numbers.* London, 1862–67

1901 LONG (A) VACATION RAMBLE IN NORWAY AND SWEDEN; by X and Y (Two Unknown Quantities). *Post* 8*vo, cloth, uncut.* Cambridge (London), 1857

1902 LONG (A) VACATION RAMBLE. ANOTHER COPY. *Post* 8*vo, cloth, uncut.* Cambridge, 1857

1903 LONGFELLOW, HENRY WADSWORTH. BALLADS AND OTHER POEMS. Third Edition. *Imperial* 8*vo, boards, rough edges.* LARGE PAPER. Cambridge, 1842

1904 LONGFELLOW, HENRY WADSWORTH. THE SPANISH STUDENT. Fifth Edition. *Post* 8*vo, boards, uncut.* Cambridge, 1844

1905 LONGFELLOW, HENRY WADSWORTH. VOICES OF THE NIGHT. Ninth Edition. *Post* 8*vo, boards, uncut.* Cambridge, 1844

1906 LONGFELLOW, HENRY WADSWORTH. THE GOLDEN LEGEND. *Foolscap* 8*vo, cloth, uncut.* D. Bogue, London, 1851

1907 LONGFELLOW, HENRY WADSWORTH. WORKS: Poems; *with portrait.* (2 *vols.*). The Golden Legend. The Song of Hiawatha. The Courtship of Miles Standish; and other Poems. Outre-Mer; a Pilgrimage beyond the Sea. Hyperion; a Romance. Kavanagh; a Tale. *Together* 8 *vols., foolscap* 8*vo, morocco, antique, gilt edges.* Boston, 1859–60

1908 LONGFELLOW, HENRY WADSWORTH. THE COMPLETE WORKS OF. Revised Edition. *Portrait on India paper.* 7 *vols., crown* 8*vo, boards, green cloth backs, red sides, uncut; uniform with "British Poets" edited by Professor Child, etc.* LARGE PAPER: *only* 100 *copies printed.* Boston, 1866

1909 LONGFELLOW, HENRY WADSWORTH. ANOTHER COPY: *the same.* 7 *vols., crown* 8*vo, boards, green cloth backs, red sides, uncut.* Boston, 1866

1910 LONGLANDE, OR, LANGLANDE, ROBERT. THE VISION AND THE CREED OF PIERS PLOUGHMAN, newly imprinted (from a MS. in the Library of Trinity College, Cambridge; edited, with Notes and a Glossary, by Thomas Wright, F. R. S., etc.). *Fac-simile frontispiece, ornate headings, etc. Printed by Whittingham.* 2 *vols., foolscap* 8*vo, cloth, uncut.* ONLY 500 COPIES PRINTED. W. Pickering, London, 1842

1911 LONGLANDE, ROBERT. ANOTHER COPY: *the same; with MS. bibliographical notes on fly-leaf.* 2 *vols., foolscap* 8*vo, cloth, uncut.* W. Pickering, London, 1842

1912 LOOKING-GLASS (THE), OR CARICATURE ANNUAL; for the Years 1830, 1831, 1832. *Numerous colored plates.* 3 *vols., folio, half morocco, neat, gilt edges.* London, 1831–33

1913 LORING, CHARLES G. CORRESPONDENCE ON THE PRESENT RELATIONS BETWEEN GREAT BRITAIN AND THE UNITED STATES OF AMERICA. (Friendly Correspondence, upon the "Trent Affair," etc.; between Edwin W. Field, of London, and Charles G. Loring, of Boston.) 8*vo, paper, uncut.* Boston, 1862

1914 LORRAIN, CLAUDE GELÉE, called LE. LIBER VERITATIS, or a Collection of (300) Prints after the Original Designs of Claude le Lorrain, in the collection of his Grace the Duke of Devonshire (and others); executed by Richard Earlom, in the Manner and Taste of the Drawings. To which is added a Descriptive Catalogue of each Print, together with the Names of those for whom, and places for which the Original Pictures were first painted (taken from the Hand-writing of Claude le Lorrain on the Back of each Drawing), and of the Present Possessors of many of the Original Pictures. *Fine impressions of this issue.* 3 *vols., folio, half crimson morocco, extra, gilt edges.* London, s. a.

1915 LOSSING, BENSON J. THE PICTORIAL FIELD-BOOK OF THE REVOLUTION; or Illustrations, by Pen and Pencil, of the History, Biography, Scenery, Relics, and Traditions of the War for Independence. *Illuminated frontispiece and several hundred wood-cuts.* 2 *vols. in* 3, *imperial* 8*vo, calf, very neat, gilt edges.* FINE ORIGINAL COPY. New York, 1851

1916 LOSSING, BENSON J. MOUNT VERNON AND ITS ASSOCIATIONS, Historical, Biographical, and Pictorial. Illustrated by Numerous Engravings, chiefly from Original Drawings by the Author, engraved by Lossing and Barritt. 8*vo, morocco, antique, gilt edges.* New York, 1859

1917 LOSSING, BENSON J. THE HOME OF WASHINGTON AND ITS ASSOCIATIONS, Historical, Biographical, and Pictorial. New Edition, revised, with Additions. Illustrated by Numerous Engravings, chiefly from Original Drawings by the Author, engraved by Lossing and Barritt. *Handsomely printed on a toned paper. Imperial* 8*vo, cloth, rough edges.* LARGE PAPER: *only* 100 *copies printed for E. French.* New York, 1865

1918 LOTHROP, SAMUEL KIRKLAND, D. D. THE NATURE AND EXTENT OF RELIGIOUS LIBERTY; a Sermon preached at the Church in Brattle Square, on Sunday Morning, June 17, 1838. 8*vo, pp.* 19, *paper; clean.* Boston, 1838

1919 LOTHROP, SAMUEL KIRKLAND, D. D. A SERMON preached January 19, 1840, on the Destruction of the Lexington by Fire, January 13th. 8*vo, pp.* 24, *paper; clean.* Boston, 1840

1920 LOTHROP, SAMUEL KIRKLAND, D. D. A HISTORY OF THE CHURCH IN BRATTLE STREET, BOSTON. *16mo, cloth.* Boston, 1851

1921 LOTHROP, SAMUEL KIRKLAND, D. D. THE CAUSES, PRINCIPLES, AND RESULTS OF THE PRESENT CONFLICT; a Discourse delivered before the Ancient and Honorable Artillery Company, on its CCXXIII. Anniversary, June 3, 1861. (With the Proceedings of the Company.) *8vo, pp. 70, paper.* Boston, 1861

1922 LOTICH, JOHANNES PIETER. HISTORIA AUGUSTA IMPERATORUM ROMANORUM; a C. Julio Cæsare, usque ad Josephum Imperatorem Augustissimum: ex Joannis Petri Lotichii Tetrastichis Mnemonicis, et Joannis Jacobi Hofmanni Tetrastichis, et ejusdem in hæc Enarrationibus Historicis. Adduntur Singulorum Imperatorum Effigies Aere Scalpto Expressæ, ex Nummis Christinæ Suecorum Reginæ. Additamenta Necessaria & Integra Omissorum Supplementa adjecit Henricus Christianus Henninius. (Adjecta est Henrici Hamelow Historia Imperatorum Romanorum Carmine Perpetuo descripta.) *Frontispiece and* 165 *portraits. Folio, old calf.* Amstelaedami, 1710

1923 LOUDON, JOHN CLAUDIUS. THE GARDENER'S MAGAZINE, and Register of Rural and Domestic Improvements. *Numerous wood-cuts.* 19 *vols., 8vo, half green morocco, neat.* COMPLETE. London, 1826–43

1924 LOUDON, JOHN CLAUDIUS. THE ARCHITECTURAL MAGAZINE, and Journal of Improvement in Architecture, Building, and Furnishing, and the Various Arts and Trades connected therewith. *Numerous wood-cuts.* 5 *vols., 8vo, half green morocco, neat.* COMPLETE. London, 1834–38

1925 LOUDON, JOHN CLAUDIUS. AN ENCYCLOPÆDIA OF GARDENING, comprising the Theory and Practice of Horticulture, Floriculture, Arboriculture, and Landscape-Gardening; including all the Latest Improvements, a General History of Gardening in all Countries, and a Statistical View of its Present State, with Suggestions for its Future Progress in the British Isles. A New Edition, considerably improved and enlarged. *Many hundred wood-cuts, by Branston.* 1 *vol. in* 2, *8vo, green morocco, neat.* London, 1835

1926 LOUDON, JOHN CLAUDIUS. AN ENCYCLOPÆDIA OF AGRICULTURE; comprising the Theory and Practice of the Valuation, Transfer, Laying-out, Improvement, and Management of Landed Property, and the Cultivation and Economy of the Animal and Vegetable Productions of Agriculture in all Countries, and a Statistical View of its Present State, with Suggestions for its Future Progress in the British Isles. Third Edition. *Above* 1,100 *wood-cuts, by Branston.* 1 *vol. in* 2, *8vo, green morocco, neat.* London, 1835

1927 LOUDON, John Claudius. An Encyclopædia of Cottage, Farm, and Villa Architecture and Furniture; containing Numerous Designs for Dwellings, from the Cottage to the Villa, including Farm Houses, Farmeries, and other Agricultural Buildings, Several Designs for Country Inns, Public Houses, and Parochial Schools, with the requisite Fittings-up, Fixtures, and Furniture, and Appropriate Offices, Gardens, and Garden Scenery, Each Design accompanied by Analytical and Critical Remarks, illustrative of the Principles of Architectural Science and Taste on which it is composed. A New Edition, with Numerous Corrections, and many of the Plates re-engraved. *Above* 2,000 *wood-cuts.* 1 *vol. in* 2, 8*vo, green morocco, neat.*
London, 1836

1928 LOUDON, John Claudius. The Suburban Gardener and Villa Companion; comprising the Choice of a Suburban or Villa Residence, or of a Situation on which to form one, the Arrangement and Furnishing of the House, and the Laying-out, Planting, and General Management of the Garden and Grounds: the Whole adapted for Grounds from One Perch to Fifty Acres and upwards in extent, and intended for the Instruction of those who know little of Gardening and Rural Affairs, and more particularly for the Use of Ladies. *Numerous wood-cuts.* 8*vo, half green morocco, neat.* London, 1838

1929 LOUDON, John Claudius. Arboretum et Fructicetum Britannicum, or the Trees and Shrubs of Britain, Native and Foreign, Hardy and Half-Hardy, Pictorially and Botanically delineated, and Scientifically and Popularly Described; with their Propagation, Culture, Management, and Uses in the Arts, in Useful and Ornamental Plantations, and in Landscape-gardening: preceded by a Historical and Geographical Outline of the Trees and Shrubs of Temperate Climates throughout the World. Second Edition. *Nearly* 3,000 *plates and wood-cuts.* 8 *vols. in* 6, 8*vo, half green morocco, neat.* London, 1854

In this copy the plates are bound in 2 vols. (usually in 4), with the quarto plates folded.

1930 LOUVET de Couvray, Jean Baptiste. Les Amours du Chevalier de Faublas. Nouvelle Édition, ornée de Huit Superbes Gravures, dessinées par Collin, élève de Girodet, gravées par les Premiers Artistes de Paris; et précédée d'une Notice sur Louvet, par M. * * *. 4 *vols.*, 8*vo, half russia, neat.* Best edition.
A. Tardieu, Paris, 1821

"Le plus belle des nombreuses éditions de ce roman licencieux." — *Brunet.*

1931 LOW, David. The Breeds of the Domestic Animals of the British Islands, described by David Low, Esq.,

F. R. S. E., Professor of Agriculture in the University of Edinburgh, etc., etc.; and illustrated with plates from drawings by Mr. W. Nicholson, R. S. A., reduced from a Series of Portraits from Life. *Contains 56 fine colored plates. 2 vols. in 1, atlas 4to, half green morocco, extra, gilt edges.* FINE COPY. London, 1842

1932 LOWELL, JAMES RUSSELL. POEMS. *Imperial 8vo, half green morocco, very neat, gilt top, uncut.* LARGE PAPER. Cambridge, 1844

1933 LOWELL, JAMES RUSSELL. MELIBŒUS-HIPPONAX: the Biglow Papers; edited, with an Introduction, Notes, Glossary, and Copious Index, by Homer Wilbur, A. M., (Prospective) Member of many Literary, Learned, and Scientific Societies (for which see page v.). Fifth Edition. *16mo, cloth.* Boston, 1862

1934 LOWELL, JAMES RUSSELL. MELIBŒUS-HIPPONAX; the Biglow Papers; Second Series. *16mo, cloth.* Boston, 1867

1935 LOWELL, ROBERT T. S. THE NEW PRIEST IN CONCEPTION BAY. [By R. T. S. Lowell.] *2 vols., 16mo, cloth.* Boston, 1858

1936 LOWNDES, WILLIAM THOMAS. THE BIBLIOGRAPHER'S MANUAL OF ENGLISH LITERATURE, containing an Account of Rare, Curious, and Useful Books, published in, or relating to, Great Britain and Ireland, from the Invention of Printing; with Bibliographical and Critical Notices, Collations of the Rarer Articles, and the Prices at which they have been sold in the Present Century. *Fine interleaved copy, with MS. notes. 4 vols. in 6, 8vo, calf, gilt.* W. Pickering, London, 1834

1937 LOWNDES, WILLIAM THOMAS. ANOTHER COPY: New Edition, revised, corrected, and enlarged [by Henry G. Bohn]. *Parts I.–VI., interleaved and bound in 6 vols., post 8vo, half morocco, neat, marbled edges.* London, 1857–61

1938 LUCAN. PHARSALIA; translated into English Verse, by Nicholas Rowe, Esq. (With Historical and Geographical Notes.) *Map, frontispiece, and numerous vignettes, after Cheron, engraved by Kirkall, etc. Royal folio, old calf, marbled edges.* J. Tonson, London, 1718

1939 LUCRETIUS. T. LUCRETIUS CARUS, OF THE NATURE OF THINGS, IN SIX BOOKS; translated into English Verse, by Tho. Creech. Explain'd and illustrated with Notes and Animadversions; being a Compleat System of the Epicurean Philosophy. *Frontispiece. 2 vols., 8vo, russia.* London, 1714–15

"A translation highly praised by Dryden. In this edition of 1714 all the verses in the text which Mr. Creech had left untranslated are supplied, and many new notes added, and intermixed by another hand." — *Lowndes.*

1940 LUCRETIUS. TITI LUCRETII CARI DE RERUM NATURA LIBRI SEX. *Royal 4to, half calf; almost free from stains.* J. Baskerville, Birminghamiæ, 1772

1941 LUCRETIUS. ANOTHER COPY: *the same.* 12*mo, old marbled calf, gilt, back cracked; clean.* J. Baskerville, Birminghamiæ, 1773

1942 LUDEWIG, HERMANN E. THE LITERATURE OF AMERICAN ABORIGINAL LANGUAGES. With Additions and Corrections, by Professor Wm. W. Turner. Edited by Nicholas Trübner. 8*vo, cloth, gilt top.* London, 1858

1943 LUDLOW, EDMUND. MEMOIRS OF EDMUND LUDLOW, ESQ., Lieutenant General of the Horse, Commander-in-Chief of the Forces in Ireland, one of the Council of State, and a Member of the Parliament which began on November 3, 1640. *Portrait.* 2 *vols.,* 8*vo, old calf; binding broken and third volume* (1699) *wanting.* Vevay, 1698

1944 LUDWIG, MOSES R., M. D. LUDWIG GENEALOGY. Sketch of Joseph Ludwig, who was born in Germany in 1699, and his Wife and Family, who settled at "Broad Bay," Waldoboro', 1753. *Portraits, etc.* 12*mo, cloth.* Augusta (Me.), 1866

1945 LUMISDEN, ANDREW. REMARKS ON THE ANTIQUITIES OF ROME AND ITS ENVIRONS; being a Classical and Topographical Survey of the Ruins of that Celebrated City. The Second Edition. *Portrait and* 48 *plates.* 4*to, calf.* London, 1812

One of the copies with 36 additional plates.

1946 LUTHER, MARTIN. LIFE OF; by John F. W. Tischer. To which is added, a Selection from the most Celebrated Sermons of Luther. *Portrait.* 8*vo, cloth.* S. S. Miles, s. l., 1841

1947 LYNDWODE, WILLIAM, BISHOP OF ST. DAVIDS, ETC. PROVINCIALE, SEU CONSTITUTIONES ANGLIE; cum Summariis atqs Justis Annotationibus Honestis Characteribus, Summaqs Accuratione rursum impresse. *First edition with notes; two columns, printed in red and black. Folio, old calf.* **Black Letter.** *Perfect copy.* (Paris), 1501

See folio cxcii, "Explicitū opus magistri wilhelmi lyndewode," etc.

1948 LYTTON, SIR EDWARD LYTTON BULWER. THE SIAMESE TWINS, a Satirical Tale of the Times; with other Poems. 12*mo, boards, rough edges.* New York, 1831

1949 LYTTON, SIR EDWARD LYTTON BULWER. LEILA, OR THE SIEGE OF GRANADA. Illustrated with Splendid Engravings from Drawings by the most Eminent Artists. *Royal* 8*vo, cloth.* Philadelphia, 1838

1950 LYTTON, SIR EDWARD LYTTON BULWER. THE NOVELS AND ROMANCES OF. A New Edition, with Illustrations by H. K. Browne, John Gilbert, etc., etc. 10 *vols., post 8vo, half calf, extra, contents lettered, marbled edges.* London, 1856

CONTENTS: Pelham, Godolphin, Disowned, Devereux, Eugene Aram, Paul Clifford, Rienzi, Last Days of Pompeii, Ernest Maltravers, Alice, Last of the Barons, Leila, Zanoni, Harold, Night and Morning, Pilgrims of the Rhine, Lucretia, Caxtons, My Novel.

1951 MACAULAY, THOMAS BABINGTON, LORD. THE HISTORY OF ENGLAND from the Accession of James II. *Portrait. Vols. I., II., royal 8vo, half morocco, neat.* London, 1849

1952 MACAULAY, THOMAS BABINGTON, LORD. LAYS OF ANCIENT ROME. With Illustrations, Original and from the Antique, drawn on Wood by George Scharf, Jun. New Edition. *Foolscap 4to, boards.* London, 1852

1953 MACAULAY, THOMAS BABINGTON, LORD. ANOTHER COPY: *the same. Foolscap 4to, smooth morocco, extra, gilt edges, by Hayday.* London, 1855

1954 MACAULAY, THOMAS BABINGTON, LORD. CRITICAL AND HISTORICAL ESSAYS, contributed to the Edinburgh Review. Tenth Edition. (3 *vols.*) — THE MISCELLANEOUS WRITINGS OF. (2 *vols.*) *Portrait. Together, 5 vols., 8vo, half calf, extra, marbled edges.* London, 1860

1955 MACFARLANE, CHARLES; and REV. THOMAS THOMSON. THE COMPREHENSIVE HISTORY OF ENGLAND; Civil and Military, Religious, Intellectual, and Social, from the Earliest Period to the Suppression of the Sepoy Revolt. The Whole revised and edited by the Rev. Thomas Thomson. Illustrated by above One Thousand Engravings. 4 *vols., royal 8vo, half morocco, marbled edges.* London, 1861

1956 MACGREGOR, JOHN. MY NOTE BOOK. *Frontispieces on India paper.* 3 *vols., post 8vo, half calf, neat.* London, 1835

A personal narrative of travels on the Continent, with the statistical information at the end of the third volume.

1957 MACKAY, CHARLES. THE SCENERY AND POETRY OF THE ENGLISH LAKES; a Summer Ramble. With Numerous Illustrations from Original Sketches, engraved by Thomas Gilks. Second Edition. 12*mo, cloth.* London, 1852

1958 MACKENZIE, ALEXANDER. VOYAGES FROM MONTREAL, on the River St. Lawrence, through the Continent of North America, to the Frozen and Pacific Oceans; in the Years 1789 and 1793. With a Preliminary Account of the Rise, Progress, and Present State of the Fur Trade of that Country. *Portrait and maps. 4to, old marbled calf, very neat.* London, 1801

1959 MACKENZIE, ALEXANDER. ANOTHER COPY: *the same. Portrait and maps. 4to, half calf.* London, 1801

1960 MACKENZIE, ALEXANDER SLIDELL. A YEAR IN SPAIN. *Wood-cuts. 2 vols., crown 8vo, half calf.* J. Murray, London, 1831

1961 MACKENZIE, ALEXANDER SLIDELL. THE AMERICAN IN ENGLAND. *2 vols. in 1, 12mo, half calf, neat.* New York, 1835

1962 MACKEY, ALBERT G. THE PRINCIPLES OF MASONIC LAW; a Treatise on the Constitutional Laws, Usages, and Landmarks of Freemasonry. *Portrait. 12mo, cloth.* New York, 1856

1963 MACKEY, ALBERT G. A LEXICON OF FREEMASONRY; containing a Definition of all its Communicable Terms, Notices of its History, Traditions, and Antiquities, and an Account of all the Rites, and Mysteries of the Ancient World. Second Edition, enlarged and improved by the Author. *12mo, cloth.* Charleston, 1852

1964 MACKEY, ALBERT G. ANOTHER COPY: new and improved Edition (the Fifth, enlarged by the Author). *Portrait. 12mo, cloth.* Philadelphia, 1860

1965 MACKLIN, CHARLES. MEMOIRS OF THE LIFE OF; Principally compiled from his own Papers and Memorandums, which contain his Criticisms on, and Characters and Anecdotes of, Betterton, Booth, Wilks, Cibber, Garrick, Barry, Mossop, Sheridan, Foote, Quin, and most of his Contemporaries: together with his Valuable Observations on the Drama, on the Science of Acting, and on Various other Subjects. The Whole forming a Comprehensive but Succinct History of the Stage, which includes a Period of One Hundred Years. By James Thomas Kirkman. *Portrait. 2 vols., old marbled calf, gilt, yellow edges.* London, 1799

1966 MACNISH, ROBERT, M. D. TALES, ESSAYS, AND SKETCHES; with the Author's Life, by his Friend, D. M. Moir. Second Edition. *Portrait. 2 vols., foolscap 8vo, cloth, uncut.* London, 1844

1967 MACOY, ROBERT. THE MASONIC MANUAL, a Pocket Companion for the Initiated; containing the Rituals of Freemasonry, Embraced in the Degrees of the Lodge, Chapter and Encampment. Together with Forms of Masonic Documents, Notes, Songs, Dates, etc., compiled and arranged by Robert Macoy. Fourth Edition. *Above 300 wood-cuts, 32mo, cloth, gilt edges.* New York, 1854

1968 MADAN, MARTIN, D. D. THELYPHTHORA: or a Treatise on Female Ruin, in its Causes, Effects, Consequences, Prevention, and Remedy; considered on the Basis of the Divine Law, under the following Heads, viz: Marriage, Whoredom, and Fornication, Adultery, Polygamy, Divorce: with many other Incidental Matters, particularly including an Examination of the Principles and Tendency of Stat. 26 Geo. II. c. 33, commonly called the Marriage Act. 3 *vols.*, 8*vo*, *old sprinkled calf, neat.* J. Dodsley, London, 1780–81

"The controversy which this singular work occasioned lasted long, and was carried on with great keenness. In it the author maintains the lawfulness of polygamy as being authorized by the Mosaic Law, and therefore obligatory on Christians." — *Lowndes.*

1969 MADDEN, Richard Robert. The Infirmities of Genius, illustrated by referring the Anomalies in the Literary Character, to the Habits and Constitutional Peculiarities of Men of Genius. 12*mo*, *cloth.* Philadelphia, 1833

1970 MADEMOISELLE Mori. A Tale of Modern Rome. *Crown* 8*vo*, *cloth.* Boston, 1860

1971 MADISON, James. Letters and other Writings. *Portrait.* 4 *vols.*, 8*vo*, *half green morocco, neat, gilt tops, rough edges.* Philadelphia, 1865

1972 MAFFEI, A., Conte. Brigand Life in Italy; a History of Bourbonist Reaction. Edited from Original and Authentic Documents. 2 *vols.*, 8*vo*, *cloth, uncut.* London, 1865

1973 MAGINN, William. The O'Doherty Papers. Annotated by Dr. Shelton Mackenzie. *Portrait.* 2 *vols.*, 12*mo*, *cloth.* New York, 1855

1974 MAGOON, Elias L., D. D. Proverbs for the People, or Illustrations of Practical Godliness drawn from the Book of Wisdom. 12*mo*, *cloth.* Boston, 1849

1975 MAINE. Reports on the Adjutant General of the State of Maine; December 1, 1860. 8*vo*, *pp.* 32, *paper.* Augusta, 1860

1976 MAINE. Reports of the Maine State Prison: of the Committee appointed by the Legislature, 1860, *and*, of the Warden, Inspectors, Physician, and Chaplain, 1863. 2 *pamphlets*, 8*vo.* Augusta, 1860–63

1977 MAINE Historical Society. Collections of. (Vol. I. reprinted for the Society, with Corrections and Additions, William Willis, Editor, 1865.) *Maps, portraits, etc.* 6 *vols.*, 8*vo*, *cloth.* Published for the Society, Portland, 1847–65

1978 MAINE (The) Register, and State Reference Book; 1852. 12*mo*, *cloth.* Hallowell, 1852

1979 MAINTENON, Françoise d'Aubigné, Marquise de. The Secret Correspondence of, with the Princess des Ursins; from the Original Manuscripts in the Possession of the Duke de Choiseul. Translated from the French [by Mrs. Charlotte Lennox]. *Portraits.* 3 *vols.*, 8*vo*, *cloth.* London, 1827

1980 MAITLAND, Samuel Roffey, D. D. The Dark Ages; a Series of Essays intended to illustrate the State of

Religion and Literature in the Ninth, Tenth, Eleventh, and Twelfth Centuries. Third Edition. *8vo, cloth.* London, 1853

1981 MALCOLM, JAMES P. AN HISTORICAL SKETCH OF THE ART OF CARICATURING; with Graphic Illustrations. *Contains* 31 *curious plates of ancient and modern caricatures. 4to, calf, very neat.* London, 1813

1982 MALIBRAN DE BERIOT, MARIA FELICIA. MEMOIRS AND LETTERS OF. By the Countess de Merlin; with Notices of the Progress of the Musical Drama in England. 2 *vols. in* 1, 12*mo, half morocco.* Philadelphia, 1840

1983 MALLING, OVE. GREAT AND GOOD DEEDS OF DANES, NORWEGIANS, AND HOLSTEINIANS, translated. *Portrait of "Frederik* (VI.), *Prince Royal of Denmark," engraved by J. Heath, after a picture by Lips. Royal 4to, calf, very neat, marbled edges.* LARGE PAPER. London, 1807

1984 MALONE, EDMOND. AN INQUIRY INTO THE AUTHENTICITY OF CERTAIN MISCELLANEOUS PAPERS AND LEGAL INSTRUMENTS, published Dec. 24, MDCCXCV., and attributed to Shakspeare, Queen Elizabeth, and Henry, Earl of Southampton; illustrated by fac-similes of the Genuine Hand-Writing of that Nobleman and of her Majesty, a New Fac-simile of the Hand-Writing of Shakspeare, never before exhibited, and other Authentic Documents. In a Letter addressed to the Right Hon. James, Earl of Charlemont. *8vo, old marbled calf, yellow edges.* London, 1796

1985 MALTA (THE) PENNY MAGAZINE. *September* 14, 1839–*December* 25, 1841. *Published weekly.* 2 *vols., post 4to, cloth.* (Valletta), 1840–41

1986 MALTE-BRUN, MALTHE CONRAD BRUUN, called. UNIVERSAL GEOGRAPHY, or a Description of all the Parts of the World, according to the Great Natural Divisions of the Globe; Improved by the Addition of the most Recent Information, derived from Various Sources. 4 *vols., 8vo, old calf.* Philadelphia, 1827–29

1987 MALTE-BRUN, MALTHE CONRAD BRUUN, called. PRÉCIS DE LA GÉOGRAPHIE UNIVERSELLE, ou Description de toutes les Parties du Monde, sur un Plan Nouveau, d'après les Grandes Divisions Naturelles du Globe; précédée de l'Histoire de la Géographie chez les Peuples Anciens et Moderns, et d'une Théorie Générale de la Géographie Mathématique, Physique, et Politique; accompagnée de Cartes, de Tableaux Analytiques, Synoptiques, Statistiques, et Élémentaires; et d'une Table Alphabétique des Noms de Lieux, de Montagnes, de Rivières, etc. Cinquième Édition, revue, corrigée, mise dans un Nouvel Ordre, et augmentée de toutes les Nouvelles Découvertes; par M. J.-J.-N.-Huot.

Numerous plates; and an atlas of 72 *colored maps of which* 14 *are double.* 6 *vols., imperial* 8*vo;* 1 *vol. imperial* 4*to; half calf, extra.* Paris, 1843

1988 MALTE-BRUN, MALTHE CONRAD BRUUN, called. A DESCRIPTION OF ALL PARTS OF THE WORLD, according to the Great Natural Divisions of the Globe, with Analytical, Synoptical, and Elementary Tables; or, Universal Geography. With Additions and Corrections, by James G. Percival. A New Edition, containing Recent Geographical Discoveries, Changes in Political Geography, and other Valuable Additions; compiled, from the late French Editions of Malte-Brun, by M. M. Huot and Lavallée, and other late Authorities, by W. A. Crafts. *Numerous large plates and colored maps.* 3 *vols.,* 4*to, half morocco.* Boston, 1863.

1989 MANDEVILLE, BERNARD DE, M. D. THE VIRGIN UNMASK'D, or Female Dialogues betwixt an Elderly Maiden Lady and her Niece, on Several Diverting Discourses: on Love, Marriage, Memoirs, and Morals, etc. The Second Edition. *Crown* 8*vo, half calf, extra, marbled edges.* London, 1724

1990 MANDEVILLE, BERNARD DE, M. D. THE FABLE OF THE BEES; or, Private Vices, Public Benefits: with an Essay on Charity and Charity-Schools, and a Search into the Nature of Society. The Ninth Edition; to which is added, a Vindication of the Book from the Aspersions contained in a Presentment of the Grand Jury of Middlesex, and an Abusive Letter to the Lord C. BOTH PARTS. 2 *vols.,* 12*mo, calf.* Edinburgh, 1755

"In a second volume, which was subsequently published (comparatively little known, though very well worth reading), the author displays his principles in a more systematic form," etc. See "Edinburgh Review," Vol. XLVIII., p. 173.

1991 MANN, HORACE. LIFE OF; by his Wife. 12*mo, cloth.* Boston, 1865

1992 MANN, HORACE. THOUGHTS SELECTED FROM THE WRITINGS OF. 16*mo, cloth, gilt edges.* Boston, (1868)

1993 MANTELL, GIDEON ALGERNON. A PICTORIAL ATLAS OF FOSSIL REMAINS, consisting of Coloured Illustrations selected from Parkinson's "Organic Remains of a Former World," and Artis's "Antedeluvian Phytology;" with Descriptions. *With seventy-four plates, containing nearly nine hundred figures.* 4*to, cloth.* H. G. Bohn, London, 1850

1994 MANUSCRIPT. A POCKET VOLUME WRITTEN UPON VELLUM, in Latin and German; *apparently the work of some alchimist of the sixteenth century. About* 100 *leaves* 3 × 4 *inches.* (Germany, cir. 1600?)

1995 MANUSCRIPT. A POETICAL TABLE BOOK OF THE SEVENTEENTH CENTURY; containing Poems, Original and Selected, in various Hands and at Various Dates, written in the Early Part of the Seventeenth Century. *4to*, $8\frac{1}{2} \times 7$ *inches, vellum covers, gilt edges.* (England, cir. 1625)

This book apparently belonged to Sir Roger Twysden, the historian, and at page 95, and elsewhere, are pieces probably in his hand. Near the end is an elegy the first two verses of which contain the acrostic "Wiliam Twysden." Among the original contributions are those of Sir Warham St. Leger, Anthony St. Leger, Laurence Ashbournham, Sir Hugh Cholmley, Sir Edward Herbert, Sir Edmond Scory, Lord Faukland, etc., etc.

1996 MANUSCRIPT. LIBRO PRIMERO DE LAS MISSAS DE LA VIRGEN NUESTRA SEÑORA; Missas Votibas de Sanctos i Fiestas Movibles. Para el Uso del Cōbento y Hospital de Nuestra Señora de Bethlem, de Mexico. BEAUTIFULLY EXECUTED, UPON VELLUM, IN RED AND BLACK GOTHIC CHARACTERS, WITH RED LINES AROUND EACH PAGE AND 57 LARGE ILLUMINATED CAPITALS. *Contains* 134 *leaves (numbered), and* 8 *leaves of music and tables.* "ASPERGES AL FIN." *Folio,* 20×14 *inches, calf over wood, with iron clasps, gilt edges.* Mexico, 1702

The Colophon is dated September 24, 1702.

1997 MAPS OF THE SOCIETY FOR THE DIFFUSION OF USEFUL KNOWLEDGE. (With an Index to the Principal Places in the World, with Reference to the Modern Maps; by the Rev. James Mickleburgh, A. M.) *Contains* 218 *colored maps, including the* 6 *maps of stars.* 2 *vols., elephant 4to, half morocco;* 1 *vol. (index), 8vo, cloth.* ORIGINAL COPY. London, 1844

The impressions are clearer in the original copies than in those of a subsequent date.

MAPS, PLANS, ETC.

1998 CARTE DE LA NAVIGATION À VAPEUR DANS LE BASSIN DE LA MEDITERRANÉE. *Colored.* $26\frac{1}{2} \times 40$ *inches, mounted on cloth. Folded and enclosed in case* $4\frac{3}{4} \times 6\frac{3}{4}$ *inches.* Publié par Andriveau-Goujon, Paris, 1851

1999 COLLINS' COMPLETE MAP OF THE CRIMEA, shewing the Military and Carriage Roads, with Distances from Various Points on the Western Coast. *Colored.* $20 \times 25\frac{1}{2}$ *inches. Folded in paper cover* 4×6 *inches.* H. G. Collins, (London,) s. a.

2000 DEUTSCHLAND, KÖNIGR. DER NIEDERLANDE Kgr. Belgien und die Schweiz, nebst Theilen der Angränzenden Länder; nach Adolf Stieler's Entwurf in Jahr 1836: besonders zum Reisegebrauch eingerichtet, mit Bezeichnung der Strassen, Eilwagen-und Extra-post-Routen, unter Mitwirkung des Geh.-Hof.-u. Finanzraths und Ober-post-Commissairs F. M. Diez. Gemeinschaftlich gezeichnet von F. v. Stülpnagel, Königl. Preuss. Hauptmann a. D., und J. C. Bär, 1838.

Colored. 34 × 42 *inches, mounted on cloth. Folded and enclosed in case* $5\frac{1}{2}$ × $8\frac{1}{2}$ *inches.*
Justus Perthes, Gotha, 1838

2001 INDIA, WITHIN AND BEYOND THE GANGES, with Tibet and the Chinese Provinces; including the Malayan and Chinese Seas. (Drawn and engraved under the Direction of J. & C. Walker.) *Colored.* 26 × 40 *inches, mounted on cloth. Folded and enclosed in case* $5\frac{1}{4}$ × 9 *inches.*
(London), s. a.

2002 KELLER'S ZWENTE REISEKARTE DER SCHWEIZ. *Colored.* $21\frac{1}{2}$ × 26 *inches, mounted on cloth. Folded and enclosed in case* $4\frac{1}{2}$ × 9 *inches.* H. Keller, Zürich, 1840

2003 MAPA SPECIAL DE LOS CAMINOS DE LOS REYNOS DE ESPAÑA Y DE PORTUGAL; indicando la Distancia de un Lugar a otro y la de Madrid y de Lisboa a las Principales Ciudades de aquellos Reynos. Por De Simencourt. $21\frac{3}{4}$ × $31\frac{3}{4}$ *inches, mounted on cloth. Folded and enclosed in case* $5\frac{1}{2}$ × $7\frac{1}{2}$ *inches.*
Paris, 1837

2004 PIANTA DI ROMA; publicata nell' Anno MDCCCLIII., da Luigi Piale. $26\frac{1}{2}$ × 36 *inches, mounted on cloth. Folded and enclosed in case* $4\frac{3}{4}$ × $6\frac{3}{4}$ *inches.* (Roma), 1853

2005 PLAN DE LA BATAILLE DE WATERLOO, ou de Mont-St.-Jean; reduit du Grand Plan de la même Bataille, dressé et publié en 1816. Par W. B. Craan. *Colored.* $17\frac{1}{2}$ × $23\frac{1}{2}$ *inches. Folded in half morocco cover* $4\frac{1}{2}$ × $6\frac{1}{2}$ *inches.*
Publié par H. Gerard, Bruxelles, 1840

2006 PLAN OF LONDON AND WESTMINSTER, with the Borough of Southwark; reduced from the Large Plan in Forty Sheets. *Colored.* 30 × 44 *inches, mounted on cloth. Folded and enclosed in case* 5 × 8 *inches.* J. Wyld, (London), 1842

2007 MARANA, GIOVANNI PAOLO. THE EIGHT VOLUMES OF LETTERS WRIT BY A TURKISH SPY, who lived Five and Forty Years, undiscover'd at Paris; giving an Impartial Account to the Divan, at Constantinople, of the most Remarkable Transactions of Europe, and Discovering Several Intrigues and Secrets of the Christian Courts (especially of that of France) from the Year 1637 to the Year 1682. Written Originally in Arabick, translated into Italian, from thence into English; and now published with a large Historical Preface and Index to illustrate the Whole, by the Translator of the First Volume. *Frontispiece by F. H. Van Hove.* 8 *vols.,* 12*mo, old calf.* London, 1718

This work was originally written (either in French or Italian) by Marana, a Genoese of noble family, while an exile residing in Paris.

2008 MARANA, GIOVANNI PAOLO. ANOTHER COPY: the Twenty-sixth Edition. *Frontispiece by J. Basire.* 8 *vols.,* 12*mo, mottled calf, green edges.* London, 1770

2009 MARCENAY DE GHUY, ANTOINE DE. ŒUVRE DE. Cet Œuvre consiste en Différens Morceaux d'Histoires, Portraits, Paisages, Batailles, &c., d'après le Poussin, Vandick, Rembrandt, le Brun, et autres Maîtres. *Contains fine impressions of 56 (large and small) plates by this artist, who was one of the most successful imitators of the style of Rembrandt. Imperial 4to, half morocco.* Paris, (1755–1778)

2010 MARLOWE, CHRISTOPHER. THE WORKS OF. (Edited, with Life, by George Robinson.) *3 vols., crown 8vo, cloth, uncut.* W. Pickering, London, 1826

2011 MARMONTEL, JEAN FRANÇOIS. MORAL TALES. (Translated by C. Dennis and R. Lloyd.) A New Edition. *Plates by Sharp, etc. 3 vols., 12mo, marbled calf, gilt, yellow edges.* London, 1800

2012 MAROLLES, MICHEL DE. TABLEAUX DU TEMPLE DES MUSES, tirez du Cabinet de Feu Mr Favereau, representant les Vertus et les Vices, sur les Plus Illustres Fables de l'Antiquité; avec les Descriptions, Remarques, & Annotations. *Portrait of Favereau, frontispiece, and 58 plates engraved by Bloemaert after designs by Diepenbeeck. Folio, calf, gilt, marbled edges.* J. du Puys, Paris, 1663

2013 MARRYAT, CAPTAIN FREDERICK. SNARLEYYOW, or the Dog Fiend. *8vo, paper.* Paris, 1837

2014 MARRYAT, CAPTAIN FREDERICK. A DIARY IN AMERICA, with Remarks on its Institutions. *3 vols., crown 8vo, half calf, extra.* FIRST SERIES. London, 1839

2015 MARRYAT, CAPTAIN FREDERICK. A DIARY IN AMERICA, with Remarks on its Institutions. PART SECOND. *Maps. 3 vols., crown 8vo, cloth, uncut.* SECOND SERIES. London, 1839

2016 MARRYAT, CAPTAIN FREDERICK. THE COMPLETE WORKS OF. *2 vols. in 1, royal 8vo, half morocco.* Philadelphia, 1850

2017 MARRYAT, JOSEPH. A HISTORY OF POTTERY AND PORCELAIN, MEDIÆVAL AND MODERN. Second Edition, revised and augmented. *With 6 fine colored plates, each representing two specimens, and numerous wood-cuts. 8vo, tree calf, gilt, marbled edges.* J. Murray, London, 1857

2018 MARRYAT, JOSEPH. ANOTHER COPY: *the same. With same plates, etc. 8vo, cloth, uncut.* J. Murray, London, 1857

2019 MARSH, GEORGE PERKINS. THE ORIGIN AND HISTORY OF THE ENGLISH LANGUAGE, and of the Early Literature it Embodies. *8vo, cloth.* New York, 1862

2020 MARSHALL, JOHN. THE LIFE OF GEORGE WASHINGTON, First President of the United States; compiled under the Inspection of the Hon. Bushrod Washington, from Original Papers bequeathed to him by his deceased Relative.

To which is prefixed, an Introduction, containing a Compendious View of the Colonies planted by the English on the Continent of North America. *Portrait by J. Fittler after Stuart, maps, plans, and plates.* 5 *vols.*, 8*vo, old calf, very neat.* R. Phillips, London, 1804–07

2021 MARSHALL, Lieut. John, R. N. Royal Naval Biography, or Memoirs of the Services of all the Flag-Officers, Superannuated Rear-Admirals, Retired-Captains, Post-Captains, and Commanders, whose Names appeared on the Admiralty List of Sea Officers at the Commencement of the Present Year (1823), or who have since been promoted; illustrated by a Series of Historical and Explanatory Notes, which will be found to contain an Account of all the Naval Actions, and other Important Events, from the Commencement of the late Reign in 1760, to the Present Period. With Copious Addenda. 12 *vols.*, 8*vo, half calf, extra, marbled edges.* London, 1823–35

2022 MARTIAL (The) Achievements of Great Britain and her Allies, from 1799 to 1815. *A series of* 53 *colored plates (including the arms of Wellington), with descriptive letter-press. Imperial* 4*to, half crimson morocco, neat, gilt top, uncut.* London, (1814–15)

2023 MARTIAL. Epigrams, with Mottos from Horace, etc.; translated, imitated, adapted, and addrest to the Nobility, Clergy, and Gentry. With Notes Moral, Historical, Explanatory, and Humorous. By the Rev. Mr. Scott. 12*mo, sheep.* London, 1773

2024 MARTIAL. The Epigrams of; translated into English Prose, each accompanied by one or more Verse Translations, from the Works of English Poets, and Various other Sources. *Post* 8*vo, cloth, uncut.* London, 1860

2025 MARTIN, Bon Louis Henri. History of France, from the most Remote Period to 1789. Authorized Translation; from the Fourth Paris Edition, by Mary L. Booth. *Map, portraits, etc.* 4 *vols., imperial* 8*vo, cloth, rough edges.* Large paper: *only* 75 *copies printed.*
Boston, 1865–66

M. Martin's history is divided into eight parts, of two volumes each, and an Index, forming seventeen volumes; the several parts, or epochs, being complete in themselves. The above four volumes contain the seventh and eighth parts (Vols. XIII.–XVI.), comprising the Age of Louis XIV., and the Decline of the French Monarchy.

2026 MARTIN, Charles. The Civil Costume of England; from the Conquest to the Present Time. Drawn from Tapestries, Monumental Effigies, Illuminated Manuscripts, Portraits, etc.; etched by Leopold Martin. *A series of* 61 *plates, highly illuminated in gold, silver, and colors. Royal* 4*to, cloth, arms of Prince Albert on side, gilt edges.*
London, 1842

2027 MARTIN, JOHN. A BIBLIOGRAPHICAL CATALOGUE OF BOOKS PRIVATELY PRINTED; including those of the Bannatyne, Maitland, and Roxburghe Clubs, and of the Private Presses at Darlington, Auchinleck, Lee Priory, Newcastle, Middle Hill, and Strawberry Hill. *Frontispiece and woodcuts. 8vo, tree calf, marbled edges.* FIRST EDITION. London, 1834

2028 MARTIN, MANUEL. EJERCICIO COTIDIANO DE DIFERENTES ORACIONES, para Antes y Despues de la Confesion y Comunion; con un Ejercicio para la Santa Misa. Recopilado de Varios Autores, por D. Manuel Martin. Nueva Edicion, adornada con 27 Láminas Finas. *Only 6 plates. 18mo, calf.* Valencia, 1821

2029 MARTIN, ROBERT MONTGOMERY. THE INDIAN EMPIRE: History, Topography, Geology, Climate, Population, Chief Cities, and Provinces; Tributary and Protected States; Military Power and Resources; Religion, Education, Crime; Land Tenures; Staple Products; Government, Finance, and Commerce. With a Full Account of the Meeting of the Bengal Army; of the Insurrection in Western India; and an Exposition of the Alleged Causes. *Maps, portraits, and views. 3 vols., imperial 8vo, half morocco, marbled edges.* London, (1859?)

2030 MARTINEAU, HARRIET. RETROSPECT OF WESTERN TRAVEL. *3 vols., 12mo, half calf, extra.* London, 1838

2031 MARTINEAU, HARRIET. HEALTH, HUSBANDRY, AND HANDICRAFT. *Crown 8vo, cloth, uncut.* London, 1861

2032 MASERES, FRANCIS. THE CANADIAN FREEHOLDER, in Two Dialogues, between an Englishman and a Frenchman, settled in Canada; shewing the Sentiments of the Bulk of the Freeholders of Canada concerning the late Quebec-Act, with some Remarks on the Boston-Charter Act, and an Attempt to shew the great Expediency of Immediately Repealing both those Acts of Parliament, and of making some other Useful Regulations and Concessions to his Majesty's American Subjects, as a Ground for Reconciliation with the United Colonies in America. *3 vols., 8vo, half calf, neat.* London, 1777–79

2033 MASIUS, DR. HERMANN. STUDIES FROM NATURE. Translated by Charles Boner. Illustrated by E. Hasse, of Leipsic. *Crown 8vo, cloth, uncut.* London, 1854

2034 MASON, GEORGE CHAMPLIN. RE-UNION OF THE SONS AND DAUGHTERS OF NEWPORT, R. I., August 23, 1859. Compiled and printed by Order of the General Committee of Arrangements. *12mo, cloth.* Newport, R. I., 1859

Contains a history of the "Redwood Library and Athenæum," from its establishment in 1730, to its enlargement in 1859.

2035 MASON, JOHN MONCK. COMMENTS ON THE PLAYS OF BEAUMONT AND FLETCHER; with an Appendix, containing some further Observations on Shakespeare, extended to the late Editions of Malone and Steevens. *8vo, boards, rough edges.* London, 1798

2036 MASON, THOMAS MONCK. AERONAUTICA, or Sketches illustrative of the Theory and Practice of Aerostation; comprising an enlarged Account of the late Aerial Expedition to Germany. *8vo, cloth, uncut.* London, 1838

2037 MASON, WILLIAM. THE WORKS OF. *Fine portraits of Mason, Robert Earl of Holdernesse, and William Burgh, engraved by Robert Cooper. 4 vols., 8vo, sprinkled calf, very neat; with MS. notes and cuttings from reviews, catalogues, etc.* London, 1811

2038 MASONIC PAMPHLETS. ADDRESSES, ETC.: — A Masonic Address at Wiscasset, June 24, A. L. 5813; by Freeman Parker. *Hallowell*, 1813. — An Address at the Annual Communication of the Grand Lodge of Maine, January 28, 1830; by Samuel Fessenden, Esq. *Portland*, 1830. — Historical Narrative, Explanation, and Vindication of the Course pursued by the Grand Lodge of the State of New York, in relation to the Unmasonic and Unconstitutional Attempt of a Portion of their Body to Revolutionize the Organization thereof; addressed to the Grand Lodges of the World, etc. *New York*, 1849. — Address delivered before the General Grand Chapter of the United States, in the City of Hartford, Connecticut, September 9, 1856; by M. E. Robert P. Dunlap, G. G. H. P. (*Portland*), 1856. — Address delivered before the Grand Lodge of Maine, in the City of Portland, May 4, 1858; by M. W. Robert P. Dunlap, Grand Master. (9 copies.) *Portland*, 1858. — A Sermon delivered in Orono, Maine, February 7, 1859, at the Funeral of Charles Oscar Russ, by Rev. L. Barstow; with an Address to the Fraternity, by Rev. J. C. Knowlton, of Oldtown. (2 copies.) *Bangor*, 1859. *Together*, 15 *pamphlets* (*including* 9 *duplicates*). Hallowell, Portland, etc., 1813–59

2039 MASONIC PAMPHLETS. PROCEEDINGS OF THE GRAND BODIES OF THE STATE OF MAINE: Grand Commandery, Annual Conclaves held at Portland; *Years*, 1853, 1854–5–6 *together* (2 *copies*), 1857, 1858 (2 *copies*), 1859, 1860. — Grand Council (Royal and Select Masters), Annual Convocations held at Portland; *Years*, 1856, 1857, 1858 (2 *copies*), 1859, 1860. — Grand Chapter, Annual Convocations held at Portland (and at Bangor in 1851); *Years*, 1851 (2 *copies*), 1853 (2 *copies*), 1856, 1857, 1858 (2 *copies*), 1859 1860. — Grand Lodge, Annual Communications held at Portland (and at Augusta 1838–46); *Years*, 1826, 1838 (2 *copies*), 1839, 1840, 1841, 1846, 1853, 1854 (2 *copies*),

1855, 1856, 1857, 1858 (2 *copies*), 1859, 1860. *Together*, 41 *pamphlets* (*including* 9 *duplicates*). Portland and Augusta, 1826–60

2040 MASONIC PAMPHLETS. BY-LAWS, CONSTITUTIONS, etc., OF VARIOUS MASONIC BODIES: Act of Incorporation (June 16, 1820) and By-Laws of the Grand Lodge of Maine, adopted January 11, 1821. *Augusta*, 1839. — Act of Incorporation (January 19, 1822) and By-Laws of the Grand Chapter of Maine (with Annual Communication held in 1845). *Portland*, 1845. — By-Laws of St. John's Encampment No. 3, Bangor, Me. *Bangor*, 1850. — Constitutions and General Regulations of the Grand Lodge of Maine, revised and adopted May 4, 1849. *Portland*, 1854. — By-Laws of King Hiram Chapter, Lewiston, Me., approved and adopted May, 1855. *Portland*, 1855. — By-Laws of Blue Mountain Lodge, Phillips, Me., adopted November, 1851. *Portland*, 1856. — By-Laws of King Solomon's Chapter, Rockland, Me., revised and adopted, 1857. *Rockland*, 1857. — By-Laws of Orient Lodge No. 15, Thomaston, Me. *Portland*, 1863. *Together*, 8 *pamphlets*. Augusta, Portland, etc., 1839–63

2041 MASONIC PAMPHLETS. PROCEEDINGS OF THE GRAND LODGE OF THE STATE OF MAINE, at its Annual Communications, Portland, 1848–56. — Address of Hon. Benjamin B. French, Grand Master of the Grand Lodge of the District of Columbia, delivered at Portland before the Grand Lodge of Maine, June 26, 1849. — Constitutions and General Regulations of the Grand Lodge of Maine, revised and adopted May 4, 1849. *Together*, 11 *pamphlets bound in* 1 *vol., thick* 8vo, *half morocco*. Portland, 1848–56

2042 MASONIC PAMPHLETS. PROCEEDINGS OF THE GRAND CHAPTER OF THE STATE OF MAINE, at its Annual Convocations held at Portland (and at Bangor in 1851) in the Years 1846–56. — By-Laws of the Grand Chapter of Maine. — Proceedings of the General Grand Chapter for the United States, held at Boston, September 10, 1850. *Together*, 12 *pamphlets bound in one vol.*, 8*vo*, *half crimson morocco*. Portland, 1847–56; Washington, 1850

2043 MASONIC SONGS. SONGS USED BY FREE-MASONS IN ALL GOOD LODGES. *Consists of pp.* 93–108 *of some old masonic work, post* 8*vo size*. (America, 17 — ?)

2044 MASSACHUSETTS. ANNUAL REPORTS OF THE ADJUTANT-GENERAL; for the Years ending December 31, 1862, 1863, and 1865. 3 *vols.*, 8*vo*, *paper and cloth*. Boston, 1863–66

2045 MASSACHUSETTS. DEBATES, RESOLUTIONS, AND OTHER PROCEEDINGS of the Convention of the Commonwealth of Massachusetts, convened at Boston, on the 9th of January,

1788, and continued until the 7th of February following, for the Purpose of Assenting to and Ratifying the Constitution recommended by the Grand Federal Convention; together with the Yeas and Nays on the Decision of the Grand Question. To which the Federal Constitution is prefixed. *Small 4to, sheep.* Boston, 1788

2046 MASSACHUSETTS. DEBATES AND PROCEEDINGS in the Convention of the Commonwealth of Massachusetts, held in the Year 1788, and which finally ratified the Constitution of the United States. [Edited by Bradford K. Peirce and Charles Hale.] *8vo, cloth.* Boston, 1856

2047 MASSACHUSETTS. JOURNAL OF DEBATES AND PROCEEDINGS in the Convention of Delegates, chosen to Revise the Constitution of Massachusetts, begun and holden at Boston, November 15, 1820, and continued by Adjournment to January 9, 1821. New Edition, revised and corrected. *8vo, cloth.* Boston, 1853

2048 MASSACHUSETTS. GENERAL LAWS AND RESOLVES passed by the Legislature of; during the Session of 1863. *Index. 8vo, pp.* 101. (Boston, 1863)

2049 MASSACHUSETTS. MANUAL FOR THE USE OF THE GENERAL COURT, containing the Rules and Orders of the Two Branches; together with the Constitution of the Commonwealth, and that of the United States. Prepared by S. N. Gifford and Wm. S. Robinson. *Plans. 16mo, cloth.* Boston, 1867

2050 MASSACHUSETTS. RECORDS OF THE GOVERNOR AND COMPANY OF THE MASSACHUSETTS BAY IN NEW ENGLAND; 1628-1686. Edited by Nathaniel B. Shurtleff, M. D., etc. *5 vols. in 6, 4to, cloth, gilt tops, uncut.* Boston, 1853-54

2051 MASSACHUSETTS. REPORTS CONCERNING PROPERTY IN TRUST, in the Commonwealth of Massachusetts, as held by Certain Corporations, and by Trustees under Acts of Incorporation. Acts of 1864, Chap. 239; and 1865, Chap. 271. Published by the Secretary of the Commonwealth. *8vo, pp.* 239, *paper.* Boston, 1866

2052 MASSACHUSETTS. STATISTICAL INFORMATION RELATING TO CERTAIN BRANCHES OF INDUSTRY in Massachusetts, for the Year ending May 1, 1865. Prepared by Oliver Warner, Secretary of the Commonwealth. *8vo, cloth.* Boston, 1866

2053 MASSACHUSETTS. THIRTEENTH ANNUAL REPORT OF THE SECRETARY OF THE MASSACHUSETTS BOARD OF AGRICULTURE, together with Reports of Committees appointed to visit the County Societies, with an Appendix containing an Abstract of the Finances of the County Societies, for the Year 1865. *Wood-cuts, 8vo, cloth.* Boston, 1866

2054 MASSEY, William. A History of England, during the Reign of George the Third. *4 vols., 8vo, half calf, extra, marbled edges.* London, 1855–63

2055 MASSINGER, Philip. The Plays of; with Notes, Critical and Explanatory, by W. Gifford, Esq. The Second Edition. *Portrait after one by T. Cross. 4 vols., royal 8vo, smooth crimson morocco, very neat, contents lettered, gilt edges, by Holloway.* Large paper: *few printed.* London, 1813

"Best edition, but not perceptibly different from the previous one of 1805, of which it has been said, 'that a more perfect edition of an old poet than this never issued from the press.'" — *Lowndes.* See Jonson, Ben.

2056 MASSINGER, Philip. Another copy: *the edition alluded to in the above note. Portrait. 4 vols., 8vo, old mottled calf, gilt.* London, 1805

2057 MASSON, David. The Life of John Milton; narrated in connection with the Political, Ecclesiastical, and Literary History of his Time. *Portraits and fac-similes. Vol. I.,* 1608–1639. *8vo, cloth.* Boston, 1859

2058 MATHER, Cotton, D. D., and Rev. Joseph Sewall. Hades Look'd Into: the Power of Our Great Saviour over the Invisible World, and the Gates of Death which lead into that World; considered in a Sermon preached at the Funeral of the Honourable Wait Winthrop, Esq., who expired 7 d. IX. m. 1717, in the lxxvi. Year of his Age. By C. Mather, D. D., & F. R. S. *Title; Preface, by Increase Mather, pp. vi.; The Keys of the Invisible World, and Epitaphium, pp.* 46. — The Character and Blessedness of the Upright; a Sermon occasion'd by the Death of the Honourable Wait Winthrop, Esq., who expired Nov. 7, 1717, Ætatis 76. By Joseph Sewall, A. M., Pastor of a Church of Christ in Boston. *Title; and pp.* 1–46. *Together, 1 vol., 16mo. paper.* Printed by T. Crump, Boston, 1717

2059 MATHER, Cotton, D. D.; and Robert Calef. The Witchcraft Delusion in New England: its Rise, Progress, and Termination, as exhibited by Dr. Cotton Mather in the Wonders of the Invisible World; and by Mr. Robert Calef, in his More Wonders of the Invisible World. With a Preface, Introduction, and Notes, by Samuel G. Drake. *3 vols., foolscap 4to, paper, rough edges.* Only 280 copies in this size, and 50 on large paper. Roxbury, Mass., 1866

Literal reprints from the editions of 1693 and 1700, printed by Joel Munsell, Albany, forming Vols. V., VI., VII. of "Woodward's Historical Series."

2060 MATHER, Increase, D. D., and Cotton, D. D. The History of King Philip's War, by the Rev. Increase Mather, D. D.; also, a History of the same War, by the Rev. Cotton Mather, D. D. To which are added an Introduction and Notes, by Samuel G. Drake. *Portraits and pedigree of the Mathers; and a fine portrait of Dr. Winslow Lewis, on India paper. Royal 4to, paper, rough edges.* LARGE PAPER: ONLY 10 COPIES IN THIS SIZE. Boston, 1862

Literal reprint of which the edition was limited to 10 copies on large paper and 250 in foolscap quarto.

2061 MATHER, INCREASE, D. D. EARLY HISTORY OF NEW ENGLAND: being a Relation of Hostile Passages between the Indians and European Voyagers and First Settlers, and a Full Narrative of Hostilities, to the Close of the War with the Pequots, in the Year 1637; also a Detailed Account of the Origin of the War with King Philip. By Increase Mather. With an Introduction and Notes, by Samuel G. Drake. *Royal 4to, paper, rough edges.* LARGE PAPER: ONLY 11 COPIES IN THIS SIZE. Boston, 1864

Edition limited to 11 copies on large paper and 250 in foolscap quarto.

2062 MATHEWS, CHARLES. MEMOIRS OF CHARLES MATHEWS, COMEDIAN; by Mrs. Mathews. (Including his Autobiography.) *Portraits and plates. 4 vols., 8vo, half blue calf, extra, marbled edges.* London, 1838–39

2063 MATHIAS, THOMAS JAMES. PURSUITS OF LITERATURE; a Satirical Poem, in Four Dialogues, with Notes. First American, from the Seventh London Edition, revised. *8vo, old marbled calf, yellow edges.* Philadelphia, 1800

"This satirical publication created a great sensation and considerable controversy." — *Lowndes.*

2064 MATHIAS, THOMAS JAMES. THE PURSUITS OF LITERATURE; a Satirical Poem, in Four Dialogues, with Notes; to which are added an Appendix, the Citations translated, and a Complete Index. The Sixteenth Edition. *Handsomely printed by W. Bulmer & Co.* ILLUSTRATED *with 77 fine portraits, engraved by Houbraken, Bartolozzi, and other celebrated engravers, after Van Dyck, Sir J. Reynolds, Sir T. Lawrence, and other eminent artists; also a fac-simile of the Death Warrant of Charles I. A few of the portraits are very neatly inlaid; many of them are on India paper, and proof impressions. Folio, half green morocco, extra, gilt edges.* LARGE PAPER; *only a few copies of this size printed, for illustration.* London, 1812

2065 MATTHIÆ, AUGUST HEINRICH. A COPIOUS GREEK GRAMMAR; translated from the German, by Edward V. Blomfield. Fifth Edition, thoroughly revised, and greatly enlarged, from the Last Edition of the Original, by John Kenrick. (With the Index of Quotations from Greek Authors contained in this Edition.) *3 vols., 8vo, boards, uncut.* J. Murray, London, 1832–33

2066 MATTHIAS, BENJAMIN. RULES OF ORDER. A Manual for Conducting Business in Town and Ward Meetings, Societies, Boards of Directors and Managers, and other

Deliberative Bodies; based on Parliamentary, Congressional, and Legislative Practice. 18*mo, cloth.* Philadelphia, 1851

2067 MATTHISSON, Friedrich von. Letters written from Various Parts of the Continent, between the Years 1785 and 1794; containing a Variety of Anecdotes relative to the Present State of Literature in Germany, and to celebrated German Literati. With an Appendix. Translated from the German by Anne Plumtre. *Title wanting.* 8*vo, old marbled calf; binding broke.* (London, 1799)

"In the appendix are included three letters of the poet Gray, never before published in this country." —*Lowndes.*

2068 MATURIN, Rev. Charles Robert. Melmoth the Wanderer; a Tale. 4 *vols.,* 12*mo, half morocco.* Edinburgh, 1820

2069 MAUNDRELL, Rev. Henry. A Journey from Aleppo to Jerusalem at Easter, A. D. 1697. The Fourth Edition, to which is now added an Account of the Author's Journey to the Banks of the Euphrates at Beer, and to the Country of Mesopotamia. *Plates.* 8*vo, old calf; with MS. notes.* Printed at the Theatre, Oxford, 1721

"Bishop Newton, in speaking of Maundrell, observes, 'whom it is a pleasure to quote as well as to read, and whose Journal from Aleppo to Jerusalem, though a little book, is yet worth a folio, and is so accurately and ingeniously written, that it might serve as a model for all writers of travels.'"—*Lowndes.*

2070 MAWE, John. Travels in the Interior of Brazil, particularly in the Gold and Diamond Districts of that Country, by Authority of the Prince Regent of Portugal; including a Voyage to the Rio de la Plata, and an Historical Sketch of the Revolution of Buenos Ayres. *Plates.* 8*vo, boards.* Philadelphia, 1816

2071 MAWE, John. A Treatise on Diamonds, and Precious Stones; including their History, Natural and Commercial: to which is added, the Methods of Cutting and Polishing. With Colored Plates. Second Edition. *Crown* 8*vo, half calf.* London, 1823

2072 MAXIMILIAN, Alexander Philipp, Prince. Travels in Brazil, in the Years 1815, 1816, 1817. *Map and plates.* 4*to, half morocco.* London, 1820

2073 MAXIMILIAN, Alexander Philipp, Prince. Travels in the Interior of North America. With Numerous Engravings on Wood, and a Large Map. Translated from the German, by H. Evans Lloyd. To accompany the Original Series of Eighty-one Elaborately-Coloured Plates; size imperial folio. With the Atlas of Illustrations. 2 *vols., imperial* 4*to, and imperial folio, half russia.* Ackermann & Co., London, 1843–44

2074 MAXWELL, Colonel Montgomery. My Adventures. *Portraits of Gen. Neil Douglas and Col. Maxwell.* 2 *vols.,* 12*mo, half calf, extra.* London, 1845

2075 MAXWELL, WILLIAM HAMILTON. LIFE OF FIELD-MARSHAL THE DUKE OF WELLINGTON. Fifth Edition. *Portraits and numerous fine plates, plans of battles, etc.* 3 *vols., 8vo, tree calf, gilt, marbled edges, by Riviere.* London, 1852

2076 MAYHEW, EDWARD. THE ILLUSTRATED HORSE DOCTOR; being an Accurate and Detailed Account of the Various Diseases to which the Equine Race are subjected, together with the Latest Mode of Treatment, and all the Requisite Prescriptions, written in Plain English. *Above* 400 *wood-cuts. 8vo, cloth.* New York, 1861

2077 MAYHEW, THE BROTHERS. THE IMAGE OF HIS FATHER; a Tale of a Young Monkey. *Wood-cuts, 12mo, half calf.* New York, 1848

2078 M'BURNEY, I.; and SAMUEL NEIL. CHRONOLOGICAL TABLES; comprehending the Chronology and History of the World, from the Earliest Records to the Close of the Russian War. First Division: Ancient and Mediæval History, A. M. 1 to A. D. 1500. Second Division: Modern History, A. D. 1501 to A. D. 1856. *Charts.* 2 *vols., crown 8vo, cloth, uncut.* London, 1857

2079 M'CALLUM, HUGH, and JOHN. AN ORIGINAL COLLECTION OF THE POEMS OF OSSIAN, Orrann, Ulin, and other Bards, who flourished in the same Age. Collected and edited by Hugh and John M'Callum. *8vo, half morocco, very neat, gilt top, uncut.* Printed for the Editors, Montrose (Scotland), 1816

2080 McIAN, R. R. THE CLANS OF THE SCOTTISH HIGHLANDS, illustrated by Appropriate Figures, displaying their Dress, Tartans, Arms, Armorial Insignia, and Social Occupations, from Original Sketches by R. R. McIan, Esq.; with accompanying Description and Historical Memoranda of Character, Mode of Life, etc., etc., by James Logan, Esq., F. S. A. Sc., etc., etc. *Illuminated frontispieces and* 72 *full-length figures,* VERY FINELY COLORED. 2 *vols., imperial folio, half morocco, extra, gilt edges.* LARGE PAPER: *fine copy.* Ackermann & Co., London, 1845–47

In the large paper copies the plates are colored with extra care.

2081 MEAD, HENRY. THE SEPOY REVOLT; its Causes and its Consequences. *16mo, boards.* London, 1858

2082 MÉDAILLES SUR LES PRINCIPAUX ÉVÉNEMENTS DU RÈGNE ENTIER DE LOUIS-LE-GRAND; avec des Explications Historiques [par F. Charpentier, P. Tallemand, J. Racine, Boileau Despréaux, etc.]. SECOND EDITION, *with the continuation by Claude Gros de Boze. Frontispiece, by Simonneau l'aîné, after A. Coypel, and* 318 *medals; each page surrounded with a different ornate border appropriate for ar-*

chitectural and decorative purposes. Large folio, red morocco, gilt, arms gilt on sides, gilt edges. Imprimerie Royale, Paris, 1723

This fine work is well printed on a thick paper, upon one side only; the borders are by Berain, Coypel, and Le Clerck; the portraits of the Medals are by Edelinck, and the reverses by Audran and Picart.

2083 MEDICAL BOTANY: or, History of Plants in the Materia Medica of the London, Edinburgh, and Dublin Pharmacopœias; arranged according to the Linnæan System. *Portrait of Linnæus and 138 finely colored plates. 2 vols., royal 8vo, calf, gilt.* London, 1821–22

2084 MEDWIN, CAPTAIN THOMAS. THE ANGLER IN WALES, or Days and Nights of Sportsmen. *Frontispieces by Landseer, and fine wood-cuts. 2 vols., 8vo, half morocco, neat, gilt tops.* London, 1834

2085 MEIER, GEORG FRIEDRICH. THE MERRY PHILOSOPHER, OR THOUGHTS ON JESTING; containing Rules by which a Proper Judgment of Jests may be formed, and the Criterion for Distinguishing True and Genuine Wit from that which is False and Spurious: together with Instructions for Improving the Taste of those who have a Natural Turn for Pleasantry and Good Humour. Now first translated into English from the German Original. *Small 8vo, new sprinkled calf, gilt, carmine edges.* FINE COPY. London, 1764

2086 MELMOTH, WILLIAM. FITZOSBORNE'S LETTERS, ON SEVERAL SUBJECTS; with the Dialogue concerning Oratory. To which is prefixed, a Memoir of the Author. *12mo, calf, extra, marbled edges.* Boston, 1815

2087 MEMOIRES DE L'INSTITUT DE FRANCE. Vols. I.–IV., Classe d'Histoire et de Littérature Ancienne; Vols. V.–XV., Académie des Inscriptions et Belles-Lettres (Vol. XI. contenant la Table Alphabétique des Matières traitées dans les Dix Premièrs Volumes). *Numerous plates. 15 vols. in 18, 4to, half calf, neat.* Paris, 1815–45

2088 MEMOIRS OF A CERTAIN ISLAND ADJACENT TO THE KINGDOM OF UTOPIA, written by a Celebrated Author of that Country; now translated into English. The Second Edition. *2 vols., 8vo, old calf.* London, 1726

2089 MEMOIRS (THE) OF A PROTESTANT, condemned to the Galleys of France for his Religion, written by himself; comprehending an Account of the Various Distresses he suffered in Slavery, and his Constancy in supporting almost every Cruelty that Bigoted Zeal could inflict or Human Nature sustain, also a Description of the Galleys and the Service in which they are employed; the Whole interspersed with Anecdotes relative to the General History of the Times, for a Period of Thirteen Years, during which the Author continued in Slavery, 'till he was at last set Free, at the Intercession of the Court of Great Britain. Translated from the Original, just published at the Hague, by James Willington [Oliver Goldsmith]. 2 *vols., small 12mo, old sprinkled calf, neat; with book-plate of David Garrick.* London, 1758

Prior says that Willington was the name of one of Goldsmith's fellow-students in Dublin.

"Goldsmith's first known publication." — *Lowndes.*

2090 MEMORABLE EVENTS IN THE LIFE OF A LONDON PHYSICIAN. *8vo, cloth, uncut.* London, 1863

2091 MEN OF THE TIME: BIOGRAPHICAL SKETCHES OF EMINENT LIVING CHARACTERS; Authors, Architects, Artists, Composers, Dramatists, Divines, Discoverers, Engineers, Journalists, Lawyers, Men of Science, Monarchs, Novelists, Painters, Philanthropists, Poets, Politicians, Savans, Sculptors, Statesmen, Travellers, Voyagers, Warriors, etc. Also Biographical Sketches of Celebrated Women of the Time. *Very thick foolscap 8vo, cloth, uncut.* London, 1857

2092 MENDELSSOHN-BARTHOLDY, FELIX. LIFE OF. From the German of W. A. Lampadius; with Supplementary Sketches by Julius Benedict, Henry F. Chorley, Ludwig Rellstab, Bayard Taylor, R. S. Willis, and J. S. Dwight. Edited and translated, by William L. Gage. *Portrait. Foolscap 8vo, cloth, gilt top.* New York, 1865

2093 MENDELSSOHN-BARTHOLDY, FELIX. ORATORIO OF ST. PAUL; in Vocal Score. Novello's revised Edition. *Imperial 8vo, boards.* Boston, s. a.

2094 MEREDITH, GEORGE. THE SHAVING OF SHAGPAT; an Arabian Tale. *12mo, cloth, uncut.* London, 1856

2095 MEREDITH, LOUISA ANNE. OVER THE STRAITS; A VISIT TO VICTORIA. With Illustrations from Photographs and the Author's Sketches. *8vo, cloth, uncut.* London, 1861

2096 MERIVALE, REV. CHARLES. HISTORY OF THE ROMANS UNDER THE EMPIRE. New Edition. *Maps. 8 vols., post 8vo, tree calf, gilt, marbled edges, by Riviere.* London, 1865

2097 MERRILL, REV. SAMUEL H. THE CAMPAIGNS OF THE FIRST MAINE AND FIRST DISTRICT OF COLUMBIA, CAVALRY. *Portraits. 12mo, cloth.* Portland, 1866

2098 MERRYLAND (THE) MISCELLANY; containing the Ten following Pieces, viz.: I. A New Description of Merryland, being a Topographical, Geographical, and Natural History of that Country; address'd to Dr. Cheyne, of Bath. II. Arbor Vitæ, or the Tree of Life, etc. III. The Potent Ally, or Succours from Merryland; address'd to Alderman Parsons. IV. Merryland Display'd, being Observations on the New Description of Merryland; written by an Eminent

Physician, and address'd to the Author of that Pamphlet. V. The Poetical History of Pandora's Box. VI. Armour, a Poem. VII. Κυνλυμογενια, a Tale. VIII. Consummation, or the Rape of Adonis. IX. The Resurrection, a Tale. X. Ερωτό Πολις, or the Present State of Bettyland; written by that great Master of Humour, Charles Cotton, Esq., Author of Virgil Travestie, etc. *Frontispiece. 8vo, half calf.* E. Curll, London, 1742

2099 MERRYWEATHER, F. SOMNER. BIBLIOMANIA IN THE MIDDLE AGES, or Sketches of Bookworms, Collectors, Bible Students, Scribes, and Illuminators, from the Anglo-Saxon and Norman Periods to the Introduction of Printing into England; with Anecdotes illustrating the History of the Monastic Libraries of Great Britain in the Olden Time. *Post 8vo, half morocco, marbled edges.* London, 1849

2100 METROPOLITAN IMPROVEMENTS, OR LONDON IN THE NINETEENTH CENTURY: displayed in a Series of Engravings of the New Buildings, Improvements, etc., by the most Eminent Artists, from Original Drawings, taken from the Objects themselves expressly for this Work, by Mr. Thos. H. Shepherd; comprising the Palace, Parks, New Churches, Bridges, Streets, River Scenery, Public Offices and Institutions, Gentlemen's Seats and Mansions, and every other Object worthy of Notice throughout the Metropolis and its Environs. With Historical, Topographical, and Critical Illustrations; by James Elmes (John Britton, and others). *Nearly 350 views, India proofs. 2 vols., 4to, purple calf, gilt, marbled edges.* London, 1828, etc.

2101 MEYRICK, SIR SAMUEL RUSH. A CRITICAL INQUIRY INTO ANTIENT ARMOUR, as it existed in Europe, particularly in Great Britain, from the Norman Conquest to the Reign of King Charles II.; with a Glossary of Military Terms of the Middle Ages. Second Edition, corrected and enlarged. *Contains 81 large plates, including the new plate of the Battle of the Locks and Keys; 71 of which, and the initial letters, are highly illuminated in gold, silver, and colors. 3 vols., imperial 4to, half crimson morocco, extra, gilt edges.* London, 1842

2102 MEYRICK, SIR SAMUEL RUSH. ENGRAVED ILLUSTRATIONS OF ANTIENT ARMS AND ARMOUR, from the Collection at Goodrich Court, Herefordshire; after the Drawings, and with the Descriptions of Sir Samuel Rush Meyrick, Kt., K. H., LL. D., F. S. A., etc., etc. By Joseph Skelton, F. S. A. *Portrait of Meyrick, engraved titles, and 154 plates of arms and armour in detail. 2 vols., imperial 4to, half crimson morocco, extra, gilt edges.* London, 1854

2103 MICHAUX, FRANÇOIS ANDRÉ. THE NORTH AMERICAN SYLVA, or a Description of the Forest Trees of the United

States, Canada, and Nova Scotia, considered particularly with Respect to their Use in the Arts, and their Introduction into Commerce; to which is added a Description of the most Useful of all the European Forest Trees. Translated from the French of F. Andrew Michaux [by Augustus L. Hillhouse]. *With* 156 *finely colored plates.* 2 *vols., thick royal* 8*vo, half russia, very neat.* FINE COPY. Paris, 1819

2104 MICHELET, JULES. LOVE ("L'AMOUR"); from the French. Translated from the Fourth Paris Edition, by J. W. Palmer, M. D. 12*mo, cloth.* New York, 1859

2105 MICHELET, JULES. WOMAN ("LA FEMME"); from the French. Translated from the Last Paris Edition, by J. W. Palmer, M. D. 12*mo, cloth.* New York, 1860

2106 MICROCOSM (THE) OF LONDON, or London in Miniature. *Wood-cut titles, engraved dedication, and* 104 *colored plates, by Rowlandson and Pugin, representing the interiors and exteriors of the principal buildings, and illustrating the manners, etc., of London.* 3 *vols., imperial* 4*to, tree calf.* R. Ackermann, London, (1811)

2107 MIDDLETON, THOMAS. THE WORKS OF; now first collected, with some Account of the Author, and Notes by the Reverend Alexander Dyce. *Portrait, on India paper, and fac-simile of engraved title to earliest editions of "A Game at Chess."* 5 *vols.,* 8*vo, polished calf, gilt, marbled edges, by Riviere.* LARGE PAPER: *only* 25 *copies printed for presentation.* E. Lumley, London, 1840

2108 MIDWIFE (THE), OR THE OLD WOMAN'S MAGAZINE: containing all the Wit, and all the Humour, and all the Learning, and all the Judgement, that has ever been, or ever will be, inserted in all the other Magazines, or the Magazine of Magazines, or the Grand Magazine of Magazines, or any other Book whatsoever; so that those who buy this Book will need no other. Publish'd pursuant to Several Acts of Parliament, and by Permission of their most Christian and most Catholic Majesties, the Great Mogul and the States General. Embellish'd with Cuts according to Custom. Printed for Mary Midnight, and sold by T. Carnan in St. Paul's Churchyard. *Engraved title to the first volume.* 3 *vols. in* 2, 12*mo, sprinkled calf, gilt, marbled edges.* London, 1751–53

2109 MIERS, JOHN. TRAVELS IN CHILE AND LA PLATA; including Accounts respecting the Geography, Geology, Statistics, Government, Finances, Agriculture, Manners and Customs, and the Mining Operations in Chile, collected during a Residence of Several Years in these Countries. *Illustrated by original maps, views, etc.* 2 *vols.,* 8*vo, cloth.* London, 1826

2110 MILL, JOHN STUART. ON LIBERTY. *Post 8vo, cloth.* Boston, 1863

2111 MILLAR, JOHN. AN HISTORICAL VIEW OF THE ENGLISH GOVERNMENT, from the Settlement of the Saxons in Britain to the Revolution in 1688; to which are subjoined, some Dissertations connected with the History of the Government, from the Revolution to the Present Time. Fourth Edition. *4 vols., royal 8vo, cloth, uncut.* London, 1818

2112 MILLEDULCIA: A THOUSAND PLEASANT THINGS, selected from Notes and Queries. *Square 12mo, cloth, gilt top.* New York, 1857

2113 MILLER, JOHN. AN ILLUSTRATION OF THE SEXUAL SYSTEM OF LINNÆUS. *Latin and English. Frontispiece, engraved title, and 108 finely colored plates, including 4 without letters and numbers and 4 of leaves. Imperial folio, half russia.* London, 1794

"This work obtained the approbation of Linnæus himself." — *Lowndes.*

2114 MILLER, JOHN. MEMOIRS OF GENERAL (WILLIAM) MILLER, in the Service of the Republic of Peru. *Portrait, maps, plans, etc. 2 vols, 8vo., half calf, very neat.* London, 1828

"An interesting description of the War of Independence of the Spanish colonies in South America." — *Lowndes.*

2115 MILLER, REV. JOHN. A DESCRIPTION OF THE PROVINCE AND CITY OF NEW YORK; with Plans of the City, and Several Forts as they existed in the Year 1695. By John Miller. A New Edition, with an Introduction and Copious Historical Notes, by John Gilmary Shea, LL. D. *Printed by Munsell. Royal 4to, cloth, uncut.* LARGE PAPER: *only 50 copies printed.* New York, 1862

No. 3 of "Gowans' Bibliotheca Americana," reprinted from the small edition published (from the Original MSS. now in the British Museum) by Thomas Rodd, London, 1843. See DENTON, and WOOLEY.

2116 MILLER, SAMUEL, D. D. A BRIEF RETROSPECT OF THE EIGHTEENTH CENTURY; Part First, containing a Sketch of the Revolutions and Improvements in Science, Arts, and Literature, during that Period. *2 vols., 8vo, sheep.* New York, 1803

2117 MILLIN, AUBIN LOUIS. PEINTURES DE VASES ANTIQUES VULGAIREMENT APPELÉS ÉTRUSQUES, tirées de Différentes Collections et gravées par A. Clener; accompagnées d'Explications par A. L. Millin. Publiées par M. Dubois Maisonneuve. *Contains 150 plates. 2 vols., atlas folio, half russia, rough edges.* FINE ORIGINAL COPY. Paris, 1808–10

2118 MILLINGEN, JAMES. PEINTURES ANTIQUES ET INÉDITES DE VASES GRECS, tirées de Diverses Collections; avec des Explications, par J. V. Millingen. *Vellum paper; with 63 plates. Imperial folio, boards, uncut.* Rome, 1813

2119 MILLINGEN, JAMES. PEINTURES ANTIQUES DE VASES GRECS, de la Collection de Sir John Coghill, Bart. Publiées par James Millingen, de la Société des Antiquaires de Londres, &c. *Vellum paper; with 52 plates. Imperial folio, paper, rough edges.* Rome, 1817

2120 MILLINGEN, JOHN GIDEON. THE PASSIONS, or Mind and Matter; illustrated by Considerations on Hereditary Insanity, etc., etc., etc. By Dr. Millingen. *8vo, cloth, uncut.* London, 1848

Second edition of the work entitled "Mind and Matter."

2121 MILLOT, CLAUDE FRANÇOIS XAVIER. ŒUVRES. Continuées par MM. Millon, Delisle de Sales, etc. — Histoire Ancienne, 3 *vols.;* Histoire Moderne, 4 *vols.;* Histoire d'Angleterre, 2 *vols.;* Histoire de France, 3 *vols. Together,* 12 *vols., 8vo, old marbled calf, gilt, marbled edges.* Paris, 1819–20

2122 MILLS, CHARLES. WORKS. AN HISTORY OF MUHAMMEDANISM: comprising the Life and Character of the Arabian Prophet, and Succinct Accounts of the Empires formed by the Muhammedan Arms; an Inquiry into the Theological, Moral, and Juridical Codes of the Muselmans, and the Literature and Sciences of the Saracens and Turks; with a View of the Present Extent and Influence of the Muhammedan Religion. [By Mills.] 1 *vol.*, 1817. — THE TRAVELS OF THEODORE DUCAS, in Various Countries in Europe, at the Revival of Letters and Art; edited [written] by Charles Mills. Part the First; Italy. [All that was published.] 2 *vols.*, 1822. — THE HISTORY OF THE CRUSADES, for the Recovery and Possession of the Holy Land; by Charles Mills. The Third Edition. 2 *vols.*, 1822. — THE HISTORY OF CHIVALRY, or Knighthood and its Times; by Charles Mills. 2 *vols.*, 1825. *Together,* 7 *vols., with maps and plates. 8vo, polished calf, gilt, yellow edges, by Riviere.* London, 1817–25

2123 MILLS, CHARLES. WORKS. HISTORY OF MUHAMMEDANISM. The Second Edition, revised and augmented. 1 *vol.*, 1818. — HISTORY OF THE CRUSADES: the Second Edition. 2 *vols.*, 1821. — HISTORY OF CHIVALRY: *second edition, with "Appendix."* 2 *vols.*, 1826. *Together,* 5 *vols., with maps and plates. 8vo, sprinkled calf, gilt, marbled edges, by Riviere.* London, 1818–26

2124 MILMAN, REV. HENRY HART. ANNE BOLEYN. A Dramatic Poem. *8vo, boards, rough edges.* J. Murray, London, 1826

2125 MILTON, JOHN. POETICAL WORKS. A New Edition, with Notes of Various Authors, by Thomas Newton, D. D. *Three portraits of Milton by Vertue, and numerous plates.* 3 *vols., 4to, old mottled calf.* London, 1749–52

2126 MILTON, JOHN. THE WORKS OF; Historical, Political, and Miscellaneous; now more correctly printed, from the Originals, than in any Former Edition, and Many Passages restored, which have been hitherto omitted: to which is prefixed an Account of his Life and Writings [by Thomas Birch]. *Portrait by Vertue. 2 vols., 4to, old sprinkled calf.* London, 1753

2127 MILTON, JOHN. THE POETICAL WORKS OF; with the Principal Notes of Various Commentators: to which are added Illustrations, with some Account of the Life of Milton; by Rev. Henry John Todd, M. A. *Portrait and plate. 6 vols., imperial 8vo, citron morocco, very neat, gilt edges, by Hering; uniform with "Prose Works by Symmons."* LARGE PAPER: *fine copy.* London, 1801

2128 MILTON, JOHN. THE PROSE WORKS OF; with a Life of the Author, interspersed with Translations and Critical Remarks, by Charles Symmons, D. D. *Beautifully printed by T. Bensley. 7 vols., imperial 8vo, citron morocco, very neat, gilt edges, by Hering; uniform with "Poetical Works by Todd."* LARGE PAPER: *fine copy of this excellent and elegant edition.* London, 1806

2129 MILTON, JOHN. L'ALLEGRO AND IL PENSEROSO. With Thirty Illustrations designed expressly for the Art-Union of London. *Printed on one side only of a fine paper. 4to, half morocco, neat.* London, 1848

2130 MINGAUD, ——. THE NOBLE GAME OF BILLIARDS; wherein are exhibited Extraordinary and Surprising Strokes which have excited the Admiration of Most of the Sovereigns of Europe. By Monsieur Mingaud, formerly Capitaine d'Infantrie in the Service of France. Translated and published by John Thurston, Billiard Table Manufacturer. Third Edition. *Engraved title and 43 plates with directions for performing nearly 70 difficult "strokes." Small folio, half morocco.* London, 1836

2131 MINOT, GEORGE RICHARDS. CONTINUATION OF THE HISTORY OF THE PROVINCE OF MASSACHUSETTS BAY, from the Year 1748; with an Introductory Sketch of Events from its Original Settlement. *2 vols. in 1, 8vo, half russia, neat.* Boston, 1798–1803

2132 MIRROR (THE) OF TASTE, and Dramatic Censor. *Nos. 1–6 (Jan.–June, 1810), with the 6 plays bound together at the end. 1 vol., 8vo, half roan.* Philadelphia, 1810

Contains biographies, criticisms, etc., and the following plays: Dimond's "Foundling of the Forest," Arnold's "Man and Wife," Lewis's "Venoni," Massinger's "New Way to Pay Old Debts," Lewis's "Alfonso," Reynolds's "Free Knights."

2133 MIRROR FOR MAGISTRATES; in Five Parts. Collated with Various Editions, and Historical Notes, etc., by Joseph

Haslewood. 3 *vols., post 4to, olive turkey morocco, extra, gilt over carmine edges, by Riviere; uniform with* PAINTER'S PALACE OF PLEASURE. ONLY 150 COPIES PRINTED. London, 1815

"Best edition of this popular production of the reign of Elizabeth." — *Lowndes.*

2134 MISCELLANEA AUREA, OR THE GOLDEN MEDLEY; consisting of: I. A Voyage to the Mountains of the Moon under the Æquator, or Parnassus reform'd. II. The Fortunate Shipwreck, or a Description of New Athens, being an Account of the Laws, Manners, Religion, and Customs of that Country; by Morris Williams, Gent., who resided there above Twenty Years. III. Alberoni, or a Vindication of that Cardinal. IV. The Secret History of the Amours of Don Alonzo, Duke of Lerma, Grandee of Spain. V. The Garden of Adonis, or Love to no Purpose; being above Twenty Copies of Verses and Love-Letters, by a Lady. VI. Mahomet no Imposter, written in Arabick by Abdulla Mahumed Omar. VII. An Account of Bad and Good Women, Ancient and Modern; among which is the Story of the Spartan Dame, the Subject of Mr. Southern's Play. With several other Epistolary Essays, in Prose and Verse, by Mr. Milton, the Lady W——, Mr. Philips, Mr. Killegrew, Author of the Chit Chat, and several others. *8vo, old calf.* London, 1720

2135 MISSALE ROMANUM, ex Decreto Sacrosancti Concilii Tridentini restitutum, Pii V. Pont. Max. Jussu editum; cum Kalendario Gregoriano: permittente Summo Pont. *Printed in red and black, with ornate initials; several large wood-cuts, and numerous small ones, and music. 4to, old calf, tooled edges; binding broken, but text in fair condition.* Black letter. Apud Johannem Variscum, & Paganinum de Pageninis, Venetiis, 1585

2136 MITCHELL, DONALD GRANT. THE LORGNETTE, or Studies of the Town; by an Opera Goer. Fourth Edition, set off with Mr. Darley's Designs. BOTH SERIES. *2 vols., 12mo, cloth.* New York, 1851

2137 MITCHELL, O. M., LL. D. POPULAR ASTRONOMY. *Plates. 12mo, cloth.* New York, 1860

2138 MITCHELL'S NEW GENERAL ATLAS; containing Maps of the Various Countries of the World, Plans of Cities, etc., embraced in Fifty-three Quarto Maps, forming a Series of Eighty-four Maps and Plans, together with Valuable Statistical Tables. *Imperial 4to, half morocco.* Philadelphia, 1865

2139 MITFORD, WILLIAM. THE HISTORY OF GREECE: with his Final Additions and Corrections. To which is prefixed, a Brief Memoir of the Author, by his Brother, the late Lord Redesdale. Carefully revised by William King, Editor of the First Posthumous Edition. *Portrait; and wood-cuts (on titles) of Grecian coins, from specimens in the British Museum. 8 vols., 8vo, tree calf, gilt, marbled edges. Seventh edition.* London, 1838

2140 M'KENNEY, Thomas L.; and James Hall. History of the Indian Tribes of North America; with Biographical Sketches and Anecdotes of the Principal Chiefs. Embellished with One Hundred and Twenty Portraits, from the Indian Gallery in the Department of War, at Washington. *The portraits finely colored. 3 vols., royal folio, half crimson morocco, extra, emblematically tooled, gilt edges, by Wright.* Philadelphia, (1838–44)

2141 M'LEVY, James. Curiosities of Crime in Edinburgh, during the Last Thirty Years. Third Edition. *Wood-cut portrait. 16mo, boards.* Edinburgh, 1861

2142 MODERN London; being the History and Present State of the British Metropolis. *Plan of London and 53 plates of views, etc., 31 of which (representing the costumes of the itinerant traders) are colored. 4to, old marbled calf; with book-plate of Sir George Staunton, Bart.* London, 1805

2143 MODERN (The) Plutarch, or Universal Biography; including Authentic Memoirs of Distinguished Public Characters of all Nations, Living and Recently Deceased, with Original Portraits. *4 vols., 12mo, half calf.* London, 1806–07

2144 MODES (Les) Parisiennes Illustrées; Journal de la Bonne Compagnie. *For the Years 1852–54. Colored plates and wood-cuts. 6 vols., 4to, boards.* Paris, 1852–54

2145 MOLIÈRE, Jean Baptiste Poquelin de. Œuvres Complètes. Édition illustrée de 140 Vignettes par Janet-Lange, augmentée d'une Vie de Molière et de Notices sur chaque Pièce, par Émile de la Bédollière. *Imperial 8vo, cloth.* Paris, s. a.

2146 MONK, Maria. Further Disclosures by Maria Monk, concerning the Hotel Dieu Nunnery of Montreal; also her Visit to Nuns' Island, and Disclosures concerning that Secret Retreat. Preceded by a Reply to the Priests' Book, by Rev. J. J. Slocum. *Portrait. 12mo, cloth.* New York, 1837

2147 MONSTRELET, Enguerrand de. The Chronicles of. Containing an Account of the Cruel Civil Wars between the Houses of Orleans and Burgundy, of the Possession of Paris and Normandy by the English, their Expulsion thence, and of other Memorable Events that happened in the Kingdom of France as well as in other Countries: a History of Fair Example and of Great Profit to the French, beginning at the Year MCCCC., where that of Sir John Froissart finishes, and ending at the Year MCCCCLXVII.; and continued by others to the Year MDXVI. Translated by Thomas Johnes, Esq. 5 *vols., royal 4to, russia, neat, marbled edges.* Hafod Press, 1809

The fifth volume contains 51 plates and Index. See ARNOLD, RICHARD.

2148 MONSTRELET, ENGUERRAND DE. ANOTHER COPY. *Second edition.* 12 *vols., 8vo, and* 1 *vol.* (*with the* 51 *plates*), *4to, half calf; with book-plate of J. Knight.* London, 1810

2149 MONTAGU, MRS. ELIZABETH. AN ESSAY ON THE WRITINGS AND GENIUS OF SHAKSPEARE, compared with the Greek and French Dramatic Poets; with some Remarks upon the Misrepresentations of Mons. de Voltaire. The Sixth Edition, corrected; to which are added, Three Dialogues of the Dead. *Royal 8vo, half morocco, marbled edges.* LARGE PAPER. London, 1810

"According to T. Warton, the most elegant and judicious piece of criticism this age has produced." — *Lowndes.*

Mrs. Montague originated the literary society known as the "Blue Stocking Club."

2150 MONTAGU, MRS. ELIZABETH. ANOTHER COPY: *the same; small paper. 8vo, half calf.* London, 1810

2151 MONTAGU, EDWARD WORTLEY. REFLECTIONS ON THE RISE AND FALL OF THE ANCIENT REPUBLICKS; adapted to the Present State of Great Britain. The Third Edition, with Additions and Corrections. *8vo, old calf, binding broken.* London, 1769

It has been said that this work, which was first published when the avowed author was travelling on the Continent in charge of a private tutor, was in reality written by his tutor, the Rev. Mr. Foster.

2152 MONTAGU, LADY MARY WORTLEY. THE WORKS OF: including her Correspondence, Poems, and Essays. Published from her Genuine Papers [in Possession of her Grandson, John First Marquis of Bute; edited, with Memoirs, by the Rev. James Dallaway]. *Portraits and fac-similes.* 5 *vols., crown 8vo, half russia; with book-plate of Folkestone.* London, 1803

2153 MONTAIGNE, MICHEL DE. THE ESSAYS OF; translated into English, with very Considerable Amendments and Improvements, from the most Accurate French Edition of Peter Coste. The Ninth Edition. *Portrait.* 3 *vols., royal 8vo, dark green turkey morocco, neat, gilt edges.* London, 1811

Fine copy of an elegantly printed edition.

2154 MONTAIGNE, MICHEL DE. WORKS OF: comprising his Essays, Journey into Italy, and Letters; with Notes from all the Commentators, Biographical and Bibliographical Notices, etc. By W. Hazlitt. A New and Carefully Revised Edition; edited by O. W. Wight. *Portrait.* 4 *vols., post 8vo, cloth.* New York, 1859

2155 MONTANUS, ARNOLDUS. ATLAS JAPANNENSIS: being Remarkable Addresses, by Way of Embassy, from the East India Company of the United Provinces, to the Emperor of Japan; containing a Description of their Several Territories, Cities, Temples, and Fortresses; their Religions, Laws, and Customs; their Prodigious Wealth, and Gorgeous Habits; the Nature of their Soil, Plants, Beasts, Hills, Rivers, and Fountains; with the Character of the Ancient and Modern Japanners. Collected out of their Several Writings and Journals. English'd and adorn'd with above a Hundred Several Sculptures, by John Ogilby, Esq., etc. *Large folio, old calf.*
Printed by Tho. Johnson, for the Author, London, 1670

2156 MONTFAUCON, BERNARD DE. L'ANTIQUITÉ EXPLIQUÉE ET REPRÉSENTÉE EN FIGURES. *French and Latin. Above 900 plates, fine impressions. 5 vols. in 10, royal folio, old calf. Without supplement.* LARGE PAPER: ORIGINAL EDITION.
Paris, 1719

"L'édition citée [celle-ci] est la meilleure, et l'on n'en trouve pas facilement de beaux exemplaires." —*Brunet.*

2157 MONTFAUCON, BERNARD DE. ANTIQUITY EXPLAINED AND REPRESENTED IN SCULPTURES; by the learned Father Montfaucon. Translated into English by David Humphreys, M. A., etc. COMPLETE WITH SUPPLEMENT, *containing all the plates in the 15 vols., of the original edition, but on a reduced scale. 7 vols. in 6, folio, old calf, gilt, red edges; with book-plate of Peter Hardy, F. R. S.* FINE COPY.
London, 1721–25

2158 MONTHLY (THE) MAGAZINE, OR BRITISH REGISTER. *Complete from commencement (February 1, 1796), to January 30, 1820, inclusive, except Vols. XLI. and XLII. Numerous maps, large plates, and wood-cuts. 46 vols., 8vo, half calf.*
London, 1796–1820

2159 MONUMENTS OF ART; SHOWING ITS DEVELOPMENT FROM THE EARLIEST ARTISTIC ATTEMPTS TO THE PRESENT PERIOD. By V. Voit, Dr. E. Guhl, Jos. Caspar and Dr. W. Luebke, in Berlin. *Engraved titles and 156 plates, containing several thousand examples, chiefly in outline, but with many highly-finished engravings and several illuminated in gold and colors. With text by Prof. Dr. Wm. Lübke, of Berlin, and Dr. Charles Fr. von Lützow, of Munich. 2 vols., oblong 4to, half morocco, marbled edges, and 1 vol. (text) 8vo, cloth.* New York, (1865)

This work was originally issued (Stuttgart. 1847–56), under the general direction of the celebrated German art-critic, Kugler.

2160 MOONEY, THOMAS. A HISTORY OF IRELAND, FROM ITS FIRST SETTLEMENT TO THE PRESENT TIME; including a Particular Account of its Literature, Music, Architecture, and National Resources; with Upwards of Two Hundred

Biographical Sketches of its most Eminent Men. *Wood-cut portraits, etc. 8vo, half morocco. Fourth edition.* Boston, s. a.

2161 MOORE, CHARLES W., and S. W. B. CARNEGY. THE MASONIC TRESTLE-BOARD; adapted to the National System of Work and Lectures, as revised and perfected by the United States Masonic Convention, at Baltimore, Maryland, A. L., 5843. *Plates. 8vo, half morocco.* Boston, 1843

2162 MOORE, EDWARD. FABLES FOR THE FEMALE SEX. The Third Edition. *With 17 plates after F. Hayman, engraved by Grignion, Mosley, etc. 8vo, cloth.* London, 1766

2163 MOORE, EDWARD. ANOTHER COPY: the Fifth Edition. *With same plates. 8vo, old calf.* London, 1783

2164 MOORE, FRANK. MATERIALS FOR HISTORY printed from Original Manuscripts; with Notes and Illustrations. FIRST SERIES. (Correspondence of Henry Laurens of South Carolina.) *Portrait of Laurens on India paper. 4to, paper, uncut.* ONLY 100 COMPLETE COPIES PRINTED. Printed for the Zenger Club, New York, 1861

Of this work, as far as page 136, there were 250 copies printed, as stated on reverse of leaf containing "Advertisement," but of the remainder of the volume, including index, only 100 copies were printed.

2165 MOORE, FRANK. WOMEN OF THE WAR; their Heroism and Self-Sacrifice. Illustrated with Steel Engravings. *8vo, cloth.* Hartford, 1866

2166 MOORE, GEORGE HENRY. "MR. LEE'S PLAN, — March 29, 1777." The Treason of Charles Lee, Major General, Second in Command in the American Army of the Revolution. *Portrait, caricature, and fac-simile. Royal 8vo, cloth, uncut.* New York, 1860

2167 MOORE, HUGH. MEMOIR OF COL. ETHAN ALLEN; containing the most Interesting Incidents connected with his Private and Public Career. *12mo, cloth.* Plattsburgh, N. Y., 1834

2168 MOORE, JOHN, M. D. ZELUCO. Various Views of Human Nature, taken from Life and Manners. The Fourth Edition. *2 vols., 8vo, half russia, extra, yellow edges.* London, 1797

2169 MOORE, JOHN, M. D. MORDAUNT. Sketches of Life, Characters, and Manners, in Various Countries; including the Memoirs of a French Lady of Quality. *3 vols., 8vo, half russia, extra, yellow edges.* London, 1800

2170 MOORE, JOHN, M. D. THE WORKS OF: with Memoirs of his Life and Writings, by Robert Anderson, M. D. *Portrait. 7 vols., 8vo, half calf.* Edinburgh, 1820

2171 MOORE, JOHN HAMILTON. A NEW AND COMPLETE COLLECTION OF VOYAGES AND TRAVELS, etc. *Above* 100 *plates of maps, charts, plans, views, etc., after Wale, Dodd, etc., engraved by Grignion, Walker, etc. 2 vols., folio, old calf.* London, s. a.

2172 MOORE, THEOPHILUS. MARRIAGE CUSTOMS and Modes of Courtship of the Various Nations of the Universe; with Remarks on the Condition of Women, Penn's Maxims, and Counsel to the Single and Married, etc., etc. Second Edition. *Frontispiece. 12mo, calf, neat.* London, 1820

2173 MOORE, THOMAS. MEMOIRS OF THE LIFE OF RICHARD BRINSLEY SHERIDAN. The Third Edition. *Portrait and fac-simile. 2 vols., 8vo, boards, rough edges.* London, 1825

2174 MOORE, THOMAS. THE POETICAL WORKS OF; complete in One Volume. *Portrait, and engraved title. Royal 8vo, green turkey morocco, extra, gilt edges, by Hayday.* Longmans & Co., London, 1846

2175 MOORE, THOMAS. LALLA ROOKH; an Oriental Romance. *Vignette on the engraved title and 12 fine plates after K. Meadows, E. Corbould, and F. P. Stephanhoff, engraved under the direction of C. Heath. Square 8vo, cloth, uncut.* Longmans & Co., London, 1853

2176 MOORE, THOMAS. MEMOIRS, JOURNAL, AND CORRESPONDENCE OF; edited by Lord John Russell. *Engraved titles, fine vignette on each, and 8 portraits. 8 vols., crown 8vo, cloth, uncut.* London, 1853–56

2177 MOORE, THOMAS. IRISH MELODIES; with Symphonies and Accompaniments by Sir John Stevenson, Mus. Doc., and Characteristic Words by Thomas Moore, Esq. New Edition, edited by J. W. Glover, Esq. *Frontispiece and engraved title; the music both vocal and instrumental. 4to, cloth, gilt edges.* Dublin, (1859)

2178 MOORMAN, JOHN J., M. D. THE VIRGINIA SPRINGS, and Springs of the South and West. With Map and Plates, and the Routes and Distances to the Various Springs. *12mo, cloth.* Philadelphia, 1859

2179 MORANT, REV. PHILIP. THE HISTORY AND ANTIQUITIES OF THE COUNTY OF ESSEX; compiled from the Best and most Ancient Historians, from Domesday-Book, Inquisitiones Post Mortem, and other the most Valuable Records and MSS., etc. The Whole digested, improved, perfected, and brought down to the Present Time. Illustrated with Copper Plates. *2 vols., folio, new sprinkled calf, gilt, carmine edges; binding slightly injured.* ORIGINAL EDITION: *fine copy.* London, 1768

Plates engraved by Vertue, etc.

2180 MORE, CRESACRE. THE LIFE OF SIR THOMAS MORE, with a Biographical Preface, Notes, and other Illustrations,

by the Rev. Joseph Hunter, F. S. A. *Portrait and wood-cut. 8vo, tree calf, gilt, marbled edges.*
W. Pickering, London, 1828

2181 MORE, SIR THOMAS. A MOST PLEASANT, FRUITFUL, AND WITTY WORK, of the Best State of a Public Weal, and of the New Isle called Utopia; written in Latin, and translated into English by Raphe Robinson, A. D. 1551. A New Edition, with Copious Notes (including the whole of Dr. Warner's), and a Biographical and Literary Introduction; by the Rev. T. F. Dibdin, F. S. A. *Portrait of More, wood-cuts, etc. 1 vol., 4to, diamond calf, gilt.* LARGE PAPER: *only 40 copies printed.* London, 1808

This copy has a wood-cut border around the title and the plate of the "Family of Sir Thomas More" in outline, which are not found in the small paper copies. In the introduction the 41 different portraits of More and the different editions of the Utopia are criticised.

2182 MORE, SIR THOMAS. ANOTHER COPY: *small paper. Portrait, etc. 2 vols., crown 8vo, russia, neat, rough edges.*
London, 1808

2183 MORELL, ANDRÉ. THESAURUS MORELLIANUS, sive Familiarum Romanarum Numismata Omnia, diligentissime undique conquisita, ad ipsorum Nummorum Fidem accuratissime delineata, & juxta Ordinem Fulvii Ursini & Caroli Patini disposita, a Celeberrimo Antiquario Andrea Morellio. Accedunt Nummi Miscellanei Urbis Romae, Hispanici, & Goltziani Dubiae Fidei Omnes. Nunc Primum edidit & Commentario Perpetuo illustravit Sigebertus Havercampus. 2 *vols.* — THESAURUS MORELLIANUS, sive Christ. Schlegelii, Sigeb. Havercampi, & Antonii Francisci Gorii Commentaria in XII. Priorum Imperatorum Romanorum Numismata Aurea, Argentea, & Aerea, cujuscumque Moduli, diligentissime conquisita, & ad ipsos Nummos accuratissime delineata, a Celeberrimo Antiquario Andrea Morellio. Accedunt Cl. Gorii Descriptio Columnæ Trajanæ, a Morellio itidem elegantissime in aes incisae; nec non Tristani, Rubenii, ac Harduini Interpretationes Pretiosissimorum aliquot Antiquitatis Monumentorum. Cum Praefatione Petri Wesselingii. *Fine impressions of the plates. Together, 5 vols., royal folio, half calf, extra, marbled edges.* LARGE PAPER: *fine copy.*
Amstelædami, 1734–52

2184 MORELL, J. D. ELEMENTS OF PSYCHOLOGY. Part I. *12mo. cloth, uncut.* W. Pickering, London, 1853

2185 MORELL, JOHN REYNELL. ALGERIA; the Topography and History, Political, Social, and Natural, of French Africa. *Map and wood-cuts. 8vo, cloth, uncut.*
London, 1854

2186 MORFORD, HENRY. OVER-SEA; or England, France, and Scotland, as seen by a Live American. *Wood-cuts, 12mo, cloth.* New York, 1867

2187 MORGAN, Sydney Owenson, Lady. The Life and Times of Salvator Rosa. *Portrait.* 2 *vols.*, 8*vo, cloth, uncut.* London, 1824

2188 MORISON, Douglas. Views of the Ducal Palaces and Hunting Seats of Saxe Coburg and Gotha. *Frontispiece and* 20 *lithographic plates, with descriptive letter-press. Imperial folio, half morocco.* London, 1846

2189 MORLEY, Henry. Palissy the Potter; the Life of Bernard Palissy, of Saintes. Second Edition. *Crown* 8*vo, cloth, uncut.* London, 1855

2190 MORLEY, Henry. Memoirs of Bartholomew Fair. With Fac-simile Drawings, engraved upon Wood, by the Brothers Dalziel. 8*vo, cloth, uncut.* London, 1859

2191 MORPHY, Paul. Morphy's Games of Chess; being the Best Games played by him in Europe and America, with Analytical and Critical Notes, by J. Löwenthal. *Portrait, etc. Post* 8*vo, half pink calf, neat.* London, 1860

2192 MORRIS, Beverley Robinson. British Game Birds and Wildfowl. *With* 60 *finely colored plates. Royal* 4*to, half crimson morocco, neat, emblematically gilt sides, gilt edges.* London, 1855

2193 MORRIS, John Payne. The Genealogies recorded in the Sacred Scriptures; according to every Family and Tribe, with the Line of Our Saviour Jesus Christ observed from Adam to the Virgin Mary. *Title and* 38 *lithographic plates. Folio, cloth.* (London), 1837

2194 MORSE, Jedidiah, D. D. An Appeal to the Public, on the Controversy respecting the Revolution in Harvard College, and the Events which have followed it; occasioned by the Use which has been made of Certain Complaints and Accusations of Miss Hannah Adams, against the Author. *Royal* 8*vo, boards, rough edges.* Printed for the Author, Charlestown, 1814

2195 MORTON, Nathaniel. New-England's Memorial; or a Brief Relation of the most Memorable and Remarkable Passages of the Providence of God, manifested to the Planters of New-England in America, with Special Reference to the First Colony thereof, called New Plymouth. As also a Nomination of Divers of the most Eminent Instruments, deceased, both of Church and Commonwealth; improved in the First Beginning, and after Progress, of Sundry of the Respective Jurisdictions in those Parts, in Reference unto Sundry Exemplary Passages of their Lives, and the Time of their Death. 12*mo, sheep.* Plymouth, Mass., 1826

2196 MOSHEIM, Johann Lorenz von. Commentaries on the Affairs of the Christians before the Time of

Constantine the Great, or an Enlarged View of the Ecclesiastical History of the First Three Centuries; with Copious Illustrative Notes and References. Translated from the Latin; by Robert S. Vidal. *3 vols. in 2, 8vo, half calf, very neat.* London, 1813

2197 MOSHEIM, Johann Lorenz von. An Ecclesiastical History, Ancient and Modern, from the Birth of Christ to the Beginning of the Eighteenth Century; in which the Rise, Progress, and Variations of Church Power are considered in their Connexion with the State of Learning and Philosophy, and the Political History of Europe during that Period. Translated from the Original Latin, and accompanied with Notes and Chronological Tables, by Archibald Maclaine, D. D.; to which is added, an Accurate Index. *6 vols., 8vo, half russia, neat.* London, 1823

2198 MOTHERWELL, William. Minstrelsy, Ancient and Modern; with an Historical Introduction and Notes. *Engraved title, plates, and music. Foolscap 4to, cloth, rough edges.* Glasgow, 1827

2199 MOTHERWELL, William. The Poetical Works of; with Memoir, by James M'Conechy, Esq. Third Edition, greatly enlarged. *Fac-similes, etc. Foolscap 8vo, cloth, uncut.* Glasgow, 1849

2200 MOTLEY, John Lothrop. The Rise of the Dutch Republic. *Portrait. 3 vols., 8vo, cloth, uncut.* New York, 1858

2201 MOTLEY, John Lothrop. History of The United Netherlands, from the Death of William the Silent to the Synod of Dort; with a Full View of the English-Dutch Struggle against Spain, and of the Origin and Destruction of the Spanish Armada. *Portraits and map. 2 vols., 8vo, cloth.* New York, 1861

2202 MOURADJA d'Ohsson, Ignace. Tableau Général de l'Empire Othoman, divisé en Deux Parties; dont l'une comprend la Législation Mahométane, l'autre l'Histoire de l'Empire Othoman. *Frontispiece (title) and 137 plates of views, customs, costumes, etc. 2 vols., imperial folio, half green morocco, gilt tops, uncut.* Paris, 1787–90

"Ouvrage fort bien exécuté, mais qui malheureusement n'est pas terminé." — *Brunet.*

2203 MOWATT, Anna Cora. Autobiography of an Actress, or Eight Years on the Stage. *Portrait. Post 8vo, cloth.* Boston, 1859

2204 MOXON, Joseph. Mechanick Exercises, or the Doctrine of Handy-Works. *Plates. Small 4to, calf.* London, 1693–94

This volume contains "Smithing," "Joinery," "House-Carpentry," and "Turning."

2205 MOZART, JOHANN CHRYSOSTOMUS WOLFGANG AMADEUS. THE LETTERS OF; (1769–1791.) Translated, from the Collection of Ludwig Nohl, by Lady Wallace. *Portrait and fac-simile of handwriting.* 2 *vols., post* 8*vo, cloth.* New York, 1866

2206 MULOCH, DINAH MARIA. A WOMAN'S THOUGHTS ABOUT WOMEN. 12*mo, cloth.* London, 1864

2207 MUNCHAUSEN. THE ADVENTURES OF BARON MUNCHAUSEN. A New and Revised Edition, with an Introduction by T. Teignmouth Shore, M. A. Illustrated by Gustave Doré. 4*to, cloth, gilt top.* Cassell, Petter, & Galpin, London, s. a.

2208 MUNDIE, ROBERT. GLEANINGS OF NATURE, containing Fifty-seven Groups of Animals and Plants; with Popular Descriptions of their Habits. *The plates of flowers finely colored. Imperial* 8*vo, cloth, uncut.* London, 1838

2209 MUNDT, MRS. CLARA MÜLLER. THE MERCHANT OF BERLIN; an Historical Novel. By L. Mühlbach [Mrs. Mundt]. Translated from the German, by Amory Coffin, M. D. 12*mo, cloth.* New York, 1867

2210 MUNDT, MRS. CLARA MÜLLER. JOSEPH II. AND HIS COURT. Translated from the German, by Adelaide de V. Chaudron. *Wood-cuts.* 8*vo, cloth.* New York, 1867

2211 MUNN, LEWIS C. AUTOGRAPHS: the American Orator Appendix, containing the Declaration of Independence, with Fac-similes of the Autographs of the Signers; the Constitution of the United States; Washington's Farewell Address; and Fac-similes of a Large Number of Distinguished Individuals. Sixth Edition. 12*mo, half morocco, gilt top, uncut.* Worcester, 1856

2212 MUNSELL, JOEL. THE EVERY DAY BOOK OF HISTORY AND CHRONOLOGY; embracing the Anniversaries of Memorable Persons and Events, in Every Period and State of the World, from the Creation to the Present Time. 8*vo, cloth.* New York, 1858

2213 MURPHY, ARTHUR. THE WORKS OF. (Dramatic.) *Portrait by Cook after Dance.* 7 *vols.* 8*vo, old sprinkled calf, gilt, red edges; with book-plate of John Exley Adams.* London, 1786

2214 MURPHY, ARTHUR. THE LIFE OF DAVID GARRICK, ESQ. 8*vo, sheep.* Dublin, 1801

2215 MURPHY, JAMES C. A GENERAL VIEW OF THE STATE OF PORTUGAL: containing a Topographical Description thereof, in which are included, an Account of the Physical and Moral State of the Kingdom; together with Observations on the Animal, Vegetable, and Mineral Productions of its Colonies. The Whole compiled from the Best Portuguese

Writers, and from Notices obtained in the Country. Illustrated with Plates. *4to, half calf, marbled edges.* London, 1798

2216 MURPHY, James C. The Arabian Antiquities of Spain. *A series of 100 highly finished line engravings by Landseer, Fittler, Le Keux, and other eminent engravers, from drawings made upon the spot by J. C. Murphy; representing the most remarkable remains of the architecture, sculpture, paintings, mosaics, etc., of the Spanish Arabs. With descriptions of the plates.* 1 *vol., elephant folio, half maroon morocco, extra, gilt edges.* Original copy : *fine impressions.* London, 1813 (1816)

2217 MURPHY, James C. The History of the Mahometan Empire in Spain: containing a General History of the Arabs, their Institutions, Conquests, Literature, Arts, Sciences and Manners, to the Expulsion of the Moors. Designed as an Introduction to the Arabian Antiquities of Spain by James Cavanah Murphy, Architect. [Compiled by John Shakespear, the Rev. Thomas Hartwell Horne, and William Mitford.] *Map, etc., 4to, polished calf, gilt, by Mackenzie.* London, 1816

2218 MURPHY, James C. Plans, Elevations, Sections, and Views of the Church of Batalha, in the Province of Estremadura in Portugal, with the History and Description of Fr. Luis de Sousa; with Remarks. To which is prefixed an Introductory Discourse on the Principles of Gothic Architecture. Illustrated with 27 Plates. *The plates engraved by Lowry. Imperial folio, half morocco.* London, 1836

2219 MURRAY'S Hand Books for Travellers; Southern Germany. 1837. Northern Germany. 1838. Switzerland, etc. 1838. *Maps, etc.* 3 *vols., 12mo, cloth.* London, 1837–38

2220 MURRAY, Lindley. Memoirs of the Life and Writings of; in a Series of Letters written by himself. With a Preface, and a Continuation of the Memoirs, by Elizabeth Frank. Second Edition. *Portrait, and fac-simile autograph "at the age of eighty years." 8vo, half calf.* York, 1827

2221 MUSÉE Français: Recueil des plus Beaux Tableaux, Statues, et Bas-Reliefs, qui existaient au Louvre avant 1815; avec l'Explication des Sujets et des Discours Historiques sur la Peinture, la Sculpture, et la Gravure, par Duchesne aîné. *With French and English letter-press.* 4 *vols., atlas folio, half crimson French morocco.* Galignani, Paris, (1829–30)

2222 MUSÉE (Le) Royal Publié par Henri Laurent, Graveur du Cabinet du Roi, ou Recueil de Gravures d'après les Plus Beaux Tableaux, Statues, et Bas-Reliefs, de la Collection Royale; avec Description des Sujets, Notices

Littéraires, et Discours sur les Arts. *2 vols., atlas folio, half crimson French morocco.* F. Didot, Paris, 1816–18

2223 MUSICAL (THE) MISCELLANY; being a Collection of Choice Songs set to the Violin and Flute, by the most Eminent Masters. *Frontispieces engraved by Vander Gucht. 6 vols., small 8vo, sheep.* London, 1729–31

2224 MUSPRATT, SHERIDAN, M. D., ETC. CHEMISTRY, Theoretical, Practical, and Analytical; as applied and relating to the Arts and Manufactures. *Numerous portraits and above 1,100 wood-cuts. 2 vols., thick imperial 8vo, morocco, extra, gilt edges.* Glasgow, (1860)

2225 MUSTON, ALEXIS. THE ISRAEL OF THE ALPS; a History of the Persecutions of the Waldenses. Translated from the French of the Rev. Dr. Alexis Muston, by William Hazlitt. *Wood-cuts. Post 8vo, cloth.* London, 1852

2226 NAPIER, HENRY EDWARD. FLORENTINE HISTORY; from the Earliest Authentic Records, to the Accession of Ferdinand the Third, Grand Duke of Tuscany. *6 vols., post 8vo, calf, gilt, marbled edges.* E. Moxon, London, 1846–47

2227 NAPIER, MARK. MONTROSE AND THE COVENANTERS; their Characters and Conduct, illustrated from Private Letters and other Original Documents hitherto unpublished: embracing the Times of Charles the First, from the Rise of the Troubles in Scotland to the Death of Montrose. *2 vols., 8vo, cloth, uncut.* London, 1838

2228 NAPIER, SIR WILLIAM FRANCIS PATRICK. HISTORY OF THE WAR IN THE PENINSULA, and in the South of France; from the Year 1807 to the Year 1814. (With the Additions, consisting of Controversial Pamphlets.) *Numerous plans, etc. 6 vols., 8vo, polished calf, gilt, yellow edges, by Bedford.* ELEGANT COPY OF BEST EDITION. London, 1832–40

2229 NAPLES AND THE CAMPAGNA FELICE; in a Series of Letters addressed to a Friend in England, in 1802. *With 18 colored plates, including maps and plans, by Rowlandson, etc. Imperial 8vo, cloth, gilt top.* R. Ackermann, London, 1815

2230 NAPOLÉON I. LIFE OF, etc., in English; *comprised in the following works:—*

THE LIFE OF NAPOLEON BUONAPARTE; by William Hazlitt. *4 vols., 8vo.* E. Wilson, etc., 1830

MEMOIRS OF NAPOLEON, his Court and Family; by the Duchess d'Abrantes. *With 1[illegible] portraits. 2 vols., 8vo.* R. Bentley, 1836

MANUSCRIPT OF 1814: Memoirs of the Invasion of France by the Allied Armies, and of the Last Six Months of the

Reign of Napoleon, including his Abdication; by Baron Fain. New Edition. *Fac-simile of abdication and map of campaign of* 1814. 1 *vol.*, 8*vo.* H. Colburn, 1834

MEMOIRS OF THE PRIVATE LIFE, Return, and Reign of Napoleon in 1815; by M. Fleury de Chaboulon. 1 *vol.*, 8*vo.* J. Murray, 1820

SECRET MEMOIRS of Napoleon Buonaparte, preceded by an Historical Survey of the Character of this Extraordinary Personage, founded on his own Words and Actions; by One who never quitted him for Fifteen Years [C. Doris]. Second Edition, to which is added an Account of the Regency at Blois, and the Itinerary of Buonaparte, from the Period of his Residence at Fontainebleau, to his Establishment on the Island of Elba. 1 *vol.*, 8*vo.* H. Colburn, etc., 1815

THE CONFIDENTIAL CORRESPONDENCE of Napoleon Bonaparte with his Brother Joseph, sometime King of Spain; selected and translated, with Explanatory Notes, from the Mémoires du Roi Joseph. 2 *vols.*, 8*vo.* J. Murray, 1855

HISTORY OF THE EXPEDITION TO RUSSIA, undertaken by the Emperor Napoleon, in the Year 1812; by General, Count Philip de Segur. *Portraits, map, etc.* 2 *vols.*, 8*vo.* Treuttel, etc., 1825

MEMOIRS OF THE HISTORY OF FRANCE during the Reign of Napoleon; dictated by the Emperor at Saint Helena to the Generals who shared his Captivity, and published from the Original Manuscripts, corrected by himself. Vols. I. and II. dictated to General Gourgaud, his Aide-de-Camp; Vols. III.–VII. dictated to the Count de Montholon (Vols. V.–VII. containing Historical Miscellanies). *Fac-similes, maps, plans, etc.* 7 *vols.*, 8*vo.* H. Colburn, etc., 1823

NARRATIVE OF THE SURRENDER of Buonaparte, and of his Residence on Board H. M. S. Bellerophon, with a Detail of the Principal Events that occurred in that Ship, between the 24th of May and the 8th of August, 1815; by Captain F. L. Maitland, C. B. Second Edition. 1 *vol.*, 8*vo.* H. Colburn, 1826

THE ISLAND EMPIRE, or the Scenes of the First Exile of the Emperor Napoleon I., together with a Narrative of his Residence on the Island of Elba, taken from Local Information, the Papers of the British Resident, and other Authentic Sources; by the Author of "Blondelle." *Colored portrait, tinted view, map, etc.* 3 *parts in* 1 *vol.*, 8*vo.* T. Bosworth, 1855

NAPOLEON IN EXILE, or a Voice from St. Helena: the Opinions and Reflections of Napoleon on the most Important Events of His Life and Government, in his Own Words;

by Barry E. O'Meara, Esq,, his late Surgeon. Fourth Edition. *Portraits, etc.* *2 vols., 8vo.* W. Simpkin, etc., 1822
HISTORY OF THE CAPTIVITY of Napoleon at St. Helena, from the Letters and Journals of the late Lieut. Gen. Sir Hudson Lowe, and Official Documents not before made public; by William Forsyth, M. A., etc. *Portrait of Lowe, map, and views.* *3 vols., 8vo.* J. Murray, 1853
HISTORY OF THE CAPTIVITY of Napoleon at St. Helena; by General, Count Montholon, the Emperor's Companion in Exile and Testamentary Executor. *Fac-simile of handwriting of Montholon.* *4 vols., 8vo.* H. Colburn, 1846–47
THE LAST DAYS of the Emperor Napoleon; by Doctor F. Antommarchi, his Physician. *2 vols., 8vo.*
H. Colburn, 1825
MEMOIRS OF THE DUKE OF ROVIGO (M. Savary), written by himself, illustrative of the History of the Emperor Napoleon. *8 parts in 4 vols., 8vo.* H. Colburn, 1828
THE MEMOIRS OF JOSEPH FOUCHÉ, Duke of Otranto, Minister of the General Police of France. Translated from the French. Second Edition, revised and corrected. *Portrait.* *2 vols., 8vo.* C. Knight, 1825
Together, 40 vols., 8vo, half calf, extra, marbled edges; with book-plate of Peter Hardy, F. R. S. London, 1815–55

The above sixteen works, uniform in size and binding, form a remarkably fine set of the "Life and Times" of Napoleon I.

2231 NAPOLÉON III. HISTORY OF JULIUS CÆSAR. [Translated from the French of Napoléon III.] *Finely printed on a heavy paper.* *2 vols., thick imperial 8vo (4to), half crimson morocco, gilt tops, arms on sides.* London, (1865–66)

2232 NAPOLÉON III. ANOTHER COPY: *the same.* *2 vols., imperial 8vo (4to), half crimson morocco, gilt tops, arms on sides.* London, (1865–66)

2233 NAPOLÉON III. ANOTHER COPY: *Vol. I. of the American reprint.* *Royal 8vo, cloth.* New York, 1865

2234 NARES, REV. ROBERT. A GLOSSARY, or Collection of Words, Phrases, Names, and Allusions to Customs, Proverbs, etc.. which have been thought to require Illustration, in the Works of English Authors, particularly Shakespeare and his Contemporaries. *4to, half morocco.* London, 1822

2235 NARRAGANSETT CLUB. PUBLICATIONS OF THE. (First Series.) *3 vols., 4to, cloth, rough edges.* EDITION LIMITED TO 250 COPIES, *only 200 of which for sale.*
Providence, 1866–67

These three volumes are composed of writings of Roger Williams (and of writings relating to the same), edited by James H. Trumbull, Reuben A. Guild, Rev. J. Lewis Diman, and Rev. Samuel L. Caldwell, D. D.; with a "Biographical Introduction," by Mr. Guild.

2236 NARRAZIONI DELLE SOLENNI REALI FESTE fatte celebrare in Napoli da sua Maestá il Re delle Due Sicilie, Carlo, Infante di Spagna, Duca di Parma, Piacenza, etc, etc., per la Nascita del suo Primogenito, Filippo, Real Principe delle Due Sicilie. VELLUM PAPER, *with* 15 *large* (*double, and folded*) *plates and some smaller ones, chiefly by Giuseppe Vasi. Atlas folio, old mottled calf.* Napoli, 1749

The engravings in this work so pleased the king (Charles III., of Naples), that Vasi was assigned apartments in the Farnese palace at Rome.

2237 NASH, JOHN, ARCHITECT. ILLUSTRATIONS OF HER MAJESTY'S PALACE AT BRIGHTON, formerly the Pavilion; executed by the Command of King George the Fourth, under the Superintendence of John Nash, Esq., Architect. To which is prefixed a History of the Palace, by Edward Wedlake Brayley, Esq., F. S. A. PROOF IMPRESSIONS *of the* 31 *plates, and a duplicate set of* 28 *of them, colored in imitation of the original drawings, mounted on thick tinted card-board.* 1 *vol. imperial folio, boards.* London, 1838

2238 NASH, JOSEPH. THE MANSIONS OF ENGLAND IN THE OLDEN TIME. FOUR SERIES COMPLETE, *containing a frontispiece and* 25 *plates in each series; in all* 104 *large and finely colored views, mounted on very thick card-board, atlas folio size. Enclosed in* 4 *portfolios, half morocco, gilt labels on sides; with descriptions of the plates in* 1 *vol.,* 8*vo, cloth.* VERY FINE SET. London, 1839–49

This work, which illustrates the domestic architecture, customs, costumes, and recreations of the Tudor Age, is one of the most beautiful, as well as instructive works of the kind ever produced.

2239 NASON, ELIAS. SIR CHARLES HENRY FRANKLAND; or, Boston in the Colonial Times. *Royal* 8*vo, paper, rough edges.* LARGE PAPER: *only* 50 *copies printed.* J. Munsell, Albany, 1865

2240 NATIONAL (THE) ALMANAC, and Annual Record for the Years 1863 and 1864. 2 *vols.,* 12*mo, half green morocco.* Philadelphia, 1863–64

2241 NATIONAL (THE) CYCLOPÆDIA OF USEFUL KNOWLEDGE. 12 *vols. in* 6, 8*vo, half calf.* Boston (London), 1853

2242 NATIONAL (THE) PORTRAIT GALLERY of Distinguished Americans; conducted by James B. Longacre, Philadelphia, and James Herring, New York, under the Superintendence of the American Academy of the Fine Arts. *Engraved titles, and* 144 *portraits.* 4 *vols.,* 4*to, morocco, extra, gilt edges.* New York, 1834–39

2243 NATIONAL (THE) PORTRAIT GALLERY, of Eminent Americans, including Orators, Statesmen, Naval and Military Heroes, Jurists, Authors, etc., etc.; from Original Full-length Paintings by Alonzo Chappel. With Biographical and Historical Narratives, by Evert A. Duyckinck. 2 *vols.*, *4to, morocco, extra, gilt edges.* New York, (1861–64)

2244 NATURAL History. A Collection of Figures of Birds, Animals, Reptiles, and Fishes; all finely colored. *Each figure very neatly cut out and mounted, in a scrap-book, with name beneath.*

2245 NAVAL (The), Achievements of Great Britain; from 1793 to 1817. *A series of* 54 *engravings, with a duplicate set of etchings, after paintings by T. Whitcombe. Plates only. Imperial 4to, calf, extra, gilt edges; back cracked.* London, 1816–17

2246 NEALE, John Preston. Views of the Seats of Noblemen and Gentlemen in England, Wales, Scotland, and Ireland. Both series complete. *Above* 700 *views engraved by LeKeux and other eminent engravers.* 11 *vols.*, *8vo, green morocco, extra, gilt edges.* Original copy. London, 1818–29

2247 NEALE, John Preston. The Mansions of England, or Picturesque Delineations of the Seats of Noblemen and Gentlemen. Arranged in Counties. *Above* 700 *views, many on India paper.* 2 *vols.*, *4to, half crimson morocco, extra, gilt tops, uncut.* London, 1847

2248 NELSON, Rev. David. The Cause and Cure of Infidelity; including a Notice of the Author's Unbelief, and the Means of his Rescue. *12mo, half roan.* New York, (1841)

2249 NEPOS. Corn. Nepotis Vitæ Excellentium Imperatorum, cum quorumdam Iconibus. *Small 12mo, one cover wanting.* Amstelodami, 1711

2250 "NEVER too Late to Learn!" Five Hundred Mistakes of Daily Occurrence in Speaking, Pronouncing, and Writing the English Language, corrected. *12mo, cloth.* New York, 1856

2251 NEW (The) American Cyclopædia; or, Popular Dictionary of General Knowledge. Edited by George Ripley and Charles A. Dana. (With Supplement.) 16 *vols.* — The American Annual Cyclopædia and Register of Important Events; embracing Political, Civil, Military, and Social Affairs; Public Documents; Biography, Statistics, Commerce, Finance, Literature, Science, Agriculture, and Mechanical Industry; for the Years 1861–1864. 4 *vols. Portraits, maps, etc. Together* 20 *vols.*, *royal 8vo, russia, very neat, marbled edges.* New York, 1863–65

2252 NEW (A) and Impartial Collection of Interesting Letters, from the Public Papers, many of them written by Persons of Eminence, on a great Variety of Important Subjects, which have occasionally engaged the Public Attention; from the Accession of his Present Majesty, in September, 1765, to May, 1767. *2 vols., 8vo, old calf; with book-plate of The Rt Honble Isaac Barré. Covers of first volume severed.* J. Almon, London, 1767

2253 NEW (THE) BATH GUIDE, OR MEMOIRS OF THE B-N-R-D FAMILY; in a Series of Poetical Epistles. A New Edition. *Plates. Small 8vo, marbled calf.* Vernor and Hood, London, 1801

2254 NEW (A) CRITICAL PRONOUNCING DICTIONARY OF THE ENGLISH LANGUAGE; ETC. With a Classical Dictionary and Chronological Table. By an American Gentleman. *Royal 8vo, sheep.* Burlington, N. J., 1813

2255 NEW (A) DICTIONARY OF QUOTATIONS FROM THE GREEK, LATIN, AND MODERN LANGUAGES; translated into English, and accompanied with Illustrations, Historical, Poetical, and Anecdotical. With an Extensive Index, referring to every Important Word. From the Last London Edition. *Crown 8vo. cloth, gilt top.* Philadelphia, 1859

2256 NEW (THE) FOUNDLING HOSPITAL FOR WIT; being a Collection of Several Curious Pieces in Verse and Prose; written by Lord Chesterfield, Lord Hardwicke, Lord Lyttleton, Sir C. H. Williams, Mr. Wilkes, Mr. Churchill, Mr. Garrick, Mr. Potter, Dr. Akenside, and other Eminent Persons. [Edited by John Almon.] *Frontispiece to each part. 6 parts in 3 vols., small 8vo, half calf; with book-plate of Saml. Ireland. Various editions.* J. Almon, London, 1769–76

2257 NEW (THE) GOSPEL OF PEACE, ACCORDING TO ST. BENJAMIN. *Books I.–IV. in 1 vol., 16mo, half roan.* New York, (*cir.* 1864)

2258 NEWCASTLE, MARGARET CAVENDISH, DUCHESS OF. The Life of the Thrice Noble, High, and Puissant Prince, William Cavendish, Duke, Marquess, and Earl of Newcastle; one of his Majesties Privy Council; who had the Honour to be Governour to our most Glorious King, in his Youth. Written by the Thrice Noble, Illustrious, and Excellent Princess, Margaret, Duchess of Newcastle, his Wife. *Small folio; part of the notes at the end of the volume wanting, but complete from title to page 196 inclusive.* London, 1667

2259 NEW ENGLAND (THE) FARMER; a Semi-Monthly (monthly from 1852) Journal, devoted to Agriculture, Horticulture, and their Kindred Arts and Sciences. *Numerous wood-cuts. December, 1848–December, 1855. 7 vols., royal 8vo, cloth.* Boston, 1849–55

2260 NEW ENGLAND HISTORICAL AND GENEALOGICAL REGISTER; published quarterly under the Direction of the New England Historic Genealogical Society. *Numerous*

portraits, etc. COMPLETE *from January,* 1847, *to October,* 1866, *inclusive.* 20 *vols.,* 8*vo ; half morocco,* 3 *cloth.*
Boston, 1847–66

2261 NEW ENGLAND HISTORICAL AND GENEALOGICAL REGISTER. ANOTHER SET : *January,* 1847–*October,* 1860, 14 *vols.,* 8*vo, half morocco, neat.* Boston, 1847–60

2262 NEW ENGLAND SCENERY, from Nature. Third and Fourth Series. *Consists of* 12 *lithographs and* 1 *wood-cut.* 2 *parts, oblong* 4*to, paper.* Boston, 1852

2263 NEW ENGLAND'S FIRST FRUITS : in Respect, First of the Conversion of Some, Conviction of Divers, Preparation of Sundry of the Indians; 2. of the Progresse of Learning, in the Colledge at Cambridge in Massachusets Bay. With Divers other Speciall Matters concerning that Countrey. Published, by the Instant Request of Sundry Friends, who desire to be satisfied in these Points, by Many New-England Men who are here Present, and were Eye or Ear-Witnesses of the Same. *Small* 4*to, pp.* 26, *morocco ; perfect.*
London, 1643

2264 NEWTON, CHARLES T., and R. P. PULLAN. A HISTORY OF DISCOVERIES AT HALICARNASSUS, CNIDUS, AND BRANCHIDÆ. *Nearly* 100 *large plates of architecture, inscriptions, sculpture, etc. Plates in* 1 *vol. imperial folio ; text in* 2 *vols., imperial* 8*vo, cloth.* ONLY 300 COPIES PRINTED FOR SUBSCRIBERS. London, 1862–63

2265 NEW YORK CITY DURING THE AMERICAN REVOLUTION ; being a Collection of Original Papers (now first published) from the Manuscripts in the Possession of the Mercantile Library Association, of New York City. *Map, etc.,* 4*to, cloth, gilt top, rough edges.* PRIVATELY PRINTED, *for the Association.* (New York,) 1861

Selections from the "Tomlinson Collection" of MSS., with an historical introduction by Henry B. Dawson.

2266 NICHOLS, JOHN. A COLLECTION OF ALL THE WILLS, now known to be extant, of the Kings and Queens of England, Princes and Princesses of Wales, and every Branch of the Blood Royal, from the Reign of William the Conqueror, to that of Henry the Seventh exclusive ; with Explanatory Notes, and a Glossary. *Post* 4*to, half calf.*
J. Nichols, London, 1780

2267 NICHOLS, JOHN. BIOGRAPHICAL ANECDOTES OF WILLIAM HOGARTH : with a Catalogue of his Works, Chronologically arranged ; and Occasional Remarks. The Third Edition, enlarged and corrected. *Engraved title, with the knife and fork etching.* 8*vo, old marbled calf, gilt ; with book-plate of Thomas Webster.* BEST EDITION.
London, 1785

2268 NICHOLS, JOHN. ANOTHER COPY : *the same.* 8*vo, half calf.* London, 1785

2269 NICHOLS, John. Literary Anecdotes of the Eighteenth Century: comprising Biographical Memoirs of William Bowyer, Printer, F. S. A., and many of his Learned Friends; an Incidental View of the Progress and Advancement of Literature in this Kingdom during the Last Century; and Biographical Anecdotes of a Considerable Number of Eminent Writers and Ingenious Artists; with a Very Copious Index. *Numerous portraits, and plates. 9 vols., 8vo, tree calf, gilt, marbled edges; uniform with "Literary Illustrations."* London, 1812–15

2270 NICHOLS, John. Illustrations of the Literary History of the Eighteenth Century: consisting of Authentic Memoirs and Original Letters of Eminent Persons; and intended as a Sequel to the Literary Anecdotes. *6 vols., 8vo, tree calf, gilt, marbled edges; uniform with "Literary Anecdotes."* London, 1817–31

2271 NICOLAS, Sir Nicholas Harris. Life of William Davison, Secretary of State and Privy Counsellor to Queen Elizabeth. *Plates of fac-similes of writing, genealogical table, etc. 8vo, tree calf, gilt, marbled edges.* London, 1823

"A minute investigation of the question as to Elizabeth's privity and consent to the death of her sister, Mary Queen of Scots." — *Gentleman's Magazine.*

2272 NICOLAS, Sir Nicholas Harris. History of the Orders of Knighthood of the British Empire, of the Order of the Guelphs of Hanover, and of the Medals, Clasps, and Crosses conferred for Naval and Military Services. (With the Addenda completing the Catalogue of Knights to 30th July, 1846.) *Elegantly printed by Whittingham. Full-length portrait of Queen Victoria, and many other large plates, beautifully colored, besides numerous wood-cuts of medals, badges, crosses, stars, clasps, etc. 4 vols., imperial 4to, half russia, extra, red edges.* London, 1842

2273 NICOLAS, Sir Nicholas Harris. Another copy: *the same. With same plates, etc. 4 vols., imperial 4to, cloth, uncut.* London, 1842

"Sir H. Nicolas has produced the first comprehensive history of the British Orders of Knighthood; and it is one of the most elaborately prepared and splendidly printed works that ever issued from the press. The author appears to us to have neglected no sources of information, and to have exhausted them — in as far as regards the general scope and purpose of the inquiry. The graphical illustrations are such as become a work of this character upon such a subject; at, of course, a lavish cost, the resources of the recently revived art of wood-engraving have been combined with the new art of printing in colours, so as to produce a rich effect, almost rivalling that of the monastic illuminations." — *Quarterly Review, Vol. LXVIII. p.* 414.

2274 NILES, Rev. Samuel. The True Scripture-Doctrine of Original Sin stated and defended: in Way of Remarks on a Late Piece intitled "the Scripture-Doctrine of Original Sin proposed to Free and Candid Examination, by John Taylor; the Second Edition." To which is premised a Brief

Discourse on the Decrees of God, in General, and on the Election of Grace, in Particular; being the Substance of many Meditations, in the Course of a Long Life, and now published as his (renewed) Dying Testimony, for Truth, and against Error, by Samuel Niles, Pastor of a Church in Braintree. 12*mo, old calf.* S. Kneeland, Boston, 1757

2275 NOLAN, EDWARD H. THE ILLUSTRATED HISTORY OF THE WAR AGAINST RUSSIA. *Engraved titles, maps, and numerous portraits and plates.* 2 *vols., imperial* 8*vo, cloth.* London, (1857)

2276 NOLAN, EDWARD H. THE ILLUSTRATED HISTORY OF THE BRITISH EMPIRE IN INDIA AND THE EAST, from the Earliest Times to the Suppression of the Sepoy Mutiny in 1859. *Engraved titles, maps, and numerous portraits and plates.* 2 *vols., imperial* 8*vo, cloth.* London, (1860)

2277 NOLAN, REV. FREDERICK. THE CHRONOLOGICAL PROPHECIES, as constituting a connected System in which the Principal Events of the Divine Dispensations are determined by the Precise Revelation of their Dates; demonstrated in a Series of Lectures delivered in the Chapel of Lincoln's Inn in 1833, 1834, 1835, 1836. *Printed by Whittingham.* 8*vo, half morocco.* W. Pickering, London, 1837

2278 NOLTE, VINCENT. FIFTY YEARS IN BOTH HEMISPHERES; or Reminiscences of the Life of a Former Merchant. Translated from the German. 12*mo, cloth.* New York, 1854

2279 NORDBERG, GORAN ANDERS. HISTOIRE DE CHARLES XII. traduite du Suèdois [par Charles Gustave Warmholtz]. (Tome IV. contenant les Preuves de cette Histoire.) 4 *vols. in* 3, 4*to, half calf; backs cracked. Autograph of Robert Rantoul, Jr.* La Haye, 1748

"The most copious, and intrinsically valuable, history of Charles XII. is that by NORDBERG, published in the French language at the Hague, in 1748, 4to, 4 vols." — *Dibdin.*

2280 NORTH-AMERICAN (THE) REVIEW. *May,* 1815–*October,* 1867, *with* INDEX *to first* 25 *vols.* 106 *vols.,* 8*vo, half russia, neat; except Vols. XCVI.–CV., which are in numbers.* Boston, 1815–67

2281 NORTHCOTE, JAMES. FABLES, Original and Selected. [Edited, with Life, by Edmund Southey Rogers.] Illustrated by Two Hundred and Seventy-five Engravings on Wood. *Foolscap* 8*vo, cloth.* London, 1857

2282 NORTHEND, CHARLES. THE TEACHER AND THE PARENT, a Treatise upon Common-School Education. Fifth Edition. 12*mo, cloth.* New York, 1856

2283 NORTHERN (THE) TRAVELLER; containing the Routes to Niagara, Quebec, and the Springs, with the Tour of New-

England, and the Route to the Coal Mines of Pennsylvania. Second Edition. *Maps and plates.* 12*mo, half bound.* New York, 1826

2284 NORTON, CAROLINE ELIZABETH S. THE CHILD OF THE ISLANDS; a Poem. *Frontispiece, engraved title, and border around each page. Royal* 8*vo, half calf.* London, 1845

2285 NORTON, CHARLES ELIOT. NOTES OF TRAVEL AND STUDY IN ITALY. *Post* 8*vo, cloth.* Boston, 1860

2286 NOTES AND QUERIES; a Medium of Inter-communication for Literary Men, Artists, Antiquaries, Genealogists, General Readers, etc. *Nov.* 3, 1849–*Dec.* 30, 1865, *with* INDEXES. *First series,* 12 *vols. and index; second series,* 12 *vols. and index; third series,* 8 *vols. Together,* 34 *vols., foolscap* 4*to, half green morocco, gilt tops, rough edges.* COMPLETE SET. London, 1850–65

2287 NOTES AND QUERIES. FIRST SERIES, *to Dec.* 30, 1854. 10 *vols., half calf, marbled edges.* London, 1850–54

2288 NOTT, JOSIAH C., M. D.; and GEORGE ROBINS GLIDDON. TYPES OF MANKIND, or Ethnological Researches; based upon the Ancient Monuments, Paintings, Sculptures, and Crania of Races; and upon their Natural, Geographical, Philological, and Biblical History: illustrated by Selections from the inedited Papers of Samuel George Morton, M. D.; and by Additional Contributions from Prof. L. Agassiz, W. Usher, M. D., and Professor H. L. Patterson, M. D. *Portrait and memoir of Dr. Morton, and numerous plates and wood-cuts.* 4*to, half russia.* Philadelphia, 1854

2289 NOUVEAU DICTIONNAIRE D'HISTOIRE NATURELLE, appliquée aux Arts, principalement à l'Agriculture et à l'Économie Rurale et Domestique; par une Société de Naturalistes et d'Agriculteurs. Avec des Figures tirées des Trois Règnes de la Nature. *Fine impressions of the numerous plates.* 24 *vols.,* 8*vo, half russia, neat.* ORIGINAL EDITION. Paris, 1803–04

A later edition of this work has been published which is more complete, but it is not so well printed, and the impressions of the plates are inferior.

2290 NOUVEAU MANUEL DU VOYAGEUR, OR THE TRAVELLER'S POCKET COMPANION; containing Copious and Familiar Conversations in English, German, French, and Italian. Together with a Complete Vocabulary, etc. Third Edition, revised and corrected. 18*mo, boards.* Heidelberg, 1837

2291 NUMISMATA CIMELII CAESAREI REGII AUSTRIACI VINDOBONENSIS, quorum Rariora Iconismis, cetera Catalogis exhibita [Operâ et Studio Josephi de France, Valentini du Val, Erasmi Frölich, et Josephi Khell]. Jussu Mariae Theresiae Imperatricis et Reginae Augustae. *Contains* 137 *fine plates, with above* 1,000 *representations of coins and medals, by Kleiner.* 2 *parts in* 1 *vol., royal folio, old mottled calf.* Vindobonae, 1755

2292 OBSERVER (THE): being a Collection of Moral, Literary, and Familiar Essays. [By Richard Cumberland and others.] 5 *vols.,* 8*vo, half calf, rough edges.* VERY WIDE MARGINS. London, 1791–95

2293 O'CALLAGHAN, EDMUND B., M. D. A LIST OF EDITIONS OF THE HOLY SCRIPTURES, and Parts thereof, printed in America previous to 1860; with Introduction and Bibliographical Notes. *Fac-similes of titles to Eliot's Indian Bible and New Testament. Imperial* 8*vo, paper, rough edges.* ONLY 150 COPIES PRINTED. Munsell & Rowland, Albany, 1861

2294 OCKLEY, REV. SIMON. THE HISTORY OF THE SARACENS; containing the Lives of Abubeker, Omar, Othman, Ali, Hasan, Moawiyah I., Yezid I., Moawiyah II., Abdolla, Merwan I., and Abdolmelick, the Immediate Successors of Mahomet; giving an Account of their most Remarkable Battles, Sieges, etc., particularly those of Aleppo, Antioch, Damascus, Alexandria, and Jerusalem; illustrating the Religion, Rites, Customs, and Manner of Living of that Warlike People. Collected from the most Authentic Arabic Authors, especially MSS. not hitherto publish'd in any European Language. The Third Edition. 2 *vols.,* 8*vo, half calf.* Cambridge, 1757

This edition contains "Sentences of Ali, Son-in-Law of Mahomet, and his Fourth Successor," translated from an Arabic MS. in the Bodleian Library. Gibbon quotes from this work and Prof. Smyth recommends it.

2295 OEHLENSCHLÄGER, ADAM GOTTLOB. THE GODS OF THE NORTH; an Epic Poem. Translated from the Original Danish into English Verse, by William E. Frye (with an Alphabetical List of the Proper Names occurring in or connected with the Poem). *Royal* 8*vo, half morocco.* Paris, 1845

2296 OGILBY, JOHN. AMERICA: being the Latest and most Accurate Description of the New World; containing the Original of the Inhabitants, and the Remarkable Voyages thither; the Conquest of the Vast Empires of Mexico and Peru, and other Large Provinces and Territories, with the Several European Plantations in those Parts; also their Cities, Fortresses, Towns, Temples, Mountains, and Rivers; their Habits, Customs, Manners, and Religions; their Plants, Beasts, Birds, and Serpents. With an Appendix, containing, besides Several other Considerable Additions, a Brief Survey of what hath been discover'd of the Unknown South-Land and the Arctick Region. Collected from most Authentick Authors, augmented with Later Observations and adorn'd with Maps and Sculptures. *With catalogue of the authors referred to. Large folio, old mottled calf, gilt.* Printed by the Author, London, 1671

2297 OGILBY, JOHN. BRITANNIA: or an Illustration of the Kingdom of England and Dominion of Wales; by a Geographical and Historical Description of the Principal Roads thereof, actually admeasured and delineated in a Century of Whole-sheet Copper-sculps, accommodated with the Iconography of the Several Cities and Capital Towns, and compleated by an Accurate Account of the more Remarkable Passages of Antiquity, together with a Novel Discourse of the Present State. *Large folio, rough calf.* ORIGINAL EDITION. Printed by the Author, London, 1675

2298 O'KEEFE, JOHN. THE DRAMATIC WORKS OF. Prepared for the Press by the Author. 4 *vols., 8vo, half morocco; with autograph of author.* London, 1798

2299 O'KEEFE, JOHN. RECOLLECTIONS OF THE LIFE OF; written by himself. *Portrait, 2 vols., 8vo, cloth, uncut.* London, 1826

2300 OLDHAM, JOHN. THE WORKS OF, together with his Remains. 1 *vol., 8vo, old calf, gilt; with a very old book-plate of Ellerker Bradshaw, Esq., of Risby, York.* London, 1686–87

2301 OLD PLAYS. THE CONSCIOUS LOVERS; a Comedy, by Sir Richard Steele. 1723. — THE BOND-MAN; a Tragi-Comedy [altered from Massinger, by Betterton]. 1719. — THE BEGGAR'S OPERA, by Mr. [John] Gay. *With engraved pages of music.* 1728. — THEMISTOCLES; a Tragedy [by Dr. Samuel Madden]. 1729. — THE PROVOK'D HUSBAND; a Comedy, by Sir John Vanbrugh and Mr. [Colley] Cibber. 1728. — COMUS; a Mask: (now adapted to the Stage) as alter'd [by Dr. John Dalton] from Milton's Mask at Ludlow-Castle, which was never represented but on Michaelmas-Day, 1634. The Principal Performers were the Lord Brackly, Mr. Tho. Egerton, the Lady Alice Egerton. The Music was Composed by Mr. Henry Lawes, who also represented the Attendant Spirit. The Second Edition. *Six old plays in* 1 *vol., 8vo, half morocco.* London, 1719–38

2302 OLD PLAYS. THE SUSPICIOUS HUSBAND, by Dr. [Benjamin] Hoadly. 1747. — THE MOTHER-IN-LAW, or the Doctor the Disease [by James Miller]. 1734. — THE ARTIFICE [by Susanna Centlivre]. *Title wanting.* (1721.) *Three old comedies in* 1 *vol., 8vo, old calf; with book-plate and autographs.* London, 1721–47

2303 OLD PLAYS. LOVE IN A VILLAGE [by Isaac Bickerstaffe]. 1764. — THE VILLAGE OPERA, by Mr. [Charles] Johnson. 1729. — THE MAID OF THE MILL; a Comic Op-

era [by Isaac Bickerstaffe]. 1765. — COMUS; a Mask [altered from Milton by Dr. John Dalton]. 1738. — ALFRED; a Masque [by David Mallet]. 1751. — EDGAR AND EMMELINE; a Fairy Tale, in a Dramatic Entertainment [by Dr. John Hawkesworth]. 1761. *Six comic operas, etc., in 1 vol., 8vo, old calf, with book-plates and autographs.*
London, 1729–65

2304 OLD PLAYS. BOADICIA, by Mr. [Richard] Glover, 1753. — THE GAMESTER [by Edward Moore]. 1753. — ALONZO, [by John Home]. 1773. — THE ROMAN FATHER, by Mr. W[illiam] Whitehead. 1750. — PAPAL TYRANNY IN THE REIGN OF KING JOHN, by Colley Cibber. 1745. *Five old tragedies, in 1 vol., 8vo, half calf.* London, 1745–73

2305 OLD PLAYS. MIDAS; an English Burletta [by Kane O'Hara]. *Frontispiece.* 1768. — MISS IN HER TEENS; a Farce [by David Garrick]. 1747. — CYMON [by David Garrick]. 1778. — THE STRATFORD JUBILEE; Comedy [by Francis Gentleman]. 1769. — ARTAXERXES; an English Opera [by Thomas Augustine Arne]. (1761.) — THE APPRENTICE; a Farce, by Mr. [Arthur] Murphy. 1756. — KNOW YOUR OWN MIND; a Comedy [by Arthur Murphy]. 1778. *Seven old plays in 1 vol., 8vo, half calf.*
London, 1747–78

2306 OLD PLAYS. LOVE IN A VILLAGE; a Comic Opera [by Isaac Bickerstaffe]. 1776. — BARBAROSSA; a Tragedy [by Dr. John Brown, of Newcastle]. 1770. — THE WIDOW'D WIFE; a Comedy, by W[illiam] Kenrick. 1768. — CLEMENTINA; a Tragedy [by Hugh Kelly]. 1771. — MAN AND WIFE, or the Shakespeare Jubilee; a Comedy [by George Colman, Sen.]. 1770. *Five old plays in 1 vol., 8vo, sheep.*
London, 1768–76

2307 OLD PLAYS. THE SCHOOL FOR WIVES [by Hugh Kelly]. 1774. — FALSE DELICACY, by Hugh Kelly. 1768. — THE WOODMAN; Comic Opera, by Mr. Bate Dudley. 1791. — KNAVE, OR NOT? by Thomas Holcroft. 1798. — FALSE IMPRESSIONS, by Richard Cumberland. 1797. *Five old comedies in 1 vol., 8vo, half calf.* London, 1768–98

2308 OLD PLAYS. HEAR BOTH SIDES; a Comedy, by Thomas Holcroft. 1803. — A HOUSE TO BE SOLD; a Musical Piece, by James Cobb, Music by Michael Kelly. Second Edition. 1802. — THE MARRIAGE PROMISE; a Comedy, by John Till Allingham. Second Edition. 1803. HAMLET. *From Vol. VIII. (pp. 129–316) of an edition (Steevens's, by Reed?) of Shakespeare's plays, in which Othello is the next play. With autograph of "Wilkinson."* (1803?) — THE WAY TO GET MARRIED; a Comedy [by Thomas Morton]. *Title wanting.* (1796.) — ARRIVED AT PORTSMOUTH! an Operatic Drama, by the Author of Hartford-Bridge, etc.

[William Pearce]. 1794. — THE NEW PEERAGE; a Comedy [by Miss Harriet Lee]. *Title wanting.* (1787.) *Seven old plays in 1 vol., 8vo, half russia.* London. 1787–1803

2309 OLD WOMAN'S DUNCIAD, ETC. THE SO MUCH TALK'D OF AND EXPECTED OLD WOMAN'S DUNCIAD, or Midwife's Master Piece; containing the most Choice Collection of Humdrums and Drivellers that was ever expos'd to Public View. By Mary Midnight. With Historical, Critical, and Explanatory Notes; by Margelina Scribelinda Macularia. 1751. — A BONE FOR THE CHRONICLERS TO PICK, or a Take-off Scene from behind the Curtain; a Poem, by a Candid Observer of Men and Things. 1758. *Two very curious old tracts, in verse, with some MS. notes. Portrait of Garrick, with two of his original play-bills* (1759 *and* 1761), *and some rare humorous prints inserted.* 1 *vol., 4to, half calf.* London, 1751–58

2310 OLDYS, WILLIAM. THE BRITISH LIBRARIAN; exhibiting a Compendious Review, or Abstract, of our most Scarce, Useful, and Valuable Books, in all Sciences, as well in Manuscript as in Print; with many Characters, Historical and Critical, of the Authors, their Antagonists, etc., in a Manner never before attempted, and Useful to all Readers. With a Complete Index to the Volume. *8vo, half calf; with autograph of F. Wrangham.* London, 1738

2311 OLIN, STEPHEN, D. D. TRAVELS IN EGYPT, Arabia, Petræa, and the Holy Land. *Map, plans, and* 12 *plates.* 2 *vols., 12mo, cloth.* New York, 1843

2312 OLIPHANT, LAWRENCE. NARRATIVE OF THE EARL OF ELGIN'S MISSION TO CHINA AND JAPAN in the Years 1857, '58, '59. *Colored frontispiece and numerous wood-cuts. 8vo, cloth.* New York, 1860

2313 OLIVER, GEORGE, D. D. A DICTIONARY OF SYMBOLICAL MASONRY, including the Royal Arch Degree; according to the System prescribed by the Grand Lodge and Supreme Grand Chapter of England. *8vo, cloth.* New York, 1855

2314 OLIVER, GEORGE, D. D. THE SYMBOL OF GLORY, shewing the Object and End of Freemasonry. *Frontispiece, 8vo, cloth.* New York, 1855

2315 OLMSTED, DENISON. COMPENDIUM OF NATURAL PHILOSOPHY. *8vo, sheep.* New Haven, 1833

2316 ONCE A WEEK; an Illustrated Miscellany of Literature, Art, Science, and Popular Information. *July* 2, 1859–*Dec.* 21, 1861. 5 *vols., royal 8vo, cloth.* London, 1859–61

2317 ORDER (THE) FOR THE ADMINISTRATION OF THE HOLY COMMUNION AND OCCASIONAL OFFICES, according to the Use of the Church of England. *Elegantly printed by Whittingham, in red and black, with ornate initials and other embellishments. Folio, half brown morocco, gilt top, rough edges.* **Black letter**: *fine copy.* W. Pickering, London, 1844

This handsome volume is printed on a thick paper in the same manner as Pickering's series of reprints of the Book of Common Prayer.

2318 ORIGIN (THE) AND PROGRESS OF DESPOTISM IN THE ORIENTAL AND OTHER EMPIRES, of Africa, Europe, and America. *Small 8vo, marbled calf.* Amsterdam (London), 1764

"An anonymous publication, printed at Wilkes' private press, and published in 1773." — *Lowndes.*
There was also an edition from the same press, in French, printed in 1763, with the name of Boulanger ("Ouvrage posthume de M. Boulanger") on the title. See Nichols's "Literary Anecdotes," Vol. IX. p. 755.

2319 ORTON, JAMES. THE ENTHUSIAST, or the Straying Angel; a Poem, by James Orton ("Alastor"), Author of "Excelsior." (With the Supplement to "Excelsior.") *Handsomely printed by Whittingham. Square crown 8vo, cloth, uncut.* W. Pickering, London, 1852

2320 OSBORN, FRANCIS. WORKS. (Containing Advice to a Son, Two Parts: Political Reflections upon the Government of the Turks, etc., etc.; Historical Memoires on the Reigns of Queen Elizabeth and King James, with a Miscellany of Sundry Essays, Paradoxes, etc., etc.). *Small 8vo, half morocco, neat.* London, 1689

2321 OSBORNE, LAUGHTON. THE VISION OF RUBETA; an Epic Story of the Island of Manhattan. With Illustrations done on Stone. *8vo, half calf, neat.* Boston, 1838

2322 OTTLEY, WILLIAM YOUNG. AN INQUIRY INTO THE ORIGIN AND EARLY HISTORY OF ENGRAVING, upon Copper and Wood, with an Account of Engravers and their Works, from the Invention of Chalcography by Maso Finiguerra, to the Time of Marc' Antonio Raimondi. *Numerous plates and wood-cuts, comprising fac-similes of early, rare, and curious prints. 2 vols., 4to, half calf.* London, 1816

2323 OTWAY, THOMAS. THE WORKS OF; consisting of his Plays, Poems, and Letters. With a Sketch of his Life, enlarged from that written by Dr. Johnson. *Portrait. 2 vols., 8vo, tree calf, gilt, marbled edges.* London, 1812

2324 OUR ENGLISH HOME: its Early History and Progress; with Notes on the Introduction of Domestic Inventions. *Post 8vo, cloth, uncut.* Oxford, etc., 1860

2325 OVID. P. OVIDII NASONIS OPERA. Metamorphoses, Fasti, Tristia, Amatoria, etc. *3 vols., small 8vo, red turkey morocco, extra, tooled edges, with vellum fly-leaves.* VERY FINE COPY. Hæredes Philippi Juntæ, Florentiæ, 1522–25–28

"Il est aussi très-difficile de réunir ces 3 volumes." — *Brunet.*

2326 OVID. THE METAMORPHOSES Englished, Mythologiz'd, and Represented in Figures. An Essay to the Translation of Virgil's Æneis. By G. S. [George Sandys]. *Folio, half calf; with autograph of Rufus Choate.* London, 1640

The translation of the Æneid occupies pp. 297–303, with note "to the Reader," on previous leaf, saying that he "gave it over, even in the first entrance." "Sandys was pronounced by Dryden the best versifier of his age."—*Lowndes.*

2327 OVID. THE METAMORPHOSES, in Fifteen Books, translated by the most Eminent Hands [Dryden, Addison, Congreve, Nicholas Rowe, Gay, Ambrose Philips, Croxall, Sewell, and Garth]; adorn'd with Sculptures. *Frontispiece, portrait of the Princess of Wales by Vertue after Kneller, and* 16 *other fine plates by R. Smith, E. Kirkall, etc. Folio, half calf, neat.* J. Tonson, London, 1717

2328 OVID. MÉTAMORPHOSES; traduites en Français, avec des Remarques et des Explications Historiques, par l'Abbé Banier. Nouvelle Édition, corrigée et augmentée de la Vie d'Ovide. *With* 16 *plates after Picart, engraved by Jourdan.* 4 *vols.,* 8*vo, old marbled calf, extra, gilt edges.* Paris, An Septième (1799)

2329 OVID. DES VORTREFFLICH-LATEINISCHEN POETEN P. OVIDII NASONIS FUNFFZEHEN VERWANDLÜNGS-BÜCHER, ehemals von einem Berühmten Meister in 150 Kupfern Vorgestellet, und mit einem Kurtzen Lateinisch-und Teutchen Vers erläutert anjetzo aber denen Künstlern und der Studierenden Fugend zum Nutzen und erleich terung mit Zulänglichen Beschreib-und Erklärungen der Sämmtlichen Kupfer aufs Neue an das Licht gegeben. *Frontispiece and* 150 *designs by John Wm. Baur, engraved by* (?) *Melchior Kusell. Oblong* 4*to, half morocco, neat, marbled edges.* Nürnberg, (1685?)

2330 OVID. EPISTLES, WITH HIS AMOURS; translated into English Verse, by the most Eminent Hands. (With the Three Epistles of Aulus Sabinus, in Answer to as many of Ovid; made English, by Mr. Salusbury.) Adorn'd with Cuts. 12*mo, old calf, neat.* London, 1736

2331 OWEN, DAVID DALE. REPORT OF A GEOLOGICAL SURVEY OF WISCONSIN, IOWA, AND MINNESOTA; and incidentally of a Portion of Nebraska Territory. Made under Instructions from the United States Treasury Department; by David Dale Owen. *Colored maps, plates, and wood-cuts. Royal* 4*to, cloth.* Philadelphia, 1852

2332 OXFORD ENGLISH PRIZE ESSAYS. A New Edition, brought down to the Present Time. 5 *vols.,* 12*mo, cloth, uncut.* Talboys, Oxford, 1836

2333 OXFORD (THE) SAUSAGE; or Select Poetical Pieces, written by the most Celebrated Wits of the University of Oxford. A New Edition. *Adorned with cuts, designed by the best masters. Small* 8*vo, half morocco.* Oxford, 1804

This edition contains portrait of "Mrs. Dorothy Spreadbury, Inventress of the Oxford Sausage."
This famous *jeu d'esprit* has been attributed to Warton.

2334 PAINE, ROBERT TREAT, JUN. THE WORKS, in Verse and Prose with Notes. To which are Prefixed, Sketches of his Life, Character, and Writings [by Charles Prentiss]. *Portrait, 8vo, half morocco.*
Boston, 1812

"THOMAS PAINE, whose name was afterwards, by an act of the legislature in 1801, changed to ROBERT TREAT PAINE, was born at Taunton, in the county of Bristol, December 9th, 1773." (Biography, p. xvii.) He died November 13th, 1811.

2335 PAINE, ROBERT TROUP. MEMOIRS OF; by his Parents. Printed for Private Distribution, especially for the Classmates of the Youth. *Portrait and colored plates. 4to, morocco, gilt edges; with autograph of Martyn Paine.* PRIVATELY PRINTED: PRESENTATION COPY.
New York, 1852

The subject of this memoir, son of Professor Martyn and Mary Ann Paine, was born August 10, 1829, and died March 8, 1851. His Christian name was derived from an early friend of his parents, Col. Robert Troup, whose distinguished military, civil, and Christian life is enshrined in history." (Note, p. 2.)

2336 PAINE, THOMAS. COMMON SENSE; addressed to the Inhabitants of America, on the following Interesting Subjects: I. Of the Origin and Design of Government in General, with Concise Remarks on the English Constitution. II. Of Monarchy and Hereditary Succession. III. Thoughts on the Present State of American Affairs. IV. Of the Present Ability of America, with some Miscellaneous Reflections. A New Edition, with Several Additions in the Body of the Work; to which is added an Appendix, together with an Address to the People called Quakers. [By Thomas Paine.] N. B. The New Edition here given increases the Work upwards of one-third. *Philadelphia, printed; London, re-printed for J. Almon,* 1776.— PLAIN TRUTH; addressed to the Inhabitants of America, containing Remarks on a Late Pamphlet, entitled Common Sense: wherein are shewn, that the Scheme of Independence is Ruinous, Delusive, and Impracticable; that were the Author's Asseverations, respecting the Power of America, as Real as Nugatory, Reconciliation, on Liberal Principles, with Great Britain would be exalted Policy; and that, circumstanced as we are, Permanent Liberty and True Happiness can only be obtained by Reconciliation with that Kingdom. Written by Candidus. *Philadelphia, printed; London, re-printed for J. Almon,* 1776. *Together in 1 vol., 8vo, old calf, gilt, gilt edges.*
London, 1776

2337 PAINE, THOMAS. THE RIGHTS OF MAN; for the Use and Benefit of Mankind. *8vo, half crimson morocco.*
London, 1795

2338 PAINTER, WILLIAM. THE PALACE OF PLEASURE, beautified, adorned, and well-furnished with Pleasant Histories and Excellent Morals, very requisite for Delight and Profit; chosen and selected out of Divers Good and Commendable Authors. From the Edition printed by Thomas Marsh, 1575. Edited by Joseph Haslewood. *Wood-cuts, with half titles, on India paper. 2 vols., post 4to, olive turkey morocco, extra, gilt over carmine edges, by Riviere; uniform with* MIRROR FOR MAGISTRATES. ONLY 165 COPIES PRINTED.
London, 1813

"Best edition of a work to which Shakespeare and several of our old dramatists were greatly indebted for their Plots." — *Lowndes.*

2339 PAINTER, WILLIAM. ANOTHER COPY: *the same. 2 vols., citron morocco, extra, gilt edges.* London, 1813

2340 PALEY, WILLIAM, D. D. NATURAL THEOLOGY; or, Evidences of the Existence and Attributes of the Deity, collected from the Appearances of Nature. *12mo, sheep.*
Albany, 1803

2341 PALEY, WILLIAM, D. D. PRINCIPLES OF MORAL AND POLITICAL PHILOSOPHY. The Fourteenth Edition. *2 vols., 8vo, calf, yellow edges.* R. Faulder, London, 1803

2842 PALEY, WILLIAM, D. D. ANOTHER COPY: *thick 18mo, boards.* Edinburgh, 1823

2343 PALEY, WILLIAM, D. D. WORKS; consisting of Evidences of Christianity, Moral and Political Philosophy, Natural Theology, and Horæ Paulinæ. Complete in One Volume. *Portrait. 8vo, boards, uncut.*
London, 1835

2344 PALFREY, JOHN GORHAM. HISTORY OF NEW ENGLAND, during the Stuart Dynasty. *Maps, etc., including photo-lithograph fac-simile of Smith's Map of New England,* 1614, *on India paper. 3 vols., imperial 8vo, cloth, rough edges.* LARGE PAPER: *only* 100 *copies printed.* Boston, 1865

2345 PALFREY, SARAH H. HERMAN, or YOUNG KNIGHTHOOD. *2 vols., 12mo, cloth.* Boston, 1866

2346 PALGRAVE, FRANCIS TURNER. THE GOLDEN TREASURY of the Best Songs and Lyrical Poems in the English Language; selected and arranged, with Notes. *Foolscap 8vo, cloth, gilt top.* Cambridge (Mass.), 1863

2347 PALLISER, MRS. BURY. HISTORY OF LACE. *Portraits and numerous illustrations of the most elaborate and beautiful patterns, many of which are in colors. 8vo, cloth, gilt edges.*
London, 1865

2348 PALMER, JOHN WILLIAMSON, M. D. FOLK SONGS; selected and edited by. Illustrated from Original Designs (and with Fac-simile Autograph Poems). *Imperial 8vo, smooth olive morocco, very neat, gilt edges.* LARGE PAPER.
New York, 1861

2349 PALMER, JOSEPH, M. D. NECROLOGY OF ALUMNI OF HARVARD COLLEGE, 1851–52 to 1862–63. *Royal 8vo, cloth, uncut.* Boston, 1864

2350 PAMPHLETS. A VINDICATION OF MR. RANDOLPH'S RESIGNATION. *Phil.*, 1795. — The Speech of Mr. Ames, April 28, 1796 (upon the Treaty between the United States and Great Britain). *Boston* (1796). — A Letter to General Hamilton, occasioned by his Letter to President Adams, by a Federalist. (Signed "Aristides.") — Observations on Certain Documents, etc., in which the charge of Speculation against Alexander Hamilton, is fully refuted; written by himself. *Phil.*, 1797. — Letters from his Excellency General Washington, to Arthur Young, Esq., F. R. S.; containing an Account of his Husbandry, with a Map of his Farm, his Opinions on Various Questions in Agriculture, etc., etc. *London*, 1801. — The Life of Thomas Paine, etc., with a Defense of his Writings; by Francis Oldys. *Boston*, 1796. — A View of the Political Conduct of Aaron Burr, Esq., by the Author of the "Narrative." *New York*, 1802. — An Address to the People of the United States, on the Subject of the Report of a Committee of the Treasury, by Oliver Wolcott. *Boston*, 1802. *Eight pamphlets in 1 vol., 8vo, half sheep.* Philadelphia, etc., 1795–1802

2351 PAMPHLETS. AN ORATION delivered (July 4, 1804), by John Pickering, Jun. *Salem*, 1804. — An Oration delivered (July 4, 1804) at Salem, by Joseph Story, Esq. *Salem*, 1804. — An Address delivered (July 4, 1806) by Major Samuel Swett. *Boston*, 1806. — An Oration delivered (July 4, 1806) by Henry Alexander S. Dearborn. *Salem*, 1806. — An Oration delivered (July 4, 1805), by Ichabod Nichols. *Salem*, 1805. — An Oration pronounced July 4, 1808, by Andrew Ritchie, Jun., Esq. (*Boston*), 1808. — An Oration delivered (July 4, 1810), by Joseph E. Sprague. (*Salem*), 1810. — Eulogy on Gen. Alexander Hamilton, July 26, by Hon. Harrison G. Otis, Esq. *Boston*, 1804. — A Poem on the Restoration of Learning in the East, which obtained Mr. Buchanan's Prize, by Charles Grant, Esq. *Salem*, 1807. — Commencement, a Poem, or rather Commencement of a Poem, recited before the Phi Beta Kappa Society, Cambridge, Aug. 29, 1811, by a Brother. *Salem*, 1811. — Letter to the Hon. Harrison Gray Otis, on the Present State of our National Affairs, with Remarks upon Mr. Pickering's Letter to the Governor, by John Quincy Adams. *Boston*, 1808. — Interesting Correspondence between Governour Sullivan and Col. Pickering, in which the latter vindicates himself against the Groundless Charges and Insinuations made by the Governour and others. *Boston*, 1808. — A Letter from the Hon. Timothy Pickering, exhibiting to his Constituents a View of the Imminent Danger of an Unnecessary and Ruinous War. *Boston,* 1808. — Letter from Alexander Hamilton, concerning the Public Conduct and Character of John Adams, Esq., written in the Year 1800. *Boston,* 1809. — Speech of the Hon. Josiah Quincy, in Relation to Maritime Protection. — A Letter to a Great Character (John Adams), printed and published for the Public, 1811. — A Correct Statement of the Whole Preliminary Controversy between Tho. O. Selfridge and Benj. Austin, also a Brief Account of the Catastrophe in State Street, Boston, on the 4th August, 1806, with some Remarks, by Tho. O. Selfridge. *Charlestown,* 1807. — A Sermon preached July 15, 1777, etc. (Caution recommended in the Application and Use of Scripture Language), by William Paley, M. A., etc. *Cambridge (Mass.),* 1809. — A Sermon preached in Boston, May 31, 1810, by Eliphalet Porter, D. D. *Boston,* 1810. A Discourse delivered at Reading, North Parish, May 19, 1811, in which Warnings of Death are considered as Excitements to Review Life, by Eliab Stone. *Boston,* 1811. — Address delivered (before the Lodges of St. John, St. Peter, and St. Mark, Newburyport) on the Anniversary Festival of St. John the Baptist, by Joseph Dana. *Newburyport,* 1807. — An Oration delivered (before Philanthropic Lodge, Marblehead, June 24, 5810) by Brother Edward Turner, to which is prefixed an Introductory Address by Brother Ralph H. French, R. W. P. M. *Salem,* 1810. — An Address to the M. W. Grand Lodge of Massachusetts, by Brother Isaiah Thomas, Esq., P. G. M., at the Close of the Constitutional Term as Grand Master, A. L. 5805. *Boston,* 1811. — An Address delivered before King Solomon's Lodge, Charlestown, June 24, A. L. 5811, by John Lothrop, A. M. *Boston,* 5811. — Thoughts on the Cherubimical Mystery, or an Attempt to prove that the Cherubims were Emblems of Salvation by the Blood of Jesus, by James Relly. *Boston,* 1808. — The Gospel Visitant, for September, 1811. *Twenty-five pamphlets in* 1 *vol.,* 8*vo, half sheep.* Salem, etc., 1804–11

2352 PANTOLOGIA: A NEW CYCLOPÆDIA, comprehending a Complete Series of Essays, Treatises, and Systems, alphabetically arranged; with a General Dictionary of Arts, Sciences, and Words: the Whole presenting a Distinct Survey of Human Genius, Learning, and Industry. By John Mason Good, Esq., F. R. S., etc.; Olinthus Gregory, LL. D., etc.; and Mr. Newton Bosworth; assisted by other Gentlemen of Eminence, in Different Departments of Literature. *Illustrated with elegant engravings, those on Natural History being from original drawings by Edwards and others, and beautifully coloured after nature.* 12 *vols., royal* 8*vo, half russia, neat, red edges.* London, 1813

2353 PARADYSE (THE) OF DAYNTIE DEVISES, aptly furnished with Sundry Pithie & Learned Inventions; devised and written, for the most Part, by M. Edwards, sometimes of her Majesties Chappel; the Rest, by Sundry Learned Gentlemen, both of Honour and Worshippe, viz. S. Barnarde, Jasper Heywood, E. O., F. K., L. Vaux, M. Bewe, D. S., R. Hill, M. Yloop, with others. Imprinted at London, by Henry Disle, dwellyng in Paules Churchyard, at the South-west Doore of Saint Paules Church, and are there to be solde. *4to, half morocco, neat, gilt edges.* 1576

This is a very neatly written transcript from the *original edition*, and has on a fly-leaf this note: "This is in the hand of my father, Mr. T. Rodd.—*Thos. Rodd.*"

Beloe says of this work, "I hardly know where a copy is to be found. It is not in the Museum. I have never seen a copy, but one in manuscript, lent me by Mr. Douce."

2354 PARDOE, JULIA. THE BEAUTIES OF THE BOSPHORUS: Illustrated in a Series of Views of Constantinople and its Environs, from Original Drawings by W. H. Bartlett. *Portraits, map, and 80 plates. 4to, cloth.* London, s. a.

2355 PARDON, GEORGE FREDERICK. TALES FROM THE OPERAS. *12mo, cloth.* New York, 1864

2356 PARENT-DUCHÂTELET, ALEXIS JEAN BAPTISTE. DE LA PROSTITUTION DANS LA VILLE DE PARIS, considérée sous le Rapport de l'Hygiène Publique, de la Morale, et de l'Administration; Ouvrage appuyé de Documens Statistiques puisés dans les Archives de la Préfecture de Police. Avec Cartes et Tableaux; Précédée d'une Notice Historique sur la Vie et les Ouvrages de l'Auteur, par Fr. Leuret. *2 vols., crown 8vo, half morocco.* Paris, 1836

2357 PARIS. VIEWS OF PARIS AND ENVIRONS. *A collection of 29 large colored views of buildings and places of interest in or near Paris, lithographed by Lemercier, from drawings by J. B. and Jules Arnout, etc. Without title. 1 vol., oblong folio, half morocco.* (Paris, 1845 ?)

2358 PARKER, JOHN HENRY. A GLOSSARY OF TERMS used in Grecian, Roman, Italian, and Gothic Architecture. The Fourth Edition, enlarged. Exemplified by Eleven Hundred Wood-cuts. *2 vols., royal 8vo, cloth, gilt tops.* Oxford, 1845

2359 PARKER, REV. THEODORE. THE TRIAL OF, for the "Misdemeanor" of a Speech in Faneuil Hall against Kidnapping, before the Circuit Court of the United States, at Boston, April 3, 1855. With the Defence. *Royal 8vo, cloth; with autograph of Rufus Choate.* Published for the Author, Boston, 1855

2360 PARKER, REV. THEODORE. EXPERIENCE AS A MINISTER, with some Account of his Early Life and Education for the Ministry. *12mo, cloth.* Boston, 1859

2361 PARKER, Rev. Theodore. Life and Correspondence of. By John Weiss. *Portraits, wood-cuts, etc., 2 vols., 8vo, cloth, uncut.* London, 1863

2362 PARKES, Mrs. William. Domestic Duties, or Instructions to Young Married Ladies, on the Management of their Households and the Regulation of their Conduct in the Various Relations and Duties of Married Life. Second Edition. *12mo, boards, rough edges.* London, 1825

2363 PARKMAN, Francis. History of the Conspiracy of Pontiac, and the War of the North American Tribes against the English Colonies after the Conquest of Canada. *8vo, calf, gilt, marbled edges.* Boston, 1855

2364 PARKMAN, Francis. Pioneers of France in the New World. *Portrait of Menendez and map. Crown 8vo, cloth, uncut.* Boston, 1865

2365 PARKMAN, Francis. The Jesuits in North America, in the Seventeenth Century. *Crown 8vo, cloth.* Boston, 1867

2366 PARR, Samuel. The Works of; with Memoirs of his Life and Writings, and a Selection from his Correspondence, by John Johnstone, M. D. *Portraits. 8 vols., thick royal 8vo, half morocco, gilt tops, rough edges.* Large paper. London, 1828

2367 PARRY, James. The True Anti-Pamela, or Memoirs of Mr. James Parry, late Organist of Ross in Herefordshire; in which are inserted, his Amours with the Celebrated Miss —— of Monmouthshire. Written by Himself. In Two Parts complete: Part I. Memoirs of His Life and Amours. Part II. A Journal of his Adventures in a Cruise against the Spaniards, on board the Revenge Privateer Capt. Wimble; with his Genuine Letters of Love and Gallantry. The Second Edition, with Additions. *Portrait and plate. 2 vols. in 1, 12mo, half morocco, neat.* London, 1770

2368 PARRY, Rev. J. D. The Legendary Cabinet: a Collection of British National Ballads, Ancient and Modern, from the Best Authorities; with Notes and Illustrations. *Frontispiece. Crown 8vo, half green morocco, gilt top.* London, 1829

2369 PARSONS, James, M. D. Remains of Japhet, being Historical Enquiries into the Affinity and Origin of the European Languages. *4to, half russia.* London, 1767

2370 PARSONS, Theophilus. Memoir of Theophilus Parsons, Chief Justice of the Supreme Judicial Court of Massachusetts; with Notices of some of his Contemporaries. By his Son. *Portrait. Crown 8vo, cloth, uncut.* Boston, 1859

2371 PARSONS, THEOPHILUS. AN ORATION DELIVERED ON THE FOURTH OF JULY, 1861, before the Municipal Authorities of the City of Boston. With an Appendix. *8vo, cloth.* Boston, 1861

2372 PARSONS, THEOPHILUS. DEUS HOMO: GOD-MAN. *Crown 8vo, cloth, gilt top.* Chicago, 1867

2373 PARSONS, WILLIAM. TRAVELLING RECREATIONS. 2 *vols., small 12mo, half red morocco, gilt edges.* London, 1807

2374 PARTON, JAMES. LIFE OF ANDREW JACKSON. *Portraits, etc. 3 vols., royal 8vo, half calf, extra, marbled edges.* New York, 1860

2375 PARTON, JAMES. GENERAL BUTLER IN NEW ORLEANS: History of the Administration of the Department of the Gulf in the Year 1862; with an Account of the Capture of New Orleans, and a Sketch of the Previous Career of the General, Civil and Military. *Thick 12mo, cloth.* New York, 1864

2376 PARTON, JAMES. LIFE AND TIMES OF BENJAMIN FRANKLIN. *Printed on a tinted paper, with the portraits on India paper. 2 vols., 4to, cloth, uncut.* LARGE PAPER: 100 *copies printed for E. French.* Mason Brothers, New York, 1865

2377 PARTON, JAMES. THE HUMOROUS POETRY OF THE ENGLISH LANGUAGE, from Chaucer to Saxe: Narratives, Satires, Enigmas, Burlesques, Parodies, Travesties, Epigrams, Epitaphs, Translations; including the most celebrated Comic Poems of the Anti-Jacobin, Rejected Addresses, the Ingoldsby Legends, Blackwood's Magazine, Bentley's Miscellany, and Punch. With more than Two Hundred Epigrams, etc. With Notes, Explanatory and Biographical. *Portraits, 12mo, cloth.* Boston, 1867

2378 PASHA (THE) PAPERS: EPISTLES OF MOHAMMED PASHA, REAR ADMIRAL OF THE TURKISH NAVY, written from New York to his Friend Abel Ben Hassen; translated into Anglo-American from the Original Manuscript. *12mo, cloth.* New York, 1859

2379 PASS, CRISPIN DE. COMPENDIUM OPERUM VIRGILIANORUM, ETC. Miroer des Œuvres de l'Excellent Poëte Virgile, etc. *A collection of 24 plates (from his work), without title, mounted in a 4to volume, vellum.* (Ultrajecti-Batavorum, 1612)

2380 PASSIONS (THE) PERSONIFY'D. In Familiar Fables (in Verse). *Frontispiece and 12 plates by J. Miller, 8vo, old calf.* London, (cir. 1760)

2381 PASTORET, EMMANUEL CLAUDE PIERRE, MARQUIS DE. Moyse, considéré comme Législateur et comme Moraliste. *8vo, old mottled calf, gilt, marbled edges.* Paris, 1788

2382 PATTERSON, John. Memoir of Joseph Train: the Antiquarian Correspondent of Sir Walter Scott. *Foolscap, 8vo, cloth, uncut.* Glasgow, 1857

2383 PAXTON, Sir Joseph; and Joseph Harrison. The Horticultural Register, and General Magazine. *July,* 1831–*June,* 1833. *Plan for a "National Garden," colored plates, and wood-cuts.* 2 *vols., half green morocco.* London and Sheffield, 1831–33

2384 PEARCE, Joseph, Jun. Violins and Violin Makers: Biographical Dictionary of the great Italian Artistes, their Followers and Imitators, to the Present Time; with Essays on Important Subjects connected with the Violin. 16*mo, cloth.* Sheffield and London, 1866

2385 PECK, Rev. Francis. Desiderata Curiosa; or a Collection of Divers Scarce and Curious Pieces relating chiefly to Matters of English History; consisting of Choice Tracts, Memoirs, Letters, Wills, Epitaphs, etc., transcribed, many of them, from the Originals themselves, and the rest, from Divers Antient MS. Copies, or the MS. Collections of Sundry Famous Antiquaries and other Eminent Persons, both of the Last and Present Age: the Whole, as near as possible, digested into an Order of Time, and illustrated with Ample Notes, Contents, Additional Discourses, and a Complete Index. By Francis Peck, M. A., etc. A New Edition, greatly corrected; with some Memoirs of the Life of Mr. Peck [by T. Evans]. *Portrait and plates.* 2 *vols. in* 1 *vol.,* 4*to, old mottled calf, gilt, back cracked. Book-plate of Charles Purton Cooper, Esq.* London, 1779

2386 PECKE, Thomas. Parnassi Puerperium, or some Well-Wishes to Ingenuity, in the Translation of Six Hundred of Owen's Epigrams; Martial de Spectaculis, or Rarities to be seen in Rome; and the most Select in Sir Tho. More. To which is annext a Century of Heroick Epigrams, Sixty whereof concern the Twelve Cæsars, and the Forty remaining, Several Deserving Persons. By the Author of that celebrated Eligie upon Cleeveland, Tho. Pecke, Gent. *Small 8vo, claret morocco, extra, gilt edges, by Murton.* Printed by J. Cottrel, for Tho. Bassett, London, 1659

2387 PEELE, George. The Works of; collected and edited, with some Account of his Life and Writings, by the Rev. Alexander Dyce, B. A. Second Edition, with Additions. *Fac-simile of handwriting.* 3 *vols., crown 8vo, crimson turkey morocco, gilt edges; with MS. notes. Uniform with* Greene *and* Webster. Only 250 copies printed. W. Pickering, London, 1829–39

"Peele and Marlowe were the contemporaries of Shakespeare; both had exquisite feelings for poetry, and excelled in description, to which the former lent beauty, the latter sublimity." — *Gifford.*

2388 PEIRCE, BENJAMIN. A HISTORY OF HARVARD UNIVERSITY, from its Foundation in the Year 1636, to the Period of the American Revolution. [Edited by John Pickering.] *Views. 8vo, boards, uncut.* Cambridge, 1833

2389 PELET DE LA LOZÈRE, JEAN, COMTE. NAPOLEON IN COUNCIL; or, the Opinions delivered by Bonaparte in the Council of State. Translated from the French of Baron Pelet (de la Lozère), by Captain Basil Hall, R. N. *12mo, half calf.* Edinburgh, 1837

2390 PELHAM, CAVENDISH. THE WORLD; or, the Present State of the Universe; being a General and Complete Collection of Modern Voyages and Travels. Selected, arranged, and digested, from the Narratives of the Latest and most Authentic Travellers and Navigators. *Embellished with upwards of one hundred and thirty beautiful engravings. 2 vols., 4to, calf, gilt.* London, 1806-08

Engravings by A. W. Warren, etc.

2391 PELLETAN, EUGÈNE. LE DROIT DE PARLER: Lettre à M. Imhaus. *8vo, pp. 46, paper.* Paris, 1862

2392 PEMAQUID PAPERS. PAPERS RELATING TO PEMAQUID AND PARTS ADJACENT in the Present State of Maine, known as Cornwall County, when under the Colony of New-York; compiled from Official Records in the Office of the Secretary of State at Albany, N. Y., by Franklin B. Hough. *8vo, paper, rough edges.* Albany, 1856

2393 PENHALLOW, SAMUEL. THE HISTORY OF THE WARS OF NEW-ENGLAND WITH THE EASTERN INDIANS; or, a Narrative of their continued Perfidy and Cruelty, from the 10th of August, 1703, to the Peace renewed 13th of July, 1713; and from the 25th of July, 1722, to their Submission, 15th December, 1725, which was ratified August 5th, 1726. By Samuel Penhallow, Esq. (With a Memoir by Nathaniel Adams; Notes; and an Appendix, comprising, "Gardener's Pequot Warres," and "The Gospel in New England.") *Reprinted from the Boston edition of* 1726. *Foolscap 4to, cloth.* ONLY 150 COPIES PRINTED. Cincinnati, 1859

2394 PENN, GRANVILLE. A COMPARATIVE ESTIMATE OF THE MINERAL AND MOSAICAL GEOLOGIES. Second Edition. *2 vols., 8vo, boards.* London, 1825

2395 PENN, WILLIAM. THE SELECT WORKS OF (with the Author's Life). The Third Edition. *5 vols., 8vo, old sprinkled calf, gilt.* London, 1782

2396 PENNA, AGOSTINO. VIAGGIO PITTORICO DELLA VILLA ADRIANA (DI TIVOLI), composto di Vedute disegnate dal Vero ed incise da Agostino Penna; con una Breve Descrizione di Ciascum Monumento. *Plan and 137 fine plates. 2 vols., oblong 4to, half morocco, yellow edges.* Roma, 1831-33

2397 PENNANT, THOMAS. THE BRITISH ZOOLOGY: Class I. Quadrupeds. II. Birds. Published under the Inspection of the Cymmrodorian Society, instituted for the Promoting Useful Charities, and the Knowledge of Nature, among the Descendants of the Ancient Britons. *Illustrated with one hundred and seven copper plates. Imperial folio, half russia, rough edges.* ORIGINAL EDITION: COLORED PLATES. London, 1766

This edition was "Printed by J. and J. March on Tower-Hill, for the Society: and Sold for the Benefit of the British Charity-School on Clerkenwell Green." This copy contains 133 plates, — 11 of quadrupeds and 122 of birds, — with 162 pages (numbered) of letter-press, besides 7 preliminary leaves (unnumbered), including title, dedication, preface, etc., and an index of 2 leaves. The numerous figures of birds are chiefly as large as life.

2398 PENNANT, THOMAS. BRITISH ZOOLOGY. Fourth Edition. *Choice impressions of the numerous plates. 4 vols., post 4to, old mottled calf, gilt, green edges; with book-plate of Charles Brooke. Back of Vol. I. broken, but otherwise a fine copy.* Warrington and London, 1776–77

2399 PENNANT, THOMAS. ARCTIC ZOOLOGY. *Fine large plates. 2 vols., post 4to, old marbled calf, gilt, yellow edges.* London, 1784–85

"The works of this celebrated traveller, naturalist, and antiquary are much esteemed." — *Lowndes.*

2400 PENNY (THE) CYCLOPÆDIA OF THE SOCIETY FOR THE DIFFUSION OF USEFUL KNOWLEDGE. *Many thousand woodcuts. 27 vols. in 14, imperial 8vo, half morocco, neat.* ORIGINAL EDITION. London, 1833–43

2401 PENNY (THE) MAGAZINE OF THE SOCIETY FOR THE DIFFUSION OF USEFUL KNOWLEDGE. *March* 31, 1832–*December* 31, 1845. *Both series complete. Numerous woodcuts. 9 vols., imperial 8vo; 5 vols., 8vo; half calf.* London, 1832–45

2402 PENNY MAGAZINE. DUPLICATES: *Vols. I.–III. of the first series. 3 vols., imperial 8vo, half calf.* London, 1832–34

2403 PEPYS, SAMUEL. DIARY AND CORRESPONDENCE OF SAMUEL PEPYS, F. R. S., Secretary to the Admiralty in the Reigns of Charles II. and James II.; from the Original Shorthand MS. With a Life and Notes, by Richard Lord Braybrooke. The Sixth Edition. *Portraits, etc. 4 vols., post 8vo, cloth, uncut.* London, 1858

2404 PERCY SOCIETY'S PUBLICATIONS. EARLY ENGLISH POETRY, BALLADS, AND POPULAR LITERATURE OF THE MIDDLE AGES; edited from Original Manuscripts and Scarce Publications. COMPLETE, *with a manuscript table of contents, and index of authors, bound in the first and last volumes. 94 parts in 30 vols., crown 8vo, crimson morocco, gilt edges.* ONLY 250 COMPLETE SETS. London, 1840–52

This fine set is from the library of the late Mr. Hosmer, who was a subscriber, and as only 250 copies of the later tracts were printed, a complete set is now extremely difficult to make up. For contents see Bohn's "Lowndes," Appendix, pp. 59-65.

2405 PERCY, THOMAS, D. D. A KEY TO THE NEW TESTAMENT; giving an Account of the Several Books, their Contents, their Authors, and of the Times, Places, and Occasions on which they were respectively written. From the Last London Edition. 12*mo, sheep.* Baltimore, 1822

2406 PERKINS, THOMAS HANDASYD. MEMOIR OF; containing Extracts from his Diaries and Letters, with an Appendix. By Thomas G. Cary. *Portrait.* 8*vo, cloth.* Boston, 1856

2407 PERRY, COMMODORE MATTHEW CALBRAITH. NARRATIVE OF THE EXPEDITION OF AN AMERICAN SQUADRON TO THE CHINA SEAS AND JAPAN, performed in the Years 1852, 1853, and 1854, under the Command of Commodore M. C. Perry, United States Navy; compiled from the Original Notes and Journals of Commodore Perry and his Officers, at his Request, and under his Supervision, by Francis L. Hawks, D. D. With Numerous Illustrations. (Vol. III., containing Observations on the Zodiacal Light, by Rev. George Jones, A. M. *Many of the plates finely colored.* 3 *vols.*, 4*to, cloth.* Washington, 1856

2408 PETRIE, HENRY: and REV. JOHN SHARPE. MONUMENTA HISTORICA BRITANNICA, or Materials for the History of Britain from the Earliest Period. Prepared, and illustrated with Notes, by the late Henry Petrie, Esq., F. S. A., Keeper of the Records in the Tower of London; assisted by the Rev. John Sharpe, B. A. *Vol. I., extending to the Norman Conquest, with engraved dedication, map, and 27 plates of old Saxon coins, fac-similes of charters, etc. Thick folio, half morocco, uncut.*
Published by Command of her Majesty, London, 1848

This work, containing all the important incidents of the Saxon period of English history, exrtacted from the chronicles of that per od, was undertaken at the command of George IV. The volume was not finished by Mr. Petrie, but was completed, since his death, and the prefatory matter added by Mr. Thomas Duffus Hardy.

2409 PETRONIUS, "ARBITER." THE SATYRICAL WORKS OF, in Prose and Verse; in Three Parts. Together with his Life and Character, written by Mons. St. Evremont; and a Key to the Satyr, by a Person of Quality. Made English by Mr. Wilson, Mr. Burnaby, Mr Blount, Mr. Tho. Brown, Capt. Ayloff, and several others. To which is added, the Charms of Liberty; a Poem, by the late Duke of D——. *Plates.* 8*vo, old calf.* London, 1708

2410 PETRONIUS, "ARBITER." THE WORKS OF, in Prose and Verse; in Three Parts. With a Critical Preface in Defence of the Author, and his Life, and Character, written by Mons. St. Evremont; and a Key to the Satyres, by a Person of Quality. The Second Edition, adorn'd with Cuts. Made English by Mr. Wilson, etc. [as above]. To which is prefix'd, the Charms of Liberty; a Poem, by the late Duke of Devonshire. *8vo, old calf, gilt.* London, 1710

This copy has a frontispiece by Vander Gucht, which is wanting in the one above.

2411 PETTIGREW, THOMAS JOSEPH. BIBLIOTHECA SUSSEXIANA: a Descriptive Catalogue, accompanied by Historical and Biographical Notices, of the Manuscripts and Printed Books contained in the Library of his Royal Highness the Duke of Sussex, in Kensington Palace. By Thomas Joseph Pettigrew, F. R. S., Librarian to the Duke of Sussex. *Portrait, view of library (inserted in second volume), and 19 plates. Describes 298 MSS. and above 1,500 printed editions of the Scriptures and parts thereof. 2 vols. (first volume in two parts), imperial 8vo, half olive morocco, uncut.* ONLY 500 COPIES PRINTED. London, 1827–39

2412 PEZRON, PAUL. THE ANTIQUITIES OF NATIONS, more particularly of the Celtæ or Gauls, taken to be originally the same People as our Ancient Britons; containing great Variety of Historical, Chronological, and Etymological Discoveries, many of them unknown both to the Greeks and Romans. Englished by Mr. Jones. *8vo, old calf, gilt; with book-plates of Elizabeth Whitfield, 1704, and Fullerton of Carstairs.* London, 1706

2413 PHALARIS. THE EPISTLES OF, translated from the Greek; to which are added, some Select Epistles of the most Eminent Greek Writers. By Thomas Francklin, M. A. *Frontispiece, by Grignion, after Worlidge. Royal 8vo, old calf, extra, marbled edges; back cracked. Old book-plate of Robert Ballard, Southampton.* LARGE PAPER: *clean copy.* R. Francklin, London, 1749

2414 PHILBRICK, JOHN D. THE AMERICAN UNION SPEAKER; with Introductory Remarks on Elocution, and Explanatory Notes. *8vo, half calf, extra, marbled edges.* Boston, 1865

2415 PHILES, GEORGE P. THE PHILOBIBLION, a Monthly Bibliographical Journal; containing Critical Notices of, and Extracts from, Rare, Curious, and Valuable Old Books. *Printed on India paper. Nos. 1–24 (Dec. 1861–Dec. 1863). 2 vols., unbound.* New York, 1862–63

No number was issued for December, 1862.

2416 PHILIPPS, J. T. THE HISTORY OF THE TWO ILLUSTRIOUS BROTHERS, Princes of Saxony; viz., their Serene Highnesses Ernestus the Pious, First Duke of Sax-Gotha, and Bernard the Great, Duke of Sax-Weimar, who won the Battle of Lutzen, after the Death of the Great Gustavus

Adolphus, King of Sweden: together with a Short History of his Serene Highness John William, Prince of Gotha, who was killed at the Siege of Toulon, in 1707. To which are added, Genealogical Tables of the Illustrious House of Sax-Gotha, shewing its Relation to all the Royal and Sovereign Families in Europe. *Portrait (inserted) of "Bernhard Duc de Saxe Weymar, etc., etc.," by P. de Jode (Junior). 8vo, old calf, gilt, red edges.* London, 1740

2417 PHILLIPS, GEORGE. RUDIMENTS OF CURVILINEAR DESIGN, illustrated by a Series of Plates in Various Styles of Ancient and Modern Ornament; with Explanatory Text in Aid of Selections applicable to the Arts and Manufactures. *Numerous embellishments in the text and 48 large and fine plates, including frontispiece. Imperial folio, cloth.* London, (1840?)

2418 PHILLIPS, SIR RICHARD. A COLLECTION OF MODERN AND CONTEMPORARY VOYAGES AND TRAVELS; containing, I. Translations from Foreign Languages, of Voyages and Travels never before translated. II. Original Voyages and Travels never before published. III. Analysis of New Voyages and Travels published in England. *Numerous maps and plates, some of which are colored. 11 vols., 8vo, half calf, neat.* R. Phillips, London, 1805–10

2419 PHILOSOPHICAL (A) HISTORICAL AND MORAL ESSAY ON OLD MAIDS; by a Friend to the Sisterhood. *3 vols., small 8vo, half calf.* T. Cadell, London, 1785

2420 PHILOSTRATUS. LES IMAGES, OU TABLEAUX DE PLATTE PEINTURE DES DEUX PHILOSTRATES, Sophistes Grecs, et les Statues de Callistrate; mis en François, par Blaise de Vigenère, Bourbonnois: enrichis d'Arguments et Annotations, reveus et corrigez sur l'Original, par un Docte Personnage de ce Temps en la Langue Grecque; et représentez en Taille Douce en cette Nouvelle Édition, avec des Épigrammes sur chacun d'Iceux, par Artus Thomas Sieur d'Embry. *Frontispiece and 68 plates engraved by Jaspar Isac, L. Gaultier, and T. de Leu. Royal folio, old red morocco, extra, gilt edges.* LARGE PAPER: *ruled throughout with red lines.* A. L'Angelier, Paris, 1615

2421 PHILOSTRATUS. ANOTHER COPY: *the same; with the 69 plates, and each page ruled in same manner. Royal folio, old red morocco, very neat, gilt edges.* Paris, 1615

2422 PHOTOGRAPHS. BRITISH MUSEUM PHOTOGRAPHS. *A series of 80 fine photographs of busts in the British Museum, mounted on card-board, $23\frac{1}{2} \times 17\frac{1}{2}$ inches, and enclosed in a strong portfolio, half morocco, gilt label on side, leather straps. Photographed by R. Fenton, and published by the Trustees of the British Museum.* (London), s. a.

2423 PHOTOGRAPHS. THE RAFFAELLE CARTOONS. I. Paul Preaching at Athens (28 × 36 inches). II. Christ's Charge to Peter ($28\frac{1}{2}$ × 44 inches). III. The Death of Ananias (28 × 44 inches). IV. Elymas the Sorcerer Struck with Blindness (28 × 36 inches). V. The Miraculous Draught of Fishes (28 × 36 inches). VI. The Sacrifice at Lystra (28 × 45 inches). VII. Peter and John Healing the Lame Man at the Beautiful Gate of the Temple (28 × 44 inches). *Seven fine large photographs mounted on card-board, 36 × 52 inches, and inclosed in a portfolio. Photographed by Caldesi & Montecchi, and published by P. & D. Colnaghi & Co., London. With the "Analysis," published by Charles B. Norton, New York. 12mo, cloth.* London, 1858; New York, 1860

2424 PHOTOGRAPHS. YO-SEMITE VALLEY: Photographic Views of the Falls and Valley of Yo-Semite, in Mariposa County, California; executed by C. E. Watkins, San Francisco. *Title, map, and 30 beautiful views, $16\frac{1}{2}$ × $20\frac{1}{2}$ inches, unmounted.* San Francisco, 1863

2425 PHOTOGRAPHS. COLLECTION OF PHOTOGRAPHS OF CELEBRATED PAINTINGS, Views of Noted Places, etc., etc. *Portfolio containing nearly 100 fine photographs, various sizes, mounted.*

2426 PICKERING, JOHN. A VOCABULARY, or Collection of Words and Phrases which have been supposed to be Peculiar to the United States of America; to which is prefixed an Essay on the Present State of the English Language in the United States. *8vo, half calf.* Boston, 1816

2427 PICKERING, TIMOTHY. A REVIEW OF THE CORRESPONDENCE between the Hon. John Adams, late President of the United States, and the late William Cunningham, Esq., beginning in 1803, and ending in 1812. Second Edition. *8vo, paper, rough edges.* Salem, 1824

2428 PICTORIAL (THE) BOOK OF ANCIENT BALLAD POETRY OF GREAT BRITAIN, Historical, Traditional, and Romantic; to which are added, a Selection of Modern Imitations, and some Translations. Edited by J. S. Moore, Esq. A New Edition, revised, and chronologically arranged, with Additions, Introductory Notices, a Glossary, etc., etc. *Thick 8vo, half morocco. gilt top, uncut.* London, 1853

2429 PICTORIAL (THE) HISTORY OF ENGLAND, being a History of the People, as well as a History of the Kingdom; illustrated with Many Hundred Wood-Engravings. A New Edition, revised and extended. *Fine colored maps in addition to the wood-cuts. 7 vols., thick imperial 8vo, cloth, uncut.* W. & R. Chambers, London, 1855–58

The "Pictorial History of England" (by G. L. Craik and C. Macfarlane), and the "History of the Thirty Years' Peace" (by Harriet Martineau), published by Charles Knight (1840, etc.) in 9 vols., are both incorporated in this work.

2430 PICTURESQUE (A) TOUR OF THE ENGLISH LAKES; containing a Description of the most Romantic Scenery of Cumberland, Westmoreland, and Lancashire, with Accounts of Antient and Modern Manners and Customs, and Elucidations of the History and Antiquities of that Part of the Country, etc., etc. Illustrated with 48 Coloured Views, drawn by Messrs. T. H. Fielding and J. Walton, during a Two Years' Residence among the Lakes. *4to, half red morocco, red paper sides, rough edges.*
R. Ackermann, London, 1821

2431 PICTURES OF THE FRENCH: a Series of Literary and Graphic Delineations of French Character; by Jules Janin, Balzac, Cormenin, and other Celebrated French Authors; with upwards of Two Hundred and Thirty Engravings, drawn on the Wood by Gavarni, H. Monnier, and Meissonier; and engraved by Lavielle, etc. INDIA PROOFS *of the cuts. Royal 8vo, cloth, uncut.*
W. S. Orr & Co., London, 1840

2432 PIERSON, A. T. C. TRADITIONS OF FREEMASONRY and its Coincidences with the Ancient Mysteries. *Frontispiece. 12mo, cloth.* New York, 1865

2433 PIETERS, CHARLES. ANNALES DE L'IMPRIMERIE DES ELSEVIER, ou Histoire de leur Famille et de leurs Éditions. Seconde Édition, revue et augmentée. *Arms, in gold and colors, on title. Royal 8vo, half morocco, gilt top.* BEST EDITION: WITH IMPORTANT CORRECTIONS. Gand, 1858

"Ouvrage le meilleur que nous ayons sur la biographie et la bibliographie de cette famille de célèbres imprimeurs. L'auteur y a fait usage du travail inédit du P. Adry sur le même sujet, travail dont il possède le manuscrit, et qu'il cite fort souvent. Ses descriptions méritent d'autant plus de confiance qu'il les a presque tojours données d'après ses propres exemplaires." — *Brunet.*

2434 PIGOTT, GRENVILLE. A MANUAL OF SCANDINAVIAN MYTHOLOGY, containing a popular account of the Two Eddas and of the Religion of Odin; illustrated by Translations from Oehlenschläger's Danish Poem, the Gods of the North. *Crown 8vo, cloth, uncut.*
W. Pickering, London, 1839

2435 PILOTY AND LÖHLE. KÖNIGL. BAYER. PINAKOTHEK ZU MÜNCHEN UND GEMÄLDE-GALLERIE ZU SCHLEISSHEIM, mit Seiner Majestät des Königs von Bayern Allerhöchster Genehmigung, in Lithographirten; abbildungen herdusgegeben in der Kunst Anstalt, von Piloty & Loehle, in München. *Portrait of Ludwig I., and 184* VERY LARGE *and beautiful plates, after paintings by Rubens, Guido, Poussin, Van Dyck, Raffaelle, Titian, A. Dürer, Wilkie, and other eminent painters.* ORIGINAL IMPRESSIONS ON INDIA PAPER, *some of them tinted and colored. 2 vols., elephant folio (34 × 24 inches), half morocco; somewhat water-stained and a few of the plates injured.* (*München,* 1840, etc.)

2436 PINDAR. ODES OF PINDAR; translated from the Greek, with Notes and Illustrations, by G. West, Esq., LL. D., and H. J. Pye, Esq. To which is prefixed a Dissertation on the Olympic Games. 2 *vols., 12mo, marbled calf; with autograph of Jno. Pickering.*
Longmans & Co., London, 1807

2437 PINDAR. PINDARI CARMINA, cum Lectionis Varietate et Adnotationibus; accedunt Interpretatio Latina Emendatior, Scholia, et Fragmenta; necnon Godofredi Hermanni Dissertationes Pindaricæ, et Indices Tres. A Chr. Gottl. Heyne. Nova Editio correcta et ex Schedis Heynianis aucta [edidit Schæfer]. 3 *vols., 8vo, calf, gilt.*
Londini, 1824

2438 PINEDA, PETER. A SHORT AND COMPENDIOUS METHOD FOR LEARNING TO SPEAK, READ, AND WRITE THE ENGLISH AND SPANISH LANGUAGES. The Third Impression, corrected and amended. *Post 8vo, half morocco.*
London, 1762

2439 PINELLI, BARTOLOMEO. ILLUSTRATIONS OF GIL BLAS, *consisting of* 300 *plates engraved, in outline, by V. Ferreri, after designs by Pinelli. Without title.* 3 *vols., royal 4to, half vellum, extra.* (Roma), s. a.

2440 PINKERTON, JOHN. THE TREASURY OF WIT, being a Methodical Selection of about Twelve Hundred, the Best, Apophthegms and Jests, from Books in Several Languages; containing Greek, Roman, Eastern, Spanish, Italian, German, French, and English, many of the Latter before unpublished. With a Discourse on Wit and Humour. By H. Bennet, M. A. [John Pinkerton]. 2 *vols., post 8vo, marbled calf.* London, 1786

2441 PINKERTON, JOHN. THE SCOTISH GALLERY, or Portraits of Eminent Persons of Scotland, many of them after Pictures by the Celebrated Jameson, at Taymouth, and other Places; with Brief Accounts of the Characters represented, and an Introduction on the Rise and Progress of Painting in Scotland. PROOF IMPRESSIONS *of the* 50 *fine portraits. Royal 4to, old marbled calf, gilt.* LARGE PAPER: *fine copy.* London, 1799

2442 PINKERTON, JOHN. A GENERAL COLLECTION OF THE BEST AND MOST INTERESTING VOYAGES AND TRAVELS in all Parts of the World, many of which are now first translated into English; digested upon a New Plan. *Maps, and above* 200 *plates, comprising views, costumes, customs, etc., engraved by W. & G. Cooke, Storer & Greig, and others.* 17 *vols., 4to, diamond russia; with book-plate of George Lennard Austen.* London, 1808–14

The seventeenth volume contains a catalogue of books of voyages and travels, and a general index.

2443 PINKERTON, ROBERT, D. D. RUSSIA, or Miscellaneous Observations on the Past and Present State of that Country and its Inhabitants; compiled from Notes made on the Spot, during Travels, at Different Times, in the Service of the Bible Society, and a Residence of many Years in that Country. *Colored plates, illustrating costumes, amusements, customs, etc. Royal 8vo, boards, uncut.* London, 1833

2444 PIROLI, TOMASSO. LE ANTICHITA DI ERCOLANO. [Copiate da T. Piroli.] PITTURE E BRONZI; Tomi I.–V. *Above 250 plates, with descriptions. 5 vols. in 2, 4to, half calf.* Roma, 1789–94

2445 PISTOLESI, ERASMO. IL VATICANO, descritto ed illustrato da Erasmo Pistolesi, con Disegni a Contorni diretti dal Pittore Camillo Guerra. *Above 800 plates of paintings, statues, marbles, ornaments, frescos, etc. 8 vols., royal folio, half crimson morocco, extra.* VELLUM PAPER: ORIGINAL IMPRESSIONS. Roma, 1829–38

" Description la plus étendue et la plus exacte que l'on ait donnée de la basilique et des palais du Vatican, ainsi que des sculptures et des peintures qui en font partie." —*Brunet.*

2446 PISTOLESI, ERASMO. ANTIQUITIES OF HERCULANEUM AND POMPEII, being a Selection of all the most Interesting Ornaments and Relics which have been excavated from the Earliest Period to the Present Time, forming a Complete History of the Eruptions of Vesuvius; to which is added a Selection of Remarkable Paintings by the Old Masters, comprising the Principal Objects preserved in the Museo Borbonico, at Naples. One Hundred and Twenty Engravings; with Descriptive Letter-Press, in Italian, French, and English. *2 vols., royal 4to, half morocco, neat, gilt edges.* Printed at the Royal Press, Naples, 1842

2447 PISTRUCCI, FILIPPO. ICONOLOGIA, ovvero Immagini di tutte le Case Principali a cui l'Umano Talento ha finto un Corpo; di Filippo Pistrucci, colla Traduzione Francese di Sergent Marçeau. *Frontispiece and 240 colored plates. 2 vols., royal 4to, boards, rough edges.* Milano, 1819–21

2448 PITCAIRN, REV. DAVID. PERFECT PEACE: Letters-Memorial of the late John Warren Howell, Esq., of Bath, M. R. C. S. With an Introduction by the Rev. John Stevenson. *18mo, cloth.* New York, 1856

2449 PITTENGER, LIEUTENANT WILLIAM. DARING AND SUFFERING; a History of the Great Railroad Adventure. With an Introduction by Rev. Alexander Clark. *Portrait and wood-cuts. 12mo, cloth.* Philadelphia, 1863

2450 PLATO. ΤΟΥ ΘΕΙΟΥ ΠΛΑΤΩΝΟΣ ΑΠΑΝΤΑ ΤΑ ΣΩΖΟΜΕΝΑ. DIVINI PLATONIS OPERA OMNIA quæ exstant; Marsilio Ficino Interprete. Græcus Contextus quàm diligentissimè cum Emendatioribus Exemplaribus collatus est, Latina

Interpretatio à quam plurimis Superiorum Editionum Mendis expurgata. Argumentis Perpetuis & Commentariis quibusdam ejusdem Marsilii Ficini, iisque nunc multo emendatiùs quàm antehac editis, Totum Opus explanatum est atque illustratum; quæ cur in Calcem Operis translata sint, & quid pro hac Trajectione repositum sit, ex Epistola ad Lectorem patet. Vita Platonis à Diogene Laertio copiosissimè descripta, item Pereruditum Timæi Locri Opusculum (quo Latina Exemplaria carebant) aliáque plurima non contemnenda, huic Editioni accesserunt. Adjectus est Index Rerum Omnium Locupletissimus. *Folio, old calf, red edges; with book-plate of William Stow and MS. marginal notes.*
Apud Guillelmum Læmarium, Lugduni, 1590

2451 PLATO. THE WORKS OF PLATO, viz.: his Fifty-five Dialogues, and Twelve Epistles, translated from the Greek; Nine of the Dialogues by the late Floyer Sydenham, and the Remainder, by Thomas Taylor; with Occasional Annotations on the Nine Dialogues translated by Sydenham, and Copious Notes, by the Latter Translator; in which is given the Substance of nearly all the existing Greek MS. Commentaries on the Philosophy of Plato, and a Considerable Portion of such as are already published. *5 vols., royal 4to, half calf, neat, marbled edges.* VERY FINE COPY.
Printed for Thomas Taylor, London, 1804

This work is dedicated to "His Grace Charles Howard, Duke of Norfolk, Earl Marshall of England," etc., etc., at whose expense it was published.

2452 PLENCK, JOSEPH JACOB. ICONES PLANTARUM MEDICINALIUM secundum Systema Linnæi digestarum; cum Enumeratione Virium et Usus Medici, Chirurgici atque Dilætetici. *Engraved title, and 600 plates, all finely colored, with the text in Latin and German. 6 vols. in 3, royal folio, half russia, very neat.* Viennæ, 1788–94

2453 PLUMER, WILLIAM, JUN. LIFE OF WILLIAM PLUMER, by his Son. Edited, with a Sketch of the Author's Life, by A. P. Peabody. *Portraits. Royal 8vo, half calf, antique, carmined edges.* Boston, 1856

2454 PLUMTRE, REV. JAMES. A COLLECTION OF SONGS, Moral, Sentimental, Instructive, and Amusing; selected and revised by the Rev. James Plumtre, M. A., etc. *3 vols., 12mo, calf, gilt, marbled edges.*
F. C. & J. Rivington, London, 1824–(1806)

2455 PLUTARCH. THE LIVES OF THE NOBLE GREEKS AND ROMAINES; the most of them compared together by that Grave Learned Philosopher and Historiographer, Plutarch of Chœronea. (To which are added, the Lives of Epaminondas, of Philip of Macedon, of Dionysius the Elder, and of Octavius Cæsar Augustus; collected out of Good Authors. Also the Lives of Nine Excellent Chieftaines of Warre, taken out of Latine from Emylius Probus, by S. G. S.; by whom also are added the Lives of Plutarch and of Seneca, gathered together, disposed, and enriched as the others. Translated into English by Sir Thomas North, Knight.) *First title wanting. Folio, pp.* 1–1244 *and table, half calf, red edges.* London, (1631)

"This Translation, which is from the French of Amyot, is styled by Warton Shakespeare's 'Storehouse of learned history.'"—*Lowndes.*

2456 PLUTARCH. Plutarch's Lives, translated from the Greek by several Hands; to which is prefixt the Life of Plutarch [by Mr. J. Dryden]. *Portraits and plates. 5 vols., thick small* 8*vo, old calf.* J. Tonson, London, 1683–86

2457 PLUTARCH. Lives of the most Select and Illustrious Characters of Antiquity; translated, with Notes, Historical and Critical, by John and William Langhorne, and others. Complete in One Volume. 8*vo, sheep.* New York, 1832

2458 PLUTARCH. Lives; the Translation called Dryden's, corrected from the Greek and revised, by A. H. Clough. 5 *vols., imperial* 8*vo, boards, cloth backs, red paper sides, rough edges.* Large paper: *only* 100 *copies printed.* Boston, 1865

2459 PLUTARCH. Plutarch's Morals; translated from the Greek, by Several Hands. The Fourth Edition, corrected and amended. *Frontispieces.* 5 *vols.,* 8*vo, old calf.* London, 1704

The second volume of this set is of a former impression (1691), and somewhat smaller than the other volumes.

2460 POCO MAS. Scenes and Adventures in Spain, from 1835 to 1840. *Frontispieces.* 2 *vols.,* 8*vo, cloth, uncut.* London, 1845

2461 POE, Edgar Allan. The Works of. (Edited, with Memoir, by the Rev. Rufus W. Griswold.) *Portrait.* 4 *vols., crown* 8*vo, half green morocco, very neat, gilt tops.* New York, 1861

2462 POEM (A) Addressed to a Young Lady; in Three Parts: Part 1. Descriptive and Moral. 2. On Love and Friendship. 3. The Caution. Written at Antigua. *Small* 4*to, calf, red edges, by Aitken.* Printed by Green & Russell, Boston, 1773

2463 POEMS. Sympathy, a Poem. [By Samuel J. Pratt.] The Fourth Edition. *London,* 1781.—Monody on Major Andrè, by Miss Seward; to which are added Letters addressed to her by Major Andrè, in the Year 1769. The Second Edition. *Lichfield,* 1781.—Elegy on Captain Cook, to which is added an Ode to the Sun, by Miss Seward. The Second Edition. *London,* 1780.—Armine and Elvira; a Legendary Tale. [By Rev. Dr. Edmund Cart-

wright. With Verses addressed to the Author, by Dr. Langhorne.] *Title wanting.* — THE DESERTED VILLAGE. [By Oliver Goldsmith.] *Title wanting. Together in 1 vol., with frontispiece inserted, 4to, old tree calf.*
London, etc., 1780, etc.

2464 POEMS ON AFFAIRS OF STATE, from the Time of Oliver Cromwell to the Abdication of K. James the Second; written by the greatest Wits of the Age, etc., etc. Now carefully examined, with the Originals, and published without any Castration. 4 *vols., post 8vo, half calf; with autograph of Robert Southey on title of first volume.* BEST EDITIONS.
London, 1703–07

The fourth volume contains some curious satirical plates.

2465 POEMS ON THE ABOLITION OF THE SLAVE TRADE; written by James Montgomery, James Grahame, and E. Benger. Embellished with Engravings from Pictures painted by R. Smirke, Esq., R. A. *Handsomely printed by T. Bensley. 4to, marbled calf, gilt, marbled edges; with book-plate of William Williams.* R. Bowyer, London, 1809

2466 POETRY OF THE WOODS: Passages from the Poets descriptive of Forest Scenes, etc., etc. Elegantly Illustrated. *Crown 8vo, morocco, extra, gilt edges.*
Philadelphia, 1867

2467 POLLARD, EDWARD A. THE LOST CAUSE; A New Southern History of the War of the Confederates: comprising a Full and Authentic Account of the Rise and Progress of the late Southern Confederacy, the Campaigns, Battles, Incidents, and Adventures. Drawn from Official Sources. *Numerous portraits. 8vo, sheep, marbled edges.*
New York, 1866

2468 PONCELIN DE LA ROCHE-TILHAC, JEAN CHARLES. CHEF-D'ŒUVRES DE L'ANTIQUITÉ SUR LES BEAUX-ARTS; Monuments Précieux de la Religion des Grecs & des Romains, de leurs Sciences, de leurs Loix, de leurs Usages, de leurs Mœurs, de leurs Superstitions, & de leurs Folies, tirés des Principaux Cabinets de l'Europe. Gravés, en Taille-Douce, par Bernard Picart; et publiés, par M. Poncelin de la Roche-Tilhac. 2 *vols., large folio, russia, gilt, gilt edges.* Paris, 1784

Most of the plates are from Stosch's "Pierres Antiques Gravées."

2469 POOLE, JOSHUA. THE ENGLISH PARNASSUS, or a Help to English Poesie; containing a Collection of all the Rhythming Monosyllables, the Choicest Epithets and Phrases, with some General Forms upon all Occasions, Subjects, and Themes, alphabetically digested. Together with a Short Institution to English Poesie, by way of Preface. *Frontispiece. Small 8vo, calf, very neat, gilt edges.*
London, 1677

2470 POOLE, WILLIAM FREDERICK. AN ALPHABETICAL INDEX TO SUBJECTS TREATED IN THE REVIEWS, and other Periodicals, to which no Indexes have been published; prepared for the Library of the Brothers in Unity, Yale College. *8vo, half morocco.* New York, 1848

The original edition, and foundation of the following work

2471 POOLE, WILLIAM FREDERICK. AN INDEX TO PERIODICAL LITERATURE. *Royal 8vo, dark blue turkey morocco, gilt top.* New York, 1853

2472 POOLE, WILLIAM FREDERICK. ANOTHER COPY: *the same. Royal 8vo, cloth, uncut.* New York, 1853

2473 POOR, JOHN A. MEMOIR OF HON. REUEL WILLIAMS, prepared for the Maine Historical Society. *Portrait, photograph, from a bust. 8vo, cloth, gilt top.* PRIVATELY PRINTED. (Riverside Press, Cambridge), 1864

2474 POPE, ALEXANDER. THE WORKS OF. *Plates. 6 vols., post 8vo, old polished calf.* Edinburgh, 1764

2475 POPE, ALEXANDER. AN ESSAY ON MAN, in Four Epistles, to Henry St. John, Lord Bolingbroke. *Full-length portrait, by J. H. Robinson, after Jervas; and 4 engravings, by Heath, Rhodes, Scott, and Warren, after Uwins;* INDIA PROOFS. *Folio, boards, uncut.* ONLY 200 COPIES PRINTED. London, 1819

Made up from the "Polyglot Edition."

2476 POPULAR (THE) EDUCATOR: comprising Lessons in English Grammar and Composition; French, German, Italian, and Spanish; Greek and Latin; Arithmetic, Algebra, Geometry, Ancient History, Geography, Geology, Natural History, Chemistry, Botany, Natural Philosophy, etc., etc. Illustrated with Numerous Engravings. *6 vols., 4to, cloth, uncut.* Cassell, Petter, and Galpin, London, (1852–55)

2477 PORTS (THE), HARBOURS, WATERING-PLACES, AND COAST-SCENERY OF GREAT BRITAIN; illustrated by Views, taken on the Spot, by W. H. Bartlett, with Descriptions by William Beattie. *Above 125 views, many of them engraved by Finden. 2 vols., 4to, half morocco, very neat, gilt edges.* London, 1842

2478 PORTS, HARBOURS, ETC. ANOTHER COPY: *the same. 2 vols., 4to, cloth, gilt edges.* London, 1842

2479 POTE, B. E. INQUIRY INTO THE PHONETIC READING OF THE ASHBURNHAM SIGNET, in reference to the Patriarch Joseph; with Doubts as to the Value of Egyptian Authorities. *Plate. 8vo, pp. 51, cloth.* W. Pickering, London, 1841

2480 POTTER, JOHN. ARCHAEOLOGIA GRAECA, or the Antiquities of Greece. A New Edition, with a Life of the Author, by Robert Anderson, M. D.; and an Appendix containing a Concise History of the Grecian States, and a Short Account of the Lives and Writings of the most Celebrated Greek Authors, by George Dunbar, F. R. S. E., etc. *Map and plates. 2 vols., 8vo, calf gilt.* Edinburgh, 1827

2481 POUCHOT, M. ——. MEMOIR UPON THE LATE WAR IN NORTH AMERICA, BETWEEN THE FRENCH AND ENGLISH, 1755-60; followed by Observations upon the Theatre of Actual War, and by New Details concerning the Manners and Customs of the Indians, with Topographical Maps. By M. —— Pouchot, Chevalier of the Royal and Military Order of St. Louis, etc., Commandant of Forts Niagara, and Levis in Canada. Translated and edited by Franklin B. Hough, with Additional Notes and Illustrations. *Printed on a thick paper by Munsell, with maps, plans, and portraits. 2 vols., royal 4to, paper, rough edges.* LARGE PAPER: *only 50 copies in this style.* Roxbury, Mass., 1866

The Edition was limited to 200 copies: 143 in royal octavo, 50 in quarto, and 7 in quarto on Whatman's drawing-paper.

2482 POWER, TYRONE. IMPRESSIONS OF AMERICA; during the Years 1833, 1834, and 1835. *2 vols. in 1, 12mo, half morocco.* Philadelphia, 1836

2483 POYNDER, JOHN. LITERARY EXTRACTS FROM ENGLISH AND OTHER WORKS; collected during Half a Century. Together with some Original Matter. BOTH SERIES. *3 vols., 8vo, calf gilt, marbled edges.* London, (1844-47)

2484 PRADT, DOMINIQUE DUFOUR, L'ABBÉ DE. LA EUROPA Y LA AMERICA EN 1821. Traducida en Castellano, por D. J. A. L[lorente]. *2 vols., 12mo, sheep, marbled edges.* Burdeos (Paris), 1822

2485 PRAED, WINTHROP MACKWORTH. THE POETICAL WORKS OF. New and enlarged Edition [edited, with Biographical Introduction, etc., by W. H. Whitmore]. *2 vols., small 4to, sheets, folded.* EDITOR'S EDITION: *only 50 copies printed.* New York, 1859-60

2486 PRECES SANCTI NERSETIS CLAJENSIS, ARMENIORUM PATRIARCHAE, Viginti-quatuor Linguis editae. *Portrait. Handsomely printed on vellum paper. Small 12mo, mottled calf extra, gilt edges.* Venetiis, 1837

2487 PRESCOTT, WILLIAM HICKLING. WORKS. *Portraits, maps, fac-similes, etc. 15 vols., 8vo, half calf extra, contents lettered, marbled edges.* Boston and Philadelphia, 1858-60

CONTENTS: Ferdinand and Isabella, 3 vols.; Conquest of Mexico, 3 vols.; Conquest of Peru, 2 vols.; Philip the Second, 3 vols.; Robertson's Charles the Fifth, 3 vols.; Biographical and Critical Miscellanies, 1 vol.

2488 PRESCOTT, WILLIAM HICKLING. ANOTHER SET: *the same. 15 vols., 8vo, cloth.* Boston, 1859

2489 PRESCOTT, WILLIAM HICKLING. HISTORY OF THE CONQUEST OF MEXICO; with a Preliminary View of the

Ancient Mexican Civilization, and the Life of the Conqueror, Hernando Cortés. *Portraits, etc.* 3 *vols.*, 8*vo, cloth. First edition.* New York, 1843

2490 PRESCOTT, William Hickling. History of the Conquest of Peru; with a Preliminary View of the Civilization of the Incas. *Portraits, etc.* 2 *vols.*, 8*vo, cloth. First edition.* New York, 1847

2491 PRESTON, William. Illustrations of Masonry. The Ninth Edition, with Considerable Additions. 12*mo, sheep.* London, 1796

2492 PRÉVOST d'Exiles, Antoine François. Histoire Générale des Voyages, ou Nouvelle Collection de toutes les Relations de Voyages par Mer et par Terre, qui ont été publiées jusqu'à Présent dans les Différentes Langues de toutes les Nations Connues: contenant ce qu'il y a de plus Remarquable, de plus Utile, et de mieux avéré dans les Pays où les Voyageurs ont pénétré; avec les Mœurs des Habitans, la Religion, les Usages, Arts, Sciences, Commerce, Manufactures, etc.; pour former un Système Complet d'Histoire & de Géographie Moderne, qui représente l'État Actuel de toutes les Nations. *Portrait, and several hundred plates.* 80 *vols.*, 12*mo, and* 2 *vols.* (*containing maps*), 4*to, sprinkled calf, neat, yellow edges; with autograph of Charlotte Auguste Matilde* (*daughter of George III.*). Paris, 1749-89

Voyages to America occupy a large part of this work.

2493 PRICE, Lake. Interiors and Exteriors in Venice. *Frontispiece and* 25 *large plates, lithographed by Joseph Nash from the original drawings by Lake Price, all finely colored. Mounted on a very thick card-board, atlas folio size, and enclosed* (*with the descriptions of the plates*) *in a fine strong portfolio, half morocco.* London, 1843

These views are executed in the same manner as Nash's Mansions of England.

2494 PRICE, Lake. Tauromachia, or the Bull-Fights of Spain; illustrated by Twenty-six Plates, representing the most Remarkable Incidents and Scenes in the Arenas of Madrid, Seville, and Cadiz. The whole drawn and lithographed from Studies made expressly for the Work, by Lake Price; with Preliminary Explanations, by Richard Ford. *Imperial folio, half morocco.* London, 1852

2495 PRICE, Sir Uvedale. The Picturesque: with an Essay on the Origin of Taste, and much Original Matter, by Sir Thomas Dick Lauder, Bart. *Sixty illustrations, designed and drawn on the wood, by Montagu Stanley, R. S. A.* 8*vo, cloth, uncut.* Edinburgh, 1842

2496 PRICHARD, James Cowles, M.D. The Natural History of Man, comprising Inquiries into the Modifying

Influence of Physical and Moral Agencies on the Different Tribes of the Human Family. Fourth Edition, edited and enlarged by Edwin Norris. *Illustrated with sixty-two colored plates engraved on steel, and one hundred engravings on wood. 2 vols., royal 8vo, cloth, uncut.* London, 1855

2497 PRIESTLEY, JOSEPH. EXPERIMENTS AND OBSERVATIONS RELATING TO VARIOUS BRANCHES OF NATURAL PHILOSOPHY; with a Continuation of the Observations on Air. *Plates. 3 vols., 8vo, half calf, neat.* London and Birmingham, 1779–86

2498 PRIESTLEY, JOSEPH. LIFE AND CORRESPONDENCE OF. By John T. Rutt. *Portrait. 2 vols., 8vo, half calf extra, marbled edges.* London, 1831

2499 PRINCE, REV. THOMAS. A CHRONOLOGICAL HISTORY OF NEW-ENGLAND, in the Form of Annals: being a Summary and Exact Account of the most Material Transactions and Occurrences relating to this Country, from the Discovery of Capt. Gosnold, in 1602, to the Arrival of Governor Belcher in 1730. With an Introduction, containing a Brief Epitome of the most Remarkable Transactions and Events Abroad, from the Creation; including the Connected Line of Time, the Succession of Patriarchs and Sovereigns of the most Famous Kingdoms and Empires, the Gradual Discoveries of America and the Progress of the Reformation, to the Discovery of New-England. *Vol. I., small 8vo, old calf, red edges; with autographs of Nath[l]. Lothrop, and Ezra S. Goodwin.* ORIGINAL EDITION. Boston, N. E., 1736

2500 PRINCE, REV. THOMAS. ANOTHER COPY: a New (second) Edition. *8vo, half calf, neat.* (Boston), 1826

2501 PRINCE, REV. THOMAS. ANOTHER COPY: Third Edition; to which is added, a Memoir of the Author, an Attempt towards a Perfect Catalogue of his Writings, a Genealogy of his Family, and the Names of Subscribers to the Original Edition, by Samuel G. Drake. *Portraits, arms, views, etc. 8vo, half morocco, gilt top.* ONLY 30 COPIES PRINTED: ILLUSTRATED COPY. Boston, 1852

This is one of the copies containing the 12 plates, besides wood-cuts.

2502 PRINCE SOCIETY. THE PUBLICATIONS OF THE PRINCE SOCIETY, established May 25, 1858: THE HUTCHINSON PAPERS. (Reprinted from the Edition published by T. & J. Fleet, Boston, 1769.) *2 vols., printed by J. Munsell, Albany,* 1865. — WOOD'S NEW ENGLAND'S PROSPECT. (Reprinted from the London Edition of 1634, etc.) *Fac-simile map, 1 vol., printed by J. Wilson & Son, Boston,* 1865. — JOHN DUNTON'S LETTERS FROM NEW ENGLAND. (Published from the Original Manuscript in the Bodleian Library, Oxford;

with Notes and an Appendix, by W. H. Whitmore.) *Wood-cuts illustrative of the appearance of Boston in the seventeenth century.* 1 *vol., printed by T. R. Marvin & Son, Boston,* 1867. *Together,* 4 *vols., foolscap* 4*to, paper, rough edges.* LIMITED EDITIONS. Boston, 1865–67

2503 PRIOR, JAMES. THE LIFE OF OLIVER GOLDSMITH, from a Variety of Original Sources. *Plate of monument in Westminster Abbey, and fac-simile of handwriting.* 2 *vols.,* 8*vo, half calf, neat.* J. Murray, London, 1837

2504 PRIOR, JAMES. MEMOIR OF THE LIFE AND CHARACTER OF EDMUND BURKE; with Specimens of his Poetry and Letters, and an Estimate of his Genius and Talents, compared with those of his Great Contemporaries. Third Edition. *Portrait and fac-simile of autographs.* 8*vo, calf gilt, marbled edges.* London, 1839

2505 PRIOR, MATTHEW. POEMS ON SEVERAL OCCASIONS. The Sixth Edition. *Portrait.* 12*mo, old calf.* J. & R. Tonson, London, 1741

2506 PRISSE, E. ORIENTAL ALBUM: Characters, Costumes, and Modes of Life in the Valley of the Nile; illustrated from Designs taken on the Spot, with Descriptive Letter-Press by James Augustus St. John. *Illuminated title, portrait of George Lloyd (in Eastern costume), and* 30 *large tinted plates, besides many fine wood-cuts. Imperial folio, half morocco, neat, gilt edges.* London, 1848

2507 PRIVY PURSE EXPENSES. THE PRIVY PURSE EXPENSES OF KING HENRY THE EIGHTH; from November MDXXIX, to December MDXXXII. With Introductory Remarks and Illustrative Notes, by Nicholas Harris Nicolas, Esq. (1827). — PRIVY PURSE EXPENSES OF ELIZABETH OF YORK; Wardrobe Accounts of Edward the Fourth. With a Memoir of Elizabeth of York, and Notes, by Nicholas Harris Nicolas, Esq. (1830). — PRIVY PURSE EXPENSES OF THE PRINCESS MARY, Daughter of King Henry the Eighth, afterwards Queen Mary. With a Memoir of the Princess, and Notes, by Frederick Madden, Esq., F. S. A., Assistant Keeper of the MSS. in the British Museum (1831). *Together,* 3 *vols.,* 8*vo, cloth, uncut.* ONLY 250 COPIES PRINTED. W. Pickering, London, 1827–31

2508 PROCEEDINGS OF THE MASSACHUSETTS HISTORICAL SOCIETY IN RESPECT TO THE MEMORY OF WILLIAM H. PRESCOTT, February 1, 1859. 8*vo, cloth.* Boston, 1859

2509 PROCTER, BRYAN WALLER. MARCIAN COLONNA, an Italian Tale; with Three Dramatic Scenes, and other Poems, by Barry Cornwall. 8*vo, boards, rough edges.* London, 1820

Presentation copy to Samuel Rogers, with autograph of author.

2510 PROCTER, BRYAN WALLER. THE LIFE OF EDMUND KEAN. *12mo, cloth.* New York, 1835

2511 PROCTER, BRYAN WALLER. ESSAYS AND TALES IN PROSE. *Portrait. 2 vols., 16mo, cloth; with autograph of Rufus Choate.* Boston, 1853

2512 PROCTER, BRYAN WALLER. CHARLES LAMB, a Memoir. *Foolscap 8vo, cloth, gilt top.* Boston, 1866

2513 PUCKLE, JAMES. THE CLUB; in a Dialogue between Father and Son. INDIA PROOFS *of the portrait and Thurston's wood-cuts. Imperial 8vo, green turkey morocco extra, gilt edges.* Printed by J. Johnson, London, 1817

2514 PÜCKLER-MUSKAU H. L. H. FÜRST VON. TUTTI FRUTTI; by the Author of "The Tour of a German Prince." (Translated from the German, with a Biographical Sketch of the Author, etc., by Edmund Spencer.) *2 vols., 12mo, calf, neat, marbled edges.* London, 1834

2515 PULSIFER, DAVID. THE STATE HOUSE, in Boston, Massachusetts. *Map of city, and wood-cuts. 12mo, pp. 24, paper.* Boston, 1865

2516 PUNCH AND LONDON CHARIVARI. *July* 17, 1841–*June* 30, 1866. *50 vols. in 25, cloth, gilt edges.* ORIGINAL COPY. London, 1841–66

2517 PUTNAM'S MONTHLY MAGAZINE OF AMERICAN LITERATURE, SCIENCE, AND ART. *January*, 1853–*April*, 1857. *Vols. I.–IX., in numbers.* New York, 1853–57

2518 PUTTENHAM, GEORGE. THE ARTE OF ENGLISH POESIE, contrived into Three Bookes: the First, of Poets and Poesie; the Second, of Proportion; and the Third, of Ornament. (A Verbal and Paginal Reprint of the Edition of 1589; edited, with Life of the Author and Notes, by Joseph Haslewood.) *Fac-similes, appendix, and index. Post 4to, calf gilt.* ONLY 200 COPIES PRINTED. R. Triphook, London, 1811

2519 PYCROFT, REV. JAMES. A COURSE OF ENGLISH READING; with Literary Anecdotes. Second Edition. *Foolscap 8vo, cloth, uncut.* London, 1850

2520 PYNE, JAMES B. THE ENGLISH LAKE DISTRICT. *A series of 25 large tinted and colored plates of English lake scenery, with introduction and descriptive letter-press. Imperial folio, half morocco.* Manchester, 1853

2521 PYNE, WILLIAM HENRY. THE COSTUMES OF GREAT BRITAIN; designed, engraved, and written by W. H. Pyne. *Vignette on title and 60 plates, all colored. Imperial 4to, russia extra, gilt edges.* LARGE PAPER: *fine copy.* W. Miller, London, 1808

2522 PYNE, WILLIAM HENRY. THE HISTORY OF THE ROYAL RESIDENCES of Windsor Castle, St. James's Palace, Carlton House, Kensington Palace, Hampton Court, Buckingham House, and Frogmore. *Illustrated by one hundred highly-*

finished and colored engravings, fac-similes of original drawings by the most eminent artists. 3 vols., imperial 4to, sprinkled calf gilt, marbled edges; back of first volume cracked. ORIGINAL COPY. London, 1819

2523 PYRAMIDS (THE) OF GIZEH, FROM ACTUAL SURVEY AND ADMEASUREMENT, by J. S. Perring, Esq., Civil Engineer; illustrated by Notes and References to the Several Plans, with Sketches taken on the Spot by E. J. Andrews, Esq. *3 parts in 1 vol., oblong elephant folio, half morocco.* London, 1839–42

The title to the third part reads: "The Pyramids to the Southward of Gizeh and at Abou Roash; also Campbell's Tomb, and a Section of the Rock at Gizeh: from Actual Survey and Admeasurement. With Notes and References by J. S. Perring, Esq., Civil Engineer. Accompanied by Remarks on the Hieroglyphics by S. Birch, Esq., of the British Museum."
This volume generally accompanies Col. Vyse's "Operations," etc.

2524 QUARTERLY (THE) REVIEW. *From February,* 1809 *(commencement), to September,* 1856, *inclusive.* 99 *vols.,* 8*vo; the first* 73 *vols., half calf, remainder in numbers.* New York, Boston, and London, 1809–56

Some of the early numbers have the American imprint, but with the same paging as the London edition. Vols. XX., XL., LX., and LXXX. are indexes.

2525 QUEEN'S (THE) CLOSET OPENED; being Incomparable Secrets in Physick, Chyrurgery, Preserving, Candying, and Cookery, etc., which were presented to the Queen by the most experienc'd Persons of the Times, many whereof were had in Esteem when she pleased to descend to Private Recreations. The Tenth Edition, corrected, with many New and Large Additions; together with Three Exact Tables. *Small 12mo, half calf.* London, 1698

Part I. The Pearl of Practice, 1698. Part II. A Queen's Delight, 1696. Part III. The Compleat Cook, 1695.

2526 QUILLET, CLAUDIUS. CALLIPÆDIA; a Poem, in Four Books. Written in Latin by Claudius Quillet; made English by N. Rowe, Esq. To which is prefix'd Mr. Bayle's Account of his Life. (Followed by his Epistle to Eudoxus, and Elegy on the Death of Gassendus.) 1760.—THE ŒCONOMY OF LOVE; a Poetical Essay. A New Edition, revised and corrected by the Author [ ]. 1768. *Together in 1 vol., 12mo, old calf, yellow edges; with autograph of Winslow Lewis.* London, 1760–68

2527 QUIN, MICHAEL J. A STEAM VOYAGE DOWN THE DANUBE; with Sketches of Hungary, Wallachia, Servia, Turkey, etc. Third Edition, with Additions. *Plates. 2 vols. in 1, 12mo, half morocco.* London, 1836

2528 QUINCY, JOSIAH. CONSIDERATIONS RELATIVE TO THE LIBRARY OF HARVARD UNIVERSITY, respectfully submitted to the Legislature of Massachusetts. *8vo, pp. 16, paper.* Cambridge, 1833

2529 QUINCY, JOSIAH. THE HISTORY OF HARVARD UNIVERSITY. *Plates and wood-cuts.* 2 *vols., royal* 8*vo, cloth, uncut.* Cambridge, 1840

2530 QUINCY, JOSIAH. A MUNICIPAL HISTORY OF THE TOWN AND CITY OF BOSTON, during Two Centuries; from September 17, 1630, to September 17, 1830. *Plates.* 8*vo, cloth.* Boston, 1852

2531 QUINCY, JOSIAH. MEMOIR OF THE LIFE OF JOHN QUINCY ADAMS. *Portrait.* 8*vo, cloth.* Boston, 1858

2532 QUINCY, JOSIAH P. MANUSCRIPT CORRECTIONS, from a Copy of the Fourth Folio of Shakspeare's Plays. [By J. P. Quincy.] 8*vo, pp.* 51, *paper.* Boston, 1854

2533 RABELAIS, FRANÇOIS. THE WORKS OF; translated from the French, with Explanatory Notes, by Du Chat, Motteaux, Ozell, and others. *Portrait.* 4 *vols.,* 12*mo, sprinkled calf, neat.* London, 1807

2534 RABELAIS, FRANÇOIS. THE ROMANCE OF GARGANTUA AND PANTAGRUEL; translated from the French of Dr. Francis Rabelais, by Sir Thomas Urquhart, of Cromarty, Knight. Reprinted from the Original Editions (with an Introductory Notice and Life of Rabelais, by Theodore Martin). *Frontispiece, after design by C. K. Sharpe.* 4*to, dark brown smooth morocco gilt, carmine edges, by Riviere.* ELEGANT COPY: *only* 100 *printed.* Edinburgh, 1838

This edition is very handsomely printed, uniform with the Bannatyne Club books, from the text of 1653.

"In the Foreign 'Quarterly Review,' Vol. XXXI. p. 314, there is an elaborate and amusing article upon this extraordinary man and his book, characterizing the translation by Urquhart as 'an instance of penetration into the spirit of a foreigner, which is perhaps not to be matched by any other book in the world.'" — *Lowndes.*

2535 RABELAIS, ROBERT, THE YOUNGER! A NINETEENTH CENTURY AND FAMILIAR HISTORY OF THE LIVES, LOVES, & MISFORTUNES OF ABEILARD AND HELOISA, a Matchless Pair, who flourished in the Twelfth Century; a Poem, in Twelve Cantos. Illustrated with Ten Engravings. 8*vo, calf extra, marbled edges.* J. Bumpus, London, 1819

2536 RADCLIFFE, ANNE. GASTON DE BLONDEVILLE, a Romance; St. Alban's Abbey, a Metrical Tale; with some Poetical Pieces. To which is prefixed a Memoir of the Author, with Extracts from her Journals. 4 *vols.,* 12*mo, half calf extra; with autographs.* London, 1826

The first volume contains this autograph: "To Sir Walter Stirling, Bart., with the respects and thanks of the Editor." See Vol. I. p. 132.

2537 RAFFLES, SIR THOMAS STAMFORD. THE HISTORY OF JAVA. Second Edition. 2 *vols.,* 8*vo, J. Murray,* 1830. — ANTIQUARIAN, ARCHITECTURAL, AND LANDSCAPE ILLUSTRATIONS OF THE HISTORY OF JAVA. With a Large Map of Java and its Dependencies, and Several Interesting Plates now first published. 1 *vol., royal 4to,* 1844. *Together,* 3 *vols., 8vo, and 4to, cloth, uncut.* London, 1830–44

2538 RAINOLDS, JOHN. THE OVERTHROW OF STAGE-PLAYERS, by the Way of Controversie betwixt D. Gager and D. Rainoldes; wherein all the Reasons that can be made for them are notably refuted, the Objections answered, and the Case so cleared and resolved, as that the Judgement of any Man, that is not Froward and Perverse, may easilie bee satisfied; wherein is manifestly proved, that it is not onely Unlawfull to be an Actor, but a Beholder of those Vanities. Whereunto are added also and annexed in the End, Certaine Latine Letters betwixt the said Maister Rainoldes and Doct. Gentiles, Reader of the Civill Law in Oxford, concerning the same Matter. The Second Edition. *Small 4to, boards, pp.* 190. PERFECT COPY. Oxford, 1629

2539 RALEIGH, SIR WALTER. AN ABRIDGMENT OF SIR WALTER RALEIGH'S HISTORY OF THE WORLD; in Five Books: I. From the Creation to Abraham. II. From Abraham to the Destruction of the Temple of Solomon. III. From the Destruction of Jerusalem, to Philip of Macedon. IV. From Philip of Macedon to the Race of Antigonus. V. From the Establishment of Alexander until the Conquest of Asia and Macedon by the Romans. Wherein the Particular Chapters and Paragraphs are succinctly abridg'd, according to his own Method in the Larger Volume. His Premonition to Princes; also, some Genuine Remains of that Learned Knight, viz.: I. Of the Invention of Shipping. II. A Relation of the Action at Cadiz. III. A Dialogue between a Jesuite and a Recusant. IV. An Apology for his Unlucky Voyage to Guiana. Published by Philip Raleigh, Esquire, the only Grandson to Sir Walter. The Third Edition; to which is added, an Account of the Author's Life, Tryal, and Death. *Portrait. 8vo, old calf.* London, 1702

2540 RAMBLES IN SWEDEN AND GOTTLAND; with Etchings by the Way-side. By Sylvanus, Author of "Pedestrian and other Reminiscences at Home and Abroad." *Portrait of Jenny Lind, etc. 8vo, cloth, uncut.* London, 1847

2541 RAMSAY, ALLAN. THE POEMS OF. A New Edition, corrected and enlarged, with a Glossary; to which are prefixed, a Life of the Author, from Authentic Documents [by George Chalmers], and Remarks on his Poems, from a Large View of their Merits [by Lord Woodhouselee]. *Portrait by T. Ryder, after Allan Ramsay (son of the author), fac-simile of handwriting, and view of the supposed scene of the "Gentle Shepherd."* 2 *vols., 8vo, dark green smooth morocco, extra, gilt edges; with book-plate of Alexander Henderson.* VERY FINE COPY. London, 1800

2542 RAMSAY, DAVID, M. D. THE HISTORY OF SOUTH-CAROLINA; from its First Settlement in 1670, to the Year 1808. 2 *vols.*, 8*vo*, *half calf.* Charleston, 1809

2543 RAMSAY, E. B. REMINISCENCES OF SCOTTISH LIFE AND CHARACTER. 12*mo*, *cloth*, *gilt top.* Boston, 1861

2544 RANKE, LEOPOLD VON. THE ECCLESIASTICAL AND POLITICAL HISTORY OF THE POPES OF ROME, during the Sixteenth and Seventeenth Centuries. Translated from the German, by Sarah Austin. Second Edition. 3 *vols.*, 8*vo*, *half calf extra, marbled edges.* J. Murray, London, 1841

2545 RAPIN, RENÉ. RENATI RAPINI HORTORUM LIBRI IV.; et Cultura Hortensis. Hortorum Historiam addidit Gabriel Brotier. *Frontispiece. Small* 12*mo*, *old calf gilt, gilt edges.* J. Barbou, Parisiis, 1780

2546 RAPIN DE THOYRAS, PAUL. THE HISTORY OF ENGLAND (from the Earliest Period to the Revolution in 1688), written in French by Mr. Rapin de Thoyras. Translated into English, with Additional Notes, by N. Tindal. The Second Edition. *Maps, chronological and genealogical tables, and numerous plates.* 2 *vols.*, 1732–33.—THE CONTINUATION of Mr. Rapin de Thoyras's History of England, from the Revolution to the Accession of King George II.; by N. Tindal. *Illustrated with thirty-six heads of the kings, queens, and several eminent persons; also with twenty maps and sea charts.* The Second Edition. 2 *vols.*, *J. and P. Knapton*, 1751.—A SUMMARY of Mr. Rapin de Thoyras's History of England, and Mr. Tindal's Continuation; from the Invasion of Julius Cæsar, to the End of the Reign of King George I. *Illustrated with medals, plans of battles, towns, and sieges.* The Second Edition. 1 *vol.*, 1751. *Together,* 5 *vols.*, *large folio, old calf gilt, red edges; with book-plate of Rev. M. Buckley.* BEST EDITION. London, 1732–51

2547 RAPIN DE THOYRAS, PAUL. ANOTHER COPY: *the same.* 5 *vols.*, *large folio, old calf.* BEST EDITION. London, 1732–47

2548 RAPIN DE THOYRAS, PAUL. ANOTHER COPY: *the same; with portraits of Rapin de Thoyras and Tyndal, and the heads and monuments of the kings, by Vertue; besides the Houbraken's heads, and other plates, contained in the two copies above.* 4 *vols.*, *large folio, old calf; with book-plates of Francis Douce and John Risdon.* BEST EDITION. London, 1732-51

2549 RASTELL, JOHN. THE PASTIME OF PEOPLE, or the Chronicles of Divers Realms, and most especially of the Realm of England; briefly compiled, and imprinted in Cheapside, by John Rastell [A. D. 1529]. Now first reprinted, and systematically arranged, with fac-simile Wood-cuts of the Portraits of Popes, Emperors, etc., and the Kings of England. [Edited by the Rev. T. F. Dibdin, D. D.] *Royal 4to, russia, neat marbled edges.* London, 1811

See ARNOLD, RICHARD.

2550 RAWLINSON, GEORGE. THE HISTORICAL EVIDENCES OF THE TRUTH OF THE SCRIPTURE RECORDS stated Anew, with Special Reference to the Doubts and Discoveries of Modern Times; in Eight Lectures delivered in the Oxford University Pulpit, in the Year 1859, on the Bampton Foundation. From the London Edition; with the Notes translated, by Rev. A. N. Arnold. 12*mo, cloth.* Boston, 1860

2551 RAY, REV. JOHN. A COMPLEAT COLLECTION OF ENGLISH PROVERBS, also the most Celebrated Proverbs of the Scotch, Italian, French, Spanish, and other Languages; the Whole methodically digested, and illustrated with Annotations and Proper Explications, by the late Rev. and Learned J. Ray, M. A., etc. To which is added (written by the same Author), a Collection of English Words not generally used, with their Signification and Original, in Two Alphabetical Catalogues, the one, of such as are Proper to the Northern, the other, to the Southern Counties; with an Account of the Preparing and Refining such Metals and Minerals as are found in England. The Third Edition; augmented with many Hundreds of Words, Observations, Letters, etc. 8*vo, calf, red edges.* BEST EDITION: *fine copy.* London, 1742

COLLATION: Title and Preface, pp. viii.; Proverbs, etc., pp. 319; Second Title, Dedication, and Preface, pp. xii.; Collection of Words, etc., pp. 150. Lowndes mentions a "third edition" bearing date of 1737, and a "fourth" (which he calls "best," containing same as this), bearing date of 1768.

2552 RAYMOND, GEORGE. MEMOIRS OF ROBERT WILLIAM ELLISTON, COMEDIAN. Second Edition. *With 5 illustrations by George Cruikshank and "Phiz" (H. K. Browne), and* 30 *fac-simile autographs. Portrait wanting.* 2 *vols.,* 8*vo, half dark calf, neat.* London, 1846

2553 READE, CHARLES. PEG WOFFINGTON; a Novel. 12*mo, cloth.* Boston, 1855

2554 READE, CHARLES. CHRISTIE JOHNSTONE; a Novel. 12*mo, cloth.* Boston, 1855

2555 READE, CHARLES. VERY HARD CASH; a Novel. With Illustrations. 8*vo, cloth.* New York, 1864

2556 REASON (THE) WHY: a Careful Collection of many Hundreds of Reasons for Things which, though generally believed, are imperfectly Understood. By the Author of "Inquire Within." *Wood-cuts.* 12*mo, cloth.* New York, s. a.

2557 RÉCAMIER, JEANNE FRANÇOISE JULIE ADÉLAIDE B. DE. MEMOIRS AND CORRESPONDENCE OF MADAME RÉCAMIER; translated from the French, and edited by Isaphene M. Luyster. Second Edition. *Portrait.* 12*mo, cloth.* Boston, 1867

2558 RECENT INQUIRIES IN THEOLOGY, by Eminent English Churchmen; being "Essays and Reviews." From the Second London Edition, with an Appendix; edited, with an Introduction, by Rev. Frederic H. Hedge, D. D. 12*mo, cloth.* Boston, 1861

2559 RECORDE, ROBERT. THE GROUNDE OF ARTES; teaching the Worke and Practice of Arithmetike, both in Whole Numbers and Fractions, after a more Easyer and Exacter Sorte then any like hath hitherto been sette forthe. Made by M. Robert Recorde, Doctor of Physik, and now of late overseen & augmented with new & and necessarie Additions. *Numerous wood-cuts comprising initial letters, etc. Small* 8*vo, diamond calf, red edges.* Black letter. Reginalde Wolfe, London, 1561

2560 RECTORY (THE) OF MORELAND; or My Duty. 12*mo, cloth.* Boston, 1860

2561 REDDING, CYRUS. A HISTORY AND DESCRIPTION OF MODERN WINES. Second Edition, with Considerable Additions, and a New Preface developing the System of the Port Wine Trade. *Wood-cuts.* 8*vo, half claret morocco, very neat, marbled edges.* London, 1836

2562 REDHOUSE, JAMES W. A LEXICON, ENGLISH AND TURKISH; shewing in Turkish, the Literal, Incidental, Figurative, Colloquial, and Technical Significations of the English Terms, indicating their Pronunciation in a New and Systematic Manner, and preceded by a Sketch of English Etymology, to facilitate to Turkish Students the Acquisition of the English Language. *Royal* 8*vo, half crimson morocco.* London, 1861

2563 REDOUTÉ, PIERRE JOSEPH. LES ROSES, par P. J. Redouté, Peintre de Fleurs, Desinateur en Titre de la Classe de Phisique de l'Institut et du Muséum d'Histoire Naturelle; avec le Texte par Cl. Ant. Thory. *Vol. I., with* 73 *beautiful colored plates. Imperial* 4*to, half crimson morocco, neat.* Paris, 1817

"Ouvrage de la plus grande beauté, et qui a mis le comble à la réputation du peintre." — *Brunet.*

2564 REED, ANDREW, D. D.; and JAMES MATHESON, D. D. A NARRATIVE OF THE VISIT TO THE AMERICAN CHURCHES, by the Deputation from the Congregational Union of England and Wales. *Map and plates.* 2 *vols.,* 8*vo, half green morocco, neat.* London, 1835

2565 REED, Isaac. The Repository; a Select Collection of Fugitive Pieces of Wit and Humour, in Prose and Verse, by the most Eminent Writers. [Edited by Isaac Reed.] The Third Edition, with Additions. *4 vols., foolscap 8vo, half morocco.* London, 1790

2566 REED, Rebecca Theresa. Supplement to "Six Months in a Convent," confirming the Narrative of Rebecca Theresa Reed, by the Testimony of more than One Hundred Witnesses, whose Statements have been given to the Committee; containing a Minute Account of the Elopement of Miss Harrison, with some Further Explanations of the Narrative, by Miss Reed. With an Appendix (of Notes and Certificates). *16mo, cloth.* Boston, 1835

2567 REES, Abraham, D. D. The Cyclopædia; or Universal Dictionary of Arts, Sciences, and Literature. By Abraham Rees, D. D., etc.; with the Assistance of Eminent Professional Gentlemen. Illustrated with Numerous Engravings, by the most Distinguished Artists. *Portrait by Holl, after painting by Opie. Vols. I.–XXIII. (A—— Monsoon), and 5 vols. of plates; also incomplete, the fifth containing part (Supplement, Balfouria-Zollikofer) of Vol. XXXIX. Together, 28 vols., 4to; 23 half-bound, and 5 (plates) in boards, uncut.* London, 1819

2568 REFLEXIONS upon Ridicule, or What it is that makes a Man Ridiculous, and the Means to avoid it; wherein are represented the Different Manners and Characters of Persons of the Present Age. The Fourth Edition. *2 vols. in 1, small 12mo, old calf.* London, 1727

2569 REGISTER (The) of the Times, or Political Museum: containing a Select, Impartial, and Interesting Collection of Political Transactions and Occurrences, divided and arranged into Domestic and Foreign Politics; comprising Debates of Parliament, etc., etc., etc., with all that relate to Battles, Sieges, Victories, etc. Embellished with Beautiful Engravings. *June* 11, 1794–*June* 30, 1795. *5 vols., 8vo, sheep; with book-plate of G. B. Godbold.* London, 1794–95

2570 REID, Thomas, D. D. An Inquiry into the Human Mind, on the Principles of Common Sense. The Second Edition. *Crown 8vo, old calf.* Edinburgh, 1765

2571 REID, Thomas, D. D. Essays on the Intellectual Powers of Man. *1 vol., pp. 766, 4to, half bound, uncut. First edition.* Edinburgh, 1785

2572 RELIGIO Bibliopolæ: the Religion of a Bookseller; after the Manner of the Religio Medici, by the late Ingenious and Learned Sir Thomas Browne, M. D. *8vo, pp. 84, half morocco.* London, s. a.

2573 RÉMY, Jules. Science des Conjugaisons, précédée d'un Traité sur les Modes, les Temps, et les Participes. *12mo, paper.* Paris, 1842

2574 RENAN, JOSEPH ERNEST. THE LIFE OF JESUS. Translated from the French, by Charles Edwin Wilbour. *12mo, cloth.* New York, 1864

2575 RENOUARD, ANTOINE AUGUSTIN. ANNALES DE L'IMPRIMERIE DES ALDE, ou Histoire des Trois Manuce et de leurs Éditions. Seconde Édition. *Portraits and fac-similes. 3 vols., 8vo, half crimson morocco, neat.* A. A. Renouard, Paris, 1825

2576 REPLY TO WEBSTER: a Letter to Daniel Webster, in Reply to his Legal Opinion to Baring, Brothers & Co., upon the Illegality and Unconstitutionality of State Bonds, and Loans of State Credit. By Junius. *12mo, pp. 79, paper.* New York, 1840

2577 REPORT OF THE SECRETARY OF THE TREASURY, ON THE STATE OF THE FINANCES, for the Year ending June 30, 1860. *8vo, cloth.* Washington, 1860

2578 REPORT OF THE TRIAL BY IMPEACHMENT OF JAMES PRESCOTT, ESQUIRE, Judge of the Probate of Wills, etc., for the County of Middlesex, for Misconduct and Maladministration in Office, before the Senate of Massachusetts, in the Year 1821; with an Appendix, containing an Account of Former Impeachments in the same State. By Octavius Pickering and William H. Gardiner. *Royal 8vo, boards, rough edges.* Boston, 1821

2579 REPORTS OF EXPLORATIONS AND SURVEYS to Ascertain the most Practicable and Economical Route for a Railroad from the Mississippi River to the Pacific Ocean, made under the Direction of the Secretary of War, etc. *Many hundred maps, plans, and plates of views, fish, reptiles, birds, animals, flowers, etc., a large number of which are finely colored. 13 vols., 4to, half morocco, marbled edges.* VERY FINE SET. Washington, 1855–61

2580 REPORTS OF EXPLORATIONS, ETC. ANOTHER COPY of Vol. X., containing the Zoological part of the reports. *The ornithological plates finely colored. 4to, half russia.* Washington, 1859

2581 REPORTS FROM THE SELECT COMMITTEE ON PUBLIC LIBRARIES; together with the Proceedings of the Committee, Minutes of Evidence, Appendixes, and Indexes. Ordered, by the House of Commons, to be printed, 23 July 1849, and 1 August 1850. (3 vols.) — REPORT OF THE COMMISSIONERS appointed to inquire into the Constitution and Government of the British Museum; with Minutes of Evidence. Presented to Both Houses of Parliament by Command of her Majesty. (1 *thick vol.*) *Together, 4 vols., folio, paper.* London, 1849–50

2582 REPORTS OF THE SUPERINTENDENT OF THE COAST SURVEY, showing the Progress of the Survey during the Years

1859, 1860, 1861, 1862, and 1863. *Nearly* 200 *maps, charts, etc.* 5 *vols.*, 4*to, cloth.* Washington, 1860–64

2583 REPORTS OF VARIOUS SOCIETIES, LIBRARIES, RAILROAD CORPORATIONS, etc., etc. 37 *pamphlets.* Boston, etc., 1858–66

2584 REPTON, HUMPHRY. ODD WHIMS, and Miscellanies. *Illustrated with designs by the author.* 2 *vols., royal* 8*vo, tree calf gilt, yellow edges.* LARGE PAPER: *colored plates.* Printed by Bulmer, for W. Miller, London, 1804

Contains the "Bashful Man," with plate representing him about to leave the dinner-table.

2585 REPTON, HUMPHRY. THE LANDSCAPE GARDENING AND LANDSCAPE ARCHITECTURE, of the late Humphry Repton, Esq.; being his Entire Works on these Subjects. A New Edition, with an Historical and Scientific Introduction, a Systematic Analysis, a Biographical Notice, and a Copious Alphabetical Index; by J. C. Loudon, F. L. S., etc. *Portrait and above* 250 *wood-cuts.* 1 *vol.*, 8*vo, half green morocco.* London, 1840

2586 REPUBLICK OF LETTERS. THE PRESENT STATE OF THE. [Edited by Andrew Reid.] *Complete from* 1728 *to* 1836, *inclusive.* 18 *vols.*, 8*vo, half calf.* London, 1728–36

This rare work gives a general view of the state of learning (during those years) throughout Europe, and contains accounts of the most valuable books then published, with abstracts, memoirs of authors, and other miscellaneous matter relative to literature.

2587 RETROSPECTIVE (THE) REVIEW, and Historical and Antiquarian Magazine; consisting of Criticisms upon, Analyses of, and Extracts from Curious, Valuable, and Scarce Old Books. THREE SERIES COMPLETE. 18 *vols.*, 8*vo.* 16 *vols., half morocco, rest (third series) in numbers.* London, 1820–26; 1827–28; 1853–54

First series, 28 parts in 14 vols.; second series, 6 parts in 2 vols.; third series, 8 numbers forming 2 vols.

"An excellent review of early literature, to which the editor of these pages has been much indebted. The criticisms in the first series were written by Geo. Robinson, Esq., W. Gray, Esq., Mr. Serj. Talfourd, Joseph Parkes, Esq., etc., the whole being under the superintendence of H. Southern, Esq. The second series, edited by Henry Southern and Nicholas Harris Nicolas, contains, besides the review of old books, some valuable historical, topographical, and genealogical information. The papers in the third series were chiefly written by Thomas Wright, Esq., J. O. Halliwell, Esq., and M. A. Lower, Esq." — *Bohn's Lowndes.*

2588 RETROSPECTIVE REVIEW. ANOTHER COPY, *of the first* 20 *parts of the first series, from the library of Dr. Parr; with MSS. marginal notes.* 10 *vols.*, 8*vo, half calf.* London, 1820–24

2589 RETZ, JEAN FRANÇOIS PAUL DE GONDI, Cardinal de. MEMOIRS OF; containing the Particulars of his own Life, with the most Secret Transactions at the French Court during the Administration of Cardinal Mazarin, and the

Civil Wars occasioned by it; to which are added, some other Pieces written by the Cardinal de Retz, or Explanatory to these Memoirs. Translated from the French, with Notes [by P. Davall]. *Portrait by Vander Gucht. 4 vols., small 12mo, old calf.* J. Tonson, London, 1723

2590 RETZSCH, FRIEDRICH AUGUST MORITZ. OUTLINES TO SHAKSPEARE: First Series: Hamlet, Seventeen Plates. Second Original Edition. *With explanations by C. A. Böttiger, in German and English. Royal 4to, cloth.* Leipzig, 1838

2591 RETZSCH, FRIEDRICH AUGUST MORITZ. GALLERY TO SHAKSPEARE'S DRAMATIC WORKS IN OUTLINES. Complete in One Volume, with Explanations [by C. A. Böttiger and others, in German and English]. *Oblong 4to, cloth, gilt edges.* New York, 1849

2592 REVOLUTIONARY MEMORIALS: embracing Poems by the Rev. Wheeler Case, published in 1778; and an Appendix, containing General Burgoyne's Proclamation (in burlesque, dated June 23, 1777; a Late Authentic Account of the Death of Miss Jane M'Crea; the American Hero, a Sapphic Ode, by Nat. Niles, A. M., etc. Edited by the Rev. Stephen Dodd. 12*mo, cloth.* New York, 1852

2593 REYNARD THE FOX; a Renowned Apologue of the Middle Age, reproduced in Rhyme. [By Samuel Naylor.] *Beautifully printed, embellished throughout with scroll capitals, in colors, after designs of the twelfth and thirteenth centuries. Square crown 8vo, cloth, gilt top, uncut.* Longmans & Co., London, 1845

A fine specimen of ornate typography.

2594 REYNARD THE FOX; after the German version of Goethe. By Thomas James Arnold, Esq. With Illustrations from the Designs of Wilhelm von Kaulbach. *Contains also the 12 plates engraved for W. Pickering,* 1853, *after designs by Joseph Wolf, and the engraved title. Imperial 8vo, half morocco, gilt top.* London, 1860

2595 REYNARD THE FOX. REINEKE FUCHS, von Wolfgang von Goethe; mit Zeichnungen von Wilhelm von Kaulbach, gestochen von R. Rahn und A. Schleich. *Engraved title, frontispiece, and 35 most expressive and finely executed plates, besides numerous vignettes. Royal 4to, calf extra, emblematically tooled, gilt edges.* München, 1846

2596 REYNOLDS, FREDERICK. THE LIFE AND TIMES OF; written by himself. Second Edition. *Portrait. 2 vols., 8vo, cloth, uncut.* London, 1827

2597 RHEES, WILLIAM J. MANUAL OF PUBLIC LIBRARIES, INSTITUTIONS, AND SOCIETIES, in the United States, and British Provinces of North America. 8*vo, cloth.* Philadelphia, 1859

2598 RHYMES WITHOUT REASON, WITH REASONS FOR RHYMING; to which are added, Two Prose Essays. By the Author of no other Publication!!! *Frontispiece. 4to, boards, uncut.* London, 1823

2599 RICHARDSON, CHARLES. A NEW DICTIONARY OF THE ENGLISH LANGUAGE. 2 *vols., 4to, half russia, marbled edges; back of second volume cracked.* W. Pickering, London, 1839

The arrangement of this dictionary is somewhat inconvenient for general use, the words being classified under their roots instead of following the usual strict alphabetical order. It is, however, very useful and interesting to the philologist, as it is devoted to words considered purely English, and shows, at a glance, the changes that have taken place in the language. The quotations, which are numerous, are chronologically arranged.

2600 RICHARDSON, SAMUEL. THE HISTORY OF SIR CHARLES GRANDISON; by the Editor of Pamela and Clarissa. 6 *vols., 8vo, calf gilt, yellow edges; with autograph of Elizabeth, Countess of Derby.* London, 1754

2601 RICHARDSON, SAMUEL. CLARISSA, or the History of a Young Lady; comprehending the most Important Concerns of Private Life, and Particularly shewing the Distresses that may attend the Misconduct, both of Parents and Children, in Relation to Marriage. A New Edition, with the Last Corrections by the Author. *Plates by Grignion, etc., after S. Wale.* 8 *vols., 12mo, old calf gilt, yellow edges.* London, 1792

2602 RICHMOND, CHARLES GORDON LENNOX, FIFTH DUKE OF. MEMOIR OF. *Portrait. 8vo, cloth, uncut.* London, 1862

2603 RICHTER, JEAN PAUL FRIEDRICH. TITAN; a Romance from the German, translated by Charles T. Brooks. *Portrait.* 2 *vols., post 8vo, cloth, gilt tops.* Boston, 1862

2604 RICHTER, LUDWIG. RICHTER-ALBUM: eine Auswahl von Holzschnitten nach Zeichnungen von Ludwig Richter in Dresden. Dritte Ausgabe in Zwei Bänden. *Portrait, and above 300 fine wood-cuts.* 2 *vols., small 4to, cloth, uncut.* Leipzig, 1855

2605 RICRAFT, JOSIAH. A SURVEY OF ENGLAND'S CHAMPIONS AND TRUTH'S FAITHFULL PATRIOTS, or a Chronologicall Recitement of the Principall Proceedings of the most Worthy Commanders of the Prosperous Armies raised for the Preservation of Religion, the Kings Majesties Person, the Priviledges of Parliament, and the Liberty of the Subject, etc.; with a most Exact Narration of the Severall Victories, as also the Number of Commanders and Souldiers that have been slain on Both Sides since these Uncivill Civill Wars began. With the Lively Pourtraitures of the Severall Commanders. By Josiah Ricraft. Published by Authority. London: printed by R. Austin, etc., etc., 1647. *With sec-*

ond title, — "*The Civill Warres of England, etc., collected by John Leycester,*" — *dated* 1649, *and the* "*Continuation.*" *Fac-simile reprint. Royal* 8*vo, smooth morocco; with book-plate of James Broughton.* LARGE PAPER: *fine copy.*
(Thomas Rodd, London, 1818)

This copy contains a portrait of the author, and *all* (21, a list of which may be found in Bohn's "Lowdnes," p. 2092) the other portraits, besides a portrait of George Wither inserted.

2606 RIDLEY, REV. JAMES. THE TALES OF THE GENII, or the Delightful Lessons of Horam, the Son of Asmar; faithfully translated from the Persian Manuscript, and compared with French and Spanish Editions, published at Paris and Madrid. The Third Edition. By Sir Charles Morell. *Plates by A. Walker, etc.* 2 *vols., small* 8*vo, half calf, neat.*
London, 1766

2607 RIDLEY, REV. JAMES. THE TALES OF THE GENII, or the Delightful Lessons of Horam, the Son of Asmar; translated from the Persian, by Sir Charles Morell. *With* 14 *fine plates, engraved by Fittler, Landseer, Heath, W. & G. Cooke, etc.* 2 *vols.,* 8*vo, old calf.* London, 1805

2608 RIEMER, JACOB DE. BESCHRYVING VAN 'S GRAVEN-HAGE, behelzende deszelfs Oorsprong, Benaming, Gelegentheid, Uitbreidingen, Onheilen en Luister; mitsgaders Stigtinge van het Hof, der Kerken, Kloosters, Kapellen, Godshuizen, en andere, Voornaame Gebouwen; Zittinge der Hooge Collegien zoo van Politie als Justitie, Instellinge van het Kapittel ten Hove; als mede de Privilegien, Handvesten, Keuren, en Wyze der Regeringe. Uit zeer veele nooit gedrukte Oorspronkelyke Charters en Beschei den getrokken, opgeheldert, en bevestigt, door Mr Jacob de Riemer, R. G. *Numerous large plates.* 2 *vols. in* 3, *folio, old calf extra, gilt edges.*
Delft & 's Graven-Hage, 1730–39

2609 RISTORI, ADELAIDE. RÉPERTOIRE OF MADAME RISTORI: comprising Medea, Phædra, Deborah, Mary Stuart, Macbeth, Judith, Myrrha, Elizabeth, Adrienne Lecouvreur, and Pia de Tolemei; as represented at New York in 1866–67, by Madame Ristori and her Italian Dramatic Company, under the Management of J. Grau. *The ten plays* (*in Italian and English*) *bound in* 1 *vol.,* 8*vo, half morocco.*
New York, 1866

2610 RITCHIE, LEITCH. WINDSOR CASTLE, and its Environs; including Eton College. Second Edition, with Additions, by Edward Jesse, Esq. Embellished with Numerous Engravings by the First Artists. 8*vo, half morocco, gilt top.*
London, 1848

2611 RITSON, JOSEPH. COLLECTIONS OF EARLY ENGLISH AND SCOTTISH POETRY; with some of his other Publications, viz: —

Remarks, Critical and Illustrative, on the Texts and Notes of the Last Edition of Shakspeare. 1 *vol.* 8*vo.* J. Johnson, 1783

"These remarks were attacked in the 'St. James' Chronicle,' June, 1783, by 'Alciphron' (George Steevens?), and defended by 'Justice' (Ritson himself)." —*Lowndes.*

The Quip Modest: a Few Words by Way of Supplement to Remarks, Critical and Illustrative, on the Text and Notes of the Last Edition of Shakspeare; occasioned by a Republication of that Edition, revised and augmented, by the Editor of Dodsley's Old Plays. — An Essay on Abstinence from Animal Food, as a Moral Duty. *Together, in* 1 *vol.*, 8*vo.* J. Johnson, 1788; R. Phillips, 1802

This copy of the "Quip Modest" contains the note (reflecting upon George Steevens) on page vii. of the preface, which in most copies was canceled.

Pieces of Ancient Popular Poetry; from Authentic Manuscripts and Old Printed Copies. Adorned with Cuts [by Bewick]. 1 *vol., crown* 8*vo.* T. & J. Egerton, 1791

Another copy: Second Edition. *With the original woodcuts by Bewick.* 1 *vol., crown* 8*vo.* W. Pickering, 1833

" Edited by Ritson's nephew, Joseph Frank, Esq., who has added a few notes, and introduced another Poem, 'Sir Peny,' from a MS. in the Cotton Library, which Ritson intended for the Collection." — *Lowndes.*

The English Anthology. *With vignettes by Stothard.* 3 *vols., crown* 8*vo.* T. & J. Egerton, 1793–94

Scottish Songs (with the Music, and an Historical Essay). *Vignettes.* 2 *vols.*, 12*mo.* J. Johnson & J. Egerton, 1794

Robin Hood: a Collection of all the Ancient Poems, Songs, and Ballads, now extant, relative to that Celebrated English Outlaw; to which are prefixed Historical Anecdotes of his Life (with Notes and Illustrations). *Wood-cuts.* 2 *vols., crown* 8*vo.* T. Egerton & J. Johnson, 1795

Bibliographia Poetica: a Catalogue of English Poets, of the Twelfth, Thirteenth, Fourteenth, Fifteenth, and Sixteenth Centuries; with a Short Account of their Works. 1 *vol., crown* 8*vo.* G. & W. Nicol, 1802

Northern Garlands. The Bishopric Garland, or Durham Minstrel; a Choice Collection of Excellent Songs. The Yorkshire Garland; a Curious Collection of Old and New Songs. The Northumberland Garland, or Newcastle Nightingale; a Matchless Collection of Famous Songs. The North-Country Chorister; an Unparalleled Variety of Excellent Songs. [Edited by Joseph Haslewood.] 1 *vol., crown* 8*vo.* R. Triphook, 1810

A Select Collection of English Songs, with their Original Airs; and a Historical Essay on the Origin and Progress of National Song, by the late Joseph Ritson, Esq. The Second Edition, with Additional Songs and Occasional Notes, by Thomas Park, F. S. A. *Wood-cuts.* 3 *vols., crown* 8*vo.* Rivingtons, etc., 1813

THE LIFE OF KING ARTHUR; from Ancient Historians and Authentic Documents. (With Preface, Notes, and Appendix.) 1 *vol., crown 8vo.* Payne & Foss, etc., 1825

MEMOIRS OF THE CELTS OR GAULS. (With an Appendix, containing a Dictionary of Celtic Words, a Bibliotheca Celtica, etc., etc.) 1 *vol., crown 8vo.* Payne & Foss, 1827

ANCIENT SONGS AND BALLADS, from the Reign of King Henry the Second to the Revolution. *Second edition.* 2 *vols., crown 8vo.* Payne & Foss, 1829

"The most curious and certainly the most interesting to antiquarian readers, of all Ritson's works. This edition is reprinted from a copy of the former one, corrected, enlarged, and much improved by the author." — *Lowndes.*

FAIRY TALES, now first collected; to which are prefixed Two Dissertations: 1. On Pygmies. 2. On Fairies. [Edited from a MS. Copy, prepared for the Press by Ritson, by his Nephew, Joseph Frank.] 1 *vol., crown 8vo.* Payne & Foss, & W. Pickering, 1831

THE LETTERS OF JOSEPH RITSON, Esq.; edited chiefly from Originals in the Possession of his Nephew. To which is prefixed a Memoir of the Author by Sir Harris Nicolas. 2 *vols., crown 8vo.* W. Pickering, 1833

Together, 23 *vols., crimson turkey morocco extra, gilt edges, by Hayday.* London, 1783–1833

The above is an unusually fine collection, being all carefully selected and clean copies, uniformly bound from the sheets, with very wide margins.

2612 RITSON, JOSEPH. SOME ACCOUNT OF THE LIFE AND PUBLICATIONS OF THE LATE JOSEPH RITSON, ESQ., by Joseph Haslewood. *Portrait; and the appendix, consisting of "Verses addressed to the Ladies of Stockton."* 1824. — NORTHERN GARLANDS. *The* 4 *as in the above collection.* 1810. — GAMMER GURTON'S GARLAND, or the Nursery Parnassus; a Choice Collection of Pretty Songs and Verses, for the Amusement of all Little Good Children who can neither Read nor Run. 1810. *Together,* 1 *vol., crown 8vo, claret turkey morocco gilt, gilt edges.* R. Triphook, London, 1810–24

2613 RITTER, HEINRICH. THE HISTORY OF ANCIENT PHILOSOPHY. Translated from the German, by Alexander J. W. Morrison, B. A., etc. 4 *vols., 8vo, half calf, very neat.* Oxford and London, 1838–46

2614 RITTER, HEINRICH. ANOTHER COPY: *the same.* 4 *vols., 8vo, tree calf gilt, marbled edges.* Oxford and London, 1838–46

2615 RIVERS, REV. DAVID. LITERARY MEMOIRS OF LIVING AUTHORS OF GREAT BRITAIN, arranged according to an Alphabetical Catalogue of their Names; and including a List of their Works, with Occasional Opinions upon their Literary Character. 2 *vols. in* 1, *8vo, half calf, neat, rough edges; with MS. notes.* London, 1798

2616 ROBERTS, DAVID. EGYPT AND NUBIA, from Drawings made on the Spot by David Roberts, R. A.; with Historical Descriptions by William Brockedon, F. R. S. *Title of Vol. I. and 19 other finely colored plates of this work, lithographed by Louis Haghe, mounted on thick card-board, atlas folio size.* London, 1846

2617 ROBERTS, HENRY. THE TRUMPET OF FAME (or Sir F. Drake's and Sir J. Hawkins' Farewell; with an Encouragement to all Sailors and Soldiers, that are minded to go in this Worthy Enterprize: with the Names of many Ships, and what they have done against our Foes). Written by H. R. [Henry Roberts], and first printed in 1595 [by T. Creede]. The Second Edition [edited by T. Park]. *Title, preface, original title, and 14 pages. 12mo, half morocco.* Printed at the Private Press of Lee Priory, by John Warwick. Kent, 1818

2618 ROBERTSON, JOSEPH CLINTON, and THOMAS BYERLEY. THE PERCY ANECDOTES, Original and Select; by Sholto [J. C. Robertson] and Reuben [T. Byerley] Percy, Brothers of the Benedictine Monastery, Mount Benger. *Numerous portraits, etc. 20 vols., 18mo, half crimson morocco.* London, 1820–23

2619 ROBERTSON, WILLIAM, D. D. THE WORKS OF. (With an Essay on his Life and Writings.) *Portraits, by Worthington, on India paper, of Robertson, Mary Queen of Scots, James VI., Charles V., and Columbus. 8 vols., royal 8vo, cloth, rough edges.* LARGE PAPER: *only 50 copies printed.* Talboys, Oxford; Pickering, London, 1825

One of the "Oxford English Classics."

2620 ROBERTSON, REV. WILLIAM. A RESIDENCE AT GIBRALTAR, and a Visit to the Peninsula; in the Summer and Autumn of 1841. *With 6 plates engraved by E. and W. Finden, after J. M. W. Turner, etc. 8vo, cloth, uncut.* Edinburgh, (1844)

2621 ROBERTUS SCOTORUM REX: A LETTER from the Nobility, Barons, and Commons of Scotland, in the Year 1320, yet extant under all the Seals of the Nobility, directed to Pope John; wherein they declare their Firm Resolutions to adhere to their King Robert the Bruce, etc. Translated from the Original, in Latine, etc. Edinburgh: reprinted in the Year 1689. *Small 4to, pp. 11, boards.* PRIVATELY PRINTED, *for R. Balmanno, by C. A. Alvord.* New York, March, 1861

2622 ROBINSON, EDWARD, D. D. BIBLICAL RESEARCHES IN PALESTINE, Mount Sinai, and Arabia Petræa; a Journal of Travels in the Year 1838, by E. Robinson and E. Smith, undertaken in Reference to Biblical Geography. *Maps and plans. 3 vols., royal 8vo, boards.* Boston, 1841

2623 ROBINSON, JAMES. THE MERCHANTS', STUDENTS', AND CLERKS' MANUAL. *8vo, cloth.* Boston, 1856

2624 ROBINSON, JOHN. PROOFS OF A CONSPIRACY AGAINST ALL THE RELIGIONS AND GOVERNMENTS OF EUROPE, carried on in the Secret Meetings of Freemasons, Illuminati, and Reading Societies; collected from Good Authorities, by John Robinson, A. M. The Fourth Edition; to which is added a Postscript. *8vo, sheep, yellow edges.* New York, 1798

2625 ROBINSON, MARY, "THE CELEBRATED PERDITA." POEMS. *Portrait (inserted) by T. Burke, after Sir J. Reynolds. Post 8vo, half russia, neat.* London, 1791

2626 ROBINSON, MARY. MEMOIRS OF, written by herself; with some Posthumous Pieces. *Portrait wanting. 4 vols. in 2, 16mo, half morocco.* London, 1801

2627 ROBINSON, P. F. DESIGNS FOR ORNAMENTAL VILLAS, in Ninety-six Plates; by P. F. Robinson, Architect, F. S. A., etc., etc. The Scenic Views chiefly by J. D. Harding. Third Edition, greatly improved. *Royal 4to, half morocco.* London, 1836

2628 ROBINSON, P. F. DESIGNS FOR FARM BUILDINGS, with a View to prove that the Simplest Forms may be rendered Pleasing and Ornamental by a Proper Disposition of the Rudest Materials. Third Edition. *Plans, elevations, views, etc., in 56 plates. Royal 4to, half morocco.* London, 1837

2629 ROBINSON, P. F. DESIGNS FOR GATE COTTAGES, LODGES, AND PARK ENTRANCES, in Various Styles, from the Humblest to the Castellated. The Landscapes drawn on Stone by J. D. Harding and T. Allom. Third Edition, greatly improved. *Contains 48 plates. Royal 4to, half morocco.* London, 1837

2630 ROBINSON, P. F. A NEW SERIES OF DESIGNS FOR ORNAMENTAL COTTAGES AND VILLAS, with Estimates of the Probable Cost of erecting them; forming a Sequel to the Works entitled Rural Architecture and Designs for Ornamental Villas. *Fifty-six plates, the landscapes drawn on stone by J. D. Harding and T. Allom. Royal 4to, half morocco.* London, 1838

2631 ROBSON, GEORGE FENNELL. SCENERY OF THE GRAMPIAN MOUNTAINS, illustrated by Forty-one Plates representing the Principal Hills from such Points as display their Picturesque Features; diversified by Lakes and Rivers: with an Explanatory Page affixed to each Plate, giving an Account of those Objects of Natural Curiosity and Historical Interest, with which the District abounds; *the engravings executed by Henry Morton, and colored from original drawings made on the spot by the author. Imperial folio, half crimson morocco, neat; binding somewhat injured.* London, 1819

2632 ROCHESTER, John Wilmot, Second Earl of. Poems, etc., on Several Occasions; with Valentinian, a Tragedy. *Portrait wanting. 8vo, old calf; with autograph of W. Knott, and book-plate of Shuttleworth Forcett.*
J. Tonson, London, 1691

2633 ROE, A. S. A Long Look Ahead, or the First Stroke and the Last. 12*mo, cloth.* New York, 1855

2634 ROGERS, Henry. Selections from the Correspondence of R. E. H. Greyson, Esq. [Henry Rogers]; edited by the Author of "the Eclipse of Faith" [himself]. 2 *vols., foolscap 8vo, cloth, uncut.* London, 1857

2635 ROGERS, Henry Darwin; and Alexander Keith Johnston. Atlas of the United States of America, Canada, New Brunswick, Nova Scotia, Newfoundland, Mexico, Central America, Cuba, and Jamaica, on a Uniform Scale, from the most Recent State Documents, Marine Surveys, and Unpublished Materials; with Plans of the Principal Cities and Sea-Ports, and an Introductory Essay on the Physical Geography, Products, and Resources of North America. *Contains 24 maps (double), and 9 plans of cities. Folio, half morocco, neat.* London, 1857

2636 ROGERS, Samuel. An Epistle to a Friend (with Notes and Illustrations); with other Poems. *Post 4to, pp. 47, boards, rough edges.* Original edition.
London, 1798

2637 ROGERS, Samuel. Italy; a Poem. *With 56 fine engravings, after Turner and Stothard. 4to, vellum, very neat, gilt edges.* Large paper: *fine copy.*
E. Moxon, London, 1838

2638 ROGERS, Rev. Timothy. Good Newes from Heaven, or Safe-Conduct; discovering many Treasons and Horrible Plots against every ones Soule, with Helpe from God against them that (escaping them all) the Soule may come safe to Heaven at Last, which else will be Lost for ever. By Timothie Rogers, Preacher of Gods Word in Essex. *Small 12mo, calf, red edges.*
Printed by G. M., for E. Brewster, London, 1627

2639 ROGET, Peter Mark. Thesaurus of English Words and Phrases, so Classified and Arranged as to Facilitate the Expression of Ideas, and Assist in Literary Composition. Revised and edited, with a List of Foreign Words defined in English, and other Additions, by Barnas Sears, D. D. 12*mo, cloth.* First impression. Boston, 1855

Printed from the same stereotype-plates as copies bearing subsequent dates but much better, as the plates are now very badly worn.

2640 ROLL of Students of Harvard College, who have served in the Army or Navy during the War of the Rebellion. *Foolscap 8vo, pp. 48, paper.* (Cambridge), 1865

2641 ROLLIN, CHARLES. THE ANCIENT HISTORY of the Egyptians, Carthaginians, Assyrians, Babylonians, Medes and Persians, Macedonians and Grecians. Translated from the French. From the Latest London Edition, carefully revised and corrected. *Portrait, maps, and plates.* 4 *vols.*, 8*vo, sheep gilt.* New York, 1828

2642 ROMANO, GIULIO PIPPI. ISTORIA DELLA VITA E DELLE OPERE DI GIULIO PIPPI ROMANO; scritta da Carlo D'Arco. *Portrait and* 63 *plates, chiefly double. Royal folio, half crimson morocco, gilt top.* A Spese dell' Autore, Mantova, 1838

2643 ROMILLY, SIR SAMUEL. THE LIFE OF, written by himself; with a Selection from his Correspondence. Edited by his Sons. Third Edition. *Portrait by E. Finden, facsimile of handwriting and index.* 2 *vols., foolscap* 8*vo, half calf, very neat, marbled edges.* J. Murray, London, 1842

2644 ROPER, WILLIAM. THE LIFE OF SIR THOMAS MORE; by his Son-in-Law, William Roper, Esq. With Notes and an Appendix of Letters. A New Edition, revised and corrected, by S. W. Singer. *Portraits.* 12*mo, green turkey morocco gilt, gilt edges.* Chiswick, 1822

This copy has a second portrait (fac-simile of the title to the Paris edition of 1626) inserted between the introductory matter and the life.

2645 ROSCOE, THOMAS. WANDERINGS AND EXCURSIONS IN NORTH WALES. *With fifty-one engravings, by Radclyffe, from drawings by Cattermole, Cox, Creswick, etc.* (1856). — WANDERINGS AND EXCURSIONS IN SOUTH WALES; including the River Wye. *Forty-eight engravings, by Radclyffe, from drawings by Cox, Harding, Fielding, Creswick, Watson, etc.* (s. a.) 2 *vols., royal* 8*vo, morocco extra, gilt edges.* London, 1836, etc.

2646 ROSCOE, WILLIAM. THE LIFE OF LORENZO DE MEDICI, CALLED THE MAGNIFICENT. The Third Edition, corrected. *Portrait and plates.* 2 *vols. in* 1, 4*to, old marbled calf extra, by Kalthoeber.* London, 1797

2647 ROSCOMMON, WENTWORTH DILLON, EARL OF. POEMS. To which is added, an Essay on Poetry, by the Earl of Mulgrave, together with Poems, by Mr. Richard Duke. 8*vo, old calf gilt.* J. Tonson, London, 1717

2648 ROSENBERG, CHARLES G. JENNY LIND IN AMERICA. *Portrait.* 12*mo, cloth.* New York, 1851

2649 ROSIER, JAMES. NARRATIVE OF WAYMOUTH'S VOYAGE TO THE COAST OF MAINE IN 1605, Complete, with Remarks by George Prince, showing the River explored to have been the Georges River, together with a Map of the same and the Adjacent Islands. 8*vo, pp.* 45, *paper.* Bath, 1860

2650 ROSS, ALEXANDER. HELENORE, OR THE FORTUNATE SHEPHERDESS; a Pastoral Tale. To which is added the

Life of the Author, comprehending a Particular Description of the Romantic Place where he lived, and an Account of the Manners and Amusements of the People of that Period; by his Grandson, the Rev. Alexander Thomson, Minister of Lenrathen. *Crown 8vo, boards, rough edges.* Dundee, 1812

This poem is in the broad Scottish dialect, and prefixed are lines (in the same dialect) addressed to the author, by Dr. Beattie.

2651 ROSS, Sir John. A Voyage of Discovery, made for the Purpose of Exploring Baffin's Bay, and Inquiring into the Probability of a North-West Passage. *With appendixes of natural history, etc., by Robert Brown, etc.; and 32 maps and plates, many of which are finely colored.* — Narrative of a Second Voyage in Search of a North-West Passage, and of a Residence in the Arctic Regions during the Years 1829, 1830, 1831, 1832, 1833; including the Reports of Commander, now Captain James Clark Ross, R. N., and the Discovery of the Northern Magnetic Pole. *With the appendix (usually bound as another volume), containing a sketch of the Boothians and the zoölogical, botanical, and scientific accounts. Portrait and 50 fine plates, many of which are colored. Together, 2 vols., 4to, tree calf gilt, marbled edges, by Riviere.* Elegant copy. London, 1819–35

2652 ROSS, Sir John. Another copy of Vol. II.: *without the appendix. Royal 4to, half calf neat, marbled edges.* Large paper. London, 1835

2653 ROSSINI, Luigi. Antichitá Romane. *A series of 101 grand views of the antiquities of Rome, similar to those of Piranesi, but taken at a later date;* proof impressions. *Without title. 1 vol., elephant folio, half morocco extra, gilt edges.* (Roma, 1819–23)

2654 ROUND (The) Table; a Saturday Review of Politics, Literature, Society and Art. *September* 9, 1865–*September* 21, 1867, *unbound.* New York, 1865–67

2655 ROUSSEAU, Jean Baptiste. Supplement aux Œuvres de Mr. Rousseau; contenant les Pieces que l'Auteur a rejettées de son Édition. Donné au Public par Mr. D. *12mo, red morocco extra, gilt edges.* Londres, 1723

2656 ROUSSEAU, Jean Jacques. Œuvres Complettes. Nouvelle Édition. *Portrait; and numerous plates, by Ponce, etc., after Marillier. 37 vols., 12mo, old mottled calf extra, gilt edges.* Paris, 1793

2657 ROUSSEAU, Jean Jacques. A Complete Dictionary of Music, consisting of a Copious Explanation of all Words necessary to a True Knowledge and Understanding of Music. Translated from the Original French of J. J. Rousseau, by William Waring. Second Edition. *Plates. 8vo, old polished calf gilt, green edges.* Dublin, 1779

2658 ROUSSEAU, JEAN JACQUES. ELOISA, or a Series of Original Letters. Translated from the French. A New Edition, to which is now First added, the Sequel of Julia or the New Eloisa (found amongst the Author's Papers after his Decease); together with a Portrait of Mons. Rousseau. 4 *vols., 12mo, old sprinkled calf, green edges; with book-plate of James Lean.* London, 1784

2659 ROUSSEAU, JEAN JACQUES. JULIE, OU LE NOUVELLE HÉLOÏSE. Vignettes par MM. Tony Johannot, E. Wattier, E. Lepoitevin, H. Baron, Karl Girardet, C. Rogier, etc.; gravées par M. Brugnot. *India proofs of the large engravings. 2 vols., imperial 8vo, half crimson morocco extra, gilt tops, uncut.* LARGE PAPER: *fine copy.* Barbier, Paris, 1845

2660 ROUSSEAU, JEAN JACQUES. PENSAMIENTOS DE JUAN-JACOBO ROUSSEAU, Ciudadano de Ginebra; ó sea el Espíritu de este Grande Hombre en sus Obras Filosóficas, Morales, y Políticas. Traducido del Francés al Español, por Santiago de Alvarado y de la Peña. 2 *vols., 12mo, sheep, marbled edges.* Madrid (Paris), 1824

2661 ROUSSEAU, JEAN JACQUES. THE CONFESSIONS OF. *Portrait. 2 vols., 12mo, cloth.* New York, 1858

2662 ROWDEN, FRANCES ARABELLA. THE PLEASURES OF FRIENDSHIP; a Poem in Two Parts. The Third Edition. *Frontispiece, after Corbould. Foolscap 8vo, boards, rough edges.* London, 1818

2663 ROWE, ELIZABETH. THE MISCELLANEOUS WORKS, IN PROSE AND VERSE; the Greater Part now first published, from her Original Manuscripts, by Mr. Theophilus Rowe. To which are added, Poems on Several Occasions, by Mr. Thomas Rowe; and to the Whole is prefix'd an Account of the Lives and Writings of the Authors. *Portrait by Vertue. 2 vols., 8vo, old calf.* London, 1739

2664 ROYAUMONT, NICOLAS FONTAINE, SIEUR DE. HISTORY OF THE BIBLE (illustrated with Sculptures delineated and engraven by Skilful Artists), translated by Mr. John Coughen, Joseph Raynor, and supervised by Dr. Anthony Horneck, Henry Wharton, and other Orthodox Divines. Printed for Robert Blome. *Frontispiece, 4 maps, and 258 plates, engraved by Kip, Van Hove, Vander Gucht, etc. Without title. 1 vol., royal folio, finely bound, sprinkled calf extra, gilt edges.* (London, 1690, etc.)

2665 RUFFINI, GIOVANNI. THE PARAGREENS ON A VISIT TO THE PARIS UNIVERSAL EXHIBITION; by the Author of "Doctor Antonio." With Illustrations by John Leech. *12mo, cloth.* New York, 1857

2666 RUFFINI, GIOVANNI. LAVINIA; a Novel. *12mo, cloth.* New York, 1861

2667 RULES (THE) OF CIVILITY; OR CERTAIN WAYS OF DEPORTMENT OBSERVED IN FRANCE, amongst all Persons of Quality. Translated out of French. *Small 12mo, half morocco.* London, 1671

2668 RULES (THE), ORDERS, AND REGULATIONS OF THE SOCIETY OF ENGRAVERS, instituted at London, 1802. *8vo, calf, lettered on side "S. Rogers, Esqr., Honorary Member."* Printed by T. Bensley, London, 1804

2669 RUPPANER, ANTOINE, M. D. HYPODERMIC INJECTIONS in the Treatment of Neuralgia, Rheumatism, Gout, and other Diseases. 16*mo, cloth.* Boston, 1865

2670 RUSH, JAMES, M. D. THE PHILOSOPHY OF THE HUMAN VOICE, embracing its Physiological History; together with a System of Principles, by which Criticism in the Art of Elocution may be rendered Intelligible, and Instruction, Definite and Comprehensive. To which is added a Brief Analysis of Song and Recitative. Third Edition, enlarged. 8*vo, sheep.* Philadelphia, 1845

2671 RUSHWORTH, JOHN. HISTORICAL COLLECTIONS OF PRIVATE PASSAGES OF STATE, Weighty Matters in Law, Remarkable Proceedings in Five Parliaments; beginning the Sixteenth Year of King James, Anno 1618, and ending the Fifth Year of King Charles, Anno 1629: digested in Order of Time. (Continued to 1648; with the Tryal of Thomas Earl of Stratford, Lord Lieutenant of Ireland, upon an Impeachment of High Treason, shewing the Form of Parliamentary Proceedings in an Impeachment of Treason, etc., etc. *Portrait, by J. Pine.* 8 *vols., folio, old calf, red edges.* BEST EDITION. London, 1721

For contents see Bohn's "Lowndes," p. 2152.

2672 RUSKIN, JOHN. THE STONES OF VENICE. The Foundations. With Illustrations drawn by the Author. *Many of the plates colored.* 8*vo, cloth, gilt top, uncut.* New York, 1851

2673 RUSKIN, JOHN. MODERN PAINTERS. VOL. I. containing Parts I. and II.; Of General Principles, and of Truth. VOL. II. containing Part III., Sections I. and II.; Of the Imaginative and Theoretic Faculties. VOL. III. containing Part IV.; Of Many Things. VOL. IV. containing Part V.; Of Mountain Beauty. VOL. V. completing the Work, and containing Parts VI.; Of Leaf Beauty.—VII.; Of Cloud Beauty.—VIII.; Of Ideas of Relation, 1. Of Invention Formal.—IX.; Of Ideas of Relation, 2. Of Invention Spiritual.—(Indexes). *Numerous beautiful plates and wood-cuts, engraved by J. H. Le Keux, J. C. Armytage, T. Lupton, J. Conson, the author, etc., after J. M. Turner, the author and other eminent artists.* 5 *vols., imperial* 8*vo, calf gilt, marbled edges, by Riviere.* ELEGANT COPY. London, 1856–60

2674 RUSKIN, JOHN. THE CROWN OF WILD OLIVE: Three Lectures; on Work, Traffic, and War. *Foolscap 8vo, cloth, gilt edges.* London, 1866

2675 RUSSELL, JOHN SCOTT. THE MODERN SYSTEM OF NAVAL ARCHITECTURE. *Letter-press pp. xxxvii. and* 723, *and* 168 *large plates.* 3 *vols., atlas folio, half red morocco, very neat, large gilt labels on sides, gilt tops, uncut.* VERY FINE COPY. London, 1865

The plates in this elaborate work are all fine line engravings executed at great expense, and drawn to a practical working scale of one eighth inch to the foot for the lines and fittings of ships and on a larger scale for the details and machinery. The work is divided into three parts: I. Naval Design; II. Practical Ship-Building; III. Steam Navigation,—and in this copy, Vol. I., contains the text, and Vols. II. and III. the plates.

2676 RUSSELL, WILLIAM HOWARD. MY DIARY IN INDIA; in the Year 1858–9. *Tinted plates.* 2 *vols., crown 8vo, cloth, uncut.* London, 1860

2677 RUSSELL, WILLIAM HOWARD. THE MARRIAGE OF THE PRINCE OF WALES and Princess Alexandra of Denmark. *8vo, pp.* 23, *from the "Times" account.* Boston, (1863)

2678 RUTTER, JOHN. DELINEATIONS OF FONTHILL AND ITS ABBEY. *Map and* 18 *plates, including extra ones and etchings, some finely colored, besides* 15 *wood-cuts;* ALL INDIA PROOFS. *Imperial 4to, boards, morocco back.* LARGE PAPER. *Richard Samuel White's subscription copy.* Shaftesbury, 1823

2679 RYALL, H. T. PORTRAITS OF EMINENT CONSERVATIVE STATESMEN; with Genealogical and Historical Memoirs. BOTH SERIES; *with* 73 *large portraits, wood-cuts of arms, etc.* 2 *vols., imperial 4to, cloth, gilt edges.* London, (1838–41)

2680 RYAN, RICHARD. DRAMATIC TABLE TALK; or, Scenes, Situations, & Adventures, Serious & Comic, in Theatrical History & Biography. *Portraits, fac-similes, etc.* 3 *vols., foolscap 8vo, half morocco, neat.* London, 1825

2681 SABRINAE COROLLA in Hortulis Regiae Scholae Salopiensis contexuerunt Tres Viri Floribus Legendis. Editio Altera. *8vo, half morocco, very neat, gilt top, uncut.* Londini, 1859

2682 SAINT-ÉVREMOND, CHARLES MARGOTELLE DE SAINT-DENYS, Seigneur de. THE WORKS OF; made English from the French Original, with the Author's Life, by Mr. Des Maizeaux. To which are added, the Memoirs of the Dutchess of Mazarin, written in her Name, by the Abbot St. Real, etc. *With* 2 *portraits (one after Parmentier by Vertue, the other after Kneller by R. White) and monument.* 3 *vols., 8vo, half green morocco, marbled edges.* London, 1714

2683 SAINT-JOHN, JAMES AUGUSTUS. THE HISTORY OF THE MANNERS AND CUSTOMS OF ANCIENT GREECE. 3 *vols., 8vo, cloth, uncut.* London, 1842

2684 SAINT-JOHN, JAMES AUGUSTUS. THERE AND BACK AGAIN, in Search of Beauty. 2 *vols.*, 12*mo, cloth, uncut.* London, 1853

2685 SAINT-JOHN, PERCY B. FRENCH REVOLUTION IN 1848: The Three Days of February 1848. *Portraits. Post* 8*vo, cloth, uncut.* London, 1848

2686 SAINT-PROSPER, AUGUSTE J. C. HISTOIRES D'ANGLETERRE; d'Espagne, de Portugal, de Hollande, et de Belgique; de Russie, de Pologne, de Suède, et de Danemark; depuis les Temps les plus Reculés jusqu'à nos Jours. *Numerous plates, comprising, views, costumes, etc., etc.* 3 *vols.*, 8*vo, half calf, neat, marbled edges.* Paris, 1844

Fourth, sixth, and eighth volumes (each complete in itself) of "Le Monde, ou Histoire de Tous Les Peuples."

2687 SAINTE-PALAYE, JEAN BAPTISTE DE LA CURNE DE. MEMOIRS OF THE LIFE OF FROISSART; with an Essay on his Works, and a Criticism on his History. Translated from the French by Thomas Johnes, Esq. *Crown* 8*vo, calf, neat; with book-plate and autograph of James Heywood Markland, F. R. S.* London, 1801

2688 SALA, GEORGE AUGUSTUS. A JOURNEY DUE NORTH; being Notes of a Residence in Russia. 12*mo, cloth.* Boston, 1858

2689 SALA, GEORGE AUGUSTUS. GASLIGHT AND DAYLIGHT; with some London Scenes they shine upon. *Crown* 8*vo, cloth, uncut.* London, 1859

2690 SALA, GEORGE AUGUSTUS. TWICE ROUND THE CLOCK; or, the Hours of the Day and Night in London. *Portrait and wood-cuts.* 8*vo, cloth.* London, (1860)

2691 SALA, GEORGE AUGUSTUS. LOOKING AT LIFE; or, Thoughts and Things. *Post* 8*vo, cloth, uncut.* London, 1860

2692 SALAMÉ, ABRAHAM. A NARRATIVE OF THE EXPEDITION TO ALGIERS IN THE YEAR 1816, under the Command of the Right Hon. Admiral Lord Viscount Exmouth; by Mr. A. Salamé, who accompanied his Lordship for the Subsequent Negotiations with the Dey. *Portrait of Salamé and plates, the costumes colored.* 8*vo, half russia.* J. Murray, London, 1819

2693 SALMON, NICHOLAS. STEMMATA LATINITATIS; or an Etymological Latin Dictionary; wherein the Whole Mechanism of the Latin Tongue is methodically and conspicuously exhibited, upon a Plan entirely New, and calculated to facilitate the Acquisition, as well as to impress the Knowledge of the Language. With a Key, or Introduction, ascertaining not only the Origin, but the Value of the Several Terminations and Prepositive Particles; also, a General Index to every Latin Derivative and Word entering into Composition. 2 *vols., royal* 8*vo, half morocco.* London, 1796

2694 SALMON, Thomas. Modern History, or the Present State of all Nations; describing their Respective Situations, Persons, Habits, and Buildings; Manners, Laws, and Customs, Religion and Policy; Arts and Sciences, Trades, Manufactures, and Husbandry; Plants, Animals, and Minerals. Illustrated with Cuts and Maps, accurately drawn according to the Geographical Part of this Work, by Herman Moll. The Third Edition, with Considerable Additions and Improvements, interspersed in the body of the Work; also, the History and Revolutions of Each Country, brought down to the Present Time. *3 vols. (2 vols.), folio, marbled calf gilt.* London, 1745–46

Imperfect, the first volume being Vol. I. of the "Universal Traveller" (1752), but uniformly bound and lettered "Modern History."

2695 SALMON, Thomas. The Universal Traveller, or a Compleat Description of the Several Nations of the World: shewing, I. the Situation, Boundaries and Face of the Respective Countries; II. Number of Provinces and Chief Towns in each; III. the Genius, Temper, and Habits of the Several People; IV. their Religion, Government, and Forces by Sea and Land. V. Their Trafic, Produce of their Soil, Animals, and Minerals. VI. an Abstract of the History of Each Nation. Brought down to the Present Time, and illustrated with a great Variety of Maps and Cuts. *2 vols., folio, calf gilt, red edges.* London, 1753–55

2696 SALT, Henry. A Voyage to Abyssinia, and Travels into the Interior of that Country, executed under the Orders of the British Government, in the Years 1809 and 1810; in which are included, an Account of the Portuguese Settlements on the East Coast of Africa, visited in the Course of the Voyage; a Concise Narrative of Late Events in Arabia Felix; and some Particulars respecting the Aboriginal African Tribes, extending from Mosambique to the Borders of Egypt; together with Vocabularies of their Respective Languages. *Map of Abyssinia, and numerous charts, views., etc. Royal 4to, half morocco, very neat, marbled edges.* London, 1814

2697 SALT, Henry. Another copy: *the same; trimmed a little closer. Royal 4to, half russia, very neat, marbled edges.* London, 1814

2698 SAMMES, Aylett. Britannia Antiqua Illustrata, or the Antiquities of Ancient Britain, derived from the Phœnicians; wherein the Original Trade of this Island is discovered; the Names of Places, Offices, Dignities; as likewise the Idolatry, Language, and Customs of the Primitive Inhabitants, are clearly demonstrated from that Nation; many Old Monuments illustrated; and the Commerce with that People, as well as the Greeks, plainly set forth and collected out of approved Greek and Latin Authors: together with a Chronological History of this Kingdom, from the first Traditional Beginning, until the Year of Our Lord 800, when the Name of Britain was changed into England; faithfully collected out of the Best Authors, and disposed in a Better Method than hitherto hath been done; with the Antiquities of the Saxons, as well as Phœnicians, Greeks, and Romans. The First Volume. *Map and plates. Complete, only one Volume published. Folio, calf, very neat, marbled edges; with book-plate of Sir Ralph Milbanke (Lady Byron's father), and MS. notes.*

Printed by Tho. Roycroft, for the Author, London, 1676

"Myles Davies, in his 'Athenæ Britannicæ,' p. 135, notices Wood's abuse, and adds, 'But Mr. Oldenburg, secretary to the Royal Society, in his "Philosophical Transactions," being more impartial, as well as a more able judge, has long since done Mr. Aylett Sammes irreversible justice, as to the merits of his "Britannia Illustrata."'" —*Lowndes.*

2699 SAMUELS, EDWARD A. ORNITHOLOGY AND OÖLOGY OF NEW ENGLAND; containing Full Descriptions of the Birds of New England and Adjoining States and Provinces, arranged by a long-approved Classification and Nomenclature; together with a Complete History of their Habits, Times of Arrival and Departure, their Distribution, Food, Song, Time of Breeding; and a Careful and Accurate Description of their Nests and Eggs: with Illustrations of many Species of the Birds, and Accurate Figures of their Eggs. *Royal 8vo, cloth.* Boston, 1867

2700 SANDERSON, JOHN. BIOGRAPHY OF THE SIGNERS TO THE DECLARATION OF INDEPENDENCE. (With an Introduction comprising a View of the British Colonies of North America, from their Origin to their Independence.) *Engraved titles, numerous portraits, fac-similes of signatures, etc. 9 vols., 8vo, polished calf, gilt, marbled edges, by Bedford.* ELEGANT COPY. Philadelphia, 1820–27

2701 SANDYS, WILLIAM; and SIMON ANDREW FOSTER. THE HISTORY OF THE VIOLIN, and other Instruments played on with the Bow, from the Remotest Times to the Present; also an Account of the Principal Makers, English and Foreign. *With numerous illustrations. Frontispiece colored. 8vo, cloth, uncut.* London, 1864

2702 SANGER, WILLIAM W., M. D. THE HISTORY OF PROSTITUTION; its Extent, Causes, and Effects throughout the World. [Being an Official Report to the Board of Alms-House Governors of the City of New York.] *Royal 8vo, cloth.* New York, 1858

2703 SARCASTIC NOTICES OF THE LONG PARLIAMENT: a List of the "Members that held Places, both Civil and Military, contrary to the Self-Denying Ordinance of April 3, 1645, with the Sums of Money and Lands which they divided among themselves;" giving many Curious Particulars about this Famous Assembly not mentioned by Historians or Biographers. Reprinted, Verbatim, from the Excessively Rare Original. *Handsomely printed, with head-pieces and ornate initials, at the Chiswick Press. Foolscap 4to, half morocco, red paper sides, gilt top.* VERY FEW COPIES PRINTED. London, 1863

The original tract is entitled, "The Mystery of the Good Old Cause briefly unfolded, etc., etc. Printed in the First Year of England's Liberty after almost Twenty Years' Slavery. 1660."

2704 SARGENT, EPES. PECULIAR; a Tale of the Great Transition. *Post 8vo, cloth.* New York, 1864

2705 SARGENT, LUCIUS MANLIUS. HUBERT AND ELLEN; with other Poems: the Trial of the Harp, Billowy Water, the Plunderer's Grave, the Tear Drop, the Billow. *Royal 8vo, boards, rough edges.* Boston, 1813

2706 SARGENT, LUCIUS MANLIUS. DEALINGS WITH THE DEAD; by a Sexton of the Old School. *2 vols., 12mo, cloth.* Boston, 1856

2707 SARGENT, WINTHROP. THE LIFE AND CAREER OF MAJOR JOHN ANDRÉ, Adjutant General of the British Army in America. *Portrait 8vo, cloth, uncut.* LARGE PAPER: *only 75 copies printed.* Boston, 1861

2708 SATIRIST (THE), OR MONTHLY METEOR. [Edited by William Jerdan.] *Vols. I.–V. and XII.–XIII. Caricature plates, some of which are colored. 7 vols., 8vo, half morocco, extra.* London, 1808–13

The first five volumes comprise the original issue, October, 1807–October, 1809; the other two form Vols. II. and III. of the "New Series," January–December, 1813.

2709 SAUER, MARTIN. AN ACCOUNT OF A GEOGRAPHICAL AND ASTRONOMICAL EXPEDITION TO THE NORTHERN PARTS OF RUSSIA; for ascertaining the Degrees of Latitude and Longitude of the Mouth of the River Kovirna, of the Whole Coast of the Tshutski to East Cape, and of the Islands in the Eastern Ocean stretching to the American Coast; performed by command of Catherine II. of Russia, by Commodore Joseph Billings, in the Years 1785–94. The whole narrated from the Original Papers, by Martin Sauer, Secretary to the Expedition. *Chart and 14 plates of views, costumes, etc. 4to, half russia, neat.* London, 1802

2710 SAUNDERS, FREDERICK. MOSAICS; by the Author of "Salad for the Solitary," etc. *12mo, cloth.* New York, 1859

2711 SAUNDERS, JOHN. PORTRAITS AND MEMOIRS OF EMINENT LIVING POLITICAL REFORMERS; the Portraits by George Hayter, Esq., and other Eminent Artists, and the Memoirs by a Distinguished Literary Character. To which is annexed a Copious Historical Sketch of the

Progress of Parliamentary Reform, from the Attempt to Repeal the Septennial Act in 1734, to the Passing of the Reform Bill in 1832; by William Howitt. *Folio, half morocco extra, gilt edges.* LARGE PAPER: INDIA PROOFS. London, 1840

2712 SAUNDERS, JOHN. ANOTHER COPY: *the same.* INDIA PROOFS. *Folio, half morocco, neat, marbled edges.* London, 1840

2713 SAURIN, JACQUES. DISCOURS HISTORIQUES, CRITIQUES, THEOLOGIQUES, ET MORAUX, sur les Evenemens les plus Memorables du Vieux, et du Nouveau Testament (continuez par M. Roques, et par M. C. S. de Beausobre). Avec des Figures, gravées sur les Desseins de Hoet, Houbraken, & B. Picart. 6 *vols., royal folio, mottled calf extra, marbled edges.* PAPIER SUPER-ROYAL: *very fine copy.* Amsterdam & La Haye, 1720–39

This copy is one of what is considered the best impression, the first volume bearing imprint of "B. Picart, le Romain, Marchand d'Estampes, Amsterdam, 1720;" and the other volumes that of "Pierre de Hondt, La Haye, 1728–39."

2714 SAURIN, JACQUES. SERMONS sur Divers Textes de l'Écriture Sainte. Nouvelle Édition, en Gros Caractères. *Frontispiece,* 12 *vols.,* 8*vo, old calf gilt, red edges.* Lausanne, 1759

2715 SAVAGE, JAMES. A GENEALOGICAL DICTIONARY of the First Settlers of New England, showing Three Generations of those who came before May, 1692, on the Basis of Farmer's Register. 4 *vols.,* 8*vo, cloth.* Boston, 1860–62

2716 SAVARY, ANNE JEAN MARIE RENÉ, DUC DE ROVIGO. MEMOIRS; Illustrative of the History of the Emperor Napoleon. Second Edition. 4 *vols.,* 8*vo, cloth, uncut.* London, 1835

2717 SAXE, JOHN GODFREY. POEMS. New Edition, enlarged. *Portrait.* 12*mo, cloth.* Boston, 1852

2718 SAXE, MAURICE, COMTE DE. REVERIES, or Memoirs upon the Art of War. To which are added some Original Letters upon Various Military Subjects, wrote by the Count to the late King of Poland, and M. de Folard, which were never before made Publick; together with his Reflections upon the Propagation of the Human Species. Translated from the French. *Numerous plates.* 4*to, calf.* London, 1757

2719 SCACCHI, FORTUNATUS. SACRORUM ELAEOCHRISMATON MYROTHECIA TRIA, in quibus exponuntur Olea, atque unguenta Divinos in Codices relata; et olim vel cunctis universim Gentibus, in Vitæ quà Quotidiano, quà Moliore cultu; vel Nominatim apud Israëlitas, tam in Sacrorum Antistibus, Locis, Supellectilibus, quam in Regibus solemniter inaugurandis usurpata. Ordinis Eremitarum S. Augustini, etc.

Opus Eruditione Multiplici conspersum, & Institua Veterum, Literasque Reconditiores, Hebraicas, Græcas, Romanas, hujus Argumenti Occasione passim illustrans. Nec antea sic emendatum. *Frontispiece, portrait, and numerous plates. Folio, vellum extra, arms gilt on sides.*
F. Halmam, Amstelaedami, 1701

2720 SCARRON, PAUL. THE WHOLE COMICAL WORKS OF. Vol. I. containing his Comical Romance of a Company of Stage-Players, in Three Parts, Complete; Vol. II. all his Novels and Histories, his Select Letters, Characters, etc., a great Part of which never before in English. Translated by Mr. Thomas Brown, Mr. Savage, and others. The Fifth Edition, revised and corrected. *Portrait and plates, by Vander Gucht, etc.* 2 *vols.,* 12*mo, old calf; with autograph and book-plate of Captain Man.* London, 1741

2721 SCARTH, JOHN. TWELVE YEARS IN CHINA; the People, the Rebels, and the Mandarins. *Map,* 12 *colored plates, and wood-cuts. Crown* 8*vo, cloth, uncut.* Edinburgh, 1860

2722 SCHEDEL, HARTMANN. LIBER CRONICARUM, ETC. *Above* 2,000 *wood-cuts, by M. Wolgemut (the master of Albert Dürer) and W. Pleydenwurff, representing the principal incidents, characters, and places described in the work. Table,* 18 *leaves; text, leaves* I.–CCXCIX. *followed by a map, on the reverse of which is the last colophon with date. Leaves* 258–261 *(which were left blank for the purpose of inserting additions, etc.), the title, and* 2 *leaves of the table, are wanting, but the* TEXT IS ALL PERFECT *and in good condition. Folio* (17+12½ *inches*), *stamped vellum, over wood, with brass claps.* NUREMBERG CHRONICLE: FIRST EDITION. **Black letter.** *Latin text.*
A. Koberger, Nuremberge, 1493

A colophon at fol. 266 denotes Schedel to be the author or compiler, and the last colophon (with date) mentions Wolgemut and Pleydenwurff as the artists. A very full Account of the work, with fac-similes, may be found in Dibdin's "Bibliotheca Spenceriana," Vol. III. pp. 255–280.

2723 SCHEUCHZER, JOHANN JACOB. PHYSIQUE SACRÉE, OU HISTOIRE-NATURELLE DE LA BIBLE; traduite du Latin [par De Varenne]. Enrichie de Figures en Taille-douce, gravées par les Soins de Jean André Pfeffel. 8 *vols., folio, old mottled calf gilt, over marbled edges.*
Amsterdam, 1732–37

"Parmi les 750 gravures assez belles dont ce livre est orné, et qui en font le principal mérite, il s'en trouve beaucoup de tout à fait inutiles; mais une autre partie de ces planches offre des sujets qui n'ont pas été gravés ailleurs; et c'en est assez pour rendre ce grand ouvrage indispensable aux naturalistes." — *Brunet.*

2724 SCHILLER, JOHANN CHRISTOPH FRIEDRICH VON. THE WORKS OF: Historical, Historical and Dramatic, Historical Dramas, etc. Early Dramas and Romances. (Translated by A. J. W. Morrison, and others, and H. G. Bohn.) *Portraits.* 4 *vols., post* 8*vo, half calf, neat, marbled edges.*
London, 1847–53

2725 SCHILLER, JOHANN CHRISTOPH FRIEDRICH VON. ANOTHER SET: *the same. Portraits.* 4 *vols., post* 8*vo, half purple calf extra, marbled edges.* London, 1853–60

2726 SCHIMMELPENNINCK, MARY ANNE. THEORY ON THE CLASSIFICATION OF BEAUTY AND DEFORMITY, and their Correspondence with Physiognomonic Expression; exemplified in various Works of Art, and Natural Objects. *Illustrated with four general charts, and thirty-eight copperplates.* 4*to, half calf extra, marbled edges.* London, 1815

2727 SCHLOSSER, FRIEDRICH CHRISTOPH. HISTORY OF THE EIGHTEENTH CENTURY, and of the Nineteenth till the Overthrow of the French Empire; with Particular Reference to Mental Cultivation and Progress. Translated, with a Preface and Notes, by D. Davison, M. A. 8 *vols.,* 8*vo, half calf extra.* London, 1843–52

2728 SCHOLA ITALICA ARTIS PICTORIÆ, sive Tabulae Insigniores in Romanis Pinacothecis adservatae; Tabulis Aere incisis nunc Primum editae. *Fine impressions of the* 40 *engravings by Volpato and others, after Michael Angelo, Raffaelle, Titian, Caracci, Guido, Parmigiano, etc. Imperial folio, half morocco.*
Sumptibus Petri Pauli Montagnani-Mirabili, Romae, 1806

This work is similar in general appearance to Hamilton's "Schola Italica Pictoriæ," to which it may be considered a sequel.

2729 SCHOOLCRAFT, HENRY ROWE. HISTORICAL AND STATISTICAL INFORMATION respecting the History, Condition, and Prospects of the Indian Tribes of the United States; collected and prepared under the Direction of the Bureau of Indian Affairs, etc. Illustrated by S. Eastman, Capt. U. S. A. (and other Officers). 6 *vols., royal* 4*to, half morocco, marbled edges.* Philadelphia, 1851–57

The title of the sixth volume, which contains portrait of the author, reads: "History of the Indian Tribes of the United States: their Present Condition and Prospects, and a Sketch of their Ancient Statutes. By Henry Rowe Schoolcraft, LL. D., etc., etc. With Illustrations by Eminent Artists. In One Volume. Part VI. of the Series."

2730 SCHROEDER, JOHN FREDERICK, D. D. LIFE AND TIMES OF WASHINGTON; containing a Particular Account of National Principles and Events, and of the Illustrious Men of the Revolution. Illustrated with highly-finished Steel Engravings, from Original Designs, of Historical Scenes, and Full-length Portraits; by Alonzo Chappel. 2 *vols.,* 4*to, morocco antique, gilt edges.* New York, (1857–59)

2731 SCOTT, JOHN. THE SPORTSMAN'S REPOSITORY: comprising a Series of highly-finished Engravings, representing the Horse and the Dog, in all their Varieties. From Original Paintings by Marshall, Reinagle, Gilpin, Stubbs, and Cooper; accompanied with a Comprehensive, Historical, and Systematic Description of the Different Species of each; their Uses, Management, and Improvement; interspersed with Anecdotes of the most Celebrated Horses and Dogs, and their Proprietors; also a Variety of Practical Information on Training, and the Amusements of the Field. *Engraved title and* 37 *plates, with as many vignettes.* 4*to, cloth, uncut.* London, 1845

2732 SCOTT, JOHN. ANOTHER COPY: *the same.* 4*to, cloth, uncut.* London, 1845

Scott was one of the most celebrated engravers of animals, and the horses and dogs in this work are considered among his best productions.

2733 SCOTT, REV. THOMAS. THE BOOK OF JOB, in English Verse; translated from the Original Hebrew, with Remarks Historical, Critical, and Explanatory. The Second Edition. *Frontispiece. Biographical and bibliographical MS. notes on fly-leaf.* 8*vo, sheep; with autograph signature of Thadd. M. Harris.* London, 1773

This author is *not* the well-known commentator. "An elegant and close version, with a valuable commentary, by a learned Arian dissenting minister." — *Lowndes.*

2734 SCOTT, SIR WALTER. THE LIFE OF JOHN DRYDEN. *Portrait, on India paper, engraved by J. Fittler.* 4*to, half russia extra, marbled edges.* LARGE PAPER: *only* 50 *copies printed.* London, 1808

Printed by James Ballantyne & Co., Edinburgh, from Scott's edition of Dryden's Works. A pencil-note on fly-leaf says, "only 25 copies printed on large paper;" but Lowndes says there were fifty.

2735 SCOTT, SIR WALTER. THE BORDER ANTIQUITIES OF ENGLAND AND SCOTLAND; comprising Specimens of Architecture and Sculpture, and other Vestiges of Former Ages, accompanied by Descriptions. Together with Illustrations of Remarkable Incidents in Border History and Tradition, and Original Poetry. *Fine impressions of the plates.* 1 *vol.,* 4*to, half red morocco, marbled edges.* ORIGINAL EDITION. London, 1814, etc.

This copy is imperfect, containing but 89 (should contain 94) plates, and part of the text wanting; but the impressions of the plates are superior to those of the subsequent issue with same date.

2736 SCOTT, SIR WALTER. THE POETICAL WORKS OF. *Portrait by C. Heath.* 12 *vols.,* 12*mo, boards, rough edges.* A. Constable & Co., Edinburgh, 1820

2737 SCOTT, SIR WALTER. ŒUVRES COMPLÈTES DE WALTER SCOTT. 51 *vols.,* 12*mo, half sheep* (2 *vols. bound in* 4, *and Vols. XIII.–XV. and XLVII. wanting*). *Should comprise* 53 *vols. in* 55. H. Nicolle, Paris, 1820–21

2738 SCOTT, SIR WALTER. THE COMPLETE WORKS OF: WAVERLEY NOVELS; with Notes, Index, and Glossary. 12 *vols.* — MISCELLANEOUS PROSE WORKS, with Notes, containing Biographical Memoirs, Essays, and Letters; Life of Napoleon; and, Tales of a Grandfather. 3 *vols.* — POETICAL

Works, with all his Introductions and Notes; also Various Readings, and the Editor's Notes. 1 *vol.* — Life of; by Lockhart. 1 *vol.* *Above* 200 *beautiful engravings on steel, and* 2,000 *on wood;* BRILLIANT IMPRESSIONS, *some on India paper. Together,* 17 *vols., thick royal* 8*vo, half green turkey morocco, contents lettered, gilt tops.* Abbotsford edition: *elegant copy of original issue.* Edinburgh, 1842–47

2739 SEBA, Albertus. Locupletissimi Rerum Naturalium Thesauri Accurata Descriptio, et Iconibus Artificiosissimis Expressio, per Universam Physices Historiam; Opus, cui, in hoc Rerum Genere, Nullum Par exstitit: ex toto Terrarum Orbe collegit, digessit, descripsit, et depingendum curavit Albertus Seba, Etzela Oostfrisius, etc., etc. *Latin and French text, with portrait by Houbraken after Quinkhard, frontispiece and other embellishments engraved by P. Tanyé, and* 449 *plates, containing several thousand figures of animals, birds, insects, fish, shells, plants, etc., etc.* 4 *vols., royal folio, olive morocco, neat, gilt edges; with book-plate of Robert Barclay, Bury Hill.* Very fine copy. Amstelaedami, 1734–65

"Livre beaucoup plus estimé pour les belles planches dont il est orné, et que citent souvent les meilleurs naturalistes modernes, que pour le texte qui les accompagne." — *Brunet.*

2740 SEDGWICK, Catherine Maria. Letters from Abroad to Kindred at Home. 2 *vols.,* 12*mo, cloth.* New York, 1841

2741 SEDGWICK, Catherine Maria. Married or Single? 2 *vols.,* 12*mo, cloth.* New York, 1857

2742 SEDGWICK, Mrs. Charles. A Talk with my Pupils. 12*mo, cloth.* New York, 1863

2743 SÉGUR, Philippe Paul, Comte de. History of the Expedition to Russia, undertaken by the Emperor Napoleon, in the Year 1812. Second Edition, carefully revised and corrected. *Map,* 4 *portraits and* 3 *plates.* 2 *vols.,* 8*vo, half calf extra.* London, 1825

2744 SELBY, Charles, Comedian. Maximums & Speciments of William Muggins, Natural Philosopher and Citizen of the World. New Edition. 16*mo, boards.* London, 1859

2745 SELBY, Prideaux John. Illustrations of British Ornithology: Vol. I., Land Birds; Vol. II., Water Birds. 2 *vols.,* 8*vo, W. H. Lizars, Edinburgh,* 1833. — Plates: *comprising* 383 *figures, in most cases of the full life-size, in* 228 *finely colored plates, and* 4 *plain ones of the anatomical sections.* 2 *vols., elephant folio, London,* 1841. *Together,* 4 *vols., half green levant morocco, extra, gilt edges, by Hammond.* Edinburgh & London, 1833–41

This work (published at £105), bears the same relation to British birds that Audubon's large work does to American. All the known species found in

Great Britain are represented, with full descriptions of plumage, habits, etc., both the scientific and familiar names being given, and references to all those who have previously figured them.

2746 SELECT (A) COLLECTION OF VIEWS AND RUINS IN ROME AND ITS VICINITY; executed from Drawings made upon the Spot, in the Year 1791. *A series of* 63 *colored plates. Atlas* 4*to, half morocco, neat.* London, (1830)

2747 SELECT MONUMENTS OF THE DOCTRINE AND WORSHIP OF THE CATHOLIC CHURCH in England before the Norman Conquest: consisting of Ælfric's Paschal Homily, and Extracts from his Epistles, etc., the Offices of the Canonical Hours, and Three Metrical Prayers or Hymns; in Anglo-Saxon, and partly in Latin. With English Translations, revised or newly executed, Notes, Collation of Ancient Manuscripts, and an Introduction, by E. Thomson, Esq. *Fac-simile plates.* 18*mo, cloth, gilt edges.* Lumley, London, 1849

This volume contains a reprint of the "Testimonie of Antiquitie" printed by John Day between the years 1566 and 1570.

2748 SELIGMANN, JOHANN MICHAEL. VERZAMELING VAN UITLANDSCHE EN ZELDZAAME VOGELEN, benevens eenige Vreemde Dieren en Plantgewassen; in't Engelsch naauwkeurig beschreeven en naar 't Leven met Kleuren afgebeeld, door G. Edwards en M. Catesby. Vervolgens ten opzigt van de Plaaten Merlyk verbeterd in't Hoogduitsch uitgegeven door J. M. Seligmann; thans in't Nederduitsch vertaald en met Aanhalingen van andere Autheuren verrykt, door M. Houttuyn. *Several hundred large plates, all well colored.* 9 *parts in* 5 *vols., folio, old mottled calf, gilt, red edges.* Amsterdam, 1772–81

2749 SENECA, LUCIUS ANNÆUS. TRAGŒDIÆ. *Small* 12*mo, vellum.* Typis Brigonciis, Venetiis, 1665

2750 SENECA, LUCIUS ANNÆUS. ŒUVRES: traduites en François par La Grange; avec des Notes de Critique, d'Histoire, et de Littérature. Précédées d'un Essai sur les Règnes de Claude et de Néron, et sur les Mœurs et les Écrits de Séneque, pour servir d'Introduction à la Lecture de ses Ouvrages [par Diderot]. *Portrait.* 6 *vols.,* 8*vo, old marbled calf gilt, marbled edges.* Paris, An III., (1795)

"Traduction estimée." — *Brunet.*

2751 SEROUX D'AGINCOURT, JEAN BAPTISTE LOUIS GEORGES. STORIA DELL' ARTE DIMOSTRATA COI MONUMENTI, dalla sua Decadenza nel IV. Secolo fino al suo Risorgimento nel XVI. Tradotta ed illustrata da Stefano Ticozzi. *Fine impressions of the* 325 *plates. Text,* 6 *vols.,* 8*vo; plates* 3 *vols. in* 2, *folio; together,* 8 *vols., half morocco, neat.* Prato, 1826–30

2752 SEROUX D'AGINCOURT, JEAN BAPTISTE LOUIS GEORGES. HISTORY OF ART BY ITS MONUMENTS, from its Decline in the Fourth Century to its Restoration in the Sixteenth; translated from the French of Seroux d'Agincourt. *In three thousand three hundred and thirty-five subjects, on three hundred and twenty-eight plates.* 3 *vols. in* 1, *folio, half morocco, neat, gilt edges.* London, 1847

2753 SEWALL, RUFUS K. ANCIENT DOMINIONS OF MAINE: embracing the Earliest Facts; the Recent Discoveries of the Remains of Aboriginal Towns; the Voyages, Settlements, Battle Scenes, and Incidents of Indian Warfare; and other Incidents of History; together with the Religious Developments of Society within the Ancient Sagadahoc, Sheepscot, and Pemaquid Precincts and Dependencies. *Wood-cuts of views, etc.* 8*vo, cloth.* Bath (Portland), 1859

2754 SEWARD, MISS ANNA. THE POETICAL WORKS OF; with Extracts from her Literary Correspondence (and a Biographical Preface). Edited by Walter Scott, Esq. 3 *vols., post* 8*vo, calf.* Edinburgh, 1810

2755 SEWARD, WILLIAM. BIOGRAPHIANA; by the Compiler of Anecdotes of Distinguished Persons [W. Seward, F. R. S.]. *Frontispiece, portraits, etc., by Holloway, and* 10 *engraved pages of music.* 2 *vols.,* 8*vo, half calf.* London, 1799

2756 SEWEL, WILLIAM. A COMPLEAT DICTIONARY, ENGLISH AND DUTCH; to which is added a Grammar for Both Languages. Originally compiled by William Sewel, but now, not only reviewed and more than the Half Part augmented: yet, according to the Modern Spelling, entirely improved; by Egbert Buys, Counsellor of their Poliss and Prussian Majesties, etc. *Frontispiece.* 2 *vols.,* 4*to, old calf, red edges.* Kornelis de Veer, Amsterdam, 1766

2757 SEYMOUR, E. H. REMARKS, CRITICAL, CONJECTURAL, AND EXPLANATORY, UPON THE PLAYS OF SHAKSPEARE; resulting from a Collation of the Early Copies, with that of Johnson and Steevens, edited by Isaac Reed, Esq. Together with some Valuable Extracts from the MSS. of the late Right Honourable John, Lord Chedworth. 2 *vols.,* 8*vo, old calf gilt.* London, 1805

2758 SEYMOUR, ROBERT. HUMOROUS SKETCHES, comprising Eighty-six Caricature Etchings; illustrated in Prose and Verse by Alfred Crowquill [A. H. Forrester]. New Edition; with a Descriptive List of the Plates, and a Biographical Notice of Robert Seymour, by Henry G. Bohn. *Royal* 8*vo, cloth, gilt edges.* London, 1866

This volume contains the best series of plates by the "Modern Hogarth," the original illustrator of "Pickwick Papers."

2759 SHAFTESBURY, ANTHONY ASHLEY COOPER, EARL OF; CHARACTERISTICKS OF MEN, Manners, Opinions, Times.

The Fourth Edition. *Full-length portrait and* 12 *vignettes by S. Gribelin.* 3 *vols.,* 8*vo, old sprinkled calf, neat.* London, 1727

2760 SHAFTESBURY, ANTHONY ASHLEY COOPER. EARL OF. ANOTHER COPY: the Fifth Edition, corrected; with the Addition of a Letter concerning Design. *Same plates as the above.* 3 *vols.,* 8*vo, old sprinkled calf, neat; with book-plate of R. M. French, Chiswell.* London, 1732

This edition, printed by John Darby, is the *first complete* edition.

2761 SHAFTESBURY, ANTHONY ASHLEY COOPER, EARL OF. ANOTHER COPY: *with engravings (arms, etc.) by Ravenet the elder.* 3 *vols.,* 12*mo, calf; with book-plate and autograph of E. Negus.* (London), 1749

2762 SHAKESPEARE, WILLIAM. THE WORKS OF MR. WILLIAM SHAKESPEARE, in Six Volumes; revis'd and corrected, with an Account of the Life and Writings of the Author, by N. Rowe, Esq. *Frontispieces, engraved by Vander Gucht, and* 44 *plates. J. Tonson,* 1709. — VOLUME THE SEVENTH, containing Venus & Adonis, Tarquin & Lucrece, and his Miscellany Poems; with Critical Remarks on his Plays, etc. To which is prefix'd an Essay on the Art, Rise, and Progress of the Stage in Greece, Rome, and England [by Charles Gildon]. *Frontispiece. E. Curll, etc.,* 1710. *Together,* 7 *vols.,* 8*vo, russia, very neat.* FIRST SMALL EDITION, AND FIRST WITH PLATES. London, 1709–10

Copies in fine condition are rarely found.

2763 SHAKESPEARE, WILLIAM. THE PLAYS AND POEMS OF. (From the Text of Johnson and Steevens, with Johnson's Preface and Glossary.) *Portrait by Worthington, after Droeshout.* 11 *vols., crown* 8*vo, cloth, rough edges.* W. Pickering, London & Oxford, 1825

2764 SHAKESPEARE, WILLIAM. THE PICTORIAL EDITION OF THE WORKS OF SHAKESPEARE. (Including his Poems, Doubtful Plays, and the Biography. With Introductory Notices, Notes, Various Readings, Glossary, Music to the Songs, etc.) Edited by Charles Knight. *Several hundred fine wood-cuts of views, costumes, scenes, etc.* 8 *vols., royal* 8*vo, half morocco, extra.* ORIGINAL EDITION: *fine copy.* London, 1838–43

2765 SHAKESPEARE, WILLIAM. THE WORKS OF. The Plays edited from the Folio of MDCXXIII., with Various Readings from all the Editions and all the Commentators, Notes, Introductory Remarks, a Historical Sketch of the Text, an Account of the Rise and Progress of the English Drama, a Memoir of the Poet, and an Essay upon his Genius. By Richard Grant White. *Portraits, on India paper, and wood-cuts.* 12 *vols.,* 8*vo, half olive morocco, red paper sides, gilt tops, rough edges.* LARGE PAPER: *only* 48 *copies printed.* Boston, 1857–66

2766 SHAKESPEARE, WILLIAM. THE DRAMATIC WORKS: with Glossarial Notes, a Sketch of his Life, and an Estimate of his Writings; newly arranged and edited. *Printed with four octavo pages on each page and illustrated, with* 100 *engravings after eminent artists. Atlas 4to, turkey morocco extra, gilt edges.* WITH BOYDELL'S "SMALL SET" OF PRINTS. London, 1832

2767 SHAKESPEARE, WILLIAM. THE PLAYS OF WILLIAM SHAKESPEARE, accurately printed from the Text of the Corrected Copies left by the late George Steevens, Esq., and Edmund Malone, Esq.: with Mr. Malone's Various Readings, a Selection of Explanatory and Historical Notes from the most Eminent Commentators, a History of the Stage and a Life of Shakespeare; by Alexander Chalmers, F. S. A. New Edition. *Portrait.* 8 *vols.*, 8*vo, cloth, uncut.* London, 1856

2768 SHAKESPEARE, WILLIAM. THE LIFE OF HENRY VIII., by Mr. William Shakespear; in which are interspersed Historical Notes, Moral Reflections and Observations, in Respect to the Unhappy Fate Cardinal Wolsey met with. Never before publish'd. Adorned with Several [6 portraits] Copper-Plates. By the Author of the History of the Life and Times of Cardinal Wolsey [Joseph Grove]. Dedicated to Colley Cibber, Esq. 8*vo, boards.* London, 1758

2769 SHAKESPEARE, WILLIAM. THE DEVONSHIRE "HAMLETS." Hamlet by William Shake-speare, 1603; Hamlet by William Shakespeare, 1604: being Exact Reprints of the First and Second Editions of Shakespeare's great Drama, from the very Rare Originals in the Possession of his Grace the Duke of Devonshire; with the Two Texts printed on Opposite Pages, and so arranged that the Parallel Passages Face each other. And a Bibliographical Preface, by Samuel Timmins. 8*vo, half olive morocco, red paper sides, gilt top.* London, 1860

2770 SHAKESPEARE, WILLIAM. THE DEVONSHIRE "HAMLETS." ANOTHER COPY: *the same.* 8*vo, cloth, uncut.* London, 1860

2771 SHAKESPEARE, WILLIAM. THE POEMS OF WILLIAM SHAKESPEARE. With Three Engravings (after H. Corbould). 12*mo, boards, rough edges; with book-plate of E. A. Hitchcock, U. S. Army.* J. F. Dove, London, s. a.

2772 SHAKESPEARE, WILLIAM. SHAKESPEARE'S WILL; copied from the Original in the Prerogative Court, preserving the Interlineations and Fac-similes of Three Autographs of the Poet. With a Few Preliminary Observations, by J. O. Halliwell, Esq., F. S. A. *Title and* 4 *quarto leaves.* London, 1851

2773 SHAKESPEARE SOCIETY'S PUBLICATIONS. (Consisting of Works Illustrative of Shakespeare, Old Plays, Poems, Curious Tracts, Memoirs, etc., either now printed for the First Time, or from their Rarity difficult to be procured. Edited by Eminent Literary Men.) COMPLETE; *the* 48 *parts in* 20 *vols.*, 8*vo, tree calf gilt, contents lettered, marbled edges, by Riviere.* ELEGANT SET. London, 1841–53

For list of the contents, and names of the editors, see Bohn's "Lowndes," pp. 2341–42.

2774 SHAKESPEARE SOCIETY'S PUBLICATIONS. ANOTHER SET: COMPLETE AS ISSUED. 48 *parts in* 47 *vols.* (*parts* 2 *and* 3 *together*), 8*vo, cloth, uncut.* London, 1841–53

2775 SHAKESPEARE (THE) PORTFOLIO: Illustrations to Shakespeare by British Artists. *A series of* 90 *fine engravings by Heath, Greatbach, Robinson, Pye, Finden, Engleheart, Armstrong, Rolls, and other celebrated engravers, after Smirke, Stothard, Stephanhoff, Cooper, Westall, Hilton, Briggs, Leslie, Corbould, and other eminent artists; suitable for illustrating an octavo edition of Shakespeare's Works. Royal* 8*vo, half morocco.* (London, 1821–29)

2776 SHALLUS, FRANCIS. CHRONOLOGICAL TABLES, for Every Day in the Year, compiled from the most Authentic Documents; to which is added an Index. 2 *vols.*, 12*mo, half morocco, gilt tops.* FINE CLEAN COPY. Philadelphia, 1817

2777 SHARP, THOMAS. A DISSERTATION ON THE PAGEANTS OF Dramatic Mysteries anciently performed at Coventry, by the Trading Companies of that City; chiefly with reference to the Vehicle, Characters, and Dresses of the Actors: compiled, in a great Degree, from Sources hitherto unexplored; to which are added the Pageant of the Shearmen and Taylors' Company, and other Municipal Entertainments of a Public Nature. *Numerous plates, three songs engraved with the music, glossary, and index. Royal* 4*to, cloth, uncut.* Coventry, 1825

An account of this work may be found in the "Retrospective Review," Vol. XIII., pp. 297–316.

2778 SHAW, CHARLES. A TOPOGRAPHICAL AND HISTORICAL DESCRIPTION OF BOSTON, from the First Settlement of the Town to the Present Period; with some Account of its Environs. *Wood-cuts of State House, Faneuil Hall, and other buildings; and fac-simile of first entry in the Town Records.* 12*mo, boards, rough edges.* Boston, 1817

2779 SHAW, GEORGE, M. D.; and FREDERICK P. NODDER. VIVARIUM NATURÆ, or the Naturalist's Miscellany. By G. Shaw, F. R. S.; the Figures by F. P. Nodder, Botanic Painter to her Majesty. *Vols. I.–XII., containing* 492 *finely colored plates.* 12 *vols. in* 6, *royal* 8*vo, half russia, neat.* London, 1790, etc.

This work, which was issued in numbers, has no title except the above (engraved) in the first volume. Each volume has two pages of dedication, one in English, the other in Latin.

2780 SHAW, GEORGE, M. D.; and JAMES FRANCIS STEPHENS. GENERAL ZOOLOGY, or Systematic Natural History; by George Shaw, M. D., F. R. S., etc. (Continued by James Francis Stephens, F. L. S., etc.) *Vols. I. pt.* 1.–*IX. pt.* 2. MAMMALIA, AMPHIBIA, PISCES, INSECTA, AND FIRST PART OF AVES. *Above* 916 *fine plates, chiefly engraved by Heath, from the best authorities and specimens.* 9 *vols.*, 8*vo, diamond russia extra, marbled edges.* London, 1800–15

The volumes below (large paper) contain what is wanting to complete this set.

2781 SHAW, GEORGE, M. D.; and JAMES FRANCIS STEPHENS. GENERAL ZOOLOGY, or Systematic Natural History; by George Shaw, M. D., F. R. S., etc. (Continued by James F. Stephens, F. L. S., etc.) *Vols. VIII. pt.* 1–*XIV. pt.* 2. BIRDS, AND GENERAL INDEX. *Above* 432 *fine plates, engraved by Mrs. Griffith, J. Le Keux, etc., from the first authorities and most select specimens.* 7 *vols. in* 14, *royal* 8*vo, boards, uncut.* LARGE PAPER: PROOF IMPRESSION. London, 1811–26

The class "Aves" commences in Vol. VII. pt. 1, which volume (containing 71 plates) is wanting; this class is otherwise complete. The second part of the last volume contains a general index to the whole work.

2782 SHAW, HENRY. SPECIMENS OF ANCIENT FURNITURE, drawn from existing authorities by Henry Shaw, F. S. A.; with descriptions by Sir Samuel Rush Meyrick, LL. D. and F. S. A. *Engraved title and* 74 *plates, many finely colored.* 4*to, half olive morocco, red paper sides.* W. Pickering, London, 1836

2783 SHAW, HENRY. THE HAND BOOK OF MEDIÆVAL ALPHABETS AND DEVICES. *A selection of* 20 *plates of alphabets, and* 17 *plates of original specimens of labels, monograms, heraldic and other devices, not heretofore figured. Finely printed in colors. Imperial* 8*vo, cloth. Second edition.* London, 1856

2784 SHAW, SIMEON. NATURE DISPLAYED, in the Heavens and on the Earth; according to the Latest Observations and Discoveries. *Numerous plates.* 6 *vols.*, 8*vo, half calf, neat.* Sir R. Phillips, London, 1823

2785 SHELLEY, PERCY BYSSHE. SHELLEY MEMORIALS, from Authentic Sources. Edited by Lady Shelley. To which is added an Essay on Christianity, by Percy Bysshe Shelley, now first printed. 12*mo, cloth.* Boston, 1859

2786 SHENSTONE, WILLIAM. THE WORKS, in Verse and Prose. The Fifth Edition. *Portrait and plates.* 3 *vols., post* 8*vo, old marbled calf, red edges.* J. Dodsley, London, 1777

The third volume contains "Letters to Particular Friends, from the Year 1739 to 1763."

2787 SHERER, JOHN. THE GOLD-FINDER OF AUSTRALIA ; how he went, how he fared, and how he made his Fortune. *Illustrated with forty-eight magnificent engravings, from authentic sketches taken in the colony. 8vo, half calf extra.* London, (1853)

2788 SHERIDAN, FRANCES. MEMOIR OF THE LIFE AND WRITINGS OF MRS. FRANCES SHERIDAN, Mother of Richard Brinsley Sheridan, and Author of "Sidney Biddulph," "Nourjahad;" with Remarks upon a late Life of the Right Hon. R. B. Sheridan; also Criticisms and Selections from the Works of Mrs. Sheridan; and Biographical Anecdotes of her Family and Contemporaries. By her Grand-daughter, Alicia Lefance. *Portrait wanting. Crown 8vo, half green morocco.* London, 1824

2789 SHERWOOD, MARY MARTHA. THE LIFE OF; chiefly Autobiographical; with Extracts from Mr. Sherwood's Journal during his Imprisonment in France and Residence in India. Edited by her Daughter, Sophia Kelly. *Portrait and vignette on title. 8vo, cloth, uncut.* London, 1857

2790 SHIRLEY, JAMES. THE DRAMATIC WORKS AND POEMS OF; now first collected. With Notes by the late William Gifford, Esq.; and Additional Notes, and some Account of Shirley and his Writings, by the Rev. Alexander Dyce. *Portrait by T. Lupton. 6 vols., royal 8vo, smooth crimson morocco, very neat, contents lettered, gilt edges, by Holloway.* LARGE PAPER: *Few printed.* J. Murray, London, 1833

See JOHNSON, BEN.

"The present edition of Shirley, commenced, and almost finished, as to the collection and the arrangement of the plays, by Mr. Gifford, and now completed by the addition of the poems, and a Life, by Mr. Dyce, closes that prolific but brilliant series of our dramatic authors, without which no library, which pretends to comprehend the more valuable body of English poetic literature, can be considered perfect. Shirley was the 'last minstrel' of the English stage. In him expired what may be properly called the School of Shakspeare. . . . . . No one, in short, who has not attempted to acquaint himself with the beauties of Shirley's Drama, through the old quartos, can appreciate the luxury of reading them in the clearer letter, and more genuine text of the present edition." —*Quarterly Rev., Vol. XLIX. pp.* 2, 3, *and* 29.

2791 SHORES (THE) AND ISLANDS OF THE MEDITERRANEAN, Drawn from Nature, by Sir Grenville Temple, Bart., W. L. Leitch, Esq., Major Irton, & Lieut. Allen, R. E.; with an Analysis of the Mediterranean and Descriptions of the Plates, by the Rev. G. H. Wright, M. A. *Map and 63 plates. 4to, half calf.* London, s. a.

2792 SIBTHORP, JOHN, M. D. FLORA GRÆCA: sive Plantarum Rariorum Historia, quas in Provinciis aut Insulis Græciæ legit, investigavit, et depingi curavit, Johannes Sibthorp, M. D., etc. Hic illic etiam insertæ sunt Pauculæ Species quas Vir idem Clarissimus, Græciam versus Navigans, in Itinere, præsertim apud Italiam et Siciliam, invenerit. Characteres Omnium, Descriptiones et Synonyma, elaboravit Jacobus Edvardus Smith, M. D., etc. (et Johannes Lindley, Ph. D., etc.) 10 *vols., royal folio, half green levant morocco, very neat, gilt edges, by Hammond.* VERY FINE COPY: *with* ALL *the plates colored.* London, 1806–40

" This magnificent work extends to ten volumes, each containing 2 fasciculi, and 100 plates, engraved and colored by Sowerby, after drawings by Ferd. Bauer, in all 966 plates. The expenses were defrayed from the proceeds of an estate left for the purpose by Dr. Sibthorp, aided by the contributions of fifty subscribers, to which number the edition was limited, price £12 12s. each fasciculus, therefore £254; but not more than twenty of the subscribers lived to continue the work to the conclusion." — *Lowndes.*

Of the last three volumes only TWENTY-EIGHT copies were colored. The cost of publication of the whole work was above THIRTY THOUSAND POUNDS.

2793 SIDDONS, HENRY. PRACTICAL ILLUSTRATIONS OF RHETORICAL GESTURE AND ACTION, adapted to the English Drama, from a Work on the same Subject by M. Engel; by Henry Siddons. Embellished with Numerous Engravings, expressive of the Various Passions, and representing the Modern Costume, of the London Theatres. *8vo, half calf, very neat.* P. Phillips, London, 1807

2794 SIDDONS, HENRY. ANOTHER COPY: *wanting* 3 *leaves* (*title, advertisement, and pp.* 1 *and* 2) *and* 2 *plates.* *8vo, half russia.* (London, 1807)

2795 SIDNEY, CHARLES AND AMBROSE, OF GLASTONBURY. THE SIDNEY ANECDOTES; selected from History, Ancient and Modern, and other Authentic Sources. *Portraits of Duke of Buckingham and Voltaire, and wood-cuts.* 2 *parts in* 1 *vol., 12mo, sheep.* London, 1830

2796 SIDNEY, SIR PHILIP. THE COUNTESSE OF PEMBROKES ARCADIA; written by Sir Philip Sidney, Knight. Now the Sixth Time published. *Wood-cut title. Small folio, half calf; with book-plate of Thomas Hog, Gent.*

Imprinted by H. L., for Simon Waterson, London, 1622

COLLATION: Title, reverse blank; 1 leaf. Dedication ("To my Deare Lady and Sister, the Countesse of Pembroke," signed "Your loving brother, Philip Sidney"); 1 leaf. "To the Reader;" 1 leaf. The five books of the Arcadia; pp. 1–482 (pp. 327–346 being "a supplement of the said defect by Sir W. A.," *i. e.* Sir William Alexander.) "Certaine Sonets never before printed;" pp. 483–502. "The Defence of Poesie;" pp. 503–530. "Astrophel and Stella;" pp. 531–581. "The May-Ladie;" pp. 582–588. The errors in paging are numerous, namely, 48 for 38, 43 for 42, 42 for 43, 37 for 47, 88 and 89 omitted, 95 and 96 repeated, 357–366 for 157–166, 377 for 167, 368 for 168, 351 for 315, 352 for 325, 323 for 332, 256 for 356, 352 for 357, 381 for 375, 498 for 398, 413 for 401.

2797 SIDNEY, SIR PHILIP. THE MISCELLANEOUS WORKS OF; with a Life of the Author and Illustrative Notes, by William Gray, Esq. *Handsomely printed at the Riverside Press.* *8vo, tree calf gilt, gilt over carmine edges, by Riviere.*

Boston, 1860

2798 SIDNEY, SIR PHILIP. ANOTHER COPY: *the same.* *8vo, tree calf gilt, gilt over carmine edges, by Riviere.*

Boston, 1860

2799 SILIUS ITALICUS. THE SECOND PUNICK WAR BETWEEN HANNIBAL AND THE ROMANES; the Whole Seventeen Books: Englished from the Latine of Silius Italicus, with a Continuation from the Triumph of Scipio to the Death of Hannibal; by Tho. Ross, Esq. *Portrait of Charles II. by Loggan, and plates. Royal folio, old calf extra, gilt edges.* LARGE PAPER. London, 1661

2800 SILLIMAN'S JOURNAL. The American Journal of Science and Arts; conducted by Benjamin Silliman, M. D., LL. D. (Prof. Benjamin Silliman, Jr., and Prof. James D. Dana, in Connection with Prof. Asa Gray, Prof. Louis Agassiz, Dr. Wolcott Gibbs, and Dr. Waldo I. Burnett, etc. etc.). From commencement in 1818 to 1862, inclusive. FIRST SERIES, 49 *vols.;* SECOND SERIES, 34 *vols. Portraits, and numerous plates and wood-cuts.* 82 *vols., 8vo, half morocco, red tops, rough edges; and* 1 *vol.* (*XI. first series*) *in numbers.* EXCEEDINGLY FINE SET. New York and New Haven, 1818–62

A complete set of the *first series* is now very difficult to make up, some of the numbers being extremely scarce. The Index (Vol. L.) of the first series is wanting, otherwise this set is PERFECT.

2801 SILLIMAN, BENJAMIN, M. D. A TOUR TO QUEBEC, in the Autumn of 1819. *Plates. 8vo, paper, rough edges.* London, 1822

2802 SILLIMAN, BENJAMIN, M. D. LIFE OF BENJAMIN SILLIMAN, M. D., LL. D., late Professor in Yale College; chiefly from his Manuscript Reminiscences, Diaries, and Correspondence. By George P. Fisher. *Portrait and view of residence.* 2 *vols., crown 8vo, cloth.* New York, 1866

2803 SILVESTRE, J. B. UNIVERSAL PALÆOGRAPHY, or Facsimiles of Writings of all Nations and Periods; copied from the most Celebrated and Authentic Manuscripts in the Libraries and Archives of France, Italy, Germany, and England, by M. J. B. Silvestre: accompanied by an Historical and Descriptive Text and Introduction, by Champollion-Figeac and Aimé Champollion, Fils. Translated from the French, and edited, with Corrections and Notes, by Sir Frederic Madden, K. H., F. R. S., etc. *Above* 300 *large and finely executed plates, illuminated in gold, silver, and colors.* 2 *vols., atlas folio, and* 2 *vols.* (*text*), *imperial 8vo, half crimson morocco, gilt edges.* FINE COPY. London, 1850

One of the most comprehensive and elaborate works ever issued upon this subject.

2804 SIMPSON, WILLIAM. THE SEAT OF WAR IN THE EAST. BOTH SERIES: *comprising* 81 *finely colored plates, representing the incidents of the siege of Sebastopol, the aspect of the country, costumes, fortifications, etc., etc.; with descriptions and key-plates.* 1 *vol., imperial folio, half morocco extra, gilt edges, arms gilt on side.* Colnaghi & Co., London, 1855–56

2805 SIMSON, WALTER. A HISTORY OF THE GIPSIES; with Specimens of the Gipsy Language. Edited, with Preface, Introduction, and Notes, and a Disquisition on the Past, Present, and Future of Gipsydom, by James Simson. *12mo, cloth.* New York, 1866

2806 SINCLAIR, SIR JOHN. THE CODE OF HEALTH AND LONGEVITY, or a Concise View of the Principles calculated for the Preservation of Health, and the Attainment of Long Life; being an Attempt to prove the Practicability of condensing, within a Narrow Compass, the most Material Information hitherto accumulated, regarding the Different Arts and Sciences, or any Particular Branch thereof. *Frontispieces consisting of appropriate portraits. 4 vols., 8vo, half calf, marbled edges; with book-plate of Sir Alexr Ramsay, of Balmain, Bart.* Edinburgh, 1807

Contains the substance of many writers upon this subject, including the entire works of Cornaro, Friar Bacon, and others.

2807 SINGER, SAMUEL WELLER. RESEARCHES INTO THE HISTORY OF PLAYING CARDS; with Illustrations of the Origin of Printing and Engraving on Wood. *Numerous plates, on India paper, and a large number of wood-cuts, from early prints, paintings on wood and ivory, packs of cards, etc., many of them colored. 4to, morocco, neat, gilt edges.* ONLY 250 COPIES PRINTED. London, 1816

2808 SINGER, SAMUEL WELLER. THE TEXT OF SHAKESPEARE VINDICATED from the Interpolations and Corruptions advocated by John Payne Collier, Esq., in his Notes and Emendations. *8vo, cloth, uncut.* W. Pickering, London, 1853

2809 SINGER, SAMUEL WELLER. ANOTHER COPY: *the same. 8vo, cloth, uncut.* London, 1853

2810 SISMONDI, JOHN CHARLES LÉONARD SIMONDE DE. HISTORICAL VIEW OF THE LITERATURE OF THE SOUTH OF EUROPE. Translated from the Original, with Notes, and a Life of the Author; by Thomas Roscoe. Third Edition, including all the Notes from the Last Paris Edition. *Portraits of Sismondi and Dante. 2 vols., post 8vo, cloth, uncut.* London, 1850

2811 SIX HUNDRED DOLLARS A YEAR: a Wife's Effort at Low Living, under High Prices. *16mo, cloth.* Boston, 1867

2812 SKELTON, JOSEPH. PIETAS OXONIENSIS; or, Records of Oxford Founders. *Arms of University on the engraved title, and 25 large plates, comprising portraits, tombs, etc., engraved by Skelton, J. Fittler, and H. Winkles. Imperial 4to, half morocco, uncut.* LARGE PAPER: *fine impressions.* J. Skelton, Oxford, 1828

2813 SKOTTOWE, AUGUSTINE. THE LIFE OF SHAKESPEARE, Enquiries into the Originality of his Dramatic Plots and

Characters, and Essays on the Ancient Theatres and Theatrical Usages. 2 *vols. in* 1, 8*vo, half calf extra.* London, 1824

2814 SLADE, SIR ADOLPHUS, CAPT. R. N., AND VICE ADMIRAL IN THE TURKISH SERVICE. RECORDS OF TRAVELS IN TURKEY, GREECE, ETC.; and of a Cruise in the Black Sea, with the Capitan Pasha, in the Years 1829, 1830, and 1831. Second Edition. *Map and colored plates.* 2 *vols.*, 8*vo, half calf, neat.* London, 1833

2815 SLEEPER, J. S. MARK ROWLAND; a Tale of the Sea. 12*mo, cloth.* Boston, 1867

2816 SLEIDAN, JOHANN. THE GENERAL HISTORY OF THE REFORMATION OF THE CHURCH, from the Errors and Corruptions of the Church of Rome, begun in Germany by Martin Luther, with the Progress thereof in all Parts of Christendom, from the Year 1517 to the Year 1556; written in Latin by John Sleidan, LL. D., and faithfully Englished: to which is added, a Continuation to the End of the Council of Trentin the Year 1562. By Edmund Bohun, Esq. *With* 6 *portraits by Faithorne. Folio, old calf.* London, 1689

2817 SMALL BOOKS ON GREAT SUBJECTS; edited by a Few Well Wishers to Knowledge. No. V. A Brief View of Greek Philosophy up to the Age of Pericles. Nos. XIX.–XXI. On the State of Man Subsequent to the Promulgation of Christianity; Parts I.–III. 4 *vols., foolscap* 8*vo, cloth, uncut.* W. Pickering, London, 1844–54

2818 SMEDLEY, FRANCIS E. LORIMER LITTLEGOOD, ESQ., a Young Gentleman who wished to see Life and saw it Accordingly. *Wood-cuts.* 12*mo, cloth.* New York, s. a.

2819 SMILES, SAMUEL. THE LIFE OF GEORGE STEPHENSON, Railway Engineer. From the Fourth London Edition. *Portrait,* 12*mo, cloth.* Boston, 1858

2820 SMILES, SAMUEL. SELF-HELP; with Illustrations of Character and Conduct. 12*mo, cloth.* Boston, 1860

2821 SMILLIE, JAMES. MOUNT AUBURN ILLUSTRATED, in highly finished Line Engravings, from Drawings taken on the Spot; with Descriptive Notices, by Cornelia W. Walter. *Imperial* 4*to, dark blue turkey morocco extra, gilt edges.* LARGE PAPER: *choice impressions.* New York, 1847

2822 SMILLIE, JAMES. THE RURAL CEMETERIES OF AMERICA: GREEN-WOOD ILLUSTRATED; with Descriptive Notices, by Nehemiah Cleaveland. MOUNT AUBURN ILLUSTRATED; with Descriptive Notices, by Cornelia W. Walter. *Vignette titles, and above* 40 *plates.* 1 *vol.,* 4*to, half morocco, marbled edges.* New York, 1847

2823 SMIRKE, ROBERT. THE ADVENTURE OF HUNCH-BACK, and the Stories connected with it (from the Arabian Nights

Entertainments); with Illustrative Prints engraved by William Daniell from Pictures painted by Robert Smirke, R. A. *Contains* 17 *fine plates. Atlas* 4*to, half russia.* LARGE PAPER: *India proofs.* London, 1814

2824 SMITH, ALBERT. WILD OATS AND DEAD LEAVES. *Crown* 8*vo, cloth, uncut.* London, 1860

2825 SMITH, ALEXANDER. DREAMTHORP; a Book of Essays written in the Country. *Post* 8*vo, cloth.* Boston, 1864

2826 SMITH, CHARLES A., D. D. MEN OF THE OLDEN TIME. 12*mo, cloth.* Philadelphia, 1858

2827 SMITH, HORACE. WALTER COLYTON, a Tale of 1688. 3 *vols.*, 12*mo, half morocco.* London, 1830

2828 SMITH, HORACE, and JAMES. HORACE IN LONDON: consisting of Imitations of the First Two Books of the Odes of Horace; by the Authors of Rejected Addresses, or the New Theatrum Poetarum. 12*mo, mottled calf gilt, marbled edges.* London, 1813

2829 SMITH, JEROME V. C., M. D. NATURAL HISTORY OF THE FISHES OF MASSACHUSETTS, embracing a Practical Essay on Angling. *Wood-cuts. Post* 8*vo, cloth.* Boston, 1833

2830 SMITH, CAPTAIN JOHN. THE TRUE TRAVELS, Adventures, and Observations of Captaine John Smith, in Europe, Asia, Africke, and America; beginning about the Yere 1593, and continued to this Present 1629. — THE GENERALL HISTORIÈ OF VIRGINIA, NEW-ENGLAND, AND THE SUMMER ISLES, with the Names of the Adventurers, Planters, and Governours, from their First Beginning, An. 1584, to this Present 1626, with the Proceedings of those Severall Colonies, and the Accidents that befell them in all their Journyes and Discoveries; also the Maps and Descriptions of those Countryes, their Commodities, People, Government, Customes, and Religion yet knowne. Divided into Sixe Bookes. By Captaine John Smith, sometimes Governour of those Countryes and Admiral of New-England. *Portrait, maps and plates.* 2 *vols.*, 8*vo, marbled calf.* Franklin Press, Richmond, 1819

Reprinted from the rare folio (London) edition of 1629 (1630).

2831 SMITH, CAPTAIN JOHN. ADVERTISEMENTS FOR THE UNEXPERIENCED PLANTERS of New England, or anywhere; or the Pathway to erect a Plantation. By Captain John Smith, sometimes Governour of Virginia, and Admirall of New-England. *Fac-simile of Smith's map of New-England with additions and corrections, as published in* 1635. 4*to, cloth, uncut.* ONLY 75 COPIES IN THIS STYLE. Boston, 1865

Reprint of the London edition of 1631.

2832 SMITH, CAPTAIN JOHN. A DESCRIPTION OF NEW ENGLAND, or Observations and Discoveries in the North of America in the Year of Our Lord 1614; with the Success of Six Ships that went the Next Year, 1615. By Captain John Smith, (Admiral of that Country.) *Fac-simile of original map. 4to, cloth uncut.* ONLY 75 COPIES IN THIS STYLE. Boston, 1865

Reprint of the London edition of 1616.

2833 SMITH, JOHN. A CATALOGUE RAISONNÉ of the Works of the most Eminent Dutch, Flemish, and French Painters: in which is included a Short Biographical Notice of the Artists, with a Copious Description of their Principal Pictures; a Statement of the Prices at which such Pictures have been sold at Public Sales on the Continent and in England; a Reference to the Galleries and Private Collections in which a Large Portion are at Present; and the Names of the Artists by whom they have been engraved. To which is added a Brief Notice of the Scholars and Imitators of the Great Masters of the above Schools. *9 vols., royal 8vo, half green morocco, neat, gilt tops, uncut.* VERY FINE COPY: COMPLETE. London, 1829–42

Indispensable to the collector of pictures.

2834 SMITH, JOHN J.; and JOHN FANNING WATSON. AMERICAN HISTORICAL AND LITERARY CURIOSITIES; consisting of Fac-similes of Original Documents relating to the Events of the Revolution, etc., etc., with a Variety of Reliques, Antiquities, and Modern Autographs. Collected and edited by J. J. Smith and John F. Watson. Fifth Edition, with Additions. *Imperial 4to, half morocco, gilt edges.* New York, 1852

2835 SMITH, S., D. D. THE HISTORY OF THE LIVES, Actions, Travels, Sufferings, and Deaths of our Blessed Saviour Jesus Christ, and His Twelve Apostles. *Portrait of author and 33 plates, by A. Jongelinx, R. Shepherd, H. Robert, etc. 2 vols., thick 8vo, old calf.* London, 1737–38

2836 SMITH, REV. SYDNEY. A MEMOIR OF. By his Daughter, Lady Holland. With a Selection from his Letters, Edited by Mrs. Austin. *2 vols., 12mo, cloth.* New York, 1855

2837 SMITH, WILLIAM, D. D. AHIMAN REZON, abridged and digested, as a help to all that are, or would be, Free and Accepted Masons; to which is added, a Sermon preached in Christ-Church, Philadelphia, at a General Communication celebrated, agreeable to the Constitutions, on Monday, December 28, 1778, as the Anniversary of St. John the Evangelist. *Frontispiece. 12mo, sheep.* Philadelphia, 1783

2838 SMITH, WILLIAM, D. D. ANOTHER COPY: *the same. 12mo, sheep.* Philadelphia, 1783

2839 SMITH, WILLIAM, LL. D. DICTIONARY OF GREEK AND ROMAN BIOGRAPHY AND MYTHOLOGY. *Numerous woodcuts. 3 vols., thick 8vo, half calf, neat.* Boston (London), 1849

2840 SMITH, WILLIAM, LL. D. DICTIONARY OF GREEK AND ROMAN ANTIQUITIES. Second Edition, improved and enlarged. *Numerous wood-cuts. Thick 8vo, half calf, neat.* Boston (London), 1859

2841 SMITH, WILLIAM. THORNDALE, or the Conflict of Opinions. 12*mo, cloth.* Boston, 1859

2842 SMOLLETT, TOBIAS, M. D. THE COMPLETE HISTORY OF ENGLAND, from the Descent of Julius Cæsar to the Treaty of Aix la Chapelle, 1748; containing the Transactions of One Thousand Eight Hundred and Three Years. *Map mounted on cloth, and numerous portraits.* 11 *vols.*, 8*vo, half morocco. Second and third editions.* London, 1758–63

2843 SMOLLETT, TOBIAS, M. D. ANOTHER COPY: *the same. First, second, and third editions; with the* CONTINUATION, *except the last volume (written by William Guthrie). Fine portraits, etc.* 15 *vols.*, 8*vo, polished calf, neat.* FINE COPY. London, 1758–61

2844 SMOLLETT, TOBIAS, M. D. THE HISTORY OF ENGLAND (from the Revolution, 1688, where Hume's History ends, to the Death of George II., 1760). *Portraits, by Worthington, on India paper, of Smollett and each of the sovereigns, including George III. and George IV. also.* 5 *vols, royal* 8*vo, cloth, rough edges.* LARGE PAPER: *only* 50 *copies printed.* Talboys, Oxford; Pickering, London, 1827

One of the "Oxford English Classics."

2845 SMOLLETT, TOBIAS, M. D. THE MISCELLANEOUS WORKS OF. To which is prefixed, Memoirs of his Life and Writings. Embellished with Twenty-six Engravings, by Rowlandson & others. 5 *vols.*, 8*vo, half calf, marbled edges.* Edinburgh, 1809

2846 SMOLLETT, TOBIAS, M. D. THE MISCELLANEOUS WORKS OF. With Memoirs of his Life and Writings, by Robert Anderson, M. D. The Fifth Edition. *Portrait and view of monument.* 6 *vols.*, 8*vo, calf gilt, contents lettered, marbled edges; with book-plate of H. G. Goltermann.* Edinburgh, 1817

2847 SMOLLETT, TOBIAS, M. D. THE MISCELLANEOUS WORKS OF; containing Roderick Random, Peregrine Pickle, Ferdinand Count Fathom, Sir Launcelot Greaves, Humphry Clinker, Adventures of an Atom, Travels through France and Italy, Expedition against Carthagena, Plays and Poems. With Memoir of the Author, by Thomas Roscoe. *Portrait and fac-simile of autograph letter. Royal* 8*vo, calf gilt, marbled edges.* London, 1841

2848 SMYTH, CHARLES PIAZZI. TENERIFFE: an Astronomer's Experiment, or Specialities of a Residence above the Clouds. Illustrated with Photo-Stereographs. *Post* 8*vo, cloth, gilt top.* London, 1858

2849 SMYTH, WILLIAM, PROF. LECTURES ON MODERN HISTORY, from the Irruption of the Northern Nations to the Close of the American Revolution. Second American, from the Second London Edition; with a Preface, List of Books on American History, Chronological Tables, etc., by Jared Sparks, LL. D. *2 vols., 8vo, half calf extra.* Cambridge (Mass.), 1843

2850 SMYTH, WILLIAM HENRY, R. N. SKETCH OF THE PRESENT STATE OF THE ISLAND OF SARDINIA. *Map, plates by E. Finden, etc., after the author's drawings, and wood-cuts. 8vo, half blue calf extra.* J. Murray, London, 1828

2851 SNOW, CALEB H., M. D. A HISTORY OF BOSTON, MASSACHUSETTS; from its Origin to the Present Period; with some Account of the Environs. Second Edition. *Plans, plates, and wood-cuts. 8vo, half morocco.* Boston, 1828

2852 SOANE, GEORGE. NEW CURIOSITIES OF LITERATURE, and Book of the Months. Second Edition. *Frontispiece and vignettes on titles. 2 vols., 12mo, cloth, uncut.* London, 1849

2853 SOCIETY OF DILETTANTI. SPECIMENS OF ANTIENT SCULPTURE, Ægyptian, Etruscan, Greek, and Roman; selected from Different Collections in Great Britain, by the Society of Dilettanti. *Nearly 150 fine engravings, with descriptions by Richard Payne Knight. 2 vols., imperial folio, crimson morocco extra, gilt edges, by J. Mackenzie.* Printed by T. Bensley, London, 1809–35

Only 200 copies of the first volume were printed, and very few of the second, for members of the society only.

2854 SOLVYNS, BALTHAZAR. THE COSTUME OF INDOSTAN; elucidated by Sixty Coloured Engravings, with Descriptions in English and French, taken in the Years 1798 and 1799. *Imperial 4to, dark blue morocco, extra, gilt edges.* London, 1830

2855 SOMERS, JOHN, LORD. A COLLECTION OF SCARCE AND VALUABLE TRACTS, on the most Interesting and Entertaining Subjects; but chiefly such as relate to the History and Constitution of these Kingdoms. Selected from an Infinite Number, in Print and Manuscript, in the Royal Cotton, Sion, and other Public, as well as Private, Libraries; particularly that of the late Lord Somers. The Second Edition, revised, augmented, and arranged, by Walter Scott, Esq. *13 vols., royal 4to, marbled calf gilt, marbled edges; with book-plate of John Arden.* BEST EDITION: VERY FINE COPY. London, 1809–15

"The Collection of Tracts relating to the Constitution of this country of which LORD SOMERS was the avowed Editor or Collector is, in truth, a splendid and lasting monument of the judgment and patriotism of that great man. The reprint has much the advantage in having the pieces arranged chronologically and according to their subject matter. The *additional* pieces are denoted by an asterisk. In no Collection, of the least historical pretense, let these Tracts of Lord Somers be found wanting." —*Dibdin.*

2856 SOMERVILLE, MRS. MARY. PHYSICAL GEOGRAPHY. A New Edition; with Notes and a Glossary, by W. S. W. Ruschenberger, M. D. 12*mo, cloth.* Philadelphia, 1855

2857 SOPHIA DOROTHEA. MEMOIRS OF SOPHIA DOROTHEA, Consort of George I., chiefly from the Secret Archives of Hanover, Brunswick, Berlin, and Vienna; including a Diary of the Conversations of Illustrious Personages of those Courts, illustrative of her History, with Letters and other Documents, now first published from the Originals [by Folkestone Williams]. Second Edition. *Portraits of Sophia Dorothea and Count Konigsmark.* 2 *vols.*, 8*vo, half green calf, neat.* London, 1846

2858 SOTHEBY, SAMUEL LEIGH. PRINCIPIA TYPOGRAPHICA: the Block-Books, or Xylographic Delineations of Scripture History, issued in Holland, Flanders, and Germany, during the Fifteenth Century, exemplified and considered in Connexion with the Origin of Printing; to which is added an Attempt to Elucidate the Character of the Paper-Marks of the Period. A Work contemplated by the late Samuel Sotheby, and carried out by his Son, Samuel Leigh Sotheby. *Illustrated with* 120 *large plates, some of which are colored, besides some smaller cuts and photographic fac-similes, all of which are exact copies from the rare originals.* 3 *vols., imperial* 4*to, half morocco, rough edges.* ONLY 250 COPIES PRINTED. Printed for the Author, London, 1858

Of 250 copies of this work (which is one of the most important upon the history of early printing), only 215 were sold, 30 being presented to public libraries, and the other 5 otherwise specially reserved, but not for sale.

2859 SOTHEBY, SAMUEL LEIGH. RAMBLINGS IN THE ELUCIDATION OF THE AUTOGRAPH OF MILTON. *Printed on a thick toned paper, with two photographic portraits, of Milton, one from the bust in Trinity College library and the other from the celebrated crayon drawing formerly in the possession of J. Richardson, Senr., and Jacob Tonson. Royal* 4*to, green turkey morocco extra* (*with designs in outline by J. L. Tupper, inserted in panels on each side, with three smaller reproductions of each design on inside covers*), *gilt top, by Wright.* Printed for the Author, London, 1861

The fac-simile autographs, which are numerous, are by the Electro Printing Block Co., as are also the designs on covers. The word autograph is not used in the sense of a signature only, but of the handwriting generally, and many of the fac-simile specimens are full-page plates.

2860 SOULIÉ, ÉDOUARD. NOTICE DES PEINTURES ET SCULPTURES composant le Musée Impérial de Versailles. IIe Partie, 1er et 2e Étages. 12*mo, pp.* 861, *paper.* Versailles, 1855

2861 SOUTHEY, Robert. Madoc. *Vignettes on titles. 4to, old marbled calf gilt, marbled edges.* London (Edinburgh), 1805

2862 SOUTHEY, Robert. Letters from England, by Don Manuel Alvarez Espriella; translated from the Spanish. [Written by Southey.] Second Edition. *3 vols., 12mo, calf gilt, marbled edges.* Longmans & Co., London, 1808

2863 SOUTHEY, Robert. The Poetical Works; collected by himself. (With Additional Notes and Prefaces.) *Portrait and 19 plates engraved by W. and E. Finden. 10 vols., foolscap 8vo, cloth, uncut.* Longmans & Co., London, 1838

2864 SOUTHEY, Robert. The Doctor, etc. *2 vols. in 1, 12mo, cloth.* New York, 1856

2865 SOUTHEY, Robert. The Life of the Rev. Andrew Bell, D. D., LL. D., etc.; comprising the History of the Rise and Progress of the System of Mutual Tuition. The First Volume by Robert Southey, Esq., edited by Mrs. Southey; the Two Last by his Son, the Rev. Charles Cuthbert Southey. *Portrait. 3 vols., 8vo, calf gilt, marbled edges.* J. Murray, London, 1844

2866 SOUTHWELL, Rev. Robert. St. Peter's Complaint, and other Poems. Reprinted from the Edition of 1595, with important Additions from an Original MS., and a Sketch of the Author's Life, by W. Jos. Walter. *Crown 8vo, boards, rough edges.* Large paper: *only 50 copies printed.* London, 1817

2867 SOUVESTRE, Émile. An Attic Philosopher in Paris, or a Peep at the World from a Garret. From the French. *12mo, cloth.* New York, 1859

2868 SOWERBY, George Brettingham, Jun. The Conchological Illustrations. *A series of 200 plates, comprising 1,500 colored figures representing 1,000 new species of shells mounted on drawing paper and bound in 1 vol., royal 4to, crimson morocco extra, gilt edges; with text in 1 vol., 12mo, half crimson morocco extra.* London, 1832–41

2869 SOYER, Alexis. A Shilling Cookery for the People. *16mo, cloth.* London, 1858

2870 SPARKS, Jared. Letters on the Ministry, Ritual, and Doctrines of the Protestant Episcopal Church; addressed to the Rev. Wm. E. Wyatt, D. D., in Reply to the Sermon exhibiting some of the Principal Doctrines of the Protestant Episcopal Church in the United States. *8vo, half blue morocco, neat.* Baltimore, 1820

2871 SPARKS, Jared. The Library of American Biography; conducted by Jared Sparks. *25 vols., post 8vo, half morocco, contents lettered, gilt tops.* Complete: *with MS. Index bound in Vol. I.* Boston, 1834–48

2872 SPARKS, JARED. CORRESPONDENCE OF THE AMERICAN REVOLUTION; being Letters of Eminent Men to George Washington, from the Time of his Taking Command of the Army to the End of his Presidency. Edited from the Original Manuscripts by Jared Sparks. *4 vols., imperial 8vo, cloth.* LARGE PAPER. Boston, 1853

2873 SPARKS, JARED. REMARKS ON A "REPRINT OF THE ORIGINAL LETTERS FROM WASHINGTON TO JOSEPH REED, during the American Revolution, referred to in the Pamphlets of Lord Mahon and Mr. Sparks." *8vo, pp. 43, paper.* Boston, 1853

2874 SPARKS, JARED. THE LIFE OF GEORGE WASHINGTON. *Portraits, fac-similes, etc. 8vo, half morocco, neat.* Boston, 1854

2875 SPECIMENS OF THE GERMAN LYRIC POETS; consisting of Translations in Verse, from the Works of Bürger, Goethe, Klopstock, Schiller, etc. Interspersed with Biographical Notices; and Ornamented with Engravings on Wood, by the First Artists. *8vo, boards, rough edges.* London, 1822

2876 SPELMAN, SIR HENRY. RELIQUIÆ SPELMANNIANÆ: the Posthumous Works of Sir Henry Spelman, Kt., relating to the Laws and Antiquities of England; published from the Original Manuscripts, with the Life of the Author. [By Edmund Gibson.] *Vignette on title and pedigrees; portrait wanting. Small folio, old calf; back cracked.* Oxford, 1698

2877 SPENCE, REV. JOSEPH. POLYMETIS, or an Enquiry concerning the Agreement between the Works of the Roman Poets, and the Remains of the Antient Artists; being an Attempt to illustrate them mutually from one another. In Ten Books. By the Rev[d] Mr. Spence. *Portrait by Vertue, 41 large plates, and several vignettes. Folio, half morocco, gilt top, rough edges.* FIRST EDITION: *fine impression of the plates.* R. Dodsley, London, 1747

This copy contains (p. 291) the caricature vignette representing Dr. Cooke, then Provost of Eton, as a pedagogue with an ass's head, standing before two of his pupils. In subsequent editions a figure of Hermes is substituted.

2878 SPENCER, CAPTAIN E. THE FALL OF THE CRIMEA. *Wood-cuts by the Dalziels. Crown 8vo, cloth, uncut.* London, 1854

2879 SPENCER, JESSE AMES, D. D. HISTORY OF THE UNITED STATES, from the Earliest Period to the Administration of James Buchanan. Illustrated with highly-finished Steel Engravings, from Original Pictures by Leutze, Weir, Powell, Chappel, and other American Artists. *3 vols., 4to, morocco antique, gilt edges.* New York, (1858)

2880 SPENSER, EDMUND. THE FAERIE QUEENE; by Edmund Spenser. With an Exact Collation of the Two Orig-

inal Editions, published by himself at London, in Quarto; the Former containing the Three First Books printed in 1590, and the Latter the Six Books in 1596. To which are now added, a New Life of the Author [by Dr. Birch], and also a Glossary. Adorn'd with Thirty-two Copper-plates, from the Original Drawings of the late W. Kent, Esq. *Fine impressions of the plates.* 3 *vols.*, 4*to, sprinkled calf, neat; with book-plate of Mr. Sharon Turner.*
J. Brindley, London, 1751

2881 SPENSER, EDMUND. THE WORKS OF; with the Principal Illustrations of Various Commentators. To which are added, Notes, Some Account of the Life of Spenser, and a Glossarial and other Indexes, by the Rev. Henry John Todd, F. A. S., etc. *Portrait.* 8 *vols., imperial* 8*vo, sprinkled calf gilt.* LARGE PAPER: *fine copy.* London, 1805

2882 SPENSER, EDMUND. THE POETICAL WORKS OF. (With an Essay on his Life and Writings, Notes, and a Glossary, by George Robinson, Esq.). *Portrait by Worthington.* 5 *vols., crown* 8*vo, green turkey morocco, neat, gilt edges.*
W. Pickering, London, 1825

2883 SPILSBURY, F. B. PICTURESQUE SCENERY IN THE HOLY LAND AND SYRIA, delineated during the Campaigns of 1799 and 1800, by F. B. Spilsbury, Surgeon in that Expedition during Both Campaigns. Second Edition. *Contains* 19 *large colored views. Royal folio, boards.*
London, 1819

2884 SPILSBURY, JOHN. A COLLECTION OF FIFTY PRINTS FROM ANTIQUE GEMS, in the Collections of the Right Honourable Earl Percy, the Honourable C. F. Greville, and T. M. Slade, Esquire; engraved by Mr. John Spilsbury. 4*to, red morocco extra, gilt edges.*
John Boydell, London, (1781–84)
Fine impressions, but stained.

2885 SPILSBURY, WILLIAM HOLDEN. LINCOLN'S INN; its Ancient and Modern Buildings, with an Account of the Library. *Frontispiece, etc. Foolscap* 8*vo, cloth, uncut.*
W. Pickering, London, 1850

2886 SPOONER, SHEARJASHUB, M. D. A BIOGRAPHICAL HISTORY OF THE FINE ARTS, or Memoirs of the Lives and Works of Eminent Painters, Engravers, Sculptors, and Architects; from the Earliest Ages to the Present Time. Alphabetically arranged and condensed from the Best Authorities, including the Works of Vasari, Lanzi, Kugler, Dr. Waagen, Bryan, Pilkington, Walpole, Sir C. Eastlake, and Mrs. Jameson, with Chronological Tables of Artists and their Schools, Plates of Monograms, etc. 2 *vols., imperial* 8*vo, cloth backs, red paper sides, gilt tops, uncut.* New York, 1865

2887 SPOTTISWOOD, JAMES. A BREEFE MEMORIALL OF THE LYFE AND DEATH OF JAMES SPOTTISWOOD, Bishop of Clogher, in Ireland; and of the Labyrinth of Troubles he fell into in that Kingdom, and the Manner of the Unhappie Accident brought such Troubles upon him. From a Manuscript in the Auchinleck Library. [Edited by Sir Alexander Boswell.] *4to, paper.* Edinburgh, 1811

2888 SPRAGUE, CHARLES. AN ORATION, Fourth of July, 1825, in Commemoration of American Independence, before the Executive of the Commonwealth, and the City Council and Inhabitants of the City of Boston. *8vo, pp.* 31; *paper; clean.* Boston, 1825

2889 SPRAGUE, CHARLES. CURIOSITY; a Poem, delivered at Cambridge, before the Phi Beta Kappa Society, August 27, 1829. *8vo, pp.* 30, *paper; clean.* Boston, 1829

2890 SPRAGUE, CHARLES. THE POETICAL AND PROSE WRITINGS OF. New and revised Edition. *Portrait, etc. Post 8vo, cloth, gilt edges.* Boston, 1850

2891 SPRAT, THOMAS, BISHOP. THE HISTORY OF THE ROYAL-SOCIETY OF LONDON, for the Improving of Natural Knowledge. *Plates. Small 4to, old calf.* London, 1667

2892 STACE, MACHELL. CROMWELLIANA: a Chronological Detail of Events in which Oliver Cromwell was engaged, from the Year 1642 to his Death, 1658; with a Continuation of other Transactions, to the Restoration. *With the 5 plates published with the work. Folio, half morocco, uncut.* M. Stace, Westminster, 1810

2893 STACKHOUSE, REV. THOMAS. A NEW HISTORY OF THE HOLY BIBLE, from the Beginning of the World to the Establishment of Christianity; with Answers to most of the Controverted Questions, Dissertations upon the most Remarkable Passages, and a Connection of Profane History all along. To which are added, Notes explaining Difficult Texts, rectifying Mistranslations, and reconciling Seeming Contradictions. *Portraits, plans, etc.* 6 *vols., 8vo, half calf, yellow edges.* Glasgow, 1795–96

2894 STAËL-HOLSTEIN, ANNE LOUISE GERMAINE N., BARONNE DE. DELPHINE. 6 *vols. in* 5, *12mo, half calf.* London, 1803

2895 STAËL-HOLSTEIN, ANNE LOUISE GERMAINE N., BARONNE DE. A TREATISE ON ANCIENT AND MODERN LITERATURE, illustrated by Striking References to the Principal Events and Characters that have distinguished the French Revolution. From the French. 2 *vols., 8vo, boards, rough edges.* London, 1803

2896 STAFFORD GALLERY. ENGRAVINGS OF THE MARQUIS OF STAFFORD'S COLLECTION OF PICTURES, IN LONDON; arranged according to Schools and in Chronological Order, with Remarks on each Picture. By William Young Ottley, Esq., F. S. A.; the Executive Part under the Management of Peltro William Tomkins, Esq. *Contains 300 fine engravings. 4 vols. in 2, atlas 4to, half calf neat, marbled edges.* Printed by Bensley, etc., London, 1818

2897 STANHOPE, PHILIP HENRY, EARL. THE LIFE OF BELISARIUS. *8vo, calf, gilt, marbled edges.* J. Murray, London, 1829

2898 STANLEY, ARTHUR PENRHYN, D. D. SINAI AND PALESTINE, in Connection with their History. New Edition, with Maps and Plans. *8vo, half calf extra, marbled edges.* New York, 1863

2899 STANLEY, ARTHUR PENRHYN, D. D. LECTURES ON THE HISTORY OF THE EASTERN CHURCH, with an Introduction on the Study of Ecclesiastical History. From the Second London Edition, revised. *8vo, half calf extra, marbled edges.* New York, 1863

2900 STANLEY, ARTHUR PENRHYN, D. D. LECTURES ON THE HISTORY OF THE JEWISH CHURCH; Part I., Abraham to Samuel. With Maps and Plans. *8vo, half calf extra, marbled edges.* New York, 1864

2901 STANLEY, THOMAS. THE HISTORY OF PHILOSOPHY; containing the Lives, Opinions, Actions, and Discourses of the Philosophers of Every Sect. The Third Edition; to which is added, the Life of the Author, never before published. *Portrait of Stanley by Faithorne, after "P. Lilly" (Lely), and many other portraits, etc. Folio, old calf; back cracked.* London, 1701

2902 STANLEY, THOMAS. POEMS BY. Reprinted from the Edition of 1651. [Edited, with Preface, by Sir S. E. Brydges.] *Foolscap 8vo, boards, rough edges.* ONLY 150 COPIES PRINTED. Private Press of Longmans & Co., London, 1814

2903 STARKE, MRS. MARIANA. TRAVELS IN EUROPE, for the use of Travellers on the Continent; and likewise in the Island of Sicily; to which is added an Account of the Remains of Ancient Italy, and also of the Roads leading to those Remains. Eighth Edition, considerably enlarged. *Map, plan, and index. 12mo, vellum.* Paris, 1834

2904 STATIUS, PUBLIUS PAPINIUS. OPERA OMNIA, ex Editione Bipontina, cum Notis et Interpretatione in Usum Delphini; Variis Lectionibus, Notis Variorum, Recensu Editionum et Codicum et Indice Locupletissimo accurate recensita. *4 vols., 8vo, russia, very neat, marbled edges.* A. J. Valpy, Londini, 1824

2905 STAUNTON, SIR GEORGE L. AN AUTHENTIC ACCOUNT OF AN EMBASSY FROM THE KING OF GREAT BRITAIN TO THE EMPEROR OF CHINA; including Cursory Observations made, and Information obtained, in travelling through that Ancient Empire, and a Small Part of Chinese Tartary: together

with a Relation of the Voyage undertaken on the Occasion by his Majesty's Ship The Lion, and the Ship Hindostan, in the East India Company's Service, to the Yellow Sea, and the Gulf of Pekin; with Notices of the Several Places where they stopped in their way Out and Home; being the Islands of Madeira, Teneriffe, and St. Jago; the Port of Rio de Janeiro in South America; the Islands of St. Helena, Tristan d'Acunha, and Amsterdam; the Coast of Java, and Sumatra, the Nanka Isles, Pulo Condore, and Cochin-China. Taken chiefly from the Papers of his Excellency the Earl of Macartney, his Majesty's Embassador; Sir Erasmus Gower; and of other Gentlemen in the Several Departments of the Embassy; by Sir George Staunton, Baronet, etc. *Portraits of Tchien Lung and the Earl of Macartney, with numerous vignettes in the text, and an atlas containing 44 large maps, charts, plans, and plates. 2 vols., imperial 4to, and 1 vol., atlas folio, boards, rough edges.* LARGE PAPER: *fine impressions of the plates.*
Printed by W. Bulmer & Co., London, 1797

2906 STEBBING, HENRY, D. D. THE CHRISTIAN IN PALESTINE; or, Scenes of Sacred History, Historical and Descriptive. Illustrated from Sketches taken on the Spot, by W. H. Bartlett. *Map and 79 plates. 4to, morocco antique.*
London, s. a.

2907 STEBBING, HENRY, D. D. ANOTHER COPY: *the same. Map and 79 plates. 4to, cloth, gilt edges.*
London, s. a.

2908 STEDMAN, EDMUND CLARENCE. THE PRINCE'S BALL; a Brochure, from "Vanity Fair." With Illustrations by Stephens. *12mo, cloth.* New York, 1860

2909 STEELE, SIR RICHARD. THE DRAMATICK WORKS OF: containing, the Conscious Lovers, the Funeral, the Tender Husband, the Lying Lover. *Plates by G. Vander Gucht. 12mo, old calf.* London, (1755)

2910 STEINMETZ, ANDREW. JAPAN AND HER PEOPLE. With Numerous Illustrations. *Post 8vo, cloth.* London, 1859

2911 STEPHENS, GEORGE. DRAMAS FOR THE STAGE. (Comprising Nero, a Historical Tragedy; Forgery, a Domestic Tragedy; Sensibility, a Tragedy; Self-Glorification, a Chinese Play for the Times; Rebecca and her Daughters, a Comedy [in Prose] for the Times; Philip Basil, or a Poet's Fate, a Tragedy for the Times; and, Remarks upon the Presentation of the Tragedy of "Martinuzzi.") *2 vols., 8vo, half green morocco, neat.* Ineditus: London, 1846

2912 STEPHENS, HENRY L. THE COMIC NATURAL HISTORY OF THE HUMAN RACE; designed and illustrated. *With 40 colored plates and wood-cuts. Imperial 8vo, cloth.*
Philadelphia, 1851

2913 STEPHENS, JAMES FRANCIS. ILLUSTRATIONS OF BRITISH ENTOMOLOGY; or a Synopsis of Indigenous Insects; containing their Generic and Specific Distinctions, with an Account of their Metamorphoses, Times of Appearance, Localities, Food, and Economy, as far as Practicable. *With nearly* 100 *finely colored plates containing about* 400 *figures.* HAUSTELLATA, 4 *vols.;* MANDIBULATA, 7 *vols.*; SUPPLEMENT, 1 *vol. Together,* 12 *vols., royal* 8*vo, half morocco, uncut.* London, 1828–46

2914 STEPHENS, JOHN LLOYD. INCIDENTS OF TRAVEL IN GREECE, TURKEY, RUSSIA, AND POLAND. With a map and engravings. Seventh Edition. 2 *vols.,* 12*mo, cloth.* New York, 1839

2915 STEPHENS, JOHN LLOYD. ANOTHER COPY: *the same.* 2 *vols.,* 12*mo, cloth.* New York, 1842

2916 STEPHENS, JOHN LLOYD. INCIDENTS OF TRAVEL IN CENTRAL AMERICA, CHIAPAS, AND YUCATAN. Twelfth Edition. *Numerous plates and wood-cuts.* 2 *vols.,* 8*vo, cloth.* New York, 1852–53

2917 STEPHENS, JOHN LLOYD. INCIDENTS OF TRAVEL IN EGYPT, ARABIA PETRÆA, AND THE HOLY LAND. With a Map and Engravings. Eleventh Edition. 2 *vols.,* 12*mo, cloth.* New York, 1860

2918 STEPHENSON, JOHN, M. D.; and JAMES MORSS CHURCHILL. MEDICAL BOTANY, or Illustrations and Descriptions of the Medicinal Plants of the London, Edinburgh, and Dublin Pharmacopœias; comprising a Popular and Scientific Account of Poisonous Vegetables indigenous to Great Britain. New Edition, edited by Gilbert T. Burnett, F. L. S., etc., etc. *Index, glossary, etc., and* 185 *colored plates.* 3 *vols., royal* 8*vo, cloth, rough edges.* London, 1834–36

2919 STERNE, REV. LAURENCE. THE WORKS OF; with a Life of the Author, written by himself. 6 *vols.,* 18*mo, claret morocco extra, gilt edges.* London, 1823

2920 STEVENS, GEORGE ALEXANDER. A LECTURE ON HEADS, with Additions by Mr. Pilon; as delivered by Mr. Charles Lee Lewes. To which is added an Essay on Satire. With Forty-seven Heads by Nesbit, from Designs by Thurston. *Foolscap* 8*vo, calf, neat.* London, 1812

2921 STEVENS, HENRY. AN ACCOUNT OF THE PROCEEDINGS AT THE DINNER GIVEN BY MR. GEORGE PEABODY, to the Americans connected with the Great Exhibition, at the London Coffee House, Ludgate Hill, on the 27th October, 1851. *Handsomely printed by Whittingham, with ornate initials and other embellishments. Imperial* 8*vo, cloth extra.* LARGE PAPER: PRINTED FOR PRIVATE DISTRIBUTION, *and but few copies.* W. Pickering, London, 1851

2922 STEWART, DUGALD. THE COLLECTED WORKS OF; edited by Sir William Hamilton. (With a Memoir of the Author and Selections from his Correspondence, by Professor John Veitch.) COMPLETE EDITION, *with a supplementary volume containing translations of the passages in foreign languages, and a general index. Portraits.* 11 *vols., 8vo, cloth, uncut.* Edinburgh, 1854–60

2923 STILLÉ, CHARLES JANEWAY. HISTORY OF THE UNITED STATES SANITARY COMMISSION; being the General Report of its Work during the War of the Rebellion. *8vo, cloth.* Philadelphia, 1866

2924 STOCKDALE, JOHN JOSEPH. THE COVENT GARDEN JOURNAL. Embellished with Four Views. 1 *vol., royal 8vo, half calf.* London, 1810

"A history of the O. P. Row, in which John Kemble took a large part." — *Lowndes.*

2925 STOCKDALE, JOHN JOSEPH. THE HISTORY OF THE INQUISITIONS; including the Secret Transactions of those Horrific Tribunals. *Appendix, addenda, and* 12 *plates. Royal 4to, blue morocco extra, gilt edges; with book-plate of Nicholas Garry.* LARGE PAPER. London, 1810

2926 STODDART, SIR JOHN. REMARKS ON LOCAL SCENERY AND MANNERS IN SCOTLAND during the Years 1799 and 1800. *Engraved titles, map, and* 32 COLORED *plates.* 2 *vols., royal 8vo, crimson morocco gilt, gilt edges.* London, 1801

2927 STOLBERG, FRIEDRICH LEOPOLD. TRAVELS THROUGH GERMANY, SWITZERLAND, ITALY, AND SICILY. Translated from the German by Thomas Holcroft. *Map, and* 18 *fine large folding plates, after Pirenesi and others.* 2 *vols, 4to, old marbled calf gilt.* London, 1796–97

2928 STORER, JAMES S.; and J. GREIG. SELECT VIEWS OF LONDON AND ITS ENVIRONS: containing a Collection of highly-finished Engravings, from Original Paintings and Drawings; accompanied by Copious Letter-press Descriptions of such Objects in the Metropolis and the Surrounding Country as are most Remarkable for Antiquity, Architectural Grandeur, or Picturesque Beauty. PROOF IMPRESSIONS *of the* 60 *plates and* 14 *vignettes, engraved by Storer and Greig, after drawings by Turner, F. Nash, and others.* 2 *vols. in* 1, *royal 4to, diamond russia, very neat, marbled edges.* LARGE PAPER. London, 1805

2929 STORER, JAMES S.; and J. GREIG. THE ANTIQUARIAN ITINERARY, comprising Specimens of Architecture, Monastic, Castellated, and Domestic, with other Vestiges of Antiquity in Great Britain; accompanied with Descriptions.

With 336 *beautiful little plates and* 163 *wood-cut vignettes.* 7 *vols., foolscap* 8*vo, green morocco extra, gilt edges.* London, 1815–18

2930 STORY (THE) OF A STOMACH; an Egotism, by a Reformed Dyspeptic [R—— D——]. 12*mo, pp.* 60, *cloth.* New York, 1867

2931 STORY, JOSEPH. LIFE AND LETTERS OF JOSEPH STORY, edited by his Son, William W. Story. *Portrait.* 2 *vols.,* 8*vo, half morocco.* Boston, 1851

2932 STORY, JOSEPH. ANOTHER COPY: *the same. Portrait.* 2 *vols.,* 8*vo, cloth.* Boston, 1851

2933 STORY, JOSEPH. THE MISCELLANEOUS WORKS OF; edited by his Son, William W. Story. 8*vo, cloth.* Boston, 1852

2934 STORY, WILLIAM W. ROBA DI ROMA. Second Edition. 2 *vols., crown* 8*vo, cloth, uncut.* London, 1863

2935 STOTHARD, CHARLES ALFRED. THE MONUMENTAL EFFIGIES OF GREAT BRITAIN; selected from our Cathedrals and Churches, for the purpose of bringing together and preserving Correct Representations of the Best Historical Illustrations extant, from the Norman Conquest to the Reign of Henry the Eighth, by C. A. Stothard. (With Historical Descriptions and Introduction, by Alfred John Kempe, F. S. A.) *Contains* 147 *beautiful etchings, all more or less tinted, and some of them illuminated in gold and colors; including the extra plates of the effigies at Fontevraud, and Geoffrey Plantagenet. Imperial folio, half morocco, uncut.* LARGE PAPER: ORIGINAL COPY; *with arms colored.* London, 1817–32

2936 STOWE, HARRIET E. BEECHER. DRED; a Tale of the Great Dismal Swamp. 2 *vols.,* 12*mo, cloth.* Boston, 1856

2937 STRAUSS, DAVID FRIEDRICH. THE LIFE OF JESUS, critically examined. Translated from the Fourth German Edition [by Marian Evans]. 3 *vols.,* 8*vo, cloth, uncut.* BEST EDITION. London, 1846

2938 STRAUSS, DAVID FRIEDRICH. ANOTHER COPY: *the same. Portrait.* 2 *vols., royal* 8*vo, cloth, uncut.* New York, 1856

2939 STRAY LEAVES FROM A FREEMASON'S NOTE-BOOK; by a Suffolk Rector [—— E——]. 12*mo, cloth, uncut.* London, 1846

2940 STRENGTH OUT OF WEAKNESSE, or a Glorious Manifestation of the Further Progresse of the Gospel among the Indians in New-England; held forth in Sundry Letters from Divers Ministers and others to the Corporation established by Parliament for Promoting the Gospel among the Heathen in New-England, and to Particular Members thereof, since the Last Treatise to that Effect, formerly set forth by

Mr. Henry Whitfield, late Pastor of Gilford in New-England. Published by the Aforesaid Corporation. *Small 4to, morocco; somewhat stained, but perfect.*
Printed by M. Simmons for John Blague & Samuel Howes, London, 1652

COLLATION: Title, in a type-metal border, reverse blank, "To the Supreame Authoritie of this Nation, the Parliament of the Common-Wealth of England," signed "John Owen" and 11 others, 4 pp.; "To the Reader," signed "W. Gouge" and 13 others, 5 pp.; "To the Christian Reader," 3 pp.; and text 40 pp., the last being "The Corporation to the Reader," signed "William Steele, Esquire, President."
There were several editions of this tract bearing the same date and printer's name, but varying slightly in the Collation.

2941 STRICKLAND, AGNES. LIVES OF THE QUEENS OF ENGLAND, from the Norman Conquest. A New Edition, revised and greatly augmented. *Engraved titles, portraits (of Miss Strickland and of each queen), fac-similes, etc. 8 vols., crown 8vo, tree calf gilt, marbled edges, by Riviere.* BEST EDITION: *fine copy.* Longmans & Co., London, 1864

2942 STRONG, CALEB. PATRIOTISM AND PIETY: the Speeches of Governor Caleb Strong, to the Senate and House of Representatives of Massachusetts; with their Answers, and other Official Publick Papers. 1800–1807. *Title wanting. 12mo, pp. iii.–xii. and 13–202, boards, rough edges.* (Newburyport, 1808)

2943 STROTHER, DAVID H. VIRGINIA ILLUSTRATED; containing a Visit to the Virginian Canaan, and the Adventures of Porte Crayon and his Cousins. Illustrated from Drawings by Porte Crayon. *Royal 8vo, cloth.* New York, 1857

2944 STROZZI, PIERO. LAMENTO CHE FA PIERO STROZZI sopra della Rotta che ebbe in le Chiane d'Arezzo dal S. Marchese di Marignano, Generale di sua Eccellentia. Con una Barzelletta che fa Siena, chiamando tutte le Potentie d'Italia a pianger seco. Con un Gioco di Primiera sopra la Guerra che occorre al Presente. (In Bologna Adistantia di Paris Mantouano detto il Fortunato.) Edizione Seconda. *8vo, pp. 28, boards, morocco back, rough edges.* PRIVATELY PRINTED: *only 12 copies.* Genevra, Nov. 1821

This is one of the publications of Sir S. E. Brydges during his residence in Geneva. In his notes he says: "The little TRACT here reprinted is one among several which Party banter produced at the moment [1555]; and is believed to be very rare." It contains title; "Lamento," etc., pp. 3–9; "Notes, by the English Editor," pp. 10–25; "Ode, the Spirit of Strozzi, written at Geneva, Nov. 1, 1821," pp. 26–28.

2945 STRUTT, JOSEPH. HORDA ANGEL-CYNNAN, or a Compleat View of the Manners, Customs, Arms, Habits, etc., of the Inhabitants of England, from the Arrival of the Saxons till the Reign of Henry the Eighth; with a Short Account of the Britons, during the Government of the Romans. *Contains 158 plates (2 No. 62 in Vol. I.), printed in brown ink.*

3 vols., royal 4to, old sprinkled calf, neat, yellow edges; with book-plate and autograph of John Arden. FINE COPY.
Printed for the Author, etc., London, 1775–76

The title of the third volume reads, "to the Present Time," in place of "till the Reign of Henry the Eighth," the work having been continued to a later date than was originally designed.

2946 STRUTT, JOSEPH. A COMPLETE VIEW OF THE DRESS AND HABITS OF THE PEOPLE OF ENGLAND, from the Establishment of the Saxons in Britain to the Present Time; to which is prefixed an Introduction, containing a General Description of the Ancient Habits in Use among Mankind, from the Earliest Period of Time to the Conclusion of the Seventh Century. A New and Improved Edition, with Critical and Explanatory Notes, by J. R. Planché, Esq., F. S. A., etc. *Handsomely printed, with 143 fine colored plates. 2 vols., royal 4to, half olive morocco, neat, gilt tops, uncut.*
London, 1842

2947 STRUTT, JOSEPH. THE REGAL AND ECCLESIASTICAL ANTIQUITIES OF ENGLAND; containing the Representations of all the English Monarchs, from Edward the Confessor to Henry the Eighth; and of many Persons that were Eminent under their Several Reigns; on Sixty Copper Plates, engraved by the Author: with a Supplement, containing Twelve Plates. The whole carefully collected from Ancient Illuminated Manuscripts. A New and Improved Edition; with Critical and Explanatory Notes, by J. R. Planché, Esq., F. S. A., etc. *Handsomely printed, with the 72 plates all finely colored. Royal 4to, half olive morocco, neat, uncut.* London, 1842

2948 STRYPE, REV. JOHN. HISTORICAL AND BIOGRAPHICAL WORKS; with a General Index. *Portraits. 27 vols., 8vo, calf, neat.* Clarendon Press, Oxford, 1812–28

This fine uniform set comprises the following works, viz.: —

MEMORIALS OF THOMAS CRANMER, Lord Archbishop of Canterbury; wherein the History of the Church, and the Reformation of it, are greatly illustrated, and many Singular Matters relating thereunto, now first published (1694). A New Edition, with Additions. 2 *vols.*, 1812.

THE LIFE OF SIR THOMAS SMITH, K[t]., D. C. L., Principal Secretary of State to King Edward the Sixth, and Queen Elizabeth, wherein are discovered many Singular Matters relating to the Kingdom, during his Time. A New Edition, with Corrections and Additions by the Author. *Portrait.* 1 *vol.*, 1820.

THE LIFE OF SIR JOHN CHEKE, K[t]., first Instructor, afterwards Secretary of State, to King Edward VI., one of the great Restorers of Good Learning and True Religion in this Kingdom; a Work wherein many Remarkable Points of

History, relating to the State of Learning and Religion in the Times of King Henry VIII., King Edward VI., and Queen Mary I. are brought to Light. To which is added, a Treatise of Superstition, writ by the said Learned Knight. A New Edition, corrected by the Author. *Portrait.* 1 *vol.*, 1821.

The Life and Acts of Matthew Parker, the First Archbishop of Canterbury, in the Reign of Queen Elizabeth. To which is added, an Appendix containing Various Transcripts of Records, Letters, Instruments, and other Papers. In Four Books. *Portrait.* 3 *vols.*, 1821.

The History of the Life and Acts of Edmund Grindal, the First Bishop of London, and the Second Archbishop of York and Canterbury successively, in the Reign of Queen Elizabeth. To which is added, an Appendix of Original MSS., faithfully transcribed out of the Best Archives. In Two Books. *Portrait.* 1 *vol.*, 1821.

Historical Collections of the Life and Acts of John Aylmer, Bp. of London in the Reign of Queen Elizabeth, wherein are explained many Transactions of the Church of England, and what Methods were then taken to preserve it, with Respect both to the Papist and Puritan. A New Edition. *Portrait.* 1 *vol.*, 1821.

Ecclesiastical Memorials, relating chiefly to Religion, and the Reformation of it, and the Emergencies of the Church of England, under King Henry VIII., King Edward VI., and Queen Mary I. With large Appendixes, containing Original Papers, Records, etc. 3 *vols. in* 6, 1822.

The Life and Acts of John Whitgift, D. D., the Third and Last Archbishop of Canterbury in the Reign of Queen Elizabeth; from Records, Registers, Original Letters, and other Authentic MSS. Together with a large Appendix of the said Papers. In Four Books. *Portrait.* 3 *vols.*, 1822.

Annals of the Reformation and Establishment of Religion, and other Various Occurrences in the Church of England, during Queen Elizabeth's Reign. Together with an Appendix of Original Papers of State, Records, and Letters. A New Edition. 4 *vols. in* 7, 1824.

A General Index to the Historical and Geographical Works. 2 *vols.*, 1828.

2949 STRYPE, Rev. John. Memorials of Thomas Cranmer, sometime Lord Archbishop of Canterbury; wherein the History of the Church, and the Reformation of it, during the Primacy of the said Archbishop, are greatly illustrated, and many Singular Matters relating thereto, now first published. Collected chiefly from Records, Registers, Authentic Letters, and other Original Manuscripts. *Portraits wanting. pp.* 467, *and Appendix, pp.* 271. *Folio, old calf.*

R. Chiswell, London, 1694

2950 STRYPE, REV. JOHN. ECCLESIASTICAL MEMORIALS, relating chiefly to Religion, and its Reformation, under the Reigns of King Henry VIII., King Edward VI., and Queen Mary the First; with the Appendixes containing the Original Papers, Records, etc. *7 vols., 8vo, half calf, very neat, marbled edges.* S. Bagster, London, 1816

2951 STUART, JOHN SOBIESKI STOLBERG and CHARLES EDWARD. THE COSTUME OF THE CLANS; with Observations upon the Literature, Arts, Manufactures, and Commerce of the Highlands and Western Isles, during the Middle Ages, and on the Influence of the Sixteenth, Seventeenth, and Eighteenth Centuries upon their Present Condition. *Contains 37 plates. Atlas folio, half crimson morocco extra, gilt edges, by Hammond.* COLORED PLATES. J. Menzies, Edinburgh, 1845

2952 STUART, MOSES, D. D. A COMMENTARY ON THE EPISTLE TO THE HEBREWS. *2 vols., royal 8vo, boards, rough edges.* Andover, 1827–28

2953 STUBBES, PHILIP. THE ANATOMIE OF ABUSES. Reprinted from the Third Edition of MDLXXXV., under the Superintendence of William B. D. D. Turnbull, Esq. *8vo, dark brown crushed morocco antique, gilt edges, by Holloway.* ONLY 100 COPIES PRINTED. W. Pickering, London; W. & D. Laing, Edinburgh, 1836

2954 SUCKLING, SIR JOHN. THE WORKS OF; containing his Poems, Letters, and Plays. *2 vols., small 8vo, calf.* T. Davies, London, 1770

2955 SUCKLING, SIR JOHN. ANOTHER COPY: *the same. 8vo, old calf gilt.* Dublin, 1766

2956 SUFFOLK, EDWARD HOWARD, EARL OF. MISCELLANIES, in Prose and Verse. *8vo, old calf extra; with book-plate of George Montagu, Esq[r].* London, 1725

2957 SULLIVAN, JAMES. THE HISTORY OF THE DISTRICT OF MAINE. *8vo, half morocco, neat; map wanting.* Boston, 1795

2958 SULLIVAN, JAMES. AN IMPARTIAL REVIEW OF THE CAUSES AND PRINCIPLES OF THE FRENCH REVOLUTION. *8vo, old calf.* Boston, 1798

2959 SULLIVAN, JAMES. LIFE OF; with Selections from his Writings. By Thomas C. Amory. *Portrait. 2 vols., 8vo, half calf antique; with autograph of Rufus Choate.* Boston, 1859

2960 SULLIVAN, WILLIAM, and G. B. EMERSON. THE POLITICAL CLASS BOOK. *12mo, sheep.* Boston, 1834

2961 SULLY, MAXIMILIEN DE BÉTHUNE, DUC DE. MEMOIRS OF. Translated from the French [by Charlotte Lennox]. A New Edition, revised and corrected; with Additional Notes, and an Historical Introduction, attributed to Sir Walter

Scott. *Appendix, general index, and* 4 *portraits.* 4 *vols., post* 8*vo, cloth, uncut.* London, 1856

2962 SULLY, Maximilien de Béthune, Duc de. Another copy: *the same. Portraits.* 4 *vols., post* 8*vo, cloth, uncut.* London, 1856

2963 SUM Notabill Thinges, excerptit frome the Auld Recordes of the Honorabill Citie of Aberdeene; 1565–1635. 8*vo, pp.* 29; *engraving inserted. With book-plate of Robert Balmanno.* Imprentit at Edinburgh, 1834

2964 SUMNER, Charles. The National Security and the National Faith. Speech at Worcester, September 14, 1865. *pp.* 14, *Boston.* — The Equal Rights of All. Speech in February 6 and 7, 1866. *pp.* 32, *Washington.* (2 *copies.* — The Metric System of Weights and Measures. Speech, July 17, 1866. *pp.* 7, *Boston.* — Art in the National Capitol. Speech, July 17, 1866. *pp.* 8, *Boston.* 4 *pamphlets.* Boston and Washington, 1865–66

2965 SURTEES, R. S. Handley Cross, or Mr. Jorrocks's Hunt; by the Author of "Mr. Sponge's Sporting Tour." With Illustrations by John Leech. *The* 17 *steel plates colored.* 8*vo, cloth, uncut.* London, 1854

2966 SUTHERLAND, Peter C., M. D. Journal of a Voyage in Baffin's Bay and Barrow's Straits, in the Years 1850–1851, performed by H. M. Ships "Lady Franklin" and "Sophia," under the Command of Mr. William Penny, in Search of the Missing Crews of H. M. Ships Erebus and Térror; with a Narrative of Sledge Excursions on the Ice of Wellington Channel, and Observations on the Natural History and Physical Features of the Countries and Frozen Seas visited. *Maps, colored plates, and wood-cuts.* 2 *vols., crown* 8*vo, cloth, uncut.* Longmans & Co., London, 1852

2967 SUYS, F. T. and L. P. Haudebourt. Palais Massimi à Rome: Plans, Coupes, Élévations, Profils, Voûtes, Plafonds, etc., des Deux Palais Massimi; dessinés et publiés par F. T. Suys et L. P. Haudebourt. (Avec une Notice sur la Vie et les Ouvrages de B. Peruzzi.) *Engraved title containing a portrait of Peruzzi, and* 43 *large plates of the plans and details, with* 2 *small plates of views. Vellum paper. Atlas folio, boards, uncut.* Paris, 1818

2968 SWAIN, Charles. The Mind; and other Poems. Second Edition. *Engraved title on India paper. Post* 8*vo, boards, uncut; with autograph of the author.* Presentation copy to Samuel Rogers. London, 1832

2969 SWAN, William D. The Critic Criticised, and Worcester Vindicated. Together with a Reply to the Attacks of Messrs. G. & C. Merriam, upon the Character of Dr. Worcester and his Dictionaries. 8*vo, pp.* 67. Boston, 1860

2970 SWARBRECK, SAMUEL DUNKINFIELD. SKETCHES IN SCOTLAND; drawn from Nature and on Stone. *Frontispiece and* 25 *plates lithographed by Hullmandel. Imperial folio, half morocco.* London, 1839

2971 SWEET, ROBERT. THE BRITISH FLOWER GARDEN, containing coloured Figures and Descriptions of the most Ornamental and Curious Hardy Flowering Plants, including Annuals, Biennials, Perennials, and Flowering Shrubs; with their Scientific and English Names, best Method of Cultivation and Propagation. *The two series complete with upwards of* 700 *colored plates from drawings by E. D. Smith, F. L. S.* 7 *vols., royal* 8*vo, cloth, uncut.* London, 1838

2972 SWETNAM THE WOMAN-HATER, arraigned by Women: A New Comedie; acted at the Red Bull by the late Queenes Servants. *Wood-cut on title. Small* 4*to, half morocco.* PERFECT COPY. London, 1620

2973 SWETT, SAMUEL. HISTORY OF BUNKER-HILL BATTLE; with a Plan. Second Edition; much enlarged with New Information derived from the Surviving Soldiers Present at the Celebration on the 17th June last. NOTES TO HIS SKETCH ON BUNKER-HILL BATTLE. 8*vo, pp.* 58 *and* 30, *rough edges.* Boston, 1826 & 1825.

2974 SWIFT, JONATHAN. THE WORKS OF; accurately revised. (With Supplement; being a Collection of Miscellanies, in Prose and Verse, by the Dean, Dr. Delany, Dr. Sheridan, Mrs. Johnson, and others, his Intimate Friends.) *Numerous plates.* 25 *vols.,* 8*vo, old marbled calf.* London, 1768–79

Vols. I.-XII., with Life of the Dean and Notes, as published by Dr. Hawkesworth in 1755, and again in 1768. Vols. XIII. and XIV., by Mr. Bowyer, improved from Mr. Faulkner, in 1764; reprinted, with many corrections, in 1768. Vols. XV. and XVI., by Deane Swift, Esq., 1765; and again, with Notes by J. Nichols, in 1775. Vol. XVII., with index to Works and Letters, by J. Nichols, 1775. Of the succeeding six volumes of Letters, the first three (XVIII.-XX.) are by Dr. Hawkesworth, and the next three (XXI.-XXIII.) by Deane Swift, Esq. Vols. XXIV. and XXV., form the Supplement, with notes on all the preceding volumes, by J. Nichols.

2975 SWIFT, JONATHAN. A TALE OF A TUB, written for the Universal Improvement of Mankind. To which is added, an Account of a Battel between the Antient and Modern Books in St. James's Library. With the Author's Apology; and Explanatory Notes, by W. W[o]tt[o]n, B. D., and others. (To which is added, a Discourse concerning the Mechanical Operation of the Spirit.) *Plates.* 12*mo, old calf.* B. Motte, London, 1733

2976 SWIFT, JONATHAN, VOYAGES DE GULLIVER, dans les Contrées Lointaines; par Swift. Édition illustrée par Grandville. Traduction Nouvelle (précédée d'une Notice, par Walter Scott). *Frontispiece on India paper, and above* 400 *other fine wood-cuts.* 2 *vols. in* 1, 8*vo, half morocco extra, marbled edges.* Paris, 1838

2977 SWINBURNE, ALGERNON C. LAUS VENERIS; and other Poems and Ballads. 12*mo, cloth, blue edges.* New York, 1866

2978 SWINBURNE, HENRY. TRAVELS IN THE TWO SICILIES, in the Years 1777–1780. 8*vo, old calf. Vol. I. only.* Dublin, 1783

2979 SWINTON, WILLIAM. RAMBLES AMONG WORDS; their Poetry, History, and Wisdom. 12*mo, cloth.* New York, 1859

2980 SYRIA, THE HOLY LAND, AND ASIA MINOR Illustrated; in a Series of One Hundred and Twenty Views, drawn from Nature by W. H. Bartlett, William Purser, and Thomas Allom: with Descriptions of the Plates, by John Carne, Esq. 3 *vols. in* 1, 4*to, turkey morocco extra, gilt edges.* London, s. a.

2981 TAAFFE, JOHN. THE HISTORY OF THE HOLY, MILITARY, SOVEREIGN ORDER OF ST. JOHN OF JERUSALEM; or Knights Hospitallers, Knights Templars, Knights of Rhodes, Knights of Malta. 4 *vols. in* 2, *thick* 8*vo, cloth.* London, 1852

2982 TABLEAUX DE LA RÉVOLUTION FRANÇAISE. COLLECTION COMPLÈTE DES TABLEAUX HISTORIQUES. Composée de Cent-treize Numéros en Trois Volumes (avec des Discours par l'Abbé Fauchet, Chamfort et Ginguené, pour les 25 Premières Livraisons, la Suite par Pagès). *With* 222 *fine engravings, including* 66 *portraits chiefly by Duplessi-Bertaux.* 3 *vols., royal folio, half russia, very neat, marbled edges.* VELLUM PAPER: *fine copy.* Auber, Paris, 1804

2983 TABLEAUX DE LA RÉVOLUTION FRANÇAISE. ANOTHER COPY: WITH THE ORIGINAL REPUBLICAN TEXT. *Titles wanting, but text perfect to page* 388 *inclusive, and plates to number* 96 *inclusive.* 2 *vols., royal folio; needs binding.* VELLUM PAPER. (Paris, 1791, etc.)

These two volumes form a desirable accompaniment to the above set, as they contain all of the text which was mollified in that issue.

2984 TACITUS, CAIUS CORNELIUS. THE WORKS OF; by Arthur Murphy, Esq. With an Essay on the Life and Genius of Tacitus, Notes, Supplements, and Maps. 4 *vols.,* 4*to, diamond russia, very neat, marbled edges.* London, 1793

"This is an excellent work, and supersedes all that has been done on this author. The lost portions of Tacitus are supplied by original compositions, and interstitial books are added to connect and complete the whole." —*Dr. Clarke.*

2985 TALES OF THE ACADEMY. *Plates and wood-cuts.* 2 *vols.,* 18*mo, half morocco.* London, 1828

2986 TALES OF OLD MR. JEFFERSON, OF GRAY'S INN; collected by Young Mr. Jefferson, of Lyon's Inn. The First Series. 2 *vols.,* 12*mo, cloth.* London, 1823

CONTENTS: The Welch Cottage, or the Woodman's Fireside; Mandeville, or the Voyage; The Creole, or The Negro Suicide.

2987 TALFOURD, SIR THOMAS NOON. THE DRAMATIC WORKS OF. To which are added, a Few Sonnets and Verses. *Foolscap 8vo, calf, very neat.* E. Moxon, London, 1852

2988 TASSO, TORQUATO. LA GERUSALEMME LIBERATA; con le Figure di Giambatista Piazzetta. Alla Sacra Real Maestà di Maria Teresa d'Austria, Regina d'Ungheria, e di Boemia, etc. *Royal folio, maroon morocco extra, gilt edges, by Hering.* Venezia, 1745

2989 TASSO, TORQUATO. LA GERUSALEMME LIBERATA: *the elegant edition containing portraits of Tasso and Prince Esterhazy, and 20 fine large plates, engraved under the direction of Raffael Morghen, after designs by Gasp. Martellini and others. 2 vols., folio, russia, very neat, gilt edges.* Firenze, 1820

2990 TASSO, TORQUATO. JERUSALEM DELIVERED; translated from the Italian, by John Hoole. The Fifth Edition, with Notes. *Plates by Sharp and Anker Smith, after Stothard.* 2 *vols.,* 8*vo, old marbled calf, yellow edges.* J. Dodsley, London, 1783

2991 TATE, WILLIAM. THE MODERN CAMBIST; forming a Manual of Foreign Exchanges, in the Direct, Indirect, and Cross Operations of Bills of Exchange and Bullion: including an Extensive Investigation of the Arbitrations of Exchange, according to the Practice of the First British and Foreign Houses. With Numerous Formulæ and Tables of the Weights and Measures of other Countries, compared with the Imperial Standards. Second Edition. *Royal 8vo, cloth, uncut.* London, 1834

2992 TATHAM, EDWARD, D. D. THE CHART AND SCALE OF TRUTH, by which to find the Cause of Error. Lectures read before the University of Oxford, at the Lecture founded by the Rev. John Bampton, M. A.; with a Memoir, Preface, and Notes; by E. W. Grinfield, M. A. 2 *vols., royal* 8*vo, cloth, uncut.* W. Pickering, London, 1840

2993 TATLER (THE). 4 *vols.,* 8*vo, red morocco extra, gilt edges; rebacked.* SECOND EDITION: LARGE TYPE. London, 1710–11

First complete edition which was published after the original issue.

2994 TAUTPHŒUS, THE BARONESS. AT ODDS. 12*mo, cloth.* Philadelphia, 1863

2995 TAVERN ANECDOTES and Reminiscences of the Origin of Signs, Clubs, Coffee-Houses, Streets, City Companies, Wards, etc.; intended as a Lounge-Book for Londoners and their Country Cousins. By One of the Old School. *Portrait of Christopher Brown. Foolscap* 8*vo, half morocco, neat, marbled edges.* London, (1825)

2996 TAYLOR, BAYARD. NORTHERN TRAVEL; Summer and Winter Pictures of Sweden, Lapland, and Norway. 12*mo, half calf extra, marbled edges.* London, 1858

2997 TAYLOR, HENRY. PHILIP VAN ARTEVELDE; a Dramatic Romance. Sixth Edition. 1 *vol., foolscap 8vo, calf, gilt.* E. Moxon, London, 1852

2998 TAYLOR, ISADORE JUSTIN SÉVERIN, BARON. VOYAGE PITTORESQUE, en Espagne, en Portugal, et sur la Côte d'Afrique, de Tanger à Tétouan. *Contains 75 plates engraved by G. Cooke, J. Byrne, E. Goodall, and other celebrated artists. Royal 4to, boards, uncut.* LARGE PAPER. *India proofs.* Paris, 1826

A complete copy should contain 110 plates.

2999 TAYLOR, JANE. THE WRITINGS OF: containing Memoirs and Correspondence; Poetical Remains; Essays in Rhyme; Contributions of Q. Q.; Correspondence between a Mother, and her Daughter at School; Original Poems for Infant Minds; and, Display, a Tale. 3 *vols., 12mo, half calf, neat, marbled edges.* New York, s. a.

3000 TAYLOR, JEREMY, BISHOP. THE WHOLE WORKS OF; with a Life of the Author, and a Critical Examination of his Writings, by the Rev. Reginald Heber, D. D., Bishop of Calcutta. *Portrait.* 15 *vols., 8vo, dark blue turkey morocco, gilt edges.* London, 1828

3001 TAYLOR, JEREMY. THE RULE AND EXERCISES OF HOLY LIVING. Together with Prayers containing the Whole Duty of a Christian, and the Parts of Devotion fitted to all Occasions. *Handsomely printed with large type, by Whittingham. Frontispiece (monumental effigy). 8vo, dark blue smooth morocco, gilt over carmine edges, by Hayday.* W. Pickering, London, 1847

3002 TAYLOR, JEREMY, ETC. THE RULE AND EXERCISES OF HOLY DYING (in which are described the Means and Instruments of Preparing Ourselves and Others respectively for a Blessed Death. Together with Prayers to be used by Sick and Dying Persons, or by Others Standing in their Attendance. To which are added Rules for the Visitation of the Sick.) *Handsomely printed, with large type, by Whittingham. 8vo, dark blue smooth morocco, gilt over carmine edges, by Hayday.* W. Pickering, London, 1847

3003 TAYLOR, JEREMY. THE GREAT EXEMPLAR OF SANCTITY AND HOLY LIFE, described in the History of the Life and Death of the Ever Blessed Jesus Christ. 3 *vols., foolscap 8vo, tree calf extra, marbled edges.* W. Pickering, London, 1849

3004 TAYLOR, JEREMY. ANOTHER COPY: *the same.* 3 *vols., foolscap 8vo, cloth, uncut.* W. Pickering, London, 1849

3005 TAYLOR, JOHN, THE "WATER POET." A LETTER SENT TO GEORGE WITHER, POETICA LICENTIA, ESQUIRE; by a Plain Dealing Friend of his, to prevent his Future Pseudography. [Signed "Alethegraphus."] Printed by Benevol. Typographus, sometimes Printer to the said Master Wither. Published for the Better Information of such who, by his Perpetuall Scribbling, have been screwed into an Opinion of his Worth, and Good Affection to the Publick; and are to be sold by the Cryers of New, New, New, and True News, in all the Streets of London: 1646. *Portrait of Wither (inserted), preface, and 4 leaves. Small 4to, half morocco.* (Reprinted, London, 1834)

"This unique little Tract is preserved in the British Museum, amongst the Pamphlets presented by King George the Third. It contains some very curious facts relative to Wither, and bears internal evidence of being from the pen of his quondam friend Taylor, the 'water poet.' — *Preface.*

3006 TAYLOR, JOHN, AUTHOR OF "JUNIUS IDENTIFIED." CURRENCY INVESTIGATED, with a View to its Scientific Principles; in a Series of Essays, published between the Years 1832 and 1845. *Introduction and 10 essays in 1 vol. 8vo, calf, neat.* S. Clarke, London, 1845

CONTENTS: I. An Essay on Money, its Origin and Use. II. The Standard and Measure of Value. III. Currency Fallacies refuted and Paper Money vindicated. IV. Who Pays the Taxes? V. The Monetary Policy of England and America. VI. The Minister Mistaken, or the Question of Depreciation erroneously stated by Mr. Huskisson. VII. Currency Explained, in Refutation of the Last Fallacy of the "Times." VIII. Letter to the Editor of the "Times." IX. What is a Pound? Letter to the Premier. X. The Labourer's Protection the Nation's Remedy.

3007 TAYLOR, JOHN, AUTHOR OF "MONSIEUR TONSON." RECORDS OF MY LIFE. Complete in One Volume. *8vo, half morocco.* New York, 1833

3008 TAYLOR, WILLIAM BENJAMIN SARSFIELD. THE ORIGIN, PROGRESS, AND PRESENT CONDITION OF THE FINE ARTS IN GREAT BRITAIN AND IRELAND. *Plates. 2 vols., crown 8vo, cloth, uncut.* London, 1841

3009 TAYLOR, WILLIAM COOKE. ILLUSTRATIONS OF THE BIBLE, from the Monuments of Egypt. *Wood-cuts. Post 8vo, cloth, uncut.* C. Tilt, London, 1838

3010 TEGETMEIER, W. B. THE POULTRY BOOK: comprising the Breeding and Management of Profitable and Ornamental Poultry; their Qualities and Characteristics; to which is added, "the Standard of Excellence in Exhibition Birds," authorized by the Poultry Club. *Illustrated by Harrison Weir with 30 plates (including title), finely printed in colors by Leighton Bros., besides numerous wood-cuts. Imperial 8vo, cloth, gilt edges.* London, 1867

3011 TELA, JOSEPHUS. THE MORALITY OF THE EAST, extracted from the Koran of Mohammed; with an Introduction, and Occasional Remarks. To which is prefixed, a Short Abstract of his Life not in the Former Edition. Reprinted from the Edition of 1766. — THE POLITICAL MISCHIEFS OF POPERY, demonstrating — I. that the Romish Religion ruins all those Countries where it is the Established Religion; II. that it occasions the Loss of above Two Hundred Millions of Livres, or Sixteen Millions Sterling, per Annum, to France in Particular. By a Person of Quality, a Native of France. Reprinted from the Edition of 1698, and edited by Josephus Tela. *Together in* 1 *vol., royal* 8*vo, boards, rough edges.* London, 1818

One of the volumes of Tela's "Philosophical Library."

3012 TENISON, Lady Louisa. Castile and Andalucia (described from Observations made during a Two Years' Residence in the Country). *Folding frontispiece* (*Alhambra*), 23 *tinted plates, and* 20 *wood-cut vignettes. Large imperial* 8*vo, cloth, uncut.* London, 1853

3013 TENISON, Lady Louisa. Another copy: *the same, with same plates, etc. Large imperial* 8*vo, half calf extra, marbled edges.* London, 1853

3014 TENNENT, Sir James Emerson. Ceylon: an Account of the Island, Physical, Historical, and Topographical; with Notices of its Natural History, Antiquities, and Productions. Fifth Edition, thoroughly revised. *Maps, plans, charts, and numerous fine wood-cuts.* 2 *vols., royal* 8*vo, cloth, uncut.* London, 1860

3015 TENNYSON, Alfred. In Memoriam. [Memoir of Arthur Henry Hallam, by Tennyson.] *Portraits. Crown* 8*vo, cloth, uncut.* Boston, 1861

Note on fly-leaf says, "one of only 17 copies printed on paper 27 years old."

3016 TENNYSON, Alfred. Enoch Arden. *Printed on a heavy paper, with wood-cut illustrations.* 4*to, half morocco, uncut.* Boston, 1865

3017 TERENCE. P. Terentius Afer a M. Antonio Mureto emendatus; ejusdem Mureti Argumenta et Scholia in Singulas Comoedias. *Small* 8*vo, claret morocco extra, gilt edges.* Very fine copy. Apud Aldum, Venetiis, 1575

"Cette édition, la neuvième du Térence de Muret, et la dixième si l'on y comprend celle des Turrisan, de 1570, est la plus estimable, parce qu'elle est d'une exécution assez soigneé, et surtout aussi parce que les nouvelles Scholies, placées en supplément dans l'Aldine de 1570, sont dans celle-ci remises à leur place." — *Renouard.*

3018 TERENCE. Pub. Terentii Comoedia, nunc Primum Italicis Versibus redditæ [a Nich. Fortiguerra], cum Personarum Figuris, Æri accurate incisis ex MS. Codicc Bibliothecæ Vaticanæ. *Fine impressions of the numerous plates. Folio, boards.* Mainardus, Urbini, 1736

3019 TERRY, Daniel, Comedian. British Theatrical Gallery: a Collection of Whole Length Portraits; with Biographical Notices. *Contains* 20 *fine colored portraits* (*in character*) *of celebrated actors and actresses, engraved by Robt. Cooper. Imperial* 4*to, turkey morocco, gilt edges.* London, 1825

3020 TERRY, DANIEL. ANOTHER COPY: *with uncolored plates, and 2 additional (Mr. Liston as Tony Lumpkin, and Mr. J. Reeve as Acres) colored lithographic plates inserted. Imperial 4to, cloth.* London, 1825

3021 TESTAMENT. NOVUM TESTAMENTUM ENNEAGLOTHUM: Greek, Latin, English, Hebrew, French, German, Italian, Portuguese, and Spanish. *The 9 Testaments, published by S. Bagster & Sons, bound in 1 vol., thick 12mo, turkey morocco, colored edges, with a different color for each language.* London, (1825, etc.)

3022 TESTAMENT. THE APOCRYPHAL NEW TESTAMENT; being all the Gospels, Epistles, and other Pieces now Extant, attributed in the First Four Centuries to Jesus Christ, his Apostles, and their Companions, and not included in the New Testament by its Compilers. Translated from the Original Tongues and now first collected into One Volume [by William Hone]. *8vo, half purple calf, neat.* Printed for W. Hone, London, 1820

3023 THACHER, JAMES, M. D. MILITARY JOURNAL, during the American Revolutionary War, from 1775 to 1783; describing the Events and Transactions of this Period, with Numerous Historical Facts and Anecdotes. To which is added an Appendix, containing Biographical Sketches of Several General Officers. *Numerous wood-cuts. 8vo, cloth.* Hartford, 1854

3024 THACKERAY, WILLIAM MAKEPEACE. THE BOOK OF SNOBS. *16mo, cloth.* New York, 1852

3025 THACKERAY, WILLIAM M. THE ENGLISH HUMOURISTS OF THE EIGHTEENTH CENTURY. *Crown 8vo, claret calf, neat.* London, 1853

3026 THACKERAY, WILLIAM M. ANOTHER COPY. *12mo, cloth.* New York, 1853

3027 THACKERAY, WILLIAM M. EARLY AND LATE PAPERS, hitherto uncollected. *Portrait. Post 8vo, cloth.* Boston, 1867

3028 THÉATRE COMPLET DES LATINS, par J.-B. Levée, et par Feu l'Abbé Le Monnier; augmenté de Dissertations, etc., par MM. Amaury Duval, et Alexandre Duval. *Text in Latin and French. 15 vols., crown 8vo, mottled calf.* Paris, 1820–23

This collection contains Plautus, by Levée, 8 vols.; Terence, by Lemannier, 3 vols.; Seneca, by Levée, 3 vols.; and Fragments (Ennius, etc.,) by Levée, 1 vol.

3029 THEORY (THE) OF AGREEABLE SENSATIONS; in which the Laws observed by Nature in the Distribution of Pleasure are investigated, and the Principles of Natural Theology and Moral Philosophy are established: including likewise,

relative to the same Subject, a Dissertation upon Harmony of Stile. A New Edition. 12*mo, old calf.*
W. Owen, London, 1774

3030 THESAURUS ANTIQUITATUM ROMANARUM ET GRÆCARUM, congestus a Joanne Georgio Grævio, a Jacobo Gronovio, ab Alberto Henrico de Sallengre, et a Joanne Poleno. *Fine impressions of the numerous plates. Together,* 33 *vols., royal folio, vellum.* LARGE PAPER: COMPLETE SET.
Venetiis, 1732–37

GRÆVIUS. THESAURUS ANTIQUITATUM ROMANARUM, in quo continentur Lectissimi quique Scriptores qui Superiori aut nostro Seculo Romanæ Reipublicæ Rationem, Disciplinam, Leges, Instituta, Sacra, Artesque Togatas ac Sagatas explicarunt & illustrarunt; congestus a Joanne Georgio Grævio, accesserunt Variæ & Accuratæ Tabulæ Æneæ. 12 *vols.*

GRONOVIUS. THESAURUS GRÆCARUM ANTIQUITATUM, in quo continentur Effigies Virorum ac Fœminarum Illustrium, quibus in Græcis aut Latinis Monumentis aliqua Memoriæ Pars datur & in quocunque Orbis Terrarum Spatio ob Historiam, vel Res Gestas, vel Inventa, vel Locis Nomina data, ac Doctrinam meruerunt cognosci; item Variarum Regionum Miranda, quæ celebrata apud Antiquos Saxisque & Ære expressa occurrunt, Omnia ex Veris Sincerisque Documentis petita, & pro Serie Temporum disposita; adjecta Brevi Descriptione Singulorum, quæ aut in eorum Vita aut in horum Proprietate Spectabilia percipi & intelligi refert; ubi Variis Occasionibus Nummi, Lapides, Inscriptiones, etiam Auctorum Loca explicantur & emendantur. (Contextus et designatus a Jacobo Gronovio; etiam Tres Indices Absolutissimi, I. Effigierum, II. Auctorum et Operum, III. Rerum et Verborum, quæ continentur in Duodecim Voluminibus.) 13 *vols.*

DE SALLENGRE. NOVUS THESAURUS ANTIQUITATUM ROMANARUM, congestus ab Alberto Henrico de Sallengre, Serenissimæ Principis Arausionensis Consiliario. Cum Figuris Æneis. 3 *vols.*

POLEN. UTRIUSQUE THESAURI ANTIQUITATUM ROMANARUM GRÆCARUMQUE NOVA SUPPLEMENTA, congesta ab Joanne Poleno. 5 *vols.*

3031 THIERS, LOUIS ADOLPHE. THE HISTORY OF THE FRENCH REVOLUTION. Translated, with Notes and Illustrations from the most Authentic Sources, by Frederick Shoberl. *Portraits and plates.* 5 *vols.,* 8*vo, half calf.* London, 1838

3032 THOMAS, GABRIEL. AN HISTORICAL AND GEOGRAPHICAL ACCOUNT OF THE PROVINCE AND COUNTRY OF PENNSILVANIA, and of West-New-Jersey, in America; the Richness of the Soil, the Sweetness of the Situation, the Wholesomness of the Air, the Navigable Rivers, and others, the Prodigious

Encrease of Corn, the Flourishing Condition of the City of Philadelphia, with the Stately Buildings, and other Improvements there; the Strange Creatures, as Birds, Beasts, Fishes, and Fowls, with the Several Sorts of Minerals, Purging Waters, and Stones, lately discovered; the Natives, Aborogmes, their Language, Religion, Laws, and Customs; the First Planters, the Dutch, Sweeds, and English, with the Number of its Inhabitants; as also a Touch upon George Keith's New Religion, in his Second Change since he left the Quakers. With a Map of Both Countries. By Gabriel Thomas, who resided there about Fifteen Years. London: printed for, and sold by A. Baldwin, at the Oxon Arms in Warwick-Lane, 1698. *Crown 8vo, cloth.*
Reprinted for H. A. Brady, New York, 1848

This fac-simile was "lithographed for Henry A. Brady, Member of the New York Historical Society, etc.," who was lost in the steamer *Arctic.*

3033 THOMAS, Isaiah. The History of Printing in America, with a Biography of Printers, and an Account of Newspapers; to which is prefixed a Concise View of the Discovery and Progress of the Art in other Parts of the World. *Portrait, and plates of fac-similes, etc. 2 vols., 8vo, sheep.* Fine copy. Worcester, 1810

3034 THOMPSON, Benjamin Franklin. History of Long Island, containing an Account of the Discovery and Settlement, with other Important and Interesting Matters to the Present Time. *Plates. 8vo, green calf.* New York, 1839

3035 THOMPSON, Charles. Travels through Turkey in Asia, the Holy Land, Arabia, Egypt, and other Parts of the World; giving a Particular and Faithful Account of what is most Remarkable in the Manners, Religion, Polity, Antiquities, and Natural History of those Countries: with a Curious Description of Jerusalem, as it now appears, and other Places mentioned in the Holy Scriptures. By Charles Thompson, Esq. Interspersed with Remarks of Several other Modern Travellers; illustrated with Notes, Historical, Geographical, and Miscellaneous, by the Editor: and adorned with Maps and Prints. The Third Edition. *2 vols., 12mo, old marbled calf gilt, yellow edges.* London, 1767

An abridgment of a larger work.

3036 THOMPSON, D'Arcy Wentworth. Day Dreams of a Schoolmaster. Second Edition. *Foolscap 8vo, cloth, uncut.* Edinburgh, 1864

3037 THOMPSON, Pishey. Collections for a Topographical and Historical Account of Boston, and the Hundred of Skirbeck, in the County of Lincoln. *Engraved dedication, 5 plates, and 20 wood-cuts. Royal 4to, half morocco, very neat, marbled edges.* Large paper: *India proofs of engravings.* London, 1820

3038 THOMS, William J., Projector of "Notes and Queries." Early English Prose Romances, with Bibliographical and Historical Introductions; edited by William J. Thoms, F. S. A. Second Edition, enlarged. *3 vols., crown 8vo, tree calf gilt, gilt edges, by Aitken.* London, 1858

Contents: Robert the Devyll; Thomas à Reading; Frier Bacon; Frier Rush; Virgilius; Robin Hood; George à Green; Tom à Lincolne; Helyas; Doctor Faustus; Second Report of Doctor Faustus.

3039 THOMSON, James. The Seasons. A New Edition, adorned with a Set of Engravings, from Original Paintings; together with an Original Life of the Author, and a Critical Essay on the Seasons, by Robert Heron [John Pinkerton?]. *Portrait, monument, engraved title, and 6 plates, after Corbould, etc. Post 4to, old tree calf gilt, yellow edges.* Perth, 1793

3040 THOMSON, James. Another copy: *the same. Post 4to, half morocco, yellow edges.* Perth, 1793

3041 THOMSON, James. The Works of; with his Last Corrections and Improvements. To which is prefixed, the Life of the Author, by Patrick Murdoch, D. D. *Portrait and 11 fine plates after Stothard, etc. 3 vols., royal 8vo, calf gilt, marbled edges.* Large paper. London, 1802

3042 THOMSON, James. The Poetical Works of. (With Memoir, by Sir N. Harris Nicolas.) *Portrait. 2 vols., foolscap 8vo, cloth, uncut.* Aldine edition. W. Pickering, London, 1847

3043 THOMSON, Katherine B. Memoirs of the Court and Times of King George the Second, and his Consort Queen Caroline; including Numerous Private Letters of the most Celebrated Persons of the Time addressed to the Viscountess Sundon, Mistress of the Robes to the Queen, and her Confidential Adviser; exhibiting much of the Secret, Political, Religious, and Literary History, and a Variety of Particulars not mentioned by our Historians. Now first published from the Originals, by Mrs. Thomson. *Portraits of Lady Sundon and Queen Caroline. 2 vols., 8vo, cloth, uncut.* London, 1850

3044 THOMSON, Katherine Byerley. Recollections of Literary Characters, and Celebrated Places. *2 vols., crown 8vo, cloth, uncut.* London, 1854

These "Recollections" originally appeared in "Bentley's Miscellany," and "Fraser's Magazine," under the signature of "A Middle-aged Man."

3045 THOMSON, Thomas, M. D. Travels in Sweden, during the Autumn of 1812. *Portrait of Charles John (Bernadotte) and Gustavus IV., maps, plans, views, etc. 4to, polished calf gilt, marbled edges.* London, 1813

3046 THOREAU, Henry David. The Maine Woods. *Post 8vo, cloth.* Boston, 1864

3047 THORNBURY, Walter. Life in Spain; Past and Present. With Illustrations. *12mo, cloth.* New York, 1860

3048 THORNTON, ROBERT JOHN, M. D. NEW ILLUSTRATION OF THE SEXUAL SYSTEM OF LINNAEUS: comprehending an Elucidation of the Several Parts of the Fructification; a Dissertation on the Sexes of Plants; a full Explanation of the Classes, and Orders, of the Sexual System; and the Temple of Flora, or Garden of Nature, being Picturesque, Botanical, Coloured Plates of Select Plants, illustrative of the same, with Descriptions. *Finely colored plates of the choicest flowers of Europe, Asia, Africa, and America, on a large scale; with numerous additional plates (uncolored) of the elements of botany, and a series of portraits of distinguished botanists; the portrait of the author, and several others, engraved by Bartolozzi. 2 vols., atlas folio, half russia; binding broken.*
Printed by T. Bensley, London, 1799–1807

3049 THORWALDSEN, BERTEL. INTERA COLLEZIONE DI TUTTE LE OPERE INVENTATE E COPITE DAL CAV. ALBERTO THORWALDSEN INCISA A CONTORNI; con Illustrazioni del Chiarissimo Abate Misserini. *Portrait and 116 plates, with Italian and French letter-press. 2 vols. in 1, royal folio, half vellum extra.* P. Aureli, Roma, 1831

3050 THOU, JACQUES AUGUSTE DE. HISTOIRE DE, des Choses arrivées de son Temps; mise en François, par P. du Ryer. *Portrait, frontispiece, etc., by René Lochon, Matheus, Daret, etc. Books I.–LIV. in 3 vols., folio, old mottled calf, red edges.* A. Coubré, Paris, 1659

3051 THOUSAND (THE) AND ONE NIGHTS; commonly called, in England, the Arabian Nights' Entertainments. A New Translation from the Arabic, with Copious Notes, by Edward W. Lane. Illustrated by many Hundred Engravings on Wood, from Original Designs by William Harvey. *3 vols., royal 8vo, crimson turkey morocco extra, gilt edges.*
C. Knight & Co., London, 1839–41

3052 THUCYDIDES. THE HISTORY OF THE PELOPONNESIAN WAR; translated from the Greek of Thucydides. To which are annexed, Three Preliminary Discourses: I. on the Life of Thucydides; II. on his Qualifications as an Historian; III. a Survey of the History. By William Smith, A. M. A New Edition. *Portrait of Dr. Smith, maps, etc. 2 vols., old sprinkled calf, neat.* London, 1812

3053 THUCYDIDES. ΘΟΥΚΥΔΙΔΗΣ. THE HISTORY OF THE PELOPONNESIAN WAR. The Text according to Bekker's Edition, with some alterations; with Notes, chiefly Historical and Geographical, by Thomas Arnold, D. D. Illustrated by Maps, taken entirely from Actual Surveys. *3 vols., 8vo, half calf extra, marbled edges; backs tooled to match Arnold's Rome and Life.* Oxford, 1830–35

3054 TIBBINS, J. DICTIONNAIRE FRANÇAIS-ANGLAIS, ET ANGLAIS-FRANÇAIS, contenant tous les Mots Généralement adoptés dans les Deux Langues; rédigé d'après les Meilleures Autorités. Édition Diamant. *24mo, morocco.* Baudry, Paris, 1838

3055 TICKNOR, GEORGE. LIFE OF WILLIAM HICKLING PRESCOTT. (With Prefatory Notice, Appendix, and Index.) *Numerous fine engravings, comprising portraits, Greenough's bust, views, etc. Handsomely printed with head and tail pieces, and ornate initials. Crown 4to cloth, gilt top, rough edges.* FINEST EDITION. Boston, 1864

3056 TICKNOR, GEORGE. HISTORY OF SPANISH LITERATURE. Third American Edition, corrected and enlarged. 3 *vols., 8vo, cloth, uncut.* LARGE PAPER: *only* 100 *copies printed.* Boston, 1866

3057 TIMBS, JOHN. CLUB LIFE OF LONDON; with Anecdotes of the Clubs, Coffee-Houses, and Taverns of the Metropolis during the 17th, 18th, and 19th Centuries. *Portraits of Capt. Charles Morris and George Colman the Elder.* 2 *vols., crown 8vo, cloth, uncut.* London, 1866

3058 TOCQUEVILLE, CHARLES ALEXIS HENRI MAURICE CLÈREL DE. DE LA DÉMOCRATIE EN AMÉRIQUE. Cinquième Édition, revue et corrigée. *Map.* 2 *vols., 12mo, half morocco, neat.* C. Gosselin, Paris, 1836

3059 TOCQUEVILLE, CHARLES A. H. M. C. DE. DEMOCRACY IN AMERICA. Translated by Henry Reeve, Esq. Edited, with Notes, the Translation revised and in great Part rewritten and the Additions made to the Recent Paris Editions now first translated, by Francis Bowen. 2 *vols., royal 8vo, cloth, rough edges.* LARGE PAPER: *only* 100 *copies printed.* Cambridge (Mass.), 1864

3060 TOCQUEVILLE, CHARLES A. H. M. C. DE. ANOTHER COPY: *small paper,* 2 *vols., 8vo, cloth, uncut.* Cambridge (Mass.), 1862

3061 TODD, REV. HENRY JOHN. ILLUSTRATIONS OF THE LIVES AND WRITINGS OF GOWER AND CHAUCER; collected from Authentick Documents. *Plates. 8vo, half calf extra; with book-plate of Philip Bliss.* London, 1810

"A curious work, displaying great industry of investigation." — *Lowndes.*

3062 TOLLET, ELIZABETH. POEMS ON SEVERAL OCCASIONS; with Anne Boleyn to King Henry VIII., an Epistle. *12mo, old mottled calf.* J. Clarke, London, 1755

In this volume "Susanna, or Innocence preserv'd; Musical Drama," occupies pp. 156–168.

3063 TOMKINS, THOMAS. RAYS OF GENIUS, collected to enlighten the Rising Generation. *Portrait by Schiavonetti.* 2 *vols., 12mo, citron morocco extra, gilt edges.* London, 1806

3064 TOMLINSON, CHARLES. CYCLOPÆDIA OF USEFUL ARTS, Mechanical and Chemical, Manufactures, Mining, and Engineering; with an Introductory Essay on the Great Exhibition of the Works of Industry of all Nations, 1851. *Illustrated by 40 steel engravings and 2,477 wood-cuts. 2 vols. in 4, royal 8vo, half morocco, marbled edges.* London, (1852, etc.)

3065 TOOKE, John Horne. ΕΠΕΑ ΠΤΕΡΟΕΝΤΑ, or the Diversions of Purley. A New Edition, revised and corrected by Richard Taylor, F. S. A.; with Numerous Additions from the Copy prepared by the Author for Republication. To which is annexed, his Letter to John Dunning, Esq. *Frontispiece. 2 vols., 8vo, half morocco.* London, 1829

3066 TOOKE, William. View of the Russian Empire, during the Reign of Catharine the Second, and to the close of the Eighteenth Century. The Second Edition. *Map and index. 3 vols., 8vo, marbled calf; with book-plate of William H. Eliot.* Longman & Rees, London, 1800

3067 TOWER (The) Menagerie: comprising the Natural History of the Animals contained in that Establishment; with Anecdotes of their Characters and History. Illustrated by Portraits of each, taken from Life, by William Harvey; and engraved on Wood by Branston and Wright. *8vo, half green morocco, red paper sides, uncut.* R. Jennings, London, 1829

3068 TOWLE, Nathaniel C. A History and Analysis of the Constitution of the United States; with a Full Account of the Confederations which preceded it, of the Debates and Acts of the Convention which formed it, of the Judicial Decisions which have construed it, with Papers and Tables illustrative of the Action of the Government and the People under it. *12mo, cloth.* Boston, 1860

3069 TOWNSEND, Francis. Calendar of Knights; containing Lists of Knights Bachelors, British Knights of Foreign Orders, also Knights of the Garter, Thistle, Bath, St. Patrick, and the Guelphic and Ionian Orders, from 1760 to the Present Time. *Crown 8vo, cloth, uncut.* W. Pickering, London, 1828

3070 TOWNSEND, George H. The Manual of Dates; a Dictionary of Reference to all the most Important Events in the History of Mankind to be found in Authentic Records. *Thick post 8vo, half morocco.* London, 1862

3071 TRADITIONARY Anecdotes of Shakespeare; collected in Warwickshire in the Year mdcxciii. Now first published from the Original Manuscript. *8vo, pp. 19, paper.* T. Rodd, London, 1838

Edited by J. Payne Collier, from a MS. letter (signed "John at Stiles") addressed to "Mr. (Edward) Southwell," and endorsed by him, — "From Mr. Dowdall, Description of Severall Places in Warwickshire."

3072 TRANSACTIONS of the Horticultural Society of London. First series, *complete. Numerous finely colored plates. 7 vols., royal 4to, half russia, uncut.* London, 1815–30

3073 TRANSACTIONS OF THE MASSACHUSETTS HORTICULTURAL SOCIETY. *Vol. I., with finely colored plates. Imperial 8vo, half morocco extra, gilt edges.* Boston, 1847

3074 TREATISE (A) ON THE POLICE OF LONDON; containing a Detail of the Various Crimes and Misdemeanors by which Public and Private Property and Security are, at Present, injured and endangered, and suggesting Remedies for their Prevention. The First American Edition. *8vo, sheep.* Philadelphia, 1798

3075 TRELAWNY, E. J. RECOLLECTIONS OF THE LAST DAYS OF SHELLEY AND BYRON. *Post 8vo, cloth.* Boston, 1858

3076 TRÉSOR DE NUMISMATIQUE ET DE GLYPTIQUE, ou Recueil Général de Médailles, Monnaies, Pierres Gravées, Bas-Reliefs, etc., tant Anciens que Modernes, les plus Intéressans sous le Rapport de l'Art et de l'Histoire; gravé par les Procédés de M. Achille Collas, sous la Direction de M. Paul Delaroche, Peintre, de M. Henriquel Dupont, Graveur, et de M. Charles Lenormant, Conservateur de la Bibliothéque Royale, etc. *With* 629 *plates, and descriptive letter-press by Lenormant.* 10 *vols., folio, half morocco, contents lettered.* Paris, 1834, etc.

This set, which is not complete, contains fine impressions of the plates of the first issued numbers, as follows: — VOL. I. Numismatique des Rois Grecs; 32 *plates.* Bas-Reliefs du Parthénon et du Temple de Phigalie, *complete;* 16 *plates.* Nouvelle Galerie Mythologique; 20 *plates.* — VOL. II. Iconographie des Empereurs Romains et de leurs Familles, *complete;* 62 *plates.* — VOL. III. Médailles coulées et ciselées en Italie aux XVe et XVIe Siècles, *complete;* 84 *plates.* — VOLS. IV. and V. Médailles Françaises, depuis le Règne de Charles VII. jusqu'à celui de Louis XIV.: Charles VII. to Henri IV., *complete;* 68 *plates:* Henri IV. to Louis XIV., *complete;* 37 *plates:* Louis XIV. to 1715; 36 *plates.* — VOL. VI. Sceaux des Rois et Reines de France, *complete;* 29 *plates.* — VOL. VII. Sceaux des Grands Feudataires de la Couronne de France, *complete;* 32 *plates.* Sceaux des Communes Communautés, Évêques, Abbés, et Barons; 28 *plates.* Choix Historique des Médailles des Papes; 44 *plates.* — VOL. VIII. Bas-Reliefs et d'Ornamens, Ivoires, Meubles, Armes, Bijoux; 20 *plates.* — VOL. IX. Médailles relatives à la Révolution, 1789–1804, *complete;* 96 *plates.* — VOL. X. Médailles de l'Empire Français et de l'Empereur Napoléon; 44 *plates.*

See MÉDAILLES DE LOUIS-LE-GRAND.

3077 TRIAL (THE) OF THE BRITISH SOLDIERS, of the 29th Regiment of Foot, for the Murder of Crispus Attucks, Samuel Gray, Samuel Maverick, James Caldwell, and Patrick Carr, on Monday Evening, March 5, 1770, before the Honorable Benjamin Lynde, John Cushing, Peter Oliver, and Edmund Trowbridge, Esquires, Justices of the Superior Court of Judicature, held at Boston, by Adjournment, November 27, 1770. *12mo, old calf.* Boston, 1824

3078 TRIAL OF LIEUTENANT JOEL ABBOT, by the General Naval Court Martial, holden on Board the U. S. Ship Independence, at the Navy Yard, Charlestown, Massachusetts, on Allegations made against him, by Capt. David Porter.

Reported by F. W. Waldo, Esq., one of his Counsel. To which is added an Appendix, containing Sundry Documents in Relation to the Management of Affairs on the Boston Station. *8vo, half morocco.* Boston, 1822

3079 TRIAL OF THOMAS O. SELFRIDGE, for Killing Charles Austin, on the Public Exchange, in Boston, August 4th, 1806. (1807.) REPORT OF THE TRIAL BY IMPEACHMENT OF JAMES PRESCOTT, Esquire, Judge of the Probate of Wills, for Misconduct and Maladministration in Office, before the Senate of Massachusetts, in the Year 1821. With an Appendix, containing an Account of Former Impeachments in the same State. By Octavius Pickering and William H. Gardiner, 1821. *Together, 1 vol., 8vo, half calf; with autograph of Rufus Choate.* Boston (1807), and 1821

3080 TRIAL OF PROFESSOR JOHN W. WEBSTER, for the Murder of Dr. George Parkman. Reported exclusively for the N. Y. Daily Globe. *Portraits, etc., and newspaper cuttings. 8vo, pp. 76; with book-plate of Robert Balmanno, F. S. A.* New York, 1850

3081 TRIBUNE (THE) ALMANAC and Political Register for 1860. *12mo, paper.* New York, 1860

3082 TRIPP, ALONZO. CRESTS FROM THE OCEAN-WORLD, or Experiences in a Voyage to Europe, principally in France, Belgium, and England, in 1847 and 1848. *Frontispiece. 12mo, cloth.* Boston, 1859

3083 TRISTRAM, REV. HENRY BAKER. THE GREAT SAHARA; Wanderings South of the Atlas Mountains. *Maps and woodcuts. 8vo, cloth, uncut.* J. Murray, London, 1860

3084 TROLLOPE, ANTHONY. DR. THORNE; a Novel. *12mo, cloth.* New York, 1858

3085 TROLLOPE, ANTHONY. THE BERTRAMS; a Novel. *12mo, cloth.* New York, 1859

3086 TROLLOPE, ANTHONY. THE WEST INDIES AND THE SPANISH MAIN. *Map. 8vo, half calf extra, marbled edges.* London, 1859

3087 TROLLOPE, ANTHONY. ANOTHER COPY: *12mo, cloth.* New York, 1860

3088 TROLLOPE, MRS. FRANCES. BELGIUM AND WESTERN GERMANY, in 1833; including Visits to Baden-Baden, Wiesbaden, Cassel, Hanover, the Harz Mountains, etc., etc. *Frontispieces. 2 vols. in 1, 12mo, half green morocco, neat, marbled edges.* Brussels, 1834

3089 TROLLOPE, MRS. FRANCES. A VISIT TO ITALY. *2 vols., 8vo, cloth, uncut.* London, 1842

3090 TROLLOPE, THOMAS ADOLPHUS. A SUMMER IN BRITTANY. Edited by Frances Trollope. *Colored frontispieces, vignettes on titles, and 10 plates, drawn and etched by A. Hervieu. 2 vols., 8vo, cloth, uncut.* London, 1840

3091 TROLLOPE, THOMAS ADOLPHUS. A SUMMER IN WESTERN FRANCE. Edited by Frances Trollope. *Colored frontispieces, vignettes on titles, 4 plates and wood-cuts, drawn and etched by A. Hervieu. 2 vols., 8vo, cloth, uncut.* London, 1841

3092 TROWBRIDGE, J. T. THE SOUTH; a Tour of its Battle-Fields and Ruined Cities, a Journey through the Desolated States, and Talks with the People: being a Description of the Present State of the Country, its Agriculture, Railroads, Business, and Finances; Political Views, Social Condition, and Prospects. Illustrated. *8vo, sheep.* Hartford, 1866

3093 TROWER, CHARLES FRANCIS. A WEBB OF LOVE, seeking to Enlist Loving Hearts; or Hotspur. *Foolscap 8vo, morocco extra, gilt edges.* London, (1852)

3094 TRUMBULL, JUDGE JOHN, POET. THE POETICAL WORKS OF. Containing M'Fingal, a Modern Epic Poem, revised and corrected, with Copious Explanatory Notes; the Progress of Dullness; and a Collection of Poems on Various Subjects, written before and during the Revolutionary War. *Portrait, and vignette on the engraved titles. 2 vols., royal 8vo, boards, rough edges.* Hartford, 1820

3095 TRUMBULL, JUDGE JOHN, POET. M'FINGAL; an Epic Poem. With Introduction and Notes, by Benson J. Lossing. *Portrait. Imperial 8vo, half olive morocco, red paper sides, gilt top.* LARGE PAPER: *only* 100 *copies printed.* New York, 1860

3096 TRUMBULL, COLONEL JOHN, PAINTER. AUTOBIOGRAPHY, REMINISCENCES, AND LETTERS OF; from 1756 to 1841. (With an Appendix of Letters, and Catalogue of 55 Paintings.) *Portrait, and 22 plates. 8vo, half morocco, neat, gilt top.* New Haven, 1841

3097 TRUSLER, REV. JOHN. MEMOIRS OF THE LIFE OF; with his Opinions on a Variety of Interesting Subjects, and his Remarks, through a Long Life, on Men and Manners, written by himself; replete with Humour, Useful Information, and Entertaining Anecdote. *Part 1. (all published), with wood-cuts by Bewick. 4to, half russia, very neat, marbled edges.* J. Browne, Bath, 1806

"The author sought the suppression of these Memoirs by destroying all the copies he could meet with." — *Lowndes.*

3098 TRYON, THOMAS. THE WAY TO HEALTH, Long Life, and Happiness, or a Discourse of Temperance and the Particular Nature of all things requisite for the Life of Man; as, all Sorts of Meats, Drinks, Air, Exercise, etc., with Special Directions how to use each of them to the best advantage of the Body and Mind: shewing from the True Ground of Nature whence most Diseases proceed, and how to prevent them. To which is added, a Treatise of most Sorts of English Herbs, etc., etc. The Third Edition; to which is added a Discourse of the Philosopher's Stone, or Universal Medicine, discovering the Cheats and Abuses of those Chymical Pretenders. *8vo, old calf.* London, 1697

3099 TRYON, THOMAS. THE KNOWLEDGE OF A MAN'S SELF the Surest Guide to the True Worship of God, and Good Government of the Mind and Body; in Opposition to Tradition, Custom, and Bigotry: or, the Second Part of the Way to Long-Life, Health, and Happiness. *Portrait by R. White. 8vo, old calf.* London, 1703

3100 TUCKERMAN, HENRY THEODORE. THE OPTIMIST; a Series of Essays. A New Edition. *12mo, cloth.* New York, 1852

3101 TUCKERMAN, HENRY THEODORE. SICILY; a Pilgrimage. *12mo, cloth.* New York, 1852

3102 TUCKERMAN, HENRY THEODORE. LEAVES FROM THE DIARY OF A DREAMER; found among his Papers. *Foolscap 8vo, calf antique, carmine edges.* W. Pickering, London, 1853

3103 TUCKERMAN, HENRY THEODORE. THE CHARACTER AND PORTRAITS OF WASHINGTON. *The portraits on India paper. 4to, cloth, uncut.* New York, 1859

3104 TUDOR, WILLIAM. THE LIFE OF JAMES OTIS; containing also, Notices of some Contemporary Characters and Events, from the Year 1760 to 1775. *Portrait and plates. 8vo, half calf.* Boston, 1823

3105 TURNBULL, GEORGE. A TREATISE ON ANCIENT PAINTING: containing Observations on the Rise, Progress, and Decline of that Art amongst the Greeks and Romans; the High Opinion which the Great Men of Antiquity had of it; its Connexion with Poetry and Philosophy; and the Use that may be made of it in Education. To which are added, some Remarks on the Peculiar Genius, Character, and Talents of Raphael, Michael Angelo, Nicholas Poussin, and other Celebrated Modern Masters; and the Commendable Use they made of the Exquisite Remains of Antiquity in Painting as well as Sculpture. The Whole illustrated and adorned with Fifty Pieces of Ancient Painting; discovered at Different Times in the Ruins of Old Rome, accurately engraved from Drawings of Camillo Paderni, lately done from the Originals with Great Exactness and Elegance. *Royal folio, old mottled calf gilt; with book-plate of Charles Shaw, Lord Cathcart,* 1763. LARGE PAPER: *with the* 4 *outline plates.* Printed for the Author, London, 1740

3106 TURNBULL, GEORGE. A CURIOUS COLLECTION OF ANCIENT PAINTINGS, accurately engraved from Excellent Drawings, lately done after the Originals; with an Account where and when they were found, and where they now are, and Several Critical, Historical, and Mythological Observations upon them. *Contains* 55 *plates, including the* 4 *outlines. Large folio, old calf, neat.*

Printed for S. Birt, etc., London, 1744

This copy contains *five* plates, unnumbered, not usually found in the work.

3107 TURNER, JOSEPH MALLORD WILLIAM. THE RIVERS OF FRANCE. *Choice impressions of the* 57 *beautiful plates, engraved by Cousen, Willmore, Radclyffe, etc. Descriptions in English and French.* *4to, cloth, gilt edges.* FIRST EDITION.

Longmans & Co., London, 1837

3108 TURNER, JOSEPH MALLORD WILLIAM. AN ANTIQUARIAN AND PICTURESQUE TOUR round the Southern Coast of England, illustrated with Eighty-four Plates, from Drawings by J. M. W. Turner, R. A., W. Collins, R. A., William Westall, R. A., S. Prout, P. DeWint, and others; engraved by George Cooke, E. Goodall, R. Wallis, Edward Finden, W. Miller, J. C. Allen, and W. B. Cooke. *All fine line engravings, the smaller ones on India paper, and* 40 *of them after Turner.* *4to, half morocco extra, gilt edges.*

M. A. Nattali, London, 1849

3109 TURNER, JOSEPH MALLORD WILLIAM. THE TURNER GALLERY: a Series of Sixty Engravings from the Principal Works of J. M. W. T.; with a Memoir and Illustrative Text, by Ralph N. Wornum. *Portrait and the* 60 *beautiful engravings all executed by the most eminent engravers. Atlas folio, half turkey morocco extra, gilt edges.* INDIA PROOFS BEFORE LETTERS: *only* 100 *copies in this size.*

London, (1860)

3110 TURNER, CAPTAIN SAMUEL. AN ACCOUNT OF AN EMBASSY TO THE COURT OF THE TESHOO LAMA IN TIBET; containing a Narrative of a Journey through Bootan, and Part of Tibet. To which are added, Views taken on the Spot, by Lieutenant Samuel Davis; and Observations Botanical, Mineralogical, and Medical, by Mr. Robert Saunders. *Printed by W. Bulmer & Co. Royal 4to, calf gilt.*

London, 1800

"THIBET should seem hardly to stand in need of another historian, after the very admirable work of the late *Mr. Samuel Turner*. This performance is among the most perfect of those which relate to the northern parts of India." — *Dibdin.*

3111 TURNER, CAPTAIN SAMUEL. ANOTHER COPY: the Second Edition. *Royal 4to, half morocco, very neat.*

London, 1806

3112 TWEEDIE, REV. W. K. SELECT BIOGRAPHIES; edited for the Wodrow Society, chiefly from Manuscripts in the Library of the Faculty of Advocates. 2 *vols.*, *8vo, half vellum extra, gilt tops, uncut.* Edinburgh, 1845–47

3113 TWISS, RICHARD. TRAVELS THROUGH PORTUGAL AND SPAIN, in 1772 and 1773; with an Appendix. *Map and 7 fine plates, including one engraved by Bartolozzi, after the painting (by Raphael) in the Escurial, called "Our Lady of the Fish." Royal 4to; needs binding.* LARGE PAPER. London, 1775

3114 TWO FRIENDS; by the Author of "the Patience of Hope" and "a Present Heaven." *Post 8vo, cloth, carmine edges.* Boston, 1863

3115 TYERMAN, REV. DANIEL; and GEORGE BENNET. JOURNAL OF VOYAGES AND TRAVELS, in the South Sea Islands, China, India, etc., between the Years 1821 and 1829. Compiled from Original Documents, by James Montgomery. From the First London Edition, revised. *Portraits and plates. 3 vols., 12mo, half morocco.* Boston, 1832

3116 TYLER, BENNET, D. D. MEMOIR OF THE LIFE AND CHARACTER OF REV. ASAHEL NETTLETON, D. D. *Portrait. 12mo, cloth.* Hartford, 1845

3117 TYNDALL, JOHN. THE GLACIERS OF THE ALPS; being a Narrative of Excursions and Ascents, an Account of the Origin and Phenomena of Glaciers, and an Exposition of the Physical Principles to which they are related. *Woodcuts. 12mo, cloth, uncut.* J. Murray, London, 1860

3118 TYTLER, PATRICK FRASER. THE HISTORY OF SCOTLAND, from the Accession of Alexander III. to the Union. New Edition. *10 vols., crown 8vo, tree calf gilt, marbled edges, by Macdonald.* ELEGANT COPY. Edinburgh, 1866

The tenth volume is a very complete index.

3119 ULRICI, HERMANN. SHAKSPEARE'S DRAMATIC ART; and his Relation to Calderon and Goethe. Translated from the German [by the Rev. A. J. W. Morrison]. *8vo, cloth, uncut.* London, 1846

3120 UNITARIAN (THE) MISCELLANY AND CHRISTIAN MONITOR. [Edited by Jared Sparks and F. W. P. Greenwood.] *6 vols., 12mo, boards, rough edges.* Baltimore, 1821–24

3121 UNITED STATES SANITARY COMMISSION. Pamphlets relating to. *8 pamphlets.* New York, etc., 1861–64

3122 UNITED STATES SANITARY COMMISSION BULLETIN. *Nov.* 1, 1862–*August* 1, 1865. *Nos.* 1–40. *3 vols., half bound; complete.* New York, 1866

3123 UNIVERSAL (AN) HISTORY, from the Earliest Account of Time to the Present; compiled from Original Authors, and illustrated with Maps, Cuts, Notes, Chronological and other Tables. *The Ancient part only, complete, with a general index and chronological table to the seven volumes. Fine impressions of the plates. 7 vols. in 9, folio, half calf, neat.* ORIGINAL FOLIO EDITION: *fine copy,* London, 1736–44

3124 UNIVERSAL HISTORY. ANOTHER SET: COMPLETE, EXCEPT ATLAS, WITH SUPPLEMENT. 69 *vols.*, 8*vo*, *half calf*. ORIGINAL OCTAVO EDITION. London, 1747–66.

This set is in good condition, and contains the four supplementary volumes of the History of England, Ireland, and Scotland, which are generally wanting. It is divided as follows: Ancient Part, 21 vols.; Modern Part, 44 vols.; Supplement, 4 vols.

3125 UNIVERSAL HISTORY. ANOTHER SET: *wanting Vol.* 21 *of the Ancient part* (*Chronological Tables*), *one vol. of the Supplement* (*History of Scotland*), *and the atlas.* 67 *vols.*, 8*vo*, *calf.* London, 1747, etc.

Professor Smyth in his "Lectures on Modern History," says: "Many histories and many political subjects have been passed by, but they who would look for more, or would think it advisable to turn aside from the course here proposed, may consult the volumes of the Modern Universal History, and they will find, either in the text or the references, every historical information they can well require." —*List of Books Recommended, etc.*

3126 UPHAM, REV. CHARLES WENTWORTH. LIFE, EXPLORATIONS, AND PUBLIC SERVICES OF JOHN C. FRÉMONT. *Portrait and wood-cuts.* 12*mo*, *cloth.* Boston, 1856

3127 UPHAM, THOMAS COGSWELL, D. D. ELEMENTS OF MENTAL PHILOSOPHY. 2 *vols.*, *royal* 8*vo*, *cloth*, *rough edges.* Portland, 1831

3128 UPHAM, THOMAS COGSWELL, D. D. PRINCIPLES OF THE INTERIOR OR HIDDEN LIFE. 12*mo*, *sheep.* Boston, 1843

3129 UPTON, JOHN. CRITICAL OBSERVATIONS ON SHAKESPEARE. *First edition, with the "Reverie"* (*commencing page* 139), *which was omitted in subsequent issues.* 8*vo*, *old calf; binding broken.* London, 1746

3130 USBORNE, T. H. A NEW GUIDE TO THE LEVANT, for the Use of Travellers in Greece, Egypt, Palestine, Syria, and Asia Minor; and Descriptions of Lisbon, Cadiz, Gibraltar, Malaga, Malta, the Ionian Islands, Syra, and Constantinople: also Full Particulars of the Overland Journey to India, etc. *Foolscap* 8*vo*, *cloth.* London, 1840

3131 VAILLANT, JEAN FOY. NUMMI ANTIQUI FAMILIARUM ROMANARUM perpetuis Interpretationibus illustrati, per J. Vaillant, Bellovacum, D. M. & S. Ducis Cenom. Antiquarium. *Frontispiece, vignettes, and* 152 *fine plates of coins, medals, etc.* 2 *vols.*, *folio*, *old calf.* Amstelædami, 1703

3132 VALENTIA, GEORGE ANNESLEY, VISCOUNT. VOYAGES AND TRAVELS to India, Ceylon, the Red Sea, Abyssinia, and Egypt, in the Years 1802, 1803, 1804, 1805, and 1806. *Maps*, 66 *large plates, and* 3 *vignettes, from drawings made on the spot by H. Solt, secretary to Lord Valentia, engraved by Fittler, Angus, Greig, Landseer, etc. Printed by W. Bulmer & Co.* 3 *vols.*, *royal* 4*to*, *old marbled calf.* London, 1809

3133 VALÉRY, ANTOINE CLAUDE. HISTORICAL, LITERARY, AND ARTISTICAL TRAVELS IN ITALY; a Complete and Methodical Guide for Travellers and Artists. Translated from the Second improved Edition; by C. E. Clinton. *Vignette on the engraved title, map, and fine index. 1 vol. in 2, 12mo, cloth.* Paris, 1839

3134 VALESIO, FRANCISCO. MUSEUM CORTONENSE, in quo Vetra Monumenta complectuntur Anaglypha, Thoreumata, Gemmæ Inscalptæ, insculptæque quæ in Academia Etrusca ceterisque Nobilium Virorum Domibus adservantur in Plurimis Tabulis Æreis distributum, atque a Francisco Valesio, Romano, Antonio Francisco Gorio, Florentino, et Rodulphino Venuti, Cortonense, Notis Illustratum. *Fine impressions of the 85 plates, ornate initials, and other embellishments. Folio, vellum, yellow edges.* Romæ, 1750

3135 VÁMBÉRY, ARMINIUS. TRAVELS IN CENTRAL ASIA: being the Account of a Journey from Teheran across the Turkoman Desert on the Eastern Shore of the Caspian to Khiva, Bokhara, and Samarcand, performed in the Year 1863. *Wood-cuts, and map in pocket. Royal 8vo, cloth, uncut.* New York, 1865

3136 VANDENHOFF, GEORGE. COMMON SENSE, a Dash at Doings of the Day. *12mo, boards.* Boston, 1858

3137 VAN EVRIE, JOHN H., M. D. NEGROES, AND NEGRO "SLAVERY:" the First, an Inferior Race; the Latter, its Normal Condition. *Wood-cuts, 12mo, cloth.* New York, 1861

3138 VASARI, GIORGIO. LE VITE DE PIÙ ECCELENTI PITTORI, SCULTORI, E ARCHITETTI, di Giorgio Vasari; publicate per Cura di una Società di Amatori delle Arti Belle. *Portraits. 13 vols. in 7, 12mo, half vellum.* F. le Monnier, Firenze, 1846–57

3139 VASI, GIUSEPPE; and ANTONIO NIBBY. NEW GUIDE OF ROME AND NAPLES and their Environs, from the Italian; containing a Description of the Monuments, Antiquities, Galleries, Churches, and Curiosities of both Capitals, etc., etc. *Map of Rome and environs, and 25 views of the principal monuments. 12mo, vellum.* Rome, 1841

3140 VAUGHAN, HENRY. SILEX SCINTILLANS: Sacred Poems and Ejaculations. (With a Biographical Sketch, by the Rev. H. F. Lyte.) *Foolscap 8vo, calf gilt, marbled edges.* W. Pickering, London, 1847

3141 VAUGHAN, HENRY. ANOTHER COPY: *the same. Foolscap 8vo, purple morocco extra, gilt edges, by Hayday.* W. Pickering, London, 1847

3142 VAUGHAN, HERBERT. THE CAMBRIDGE GRISETTE. Illustrated by Charles Keene. *Square crown 8vo, cloth, gilt edges.* London, 1862

3143 VAUGHAN, ROBERT, D. D. THE LIFE AND OPINIONS OF JOHN DE WYCLIFFE, D. D.; illustrated principally from his Unpublished Manuscripts. With a Preliminary View of the Papal System, and of the State of the Protestant Doctrine in Europe, to the Commencement of the Fourteenth Century. Second Edition, much improved. *Portrait. 2 vols., 8vo, cloth, uncut.* London, 1831

3144 VENABLES, COLONEL ROBERT. THE EXPERIENCED ANGLER, or Angling Improved; imparting many of the Aptest Ways and Choicest Experiments for the Taking of most Sorts of Fish in Pond or River. (Sixth Edition, with a Memoir.) *Fac-similes of the frontispiece by Vaughn, and title of the edition of 1662; and 18 plates on India paper, of the fish. Foolscap 8vo, boards, rough edges.* S. Prowett, London, 1825

3145 VENABLES, COLONEL ROBERT. ANOTHER COPY: *the same; with a different title, and 3 extra plates inserted. Foolscap 8vo, half morocco, gilt top, rough edges.* T. Gosden, London, 1827

3146 VENUTI, RIDOLFINO. ANTIQUA NUMISMATA Maximi Moduli, Aurea, Argentea, Aerea, ex Museo Alexandri S. R. E. Card. Albani in Vaticanum Bibliothecam a Clemente XII. Pont. Opt. Max. translata, et a Rodulphino Venuto, Cortonensi Notis Illustrata. *Vol. I., containing 62 large plates of medals, etc., besides numerous small views of ruins, landscapes, etc., finely etched by S. Della Bella. Folio, old calf, arms gilt on sides.* Romæ, 1739

3147 VERRAL, CHARLES. THE PLEASURES OF POSSESSION, or the Enjoyment of the Present Moment contrasted with those of Hope and Memory; a Poem. *Frontispiece. Foolscap 8vo, boards, rough edges.* London, 1810

3148 VERTOT D'AUBŒUF, RENÉ AUBERT DE. THE HISTORY OF THE KNIGHTS OF MALTA. Illustrated with LXXI. Heads of the Grand Masters, etc., engraved by the Best Hands in France, from the Original Paintings, under the Inspection of Mons. Bologne, Director of the Royal Academy of Painting; with Maps by Mons. de Lille, and the Plans and Fortifications of Malta by the Chevallier de Tigné; and a Complete Index. *2 vols., folio, old calf gilt, red edges.* LARGE PAPER: *fine copy.* London, 1728

The second title reads: "The History of the Knights Hospitallers of S. John of Jerusalem, styled afterwards, the Knights of Rhodes, and at Present, the Knights of Malta." The work was compiled at the invitation of the Order, with full access to their archives, which renders the information authentic and valuable.

3149 VERTOT D'AUBŒUF, RENÉ AUBERT DE. ANOTHER COPY: *with title like second title of the above copy. 5 vols., 12mo, calf, yellow edges.* London, 1775

3150 VETUSTA MONUMENTA: quae ad Rerum Britannicarum Memoriam Conservandam Societas Antiquariorum Londini Sumptu suo edenda curavit. *4 vols. in 3, imperial folio, polished calf extra, yellow edges; with book-plate of William Clark.* Londini, 1747–1815

3151 VICTOR, BENJAMIN. THE HISTORY OF THE THEATRES OF LONDON AND DUBLIN, from the Year 1730 to the Present Time; to which is added, an Annual Register of all the Plays, etc., performed at the Theatres-Royal in London, from the Year 1712: with Occasional Notes and Anecdotes. *Vols. I. and II. 12mo, calf.* London, 1761

3152 VICTORIA, ALEXANDRINA, QUEEN. THE EARLY YEARS OF HIS ROYAL HIGHNESS THE PRINCE CONSORT; compiled, under the Direction of her Majesty, by Lieut.-General the Hon. C. Grey. Third Edition. *Portraits. Thick 8vo, cloth, uncut.* London, 1867

3153 VIDAL, E. E. PICTURESQUE ILLUSTRATIONS OF BUENOS AYRES AND MONTE VIDEO, consisting of Twenty-four Views; accompanied with Descriptions of the Scenery, and of the Costumes, Manners, etc., of the Inhabitants of those Cities and their Environs. *Colored plates. Imperial 4to, boards, rough edges.* London, 1820

3154 VIDOCQ, EUGÈNE FRANÇOIS. MEMOIRS OF. Written by himself, and translated from the Original French, expressly for this Edition. With Illustrative Engravings, from Original Designs by Cruikshank. *Post 8vo, cloth.* Philadelphia, (1859)

3155 VIDUA, CARLO, CONTE. INSCRIPTIONES ANTIQUAE a Comite Carolo Vidua in Turcico Itinere collectae. *With 51 lithographic plates. 8vo, paper, rough edges; with autograph of John Pickering.* Lutetiæ Parisiorum, 1826

"Cet ouvrage a été l'objet de deux articles de M. Letronne, dans le 'Journal de Savants,' 1827." —*Brunet.*

3156 VIE (LA) DE DON ALPHONSE BLAS DE LIRIAS, Fils de Gil Blas de Santillane. *Plates by J. Punt. 12mo, calf gilt, marbled edges.* Amsterdam, 1744

3157 VIGNY, ALFRED VICTOR, COMTE DE. CINQ-MARS, or a Conspiracy under Louis XIII.; an Historical Romance. Translated by William Hazlitt, Esq. *Portrait. Post 8vo, cloth, uncut.* D. Bogue, London, 1847

3158 VIRGIL. PUBLII VIRGILII MARONIS OPERA, per Johannum Ogilvium edita; et Sculpturis Æneis adornata. *Fine impressions of the numerous plates by Lombart, Faithorne, Hollar, etc. Royal folio, old calf; with book-plates.* Typis, Thomæ Roycroft, Londini, 1663

3159 VIRGIL. P. VIRGILII MARONIS OPERA, Varietate Lectionis et Perpetua Adnotatione illustrata, a Chr. Gottl. Heyne, Georgiæ Augustæ Prof. et Bibliothecario M. Britann. Regia

Consil. Aul. accedit Index Uberrimus. Editio Tertia Emendatior et Auctior. *Numerous beautiful vignettes, after designs by Fiorillo from antique monuments, etc. 4 vols., thick royal 4to, calf, gilt edges, by Hering.* LARGEST PAPER: *very few copies printed.* London, 1793

"The London edition of 1793, which is merely a reimpression of the Leipsic edit. of 1788, is the most popular in this country. Some copies are struck off on LARGE PAPER, in royal octavo and quarto, ornamented with beautiful vignettes. Of the *quarto size*, only very few were printed, and they sell at a great price: the splendor of the paper, and elegance of the execution, render it a truly interesting publication. It is said that the entire expenses of bringing out this London edition of 1793 amounted to £4,000 — a great sum!" — *Dibdin (Gr. and Latin Class. vii. p.* 561).

3160 VIRGIL. P. VIRGILIUS MARO VARIETATE LECTIONIS ET PERPETUA ADNOTATIONE ILLUSTRATUS a Chr. Gottl. Heyne, accedunt Indices. Editio Novis Curis emendata et aucta. *Bust of Heyne, frontispiece, and above* 200 *beautiful vignettes, by Geyser after Fiorillo.* 6 *vols., royal* 8*vo, olive morocco, gilt edges.* VELLUM PAPER: *fine copy.* Sumptibus C. Fritsch, Lipsiæ, 1800

"Édition regardée comme un des chefs-d'œuvre de la critique classique, et qui, chose remarquable dans un livre imprimé à Leipzig à cette époque-là, se distingue par sa belle exécution typographique, ainsi que par les 204 jolies vignettes dont elle est décorée." — *Brunet.*

3161 VIRGIL. THE WORKS OF PUBLIUS VIRGILIUS MARO; Translated, adorned with Sculptures, and illustrated with Annotations, by John Ogilby, Esq., etc. The Third Edition. *Small thick* 8*vo, old calf.* Printed by the Author, London, 1675

3162 VIRGIL. THE WORKS OF VIRGIL: containing his Pastorals, Georgics, and Æneis; translated into English Verse, by Mr. Dryden. Adorn'd with a Hundred Sculptures. *Fine impressions of the plates, engraved by Hollar, Lombart, etc. Royal folio, old calf gilt.* LARGE PAPER: *original edition.* J. Tonson, 1697

Although the impressions of the plates are fine for *this issue*, they are not so brilliant as the *original impressions* of the same in Ogilby's edition. See first copy "Virgilii Opera" above.

3163 VIRGIL. THE WORKS OF VIRGIL; translated by John Dryden, Esq. *Portrait and map.* 3 *vols.,* 18*mo, old calf gilt.* A. Foulis, Glasgow, 1769

3164 VIRGIL. THE WORKS OF VIRGIL; translated into English Verse, by Mr. Dryden. A New Edition, revised and corrected by John Carey, LL. D. *Plates by Bartolozzi, Sharp, Fittler, etc.* 3 *vols.,* 8*vo, polished calf gilt, marbled edges; with book-plate of John Clifford.* London, 1806

3165 VIRGIL, ŒUVRES DE VIRGILE; traduites en François, le Texte vis-à-vis la Traduction, avec des Remarques par M. l'Abbé Desfontaines. Nouvelle Édition. *Portrait, and* 17 *fine plates after Moreau and Zocchi.* 4 *vols.,* 8*vo, calf. A page, or more, wanting (Remarques sur le livre viii.) at the end of third volume.* P. Plassan, Paris, 1796

3166 VIRGIL. P. VIRGILII MARONIS BUCOLICA: the Eclogues of Virgil; with an English Translation and Notes. New Edition. By John Martyn, F. R. S., etc. *With* 37 *finely colored botanical plates. Imperial* 8*vo, maroon morocco, gilt edges.* LARGE PAPER: *elegant copy.*
Printed by T. Bensley, London, 1813

3167 VIRGIL. ANTIQUISSIMI VIRGILIANI CODICIS FRAGMENTA ET PICTURAE, ex Bibliotheca Vaticana, ad Priscas Imaginum Formas a Petro Sancte Bartholi incisae. *Fine impressions of the* 58 *plates. Folio, vellum, red edges.* VELLUM PAPER; *with the* 3 *additional plates.* Romae, 1741

3168 VISCONTI, ENNIO QUIRINO. ICONOGRAPHIE ANCIENNE, ou Recueil des Portraits Authentiques des Empereurs, Rois, et Hommes Illustres de l'Antiquité. TOME PREMIER: ICONOGRAPHIE GRECQUE. 3 *vols., atlas folio, half red French morocco, uncut.* P. Didot l'Aîné, Paris, 1808

3169 VOLNEY, C. F. C., COMTE DE. RUINS, or Meditation on the Revolutions of Empires. Translated; to which is added, the Law of Nature, and a Short Biographical Notice by Count Daru. Also, the Controversy between Dr. Priestley and Volney. *Wood-cut.* 16*mo, boards.*
Boston, 1835

3170 VOLTAIRE, FRANÇOIS MARIE AROUËT DE. ŒUVRES COMPLÈTES DE; avec des Remarques et des Notes Historiques, Scientifiques, et Littéraires, par MM. Auguis, Clogenson, Daunou, Louis du Bois, Étienne, Charles Nodier, etc. 94 *vols.* — TABLE ANALYTIQUE DES MATIÈRES, par P. A. M. Miger. 2 *vols. Plates after Moreau, etc.* 96 *vols.,* 8*vo, half blue calf, marbled edges.*
Delangle Frères, Paris, 1825–34

Should comprise 97 vols., including the two volumes of indexes, but Vol. XIV. (La Pucelle d'Orléans) is wanting.

"Cette édition, trop volumineuse, est sans contredit une des plus belles et des plus complètes des œuvres du philosophe de Ferney." — *Brunet.*

3171 VOLTAIRE, FRANÇOIS MARIE AROUËT DE. ŒUVRES COMPLÈTES DE; avec des Notes et Une Notice Historique sur la Vie de Voltaire. *Printed in two columns; with* 9 *portraits and* 38 *plates engraved by Lefèvre, Blanchard, Hopwood, etc., after Moreau and others, besides fac-simile of autograph, etc.* 13 *vols., royal* 8*vo, half calf.*
Paris, 1835–38

3172 VOLTAIRE, FRANÇOIS MARIE AROUËT DE. LA PUCELLE D'ORLÉANS; Poëme en Vingt-un Chants. Édition ornée de Figures gravées par les Meilleurs Artistes de Paris. *Portrait of Jeanne d'Arc, and* 21 *fine plates, engraved by M. Ponce, etc., after Monsiau, Monnet, Marillier, etc.* 2 *vols., imperial* 4*to, marbled calf gilt, gilt edges.*
Didot le Jeune, Paris, An. III. (1795)

3173 VOLTAIRE, François Marie Arouët de. Histoire de Charles XII., Roi de Suede. *Title wanting.* *18mo, half sheep.* (Paris)

3174 VOYAGE Pittoresque et Historique de l'Espagne; par Alexandre de Laborde, et une Société de Gens de Lettres et d'Artistes de Madrid. *Fine impressions of the plates. Vols. I. and II. Atlas folio, half maroon morocco, neat, gilt tops.* Vellum paper.
P. Didot l'Aîné, Paris, 1806–11

"Ce magnifique ouvrage a été publié en 48 livrais de 6 pl., avec un texte. La 46e livraison ne contenait que 4 planches, et les deux dernières n'en renfermaient les titres et vignettes, et la table des 4 vol. Le prix des exemplaires complets était de 1,008 fr. — en pap. vél. 1,728 fr." — *Brunet.*

3175 WACE, Robert. Master Wace his Chronicle of the Norman Conquest, from the Roman de Rou; translated, with Notes and Illustrations, by Edgar Taylor, Esq., F. S. A. *Map, 34 full-page wood-cuts, and many smaller ones, comprising outlines from the Bayeux Tapestry, etc. 8vo, calf gilt, marbled edges.* Only 262 copies printed: 12 *of which on large paper, with engravings colored.*
W. Pickering, London, 1837

3176 WALCOTT, Rev. James. The History of the Pious Indian Convert, or the New Pilgrim's Progress; containing a Faithful Account of Hattain Gelashmin, a Heathen, who was baptiz'd into the Christian Faith by the Name of George James, and by that means brought from the Darkness of Paganism to the Light of the Gospel, of which he afterwards became an Able and Worthy Minister: together with a Narrative of his Laborious and Dangerous Travels among the Savage Indians for their Conversion, his many Sufferings and Miraculous Deliverances, and the Wonderful Things which he saw in a Vision. Publish'd for the Instruction of Mankind in General, but more particularly for the Impenitent and Unreformed. *8vo, half calf.*
Blackburn, 1792

A part of this work is styled "The Journal of George James in his Pilgrimage amongst the Inland Natives of the Countries adjoining to South Carolina."

3177 WALDRON, Francis Godolphin. The Literary Museum, or Ancient and Modern Repository; comprising Scarce and Curious Tracts, Poetry, Biography, and Criticism. [Edited by F. G. Waldron.] *8vo, half olive morocco, red paper sides.* Printed for the Editor, London, 1792

This curious collection is dedicated "to J. P. Kemble, Esq., generally known to unite the elegant antiquary with the accomplished Actor."

3178 WALDRON, Francis Godolphin. The Literary Museum, or a Selection of Scarce Old Tracts; viz., 1. the Right Renoumyde Ladies, translated from Boccace; 2. a

Delicate Diet for Dainty-mouthed Droonkardes, by Gascoyne; 3. Poems of Spenser, not in any Edition; 4. Peacham's Period of Mourning, in Six Vissions; 5. Specimen of a New Edition of Ben Jonson; 6. Ceremonies used for healing the King's Evil, consecrating Cramp Rings, etc.; 7. On Lydgate's Travelling into France; 8. the New Arcadia, by Belcher; 9. Downe's Roscius Anglicus, or Theatrical History, etc., etc. [Edited by F. G. Waldron.] *8vo, half green morocco, gilt top.*
Printed for the Editor, London, 1792

The above two copies differ not only in the title, but each contains several pages not in the other.

3179 WALKER, ALEXANDER. BEAUTY ILLUSTRATED by an Analysis and Classification of Beauty in Woman, with a Critical View of the Hypotheses of Hume, Hogarth, Burke, Knight, Alison, etc.; and of the Hypotheses of Beauty in Sculpture and Painting, by Leonardo da Vinci, Winckelmann, Mengs, Bossi, etc. *With 24 tinted plates by M. Gauci and R. J. Lane, after drawings from life by Henry Howard. Imperial 8vo, cloth, uncut.* London, 1852

3180 WALKER, ALEXANDER. ANOTHER COPY: *the same; with plates plain, India proofs. Imperial 8vo, cloth, uncut.* London, 1852

3181 WALKER, JAMES, D. D. SERMONS. *12mo, cloth.* Boston, 1861

3182 WALKER, WILLIAM SIDNEY. SHAKESPEARE'S VERSIFICATION, and its Apparent Irregularities, explained by Examples from Early and Late English Writers. *Foolscap 8vo, cloth, uncut.* London, 1854

3183 WALLER, EDMUND. POEMS, etc., written upon Several Occasions, and to Several Persons. The Eighth Edition, with Additions, to which is prefix'd the Author's Life. *Portrait of Waller, aged 23, and monument; other portraits wanting. 8vo, old calf, red edges.* J. Tonson, London, 1711

3184 WALLER, EDMUND. THE WORKS OF. In Verse and Prose; published by Mr. Fenton. *Engraved title, portraits, monument, and many other plates, engraved by Vertue. 4to, smooth morocco extra, gilt over marbled edges.* FINE COPY OF THIS ELEGANT EDITION. J. Tonson, London, 1729

3185 WALLER, EDMUND. THE WORKS OF. In Verse and Prose; to which is Prefixed the Life of the Author, by Percival Stockdale. *Small 8vo, half russia.* T. Davies, London, 1772

3186 WALPOLE, B. C. RECOLLECTIONS OF THE LIFE OF CHARLES JAMES FOX, exhibiting a Faithful Account of the most Remarkable Events of his Political Career, and a Delineation of his Character as a Statesman, Senator, and Man of Fashion; comprehending Numerous Anecdotes of his Public and Private Life: and an Accurate Description of the Ceremonies which took place at his Funeral, in Westminster Abbey, on the 10th October, 1806 (with a Supplement containing his Will). *Portrait and engraved title.* 16*mo, half morocco.* London, 1806

3187 WALPOLE, LIEUTENANT FREDERICK, R. N. THE ANSAYRII, (or Assassins,) with Travels in the Further East, in 1850–51; including a Visit to Nineveh. 3 *vols.*, 8*vo, half calf, very neat.* London, 1851

3188 WALPOLE, HORACE, EARL OF ORFORD. THE WORKS OF; in Five Volumes. (With Letters to George Montagu, 1736–1770; and to the Rev. William Cole, and others, 1745–1782. *Two vols. in one*, 1818, *forming a sixth volume.*) *Fine impressions of the numerous portraits and plates.* 6 *vols., royal* 4*to, russia, very neat, marbled edges.* LARGE PAPER: *very fine copy.* London, 1798–1818

3189 WALPOLE, HORACE, EARL OF ORFORD. A CATALOGUE OF ENGRAVERS, who have been born, or resided in England; digested from the MSS. of Mr. George Vertue. To which is added an Account of the Life and Works of the Latter. *Fine impressions of the* 9 *plates comprising* 17 *portraits.* 4*to, half calf, rough edges.* ORIGINAL EDITION: *fine copy.* Strawberry Hill, 1763

3190 WALPOLE, HORACE, EARL OF ORFORD. A CATALOGUE OF THE ROYAL AND NOBLE AUTHORS of England, Scotland, and Ireland; with Lists of their Works. Engraved and continued to the Present Time, by Thomas Park, F. S. A. *Fine impressions of the* 150 *portraits, etc.* 5 *vols.*, 8*vo, calf, marbled edges.* London, 1806

3191 WALPOLE, HORACE, EARL OF ORFORD. ANECDOTES OF PAINTING IN ENGLAND, with some Account of the Principal Artists, and Incidental Notes on other Arts; also a Catalogue of Engravers who have been born or resided in England, collected by the late George Vertue, digested and published from his Original MSS.; with Additions, by the Rev. James Dallaway. A New Edition, revised, with Additional Notes, by Ralph N. Wornum. *Illustrated edition, with* 88 *portraits by Worthington, Warren, Cooper, etc.; and numerous wood-cuts.* 3 *vols.*, 8*vo, cloth, uncut.* London, 1849

3192 WALPOLE, HORACE, EARL OF ORFORD. THE LETTERS OF; edited by Peter Cunningham. Now first chronologically arranged (illustrated with Notes and accompanied by a General Index). *Numerous portraits, views, etc.* 9 *vols.*, 8*vo, half calf antique, marbled edges.* R. Bentley, London, 1857–59

This edition contains the entire series of Walpole's correspondence, comprising his Letters to George Montagu, the Rev. Wm. Cole, the Earl of Hertford, Sir Horace Mann (both series), the Countess of Ossory, the Rev. Wm. Mason, and others.

3193 WALSH, Edward. Irish Popular Songs; with English Metrical Translations, and Introductory Remarks and Notes. *The Irish printed with Hibernian type.* 16*mo, paper.* Dublin, 1847

3194 WALSH, Rev. Robert. A Residence at Constantinople, during a Period including the Commencement, Progress, and Termination of the Greek and Turkish Revolutions. *Portrait, plates, maps, and wood-cuts.* 2 *vols.*, 8*vo, half calf extra.* London, 1836

3195 WALSH, Rev. Robert. Constantinople, and the Scenery of the Seven Churches of Asia Minor, illustrated in a Series of Drawings from Nature, by Thomas Allom; with an Historical Account of Constantinople and Descriptions of the Plates. *Maps, vignettes on titles, and* 93 *plates.* 2 *vols.*, 4*to, dark green turkey morocco extra, gilt edges.* London, (1846)

3196 WALSH, Rev. Robert. Another copy: *the same; both series in* 1 *vol.*, 4*to, crimson turkey morocco extra, gilt edges.* London, (1846)

3197 WALTON, Izaak. The Lives of Dr. John Donne, Sir Henry Wotton, Mr. Richard Hooker, Mr. George Herbert, and Dr. Robert Sanderson. A New Edition. 8*vo, tree calf gilt, marbled edges.* Clarendon Press, Oxford, 1824

3198 WALTON, Izaak; and Charles Cotton. The Complete Angler, or the Contemplative Man's Recreation; being a Discourse of Rivers, Fish-Ponds, Fish, and Fishing, written by Izaak Walton: and, Instructions how to Angle for a Trout or Grayling in a Clear Stream, by Charles Cotton. With Original Memoirs and Notes, by Sir Harris Nicolas. *Beautifully printed by Whittingham. Portraits, views, and engravings of fish, after Stothard, Inskipp, etc.* 2 *vols., imperial* 8*vo, dark blue crushed morocco gilt, gilt edges, by Wright.* Elegant copy: *India proofs of the engravings.* W. Pickering, London, 1836

3199 WALTER, Izaak; and Charles Cotton. The Complete Angler. New Edition, edited by "Ephemera" [Edward Fitzgibbon], of "Bell's Life in London." *Numerous wood-cuts, crown* 8*vo, cloth.* London, 1853

3200 WALTON, Izaak; and Charles Cotton. The Complete Angler, or Contemplative Man's Recreation; Edited by John Major. *Portraits and* 10 *plates on India paper, and* 74 *wood-cuts.* 8*vo, boards, rough edges.* Large paper: *only* 100 *copies printed.* Boston, 1866

3201 WARBURTON, Eliot Bartholomew George. The Conquest of Canada; by the Author of "Hochelaga." 2 *vols.*, 8*vo, cloth, uncut.* London, 1849–50

3202 WARBURTON, John; Rev. James Whitelaw, and Rev. Robert Walsh. History of the City of Dublin, from

the Earliest Accounts to the Present Time; containing its Annals, Antiquities, Ecclesiastical History, and Charters; its Present Extent, Public Buildings, Schools, Institutions, etc.; to which are added Biographical Notices of Eminent Men, and Copious Appendices of its Population, Revenue, Commerce, and Literature. Illustrated with Numerous Plates, Plans, and Maps. 2 *vols.*, 4*to*, *cloth*, *uncut.*
Printed by W. Bulmer & Co., London, 1818

3203 WARD, EDWARD. NUPTIAL DIALOGUES AND DEBATES, or an Useful Prospect of the Felicities and Discomforts of a Marry'd Life, incident to all Degrees, from the Throne to the Cottage: containing many great Examples of Love, Piety, Prudence, Justice, and all the Excellent Vertues that largely contribute to the True Happiness of Wedlock; drawn from the Lives of our own Princes, Nobility, and other Quality, in Prosperity and Adversity. Also the Fantastical Humours of all Fops, Coquets, Bullies, Gilts, Fond Fools, and Wantons; Old Fumblers, Barren Ladies, Misers, Parsimonious Wives, Ninnies, Sluts, and Termagants; Drunken Husbands, Toaping Gossips, Schismatical Precisians, and Devout Hypocrites of all Sorts. Digested into Serious, Merry, and Satyrical Poems, wherein Both Sexes, in all Stations, are reminded of their Duty, and taught how to be Happy in a Matrimonial State. By the Author of the London Spy ["Ned" Ward]. *Portrait by M. Vander Gucht (inserted), and plates by J. Pine.* 2 *vols.*, 12*mo*, *half calf.*
London, 1723

3204 WARD, EDWARD. FEMALE POLICY DETECTED, or the Arts of a Designing Woman Laid Open; treating I. of the Allurements, Inconstancy, Love, Revenge, Pride, and Ingratitude; II. a Pleasant and Profitable Discourse in Defence of Married Men against Peevish, Fretful, Scolding Wives, with Several Notable Examples of the Mischiefs and Miseries which have attended their Lust and Pride; III. a True Character of a Vertuous Woman, or Wife indeed, with a Poetical Description of a Maid, Wife, and Widow. To which is added, the Bachelor's Estimate of the Expences of a Married Life. 12*mo*, *new sprinkled calf gilt, gilt edges, closely trimmed but perfect.* London, s. a.

3205 WARE, JOHN F. W. HOME LIFE; What it is, and What it Needs. 12*mo*, *green morocco extra, gilt edges.*
Boston, 1864

3206 WARE, WILLIAM. JULIAN, or Scenes in Judea. *Woodcut.* 16*mo*, *cloth*, *uncut.* Edinburgh, 1860

3207 WARING, EDWARD SCOTT. A TOUR TO SHEERAZ, by the Route of Kazroon and Feerozabad; with Various Remarks on the Manners, Customs, Laws, Language, and

Literature of the Persians: to which is added, a History of Persia, from the Death of Kureem Khan to the Subversion of the Zund Dynasty. *Portraits, 4to, old calf, marbled edges.* Printed by Bulmer, London, 1807

3208 WARNER, REBECCA. ORIGINAL LETTERS, from Richard Baxter, Matthew Prior, Lord Bolingbroke, Alexander Pope, Dr. Cheyne, Dr. Hartley, Dr. Samuel Johnson, Mrs. Montague, Rev. William Gilpin, Rev. John Newton, George Lord Lyttleton, Rev. Dr. Claudius Buchanan, etc., etc.; with Biographical Illustrations. Edited by Rebecca Warner, of Beech Cottage near Bath. — EPISTOLARY CURIOSITIES, Series the Second, and Last; consisting of Unpublished Letters, of the Eighteenth Century, illustrative of the Herbert Family, and of the Latter Part of King William's and the Earlier Part of Queen Anne's Reigns: from Lord Herbert, King William, Duke of Shrewsbury, Duke of Newcastle, Queen Anne, Lord Godolphin, Sir Robert Sutton, Lord Somers, Lady Inchiquin, Duke of Marlborough, Joseph Addison, Dr. Robinson Envoy to Sweden, William Greg, George Stepney, etc., etc. With Notes. Edited by Rebecca Warner, of Beech Cottage, Bath. *2 vols., 8vo, half green morocco, gilt tops.* Bath, 1817–18

3209 WARREN, IRA, M. D. THE HOUSEHOLD PHYSICIAN, for the Use of Families, Planters, Seamen, and Travellers; being a Brief Description, in Plain Language, of all the Diseases of Men, Women, and Children, with the Newest and most Approved Methods of curing them. *Portrait, 8 colored plates, and 236 wood-cuts. Thick royal 8vo, sheep.* Boston, 1866

3210 WARREN, JOHN COLLINS, M. D. THE PRESERVATION OF HEALTH; with Remarks on Constipation, Old Age, Use of Alcohol in the Preparation of Medicines. *16mo, cloth.* Boston, 1854

3211 WARREN, JOHN COLLINS, M. D. THE GREAT TREE ON BOSTON COMMON. *View of the tree, and plan of Boston, 1722. 8vo, pp. 20, cloth.* Boston, 1855

3212 WARREN, MRS. MERCY. HISTORY OF THE RISE, PROGRESS, AND TERMINATION OF THE AMERICAN REVOLUTION; interspersed with Biographical, Political, and Moral Observations. *3 vols., 8vo, sheep, yellow edges.* Boston, 1805

3213 WARREN, SAMUEL. WORKS. *Wood-cuts, by the Dalziels etc., after John Gilbert, Birket Foster, etc. 5 vols., post 8vo, polished calf gilt, contents lettered, marbled edges, by Hayday.* Edinburgh, 1854–55

CONTENTS: Diary of a Late Physician, 1 vol.; Ten Thousand a-Year, 2 vols.; Now and Then, The Lily and the Bee, Intellectual and Moral Development, 1 vol.; Miscellanies, 1 vol.

3214 WARTON, Thomas. Observations on the Fairy Queen of Spenser. The Second Edition, corrected and enlarged. *2 vols., small 8vo, sprinkled calf gilt; with autograph of Henry Pelham.* R. & J. Dodsley, London, 1762

3215 WARTON, Thomas. The History of English Poetry, from the Close of the Eleventh, to the Commencement of the Eighteenth Century; to which are prefixed Two (Three) Dissertations: I. on the Origin of Romantic Fiction in Europe; II. on the Introduction of Learning into England, (III. on the Gesta Romanorum). With Ritson's "Observations." *3 vols., 4to, sprinkled calf gilt, yellow edges; with book-plate of Jeremiah Milles, D. D.* J. Dodsley, London, 1775–82

At the end of the first volume is bound "Observations on the Three First Volumes of the History of English Poetry, in a Familiar Letter to the Author," by Joseph Ritson. (J. Stockdale, etc., London, 1782.) Of these "Observations," Lowndes says: "Full of the grossest abuse and most illiberal invective. It is said that Ritson, at the latter period of his life, bought up and destroyed many copies."

3216 WARWICK, Sir Philip. Memoires of the Reigne of King Charles I., with a Continuation to the Happy Restauration of King Charles II. Published from the Original Manuscript, with an Alphabetical Table. *With the Address "To the Reader," but portrait wanting. 8vo, old calf; back cracked.* Original edition; *without preface.* Ri. Chiswell, London, 1701

"A candid and valuable historical work." — *Lowndes.*

3217 WASHBOURN, John, Jun. Bibliotheca Gloucestrensis; a Collection of Scarce and Curious Tracts, relating to the County and City of Gloucester, illustrative of and published during the Civil War. With an Historical Introduction, Notes, and an Appendix. *Portrait of Edward Massey, maps, and plates. 3 parts in 1 vol., post 4to, half russia, neat, marbled edges.* Privately printed. Gloucester, 1825

3218 WASHBURN, Israel, Jun. The Republican Party: Speech, delivered in the House of Representatives, January 10, 1859. *8vo, pp. 8.* (Washington, 1859)

3219 WASHINGTON, George. The Writings of; being his Correspondence, Addresses, Messages, and other Papers, Official and Private, selected from the Original Manuscripts, with a Life of the Author, Notes and Illustrations, by Jared Sparks. *Portraits, plans, fac-similes, etc., some of which are on India paper. 12 vols., imperial 8vo, calf.* Large paper. Boston, 1834–37

3220 WASHINGTON, George. Another copy: *the same; small paper. 12 vols., 8vo, cloth.* Boston, 1858

3221 WASHINGTON, George. Fac-Similes of Letters from George Washington to Sir John Sinclair, Bart., M. P., on Agricultural and other Interesting Topics; engraved from the Original Letters, so as to be an Exact Fac-simile of the Handwriting. *Portrait and views.* *4to, half morocco.* Washington, 1844

3222 WASHINGTON, GEORGE. DOMESTIC LIFE; from Original Letters and Manuscripts. By Richard Rush. *8vo, cloth, uncut.* Philadelphia, 1857

3223 WASHINGTON, GEORGE. THE DIARY OF; from 1789 to 1791, embracing the Opening of the First Congress, and his Tours through New-England, Long Island, and the Southern States; together with his Journal of a Tour to the Ohio, in 1753. Edited by Benson J. Lossing. *Portrait.* *12mo, cloth.* New York, 1860

3224 WASHINGTON, GEORGE. MONUMENTS OF PATRIOTISM: being a Collection of the most Interesting Documents, connected with the Military Command and Civil Administration of the American Hero and Patriot; to which is annexed, an Eulogium on his Character, by Major William Jackson. *Portrait, and plate (inserted).* *8vo, old calf.* J. Ormrod, Philadelphia, 1800

3225 WASHINGTON, GEORGE. MONUMENTS OF WASHINGTON'S PATRIOTISM; containing a Fac-simile of his Public Accounts, kept during the Revolutionary War, and some of the most Interesting Documents connected with his Military Command and Civil Administration. Third Edition, with Additions and Embellishments. *Portraits, views, etc.* *Folio, morocco extra, marbled edges.* Washington, 1841

3226 WASHINGTON, GEORGE. EULOGIES AND ORATIONS ON the Life and Death of General George Washington (by Major General Henry Lee, Hon. George Richards Minot, Jonathan Mitchel Sewall, Hon. John Brooks, Hon. David Ramsay, George Blake, Hon. Fisher Ames, Hon. Timothy Bigelow, John Davis, Rev. Dr. William Linn, Hon. Jeremiah Smith, Dr. Joseph Blyth, Hon. Isaac Parker, Rev. John M. Mason, Major William Jackson, Charles Pinckney Sumner, Josiah Dunham, Rev. John Thornton Kirkland). *8vo, sheep.* Boston, 1800

3227 WASHINGTON, GEORGE. THE WASHINGTONIANA: containing a Biographical Sketch of the late Gen. George Washington, with Outlines of his Character, from the Pens of Different Eminent Writers, both in Europe and America; and an Account of the Various Funeral Honors devoted to his Memory. To which are annexed his Will and Schedule of his Property. *Portrait wanting.* *12mo, old calf.* S. Sower, Baltimore, 1800

3228 WATERBURY, JARED B., D. D. SABBATHS ABROAD. *Wood-cuts.* *16mo, cloth.* Boston, (1856)

3229 WATKINS, JOHN; and FREDERICK SHOBERL. A BIOGRAPHICAL DICTIONARY of the Living Authors of Great Britain and Ireland: comprising Literary Memoirs and Anecdotes of their Lives, and a Chronological Register of their Publications, with the Number of Editions printed; including Notices of some Foreign Writers whose Works have been occasionally published in England. Illustrated by a Variety of Communications from Persons of the First Eminence in the World of Letters. *8vo, boards, rough edges.* H. Colburn, London, 1816

"As accurate a list of the works of the authors living in 1816, as could possibly be compiled." — *Lowndes.*

In Bohn's "Lowndes" this work is attributed to Wm. Upcott and Fred. Shoberl, but in "Notes and Queries" (first series, vol. xi. p. 34, et al.), may be found authority for assigning it to Dr. Watkins and Mr. Shoberl.

3230 WATKINS, JOHN. THE UNIVERSAL BIOGRAPHICAL DICTIONARY, or an Historical Account of the Lives, Characters, and Works of the most Eminent Persons in every Age and Nation, from the Earliest Times to the Present; particularly the Natives of Great Britain and Ireland. A New Edition, corrected to the Present Time. *Thick 8vo, cloth, rough edges.* London, 1826

3231 WATSON, MISS EMILY. CHILD-LIFE IN ITALY; a Story of Six Years Abroad. *Post 8vo, cloth.* Boston, 1866

3232 WATSON, SIR FREDERICK BEILBY. RELIGIOUS AND MORAL SENTENCES culled from the Works of Shakspeare, compared with Sacred Passages drawn from Holy Writ; being a Selection of Religious Sentiments, and Moral Precepts, blended in the Dramatic Works, etc., of our Immortal Bard. Compiled for the Benefit of the Benevolent Funds of the Theatres Royal, Drury Lane, and Covent Garden. *Portraits of Shakespeare and Earl of Southampton, and engraving after Stothard's painting of Shakespeare's interview with Queen Elizabeth. 8vo, half green morocco, marbled edges.* London, 1843

3233 WATSON, SIR FREDERICK BEILBY. ANOTHER COPY: Second Edition. *8vo, cloth, gilt top.* London, 1847

3234 WATSON, SIR FREDERICK BEILBY. ANOTHER COPY: from the English Edition, with an Introduction by Frederic D. Huntington, D. D. *Portrait from the Chandos portrait. Foolscap 8vo, cloth.* Boston, 1859

3235 WATTS, ALARIC ALEXANDER. LYRICS OF THE HEART; with other Poems. *With forty-one engravings on steel.* PROOF IMPRESSIONS *of the plates, engraved by Greatbach, Wallis, Rolls, Finden, etc., after Stothard, Westall, Sir T. Lawrence, etc. 8vo, purple morocco extra, gilt edges.* Longmans & Co., London, 1851

3236 WATTS, ISAAC, D. D. THE WORKS of the Reverend and Learned Isaac Watts, D. D.; containing, besides his Ser-

mons, and Essays on Miscellaneous Subjects, Several Additional Pieces, selected from his Manuscripts by the Rev. Dr. Jennings, and the Rev. Dr. Doddridge, in 1753: to which are prefixed, Memoirs of the Life of the Author compiled by the Rev. George Burder. *Portrait.* 6 *vols., royal 4to, half morocco, rough edges.* LARGE PAPER: *fine copy.*
J. Barfield, London, 1810–11

3237 WATTS, ISAAC, D. D. ORTHODOXY AND CHARITY UNITED: in Several Reconciling Essays on the Law and Gospel, Faith and Works; viz. Essay I. The Substance or Matter of the Gospel. II. The Form of the Gospel. III. The Use of the Law under the Gospel. IV. Mistaken Ways of coming to God without Christ. V. A Plain and Easy Account of Saving Faith, or coming to God by Jesus Christ. VI. A Reconciling Thought on Various Controversies about Faith and Salvation. VII. Against Uncharitableness. VIII. The Difficulties in Scripture, and the Different Opinions of Christians. IX. An Apology for Christians of Different Sentiments. The Second Edition. *8vo; needs binding.*
Rogers & Fowle, Boston, 1749

3238 WATTS, ISAAC, D. D. DIVINE AND MORAL SONGS for the Use of Children. *With thirty illustrations drawn on wood by C. W. Cope, A. R. A., and engraved by John Thompson. Foolscap 4to, cloth, gilt edges.*
J. Van Voorst, London, 1848

3239 WEALE, JOHN. DIVERS WORKS OF EARLY MASTERS IN CHRISTIAN DECORATION; with an Introduction containing the Biography, Journal of Travel, Contemporaneous Association in Art, and a Critical Account of the Works of Albert Durer; Notices of his Master, Wohlgemuth, and his Friend, Pirckheymer; Adam Krafft, and his Sacrament-House at Nuremburg; with Examples of Ancient painted and stained Glass, from York, West Wickham, Kent, and St. George's Chapel, Windsor; the Ancient Church and Sacrament-House at Limbourg; the Works of Dirk and Wouter Crabeth, etc.; also, a Succinct Account, with Illustrations of painted and stained Glass at Gouda, in Holland, and the Church of St. Jacques at Liége. Edited by John Weale. *With 75 plates engraved by Le Keux and others, most of them finely colored.* 2 *vols., imperial folio, half olive morocco extra, gilt edges.* London, 1846

3240 WEBER, HENRY WILLIAM. METRICAL ROMANCES of the Thirteenth, Fourteenth, and Fifteenth Centuries: published from Ancient Manuscripts, with an Introduction, Notes, and a Glossary. 3 *vols., crown 8vo, crimson turkey morocco, gilt edges; uniform with* HARTSHORNE.
Edinburgh, 1810

A supplementary collection to those of Ritson, Percy, and Ellis.

3241 WEBER, Henry William. Another copy: *the same. 3 vols., crown 8vo, half russia, marbled edges.* Edinburgh, 1810

3242 WEBSTER, Daniel. The Works of. (With Biographical Memoir, by Edward Everett.) *Portraits and plates.* 6 *vols., imperial 8vo, dark blue turkey morocco extra, gilt edges. Uniform with "Private Correspondence" and* Everett's Orations. Large paper: *subscriber's copy.* Boston, 1851

3243 WEBSTER, Daniel. Another copy: *the same. Portrait from Powers's bust, and view of birthplace.* 6 *vols., imperial 8vo, cloth, uncut.* Large paper: *subscriber's copy, with Webster's autograph.* Boston, 1851

3244 WEBSTER, Daniel. The Private Correspondence of; edited by Fletcher Webster. *Portraits.* 2 *vols., imperial 8vo, dark blue turkey morocco extra, gilt edges.* Large paper. Boston, 1857

In the first volume of this copy (uniform with "Works," and Everett's "Orations") is a leaf, on which is printed "Subscriber's Copy," with Webster's autograph, which should have been bound in the "Works."

3245 WEBSTER, Daniel. Another copy: *the same. Portraits.* 2 *vols., imperial 8vo, cloth, uncut.* Large paper. Boston, 1857

3246 WEBSTER, Daniel. Speech of Daniel Webster in Reply to Mr. Hayne, of South Carolina; the Resolution offered by Mr. Foot, relative to the Public Lands, being under Consideration. Delivered in the Senate, January 26, 1830. *12mo, pp.* 76, *folded; clean.* Washington, 1830

3247 WEBSTER, Daniel. Speech of Daniel Webster, on Mr. Clay's Resolutions, in the Senate of the United States, March 7, 1850. (On the Subject of Slavery; Edition revised and corrected by himself.) *8vo, pp.* 39, *paper; clean.* Boston, 1850

3248 WEBSTER, Memorial. A Memorial of Daniel Webster, from the City of Boston. [Edited by Geo. S. Hillard.] *Portrait and view. 8vo, cloth, uncut.* Boston, 1853

3249 WEBSTER, John. The Works of; now first collected, with some Account of the Author, and Notes, by the Rev. Alexander Dyce. 4 *vols., crown 8vo, crimson turkey morocco, gilt edges; uniform with* Greene *and* Peele. Only 250 copies printed. W. Pickering, London, 1830

3250 WEBSTER, John. Another copy: *the same.* 4 *vols., crown 8vo, cloth, uncut.* W. Pickering, London, 1830

3251 WEDGWOOD, Josiah. The Life of: from his Private Correspondence and Family Papers, in the Possession of Joseph Mayer, Esq., F. S. A., F. Wedgwood, Esq., C. Darwin, Esq., M. A., F. R. S., Miss Wedgwood, and other Original Sources. With an Introductory Sketch of the Art of

Pottery in England. By Eliza Meteyard. *Portraits of Wedgwood and Bentley, and numerous fine wood-cuts. Finely printed on a thick laid paper.* 2 *vols., royal* 8*vo, cloth, uncut.* London, 1865–66

3252 WEEMSE, JOHN. A TREATISE OF THE FOURE DEGENERATE SONNES; viz., the Atheist, the Magician, the Idolater and the Jew: wherein are handled many Profitable Questions concerning Atheisme, Witchcraft, Idolatry, and Judaisme; and Sundry Places of Scripture cleared out of the Originall Tongues. Being the Fourth Volume of the Workes of Mr. Joh. Weemse, of Lathocker in Scotland, and Prebend of Dunelm. 4*to, old calf.* London, 1636

3253 WEEVER, JOHN. ANCIENT FUNERALL MONUMENTS, within the United Monarchie of Great Britaine, Ireland, and the Islands adjacent, with the Dissolved Monasteries therein contained, their Founders, and what Eminent Persons have beene in the same interred; as also the Death and Buriall of Certaine of the Bloud Royall, the Nobilitie and Gentrie of these Kingdomes entombed in Forraine Nations. A Worke reviving the Dead Memory of the Royall Progenie, the Nobilitie, Gentrie, and Communalitie of these his Majesties Dominions; intermixed and illustrated with Variety of Historicall Observations, Illustrations, Annotations and Briefe Notes, extracted out of Approved Authors, Infallible Records, Lieger Bookes, Charters, Rolls, Old Manuscripts, and the Collections of Judicious Antiquaries. Whereunto is prefixed a Discourse of Funerall Monuments, of the Foundation and Fall of Religious Houses, of Religious Orders, of the Ecclesiasticall Estate of England, and of other Occurrences touched upon by the Way, in the Whole Passage of these Intended Labours. Composed by the Studie and Travels of John Weever. *Portrait and engraved title by T. Cecill, and wood-cuts in the text. Small folio, russia, very neat, gilt edges.* ORIGINAL EDITION: *with the* INDEX *added.* T. Harper, London, 1631

This *perfect* copy contains the index (published after the work) which is generally wanting. For an analysis of this work, "of great utility to antiquarians and historians," see Oldys's "British Librarian," pp. 344–64.

3254 WEHNERT, E. H. REMINISCENCES OF MADAME MALIBRAN DE BERIOT; in a Series of Illustrations of her Principal Characters, designed and drawn on Stone by E. H. Wehnert. *No.* 1, *containing* 10 *illustrations* (*in outline*) *of Fidelio, India proofs. Portrait wanting. Oblong* 4*to, paper.* (London), 1836

3255 WEISS, REV. JOHN. A DISCOURSE UPON CAUSES FOR THANKSGIVING, preached at Watertown, Nov. 20, 1862. 8*vo, pp.* 24, *paper.* (Boston, 1862)

3256 WELCOME (THE) GUEST; a Magazine of Recreative Reading for all. Illustrated with Numerous Engravings on

Wood. *Vols. I. and II., imperial 8vo, cloth; Vols. III. and IV., 8vo, half bound; and numbers* 54–66, 76–79, *and* 821. London, (1859–61)

3257 WELD, ISAAC, JUN. TRAVELS THROUGH THE STATES OF NORTH AMERICA, and the Provinces of Upper and Lower Canada, during the Years 1795, 1796, and 1797. Fourth Edition. *Illustrated and embellished with eight plates. 8vo, boards, rough edges.* J. Stockdale, London, 1800

Of this work there was an edition ("Third") in two volumes, published same year; and Bohn's "Lowndes" designates an edition, in two volumes, published in 1807 as the "Fourth."

3258 WELLESLEY, RICHARD COLLEY WESLEY, MARQUESS. MEMOIRS AND CORRESPONDENCE of Richard Marquess Wellesley, successively Governor-General of India, British Ambassador in Spain, Secretary of State for Foreign Affairs, and Lord-Lieutenant of Ireland; comprising Numerous Letters and Documents, now first published from Original MSS. By Robert R. Pearce, Esq. *Portraits. 3 vols., 8vo, half calf extra, marbled edges.* London, 1846

3259 WELLINGTON, ARTHUR WELLESLEY, DUKE OF. SUPPLEMENTARY DESPATCHES, and Memoranda of Field Marshall Arthur, Duke of Wellington, K. G. India, 1797–1805. Edited by his Son, the Duke of Wellington. *Maps of India, with pockets for same at the end of each volume. 4 vols., 8vo, cloth, uncut.* J. Murray, London, 1858–59

3260 WELLS, WILLIAM V. THE LIFE AND PUBLIC SERVICES OF SAMUEL ADAMS, being a Narrative of his Acts and Opinions, and of his Agency in Producing and Forwarding the American Revolution; with Extracts from his Correspondence, State Papers and Political Essays. *Portraits on India paper, after paintings by Copley and Johnston, and an engraving by Paul Revere. 3 vols., imperial 8vo, cloth, rough edges.* LARGE PAPER: *only 100 copies printed.* Boston, 1866

3261 WESLEY, REV. SAMUEL. THE HISTORY OF THE NEW TESTAMENT, representing the Actions and Miracles of Our Blessed Saviour and His Appostles, attempted in Verse; and adorn'd with CLII. Sculptures; the Cuts done by J. Stuart. *Small 8vo, calf, neat.* C. Harper, London, 1701

3262 WESTALL, WILLIAM; and SAMUEL OWEN. PICTURESQUE TOUR OF THE RIVER THAMES. *Illustrated by twenty-four colored views, a map, and vignettes, from original drawings taken on the spot. Imperial 4to, cloth, gilt labels.* R. Ackerman, London, 1828

3263 WESTCOTT, THOMPSON. LIFE OF JOHN FITCH, the Inventor of the Steamboat. *12mo, half calf extra, marbled edges; with newspaper cuttings and autograph of the author.* Philadelphia, 1857

3264 WESTMACOTT, CHARLES MOLLOY. THE ENGLISH SPY: an Original Work, Characteristic, Satirical, and Humorous; comprising Scenes and Sketches in Every Rank of Society, being Portraits of the Illustrious, Eminent, Eccentric, and Notorious drawn from the Life. By Bernard Blackmantle [C. M. Westmacott]. *The illustrations designed by Robert Cruikshank. Colored plates and wood-cuts. 2 vols., royal 8vo, half morocco.* London, 1825

3265 WESTMACOTT, CHARLES MOLLOY. ANOTHER COPY: *the same. 2 vols., royal 8vo, half calf.* London, 1825

3266 WHEARE, DEGORY. THE METHOD AND ORDER OF READING BOTH CIVIL AND ECCLESIASTICAL HISTORIES; in which the most Excellent Historians are reduced into the Order in which they are successively to be read, and the Judgments of Learned Men, concerning each of them, subjoin'd. To which is added, an Appendix concerning the Historians of Particular Nations, as well Ancient as Modern; by Nicholas Horseman. Made English and enlarged by Edmund Bohun, Esq. *Small 8vo, half calf.* Printed by M. Flesher, for C. Brome, London, 1685

3267 WHIG REVIEW. THE AMERICAN REVIEW; a Whig Journal of Politics, Literature, Art, and Science. *Numerous portraits, etc. From 1845 to 1852, inclusive. 16 vols., 8vo, half morocco, neat.* New York, 1845–52

3268 WHITAKER, THOMAS DUNHAM. DUCATUS LEODIENSIS, or the Topography of the Ancient and Populous Town and Parish of Leeds, and Parts adjacent, in the West-Riding of the County of York; with the Pedigrees of many of the Nobility and Gentry, and other Matters relating to those Parts, extracted from Records, Original Evidences, and Manuscripts. By Ralph Thoresby, F. R. S. To which is added, at the Request of Several Learned Persons, a Catalogue of his Museum, with the Curiosities, Natural and Artificial, and the Antiquities; particularly the Roman, British, Saxon, Danish, Norman, and Scotch Coins, with Modern Medals: also, a Catalogue of Manuscripts; the Various Editions of the Bible; and of Books in the Infancy of the Art of Printing. With an Account of some Unusual Accidents that have attended some Persons, attempted after the Method of Dr. Plot. The Second Edition, with Notes and Additions by Thomas D. Whitaker, LL. D., F. S. A., etc. — LOIDIS AND ELMETE; or, an Attempt to illustrate the Districts described in those Words by Bede, and supposed to embrace the Lower Portions of Aredale and Wharfdale, together with the Entire Vale of Calder, in the County of York. (With the APPENDIX published in 1820.) *Fine portraits by Holl, and large plates by Le Keux and others, besides vignettes, tables of pedigrees, wood-cut initials, etc.*

2 vols., large folio, russia gilt, gilt edges, by Wright. VERY FINE COPY. Leeds (London), 1816 (and 1820)

3269 WHITE, COLONEL CHARLES. THREE YEARS IN CONSTANTINOPLE, or Domestic Manners of the Turks in 1844. Second Edition. *Maps, plates, and wood-cuts. 3 vols., 12mo, purple diamond calf gilt, marbled edges.* London, 1846

3270 WHITE, REV. GILBERT. THE NATURAL HISTORY AND ANTIQUITIES OF SELBORNE (in the County of Southampton). With the Naturalist's Calendar; and Miscellaneous Observations, extracted from his Papers. A New Edition; with Notes, by Edward T. Bennett, Esq., F. L. S., etc., and others. *Numerous wood-cuts by Jackson, etc. 8vo, calf, very neat, gilt edges, by Hayday.*
Printed by Whittingham, London, (1837)

3271 WHITE, HENRY KIRKE. THE REMAINS OF, with an Account of his Life, by Robert Southey. The Tenth Edition. *Portrait and engraved titles. 2 vols., 8vo, pink calf extra, gilt edges.* London, 1823

3272 WHITE, HENRY KIRKE. THE POETICAL WORKS OF. (With Memoir, by Sir N. Harris Nicolas, and Tributary Verses.) *Portrait. Foolscap 8vo, cloth, uncut.* ALDINE EDITION. W. Pickering, London, 1840

3273 WHITE, RICHARD GRANT. COMPANION TO THE BRYAN GALLERY OF CHRISTIAN ART, containing Critical Descriptions of the Pictures, and Biographical Sketches of the Painters; with an Introductory Essay, and an Index. *Royal 8vo, cloth, gilt top, uncut; with autograph of author.* LARGE PAPER: *presentation copy.* New York, 1853

This copy was presented, by the author, to Robert Balmanno, and contains the letter which accompanied it.

3274 WHITE, RICHARD GRANT. SHAKESPEARE'S SCHOLAR; being Historical and Critical Studies of his Text, Characters, and Commentators, with an Examination of Mr. Collier's Folio of 1632. *8vo, half olive morocco, red paper sides, gilt top, uncut.* New York, 1854

2375 WHITE, RICHARD GRANT. NATIONAL HYMNS; how they are written, and how they are not written: a Lyric and National Study for the Times. With a Letter to the Saturday Review. *Frontispiece and music. 12mo, cloth, uncut.* PRIVATELY PRINTED: *only 30 copies, see autograph of Mr. White on fly-leaf.* New York, 1862

This edition has an "Appendix" containing, I. a Letter to the "Saturday Review"; II. Leader from the "World," Jan. 5, 1861.

3276 WHITEFIELD, REV. GEORGE. MEMOIRS OF; by John Gillies, D. D. Revised and corrected, with Large Additions and Improvements; to which is appended an Extensive Collection of his Sermons and other Writings. *Portrait and wood-cuts. 8vo, roan gilt, marbled edges.*
Hartford, 1847

3277 WHITMAN, William E. S., and Charles H. True. Maine in the War for the Union; a History of the Part borne by Maine Troops in the Suppression of the American Rebellion. *Portraits of Major Generals O. O. Howard and H. G. Berry. Thick 8vo, cloth.* Lewiston, 1865

3278 WHITMAN, Zacheriah G. An Historical Sketch of the Ancient and Honourable Artillery Company, from its Formation in the Year 1637 to the Present Time; compiled and arranged from Ancient Records, by a Member of the Company. *8vo, boards, rough edges.* Boston, 1820

3279 WHITMORE, William Henry. A Handbook of American Genealogy; being a Catalogue of Family Histories and Publications containing Genealogical Information, chronologically arranged. *Rubricated title, head-pieces, and initials. Foolscap 4to, cloth, gilt top, rough edges.* Only 200 copies printed: 10 *of which on large paper.* J. Munsell, Albany, 1862

3280 WHITMORE, William Henry. The Elements of Heraldry: containing an Explanation of the Principles of the Science and a Glossary of the Technical Terms employed; with an Essay upon the Use of Coat-Armor in the United States. • *Printed on a heavy paper, with numerous wood-cuts. Imperial 8vo, cloth, uncut.* Boston, 1866

3281 WHITNEY, Mrs. A. D. T. Faith Gartney's Girlhood. Fifth Edition. *12mo, cloth.* Boston, 1863

3282 WHITTIER, John Greenleaf. In War Time; and other Poems. *Post 8vo, cloth, gilt top.* Boston, 1864

3283 WHITTIER, John Greenleaf. The Tent on the Beach; and other Poems. *Post 8vo, cloth.* Boston, 1867

3284 WIFFEN, Jeremiah Holme. Historical Memoirs of the House of Russell, from the Time of the Norman Conquest (and of the First Race of Ancestry whence the House of Russell had its Origin, from the Subjugation of Norway to the Norman Conquest). *Portraits (of first Earl of Bedford, after Holbein, and of John Duke of Bedford, after Sir T. Lawrence) and plates on India paper. 2 vols., royal 8vo, crimson morocco extra, gilt edges, by Hayday.* Large paper: *only 250 copies in this size.* London, 1833

3285 WIGHT, John. More Mornings at Bow Street: a New Collection of Humorous and Entertaining Reports; by John Wight, of the Morning Herald. *With twenty-five illustrations by George Cruikshank. Post 8vo, half green morocco.* London, 1827

3286 WILBRAHAM, Captain Richard. Travels in the Trans-Caucasian Provinces of Russia, and along the

Southern Shore of the Lakes of Van and Urumiah, in the Autumn and Winter of 1837. *Map and 5 views. 8vo, half calf extra.* J. Murray, London, 1839

3287 WILDE, WILLIAM R. THE CLOSING YEARS OF DEAN SWIFT'S LIFE, with Remarks on Stella and on some of his Writings hitherto unnoticed. Second Edition, revised and enlarged. *Portrait of Esther Johnson (" Stella "), and wood-cuts. 8vo, cloth, uncut.* London, 1849

3288 WILKES, CHARLES. NARRATIVE OF THE UNITED STATES EXPLORING EXPEDITION; during the Years 1838, 1839, 1840, 1841, 1842. *Portraits, maps, and numerous fine plates and wood-cuts. 6 vols. (sixth being the atlas), royal 4to, half morocco extra, arms gilt on sides, marbled edges.* LARGE PAPER: *less than 100 copies printed.* Philadelphia, 1845

On a fly-leaf of first volume is this autograph, "Louise Adèle Watson, from her friend, Charles Wilkes; August, 1854."

3289 WILKES, JOHN. A CELEBRATED LETTER, sent from John Wilkes, Esq., at Paris, to the Electors of Aylesbury, in the Year 1764. *Crown 8vo, pp. 23.* London, 1768

3290 WILKIE (THE) GALLERY: a Selection of the Best Pictures of the late Sir David Wilkie, R. A., introducing his Spanish and Oriental Sketches; with Notices, Biographical and Critical. *Portrait, engraved title, and 65 plates. Imperial 4to, half morocco, very neat, gilt edges.* G. Vertue, London, 1853

3291 WILKINS, JOHN, BISHOP. THE FIRST BOOK: the Discovery of a New World, or a Discourse tending to prove that 'tis Probable there may be Another Habitable World in the Moone; with a Discourse concerning the Possibility of a Passage thither. The Third Impression, corrected and enlarged. — A DISCOURSE CONCERNING A NEW PLANET, tending to prove that 'tis Probable our Earth is one of the Planets: the Second Booke, now first published. *Frontispiece by W. Marshall. 1 vol., small 8vo, old calf; with bookplate of Thos. Jolley, Esq., F. S. A.* J. Maynard, London, 1640

3292 WILKINSON, GENERAL JAMES. MEMOIRS OF MY OWN TIMES. Diagrams and Plans, Illustrative of the Principal Battles and Military Affairs, treated of in Memoirs of my Own Times. *3 vols., 8vo; 1 vol., 4to; half morocco neat, gilt tops.* Philadelphia, 1816

3293 WILKINSON, SIR JOHN GARDNER. A POPULAR ACCOUNT OF THE ANCIENT EGYPTIANS; revised and abridged from his Larger Work. *Illustrated with five hundred wood-cuts. 2 vols., crown 8vo, cloth, uncut.* J. Murray, London, 1854

3294 WILKINSON, TATE. MEMOIRS OF HIS OWN LIFE; by Tate Wilkinson, Patentee of the Theatres-Royal. York & Hull, 4 *vols.*, 12*mo*, *half green calf.* York, 1790

"Materials will be found in this work towards a compilement of a general history of the English stage." — *Lowndes.*

3295 WILLARD, REV. SAMUEL. A COMPLEAT BODY OF DIVINITY, in Two Hundred and Fifty Expository Lectures on the Assembly's Shorter Catechism; wherein the Doctrines of the Christian Religion are unfolded, their Truth confirm'd, their Excellence display'd, their Usefulness improv'd, contrary Errors & Vices refuted & Expos'd, Objections answer'd, Controversies settled, Cases of Conscience resolv'd, and a great Light thereby reflected on the Present Age. By the Rev. & Learned Samuel Willard, M. A., late Pastor of the South Church, in Boston, and Vice-President of Harvard College in Cambridge, in New-England. Prefac'd by the Pastors of the same Church (Joseph Sewall and Thomas Prince). *Folio, old calf; with autograph of James Allen.* Printed by B. Green and S. Kneeland, for B. Eliot and D. Henchman. Boston, 1726

This work was the first folio on divinity published in America. The volume contains an alphabetical list of subscribers, and a catalogue of the author's works.

3296 WILLIAMS, LIEUT.-COLONEL. ENGLAND'S BATTLES BY SEA AND LAND, from the Commencement of the Great French Revolution to the Present Time; with a Retrospective View of the Celebrated Epochs of British Military History. Including our Indian Campaigns, and the Present Expedition against Russian Aggression in the East. *Numerous maps, plans, portraits, views of places, battle-scenes, etc.* 6 *vols.*, *imperial* 8*vo*, *half morocco extra, gilt edges.* London, (*cir* 1859)

The title of the last three volumes reads, "The History of the War with Russia, giving Full Details of the Operations of the Allied Armies, by Henry Tyrrell, Esq."

3297 WILLIAMS, SIR CHARLES HANBURY. THE ODES OF. 12*mo*, *half morocco, yellow edges.* D. Lynch, London, 1768

3298 WILLIAMS, FREDERICK SIMS. OUR IRON ROADS; their History, Construction, and Social Influences. *Wood-cuts.* 8*vo*, *cloth, uncut.* London, 1852

3299 WILLIAMS, HELEN MARIA. A TOUR IN SWITZERLAND, or a View of the Present State of the Governments and Manners of those Cantons; with Comparative Sketches of the Present State of Paris. 2 *vols.*, 8*vo*, *half calf, very neat, marbled edges.* London, 1798

3300 WILLIAMS, ROGER. EXPERIMENTS OF SPIRITUAL LIFE AND HEALTH, and their Preservatives; in which the Weakest Child of God may get Assurance of his Spirituall Life and Blessednesse, and the Strongest may finde Proportionable Discoveries of his Christian Growth, and the Means of it. By Roger Williams of Providence, in New-England. London, printed in the Second Month, 1652. *Foolscap 4to, boards.* Reprinted, Providence, 1863

A literal reprint of a tract, of the original of which only *two* copies are known. See NARRAGANSETT CLUB.

3301 WILLIAMSON, CAPTAIN THOMAS. ORIENTAL FIELD SPORTS: being a Complete, Detailed, and Accurate Description of the Wild Sports of the East; and exhibiting, in a Novel and Interesting Manner, the Natural History of the Elephant, Rhinoceros, Tiger, Leopard, Bear, Deer, Buffalo, Wolf, Wild Hog, Jackall, Wild Dog, Civet, and other Domesticated Animals; as likewise the Different Species of Feathered Game, Fishes, and Serpents. The whole interspersed with a Variety of Original, Authentic, and Curious Anecdotes. *The drawings by Samuel Howitt, made uniform in size, and engraved by the first artists. Frontispieces and 40 finely colored plates. 2 vols., imperial 4to, green morocco extra, emblematically tooled, gilt edges.* LARGE PAPER: *fine copy.* E. Orme, London, 1807

3302 WILLIAMSON, WILLIAM D. THE HISTORY OF THE STATE OF MAINE, from its First Discovery, A. D. 1602, to the Separation A. D. 1820, inclusive; with an Appendix and General Index. A New Impression. *Portrait and view of State House. 2 vols., 8vo, sheep.* Hallowell, 1839

3303 WILLICH, A. F. M., M. D. THE DOMESTIC ENCYCLOPÆDIA, or a Dictionary of Facts and Useful Knowledge: comprehending a Concise View of the latest Discoveries, Inventions, and Improvements, chiefly applicable to Rural and Domestic Economy; together with Descriptions of the most interesting Objects of Nature and Art; the History of Men and Animals, in a State of Health or Disease; and Practical Hints respecting the Arts and Manufactures, both Familiar and Commercial. *Numerous plates and wood-cuts. 4 vols., 8vo, sheep, yellow edges.* London, 1802

3304 WILLIS, NATHANIEL PARKER. AMERICAN SCENERY, or Land, Lake, and River Illustrations of Transatlantic Nature, from Drawings by W. H. Bartlett; the Literary Department by N. P. Willis, Esq. *Portrait, map, and 118 views. 2 vols., 4to, half green morocco, neat, gilt edges.* G. Virtue, London, 1840

3305 WILLIS, NATHANIEL PARKER. ANOTHER COPY: *the same. 2 vols., 4to, cloth, gilt edges.* G. Virtue, London, 1840

3306 WILLIS, NATHANIEL PARKER. CANADIAN SCENERY, illustrated from Drawings by W. H. Bartlett; the Literary Department by N. P. Willis, Esq. *Portrait, map, and 118 views. 2 vols. in 1, 4to, morocco antique, gilt edges.* G. Virtue, London, 1842

3307 WILLIS, NATHANIEL PARKER. ANOTHER COPY: *the same. 2 vols., 4to, cloth, gilt edges.* G. Virtue, London, 1842

3308 WILLIS, NATHANIEL PARKER. POEMS OF EARLY AND AFTER YEARS. Illustrated by E. Leutze. Fifth Edition. *Royal 8vo, morocco extra, gilt edges.* Philadelphia, 1850

3309 WILLIS, WILLIAM. A HISTORY OF THE LAW, THE COURTS, AND THE LAWYERS OF MAINE, from its First Colonization to the Early Part of the Present Century. *Portraits. Thick 8vo, half morocco.* Portland, 1863

3310 WILLIS, WILLIAM. THE HISTORY OF PORTLAND, from 1632 to 1864; with a Notice of Previous Settlements, Colonial Grants, and Changes of Government in Maine. Second Edition, revised and enlarged. *Portrait, maps, views, etc. Thick 8vo, cloth.* Portland, 1865

3311 WILLOUGHBY. GOLDSMITH. HERVEY. SO MUCH OF THE DIARY OF LADY WILLOUGHBY as relates to her Domestic History, and to the Eventful Period of the Reign of Charles the First. — THE VICAR OF WAKEFIELD; a Tale. — THE BOOK OF CHRISTMAS, descriptive of the Customs, Ceremonies, Traditions, Superstitions, Fun, Feeling, and Festivities of the Christmas Season. *The three works bound together in 1 volume. 12mo, half calf extra.* New York, 1845

3312 WILLSON, FORCEYTHE. THE OLD SERGEANT; and other Poems. *Post 8vo, cloth, gilt top.* Boston, 1867

3313 WILLYAMS, REV. COOPER. AN ACCOUNT OF THE CAMPAIGN IN THE WEST INDIES, in the Year 1794, under the Command of their Excellencies Lieutenant General Sir Charles Grey, K. B. and Vice Admiral Sir John Jervis, K. B.; with the Reduction of the Islands of Martinique, St. Lucia, Guadaloupe, Marigalante, Desiada, etc., and the Events that followed those unparalleled Successes, and caused the Loss of Guadaloupe. By the Rev. Cooper Willyams, A. M., Chaplain of his Majesty's Ship Boyne. *Map, plan and colored plates,* THE LARGEST OF WHICH ARE NOT FOLDED. *Royal folio, half calf.* LARGEST PAPER: *only* 100 *copies printed.* Printed by T. Bensley, London, 1796

3314 WILLYAMS, REV. COOPER. A VOYAGE UP THE MEDITERRANEAN, in his Majesty's Ship the Swiftsure, one of the Squadron under the Command of Rear-Admiral Sir Horatio Nelson, K. B., etc.; with a Description of the Battle of the Nile, on the First of August, 1798, and a Detail of Events that occurred Subsequent to the Battle, in Various Parts of the Mediterranean. *Engraved dedication, chart, plan of battle, and 40 views; all finely* COLORED, *and very neatly inlaid with border around each plate. Royal folio, crimson morocco extra, emblematically tooled, gilt edges, by Staggemeier.* LARGEST PAPER: *only* 100 *copies printed.*
Printed by T. Bensley, London, 1802

3315 WILLYAMS, REV. COOPER. ANOTHER COPY: *the same; with same plates,* TINTED. *4to, boards, uncut.* London, 1802

3316 WILLYAMS, REV. COOPER. ANOTHER COPY: *the same; with same plates,* COLORED. *4to, half russia.* London, 1802

3317 WILSON, ALEXANDER; and CHARLES LUCIEN BONAPARTE. AMERICAN ORNITHOLOGY, or the Natural History of the Birds of the United States; illustrated with Plates engraved and colored from Original Drawings taken from Nature. 9 *vols.* — AMERICAN ORNITHOLOGY, or the Natural History of Birds inhabiting the United States, not given by Wilson; with Figures drawn, engraved, and coloured from Nature. 3 *vols. Together,* 12 *vols., imperial 4to, half red morocco, rough edges.* ORIGINAL EDITIONS: *unstained.* Philadelphia, 1808–28

3318 WILSON, CHARLES HENRY. THE POLYANTHEA, or a Collection of Interesting Fragments, in Prose and Verse; consisting of Original Anecdotes, Biographical Sketches, Dialogues, Letters, Characters, etc., etc. 2 *vols., 8vo, half calf, neat, yellow edges.* J. Budd, London, 1804

This work was reissued with another title, "Anecdotes of Eminent Persons," Lackington & Co., 1804.

The second volume contains an abridgment of Dr. Stiles's "History of Three of the Judges of King Charles I.," pp. 75–194; and a "Life of Captain John Smith, sometime President of Virginia, and Admiral of New England, etc.; by Jeremy Belknap, D. D.," pp. 267–350.

3319 WILSON, ERASMUS. THE EASTERN, OR TURKISH BATH; its History, Revival in Britain, and Application to the Purposes of Health. *Wood-cuts. 16mo, paper.* London, 1861

3320 WILSON, GEORGE, M. D. THE FIVE GATEWAYS OF KNOWLEDGE. *16mo, cloth.* Philadelphia, 1857

3321 WILSON, HARRIETTE. MEMOIRS OF; written by herself. (With an Index, Analytical, Referential, and Explanatory of Persons and Matter; by Thomas Little, Esq.). *Colored plates. A few pages wanting and 4 replaced in MS.* 9 *vols., 12mo, half dark calf extra, marbled edges.* J. J. Stockdale, London, 1831

3322 WILSON, JAMES. ILLUSTRATIONS OF ZOÖLOGY; being Representations of New, Rare, or Remarkable Subjects of the Animal Kingdom, drawn and coloured after Nature, with Historical and Descriptive Details. *Contains 36 plates, uncolored. Atlas 4to, half red morocco, gilt top, uncut.* Edinburgh, 1831

3323 WILSON, JESSIE AITKEN. MEMOIR OF GEORGE WILSON, M. D., F. R. S. E., etc.; by his Sister. *Portrait, 8vo, cloth, uncut.* Edinburgh, 1860

3324 WILSON, John. Shaksperiana: Catalogue of all the Books, Pamphlets, etc., relating to Shakspeare; to which are subjoined, an Account of the Early Quarto Editions of the Great Dramatist's Plays and Poems, the Prices at which many Copies have sold in Public Sales, together with a List of the Leading and Esteemed Editions of Shakspeare's Collected Works. *8vo, boards, rough edges.* Large paper: *very few printed.* J. Wilson, London, 1827

"The preface to this little volume contains a curious account of the fabricated portraits of Shakespeare." — *Lowndes.*

3325 WILSON, Rev. Joseph. A French and English Dictionary; containing Full Explanations, Definitions, Synonyms, Idioms, Proverbs, Terms of Art and Science, and Rules of Pronunciation in Each Language. *Treble columns, thick imperial 8vo, cloth, uncut.* London, 1863

3326 WILSON, Thomas, Bishop. Sacra Privata: the Private Meditations and Prayers. *Foolscap 8vo, cloth, uncut.* Large type: *beautiful edition.* W. Pickering, London, 1848

3327 WILSON, William Rae. Travels in Russia, etc., etc. *Illustrated by engravings. 2 vols. in 1, 8vo, half morocco.* London, 1828

This work contains an "Appendix" of Documents relative to Mary Queen of Scots, consisting of letters copied from the originals in the Imperial Library at St. Petersburg.

3328 WINSLOW, Forbes, M. D. The Anatomy of Suicide. *Frontispiece. 8vo, cloth, uncut.* London, 1840

3329 WINSLOW, Hubbard, D. D. Elements of Intellectual Philosophy. *12mo, cloth.* Boston, 1850

3330 WINSTANLEY, William. The Lives of the most Famous English Poets; or the Honour of Parnassus; in a Brief Essay of the Works and Writings of above Two Hundred of them, from the Time of K. William the Conqueror, to the Reign of his Present Majesty King James II. *Frontispiece, containing portrait, by F. H. Van Hove. Small 8vo, calf gilt.* London, 1687

3331 WINTHROP, Lieut.-Colonel Grenville Temple. Trial by Court Martial of; on Charges preferred against him by Adjutant Gen. William H. Sumner, in pursuance of Orders from his Excellency Levi Lincoln, Governor of the Commonwealth of Massachusetts. Printed for the Respondent. *Royal 8vo, boards, rough edges.* Boston, 1832

3332 WINTHROP, John, First Governor of the Colony of Massachusetts Bay. The History of New-England, from 1630 to 1649; from his Original Manuscripts. With Notes to illustrate the Civil and Ecclesiastical Concerns, the Geography, Settlement, and Institutions of the Country, and the Lives and Manners of the Principal Planters; by James

Savage. A New Edition, with Additions and Corrections by the Former Editor. *Portrait and fac-simile letter.* 2 *vols., 8vo, tree calf gilt, marbled edges, by Riviere.*
Boston, 1853

3333 WIRT, William. Sketches of the Life and Character of Patrick Henry. Ninth Edition, corrected by the Author. *Portraits. 8vo, sheep, marbled edges; with autograph of Rufus Choate.* Philadelphia, 1845

In this copy is inserted an autograph signature of Patrick Henry.

3334 WISEMAN, Nicholas, Cardinal. Four Lectures on the Offices and Ceremonies of Holy Week, as performed in the Papal Chapels; delivered in Rome in the Lent of MDCCCXXXVII. *Wood-cuts. 8vo, cloth.* London, 1854

3335 WISNER, Rev. Benjamin B. The History of the Old South Church in Boston; in Four Sermons, delivered May 9 and 16, 1830, being the First and Second Sabbaths after the Completion of a Century from the First Occupancy of the Present Meeting House. *Notes (pp.* 69–122), *and plan of the lower floor in* 1730. *8vo, pp.* 122, *paper, rough edges.* Fine clean copy. Boston, 1830

3336 WOLCOTT, John. The Works of Peter Pindar, Esq. *Portrait.* 5 *vols., 8vo, old marbled calf extra, marbled edges.*
London, 1794–1801

3337 WOLCOTT, John, M. D. Another copy: *the works, as published, with portrait (published* 1798) *by Mackenzie after Opie, and* 7 *satirical plates; collected and bound in* 3 *vols., 4to, boards.* London, 1765–95

Contents: Epistle to the Reviewers; Lyric Odes to the Royal Academicians, for 1782, 1783, 1785; Farewell Odes, for 1786; The Lousiad, Cantos I.-V.; Congratulatory Epistle to James Boswell; Bozzy and Piozzi; Ode upon Ode; An Apologetic Postscript to Ode upon Ode; Odes to Mr. Paine, Author of "Rights of Man." The Remonstrance, etc.; Commiserating Epistle to Lord Lonsdale; More Money! or, Odes of Instruction to Mr. Pitt, etc.; Odes of Importance, etc.; Tears of St. Margaret, etc.; Pair of Lyric Epistles to Lord Macartney and his Ship; Odes to Kien Long, etc.; Epistles to the Pope, etc. Pathetic Odes; The Royal Tour, etc.; Celebration; Instructions to a Celebrated Laureat; Brother Peter to Brother Tom; Peter's Pension; Peter's Prophecy; Sir Joseph Banks and the Emperor of Morocco; Epistle to a Falling Minister, etc.; Subjects for Painters; Expostulatory Odes to a Great Duke and a Little Lord; Benevolent Epistle to Sylvanus Urban, etc.; A Rowland for an Oliver, etc.; Advice to the Future Laureat; Complimentary Epistle to James Bruce; Rights of Kings.

3338 WOLF, Joseph. Zoölogical Sketches. *A series of* 40 *beautiful colored plates, mounted on a thick card-board and enclosed in a fine box portfolio, label on side, imperial folio size.* London, s. a.

These fine drawings were all made from the living animals in the Vivarium of the London Zoölogical Society, and rank among the finest sketches of the kind ever published.

3339 WOLLASTON, Rev. William. The Religion of Nature Delineated. *4to, old calf.*
Printed by Samuel Palmer, London, 1726

A note on the first cover says: "This scarce edition was set by Benjamin Franklin when a journeyman compositor in Palmer's printing-office, and called forth a reply from him."

3340 WOMEN AS THEY ARE, by one of them; by the Author of "Margaret, or Prejudice at Home." 2 *vols.*, 16*mo, half crimson morocco.* London, 1854

3341 WOOD, ANTHONY À. ATHENÆ OXONIENSES: an Exact History of all the Writers and Bishops who have had their Education in the University of Oxford; to which are added the Fasti, or Annals of the said University. By Anthony à Wood, M. A., of Merton College. A New (Third) Edition; with Additions, and a Continuation, by Philip Bliss, Fellow of St. John's College. 4 *vols. in* 5, *royal* 4*to, crimson turkey morocco extra, gilt edges.* London, 1813–1820

Dibdin in speaking of this edition says, "And if this work be '*thrice* welcome,' in any shape, it is *nine* times welcome in the recent impression just alluded to! — for more care, attention, accuracy, and valuable enlargement from an inexhaustible stock of materials (some of them contemporaneous, has rarely been witnessed, than in the editorial labours of Dr. Bliss upon the) text of his beloved ANTHONY À WOOD."

3342 WOOD, ANTHONY À. ANOTHER COPY: *the same.* 4 *vols., royal* 4*to, half calf, very neat, marbled edges; with book-plate of Henry Thomas Buckle.* London, 1813–20

3343 WOOD, JOHN. THE SUPPRESSED HISTORY OF THE ADMINISTRATION OF JOHN ADAMS (from 1797 to 1801), as printed and suppressed in 1802. Now republished with Notes, and an Appendix, by John Henry Sherburne. *Portrait.* 12*mo, cloth.* Published for the Editor, Philadelphia, 1846

3344 WOOD, REV. JOHN GEORGE. THE ILLUSTRATED NATURAL HISTORY. With Four Hundred and Eighty Original Designs, by William Harvey. New Edition, corrected and considerably enlarged. *Post* 8*vo, cloth, uncut.* London, 1855

3345 WOOD, REV. JOHN GEORGE. HOMES WITHOUT HANDS; being a Description of the Habitations of Animals, classed according to their Principle of Construction. With New Designs, by W. F. Keyl and E. Smith, engraved by Messrs. Pearson. *Royal* 8*vo, cloth.* New York, 1866

3346 WOOD, ROBERT. THE RUINS OF PALMYRA AND BALBEC. *With* 104 *plates.* 1 *vol. royal folio, half morocco, gilt top, uncut.* W. Pickering, London, 1827

3347 WOOD, WILLIAM MAXWELL, M. D. FANKWEI, or the San Jacinto in the Seas of India, China, and Japan. 12*mo, cloth.* New York, 1869

3348 WOODWARD, BERNARD BOLINGBROKE. THE HISTORY OF WALES, from the Earliest Times to its Final Incorporation with the Kingdom of England; with Notices of its Physical Geography and Mineral Wealth, and of the Religion and Literature, Laws, Customs, Manners, and Arts of the Welsh. *Vignette title and* 75 *plates.* 1 *vol. in* 2, *imperial* 8*vo, cloth, uncut.* London, 1853

3349 WOOLEY, Rev. Charles. A Two Years' Journal in New York, and Part of its Territories, in America. A New Edition, with an Introduction and Copious Historical Notes by E. B. O'Callaghan, M. D. *Printed by Munsell & Rowland. Royal 4to, cloth, uncut.* Large paper.
W. Gowans, New York, 1860

This work, No. 2 of "Gowans' Bibliotheca Americana," is a reprint of the London edition of 1701, which Rich styles "a very curious and uncommon little book."

3350 WOOLRYCH, Humphry William. Memoirs of the Life of Judge Jeffreys, sometime Lord High Chancellor of England. *Portrait. 8vo, half calf, neat.*
London, 1827

3351 WORCESTER, Joseph Emerson. A Dictionary of the English Language. *The new pictorial edition. 2 vols., 4to, half russia, neat, marbled edges.* Boston, 1860

3352 WORDSWORTH, Christopher, D. D., Master of Trinity College, Cambridge, etc. Ecclesiastical Biography, or Lives of Eminent Men connected with the History of Religion in England, from the Commencement of the Reformation to the Revolution; selected and illustrated with Notes. Third Edition; with a Large Introduction, some New Lives, and many Additional Notes. *4 vols., 8vo, tree calf gilt, gilt edges, by Clarke & Bedford.* Elegant copy. J. G. & F. Rivington, London, 1839

3353 WORDSWORTH, Christopher, D. D. Greece: Pictorial, Descriptive, and Historical. A New Edition, carefully revised; with Numerous Engravings on Wood and Steel, illustrative of the Scenery, Architecture, Costume and Fine Arts of that Country, by Copley Fielding, F. Creswick, D. Cox, Jun., Harvey, Paul Huet, Meissonier, Sargent Daubigny, Jaques, and other Artists. And a History of the Characteristics of Greek Art, illustrated by George Scharf, Jun'r, Esq. *Imperial 8vo, half green morocco extra, marbled edges.* London, 1853

3354 WORDSWORTH, William. The Poetical Works of. A New Edition. *Portrait. 6 vols., foolscap 8vo, cloth, uncut.*
E. Moxon, London, 1836–37

3355 WORKS (The) of Celebrated Authors, of whose Writings there are but small Remains: containing the Works of the Earl of Roscommon, the Earl of Dorset, the Earl of Halifax, and Sir Samuel Garth; George Stepney, Esq., William Walsh, Esq., Thomas Tickell, Esq., and Poems by Bishop Sprat. *2 vols., 12mo, calf, neat.*
J. & R. Tonson, etc., London, 1750

"The reader will find some material alterations in the Translation of *Horace's* Art of Poetry, which were communicated by *Dr. Rawlinson* from a Copy corrected by his Lordship's Own Hand." — *Advertisement.*

3356 WOTTON (WILLIAM, D. D.?). BART'LEMY FAIR, or an Enquiry after Wit; in which Due Respect is had to a Letter concerning Enthusiasm, to my Lord * * *. By Mr. Wotton. *Dedicated "To the most Illustrious Society of the Kit-Cats;" pp.* 175, *including title and dedication.* 8*vo, old calf.* R. Wilkin, London, 1709

An attack upon the first treatise (published, 1708) in the Earl of Shaftesbury's "Characteristicks." See SHAFTESBURY.

3357 WOUVVERMAN, PHILIP. ŒUVRES DE. Gravées d'après ses Meilleurs Tableaux qui sont dans les plus beaux Cabinets de Paris et ailleurs. Dédiées a son Altesse Serenissime Monseigneur le Comte de Clermont, Prince du Sang, par son tres Humble et tres Obeissant Serviteur, J. Moyreau, Graveur du Roy, 1737. *Engraved title, portrait, and* 104 *fine large plates. Atlas folio, half maroon morocco extra, gilt top.* VERY FINE COPY. (Paris, 1737, etc.)

3358 WRIGHT, EDWARD, M. D. SOME OBSERVATIONS MADE IN TRAVELLING THROUGH FRANCE, ITALY, ETC., in the Years MDCCXX., MDCCXXI., and MDCCXXII. The Second Edition. *Numerous plates by Vander Gucht.* 2 *vols. in* 1, 4*to, old sprinkled calf gilt, yellow edges.* A. Millar, London, 1764

3359 WRIGHT, REV. GEORGE NEWNHAM. LIFE AND CAMPAIGNS OF ARTHUR, DUKE OF WELLINGTON, K. G., ETC. *Engraved titles and numerous portraits, plans, etc.* 4 *vols.,* 8*vo, half calf, neat.* London, (1839–41)

3360 WRIGHT, THOMAS. QUEEN ELIZABETH AND HER TIMES; a Series of Original Letters, selected from the inedited Private Correspondence of the Lord Treasurer Burghley, the Earl of Leicester, the Secretaries Walsingham and Smith, Sir Christopher Hatton, and most of the Distinguished Persons of the Period. *Portraits, fac-simile and index.* 2 *vols.,* 8*vo, half calf, neat.* London, 1838

3361 WRIGHT, THOMAS. THE HISTORY OF IRELAND; from the Earliest Period of the Irish Annals to the Present Time. *Illustrated with beautiful steel engravings, from original drawings, executed expressly for this work, by H. Warren, Esq., president of the New Water Colour Society, London.* 3 *vols., imperial* 8*vo, half morocco.* London, (cir. 1853)

3362 WYATT, MATTHEW DIGBY. THE INDUSTRIAL ARTS OF THE NINETEENTH CENTURY; a Series of Illustrations of the Choicest Specimens produced by Every Nation at the Great Exhibition of Works of Industry, 1851. *Frontispiece for each volume, and* 158 *elaborate plates of sculpture, embroidery, lace, textile fabrics, metal-work, porcelain, wood and ivory carving, etc., etc., executed in the exact colors of the originals.* 5 *parts, with two titles for binding in* 2 *vols., royal folio, boards.* FINE ORIGINAL COPY. London, 1851

3363 WYCLIFFE, JOHN DE. THE LAST AGE OF THE CHURCH; now first printed from a Manuscript in the University Library, Dublin. Edited, with Notes, by James H. Todd, D. D. *Handsomely printed, the tract itself in fac-simile. Square foolscap 8vo, half morocco, red paper sides.* University Press, Dublin, 1840

3364 WYLDE, JAMES. THE MAGIC OF SCIENCE; a Manual of Easy and Instructive Scientific Experiments. *Numerous wood-cuts. Post 8vo, cloth.* London, 1861

3365 WYNNE, JAMES, M. D. PRIVATE LIBRARIES OF NEW YORK. *View of Wm. Curtis Noyes's library, with a duplicate impression (on India paper) of the same plate. Imperial 8vo, cloth, uncut.* LARGE PAPER: *only 100 copies printed.* New York, 1860

3366 YONGE, CHARLOTTE M. A BOOK OF GOLDEN DEEDS of all Times and all Lands; gathered and narrated by the Author of the "Heir of Redclyffe." *Foolscap 8vo, cloth, gilt top, uncut.* Cambridge (Mass.), 1865

3367 YOUNG, ALEXANDER, D. D. CHRONICLES OF THE FIRST PLANTERS OF THE COLONY OF MASSACHUSETTS BAY, from 1623 to 1636; now first collected from Original Records and Contemporaneous Manuscripts, and illustrated with Notes, by Alexander Young. *Portrait of Gov. Winthrop, and fac-simile of Wood's map, 1633. 8vo, cloth.* Boston, 1846

3368 YOUNG, EDWARD. NIGHT THOUGHTS on Life, Death, and Immortality. With Notes, Critical and Illustrative, by the Rev. C. E. DeCoetlogon, A. M. To which is prefixed the Life of the Author. *Engraved title, portrait, and plates after Corbould, etc. Royal 8vo, old tree calf gilt, yellow edges.* LARGE PAPER. Chapman & Co., London, (1793)

3369 YOUNG, EDWARD. THE WORKS OF; revised and corrected by himself. A New Edition. (With Life of Dr. Young.) *Portrait and 16 plates after Stothard and Wheatley. 3 vols., 8vo, old marbled calf extra, yellow edges.* London, 1802

3370 YOUNG, EDWARD. THE WORKS OF; revised and corrected by himself. (With Life of the Author.) *Portrait and 15 plates after Stothard and Wheatley. 3 vols., 8vo, calf gilt, marbled edges.* London, 1813

3371 YOUNG, EDWARD. THE POETICAL WORKS OF (with Life, by the Rev. John Mitford). *Portrait. 2 vols., foolscap 8vo, cloth, uncut.* ALDINE EDITION. W. Pickering, London, 1852

3372 YOUNG, EDWARD. THE POETICAL WORKS OF. *Portrait. 2 vols., foolscap 8vo, calf gilt, carmine edges.* Boston, 1854

3373 YRIARTE, TOMAS DE. FÁBULAS LITERARIAS de Don Tomas de Iriarte. *Edited by Charles Folsom.* 18*mo, half roan.* Cambrigia (Mass.), 1830

"Yriarte's fables are, however, not only remarkable for their classic language and excellent versification, but they possess a peculiar charm of style which may be mistaken for a happy imitation of Lafontaine, though it may be traced to a different source." — *Bouterwek, Vol. I. p.* 588, *Ed'n,* 1823.

3374 ZANETTI, ALLESANDRO. ANCIENT STATUES, Greek and Roman; designed from the Celebrated Originals in St. Mark's, and other Public Collections, in Venice, by A. Zanetti; and engraved by the First Italian Masters. *Frontispiece, portrait on title, and* 100 *plates. Atlas folio, half morocco, rough edges.* Lackington, Allen & Co., London, 1797

3375 ZARATE, AUGUSTIN DE. HISTOIRE DE LA DECOUVERTE ET DE LA CONQUETE DU PEROU; traduite de l'Espagnol, par S. D. C. [B. — A. de Broë, Seigneur de Citry de La Guette]. *Frontispieces, map, and* 13 *plates.* 2 *vols.,* 12*mo, morocco antique.* FINE COPY. J. Louis de Lorme, Amsterdam, 1700

3376 ZENTNER, J. L. A SELECT COLLECTION OF LANDSCAPES, from the Best Old Masters, one of each, engraved by L. Zentner, after Drawings made by him from Original Pictures, in Different Cabinets, during his Residence in Germany, France, Holland, etc.; to which are added Portraits of the Artists and Short Biographical Accounts of each. *Contains* 57 *fine plates (the last, "Fête Flammande," after Teniers, engraved by Le Bas), with letter-press in French and English. Oblong* 4*to, half morocco, neat, gilt label on side.* London, 1791

3377 ZSCHOKKE, JOHANN HEINRICH DANIEL. MEDITATIONS ON DEATH AND ETERNITY; translated from the German, by Frederica Rowan. *Post* 8*vo, calf gilt, gilt edges, by Hayday.* London, 1863

These "Meditations" form a part of the well-known German devotional work, "Stunden der Andact," which was published anonymously, and notwithstanding its brilliant success, Zschokke was with great difficulty prevailed upon to disclose the secret of his authorship.

Engravings.

3378 [ABSOLON.] SATURDAY NIGHT: Threading the Needle. SUNDAY MORNING IN THE LAST CENTURY. INDIA PROOFS BEFORE LETTERS. *A fine pair*, 17 × 35 *and* 27½ × 40 *inches*.

3379 ANSDELL. THE HALT. After R. Ansdell and W. P. Frith, by H. T. Ryall. *Open letter*, 31 × 24 *and* 43½ × 30½ *inches*.

3380 ANSDELL. JUST CAUGHT. After R. Ansdell, by H. T. Ryall. INDIA PROOF BEFORE TITLE. 22 × 34 *and* 30½ × 43 *inches*.

3381 ANSDELL. DEER STALKING: Examining the Ground. After R. Ansdell, by A. Lucas. *Open letter*, 14 × 26 *and* 24 × 35 *inches*.

3382 ANSDELL. HUNTING: the Death of the Fox. After R. Ansdell, by F. Stackpoole. *Open letter*, 14 × 26 *and* 24 × 35 *inches*.

3383 ANSDELL. SHOOTING: Waiting for the Guns. After R. Ansdell, by G. Paterson. *Open letter*, 14 × 26 *and* 24 × 35 *inches*.

3384 ANSDELL. FISHING: Gaffing a Salmon. After R. Ansdell, by W. H. Simmons. *Open letter*, 14 × 26 *and* 24 × 35 *inches*.

3385 BAXTER. THE ROSE OF SEVILLE. After C. Baxter, by Jouanin. *Oval*, 12 × 9½ *and* 27½ × 20 *inches*.

3386 BOUVIER. THE WILD HONEYSUCKLE. THE FORGET-ME-NOT. THE ROSE. THE LILY. THE DEW DROP. After A. Bouvier, by Hunt & C. Holl, W. H. Mote, W. & C. Hall. *Set of* 5, *open letter*, 12 × 9 *and* 22 × 15 *inches*.

3387 BOXALL. THE FAREWELL LOOK. After W. Boxall, by John Bromley. *Open letter*, 14½ × 12 *and* 27½ × 20 *inches*.

3388 BRIDGES. LORD WILLIAM RUSSELL TAKING LEAVE OF HIS CHILDREN. After John Bridges, by Samuel Bellin. INDIA PROOF BEFORE TITLE. 20 × 26 *and* 27½ × 40½ *inches*.

3389 BRIDGES. ANOTHER COPY: *the same*.

3390 BROOKS. THE ORPHANS. After T. Brooks, by S. Bellin. *Open letter*, 23½ × 18 *and* 35 × 24 *inches*.

3391 [CARLOS.] THE LETTER WRITER ("IT'S FOR YOU TO SAY, I'LL WRITE"). INDIA PROOF BEFORE LETTERS. 18 × 21½ *and* 27½ × 40 *inches*.

3392 CATTERMOLE. THE FIRST REFORMERS PRESENTING THEIR FAMOUS PROTEST AT THE DIET OF SPIRES ON THE 19TH OF APRIL, 1592. After George Cattermole, by William Walker. *India paper*, 23 × 32 *and* 30½ × 40½ *inches.*

3393 COLLINS. FETCHING THE DOCTOR. After William. Collins, by C. E. Wagstaff. *Open letter*, 17½ × 23 *and* 24 × 35 *inches.*

3394 COLLINSON. TO LET: A PLEASANT PROSPECT SIR! After G. W. Collinson, by W. T. Davey. *Oval, open letter*, 13 × 10½ *and* 27½ × 20 *inches.*

3395 COLLINSON. GOOD FOR A COLD. After J. Collinson, by W. H. Simmons. *Oval, open letter*, 13 × 10½ *and* 27½ × 20 *inches.*

3396 DRUMMOND. THE CRICKET MATCH BETWEEN SUSSEX AND KENT, AT BRIGHTON. After Wm. Drummond and Chas. J. Basébe, by G. H. Phillips. *Open letter*, 23½ × 36 *and* 30½ × 43½ ; *with key.*

3397 DUVAL. LUTHER BURNING THE POPE'S BULL OF EXCOMMUNICATION. After C. A. Duval, by T. O. Barlow. INDIA PROOF BEFORE TITLE. 21 × 33½ *and* 30½ × 40½ *inches.*

3398 EASTLAKE. THE SALUTATION. After Sir C. L. Eastlake, by Samuel Bellin. INDIA PROOF BEFORE TITLE. 22½ × 28½ *and* 30½ × 43½ *inches.*

3399 ELMORE. REBEKAH SEES THE APPROACH OF ABRAHAM'S SERVANT. After Alfred Elmore, by Francis Holl. *Open letter*, 21 × 15 *and* 35 × 24 *inches.*

3400 ETTY. THE JUDGMENT OF PARIS. After W. Etty, by C. W. Wass. INDIA PROOF BEFORE TITLE. 20 × 30 *and* 27½ × 40 *inches.*

3401 FRASER. THE EXPECTED PENNY. After Alex[r]. Fraser, by Robert Bell. *Open letter*, 16 × 12½ *and* 27 × 19 *inches.*

3402 [FRITH.] HOGARTH AT CALAIS. INDIA PROOF BEFORE LETTERS. 22 × 30½ *and* 30½ × 43½ *inches.*

3403 FRITH. DID YOU RING, SIR? SHERRY, SIR? After W. P. Frith, by Fra's Holl. *A fine pair, ovals, open letter*, 13 × 11 *and* 24 × 17½ *inches.*

3404 FRITH. BED TIME. After W. P. Frith, by Lumb Stocks. *Open letter*, 17 × 13½ *and* 30½ × 22 *inches.*

3405 FRITH. RUTH IN THE FIELDS OF BOAZ. After W. P. Frith, by W. Holl. *Open letter*, 21 × 15½ *and* 35 × 24 *inches.*

3406 GLASS. THE LAST RETURN FROM DUTY. After James W. Glass, by James Faed. INDIA PROOF BEFORE TITLE. 23 × 35 *and* 30½ × 43½ *inches.*

3407 HANNAH. CUPBOARD LOVE. After R. Hannah, by T. O. Barlow. *Open letter*, 10½ × 12 *and* 20 × 27½ *inches.*

3408 HAYDON. PORTRAIT OF THE DUKE OF WELLINGTON. After B. R. Haydon, by C. E. Wagstaff. INDIA PROOF: *with fac-simile autograph*, 14½ × 12 *and* 30½ × 22 *inches.*

3409 HAYTER. THE MARRIAGE OF HER MOST GRACIOUS MAJESTY QUEEN VICTORIA. After Sir George Hayter, by Charles Eden Wagstaff. *Open letter*, 22½ × 34 *and* 30 × 43 *inches.*

3410 HAYTER. THE CORONATION OF HER MOST GRACIOUS MAJESTY QUEEN VICTORIA. After Sir George Hayter, by H. T. Ryall. *Open letter*, 22½ × 34 *and* 30 × 43 *inches.*

3411 HENNING. MOUNT VERNON IN THE OLDEN TIME: WASHINGTON AT 30 YEARS OF AGE. After A. Henning, by H. B. Hall. *Open letter*, 19 × 24½ *and* 24 × 30 *inches.*

3412 HERBERT. THE ASSERTION OF LIBERTY OF CONSCIENCE BY THE INDEPENDENTS. After J. R. Herbert, by Saml. Bellin. INDIA PROOF BEFORE TITLE. 21 × 33 *and* 30½ × 40 *inches.*

3413 HERRING. A GLIMPSE OF AN ENGLISH HOMESTEAD. After J. F. Herring, Senr., by G. Patterson. INDIA PROOF BEFORE TITLE. 22½ × 34½ *and* 30½ × 43½ *inches.*

3414 HERRING. A FARM YARD. After J. F. Herring, Senr by G. Paterson. INDIA PROOF BEFORE TITLE. 22½ × 34½ *and* 30½ × 43½ *inches.*

3415 HERRING. FEEDING THE HORSE. After J. F. Herring, Senr., by T. L. Atkinson. *Open letter*, 31 × 24 *and* 43½ × 30½ *inches.*

3416 HUNT. CYMON AND IPHIGENIA, OR LOVE AT FIRST SIGHT. After William Hunt, by Samuel Bellin. 17½ × 24 *and* 27½ × 40 *inches.*

3417 JENKINS. GOING WITH THE STREAM. GOING AGAINST THE STREAM. After J. J. Jenkins, by H. Robinson. *A fine pair, open letter*, 20 × 28 *and* 27½ × 40 *inches.*

3418 JONES. THE DAUGHTER OF ERIN. After T. A. Jones, by F. Holl. 9 × 7½ *and* 27½ × 20 *inches.*

3419 LANDSEER. FAVORITE PONY AND SPANIELS. After Edwin Landseer, by Thomas Landseer. *Open letter*, 20 × 25½ *and* 27½ × 40 *inches.*

3420 LANDSEER. FAVORITES (Prince George's). After Edwin Landseer, by W. Gilder. *Open letter*, 20 × 25½ *and* 27½ × 40 *inches.*

3421 LANDSEER. A DISTINGUISHED MEMBER OF THE HUMANE SOCIETY. After Edwin Landseer, by Thomas Landseer. *Open letter*, 19 × 24½ *and* 27½ × 40 *inches.*

3422 [LANDSEER.] THE MONKEY THAT HAD SEEN THE WORLD. INDIA PROOF BEFORE LETTERS. 13½ × 15½ *and* 22 × 30½ *inches.*

3423 LUCY. CROMWELL'S LAST INTERVIEW WITH HIS FAVORITE DAUGHTER. After Charles Lucy, by Charles Tompkins. *Open letter*, 22½ × 18 *and* 40 × 27½ *inches.*

3424 MARTIN. BELSHAZZAR'S FEAST. DEATH OF THE FIRST BORN. THE FALL OF BABYLON. THE FALL OF NINEVEH. *Set of* 4 *finely colored.* 21½ × 32 *and* 30½ × 43½ *inches.*

3425 MARTIN. THE PAPHIAN BOWER. After J. Martin, by G. H. Phillips. *Open letter*, 17 × 23½ *and* 25 × 32 *inches*.

3426 RICHTER. THE BRUTE OF A HUSBAND. After H. Richter, by W. Nicholas. *Open letter*, 14 × 18½ *and* 22 × 30½ *inches*.

3427 SCHLOSSER. LE FRUIT DÉFENDU. After Karl Schloesser, by Durand. *Open letter*, 17½ × 26½ *and* 27½ × 40 *inches*.

3428 SOLOMON. MORNING. EVENING. After A. Solomon, by W. and F. Holl. *A fine pair, open letter*, 13½ × 9 *and* 27½ × 20 *inches*.

3429 STONE. THE FIRST APPEAL. THE LAST APPEAL. After Frank Stone, by Samuel Bellin. *A fine pair, open letter*, 24 × 18½ *and* 35 × 24 *inches*.

3430 [STONE.] IMPENDING MATE. MATED. PROOFS BEFORE LETTERS. *A fine pair*, 19 × 24½ *and* 27½ × 40 *inches*.

3431 TAYLOR. HADDON HALL ON THE MORNING OF THE CHASE. After Fredrick Taylor, by H. T. Ryall. INDIA PROOF BEFORE TITLE. 22½ × 34½ *and* 30½ × 43½ *inches*.

3432 THOMPSON. THE HIGHLAND FERRY BOAT. After Jacob Thompson, by J. T. Willmore. INDIA PROOF BEFORE TITLE. 18 × 34½ *and* 27½ × 43½ *inches*.

3433 WEBSTER. SEE-SAW. After Thomas Webster, by W. Holl. INDIA PROOF BEFORE TITLE. 16 × 26½ *and* 27½ × 40 *inches*.

3434 WRIGHT. THE AFTERNOON'S NAP. After J. M. Wright, by T. W. Huffam. *Open letter*, 18 × 24½ *and* 24 × 35 *inches*.

The above 70 engravings (Nos. 3379–3434) are all the finest impressions. The sizes are given, both with and without margin, height first.

www.ingramcontent.com/pod-product-compliance
Lightning Source LLC
LaVergne TN
LVHW021130110826
845150LV00005B/986